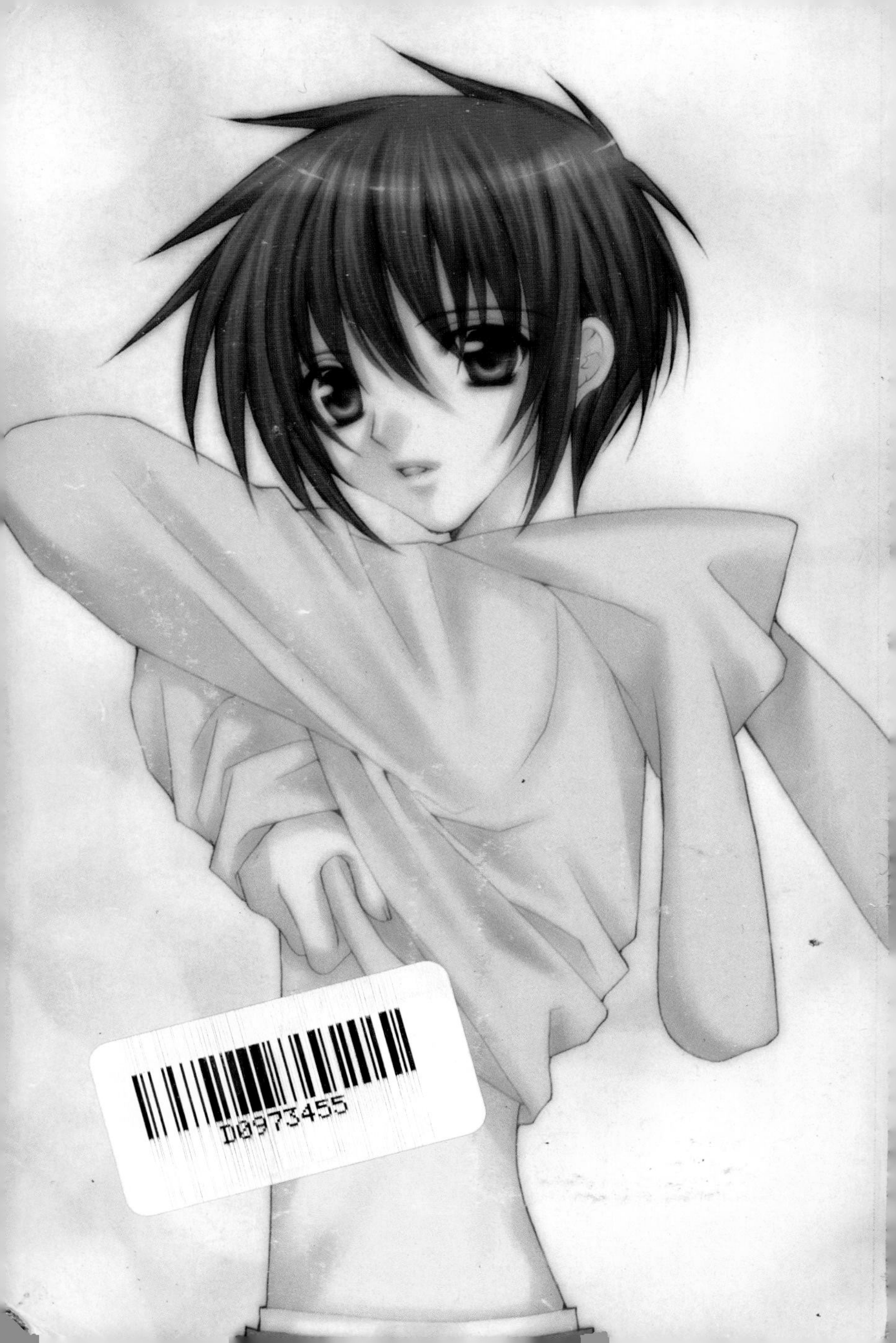

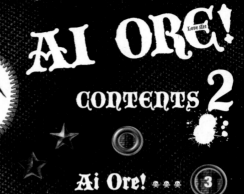

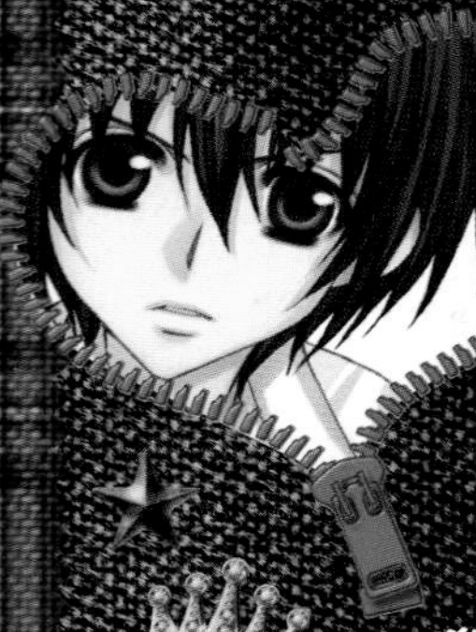

AI ORE! Love Me

CONTENTS 2

Story Thus Far

☠ Mizuki Sakurazaka, the lead guitarist of indie girl band Blaue Rosen, is an extremely handsome girl. She is treated like a "prince" at St. Nobara Girls Academy. Akira Shiraishi, a cute boy who is considered to be the "princess" of Dankaisan Boys School, wants to join her band.

☠ Akira dresses like a girl and sneaks into the audition (held at St. Nobara) for the new lead singer of Blaue Rosen. He succeeds in becoming the new lead singer, but he did it to get closer to Mizuki! Mizuki finds herself attracted to Akira, and her feelings grow stronger after she finds out Akira was her first love.

☠ But at the St. Nobara retreat, Misaki Dojima, the "prince" of the third-year students, drugs Mizuki and forces herself on her! Misaki is saved at the last minute, but an enraged Akira calls on a friend to help him get revenge on Misaki. Akira is truly in his dark mode...

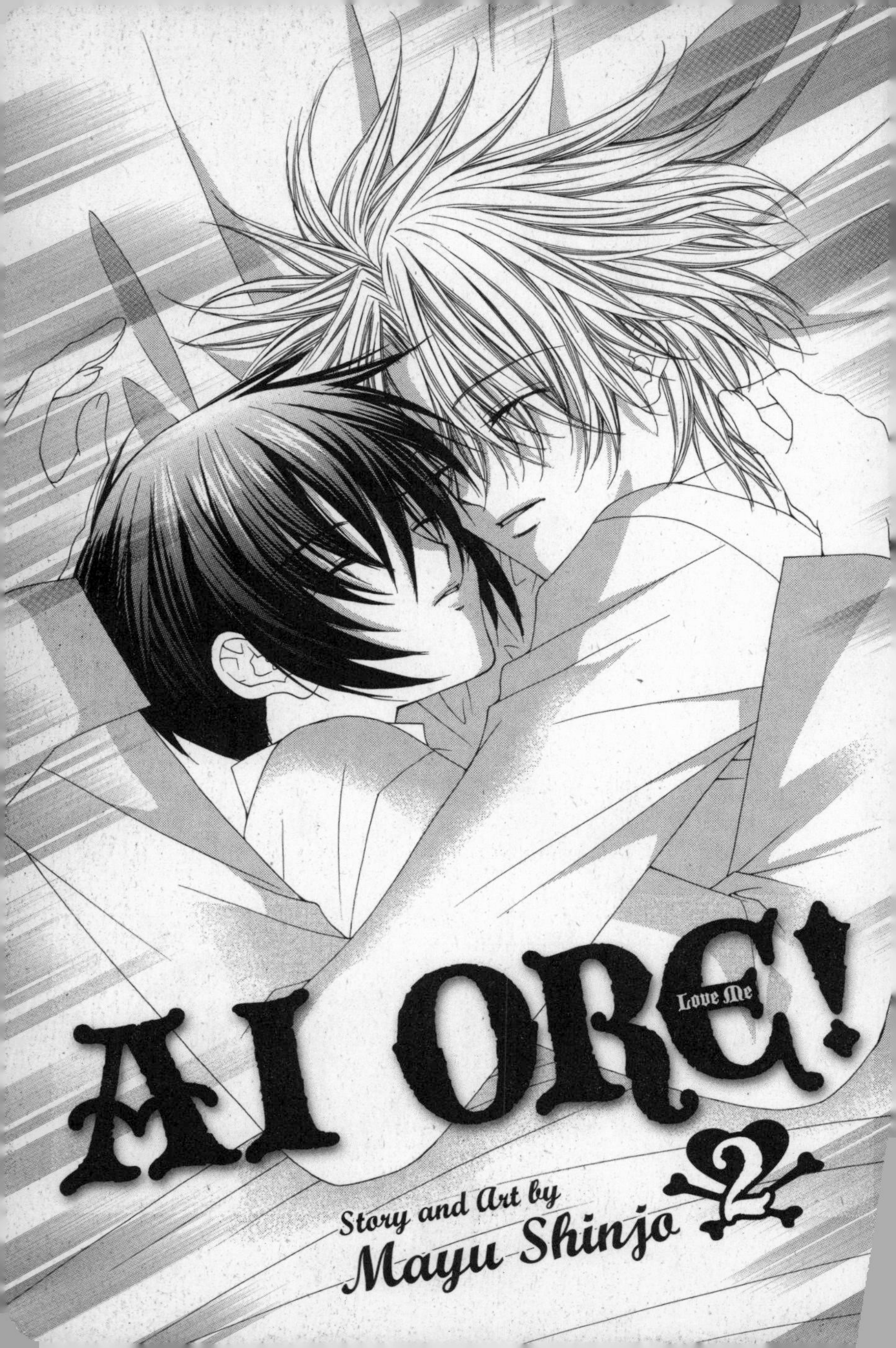
AI ORE!
Love Me
2
Story and Art by
Mayu Shinjo

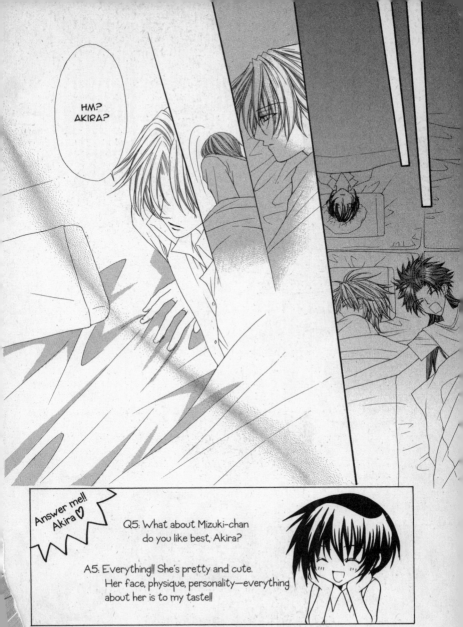

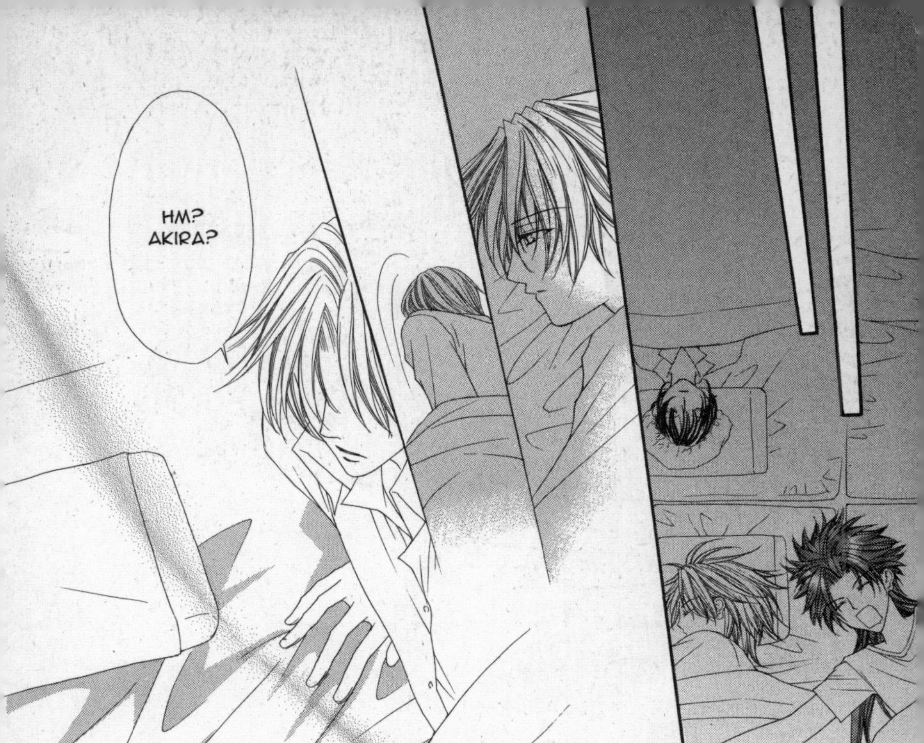
HM? AKIRA?

Answer me!! Akira♡

Q5: What about Mizuki-chan do you like best, Akira?

A5: Everything!! She's pretty and cute. Her face, physique, personality—everything about her is to my taste!!

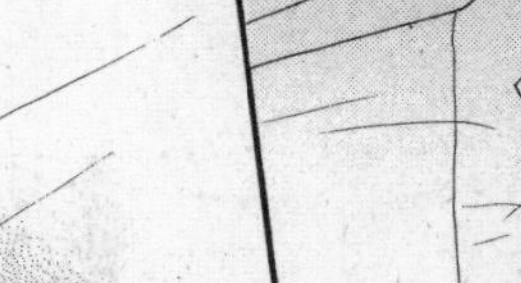

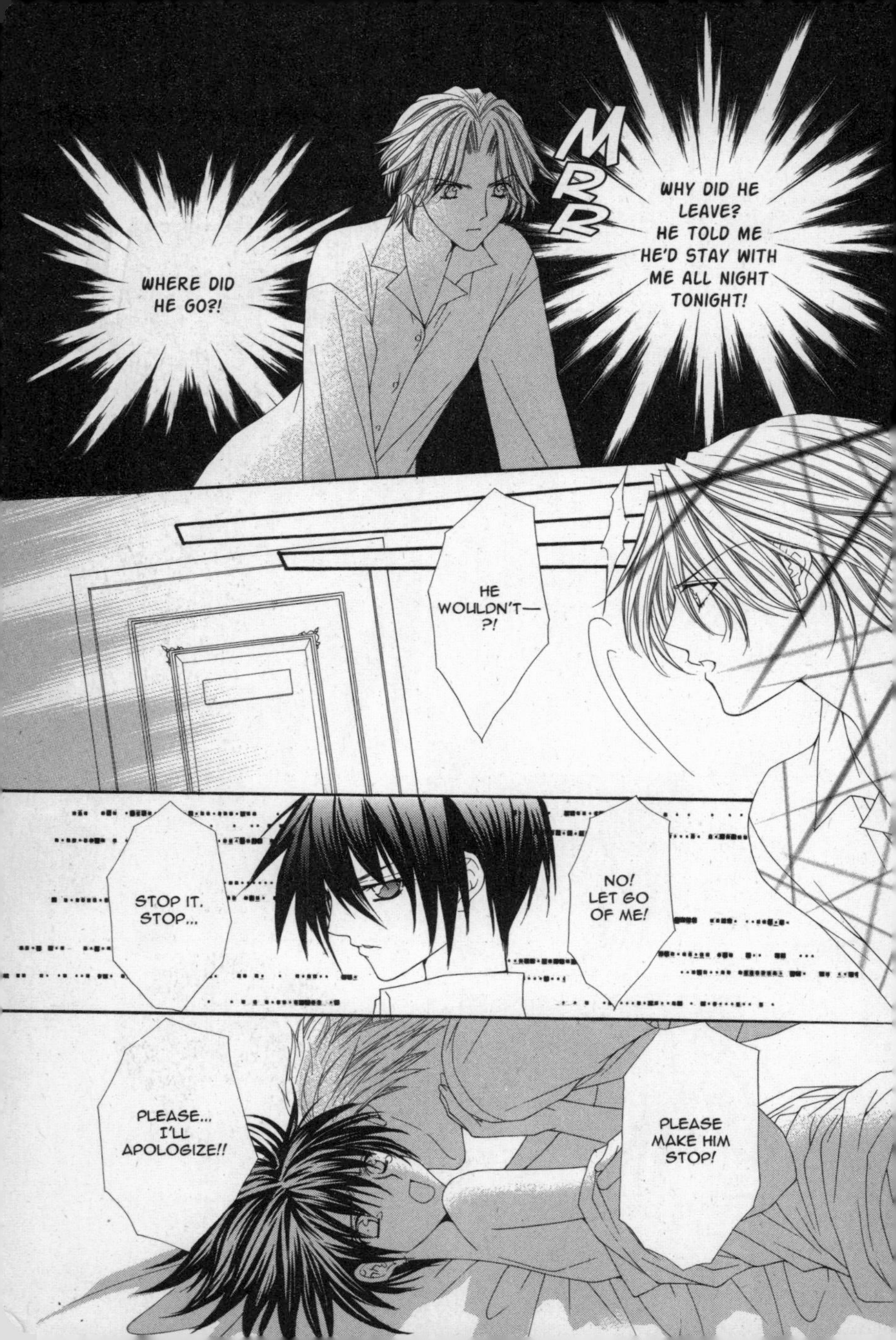
MRR
WHY DID HE LEAVE? HE TOLD ME HE'D STAY WITH ME ALL NIGHT TONIGHT!
WHERE DID HE GO?!
HE WOULDN'T— ?!
NO! LET GO OF ME!
STOP IT. STOP...
PLEASE MAKE HIM STOP!
PLEASE... I'LL APOLOGIZE!!

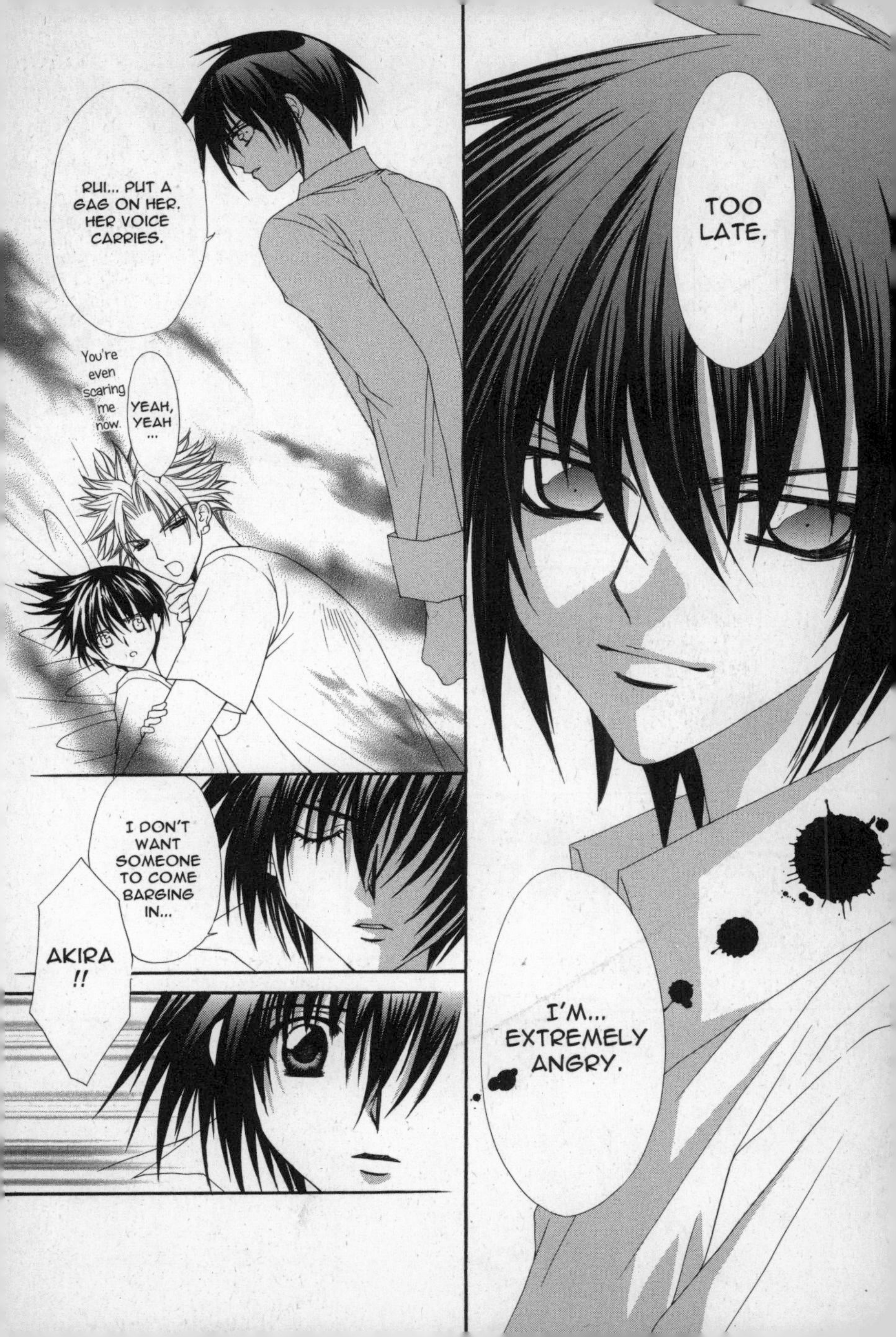
TOO LATE.
I'M... EXTREMELY ANGRY.
RUI... PUT A GAG ON HER. HER VOICE CARRIES.
YEAH, YEAH ...
You're even scaring me now.
I DON'T WANT SOMEONE TO COME BARGING IN...
AKIRA !!

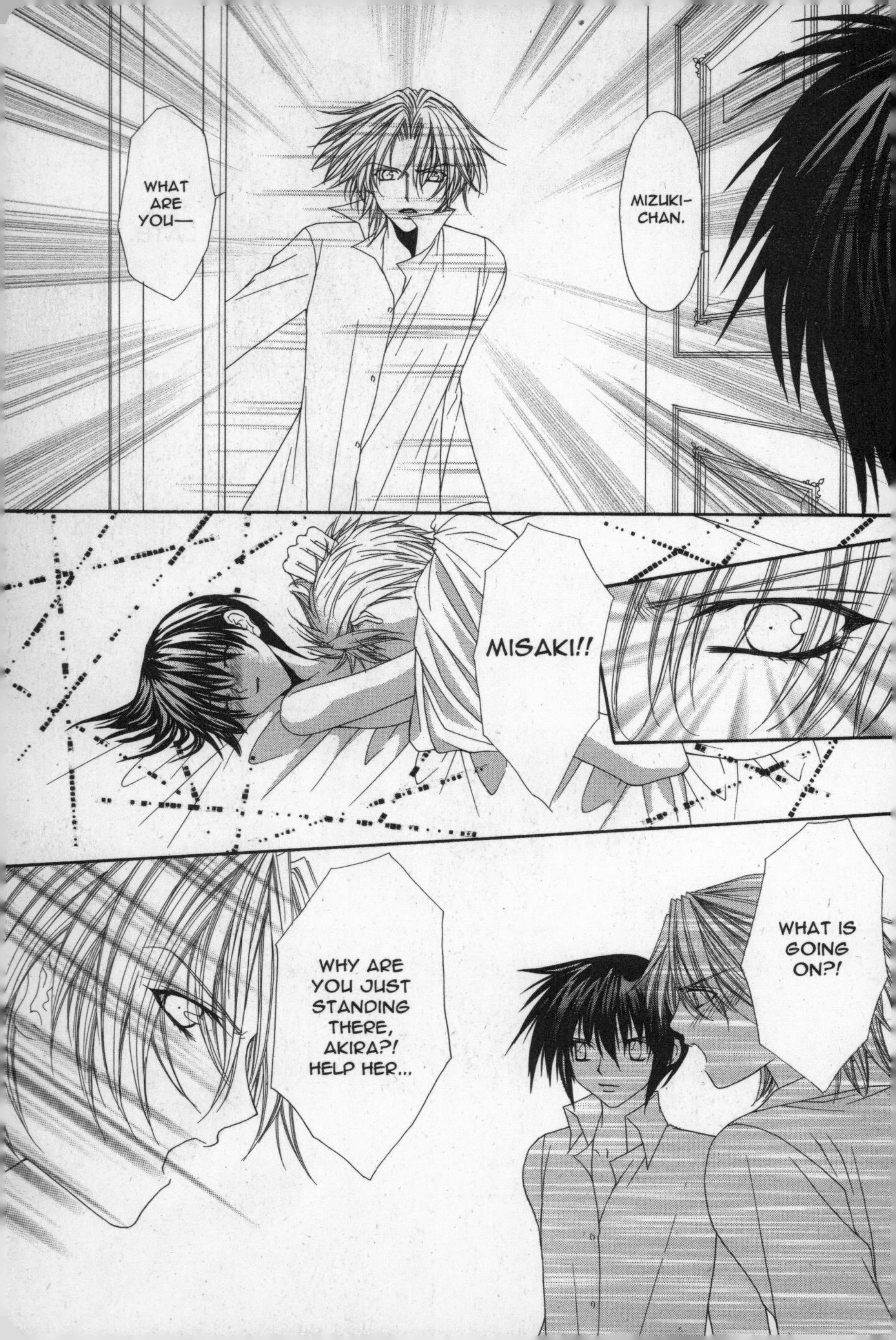
MIZUKI-CHAN.
WHAT ARE YOU—
MISAKI!!
WHAT IS GOING ON?!
WHY ARE YOU JUST STANDING THERE, AKIRA?! HELP HER...

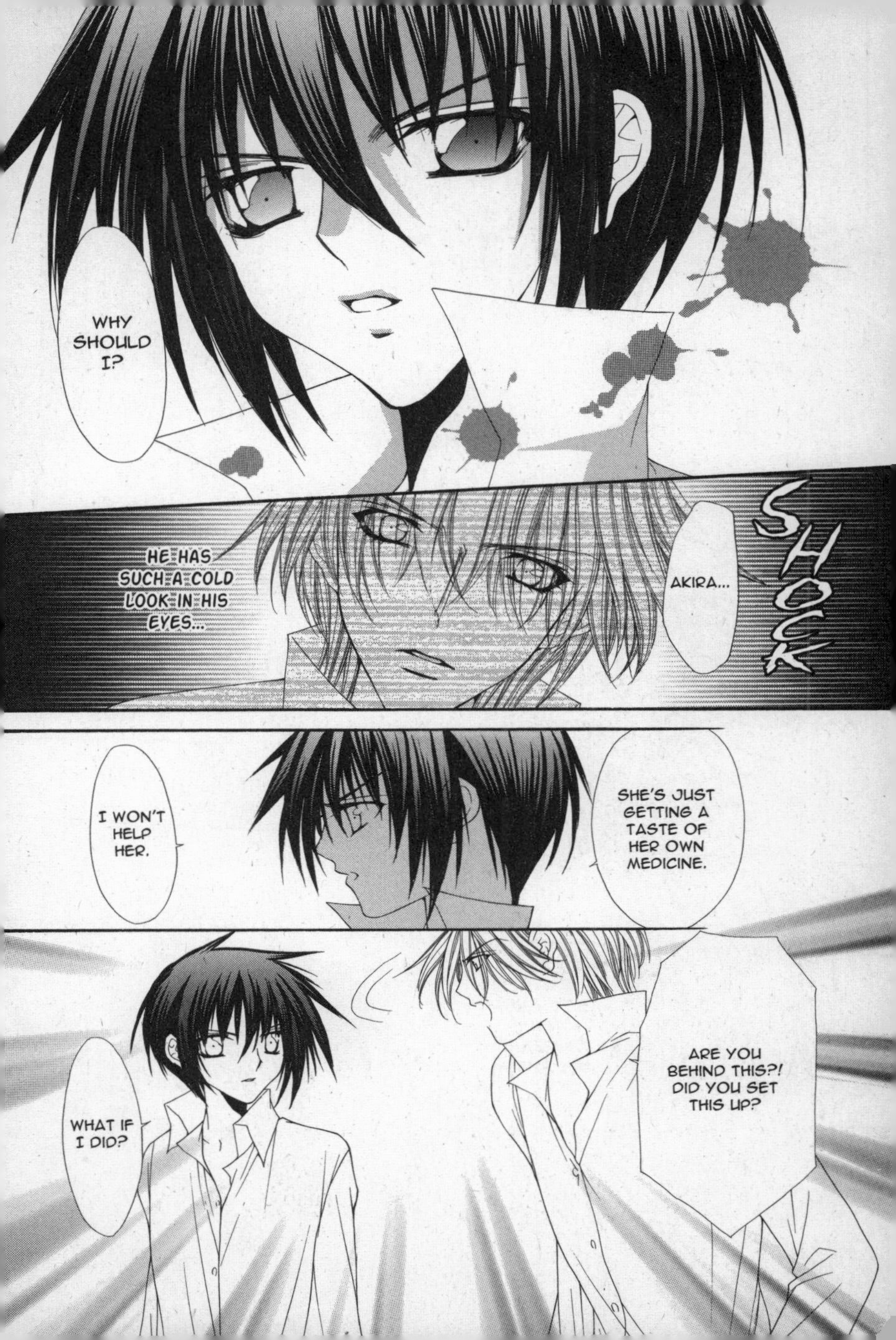
WHY SHOULD I?
SHOCK
AKIRA...
HE HAS SUCH A COLD LOOK IN HIS EYES...
SHE'S JUST GETTING A TASTE OF HER OWN MEDICINE.
I WON'T HELP HER.
ARE YOU BEHIND THIS?! DID YOU SET THIS UP?
WHAT IF I DID?

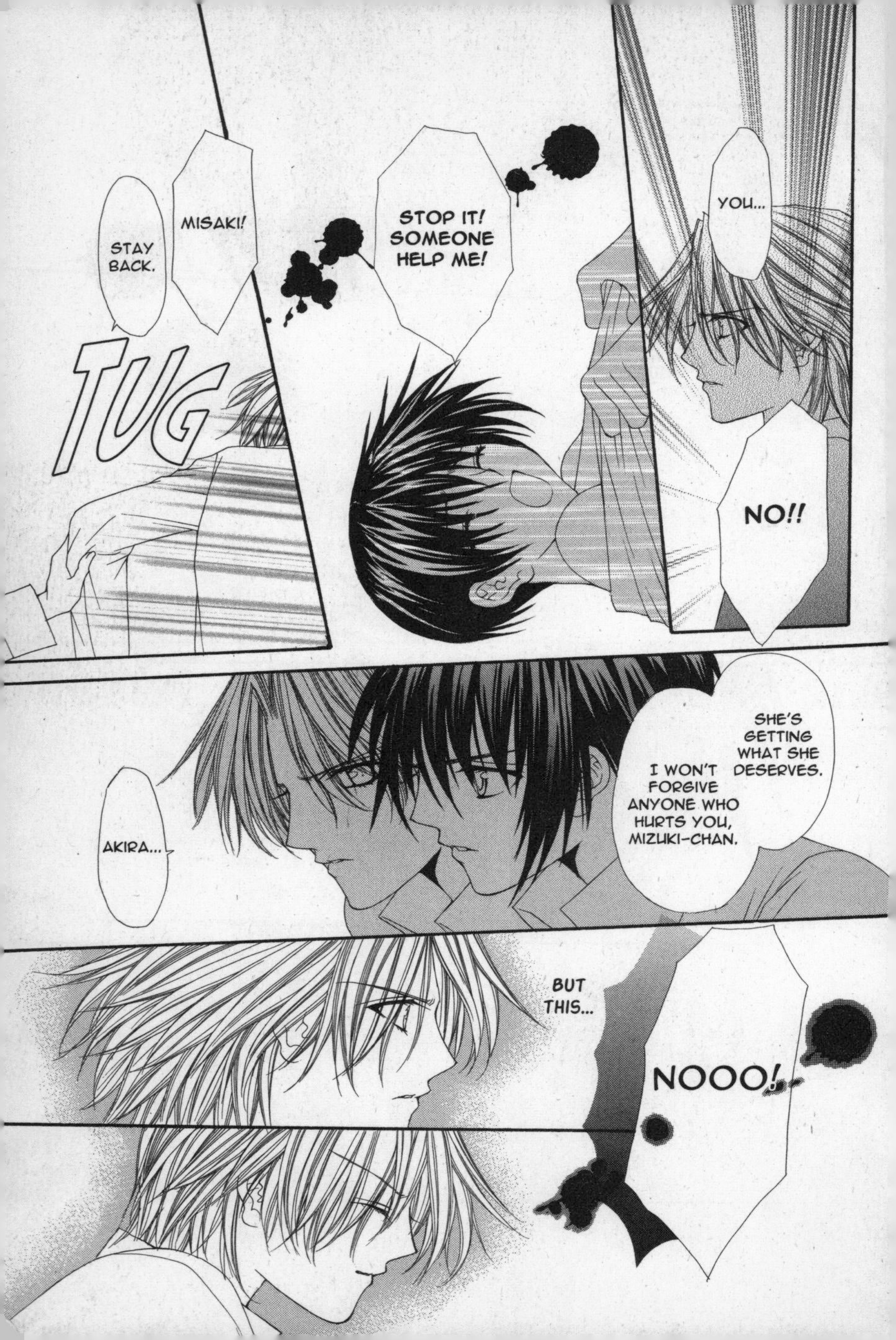
YOU...
NO!!
STOP IT! SOMEONE HELP ME!
MISAKI!
STAY BACK.
TUG
SHE'S GETTING WHAT SHE DESERVES.
I WON'T FORGIVE ANYONE WHO HURTS YOU, MIZUKI-CHAN.
AKIRA...
NOOO!
BUT THIS...

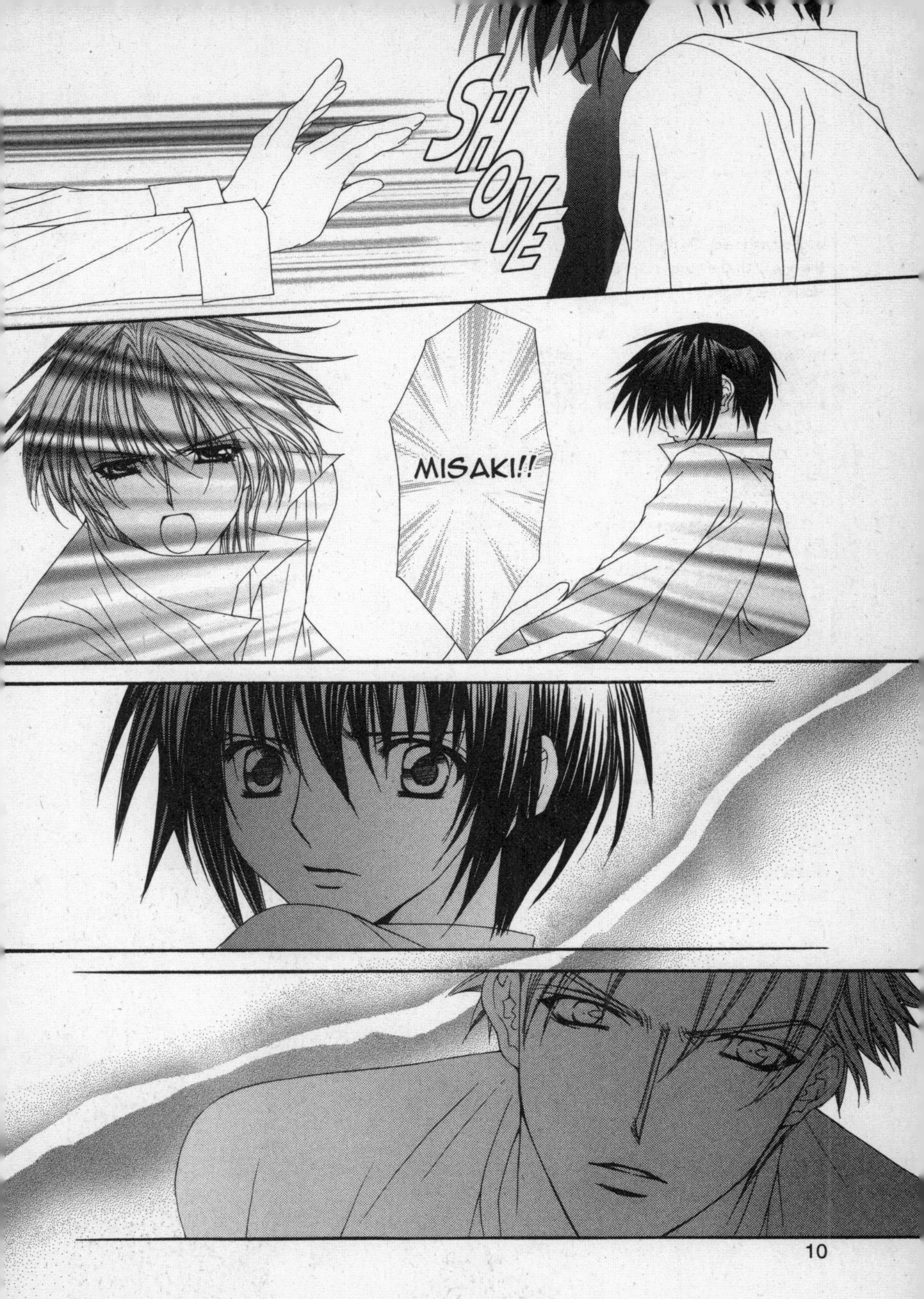
SHOVE
MISAKI!!

After that, I felt bad for Ishida-san because Ran is such a pervert. I told him, "I'm sorry you have to do such a tough role," but he just laughed and said, "Oh no, I'm not the one with the tough role. It's Hoshi." He's right...

Shinjo's selection of moe lines said by Ran:
"You're the solitary rose blooming in this crap heap that is Dankaisan Boys High School. You are our dream, our hope, our Princess!"
"Our Akira is so cute!!"
"You're going to let what despoil Akira's chastity?!"
...Oh? Shinjo-san? You sound like a fujoshi. (laugh)

Next up is Takahiro Sakurai, whom you all know as Santa from *Sensual Phrase*. It had been some time since I last met him, so we had a long conversation. I'll write about that on another page!!
And... On the topic of *Sensual Phrase*, Λucifer's Makoto makes a cameo appearance in this drama CD!!
And although this isn't something I like to admit, I too have a small part in it... (Ack!) I'd like you to fast-forward my part and just skip it completely!! (laugh)
The Ai Ore drama CD "On the Verge of Drowning?! A Hot-Spring Vacation with Friends" will come out from Sony Music Aniplex on October 18th!!

[The drama CDs are Japanese-only, but you can purchase them from online retailers. -Ed]

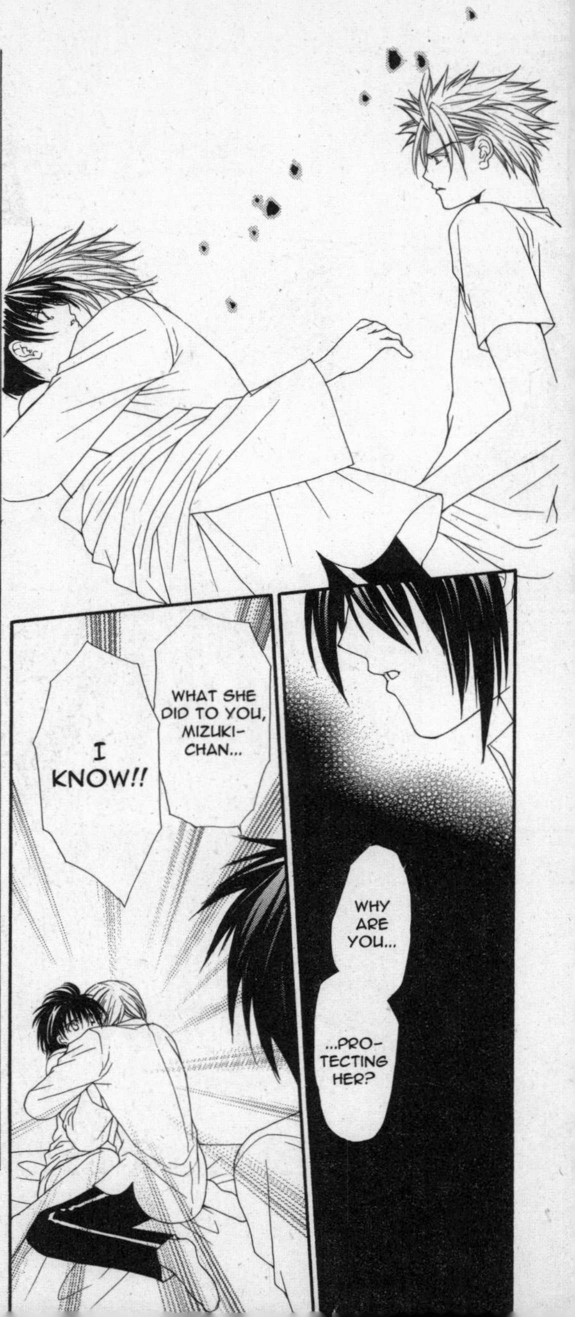
WHY ARE YOU...
...PROTECTING HER?
WHAT SHE DID TO YOU, MIZUKI-CHAN...
I KNOW!!

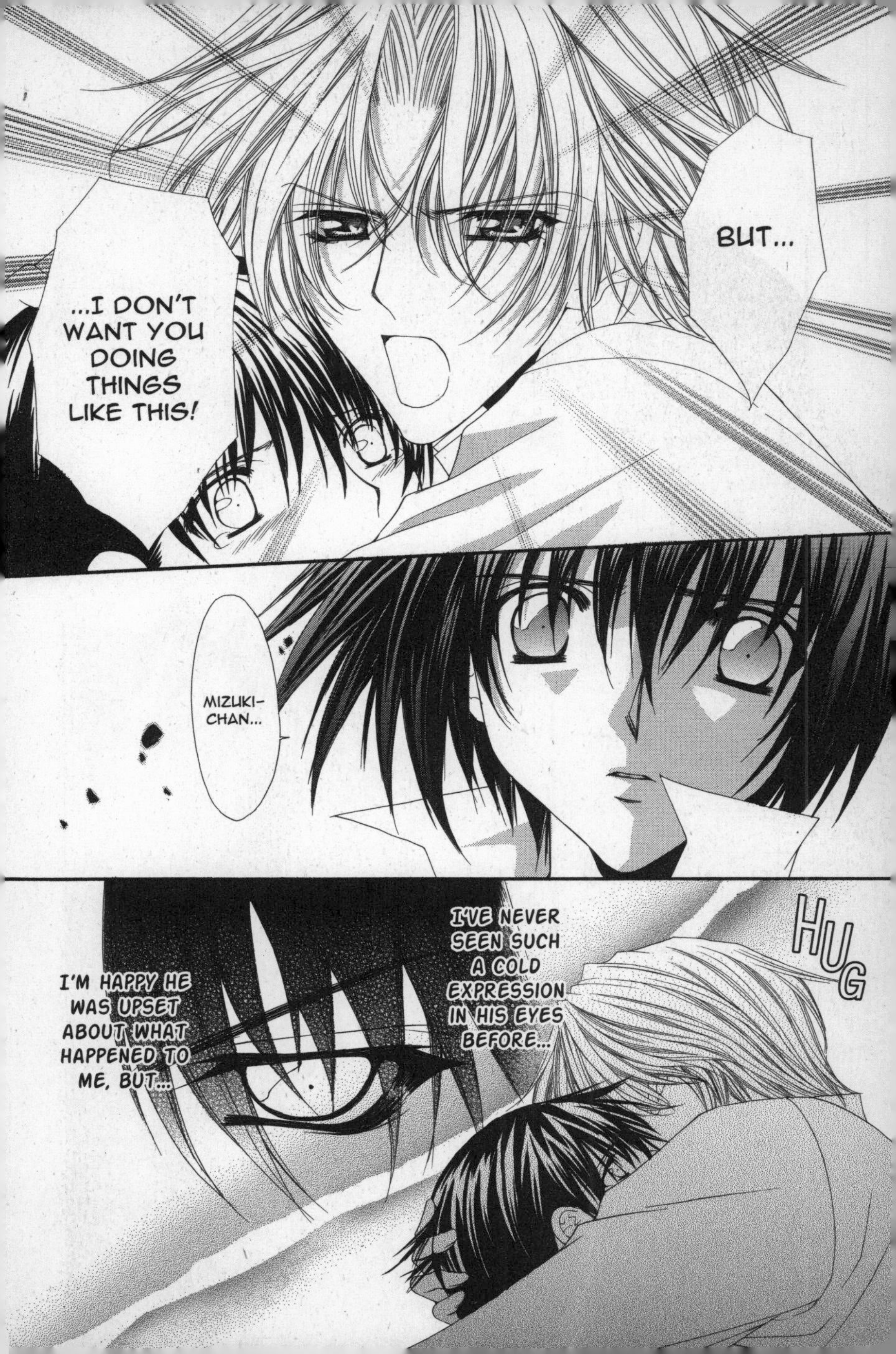
BUT...
...I DON'T WANT YOU DOING THINGS LIKE THIS!
MIZUKI-CHAN...
HUG
I'VE NEVER SEEN SUCH A COLD EXPRESSION IN HIS EYES BEFORE...
I'M HAPPY HE WAS UPSET ABOUT WHAT HAPPENED TO ME, BUT...

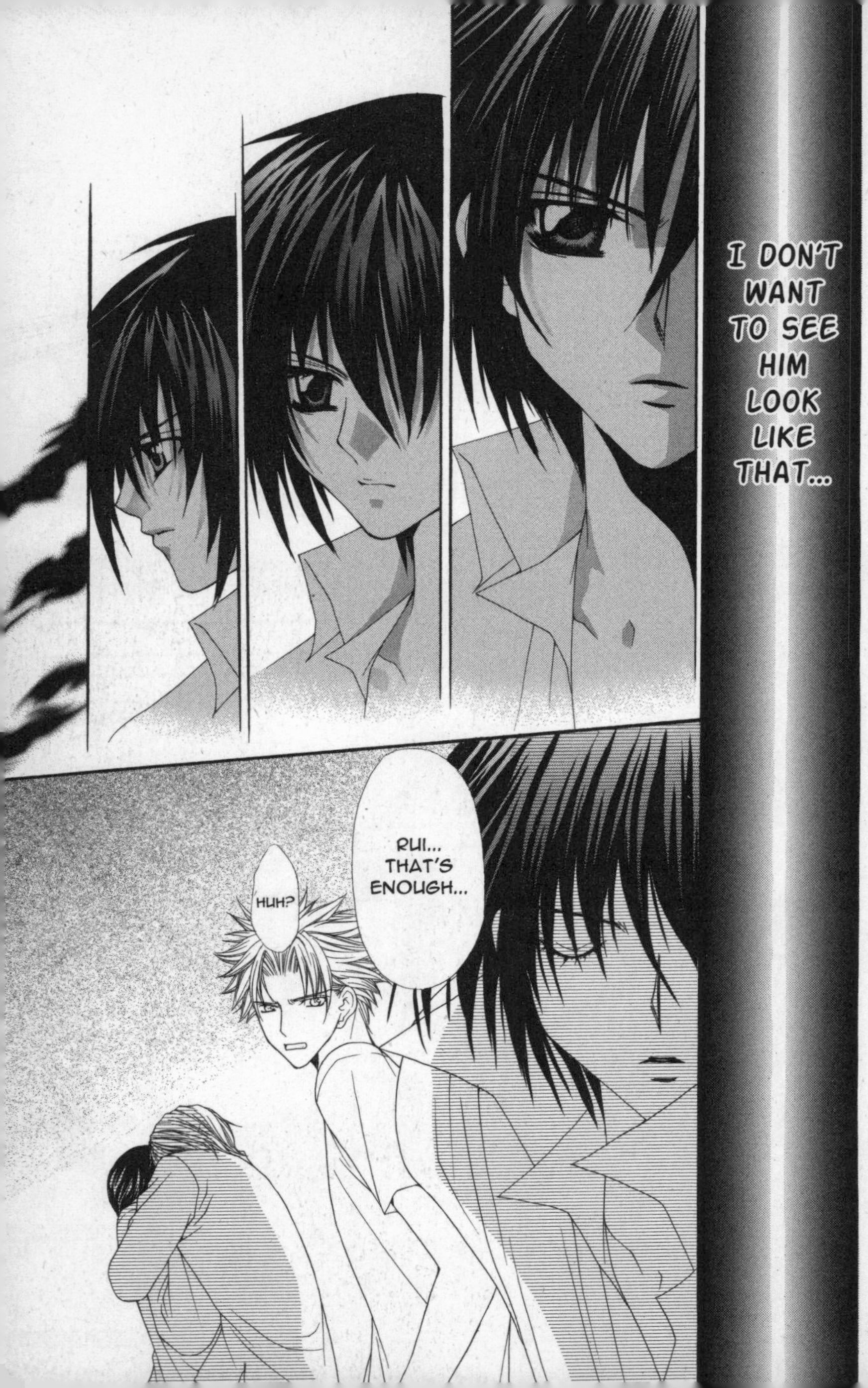
I DON'T WANT TO SEE HIM LOOK LIKE THAT...
RUI... THAT'S ENOUGH...
HUH?

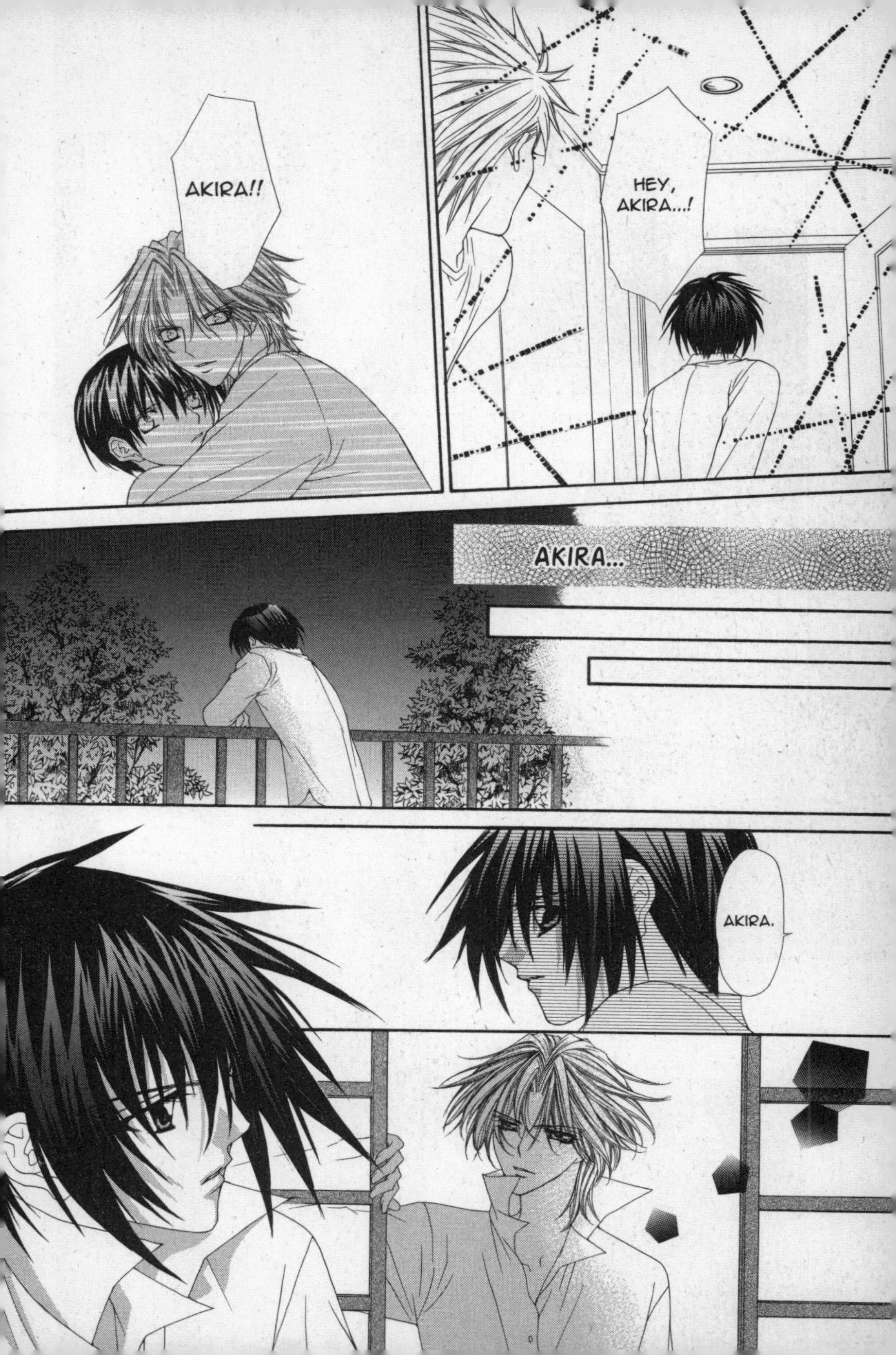
HEY, AKIRA...!
AKIRA!!
AKIRA...
AKIRA.

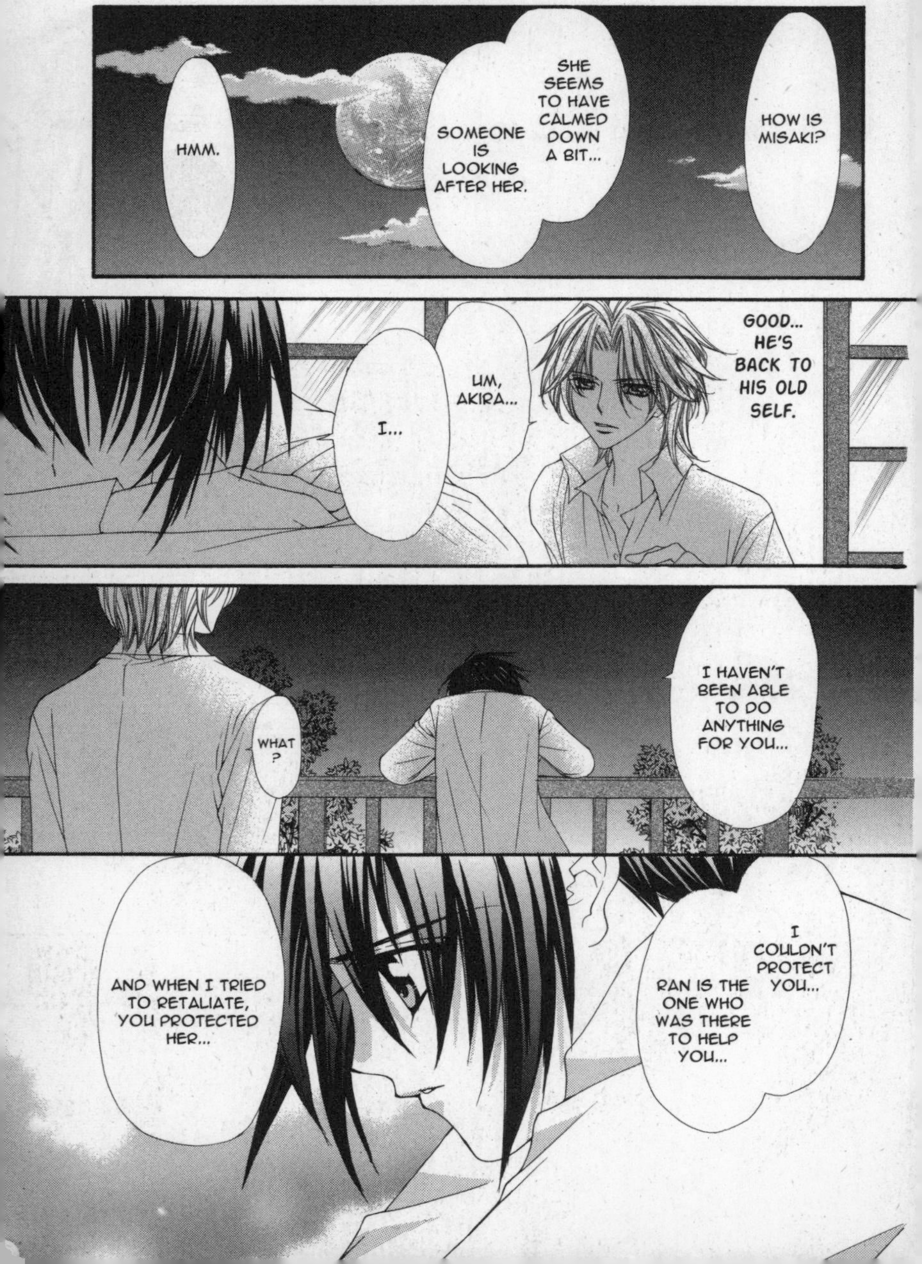
HOW IS MISAKI?
SHE SEEMS TO HAVE CALMED DOWN A BIT...
SOMEONE IS LOOKING AFTER HER.
HMM.
GOOD... HE'S BACK TO HIS OLD SELF.
UM, AKIRA...
I...
I HAVEN'T BEEN ABLE TO DO ANYTHING FOR YOU...
WHAT?
I COULDN'T PROTECT YOU...
RAN IS THE ONE WHO WAS THERE TO HELP YOU...
AND WHEN I TRIED TO RETALIATE, YOU PROTECTED HER...

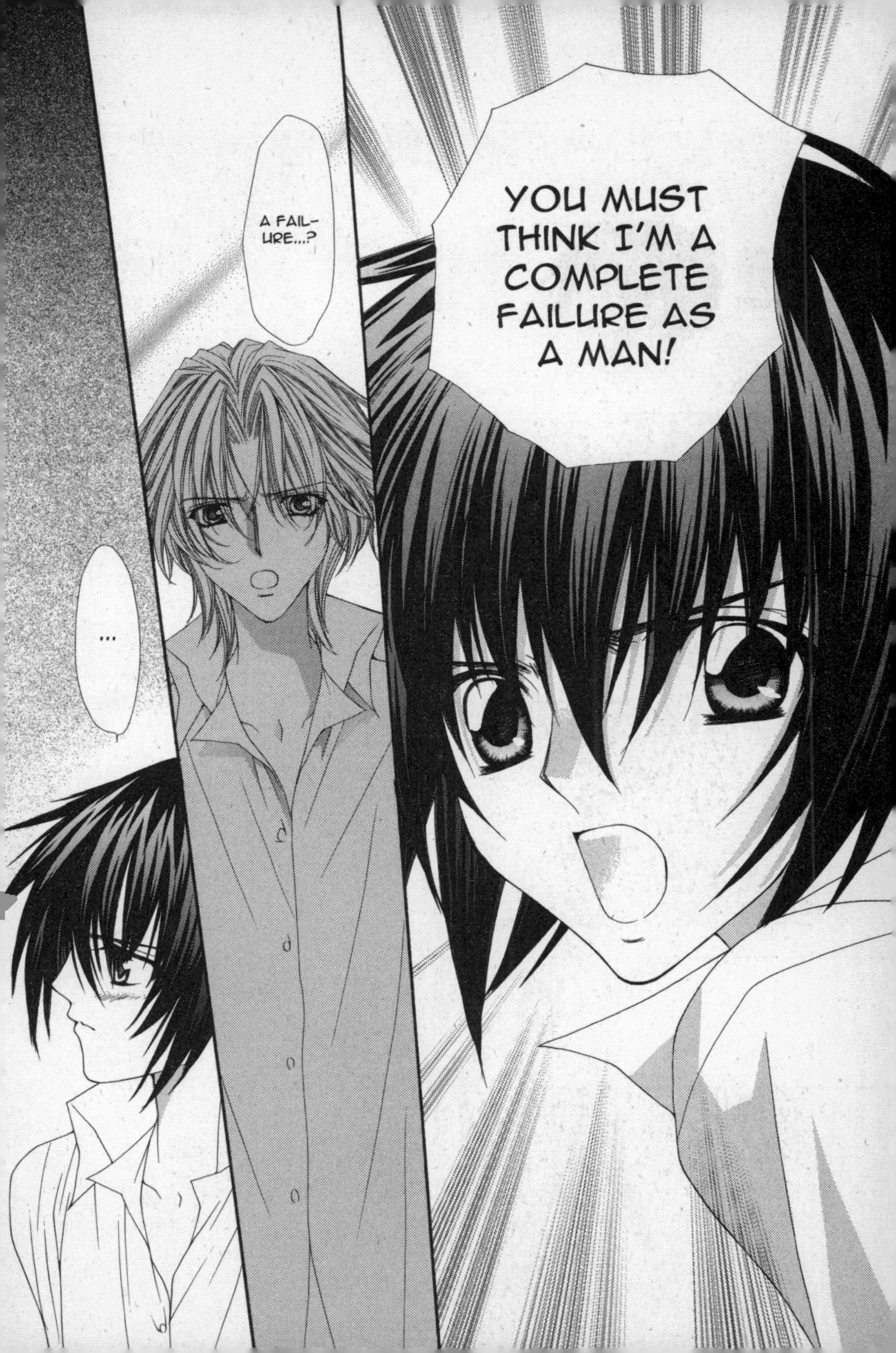
YOU MUST THINK I'M A COMPLETE FAILURE AS A MAN!
A FAIL-URE...?
...

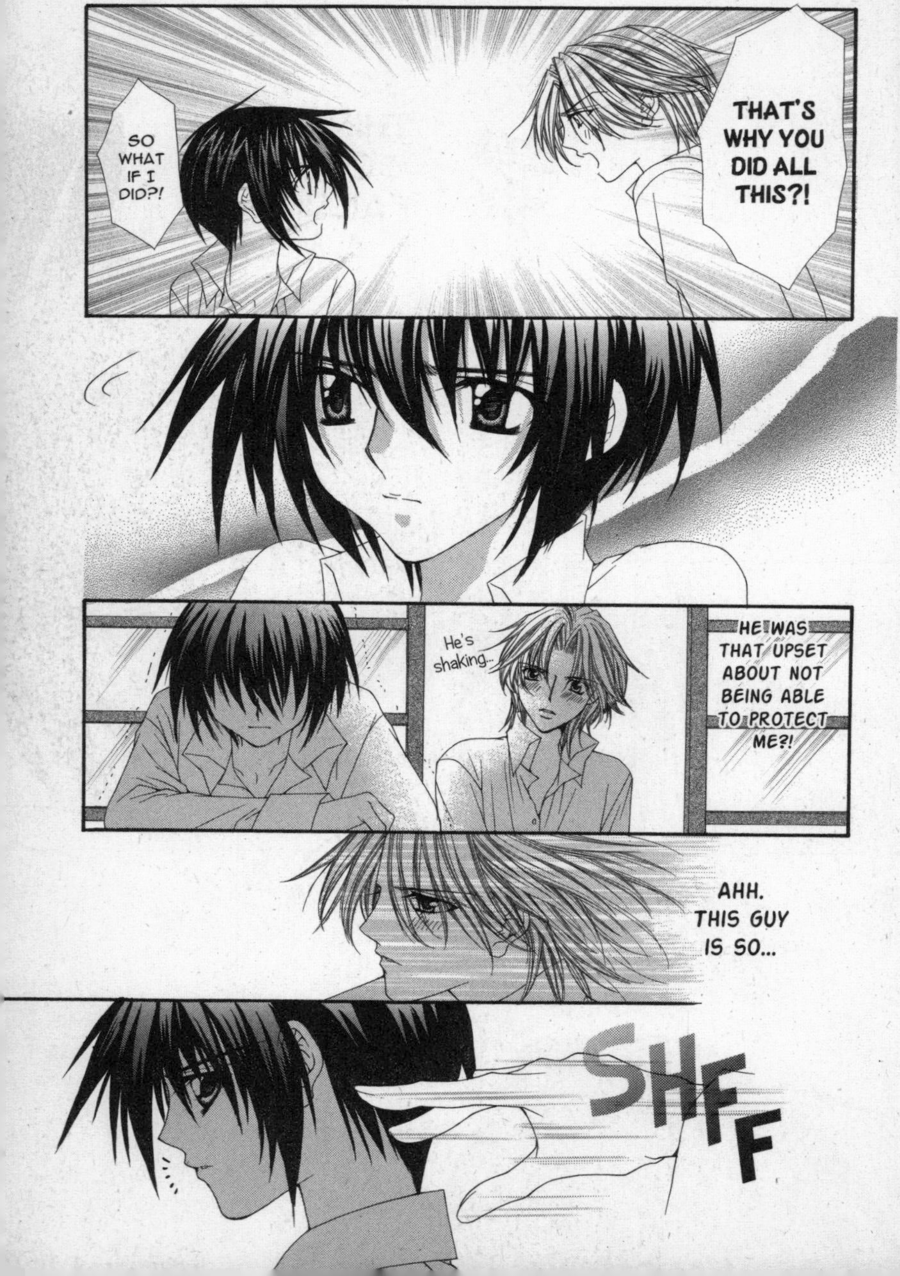
THAT'S WHY YOU DID ALL THIS?!
SO WHAT IF I DID?!
HE WAS THAT UPSET ABOUT NOT BEING ABLE TO PROTECT ME?!
He's shaking...
AHH. THIS GUY IS SO...
SHFF

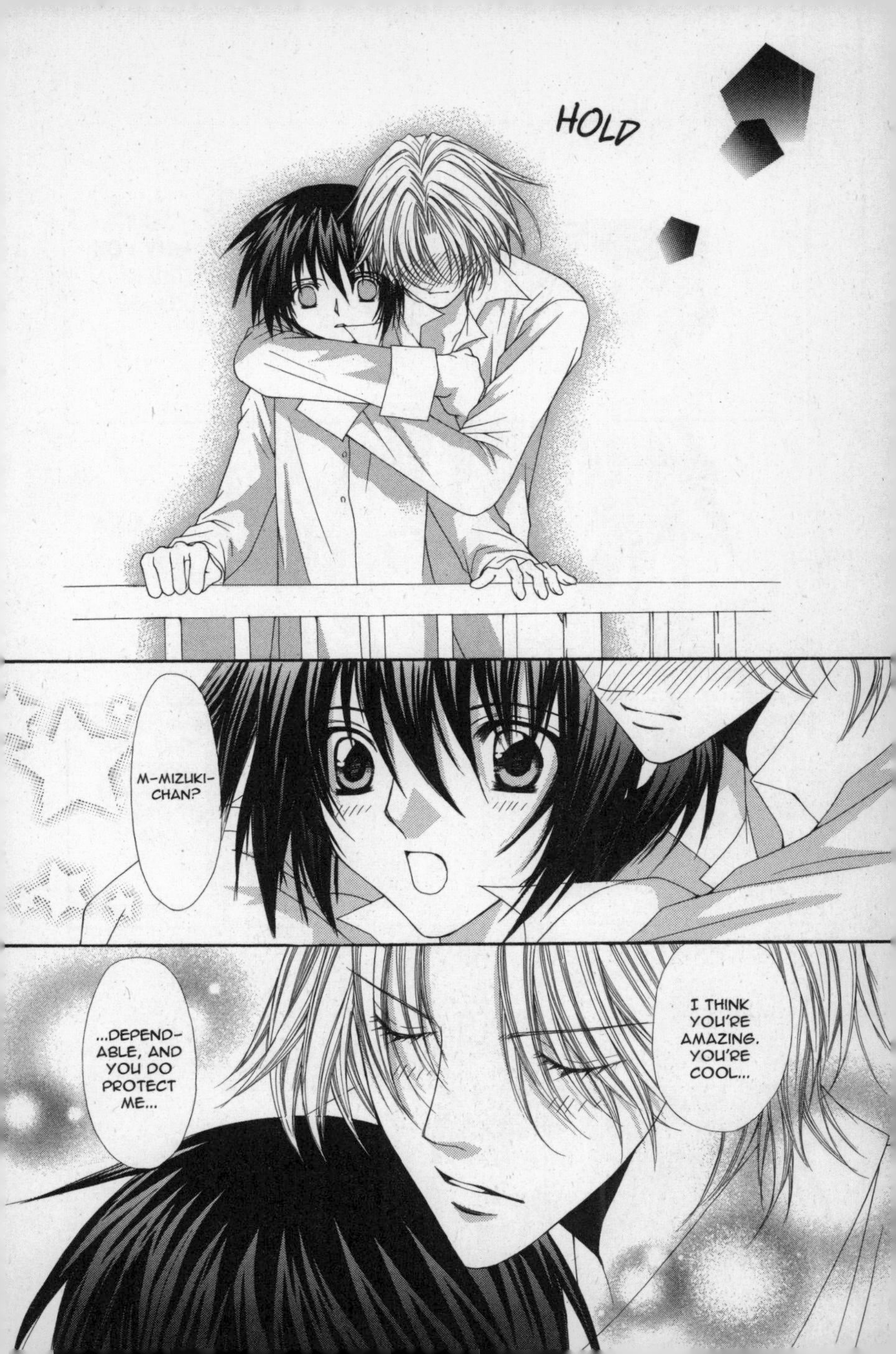
HOLD
M-MIZUKI-CHAN?
I THINK YOU'RE AMAZING. YOU'RE COOL...
...DEPEND-ABLE, AND YOU DO PROTECT ME...

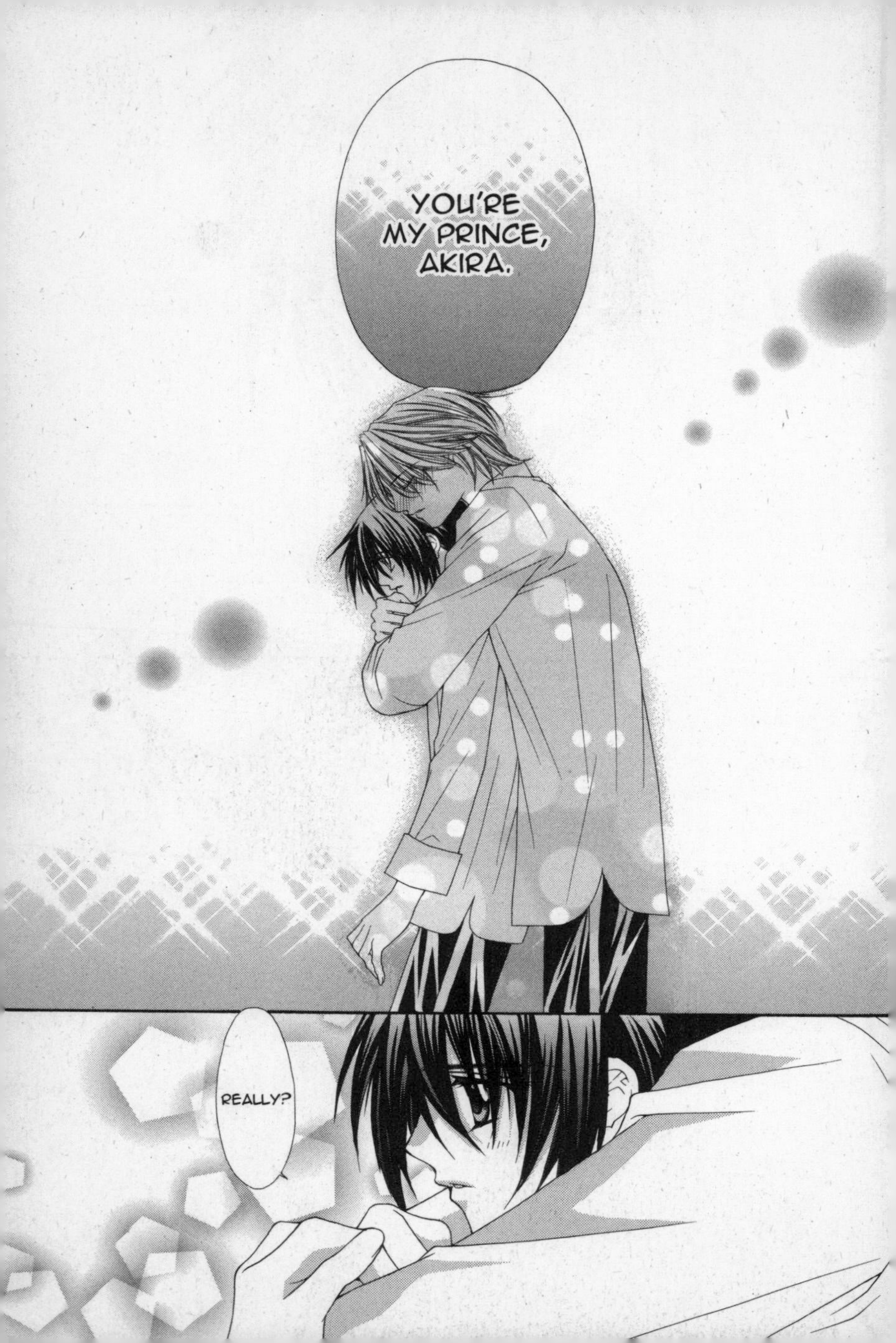
YOU'RE MY PRINCE, AKIRA.
REALLY?

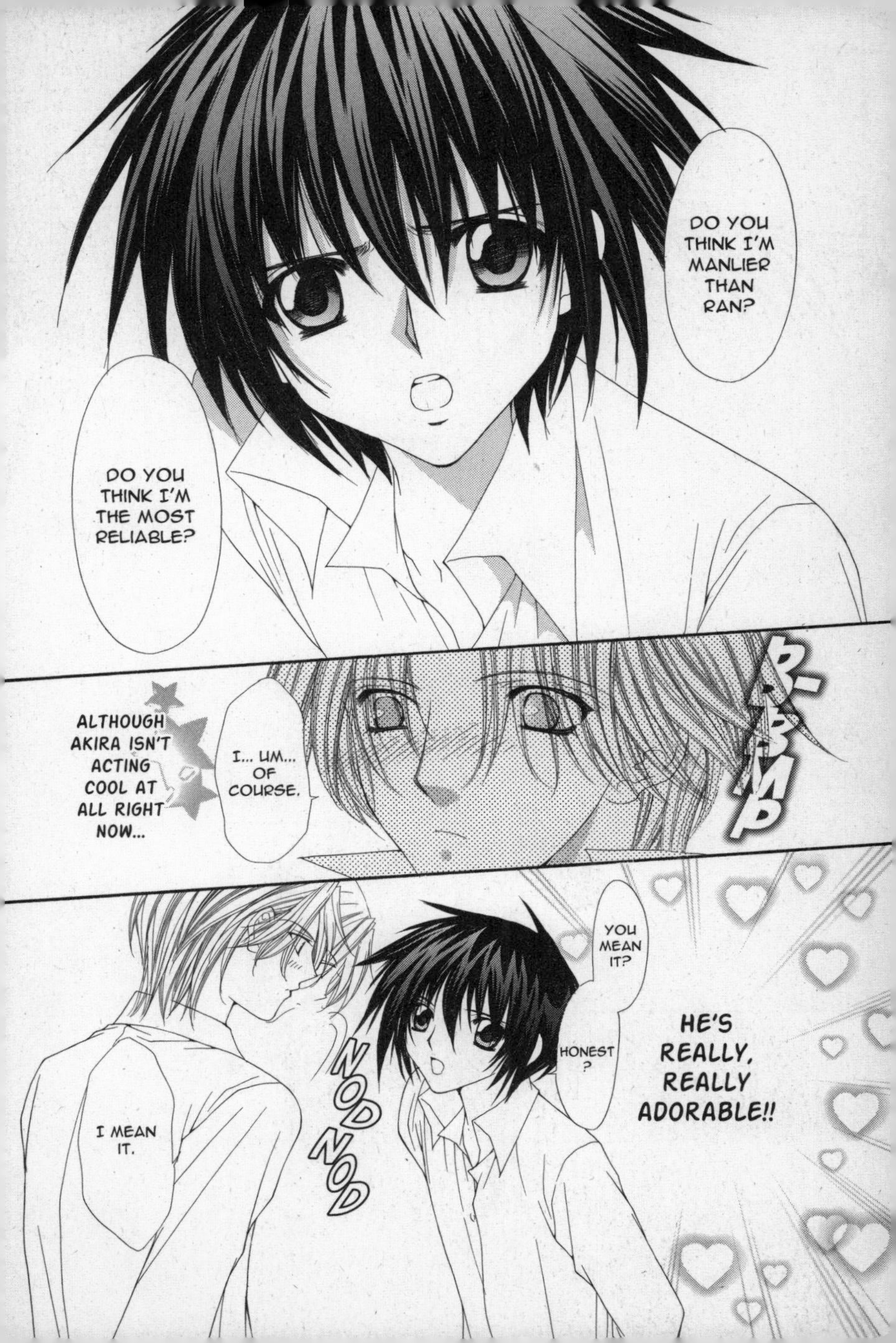
DO YOU THINK I'M MANLIER THAN RAN?
DO YOU THINK I'M THE MOST RELIABLE?
B-BMP
I... UM... OF COURSE.
ALTHOUGH AKIRA ISN'T ACTING COOL AT ALL RIGHT NOW...
YOU MEAN IT?
HE'S REALLY, REALLY ADORABLE!!
HONEST?
NOD NOD
I MEAN IT.

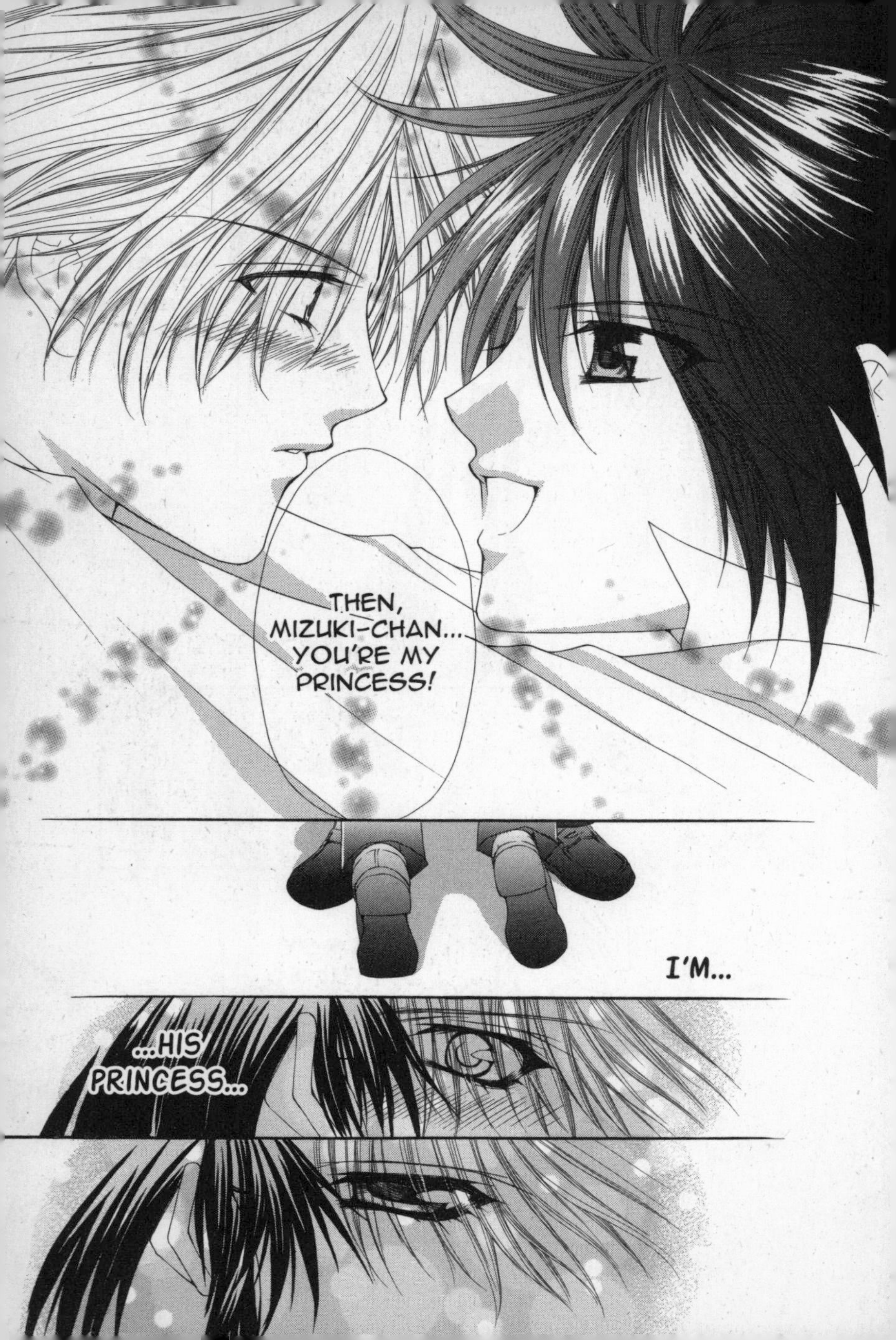
THEN, MIZUKI-CHAN... YOU'RE MY PRINCESS!
I'M...
...HIS PRINCESS...

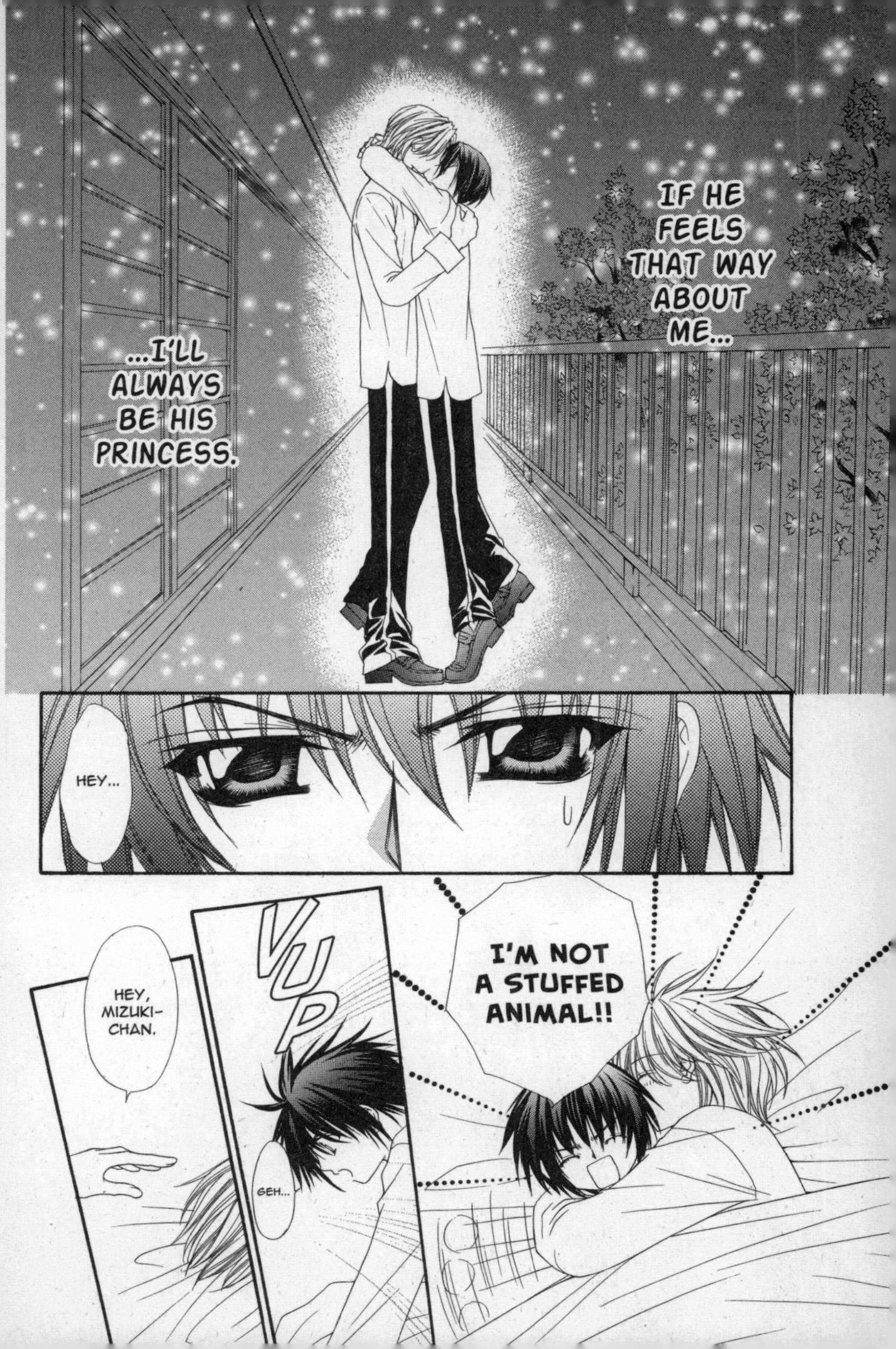
IF HE FEELS THAT WAY ABOUT ME...
...I'LL ALWAYS BE HIS PRINCESS.
HEY...
I'M NOT A STUFFED ANIMAL!!
VUP
GEH...
HEY, MIZUKI-CHAN.

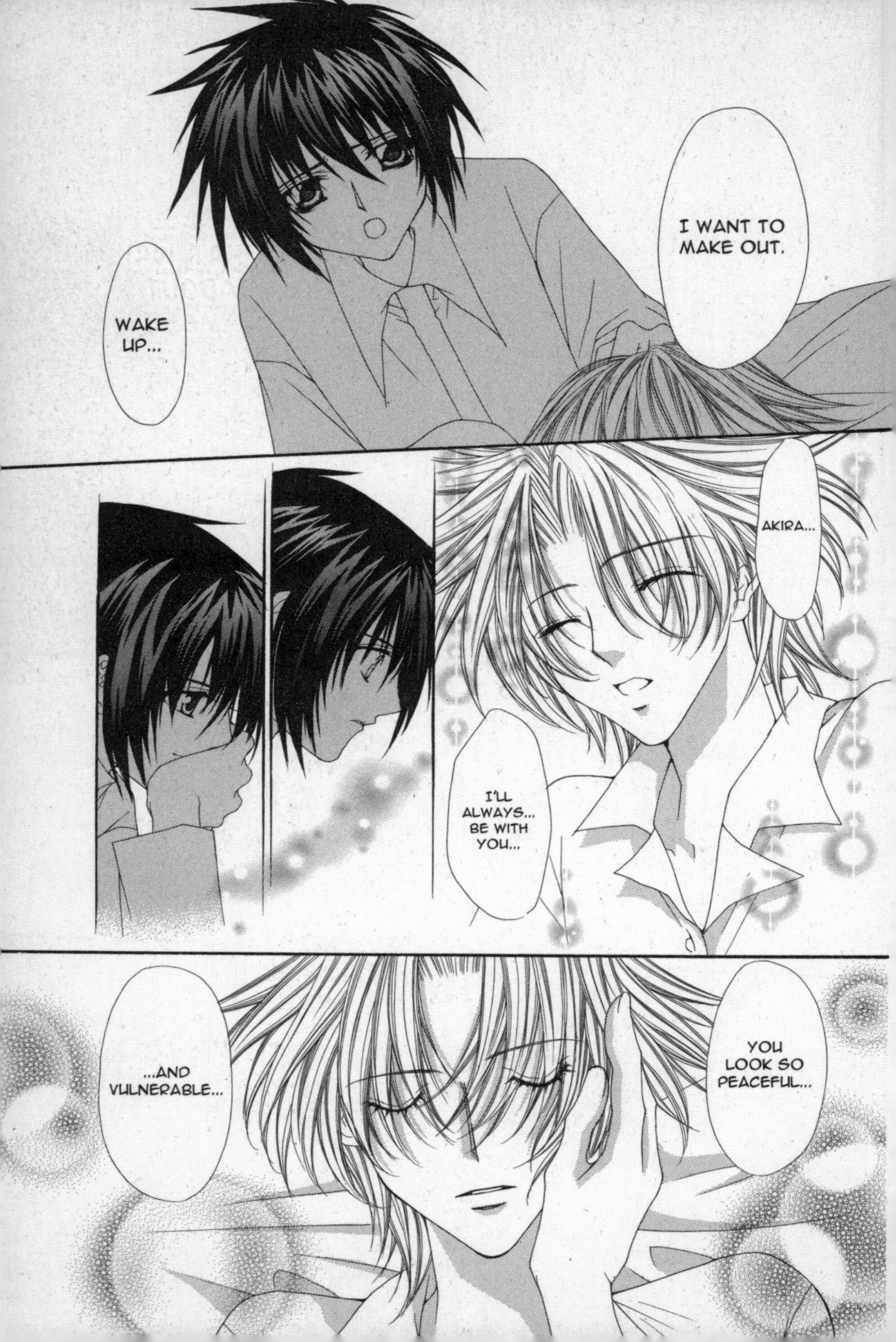
I WANT TO MAKE OUT.
WAKE UP...
AKIRA...
I'LL ALWAYS... BE WITH YOU...
YOU LOOK SO PEACEFUL...
...AND VULNERABLE...

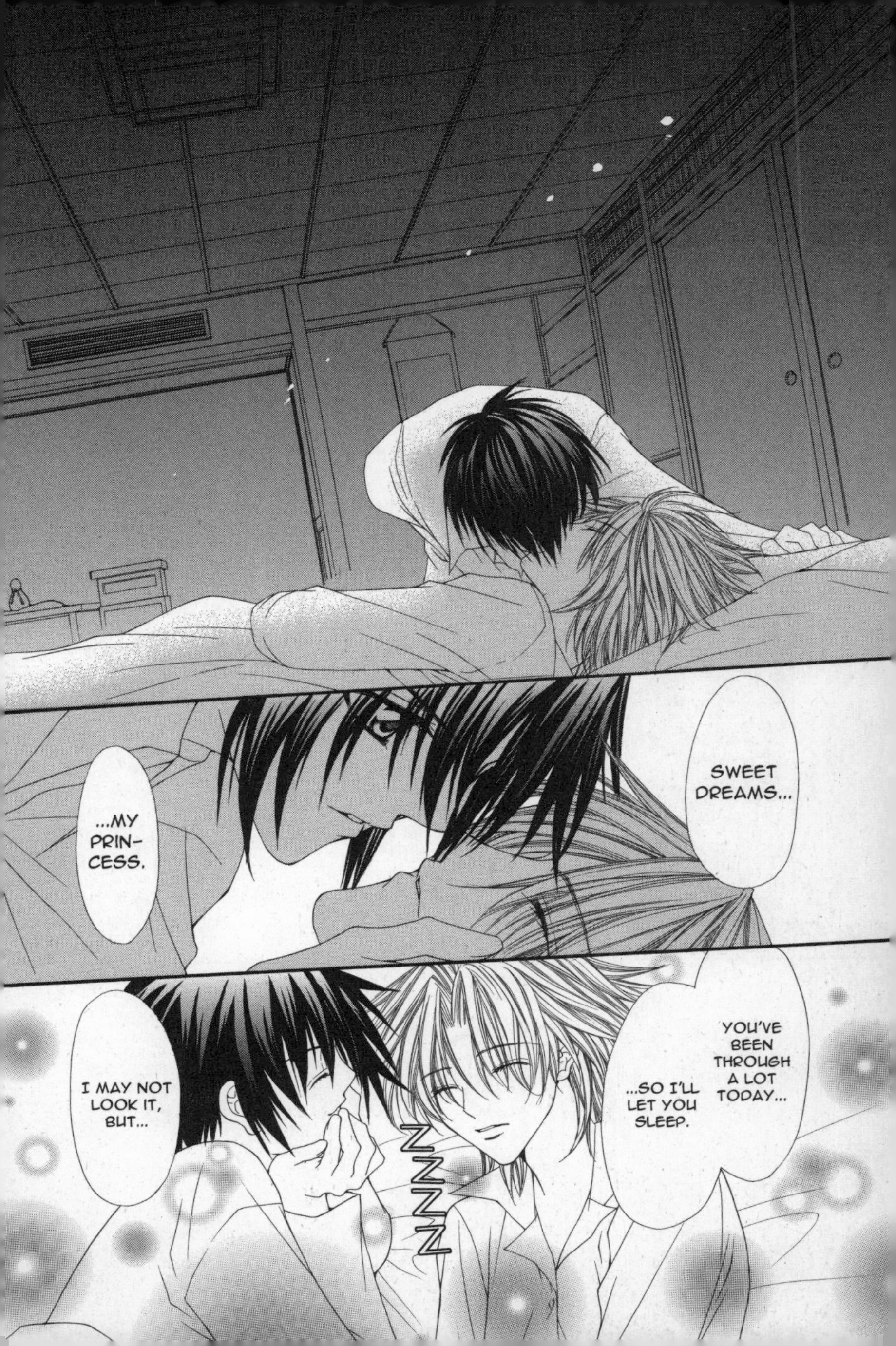
SWEET DREAMS...
...MY PRINCESS.
YOU'VE BEEN THROUGH A LOT TODAY...
...SO I'LL LET YOU SLEEP.
ZZZZ
I MAY NOT LOOK IT, BUT...

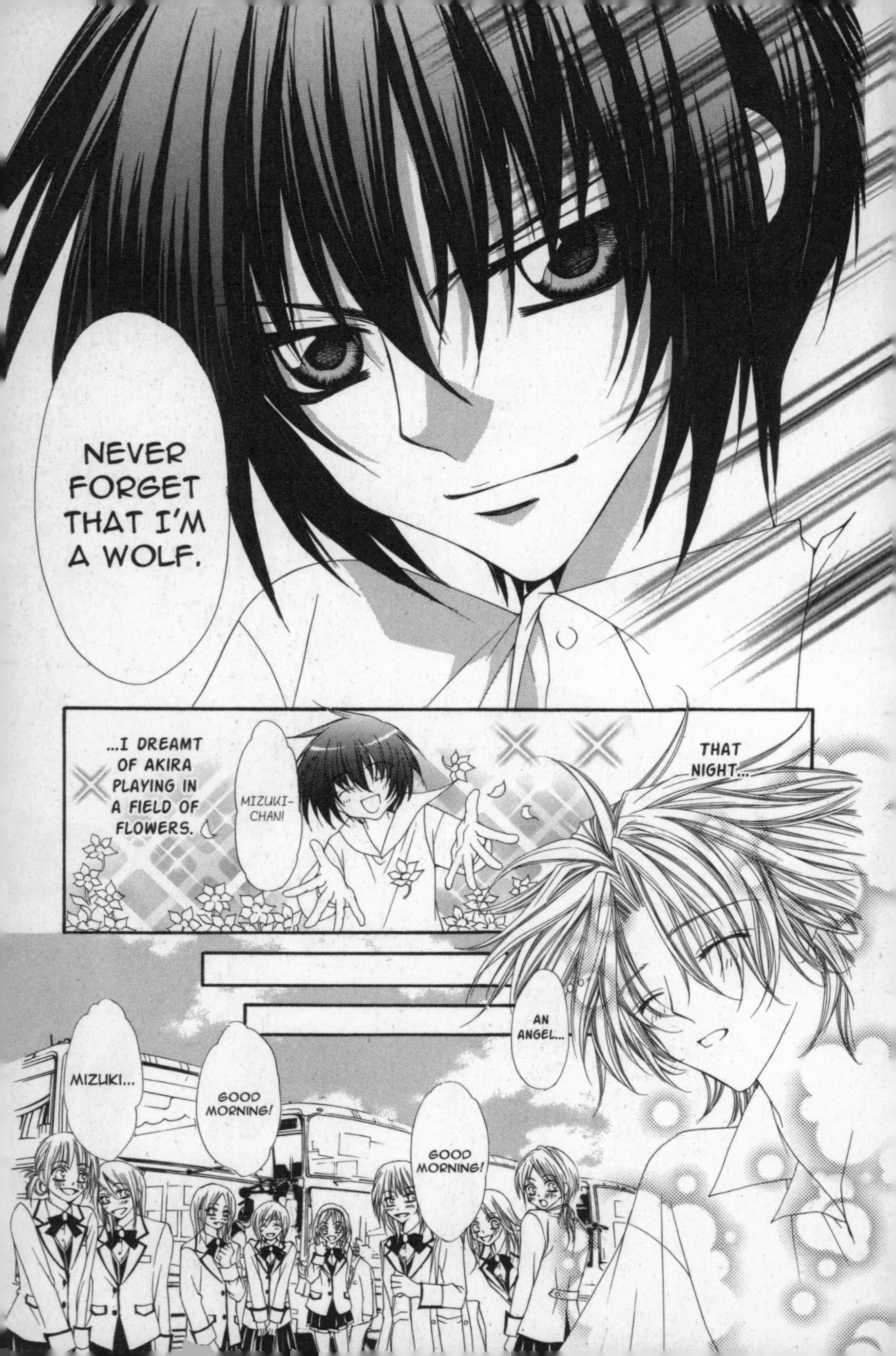
NEVER FORGET THAT I'M A WOLF.
THAT NIGHT...
...I DREAMT OF AKIRA PLAYING IN A FIELD OF FLOWERS.
MIZUKI-CHAN!
AN ANGEL...
GOOD MORNING!
GOOD MORNING!
MIZUKI...

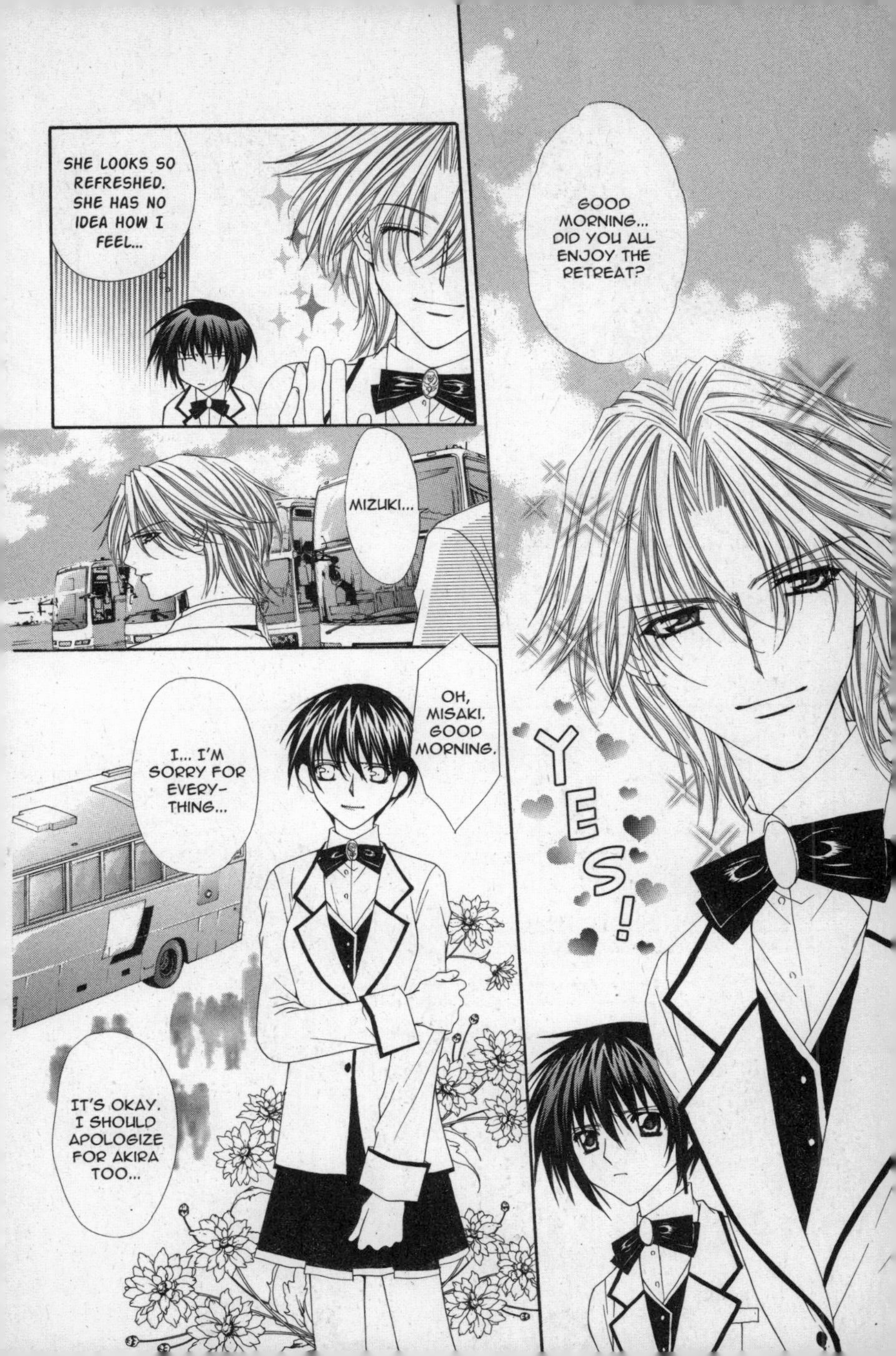
GOOD MORNING... DID YOU ALL ENJOY THE RETREAT?
YES!
SHE LOOKS SO REFRESHED. SHE HAS NO IDEA HOW I FEEL...
MIZUKI...
OH, MISAKI. GOOD MORNING.
I... I'M SORRY FOR EVERY-THING...
IT'S OKAY. I SHOULD APOLOGIZE FOR AKIRA TOO...

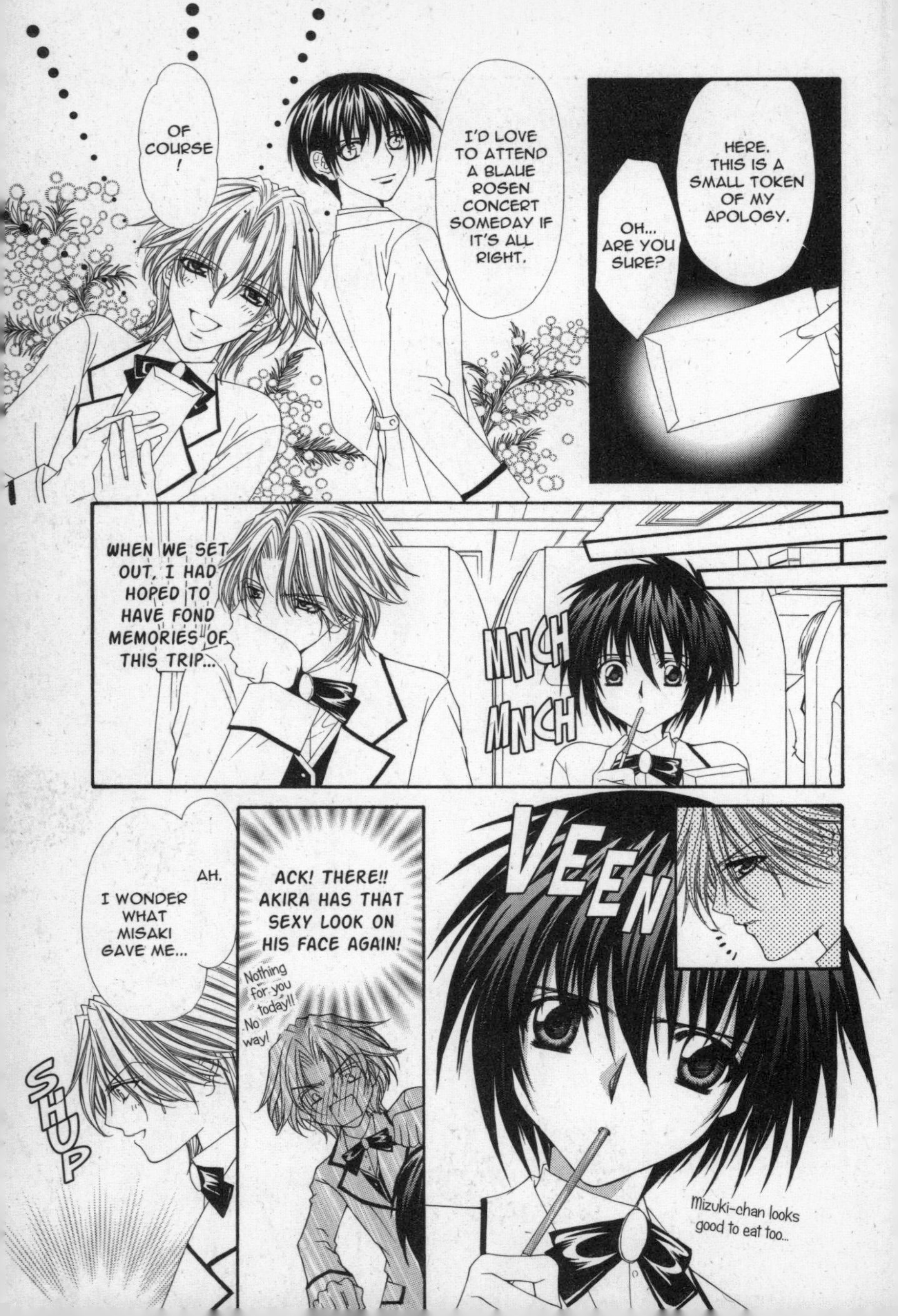
HERE. THIS IS A SMALL TOKEN OF MY APOLOGY.
OH... ARE YOU SURE?
I'D LOVE TO ATTEND A BLAUE ROSEN CONCERT SOMEDAY IF IT'S ALL RIGHT.
OF COURSE!
MNCH MNCH
WHEN WE SET OUT, I HAD HOPED TO HAVE FOND MEMORIES OF THIS TRIP...
VEEN
...
Mizuki-chan looks good to eat too...
ACK! THERE!! AKIRA HAS THAT SEXY LOOK ON HIS FACE AGAIN!
Nothing for you today!!
No way!
AH. I WONDER WHAT MISAKI GAVE ME...
SHUP

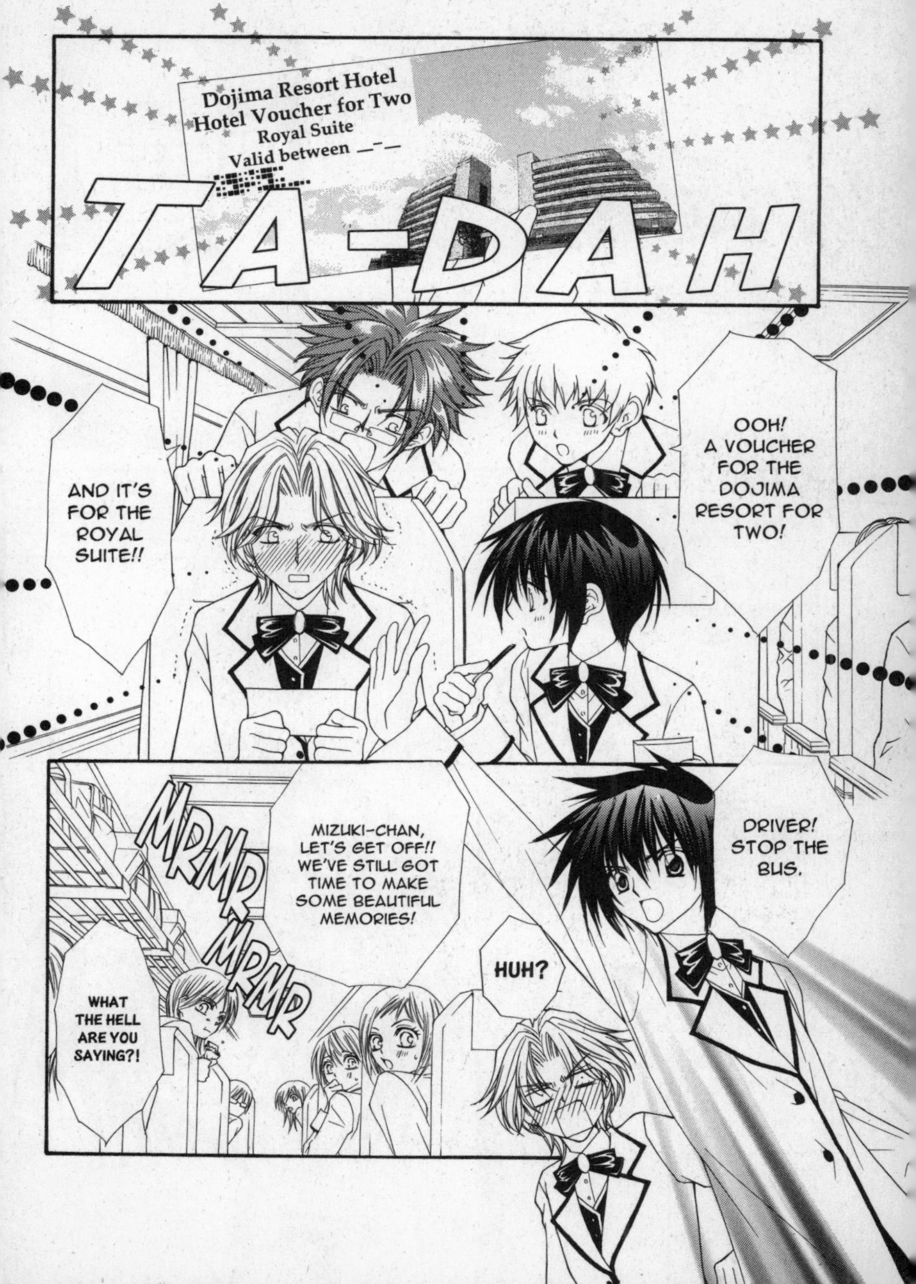
Dojima Resort Hotel
Hotel Voucher for Two
Royal Suite
Valid between _-_
TA-DAH
OOH! A VOUCHER FOR THE DOJIMA RESORT FOR TWO!
AND IT'S FOR THE ROYAL SUITE!!
DRIVER! STOP THE BUS.
HUH?
MIZUKI-CHAN, LET'S GET OFF!! WE'VE STILL GOT TIME TO MAKE SOME BEAUTIFUL MEMORIES!
MRMR MRMR
WHAT THE HELL ARE YOU SAYING?!

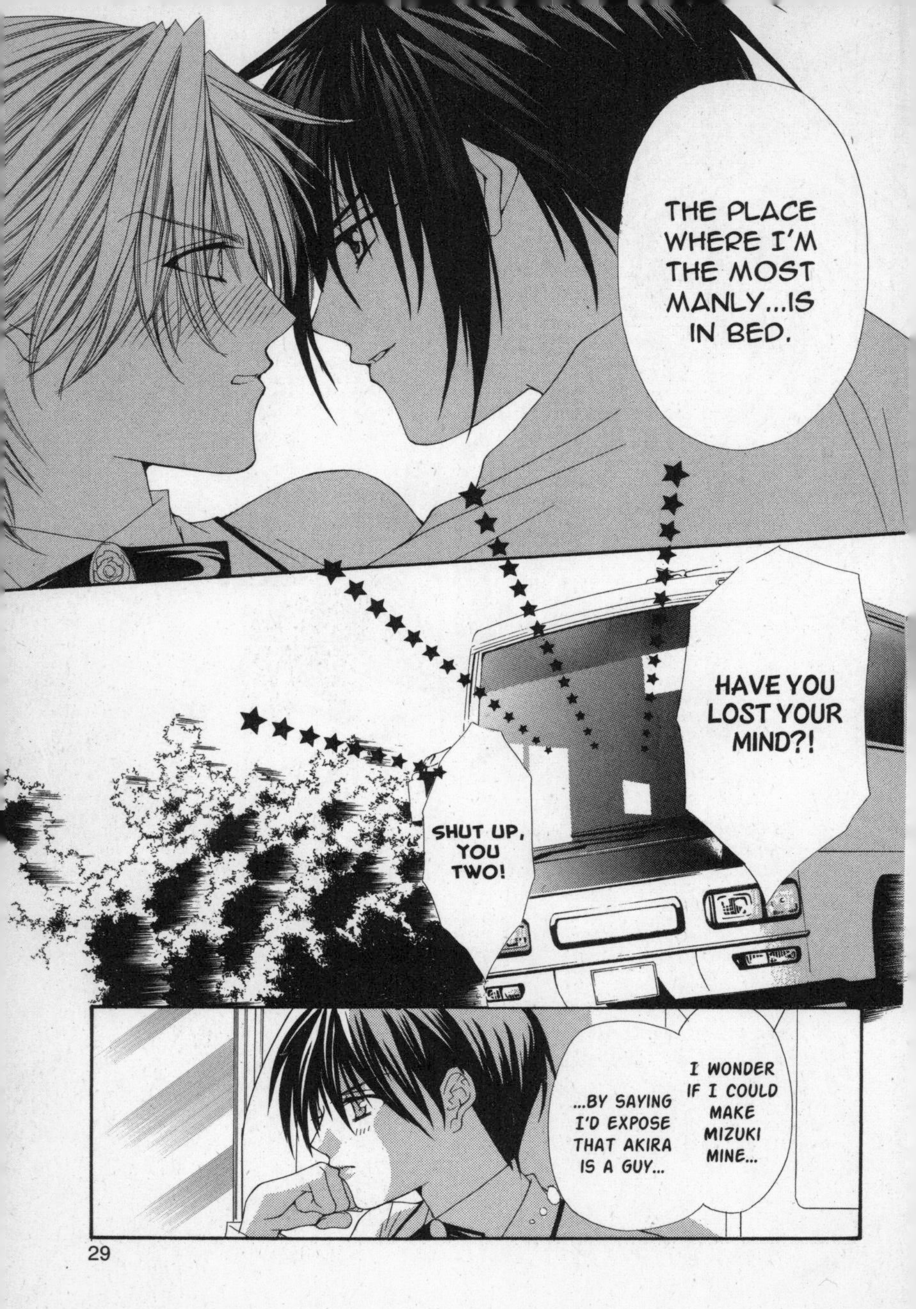
THE PLACE WHERE I'M THE MOST MANLY...IS IN BED.
HAVE YOU LOST YOUR MIND?!
SHUT UP, YOU TWO!
I WONDER IF I COULD MAKE MIZUKI MINE...
...BY SAYING I'D EXPOSE THAT AKIRA IS A GUY...

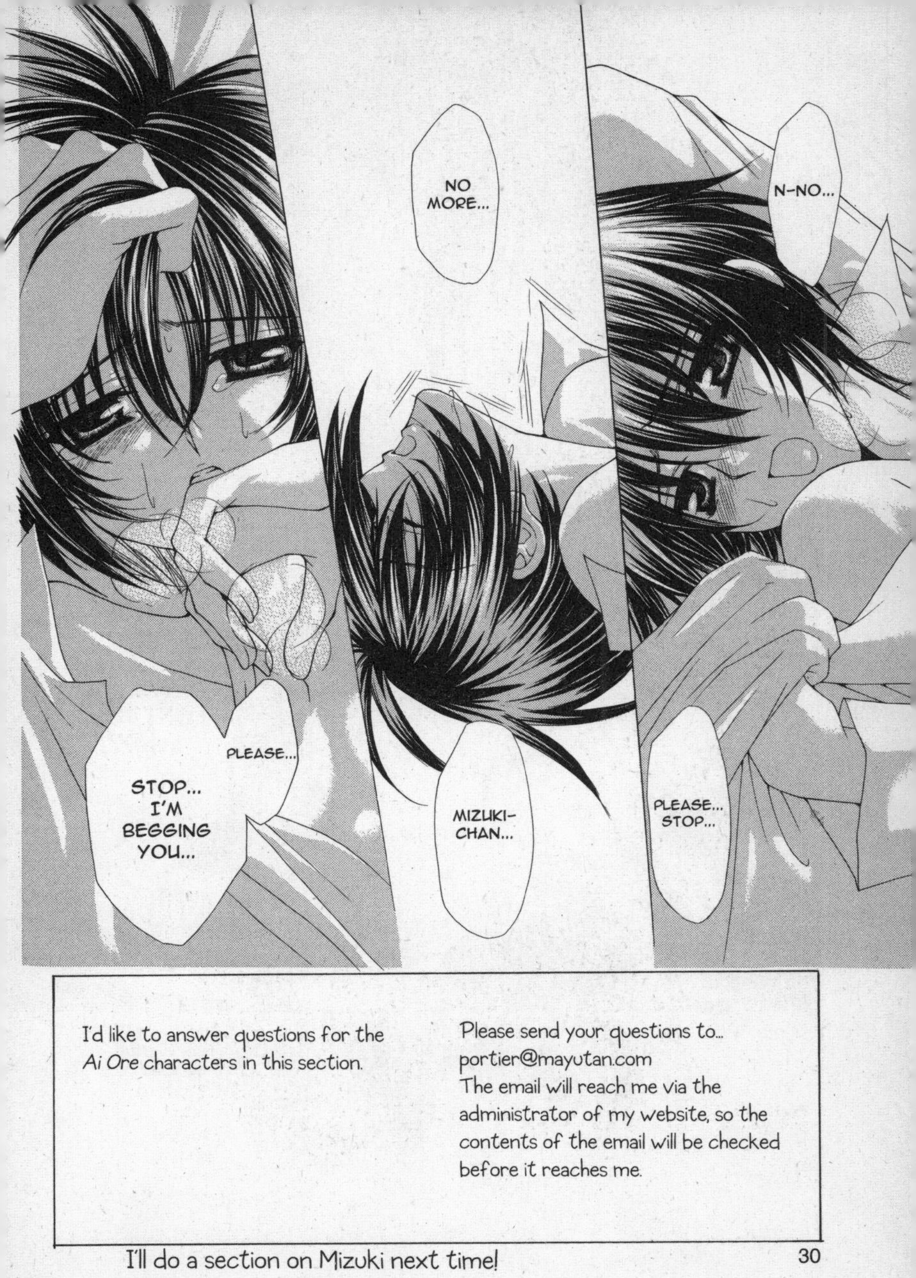
N-NO...
PLEASE... STOP...
NO MORE...
MIZUKI-CHAN...
PLEASE...
STOP... I'M BEGGING YOU...

I'd like to answer questions for the *Ai Ore* characters in this section.

Please send your questions to...
portier@mayutan.com
The email will reach me via the administrator of my website, so the contents of the email will be checked before it reaches me.

I'll do a section on Mizuki next time!

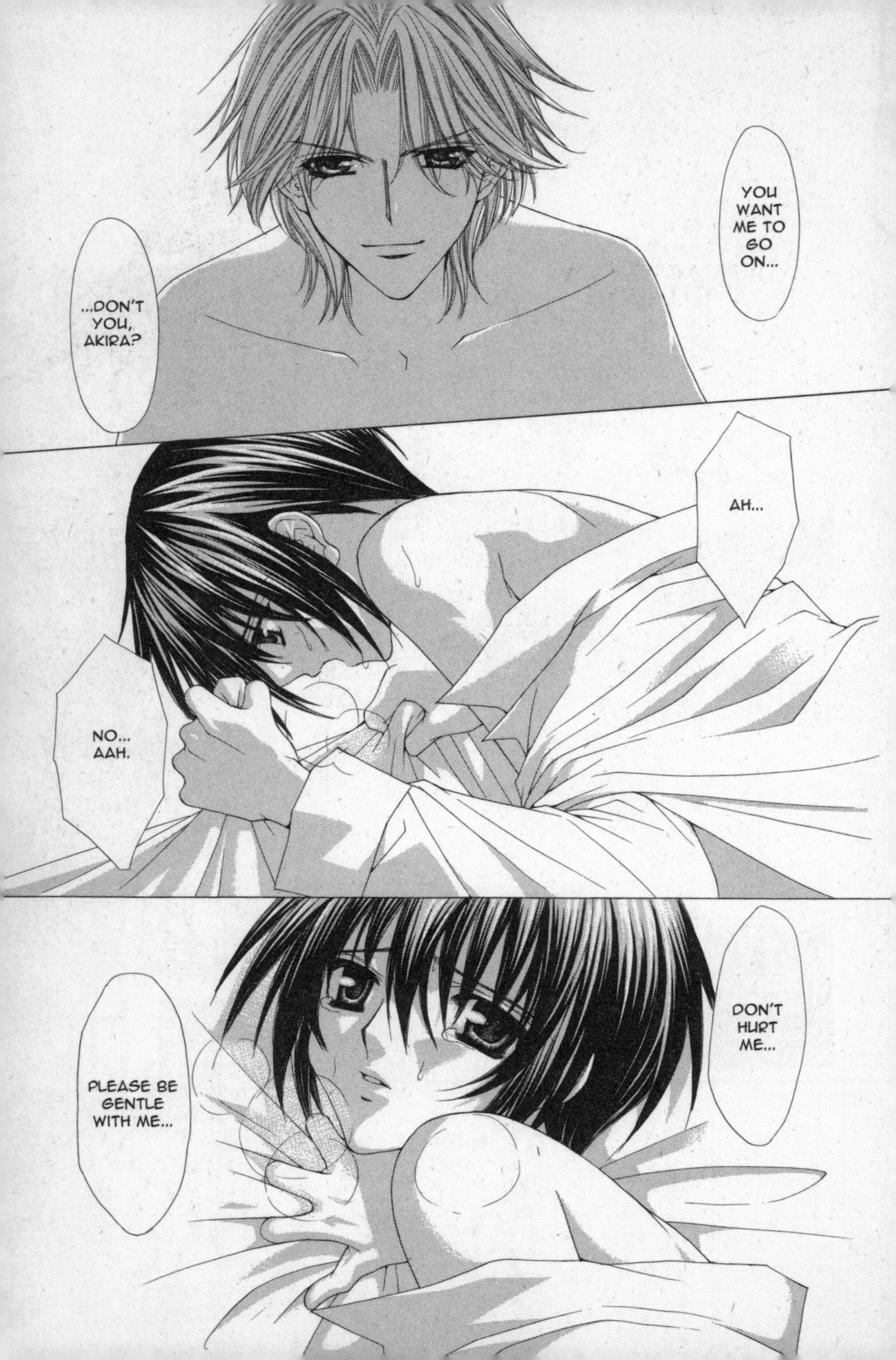
YOU WANT ME TO GO ON...
...DON'T YOU, AKIRA?
AH...
NO... AAH.
DON'T HURT ME...
PLEASE BE GENTLE WITH ME...

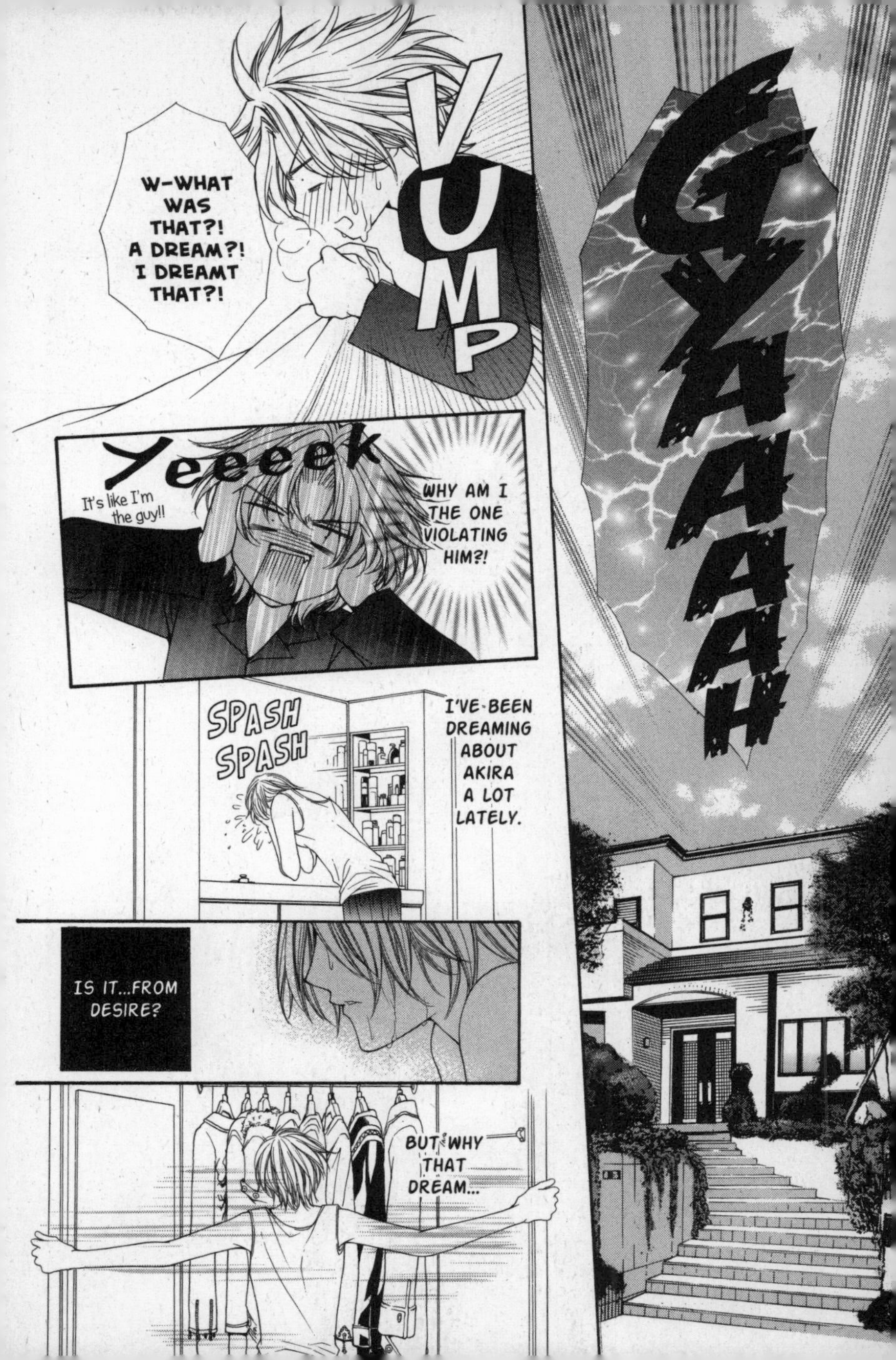
GYAAAAH
VUMP
W-WHAT WAS THAT?! A DREAM?! I DREAMT THAT?!
Yeeeek
WHY AM I THE ONE VIOLATING HIM?!
It's like I'm the guy!!
I'VE BEEN DREAMING ABOUT AKIRA A LOT LATELY.
SPASH SPASH
IS IT...FROM DESIRE?
BUT WHY THAT DREAM...

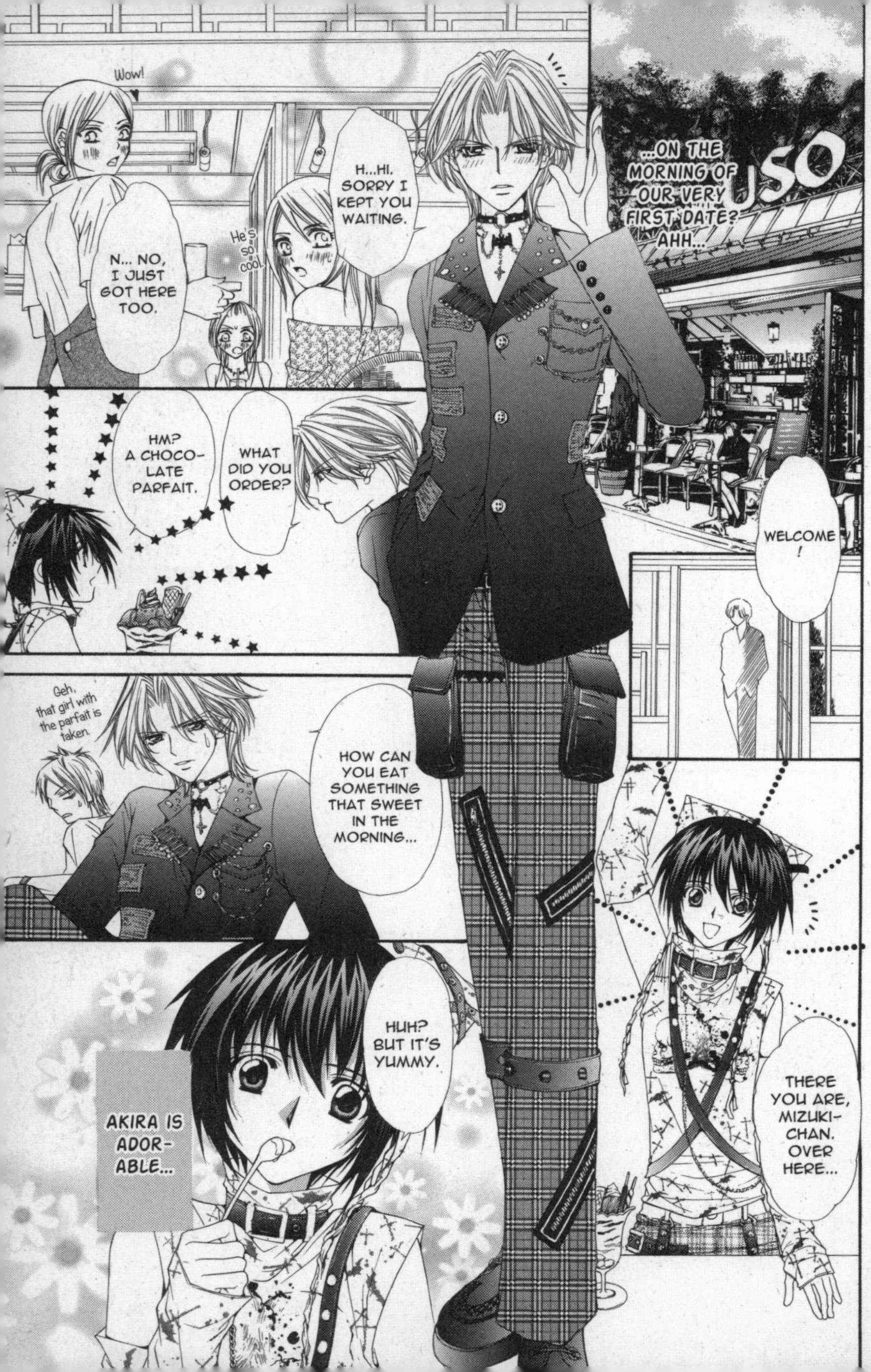

...ON THE MORNING OF OUR VERY FIRST DATE? AHH...
USO
WELCOME!
THERE YOU ARE, MIZUKI-CHAN. OVER HERE...
H...HI. SORRY I KEPT YOU WAITING.
Wow!
He's so cool.
N... NO, I JUST GOT HERE TOO.
WHAT DID YOU ORDER?
HM? A CHOCOLATE PARFAIT.
HOW CAN YOU EAT SOMETHING THAT SWEET IN THE MORNING...
Geh, that girl with the parfait is taken.
HUH? BUT IT'S YUMMY.
AKIRA IS ADORABLE...

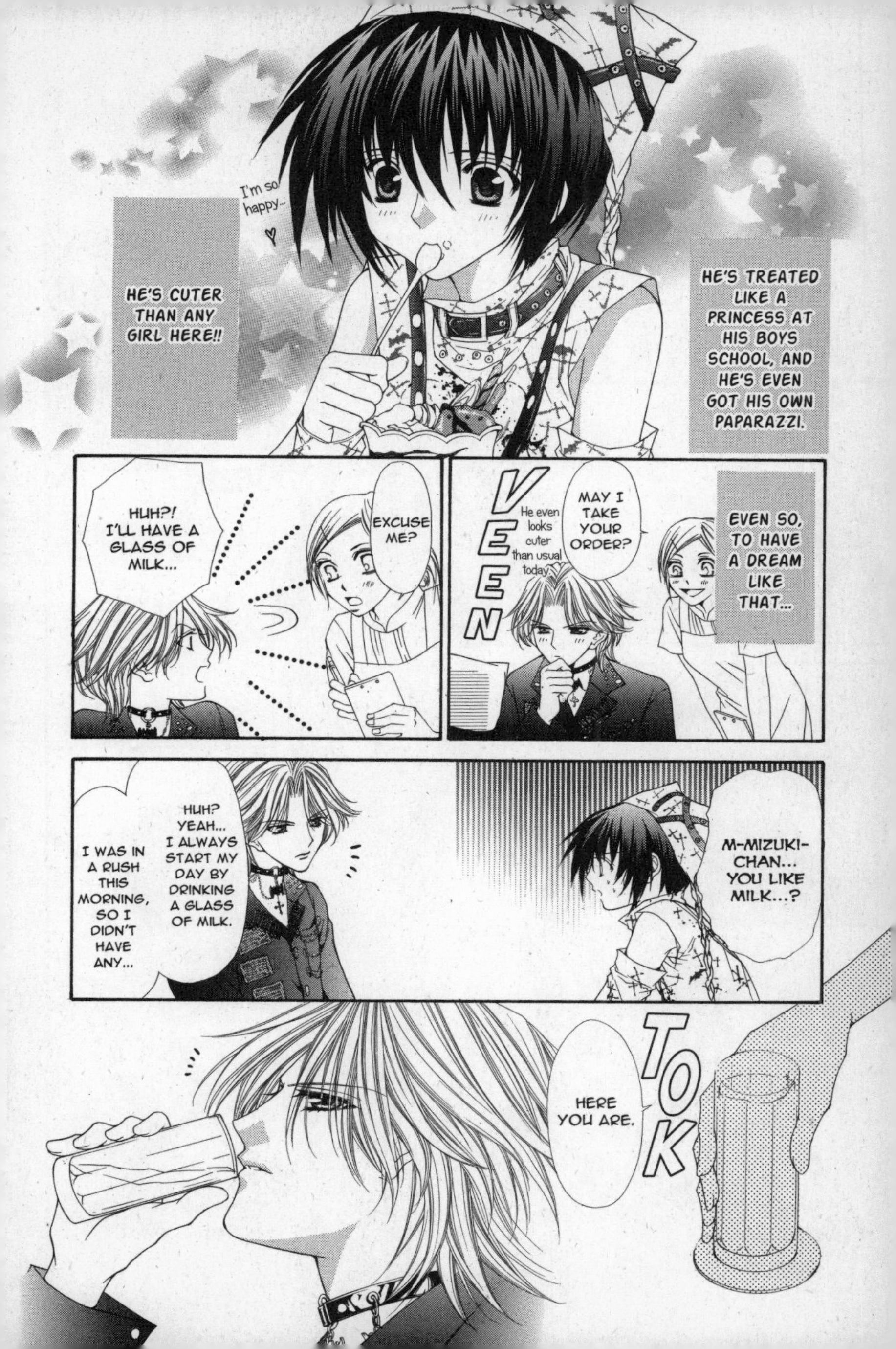
HE'S TREATED LIKE A PRINCESS AT HIS BOYS SCHOOL, AND HE'S EVEN GOT HIS OWN PAPARAZZI.
I'm so happy... ♥
HE'S CUTER THAN ANY GIRL HERE!!
EVEN SO, TO HAVE A DREAM LIKE THAT...
MAY I TAKE YOUR ORDER?
He even looks cuter than usual today.
VEEN
EXCUSE ME?
HUH?! I'LL HAVE A GLASS OF MILK...
M-MIZUKI-CHAN... YOU LIKE MILK...?
HUH? YEAH... I ALWAYS START MY DAY BY DRINKING A GLASS OF MILK.
I WAS IN A RUSH THIS MORNING, SO I DIDN'T HAVE ANY...
TOK
HERE YOU ARE.

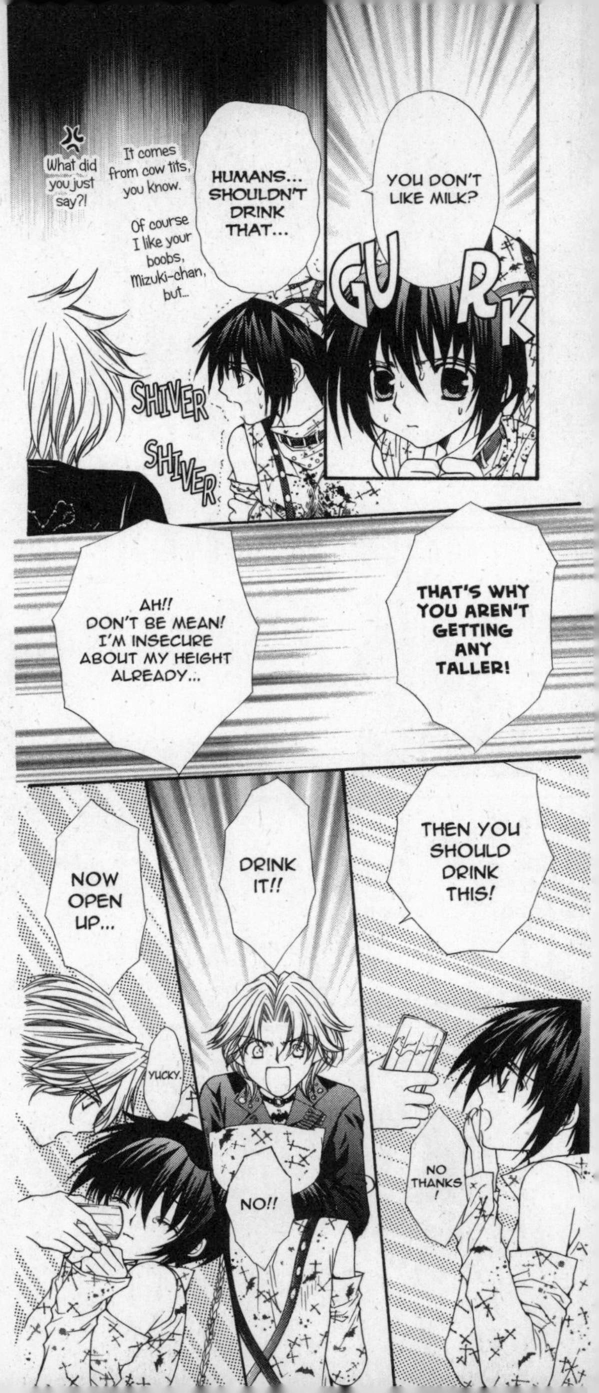
YOU DON'T LIKE MILK?
GURK
HUMANS... SHOULDN'T DRINK THAT...
It comes from cow tits, you know.
Of course I like your boobs, Mizuki-chan, but...
What did you just say?!
SHIVER
SHIVER
THAT'S WHY YOU AREN'T GETTING ANY TALLER!
AH!! DON'T BE MEAN! I'M INSECURE ABOUT MY HEIGHT ALREADY...
THEN YOU SHOULD DRINK THIS!
NO THANKS!
DRINK IT!!
NO!!
NOW OPEN UP...
YUCKY.

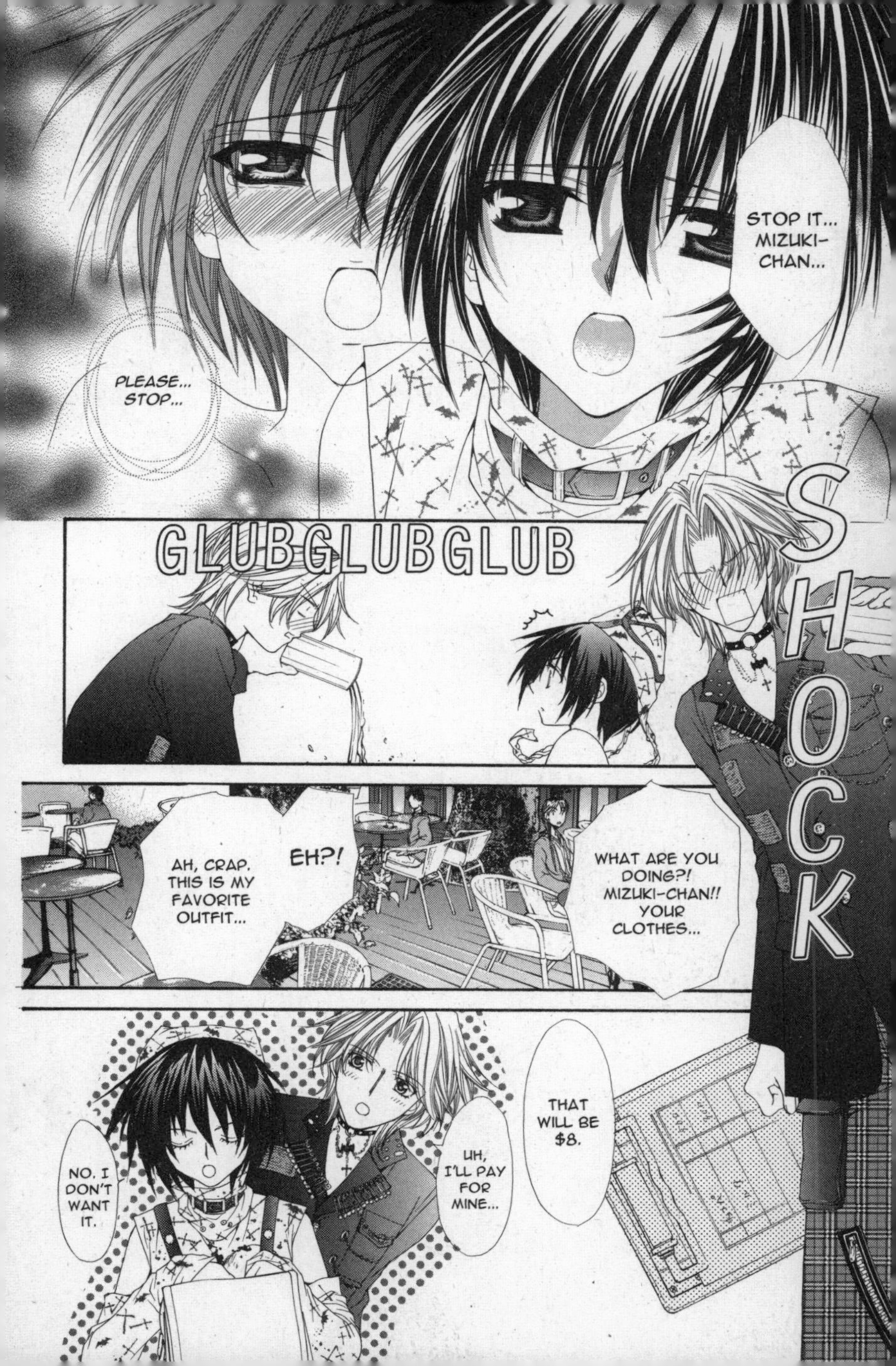

STOP IT... MIZUKI-CHAN...
PLEASE... STOP...
GLUBGLUBGLUB
SHOCK
WHAT ARE YOU DOING?! MIZUKI-CHAN!! YOUR CLOTHES...
EH?!
AH, CRAP. THIS IS MY FAVORITE OUTFIT...
THAT WILL BE $8.
UH, I'LL PAY FOR MINE...
NO. I DON'T WANT IT.

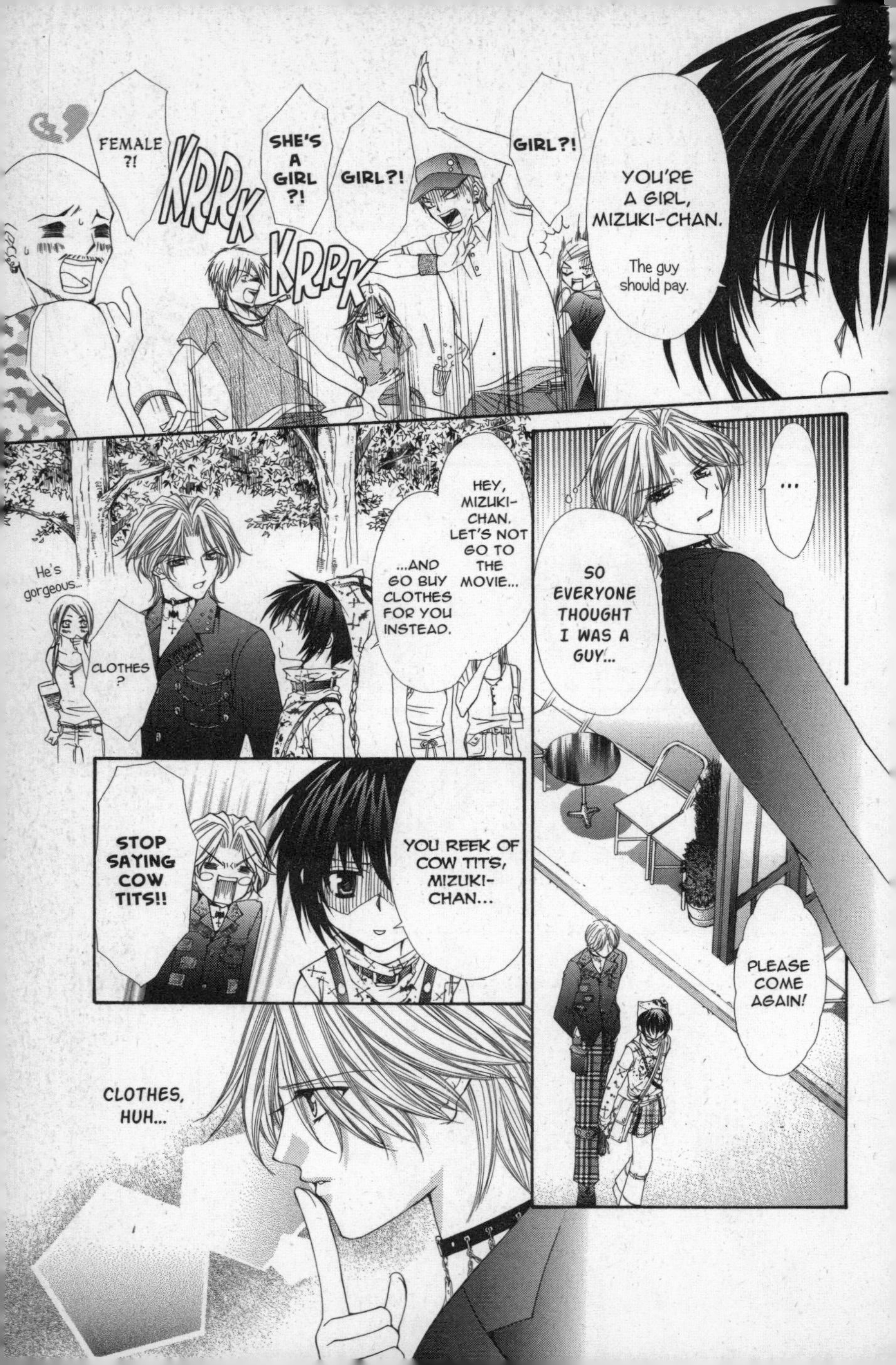
YOU'RE A GIRL, MIZUKI-CHAN.
The guy should pay.
GIRL?!
GIRL?!
SHE'S A GIRL ?!
KRRK
KRRK
FEMALE ?!
...
SO EVERYONE THOUGHT I WAS A GUY...
PLEASE COME AGAIN!
HEY, MIZUKI-CHAN. LET'S NOT GO TO THE MOVIE...
...AND GO BUY CLOTHES FOR YOU INSTEAD.
CLOTHES ?
He's gorgeous...
YOU REEK OF COW TITS, MIZUKI-CHAN...
STOP SAYING COW TITS!!
CLOTHES, HUH...

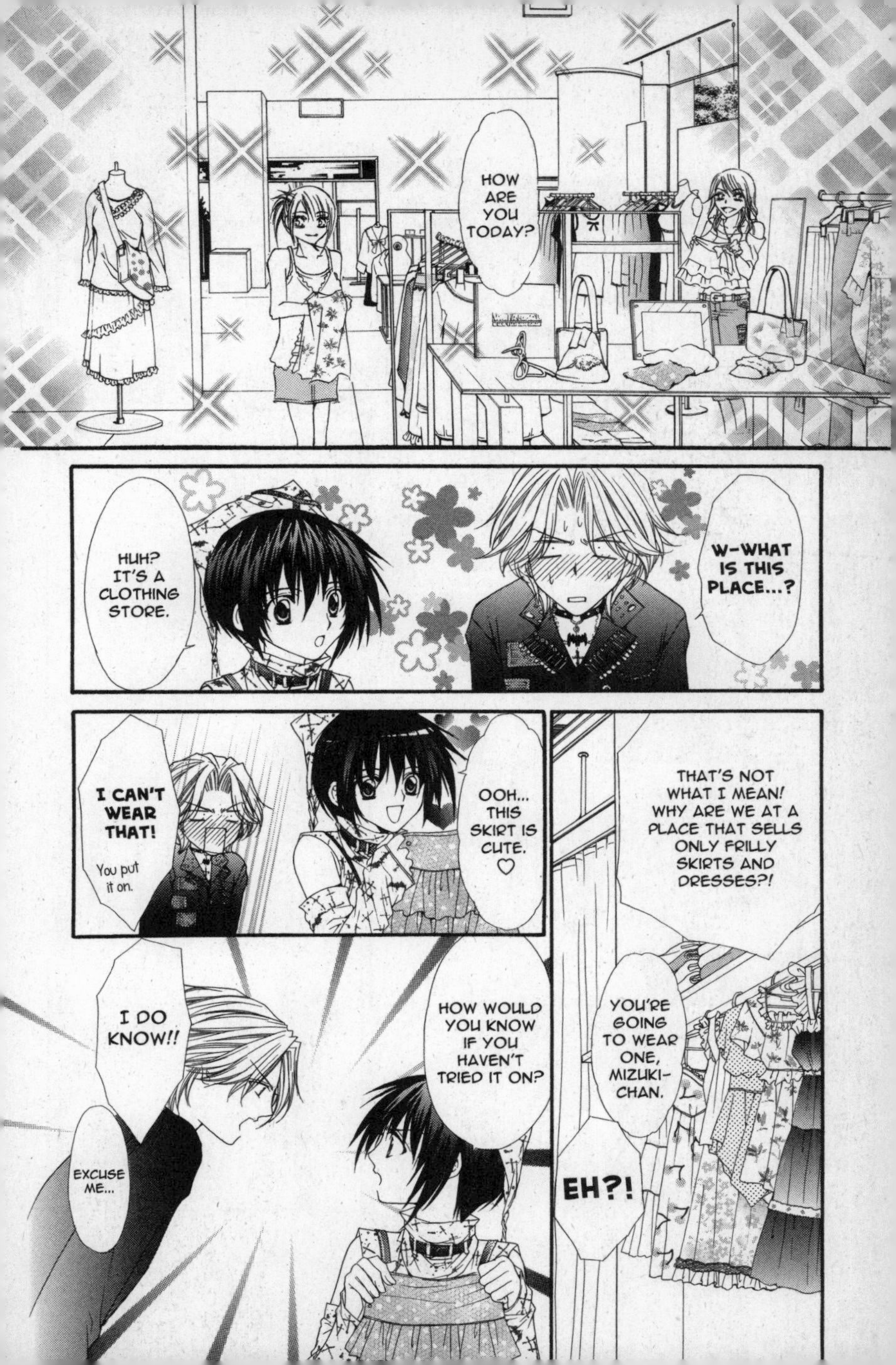
HOW ARE YOU TODAY?
W-WHAT IS THIS PLACE...?
HUH? IT'S A CLOTHING STORE.
THAT'S NOT WHAT I MEAN! WHY ARE WE AT A PLACE THAT SELLS ONLY FRILLY SKIRTS AND DRESSES?!
YOU'RE GOING TO WEAR ONE, MIZUKI-CHAN.
EH?!
OOH... THIS SKIRT IS CUTE. ♡
I CAN'T WEAR THAT!
You put it on.
HOW WOULD YOU KNOW IF YOU HAVEN'T TRIED IT ON?
I DO KNOW!!
EXCUSE ME...

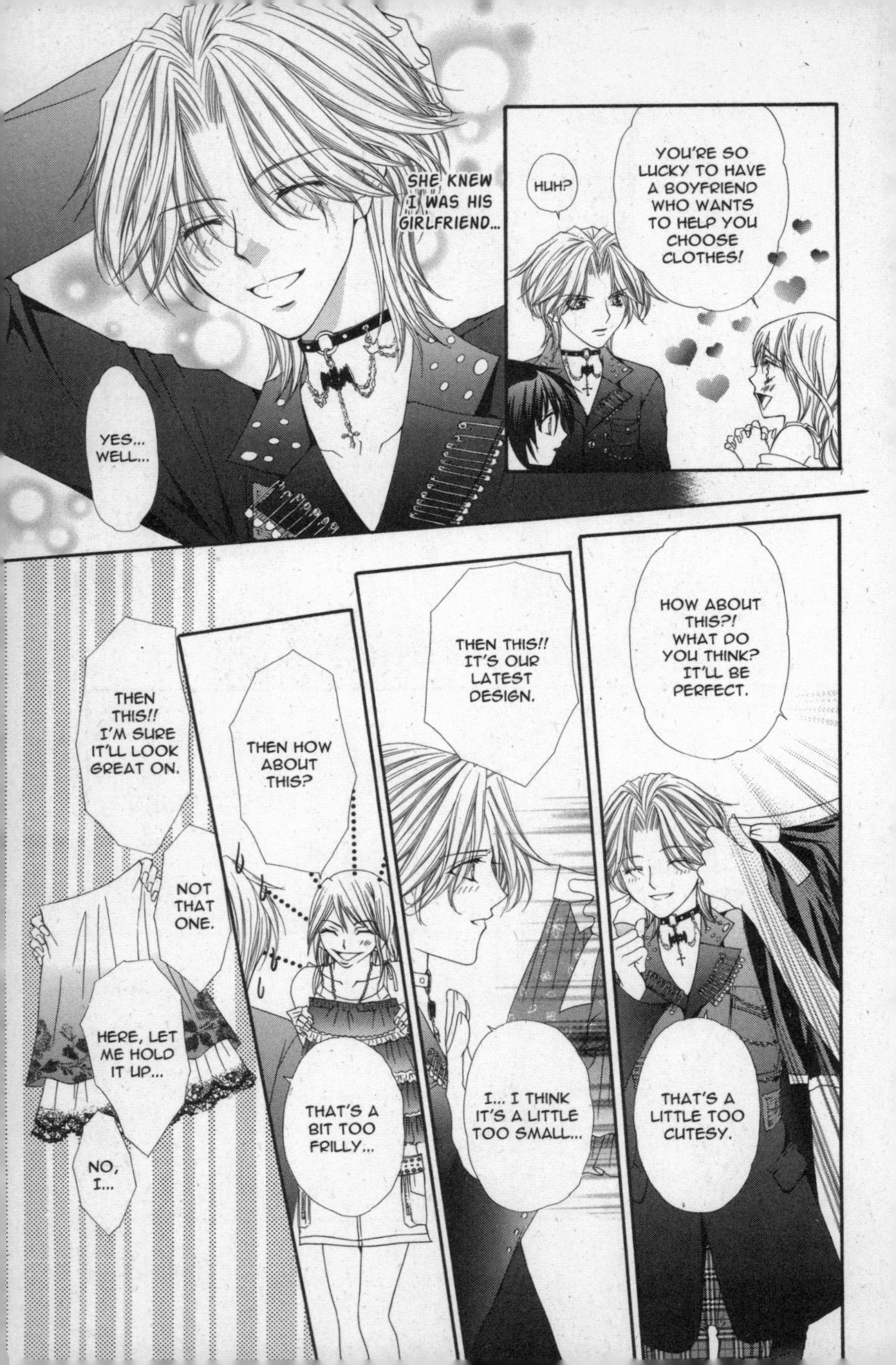
YOU'RE SO LUCKY TO HAVE A BOYFRIEND WHO WANTS TO HELP YOU CHOOSE CLOTHES!
HUH?
SHE KNEW I WAS HIS GIRLFRIEND...
YES... WELL...
HOW ABOUT THIS?! WHAT DO YOU THINK? IT'LL BE PERFECT.
THAT'S A LITTLE TOO CUTESY.
THEN THIS!! IT'S OUR LATEST DESIGN.
I... I THINK IT'S A LITTLE TOO SMALL...
THEN HOW ABOUT THIS?
THAT'S A BIT TOO FRILLY...
THEN THIS!! I'M SURE IT'LL LOOK GREAT ON.
NOT THAT ONE.
HERE, LET ME HOLD IT UP...
NO, I...

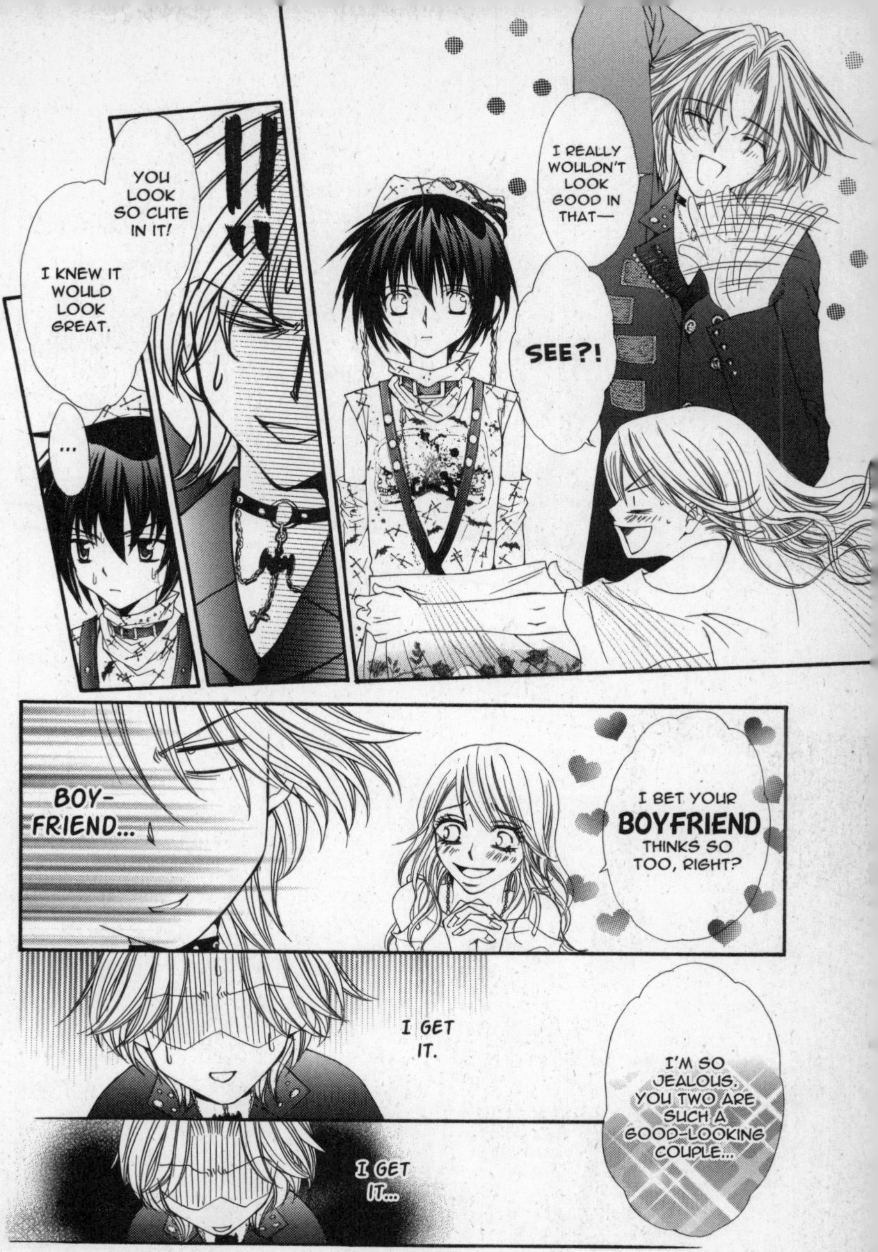
I REALLY WOULDN'T LOOK GOOD IN THAT—
SEE?!
YOU LOOK SO CUTE IN IT!
I KNEW IT WOULD LOOK GREAT.
...
I BET YOUR BOYFRIEND THINKS SO TOO, RIGHT?
BOY-FRIEND...
I'M SO JEALOUS. YOU TWO ARE SUCH A GOOD-LOOKING COUPLE...
I GET IT.
I GET IT...

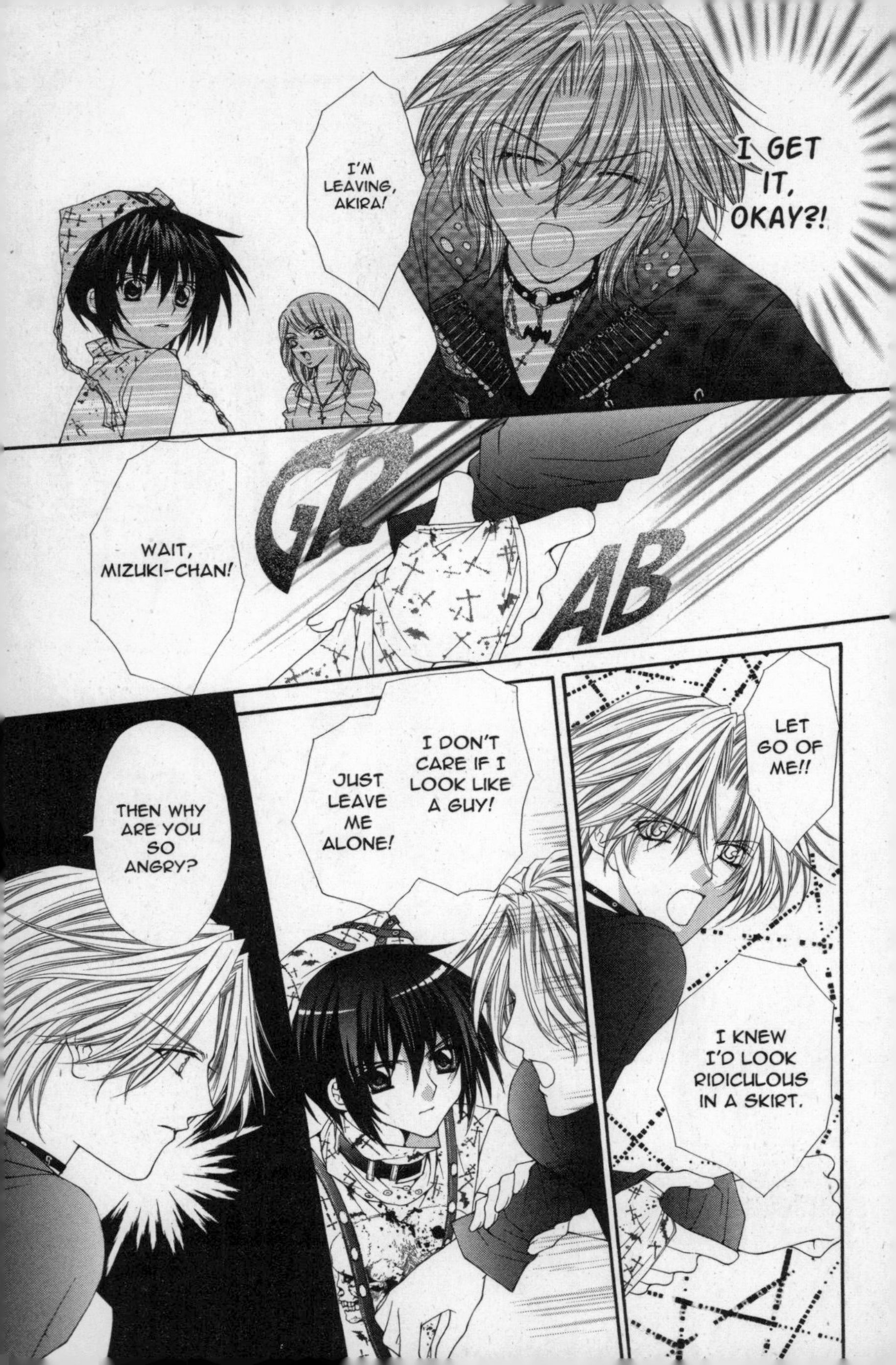
I GET IT, OKAY?!
I'M LEAVING, AKIRA!
GRAB
WAIT, MIZUKI-CHAN!
LET GO OF ME!!
I KNEW I'D LOOK RIDICULOUS IN A SKIRT.
I DON'T CARE IF I LOOK LIKE A GUY!
JUST LEAVE ME ALONE!
THEN WHY ARE YOU SO ANGRY?

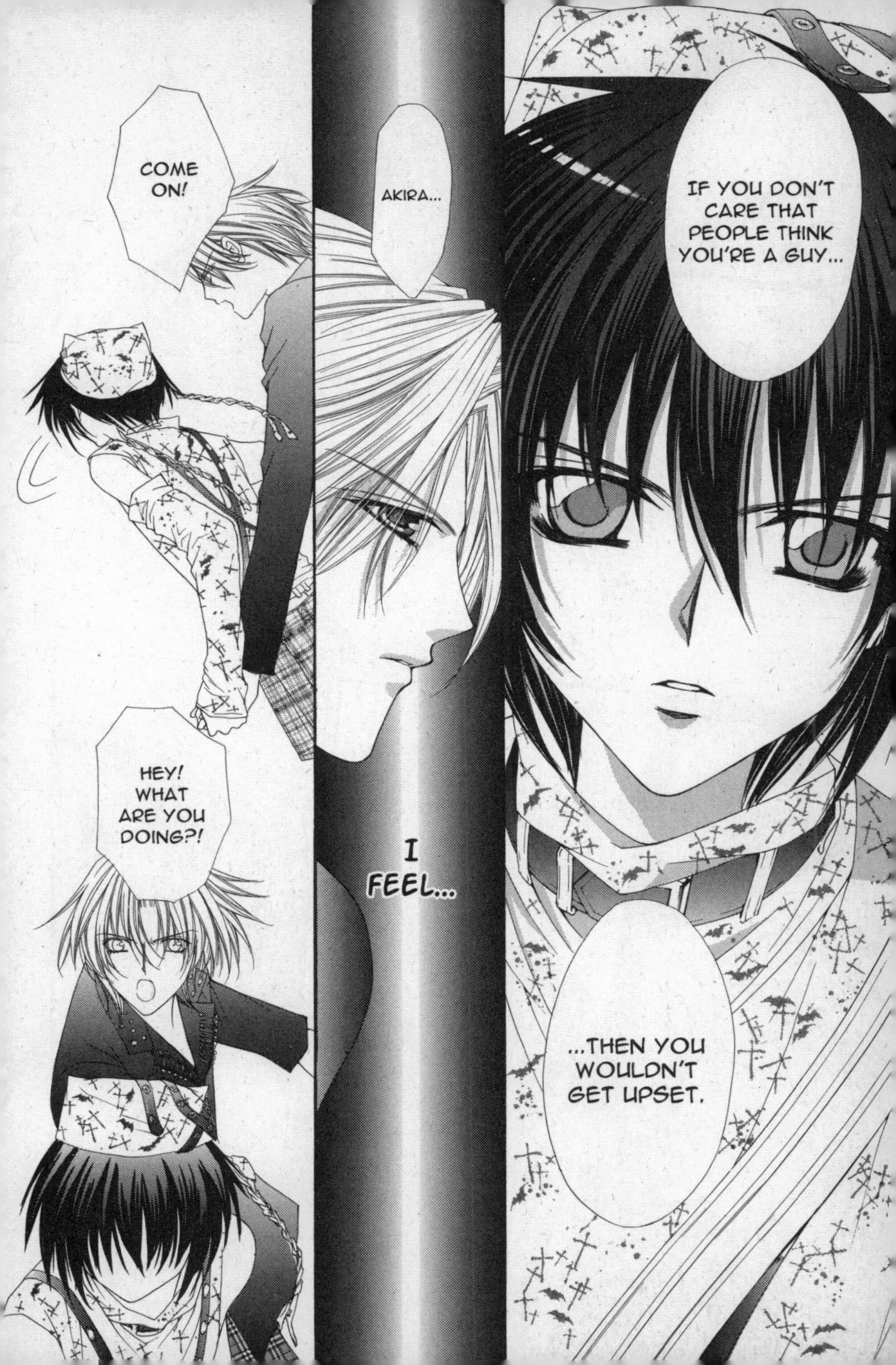
IF YOU DON'T CARE THAT PEOPLE THINK YOU'RE A GUY...
...THEN YOU WOULDN'T GET UPSET.
AKIRA...
I FEEL...
COME ON!
HEY! WHAT ARE YOU DOING?!

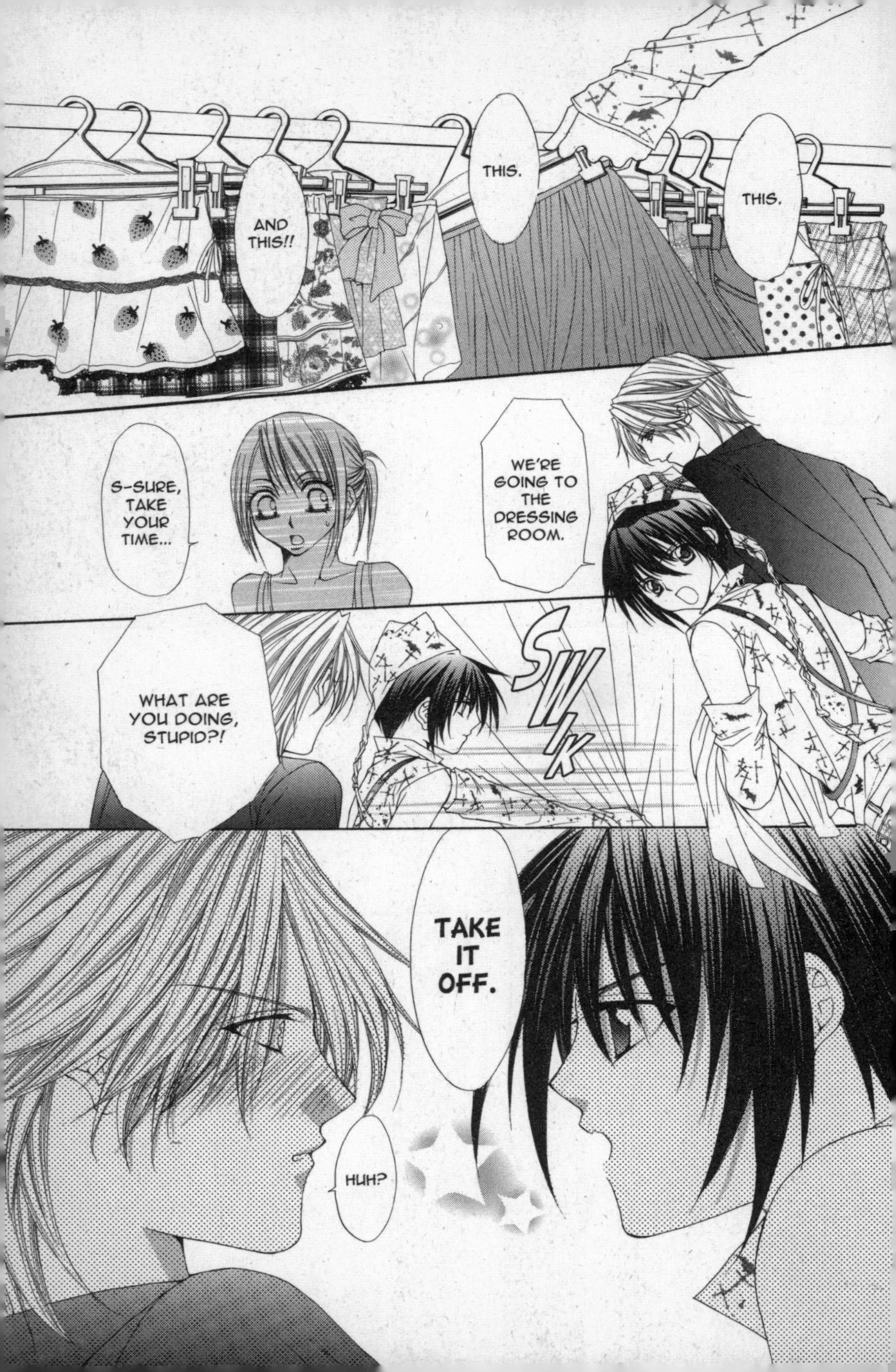
THIS.
THIS.
AND THIS!!
WE'RE GOING TO THE DRESSING ROOM.
S-SURE, TAKE YOUR TIME...
SLIK
WHAT ARE YOU DOING, STUPID?!
TAKE IT OFF.
HUH?

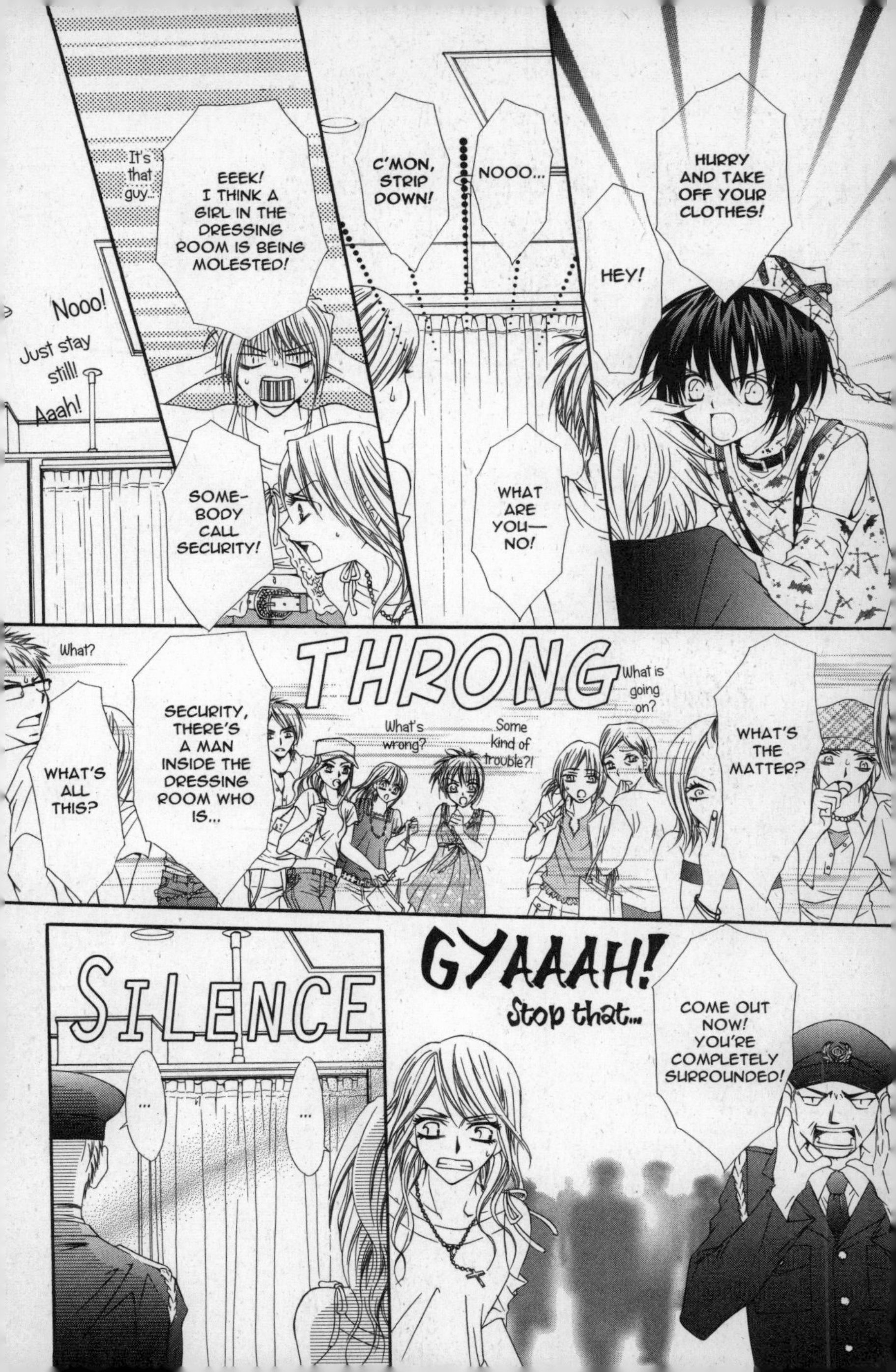
HURRY AND TAKE OFF YOUR CLOTHES!
HEY!
WHAT ARE YOU— NO!
C'MON, STRIP DOWN!
NOOO...
EEEK! I THINK A GIRL IN THE DRESSING ROOM IS BEING MOLESTED!
It's that guy...
Nooo!
Just stay still!
Aaah!
SOME-BODY CALL SECURITY!
WHAT'S THE MATTER?
What is going on?
THRONG
Some kind of trouble?!
What's wrong?
SECURITY, THERE'S A MAN INSIDE THE DRESSING ROOM WHO IS...
What?
WHAT'S ALL THIS?
COME OUT NOW! YOU'RE COMPLETELY SURROUNDED!
GYAAAH!
Stop that...
SILENCE
...
...

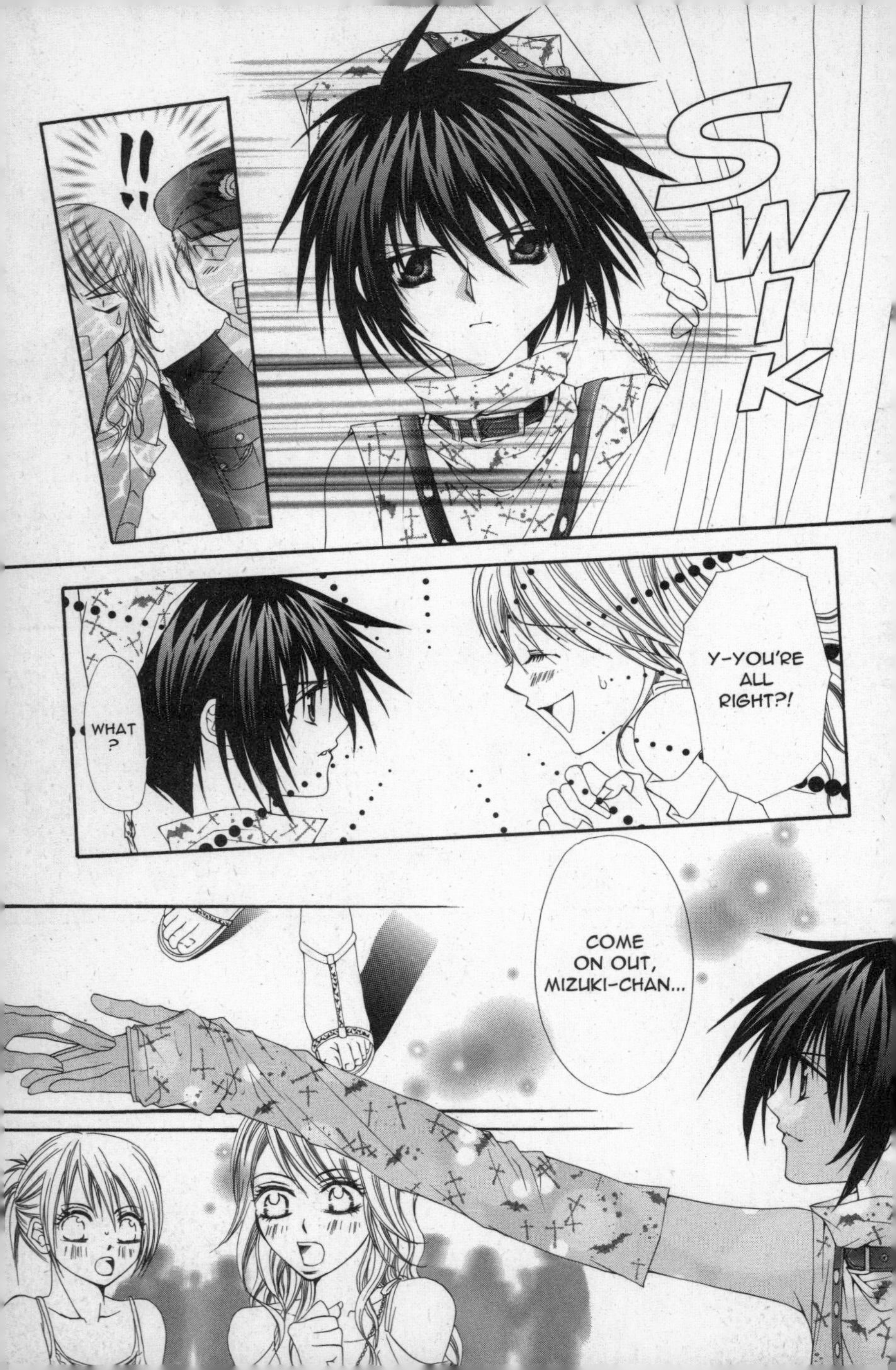
SWIK
!!
Y-YOU'RE ALL RIGHT?!
WHAT?
COME ON OUT, MIZUKI-CHAN...

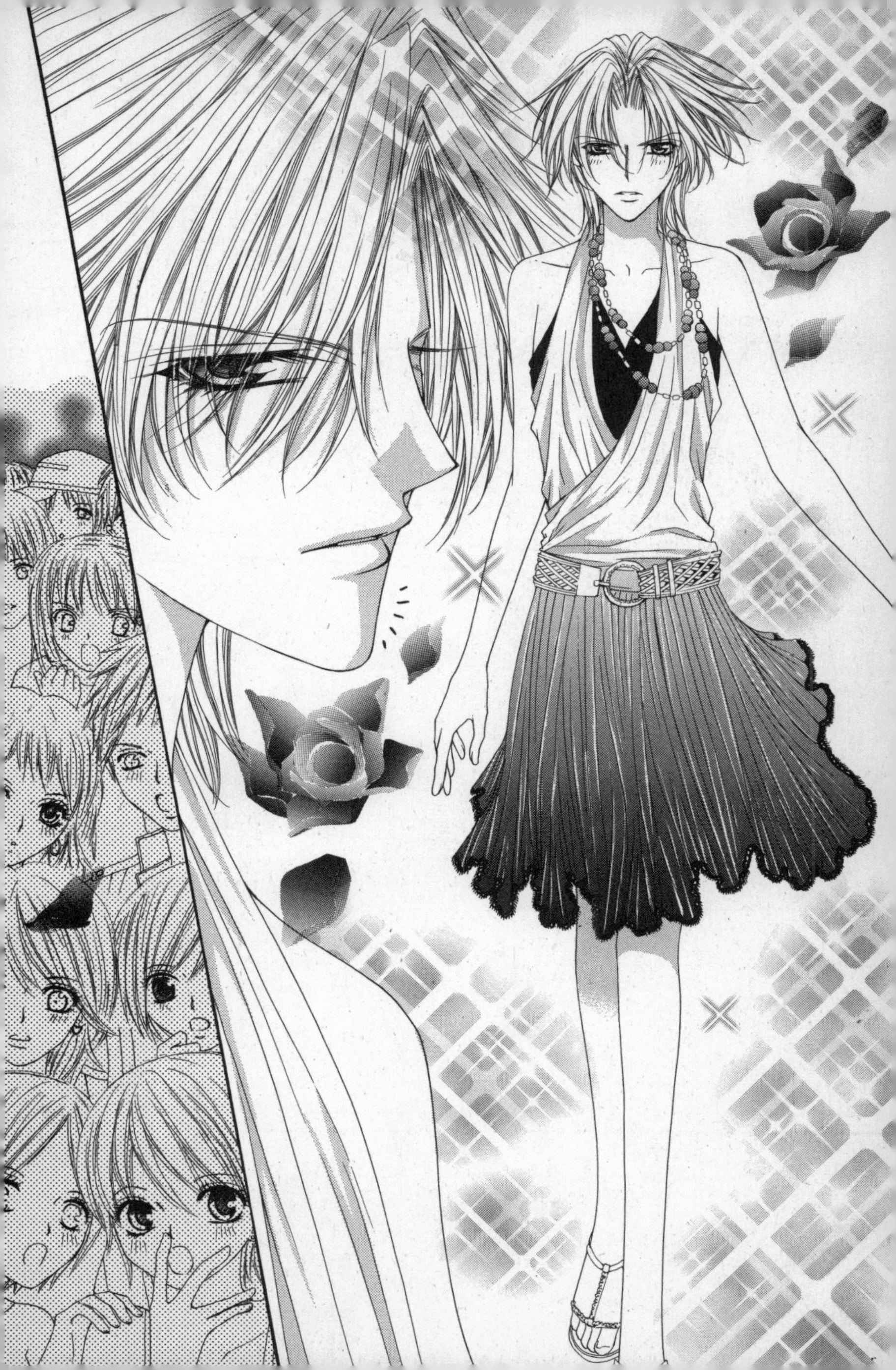

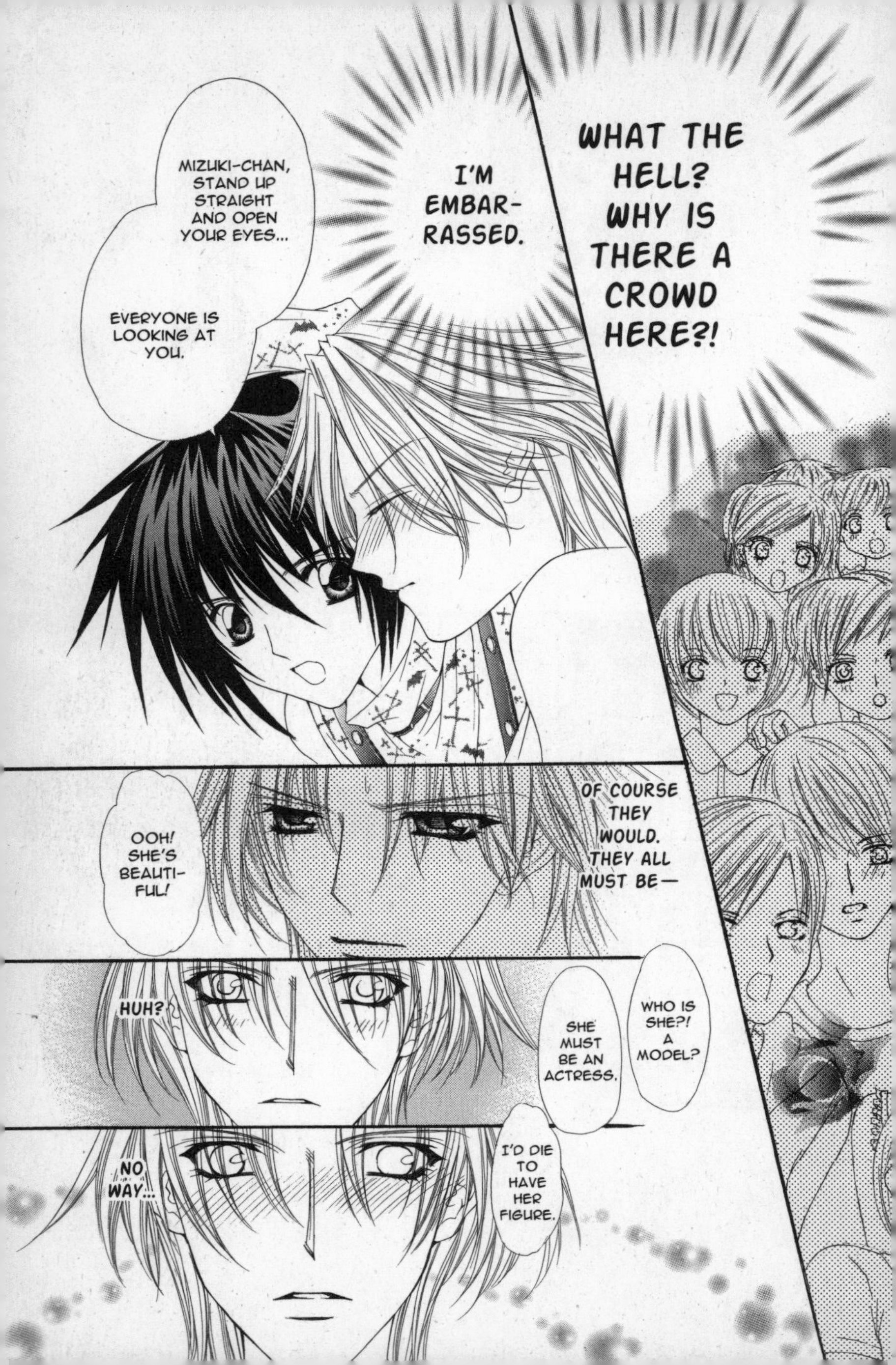
WHAT THE HELL? WHY IS THERE A CROWD HERE?!
I'M EMBARRASSED.
MIZUKI-CHAN, STAND UP STRAIGHT AND OPEN YOUR EYES...
EVERYONE IS LOOKING AT YOU.
OF COURSE THEY WOULD. THEY ALL MUST BE—
OOH! SHE'S BEAUTIFUL!
WHO IS SHE?! A MODEL?
SHE MUST BE AN ACTRESS.
HUH?
I'D DIE TO HAVE HER FIGURE.
NO WAY...

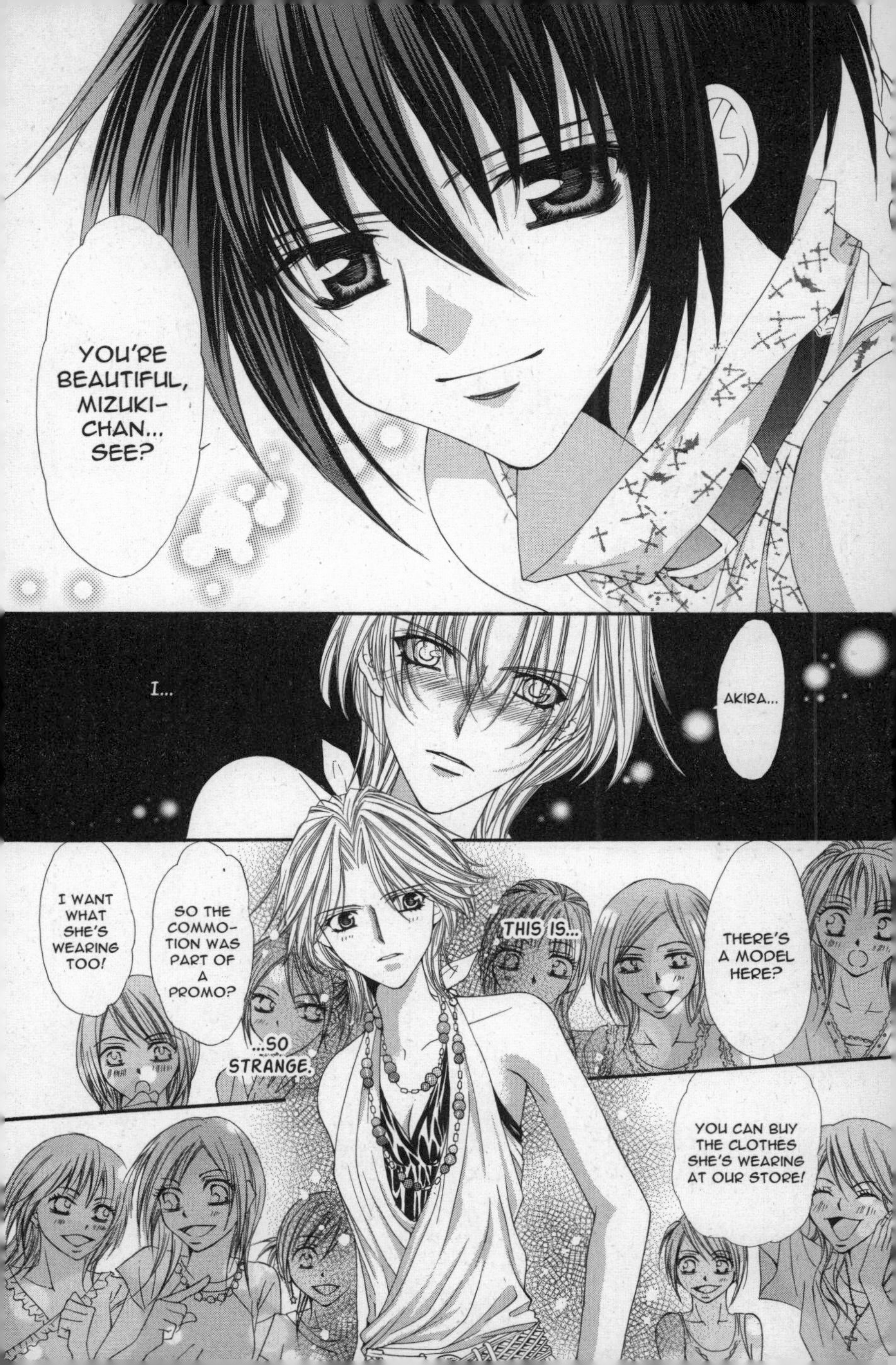
YOU'RE BEAUTIFUL, MIZUKI-CHAN... SEE?
AKIRA...
I...
THERE'S A MODEL HERE?
THIS IS...
SO THE COMMOTION WAS PART OF A PROMO?
I WANT WHAT SHE'S WEARING TOO!
...SO STRANGE.
YOU CAN BUY THE CLOTHES SHE'S WEARING AT OUR STORE!

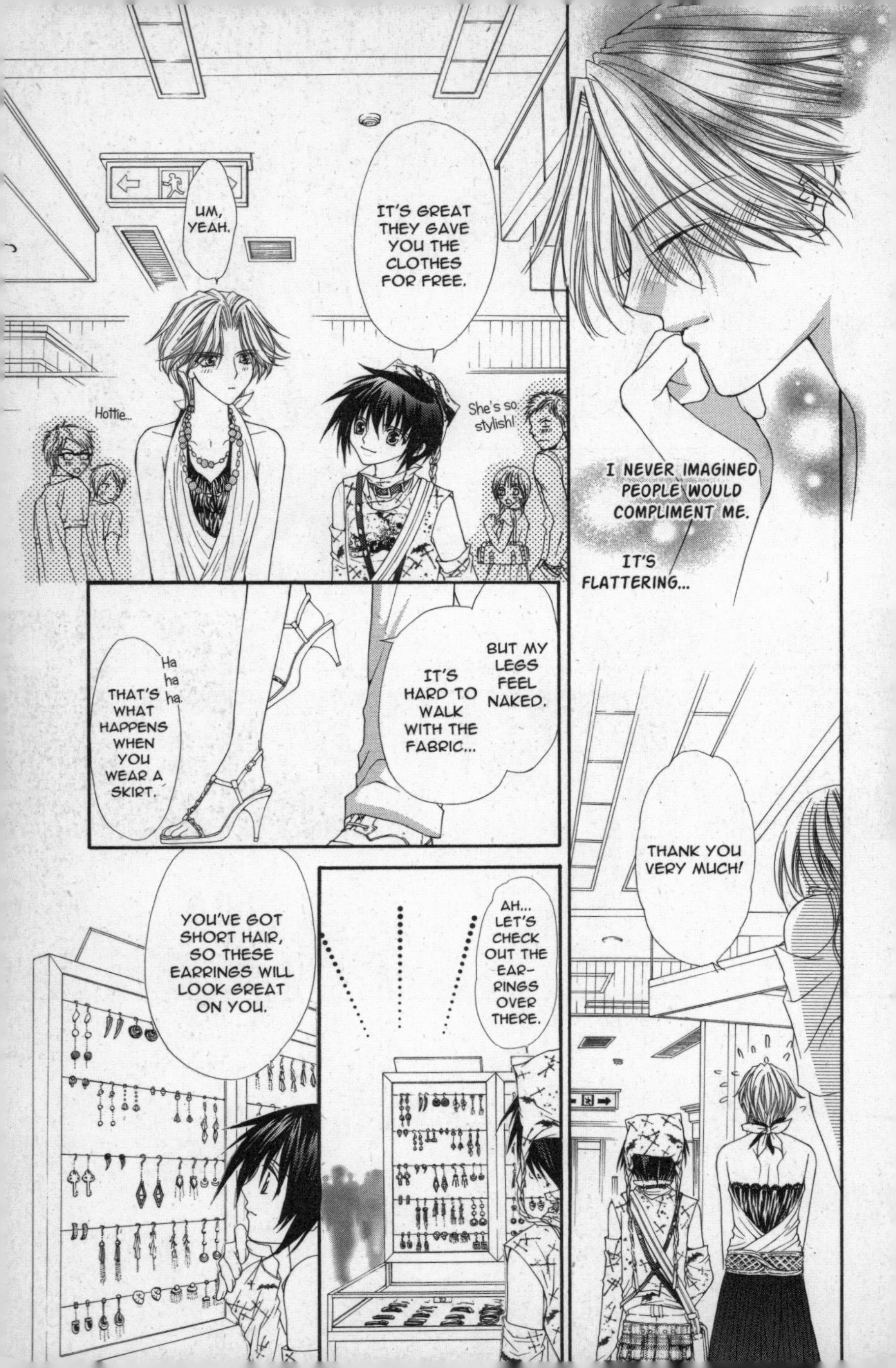
I NEVER IMAGINED PEOPLE WOULD COMPLIMENT ME.
IT'S FLATTERING...
IT'S GREAT THEY GAVE YOU THE CLOTHES FOR FREE.
UM, YEAH.
She's so stylish!
Hottie...
BUT MY LEGS FEEL NAKED.
IT'S HARD TO WALK WITH THE FABRIC...
Ha ha ha.
THAT'S WHAT HAPPENS WHEN YOU WEAR A SKIRT.
THANK YOU VERY MUCH!
AH... LET'S CHECK OUT THE EAR-RINGS OVER THERE.
......
YOU'VE GOT SHORT HAIR, SO THESE EARRINGS WILL LOOK GREAT ON YOU.

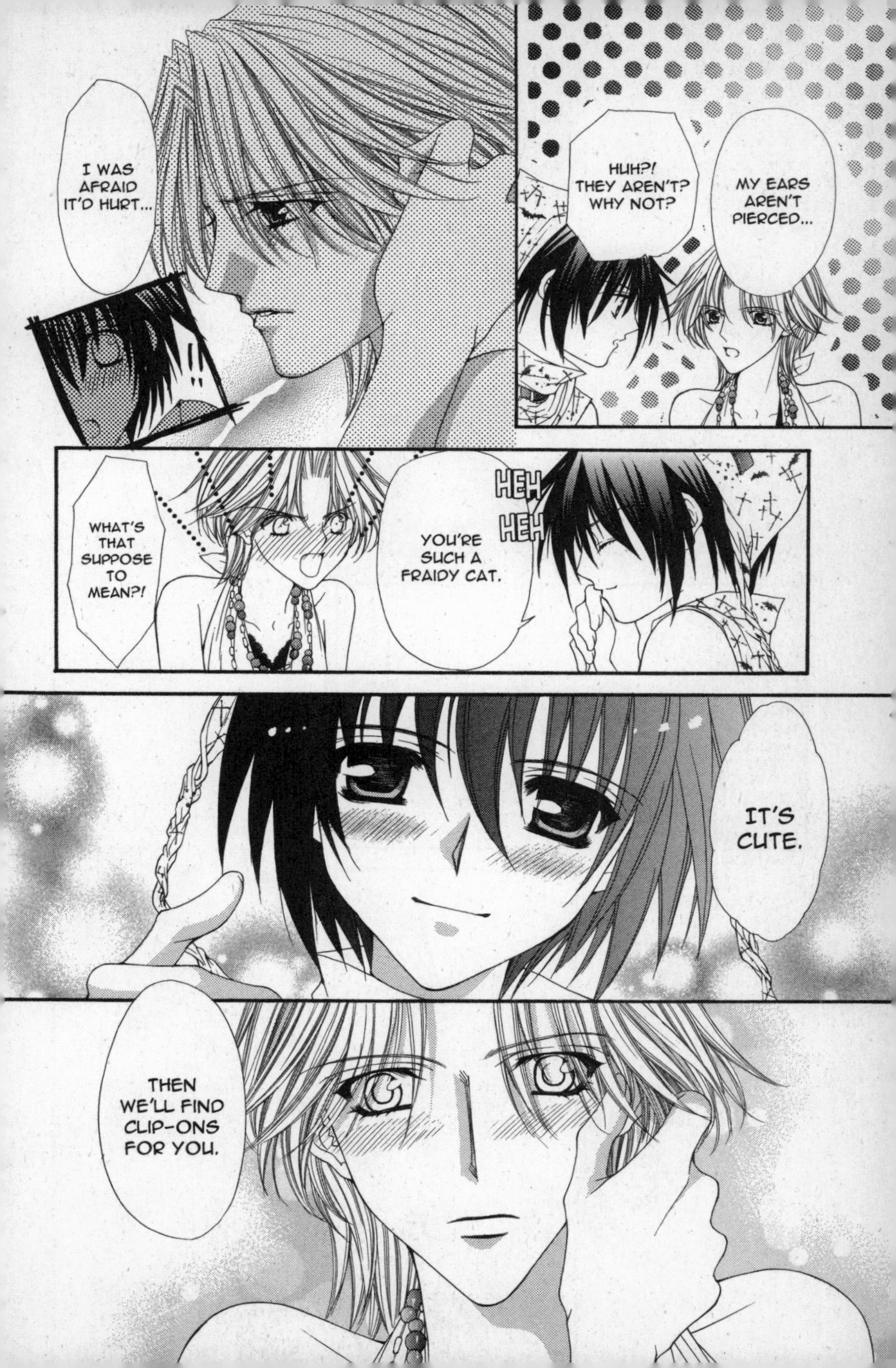
MY EARS AREN'T PIERCED...
HUH?! THEY AREN'T? WHY NOT?
I WAS AFRAID IT'D HURT...
HEH HEH
YOU'RE SUCH A FRAIDY CAT.
WHAT'S THAT SUPPOSE TO MEAN?!
IT'S CUTE.
THEN WE'LL FIND CLIP-ONS FOR YOU.

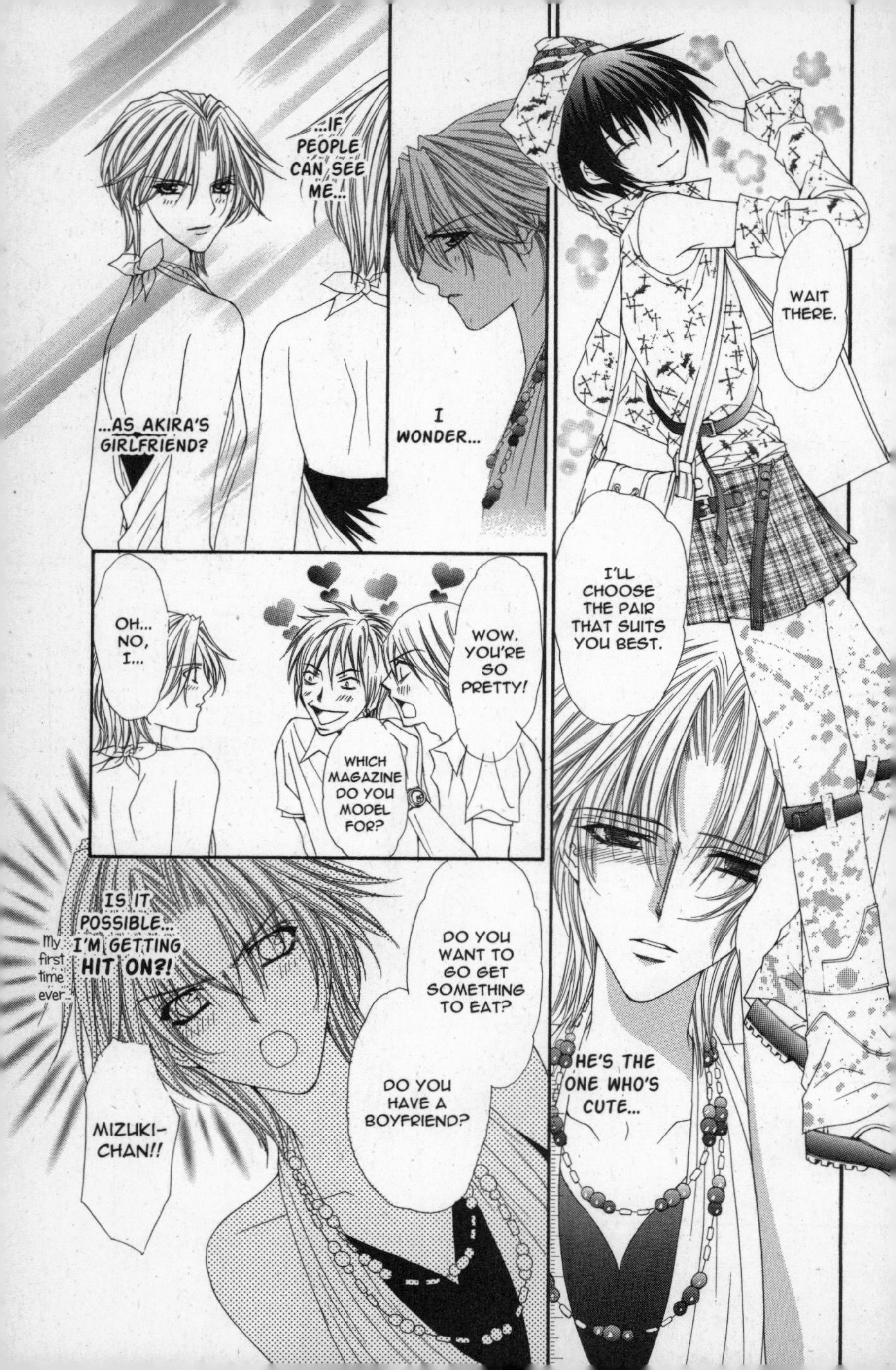
WAIT THERE.
I'LL CHOOSE THE PAIR THAT SUITS YOU BEST.
HE'S THE ONE WHO'S CUTE...
I WONDER...
...IF PEOPLE CAN SEE ME...
...AS AKIRA'S GIRLFRIEND?
WOW. YOU'RE SO PRETTY!
WHICH MAGAZINE DO YOU MODEL FOR?
OH... NO, I...
DO YOU WANT TO GO GET SOMETHING TO EAT?
DO YOU HAVE A BOYFRIEND?
IS IT POSSIBLE... I'M GETTING HIT ON?!
My first time ever...
MIZUKI-CHAN!!

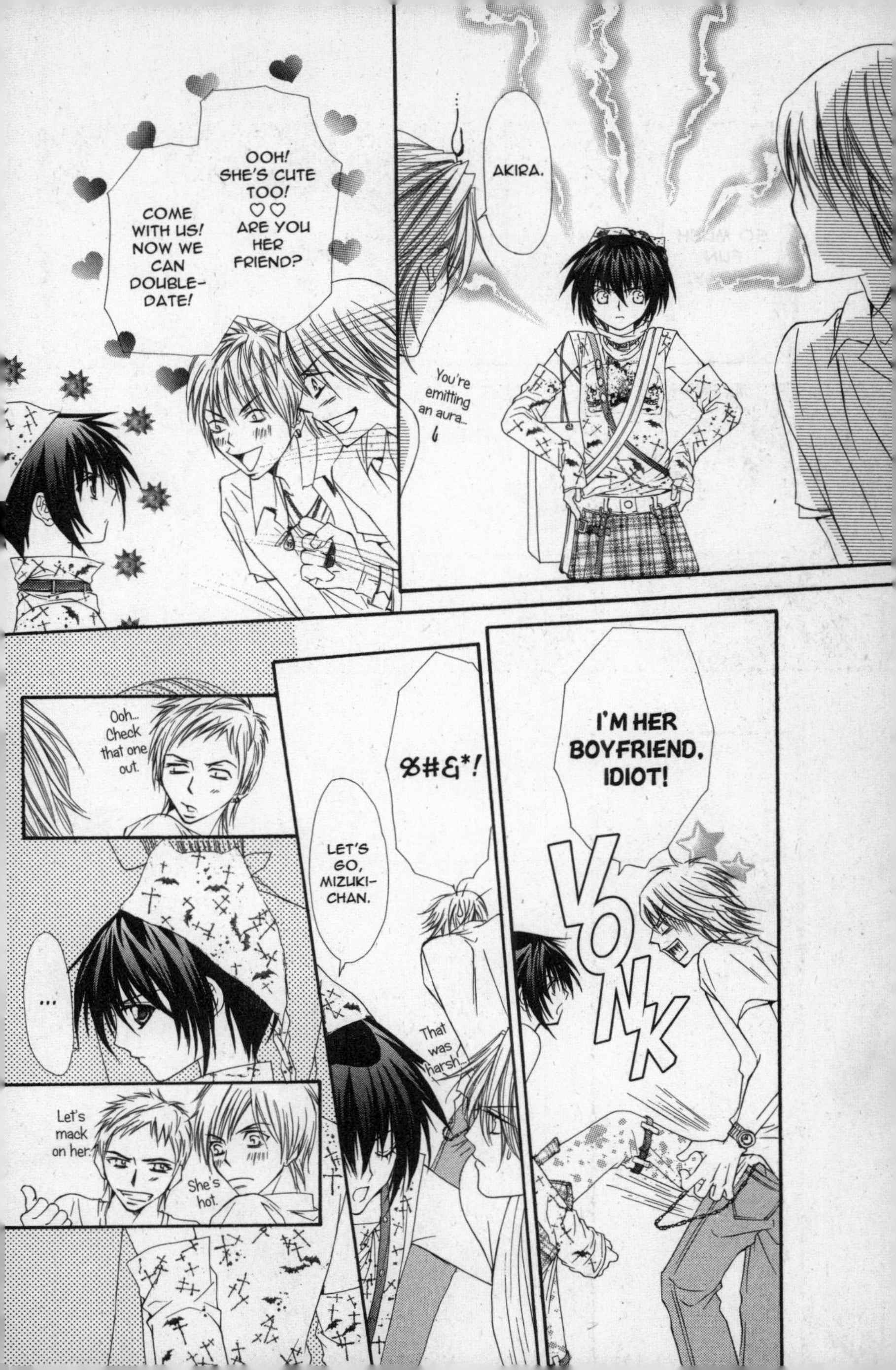
AKIRA.
You're emitting an aura...
OOH! SHE'S CUTE TOO! ♡♡ ARE YOU HER FRIEND?
COME WITH US! NOW WE CAN DOUBLE-DATE!
I'M HER BOYFRIEND, IDIOT!
VONK
&#Ɛ*!
LET'S GO, MIZUKI-CHAN.
That was harsh...
Ooh... Check that one out.
...
Let's mack on her.
She's hot.

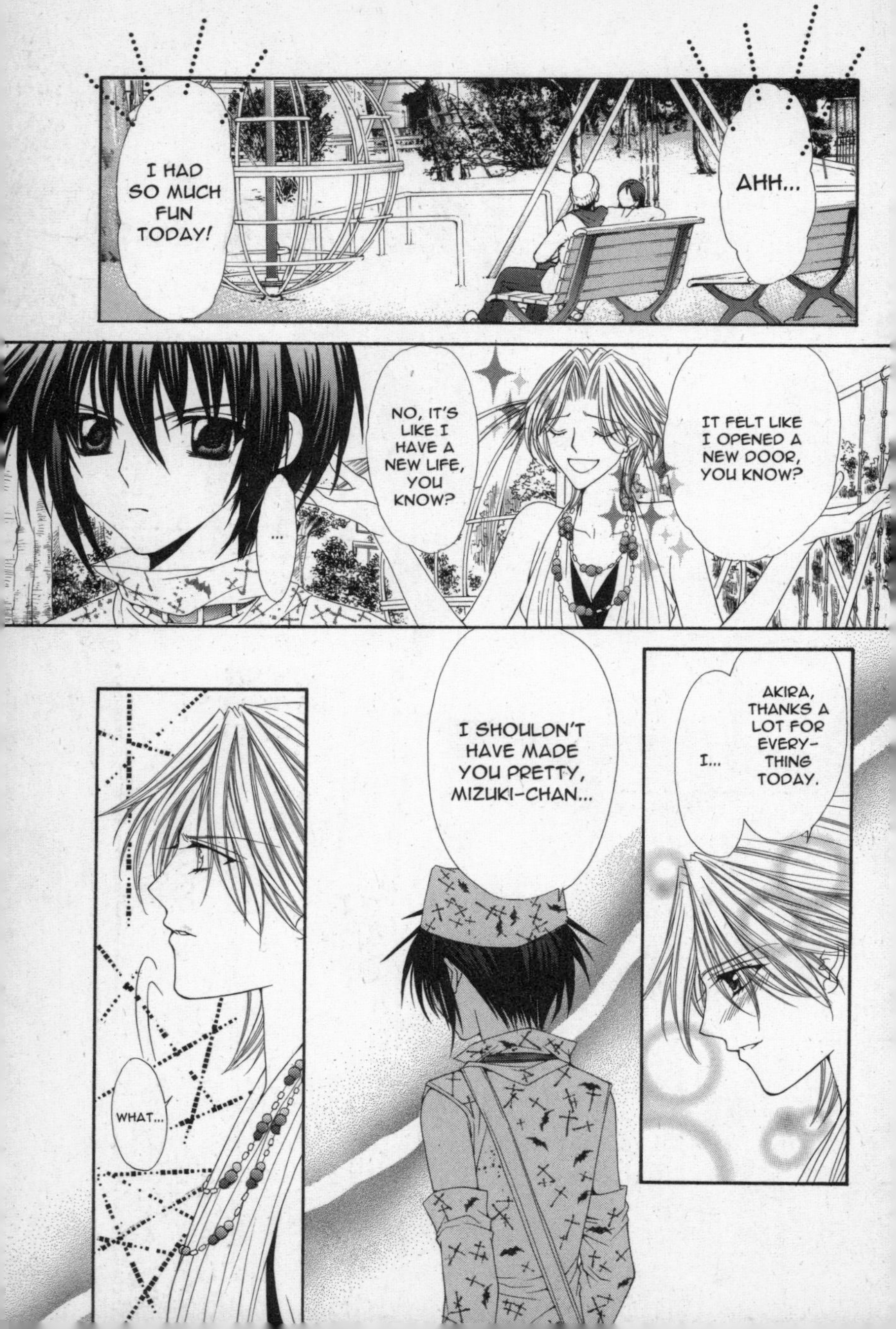
AHH...
I HAD SO MUCH FUN TODAY!
IT FELT LIKE I OPENED A NEW DOOR, YOU KNOW?
NO, IT'S LIKE I HAVE A NEW LIFE, YOU KNOW?
...
AKIRA, THANKS A LOT FOR EVERY-THING TODAY.
I...
I SHOULDN'T HAVE MADE YOU PRETTY, MIZUKI-CHAN...
WHAT...

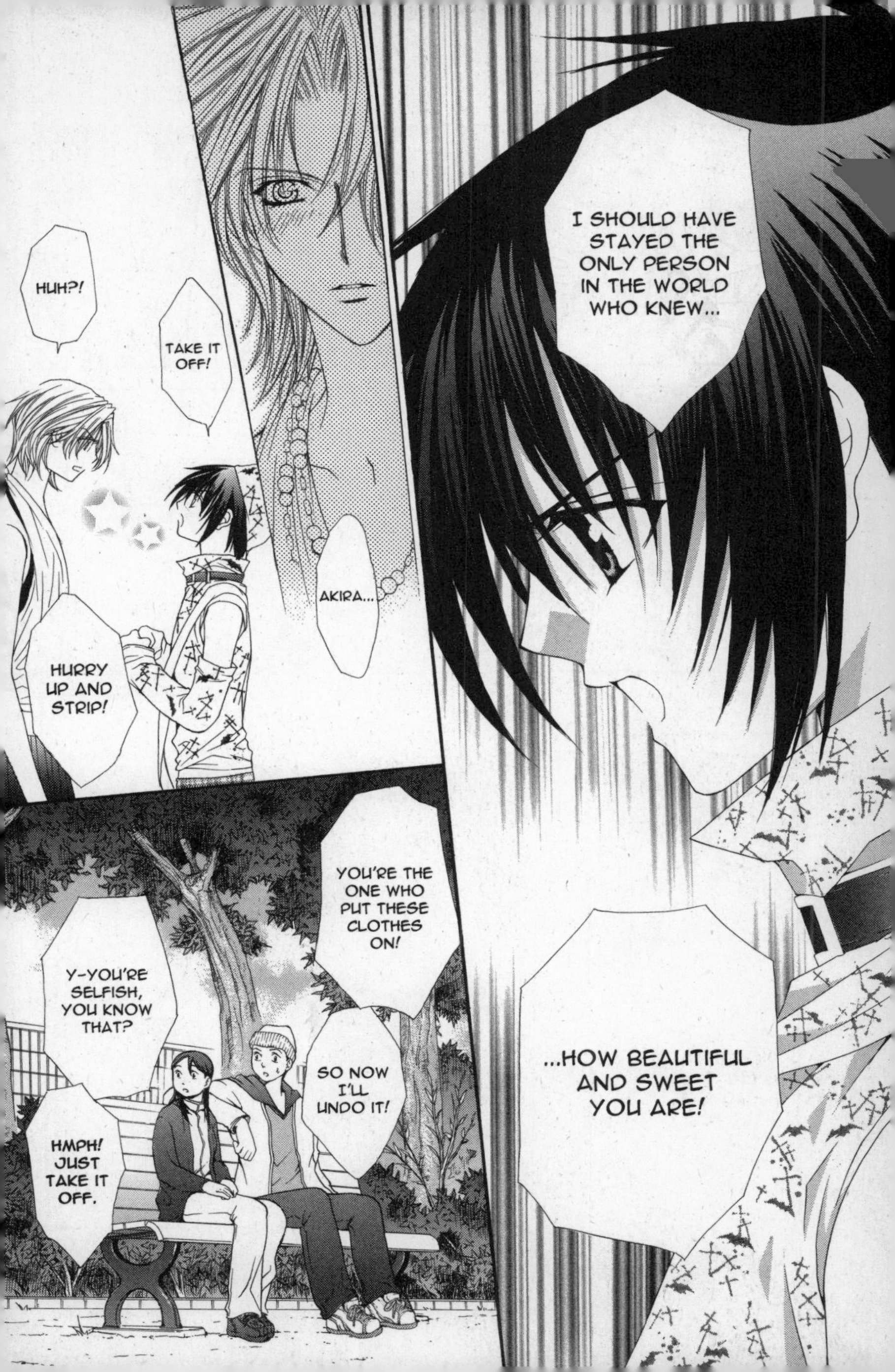
I SHOULD HAVE STAYED THE ONLY PERSON IN THE WORLD WHO KNEW...
...HOW BEAUTIFUL AND SWEET YOU ARE!
AKIRA...
TAKE IT OFF!
HUH?!
HURRY UP AND STRIP!
YOU'RE THE ONE WHO PUT THESE CLOTHES ON!
Y-YOU'RE SELFISH, YOU KNOW THAT?
SO NOW I'LL UNDO IT!
HMPH! JUST TAKE IT OFF.

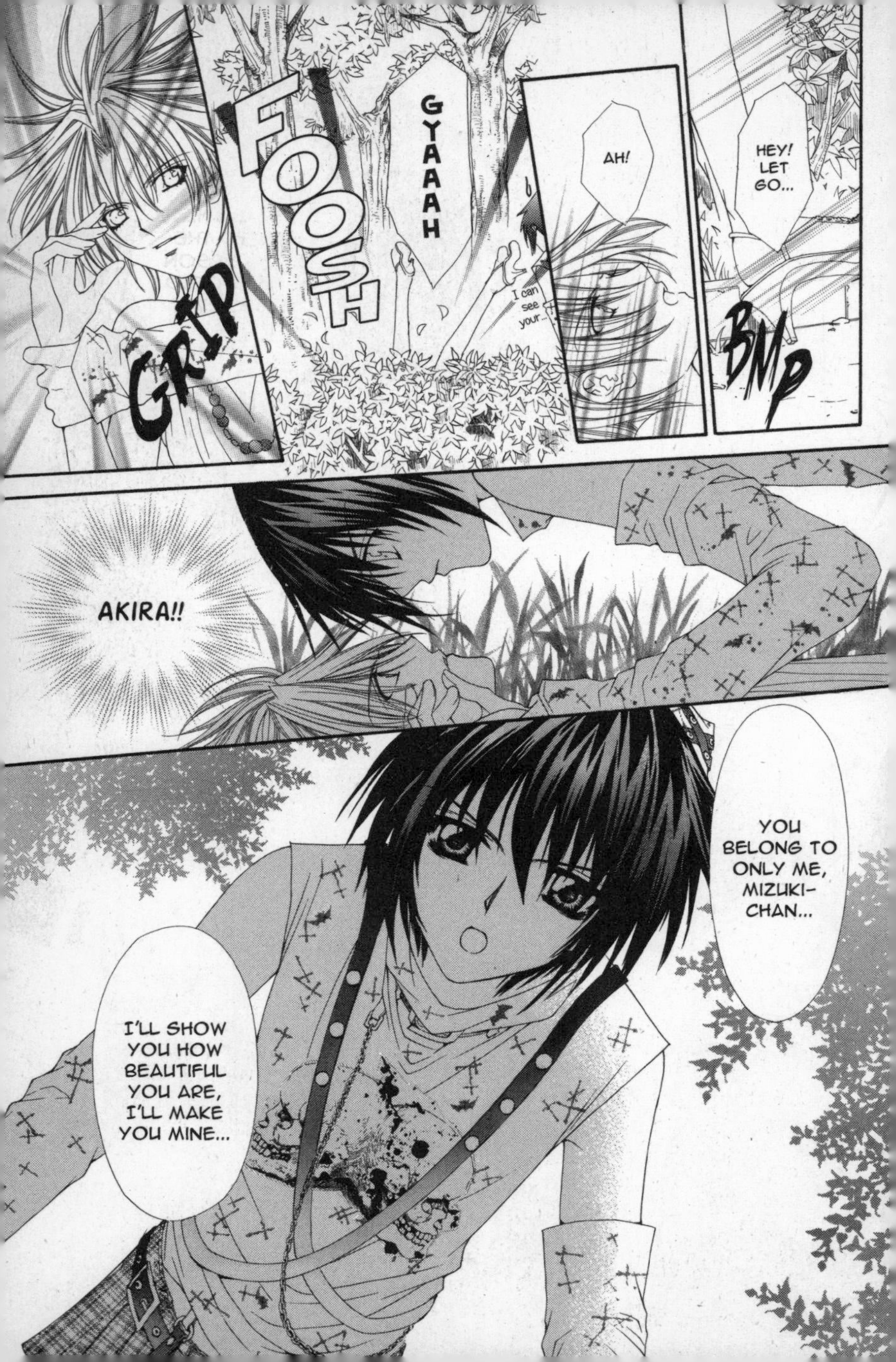
HEY! LET GO...
BMP
AH!
I can see your...
GYAAAH
FOOSH
GRIP
AKIRA!!
YOU BELONG TO ONLY ME, MIZUKI-CHAN...
I'LL SHOW YOU HOW BEAUTIFUL YOU ARE, I'LL MAKE YOU MINE...

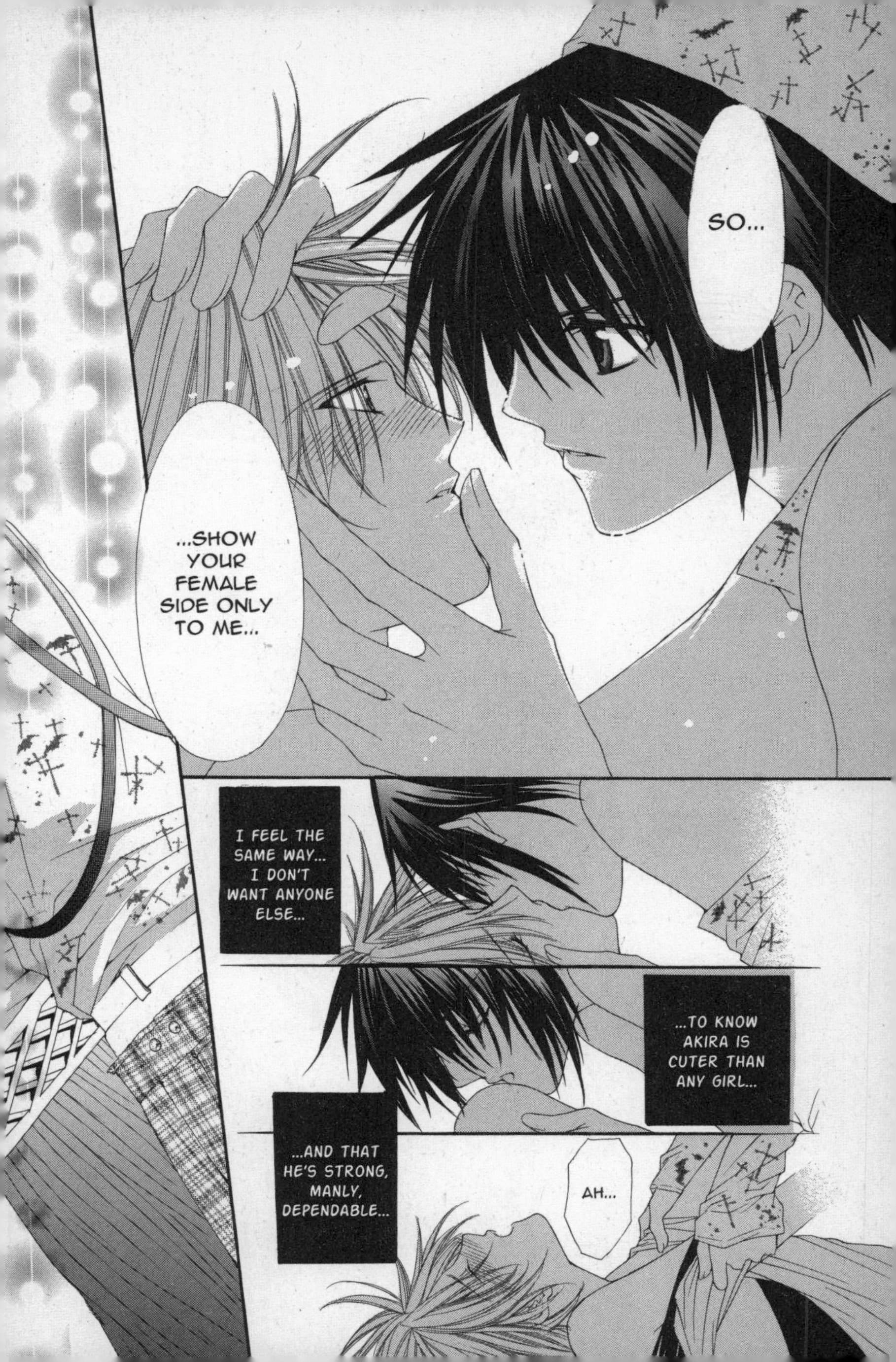
SO...
...SHOW YOUR FEMALE SIDE ONLY TO ME...
I FEEL THE SAME WAY... I DON'T WANT ANYONE ELSE...
...TO KNOW AKIRA IS CUTER THAN ANY GIRL...
...AND THAT HE'S STRONG, MANLY, DEPENDABLE...
AH...

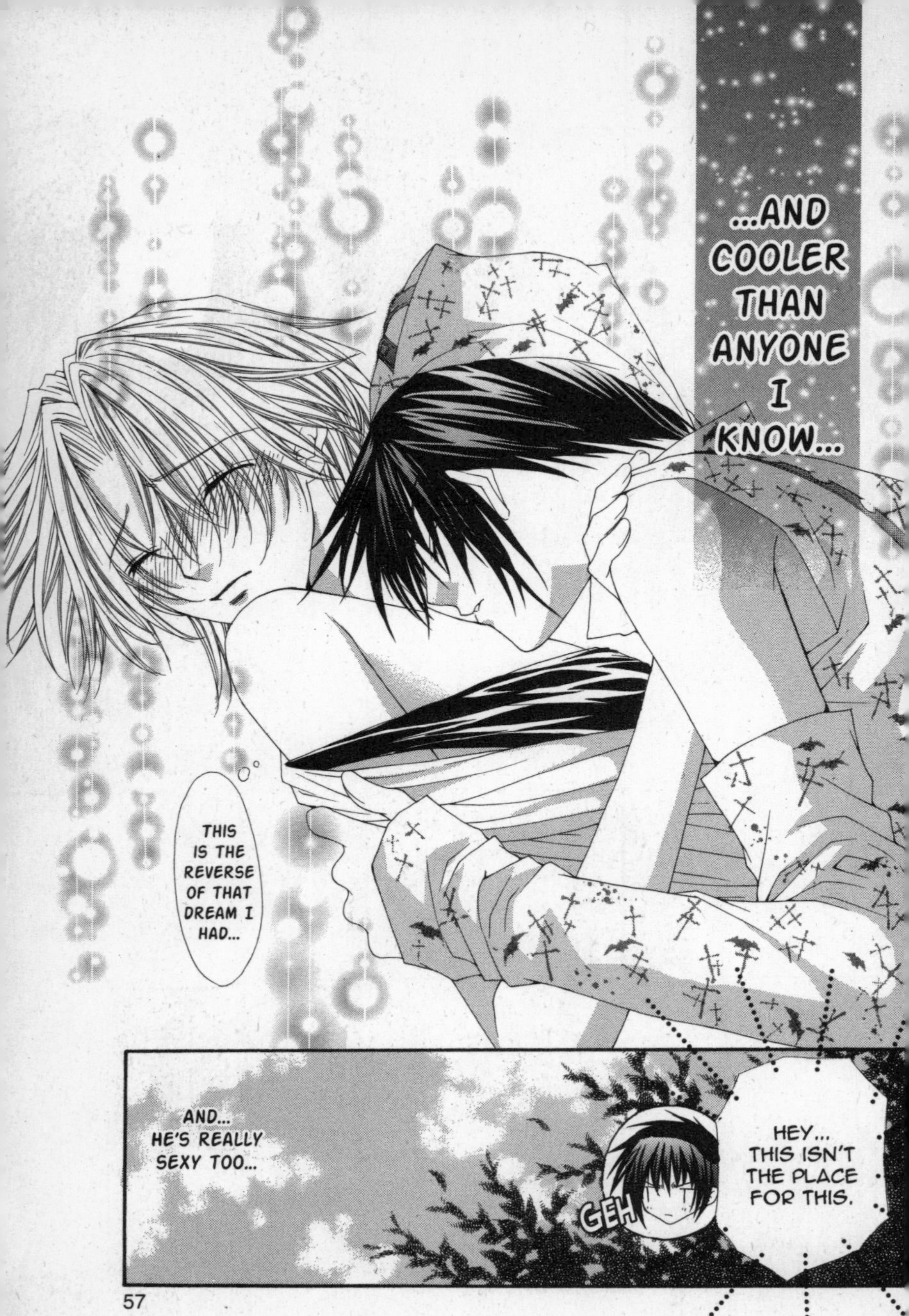
...AND COOLER THAN ANYONE I KNOW...
THIS IS THE REVERSE OF THAT DREAM I HAD...
HEY... THIS ISN'T THE PLACE FOR THIS.
GEH
AND... HE'S REALLY SEXY TOO...

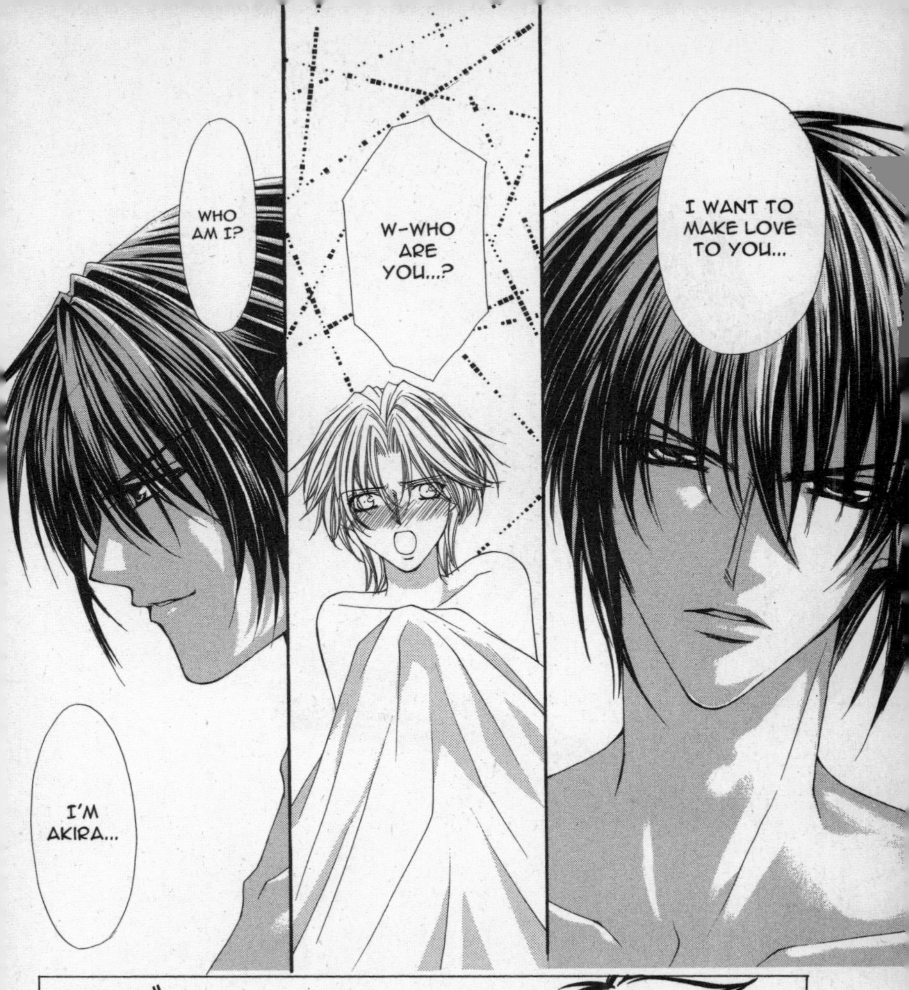
I WANT TO MAKE LOVE TO YOU...
W-WHO ARE YOU...?
WHO AM I?
I'M AKIRA...

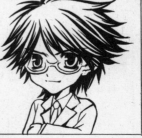

Answer me!! Ran ♥

Q1: What about Akira do you like best?

A1: His **body**.

Kidding. His pretty face, I guess.

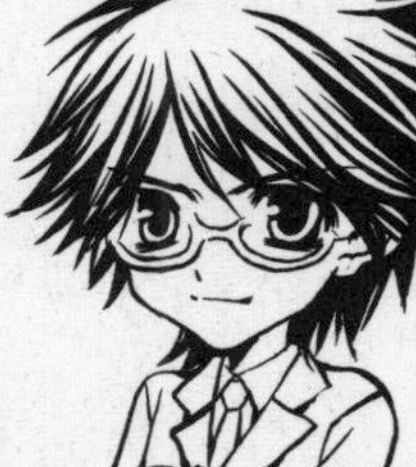

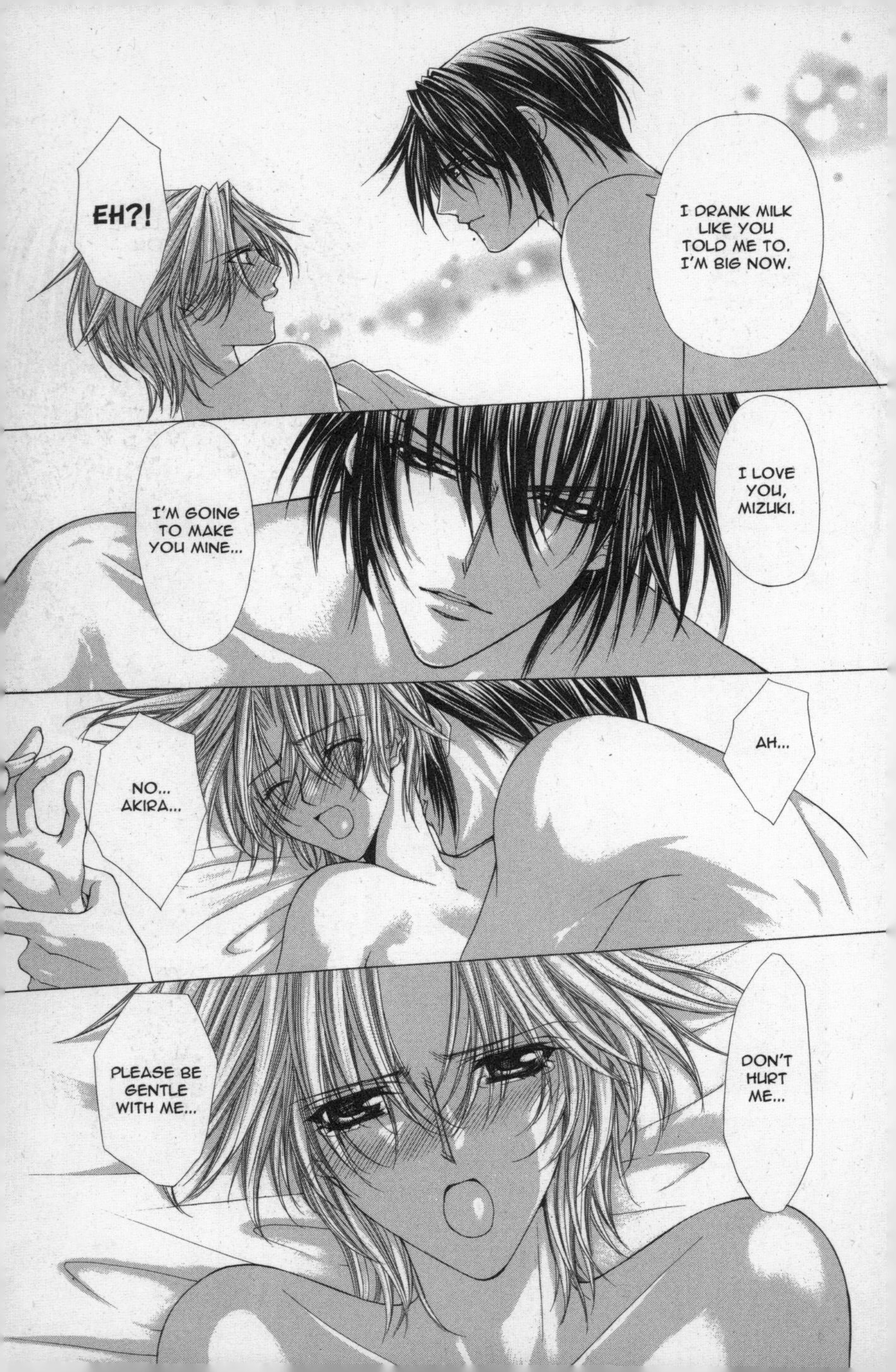
I DRANK MILK LIKE YOU TOLD ME TO. I'M BIG NOW.
EH?!
I LOVE YOU, MIZUKI.
I'M GOING TO MAKE YOU MINE...
AH...
NO... AKIRA...
DON'T HURT ME...
PLEASE BE GENTLE WITH ME...

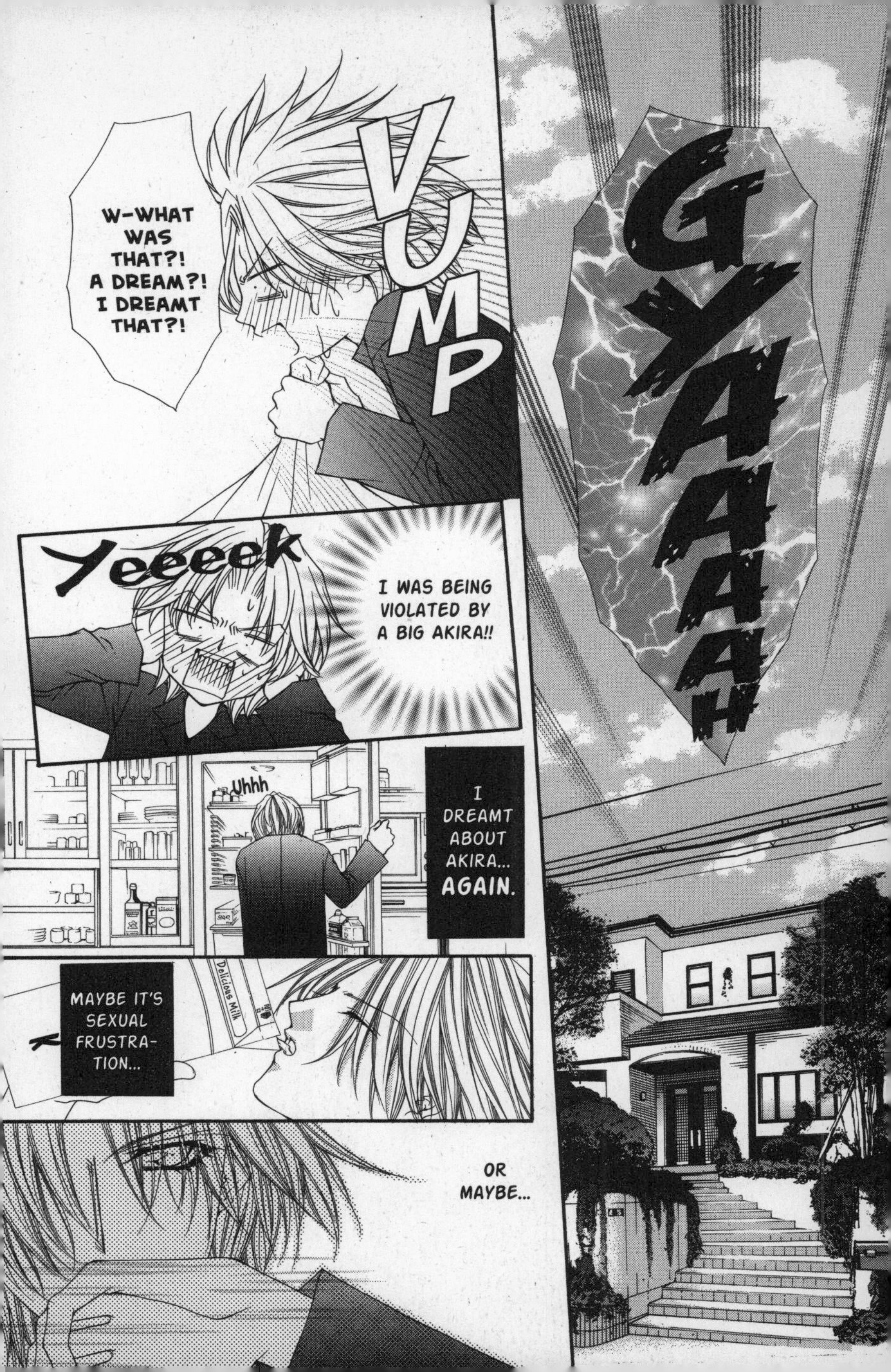
GYAAAAH
VUMP
W-WHAT WAS THAT?! A DREAM?! I DREAMT THAT?!
I WAS BEING VIOLATED BY A BIG AKIRA!!
Yeeeek
I DREAMT ABOUT AKIRA... AGAIN.
Uhhh
Delicious Milk
MAYBE IT'S SEXUAL FRUSTRA-TION...
OR MAYBE...

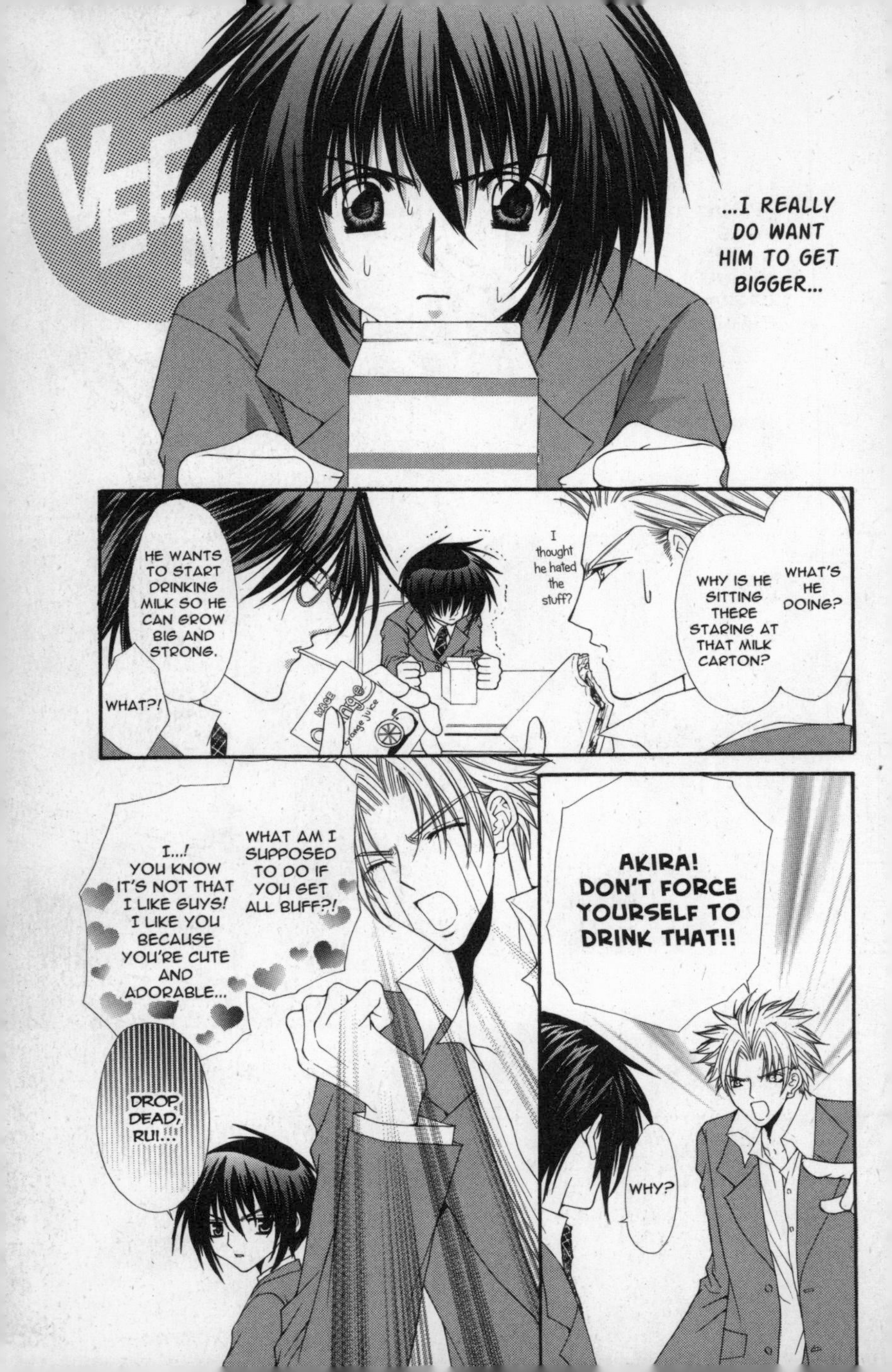
...I REALLY DO WANT HIM TO GET BIGGER...
WHAT'S HE DOING?
WHY IS HE SITTING THERE STARING AT THAT MILK CARTON?
I thought he hated the stuff?
HE WANTS TO START DRINKING MILK SO HE CAN GROW BIG AND STRONG.
WHAT?!
AKIRA! DON'T FORCE YOURSELF TO DRINK THAT!!
WHY?
WHAT AM I SUPPOSED TO DO IF YOU GET ALL BUFF?!
I...! YOU KNOW IT'S NOT THAT I LIKE GUYS! I LIKE YOU BECAUSE YOU'RE CUTE AND ADORABLE...
DROP, DEAD, RUI...

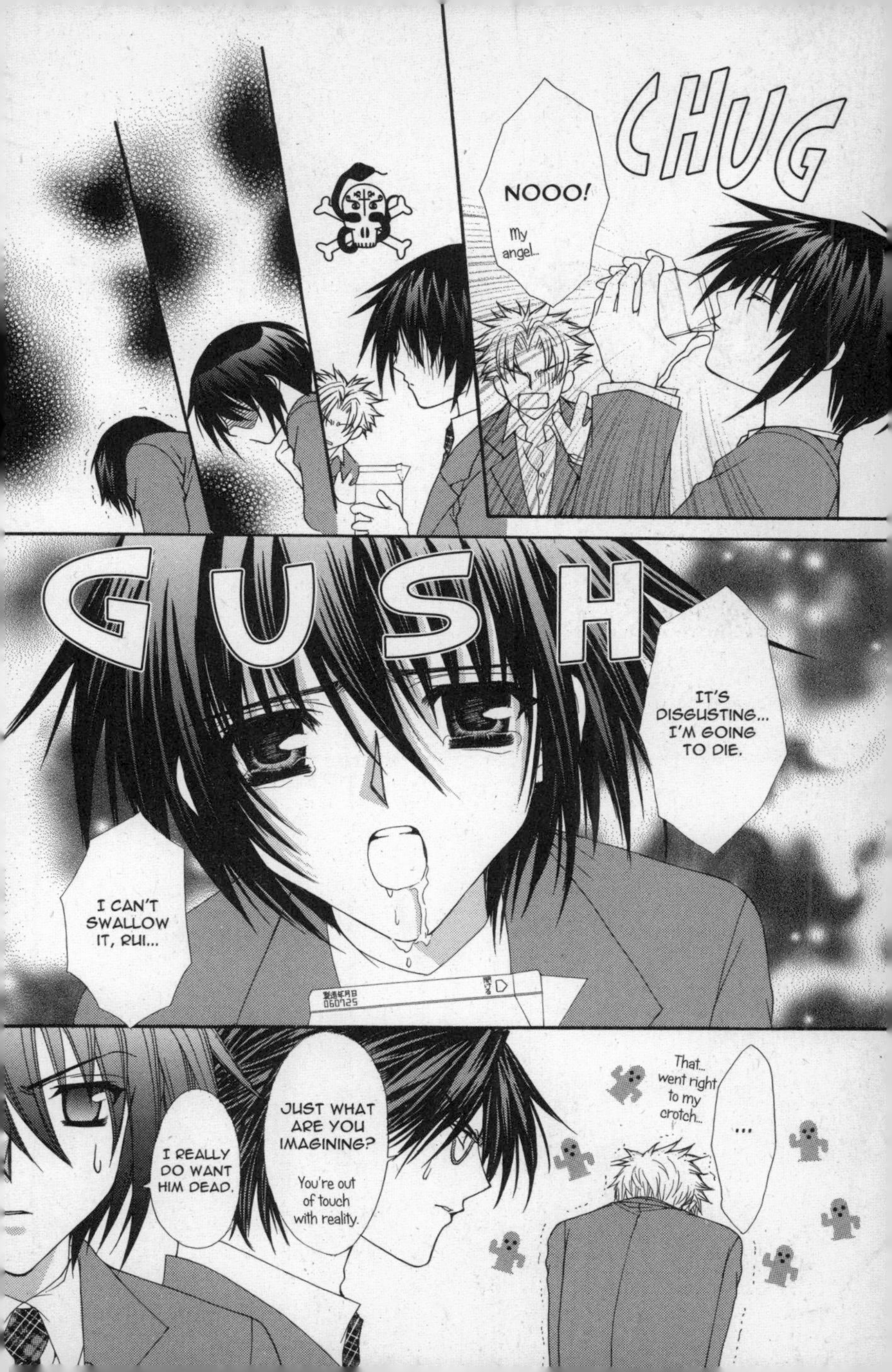
CHUG
NOOO!
My angel...
GUSH
IT'S DISGUSTING... I'M GOING TO DIE.
I CAN'T SWALLOW IT, RUI...
That... went right to my crotch...
...
JUST WHAT ARE YOU IMAGINING?
You're out of touch with reality.
I REALLY DO WANT HIM DEAD.

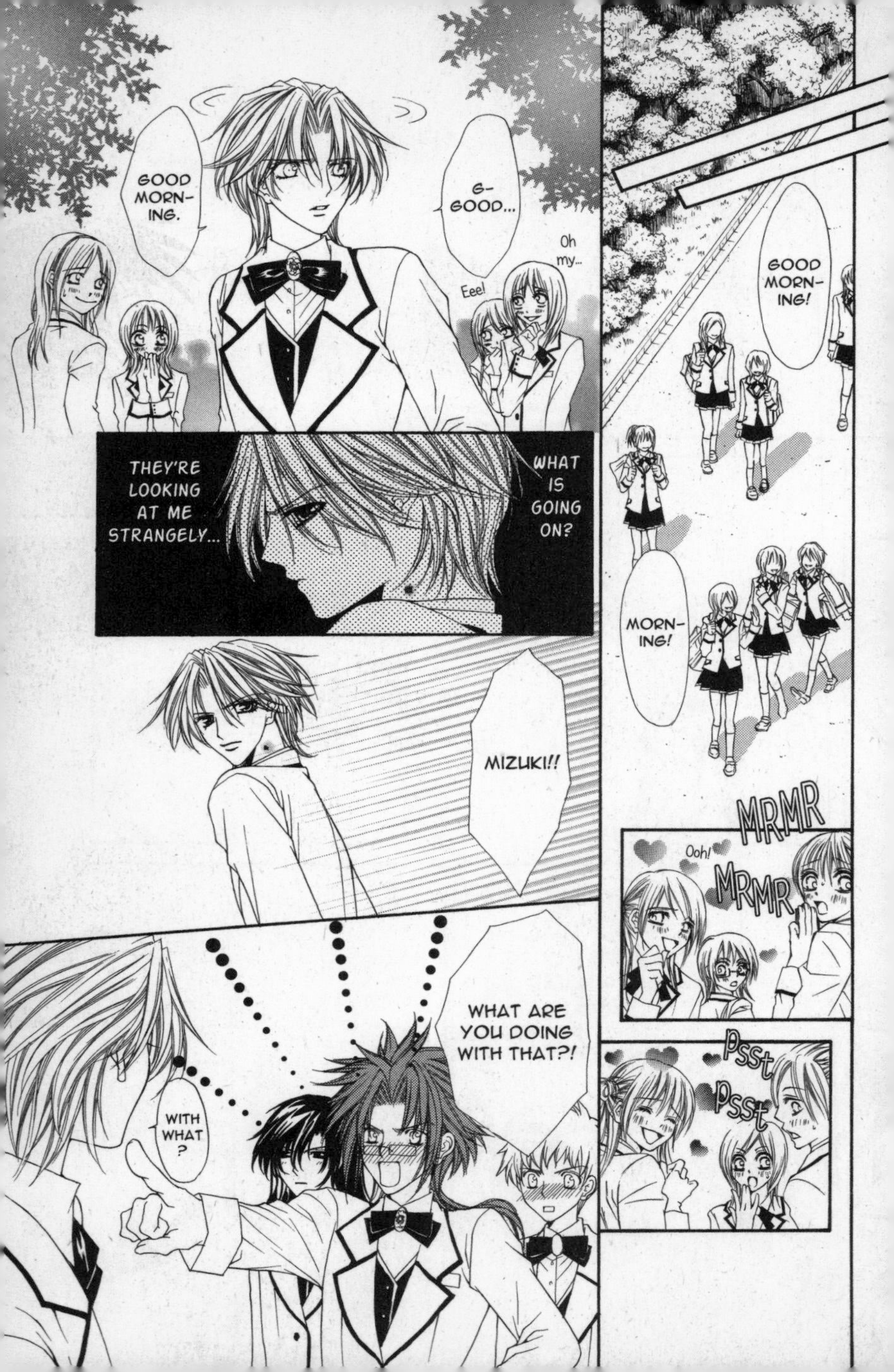
GOOD MORNING!
MORNING!
MRMR
Ooh!
MRMR
Psst
Psst
G-GOOD...
Oh my...
Eee!
GOOD MORNING.
WHAT IS GOING ON?
THEY'RE LOOKING AT ME STRANGELY...
MIZUKI!!
WHAT ARE YOU DOING WITH THAT?!
WITH WHAT?

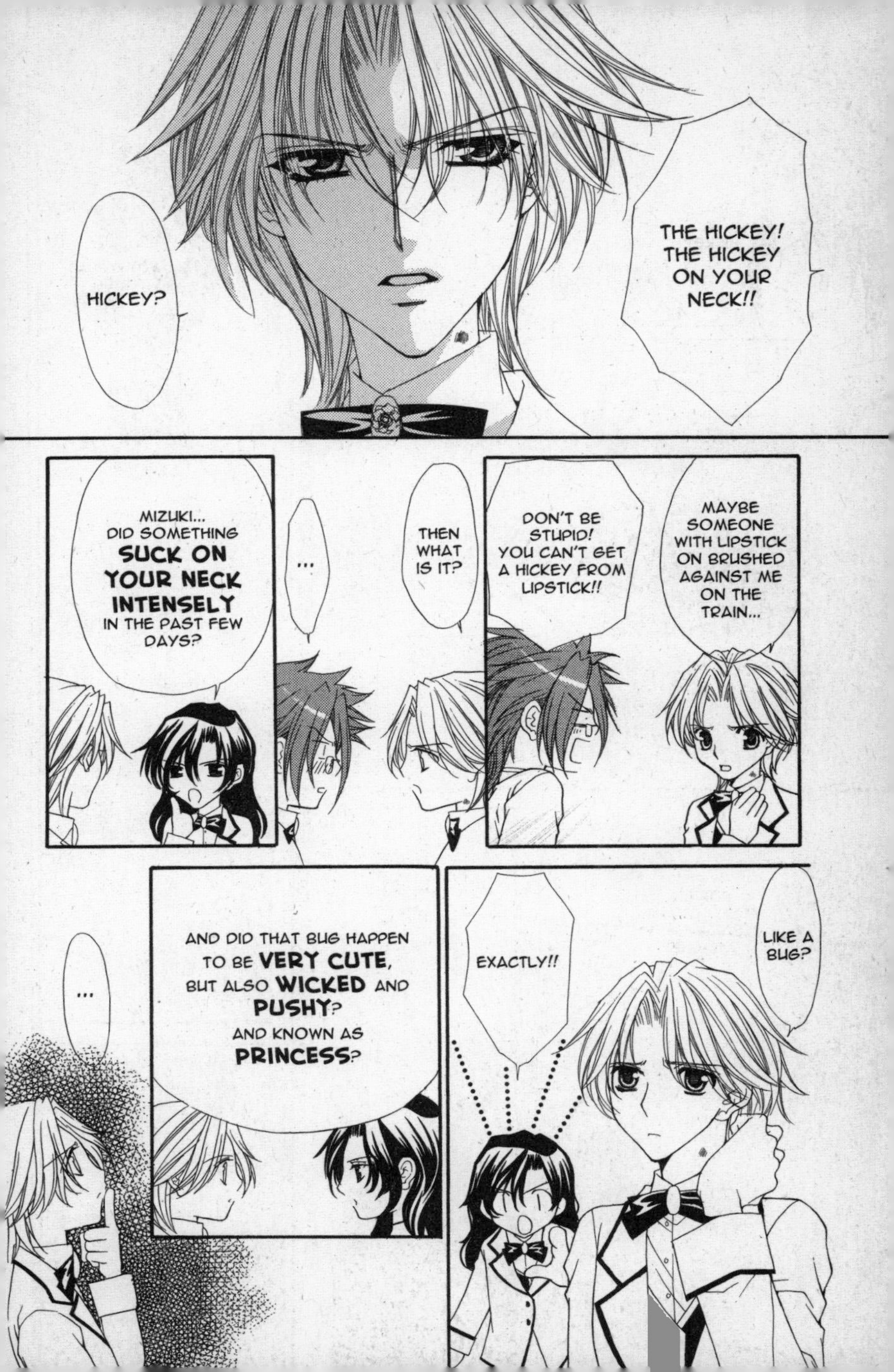
THE HICKEY! THE HICKEY ON YOUR NECK!!
HICKEY?
MAYBE SOMEONE WITH LIPSTICK ON BRUSHED AGAINST ME ON THE TRAIN...
DON'T BE STUPID! YOU CAN'T GET A HICKEY FROM LIPSTICK!!
THEN WHAT IS IT?
...
MIZUKI... DID SOMETHING SUCK ON YOUR NECK INTENSELY IN THE PAST FEW DAYS?
LIKE A BUG?
EXACTLY!!
AND DID THAT BUG HAPPEN TO BE VERY CUTE, BUT ALSO WICKED AND PUSHY? AND KNOWN AS PRINCESS?
...

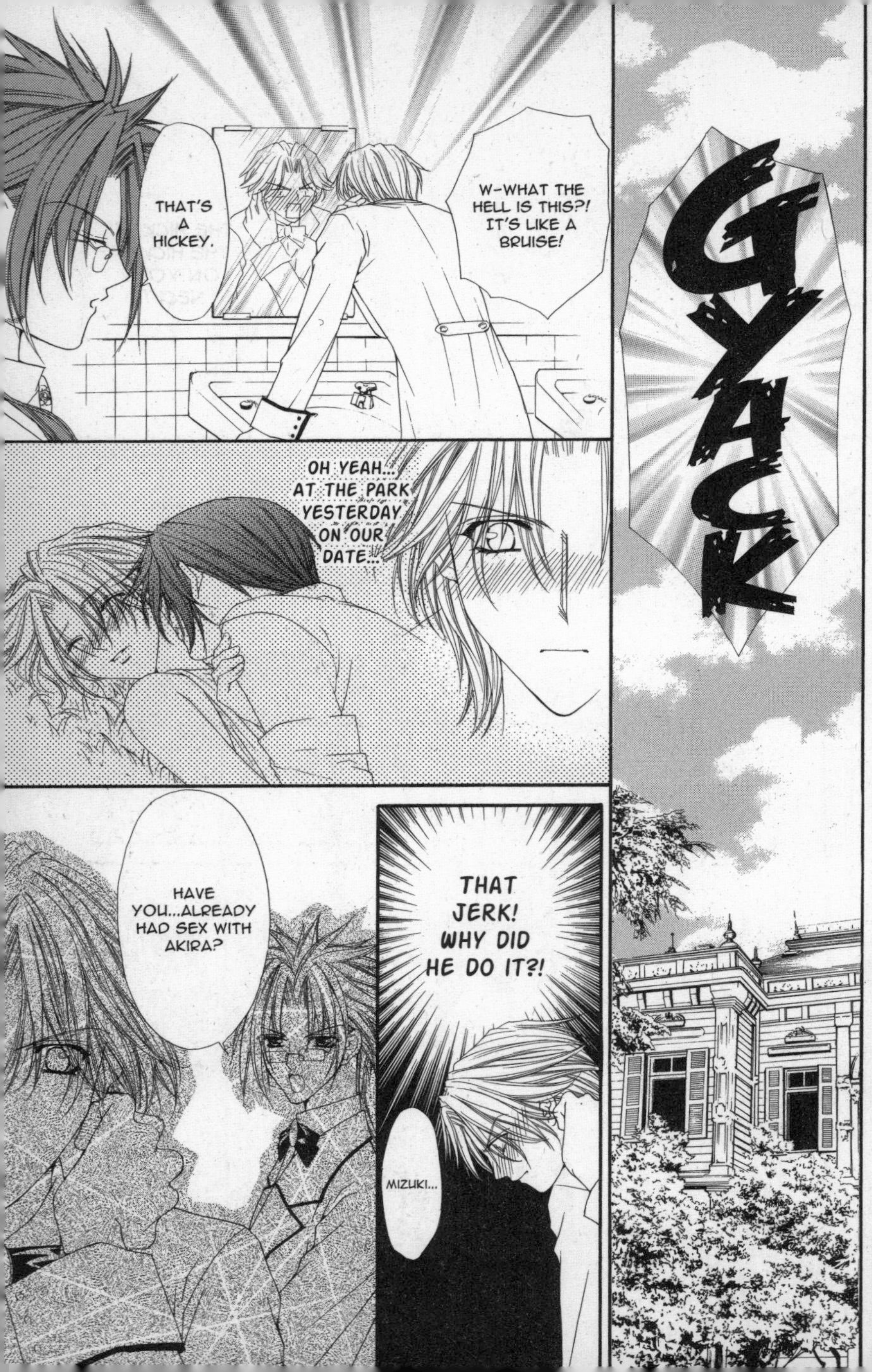
GYACK
W-WHAT THE HELL IS THIS?! IT'S LIKE A BRUISE!
THAT'S A HICKEY.
OH YEAH... AT THE PARK YESTERDAY ON OUR DATE...
THAT JERK! WHY DID HE DO IT?!
MIZUKI...
HAVE YOU...ALREADY HAD SEX WITH AKIRA?

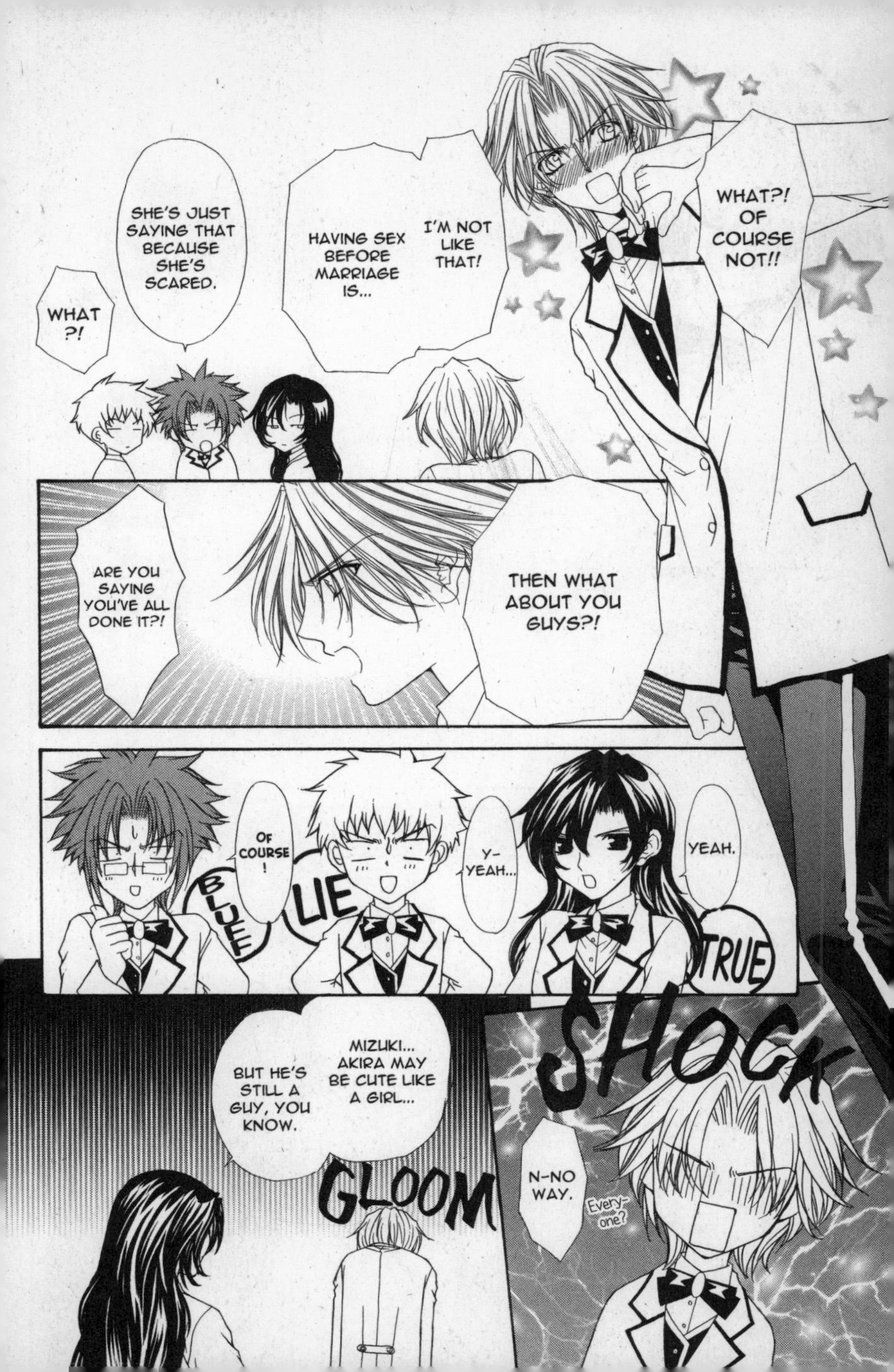
WHAT?! OF COURSE NOT!!
I'M NOT LIKE THAT!
HAVING SEX BEFORE MARRIAGE IS...
SHE'S JUST SAYING THAT BECAUSE SHE'S SCARED.
WHAT ?!
THEN WHAT ABOUT YOU GUYS?!
ARE YOU SAYING YOU'VE ALL DONE IT?!
YEAH.
TRUE
Y-YEAH...
LIE
OF COURSE!
BLUFF
SHOCK
N-NO WAY.
Every-one?
MIZUKI... AKIRA MAY BE CUTE LIKE A GIRL...
BUT HE'S STILL A GUY, YOU KNOW.
GLOOM

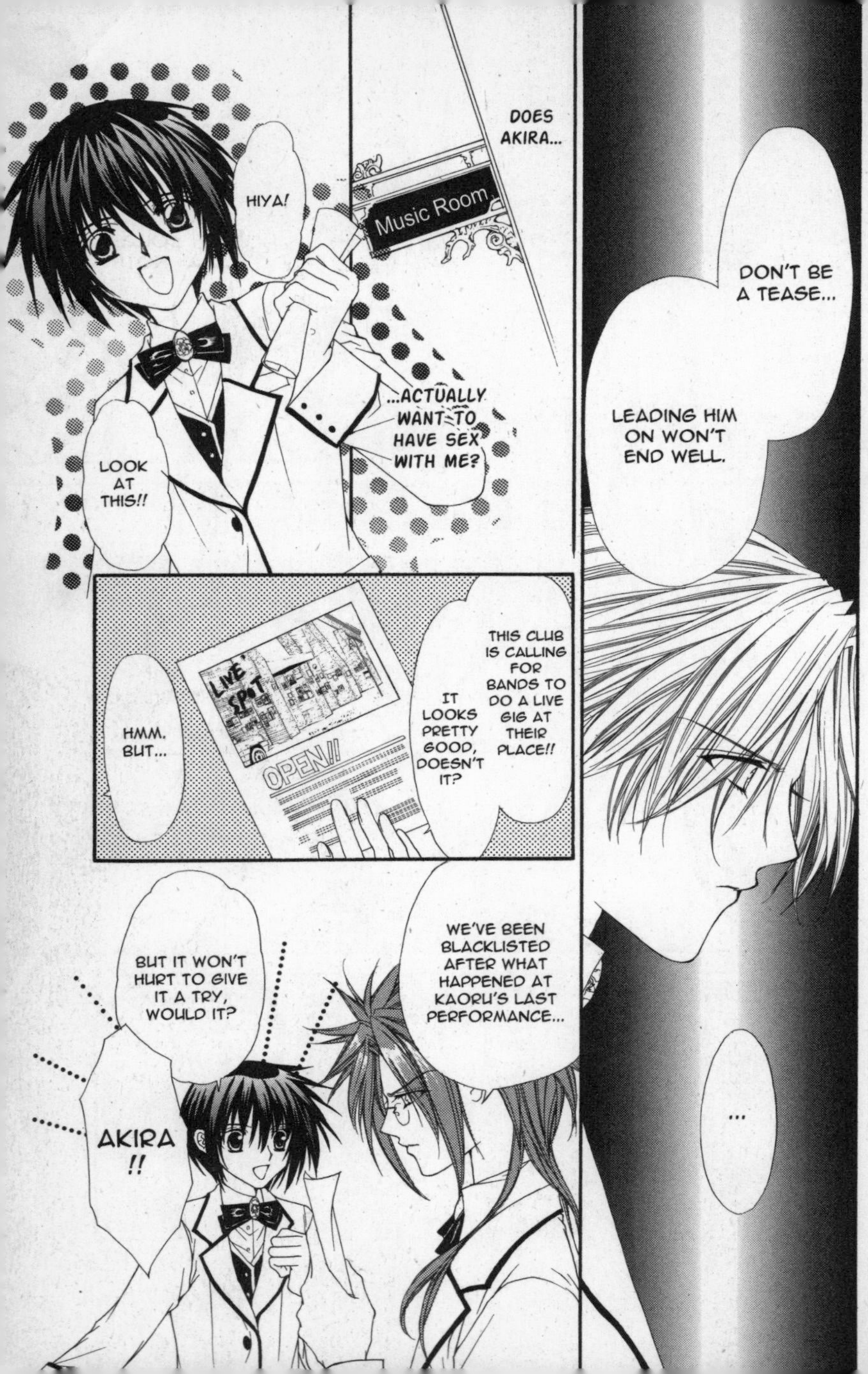
DON'T BE A TEASE...
LEADING HIM ON WON'T END WELL.
...
DOES AKIRA...
HIYA!
Music Room
...ACTUALLY WANT TO HAVE SEX WITH ME?
LOOK AT THIS!!
THIS CLUB IS CALLING FOR BANDS TO DO A LIVE GIG AT THEIR PLACE!!
IT LOOKS PRETTY GOOD, DOESN'T IT?
HMM. BUT...
LIVE SPOT
OPEN!!
WE'VE BEEN BLACKLISTED AFTER WHAT HAPPENED AT KAORU'S LAST PERFORMANCE...
BUT IT WON'T HURT TO GIVE IT A TRY, WOULD IT?
AKIRA !!

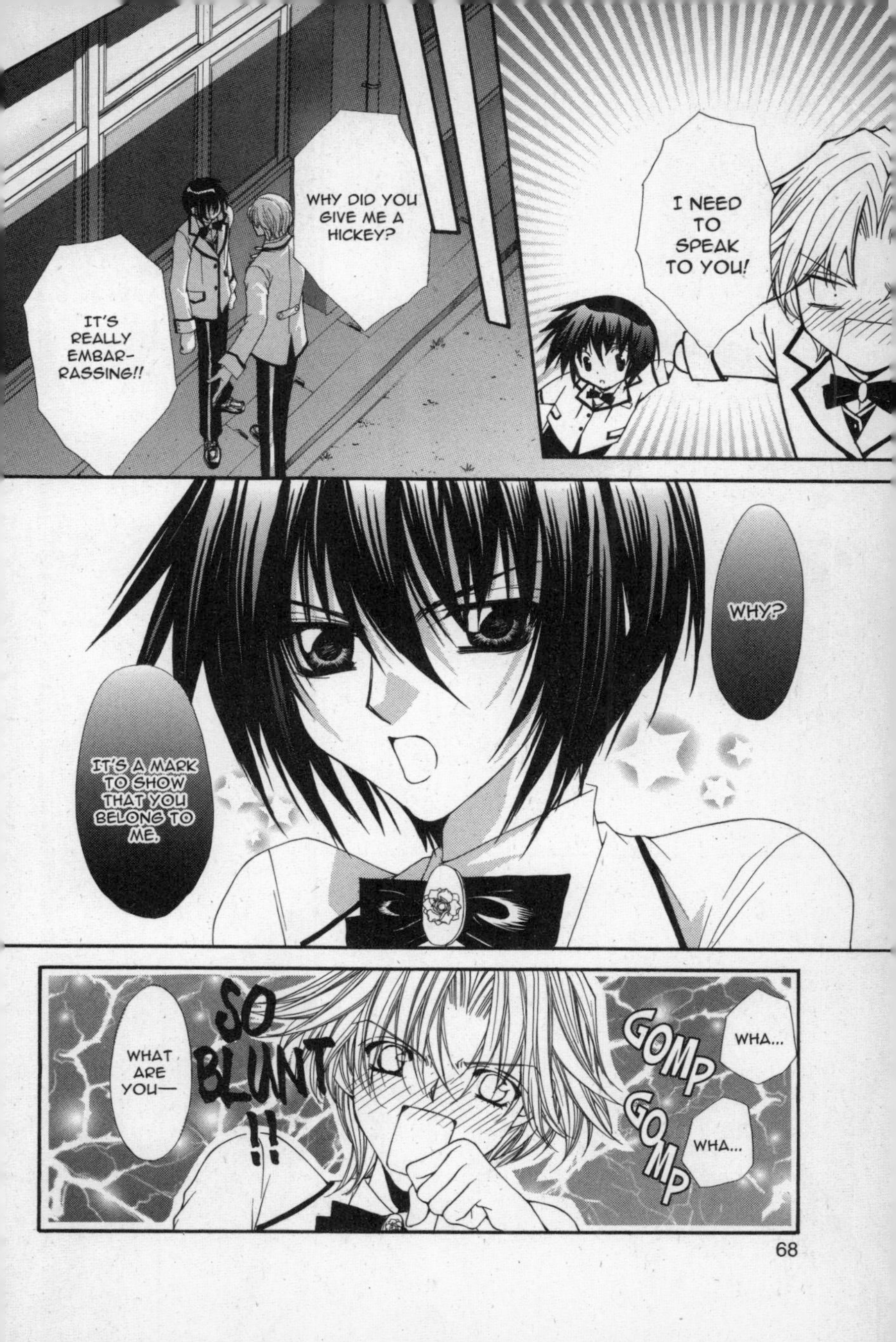
I NEED TO SPEAK TO YOU!
WHY DID YOU GIVE ME A HICKEY?
IT'S REALLY EMBARRASSING!!
WHY?
IT'S A MARK TO SHOW THAT YOU BELONG TO ME.
WHA...
GOMP GOMP
WHA...
SO BLUNT!!
WHAT ARE YOU—

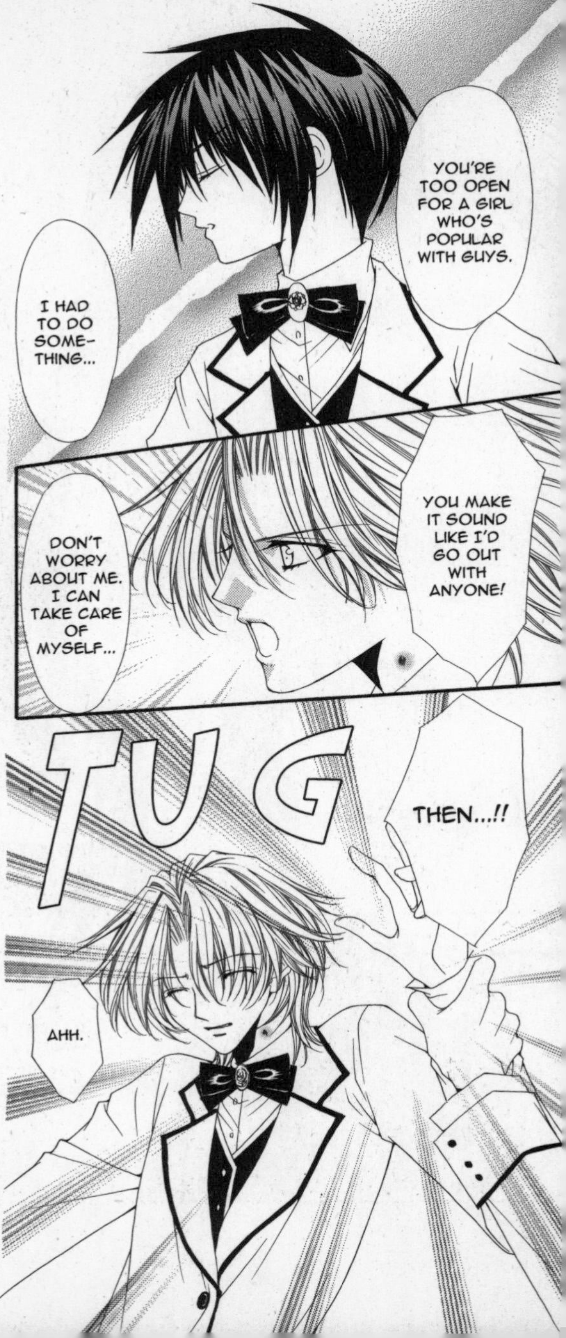
YOU'RE TOO OPEN FOR A GIRL WHO'S POPULAR WITH GUYS.
I HAD TO DO SOME-THING...
YOU MAKE IT SOUND LIKE I'D GO OUT WITH ANYONE!
DON'T WORRY ABOUT ME. I CAN TAKE CARE OF MYSELF...
THEN...!!
TUG
AHH.

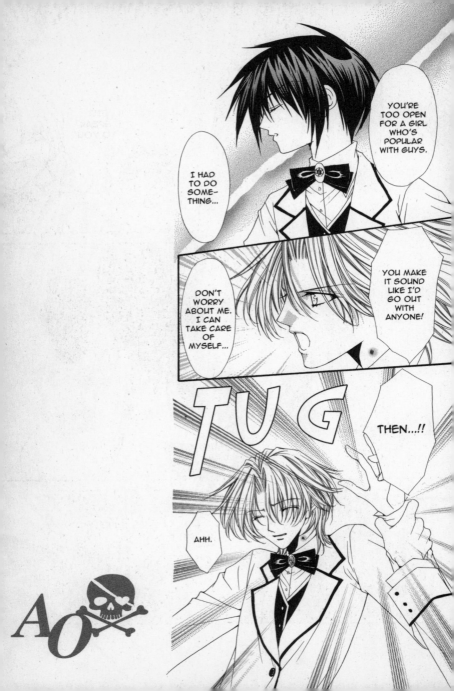

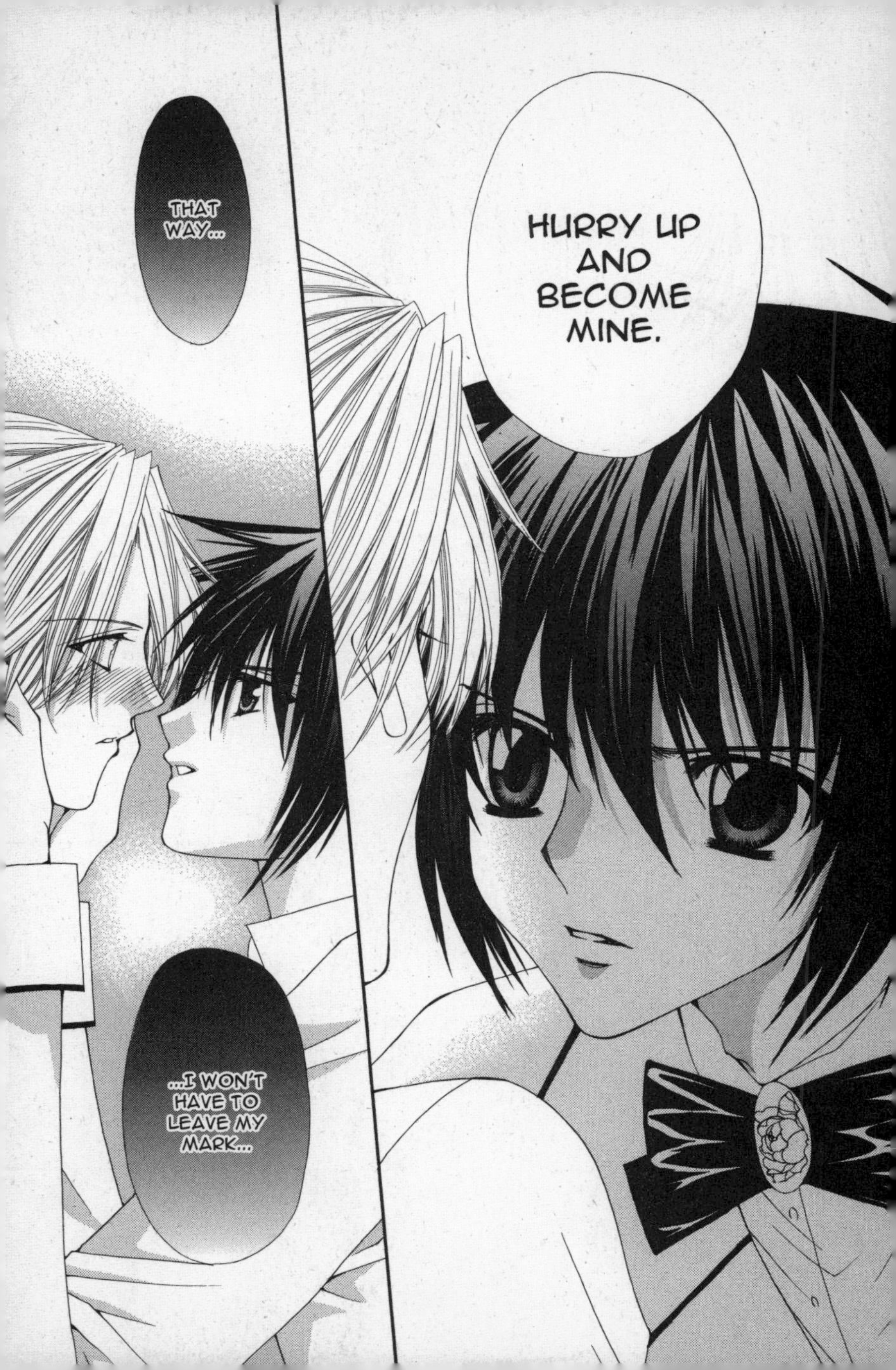
HURRY UP AND BECOME MINE.
THAT WAY...
...I WON'T HAVE TO LEAVE MY MARK...

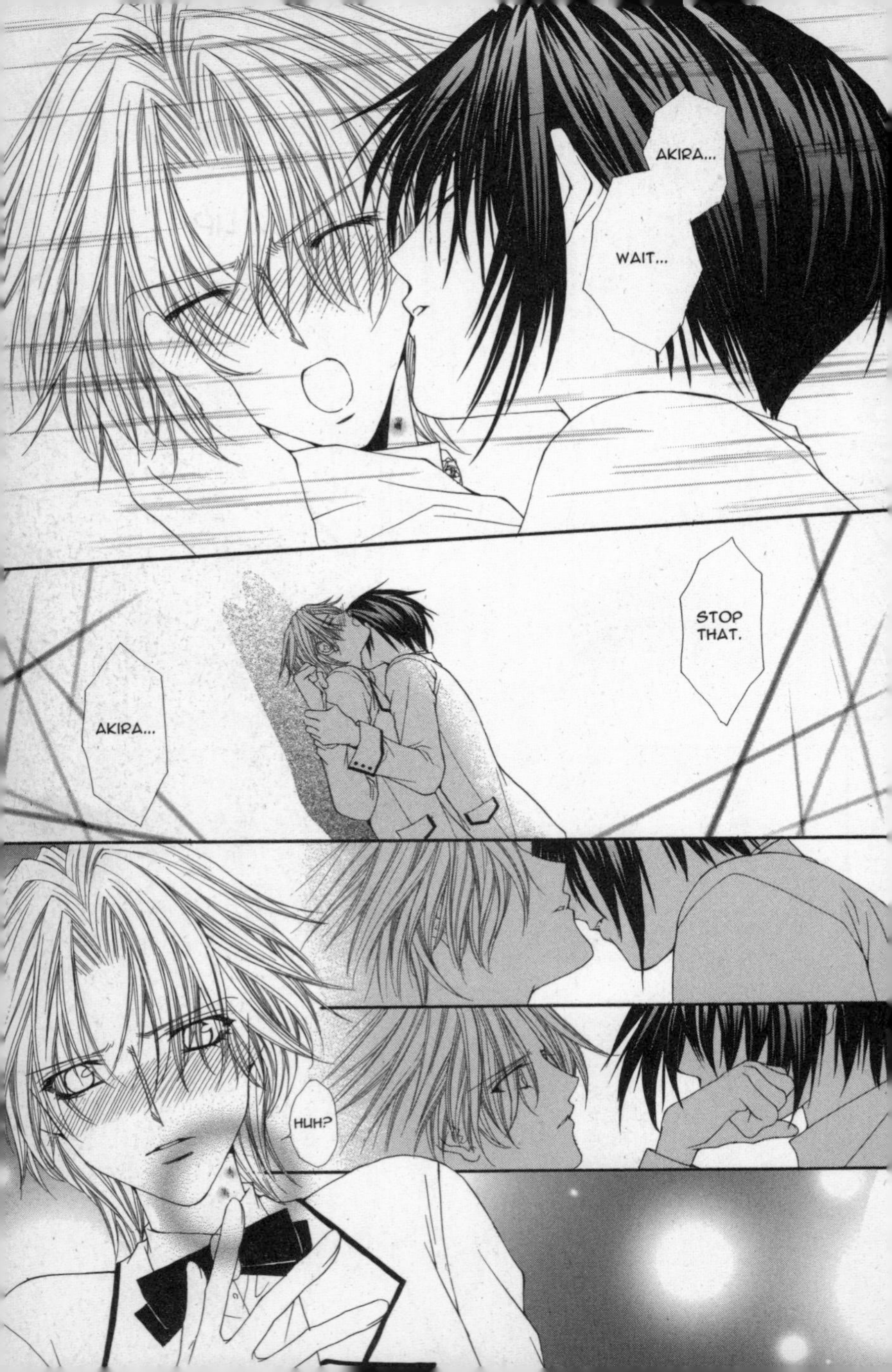
AKIRA...
WAIT...
STOP THAT.
AKIRA...
HUH?

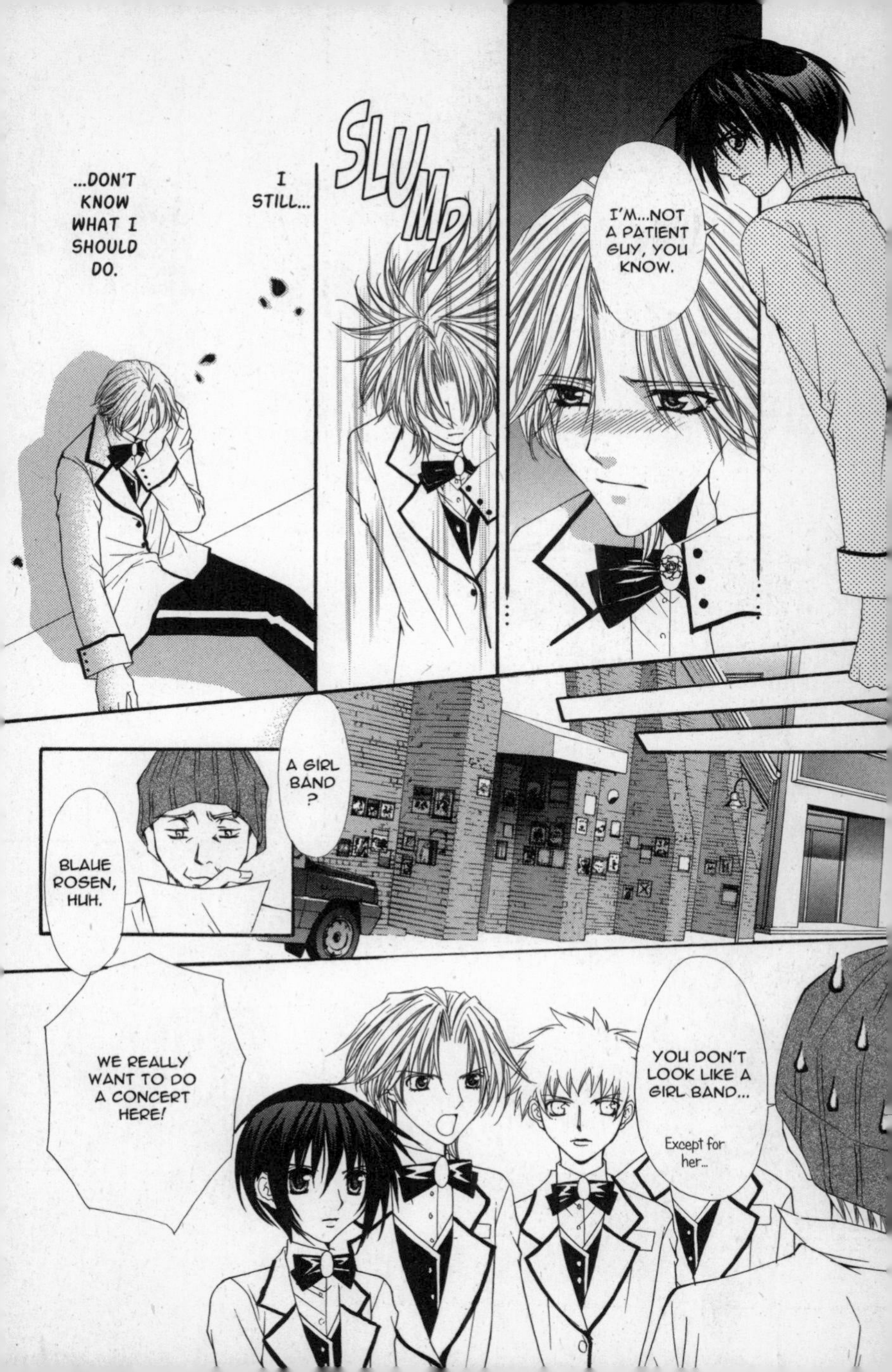
I'M...NOT A PATIENT GUY, YOU KNOW.
SLUMP
I STILL...
...DON'T KNOW WHAT I SHOULD DO.
A GIRL BAND?
BLAUE ROSEN, HUH.
YOU DON'T LOOK LIKE A GIRL BAND...
Except for her...
WE REALLY WANT TO DO A CONCERT HERE!

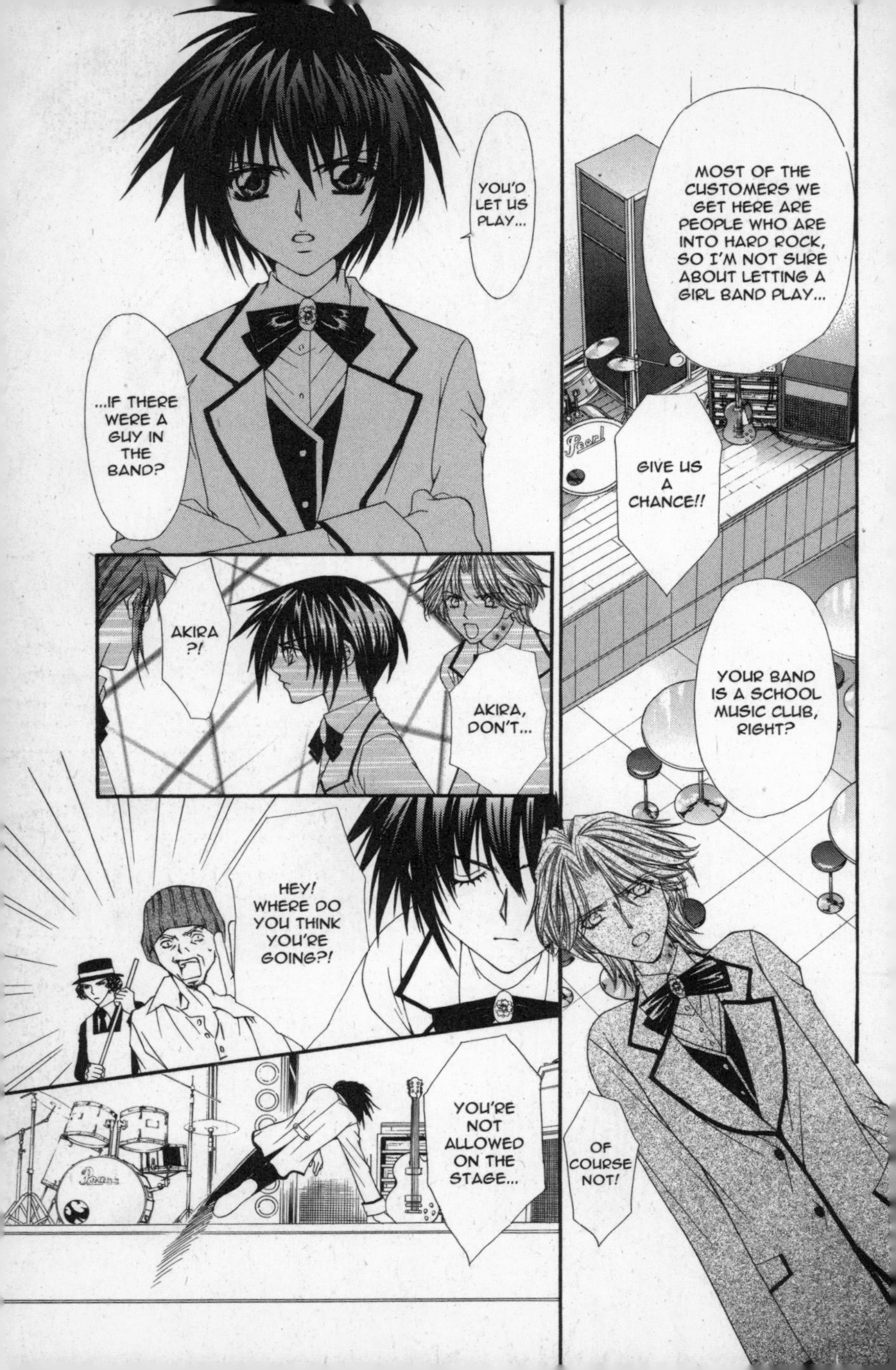
MOST OF THE CUSTOMERS WE GET HERE ARE PEOPLE WHO ARE INTO HARD ROCK, SO I'M NOT SURE ABOUT LETTING A GIRL BAND PLAY...
GIVE US A CHANCE!!
YOUR BAND IS A SCHOOL MUSIC CLUB, RIGHT?
OF COURSE NOT!
YOU'D LET US PLAY...
...IF THERE WERE A GUY IN THE BAND?
AKIRA?!
AKIRA, DON'T...
HEY! WHERE DO YOU THINK YOU'RE GOING?!
YOU'RE NOT ALLOWED ON THE STAGE...

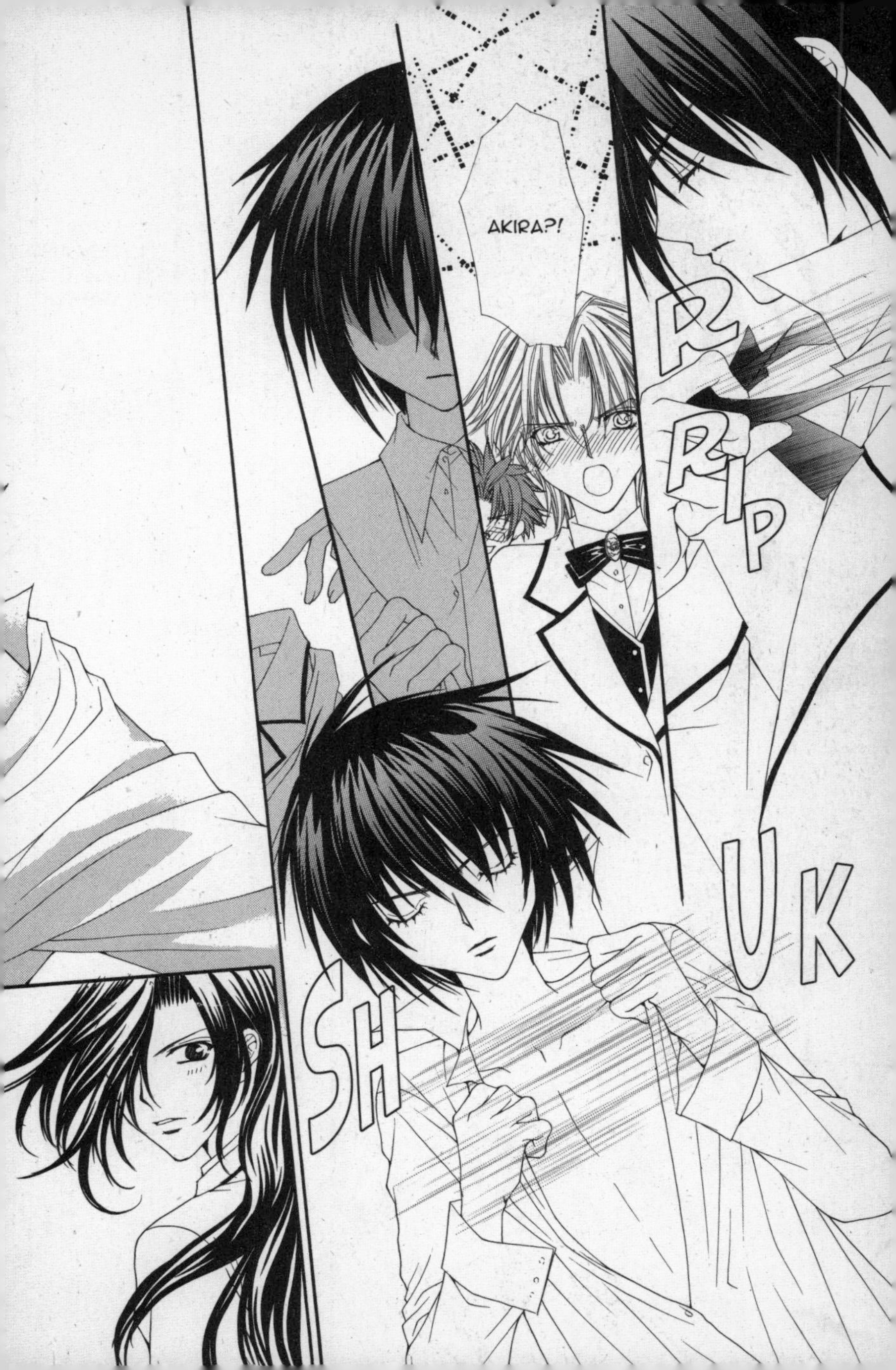
RRIP
AKIRA?!
SHUK

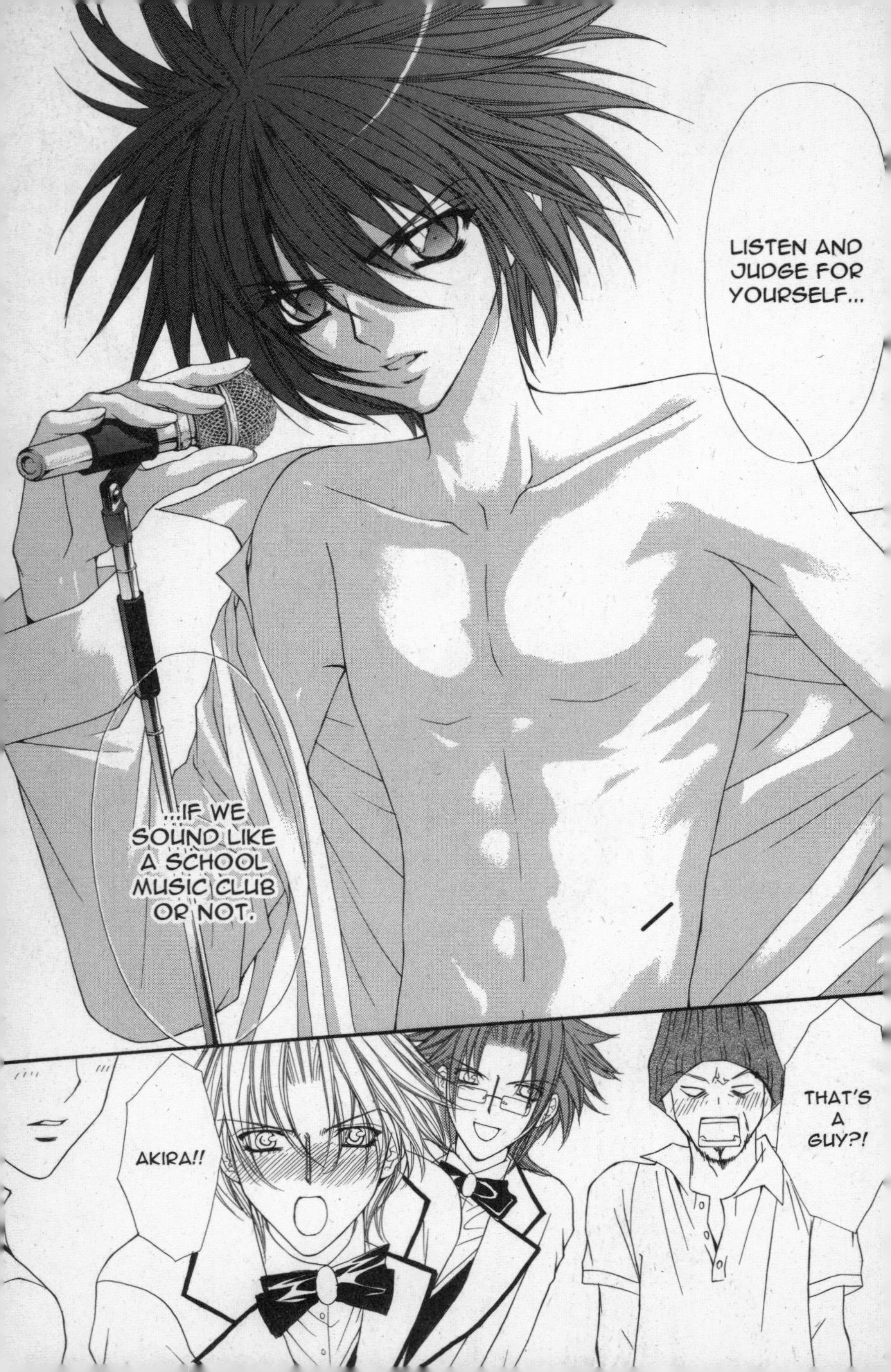
LISTEN AND JUDGE FOR YOURSELF...
...IF WE SOUND LIKE A SCHOOL MUSIC CLUB OR NOT.
THAT'S A GUY?!
AKIRA!!

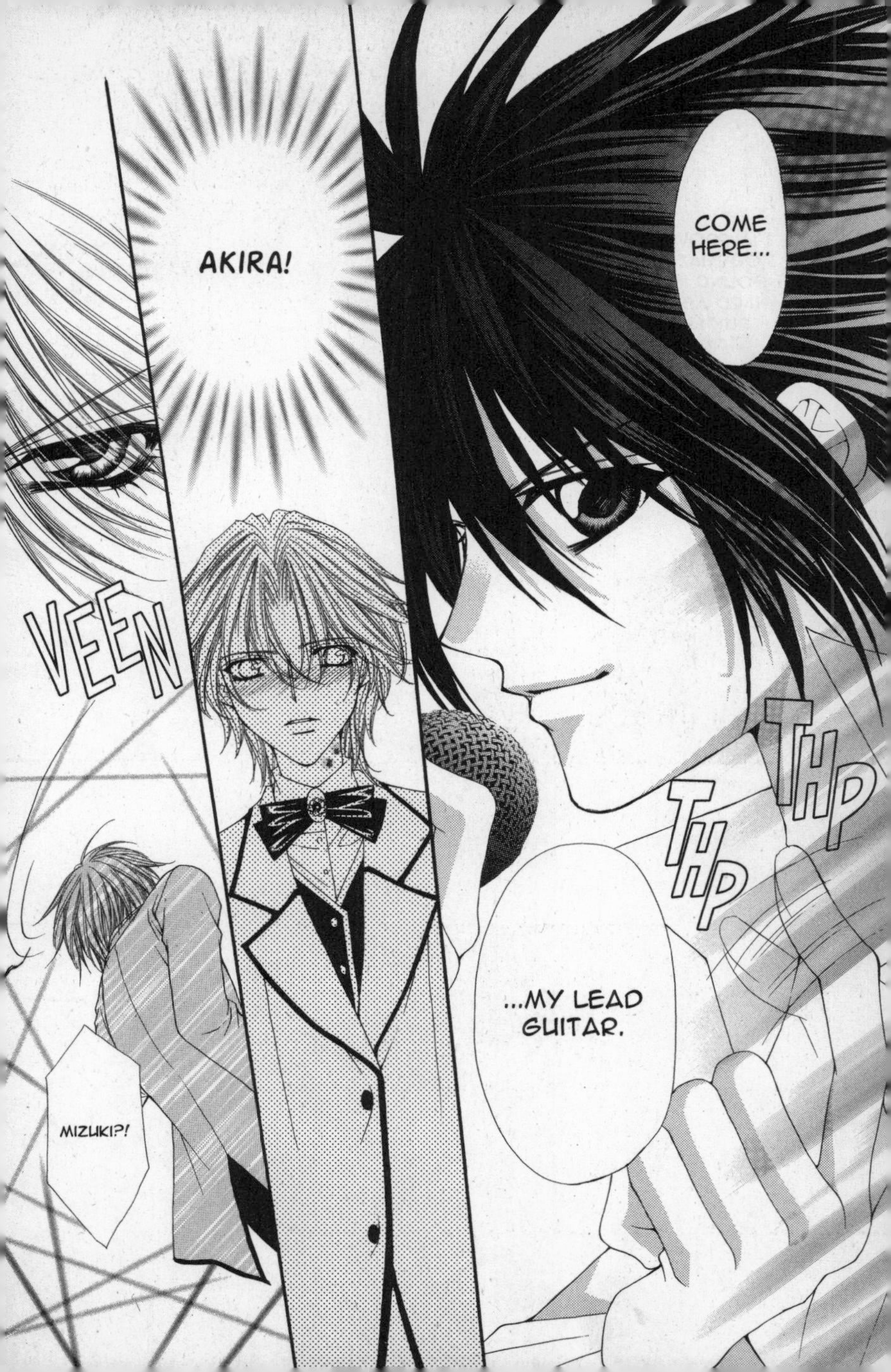
COME HERE...
THP THP
...MY LEAD GUITAR.
AKIRA!
VEEN
MIZUKI?!

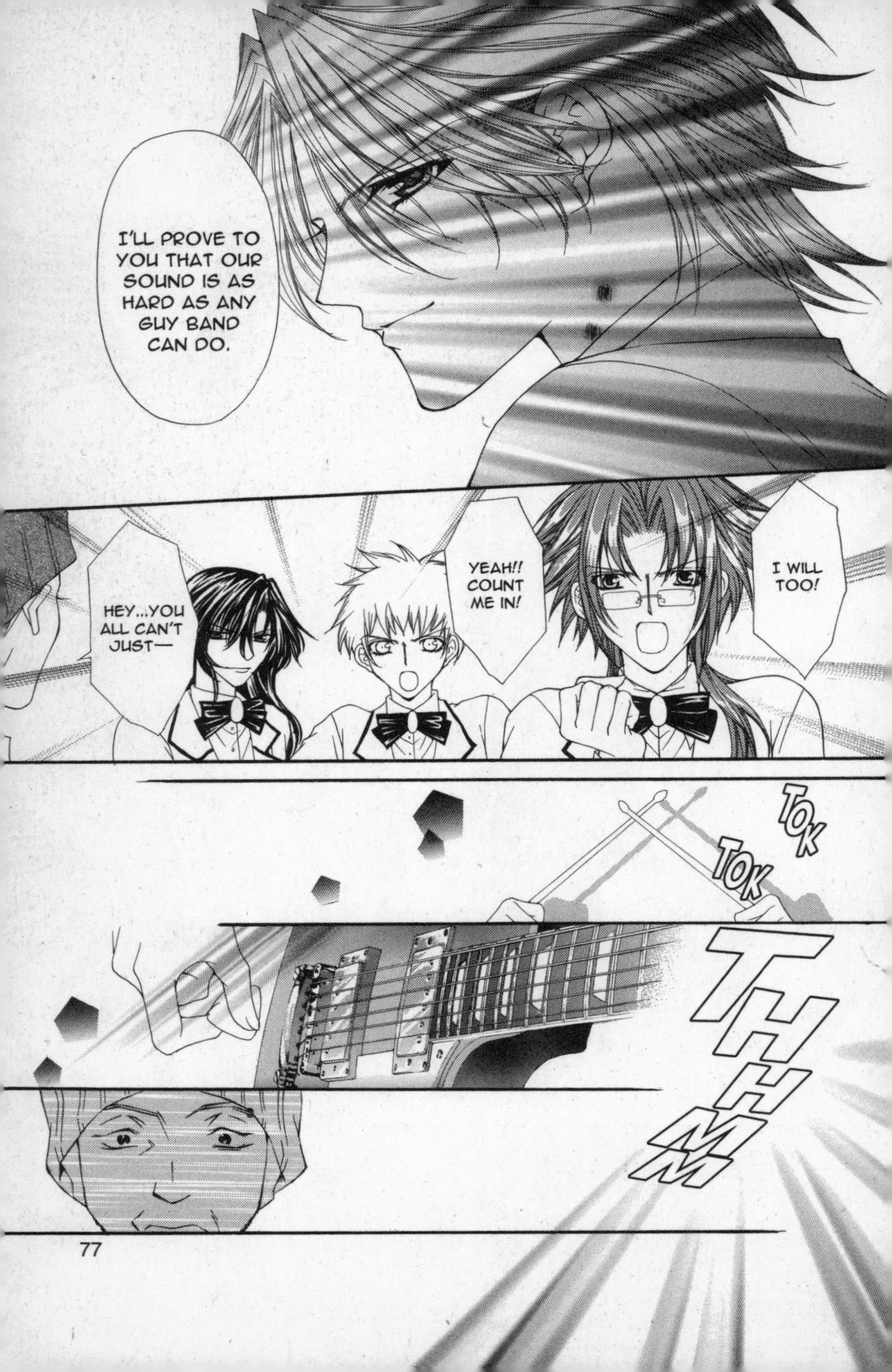
I'LL PROVE TO YOU THAT OUR SOUND IS AS HARD AS ANY GUY BAND CAN DO.
I WILL TOO!
YEAH!! COUNT ME IN!
HEY...YOU ALL CAN'T JUST—
TOK
TOK
THHMM

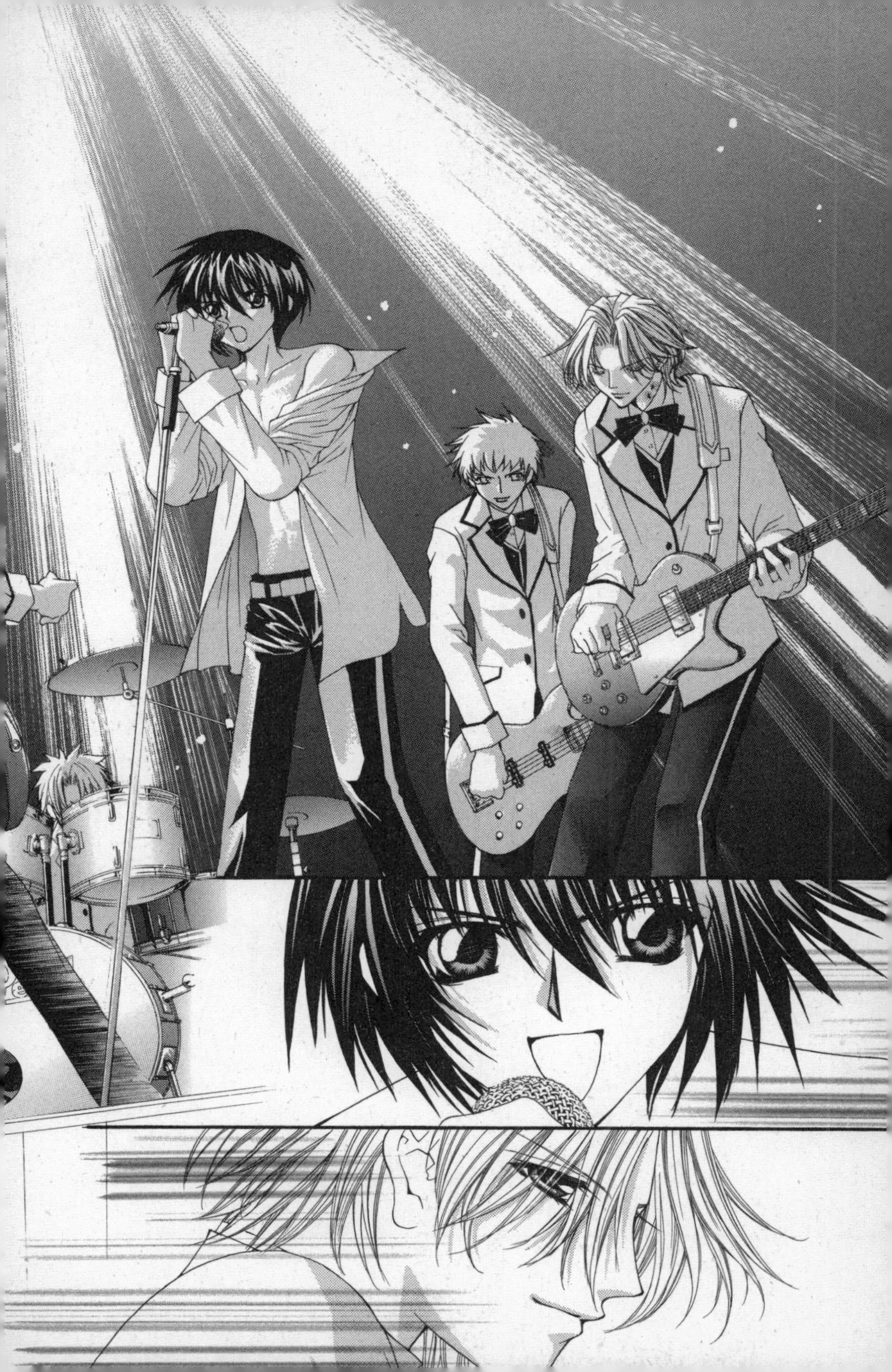

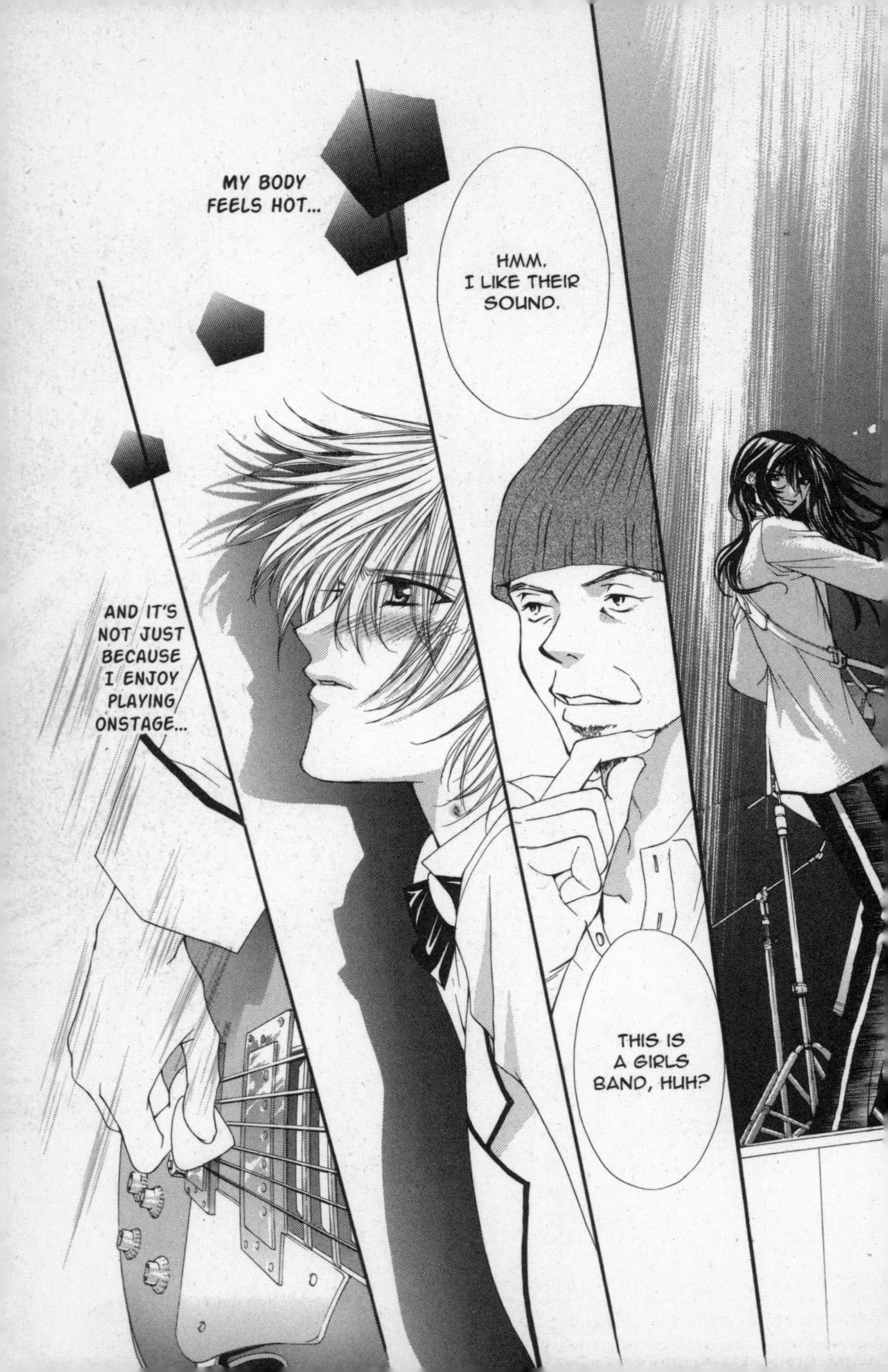
HMM. I LIKE THEIR SOUND.
THIS IS A GIRLS BAND, HUH?
MY BODY FEELS HOT...
AND IT'S NOT JUST BECAUSE I ENJOY PLAYING ONSTAGE...

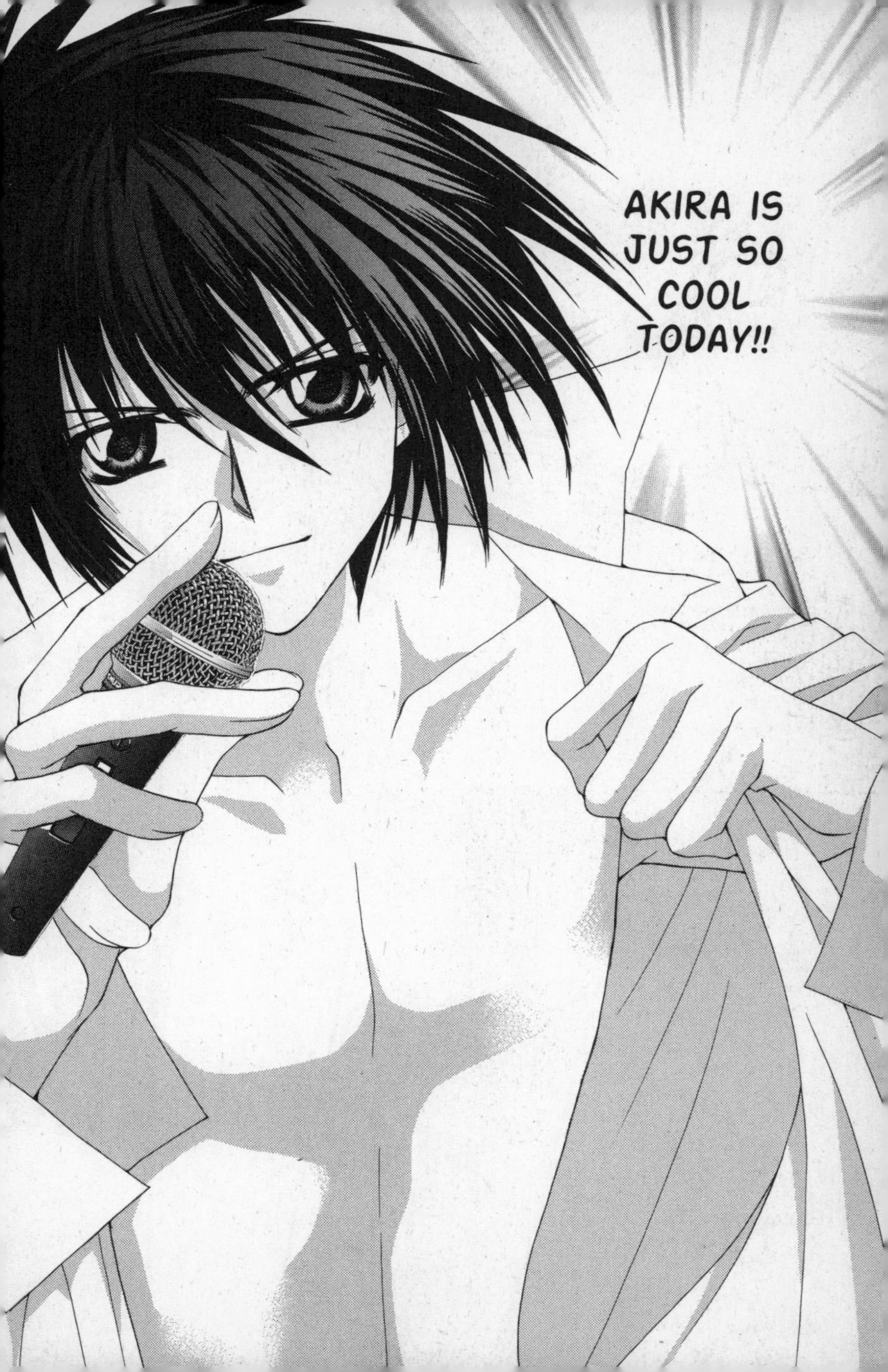
AKIRA IS JUST SO COOL TODAY!!

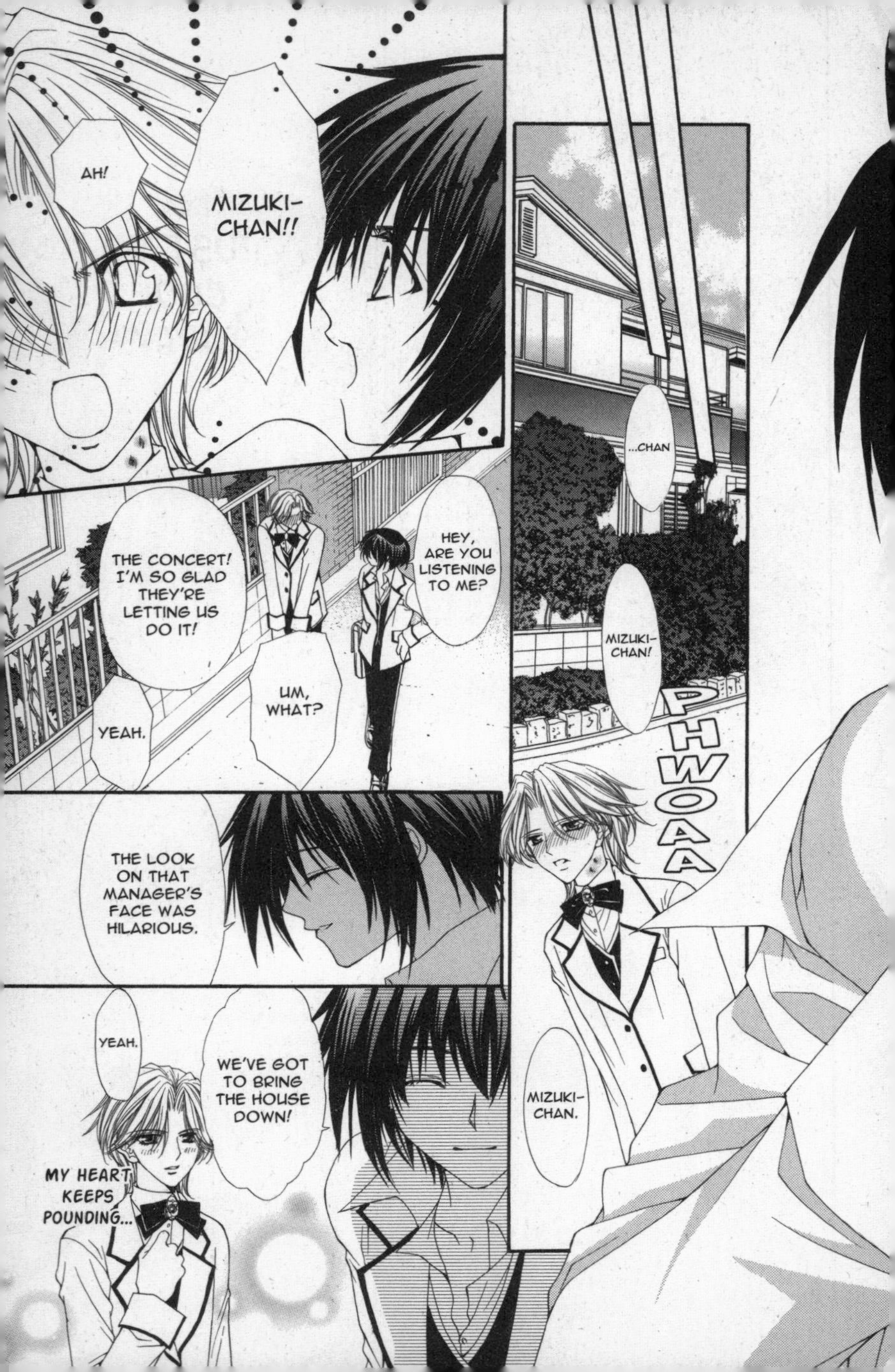
...CHAN
MIZUKI-CHAN!
PHWOAA
MIZUKI-CHAN.
MIZUKI-CHAN!!
AH!
HEY, ARE YOU LISTENING TO ME?
THE CONCERT! I'M SO GLAD THEY'RE LETTING US DO IT!
UM, WHAT?
YEAH.
THE LOOK ON THAT MANAGER'S FACE WAS HILARIOUS.
WE'VE GOT TO BRING THE HOUSE DOWN!
YEAH.
MY HEART KEEPS POUNDING...

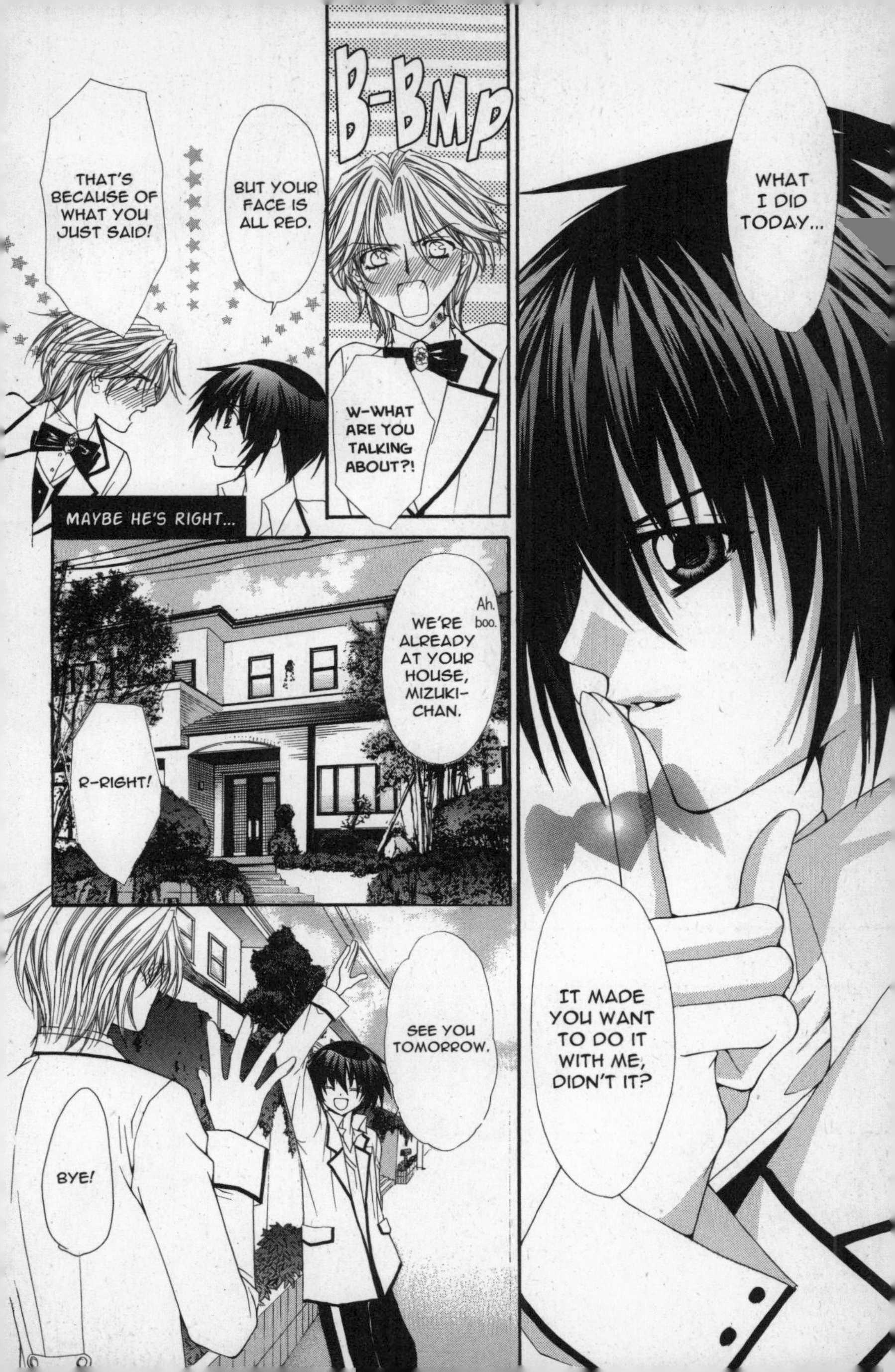
WHAT I DID TODAY...
IT MADE YOU WANT TO DO IT WITH ME, DIDN'T IT?
B-BMP
W-WHAT ARE YOU TALKING ABOUT?!
BUT YOUR FACE IS ALL RED.
THAT'S BECAUSE OF WHAT YOU JUST SAID!
MAYBE HE'S RIGHT...
WE'RE ALREADY AT YOUR HOUSE, MIZUKI-CHAN.
Ah. boo.
R-RIGHT!
SEE YOU TOMORROW.
BYE!

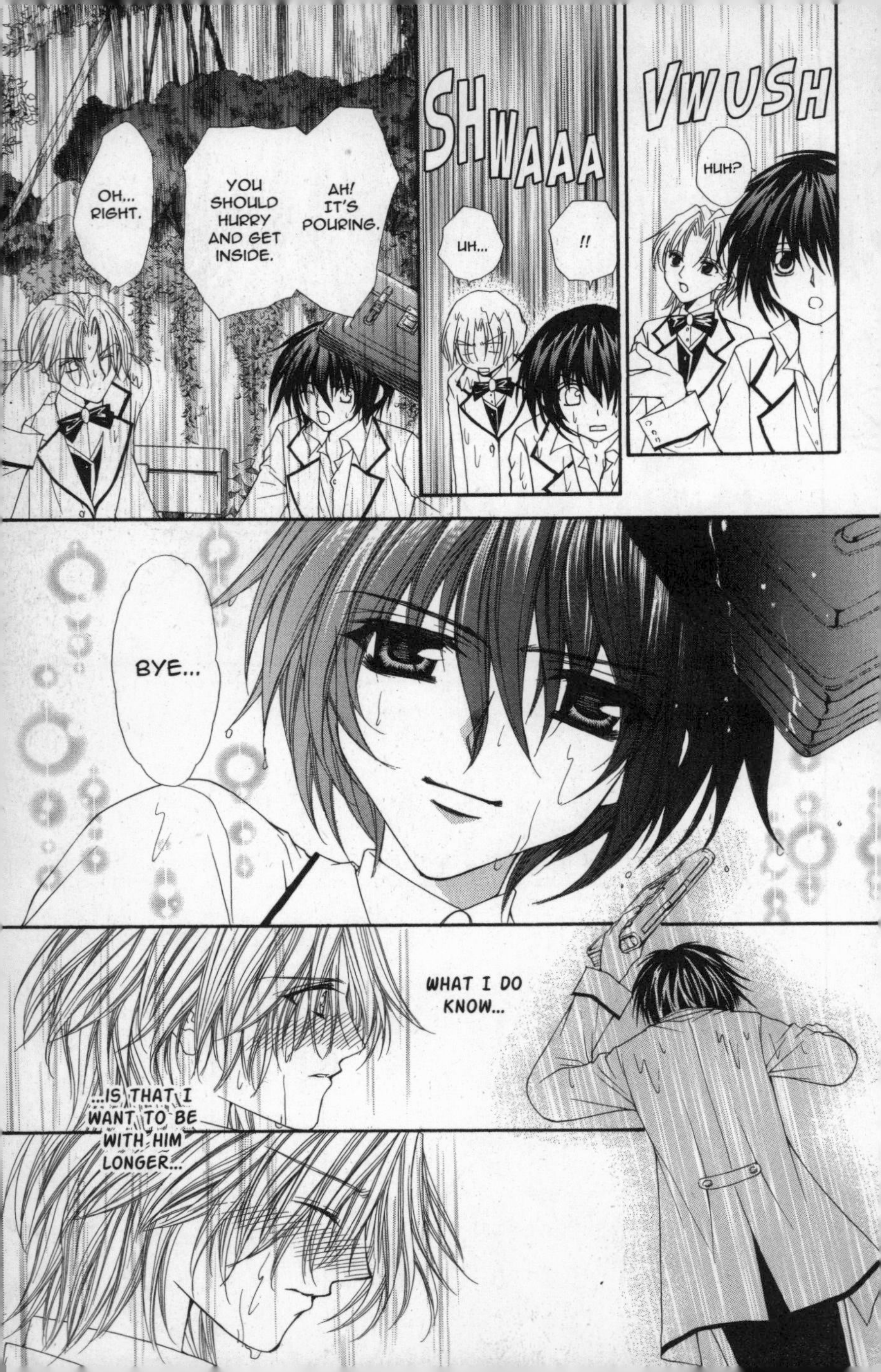
VWUSH
HUH?
SHWAAA
!!
UH...
AH! IT'S POURING.
YOU SHOULD HURRY AND GET INSIDE.
OH... RIGHT.
BYE...
WHAT I DO KNOW...
...IS THAT I WANT TO BE WITH HIM LONGER...

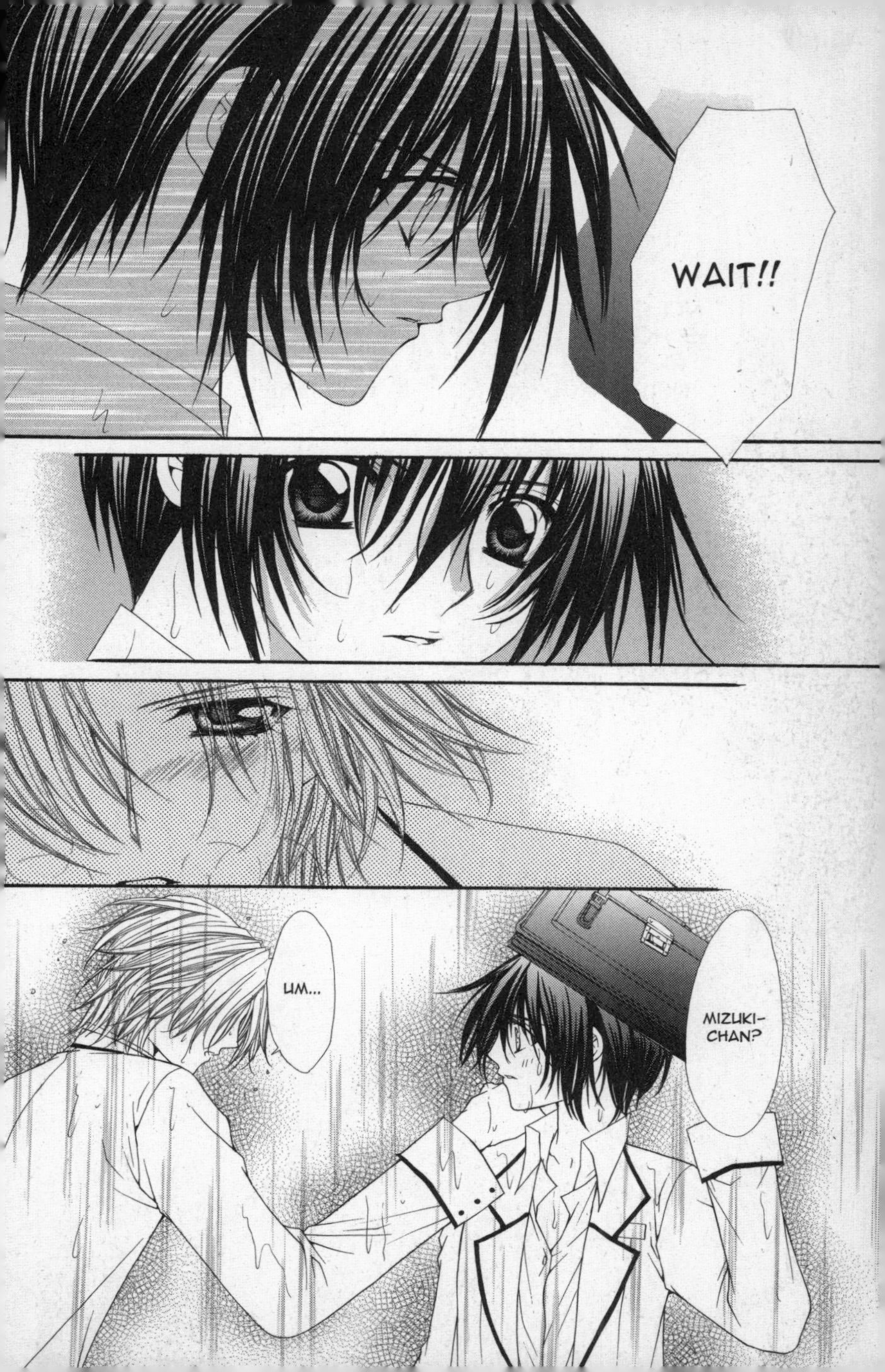
WAIT!!
MIZUKI-CHAN?
UM...

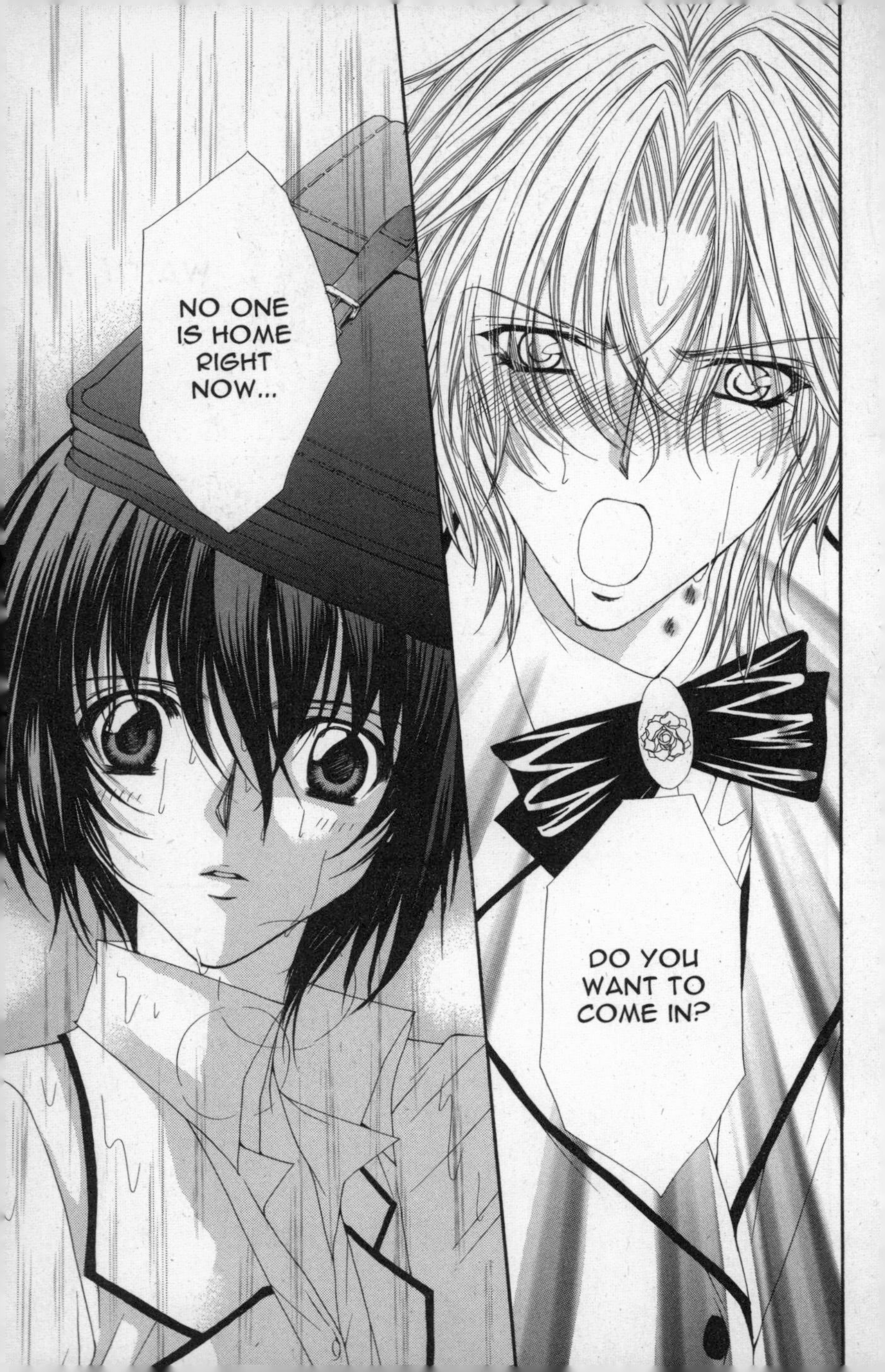
DO YOU WANT TO COME IN?
NO ONE IS HOME RIGHT NOW...

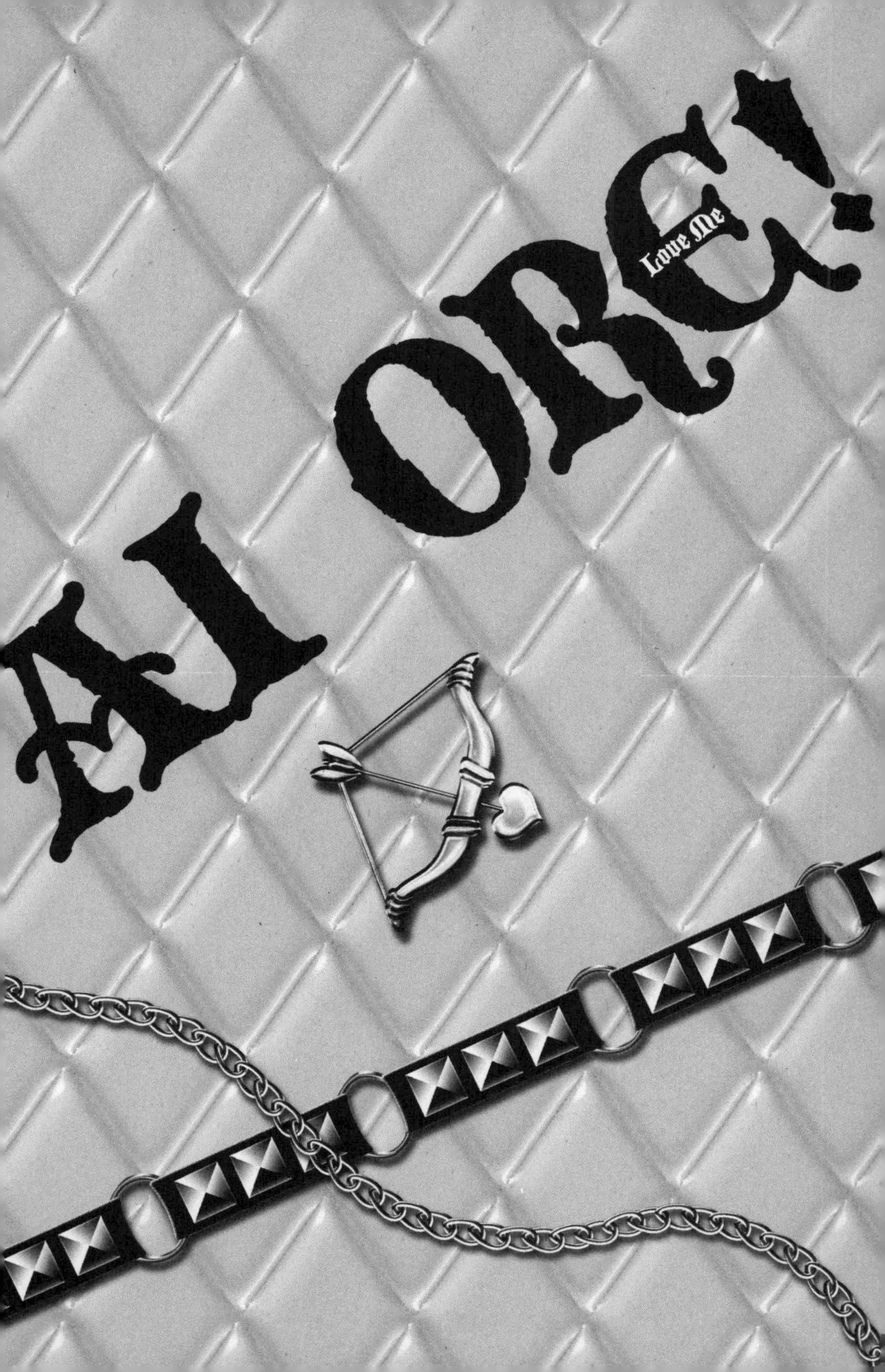
AI ORE!
Love Me

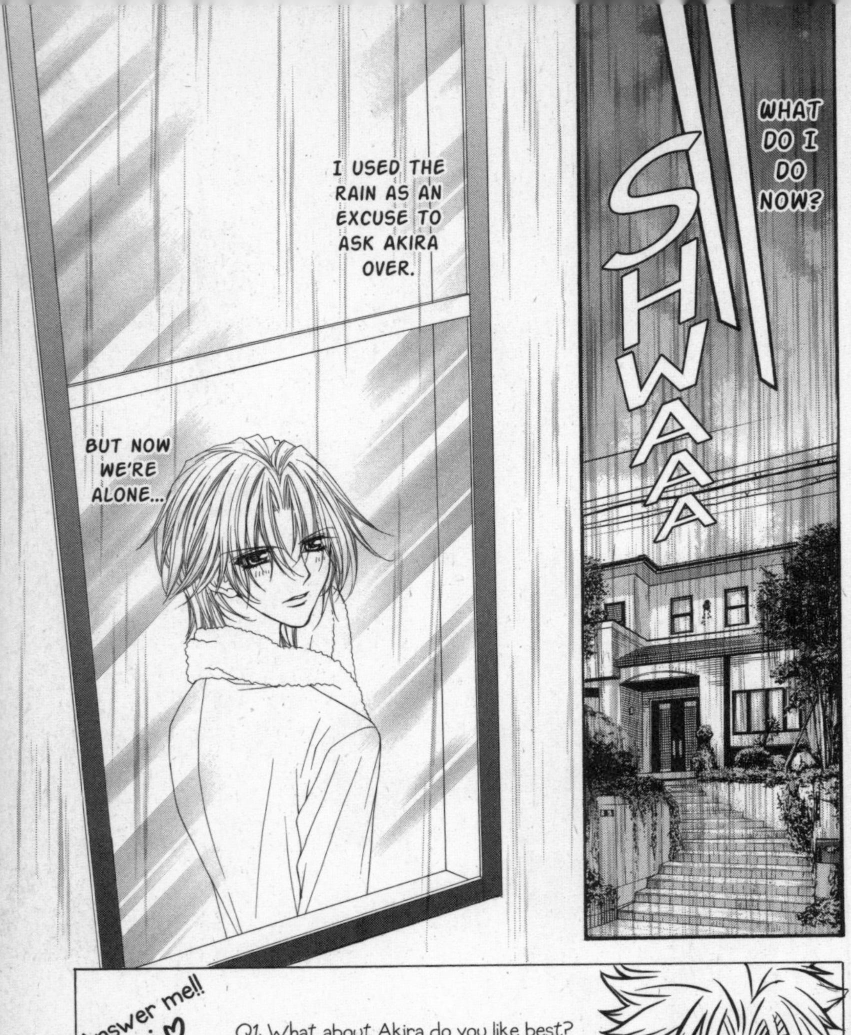
SHWAAA
WHAT DO I DO NOW?
I USED THE RAIN AS AN EXCUSE TO ASK AKIRA OVER.
BUT NOW WE'RE ALONE...

Answer me!! Rui ♡

Q1: What about Akira do you like best?

A1: Everything, of course. Everything!!
Well, the only thing I don't like about him is that he's a guy...
Aaah! I don't want to even think about it!!

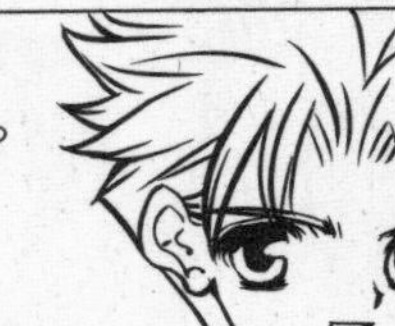

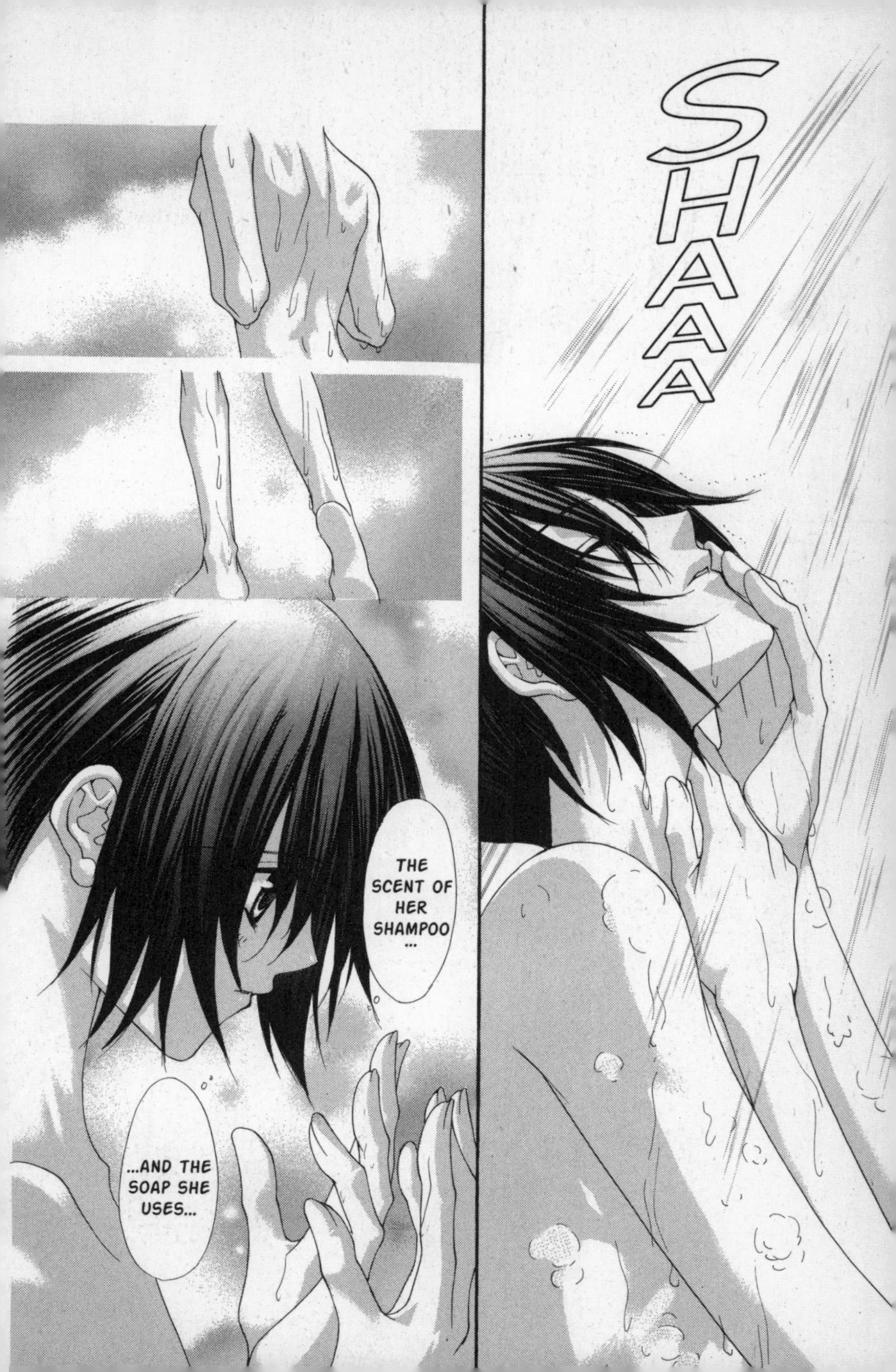
SHAAA
THE SCENT OF HER SHAMPOO ...
...AND THE SOAP SHE USES...

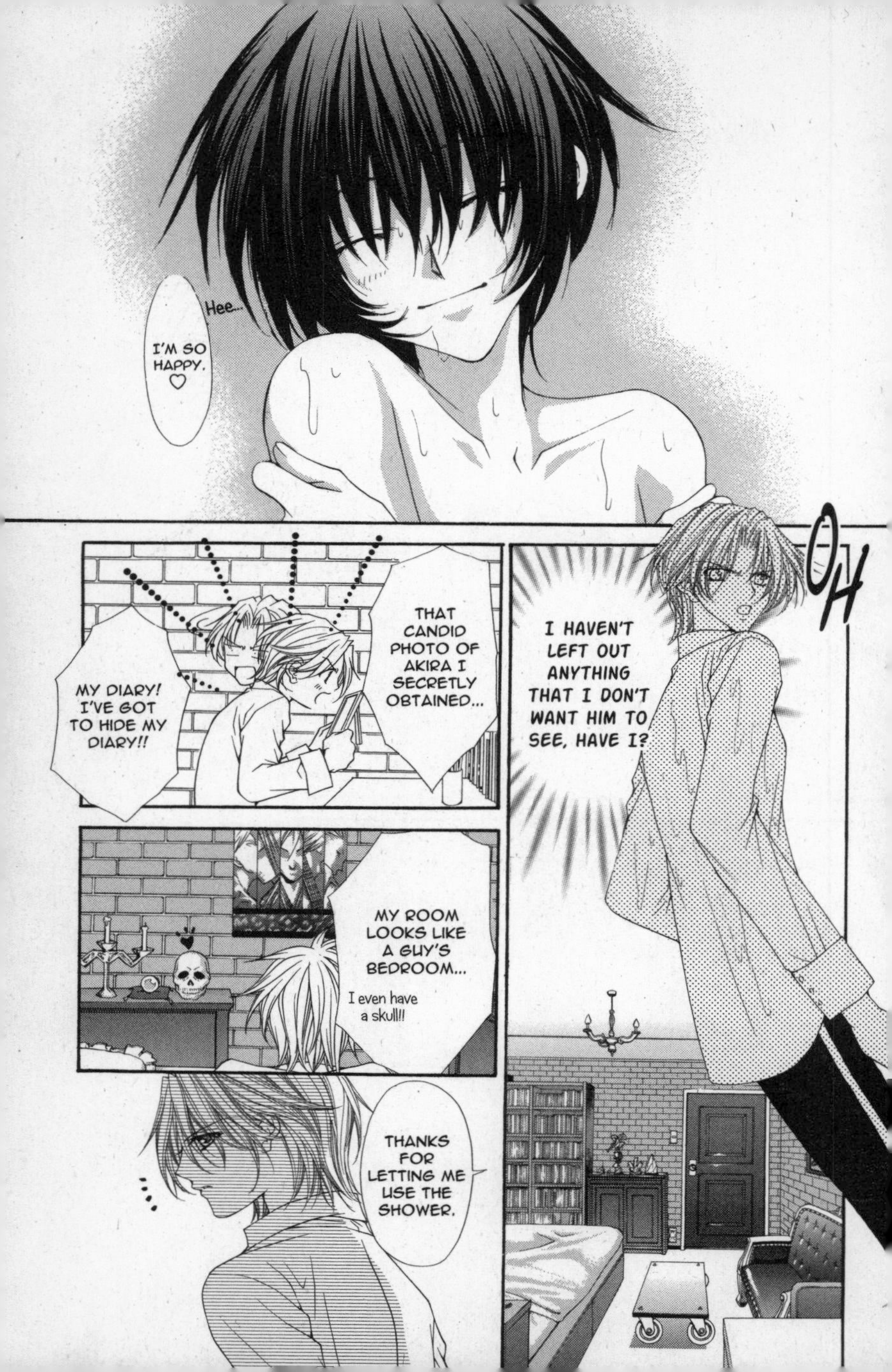
Hee...
I'M SO HAPPY. ♡
OH
I HAVEN'T LEFT OUT ANYTHING THAT I DON'T WANT HIM TO SEE, HAVE I?
THAT CANDID PHOTO OF AKIRA I SECRETLY OBTAINED...
MY DIARY! I'VE GOT TO HIDE MY DIARY!!
MY ROOM LOOKS LIKE A GUY'S BEDROOM...
I even have a skull!!
...
THANKS FOR LETTING ME USE THE SHOWER.

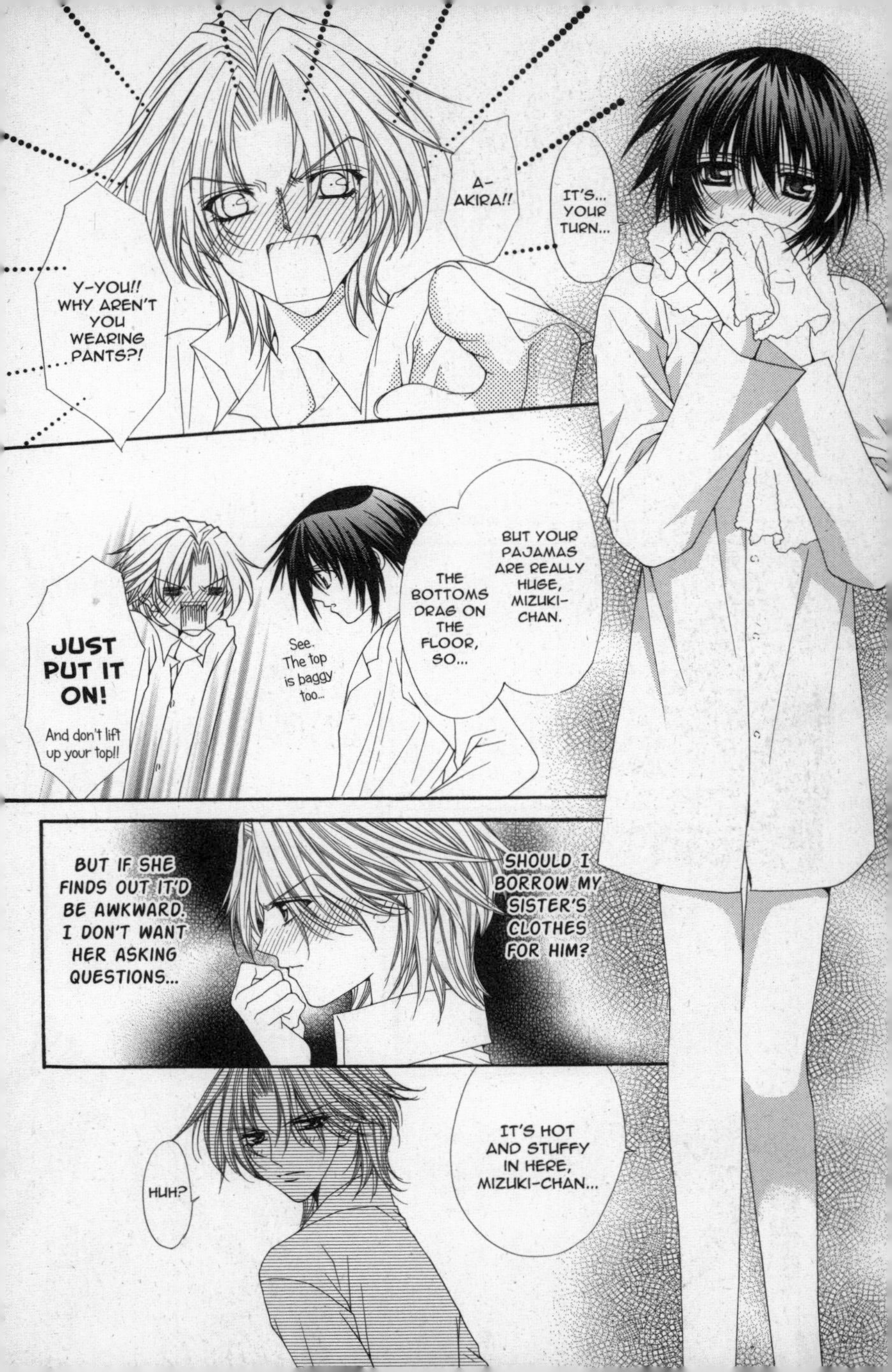
IT'S... YOUR TURN...
A-AKIRA!!
Y-YOU!! WHY AREN'T YOU WEARING PANTS?!
BUT YOUR PAJAMAS ARE REALLY HUGE, MIZUKI-CHAN.
THE BOTTOMS DRAG ON THE FLOOR, SO...
See. The top is baggy too...
JUST PUT IT ON!
And don't lift up your top!!
SHOULD I BORROW MY SISTER'S CLOTHES FOR HIM?
BUT IF SHE FINDS OUT IT'D BE AWKWARD. I DON'T WANT HER ASKING QUESTIONS...
IT'S HOT AND STUFFY IN HERE, MIZUKI-CHAN...
HUH?

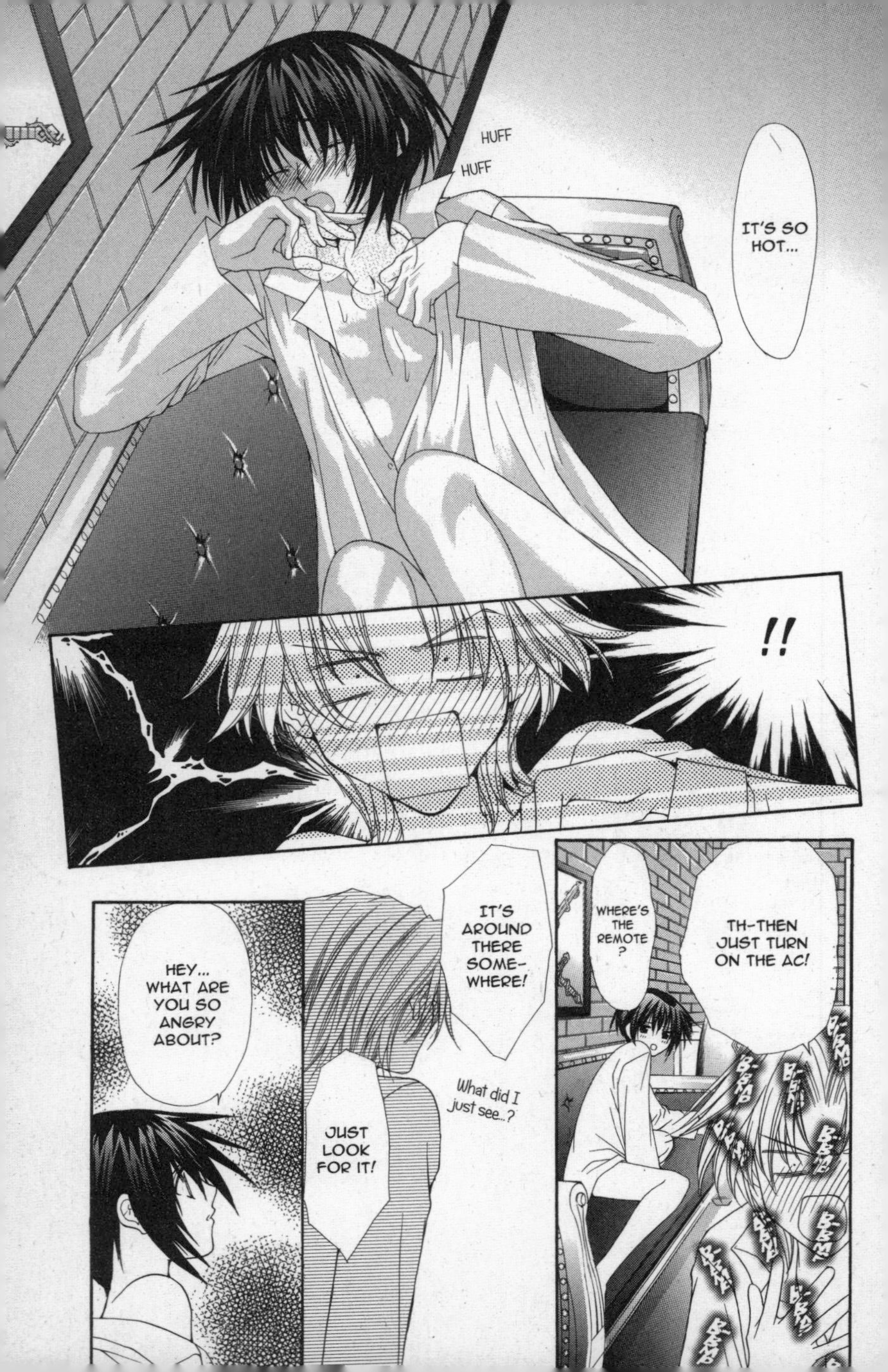
IT'S SO HOT...
HUFF
HUFF
!!
TH-THEN JUST TURN ON THE AC!
WHERE'S THE REMOTE?
IT'S AROUND THERE SOME-WHERE!
What did I just see...?
JUST LOOK FOR IT!
HEY... WHAT ARE YOU SO ANGRY ABOUT?

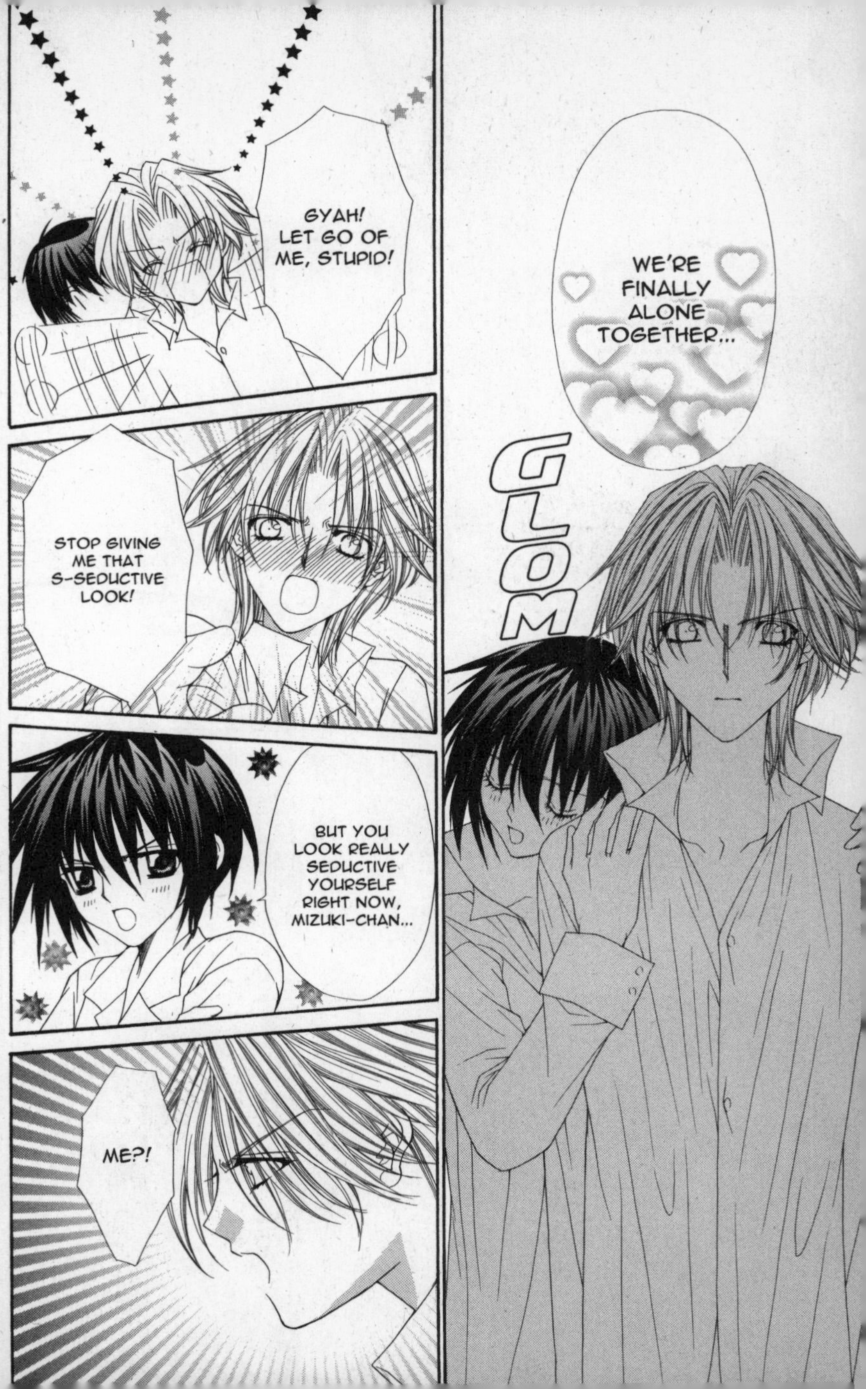
WE'RE FINALLY ALONE TOGETHER...
GLOM
GYAH! LET GO OF ME, STUPID!
STOP GIVING ME THAT S-SEDUCTIVE LOOK!
BUT YOU LOOK REALLY SEDUCTIVE YOURSELF RIGHT NOW, MIZUKI-CHAN...
ME?!

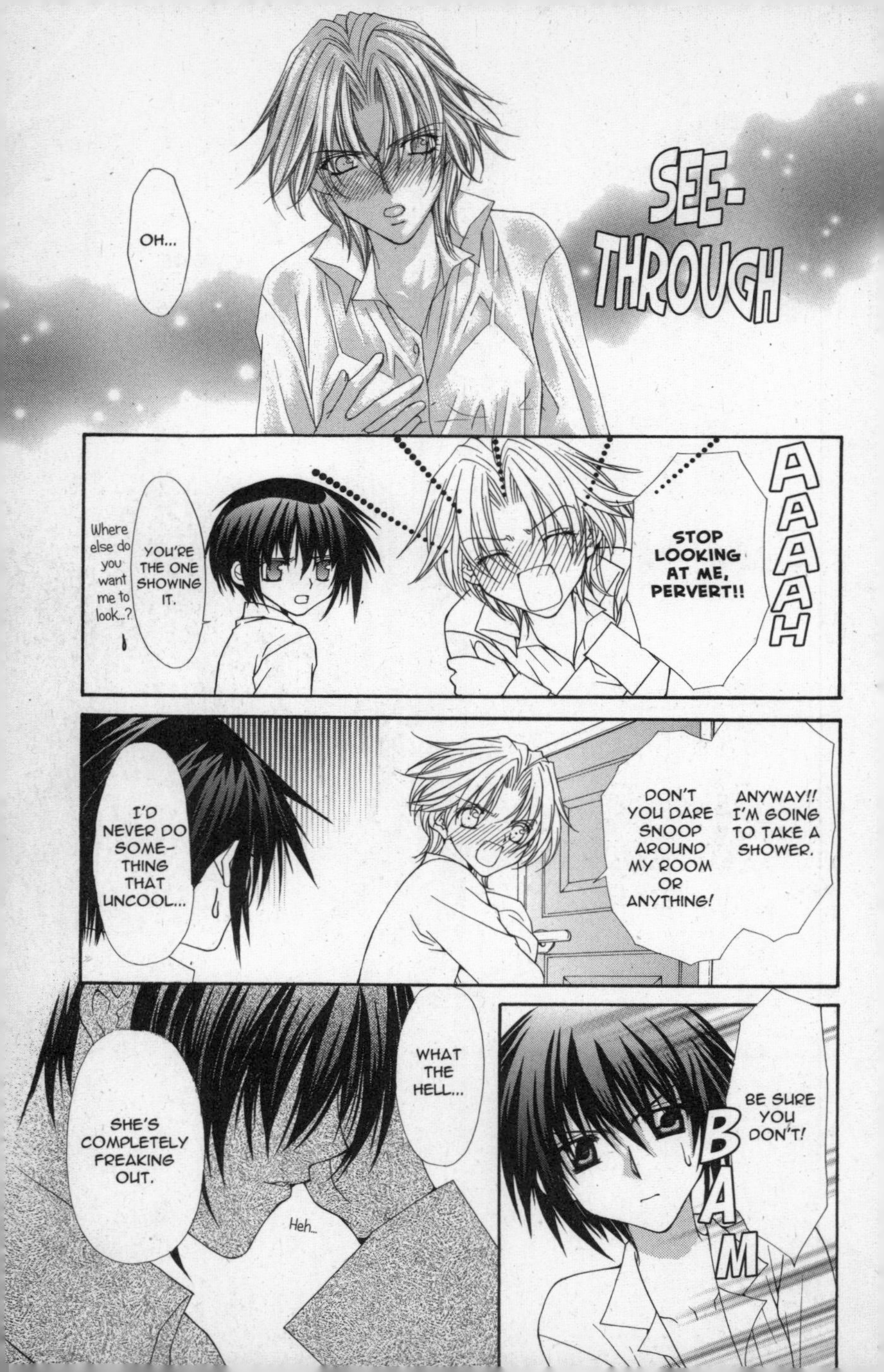
SEE-THROUGH
OH...
AAAAAH
STOP LOOKING AT ME, PERVERT!!
YOU'RE THE ONE SHOWING IT.
Where else do you want me to look...?
ANYWAY!! I'M GOING TO TAKE A SHOWER.
DON'T YOU DARE SNOOP AROUND MY ROOM OR ANYTHING!
I'D NEVER DO SOMETHING THAT UNCOOL...
BE SURE YOU DON'T!
BAM
WHAT THE HELL...
SHE'S COMPLETELY FREAKING OUT.
Heh..

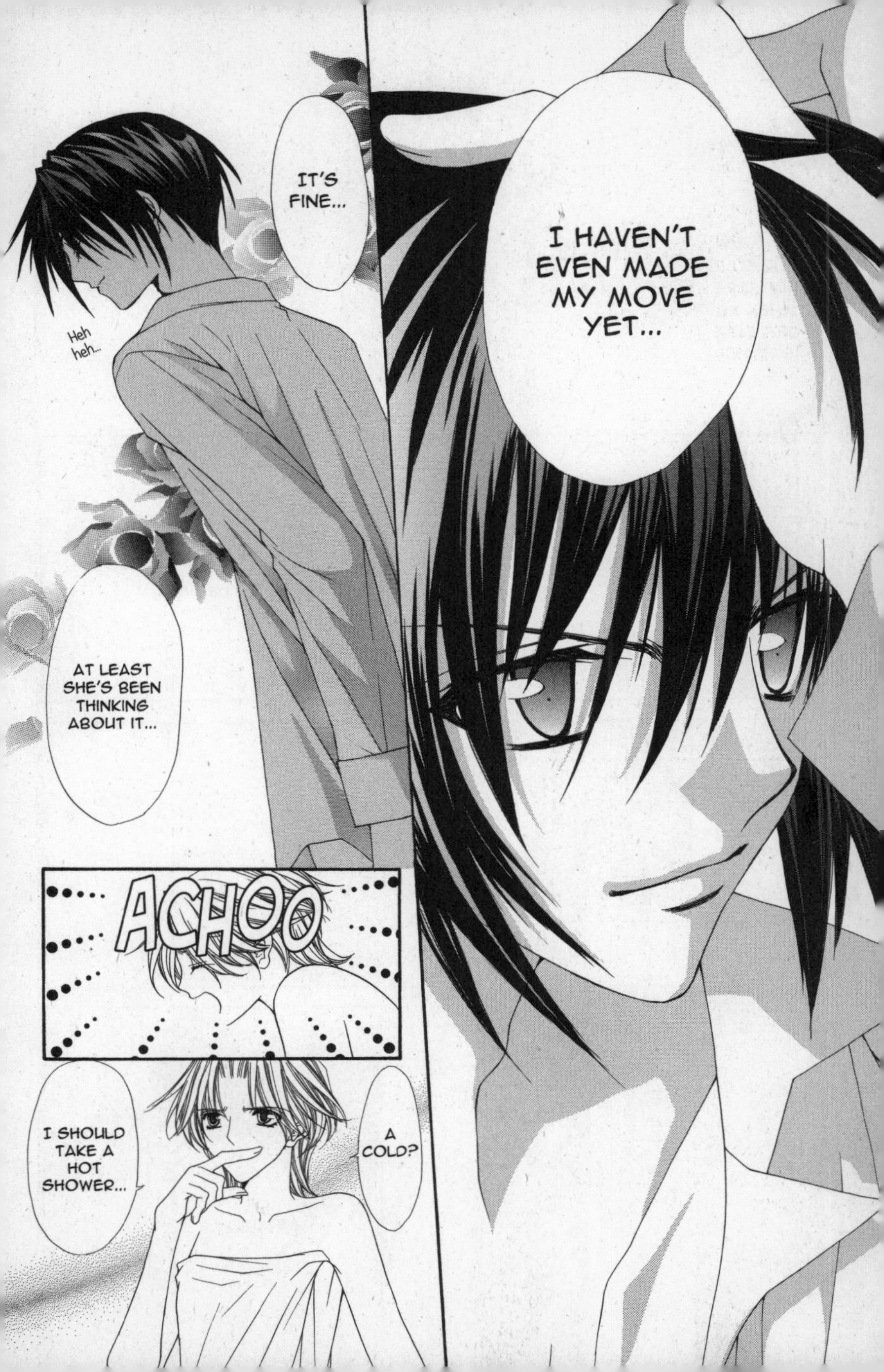
I HAVEN'T EVEN MADE MY MOVE YET...
IT'S FINE...
Heh heh...
AT LEAST SHE'S BEEN THINKING ABOUT IT...
ACHOO
A COLD?
I SHOULD TAKE A HOT SHOWER...

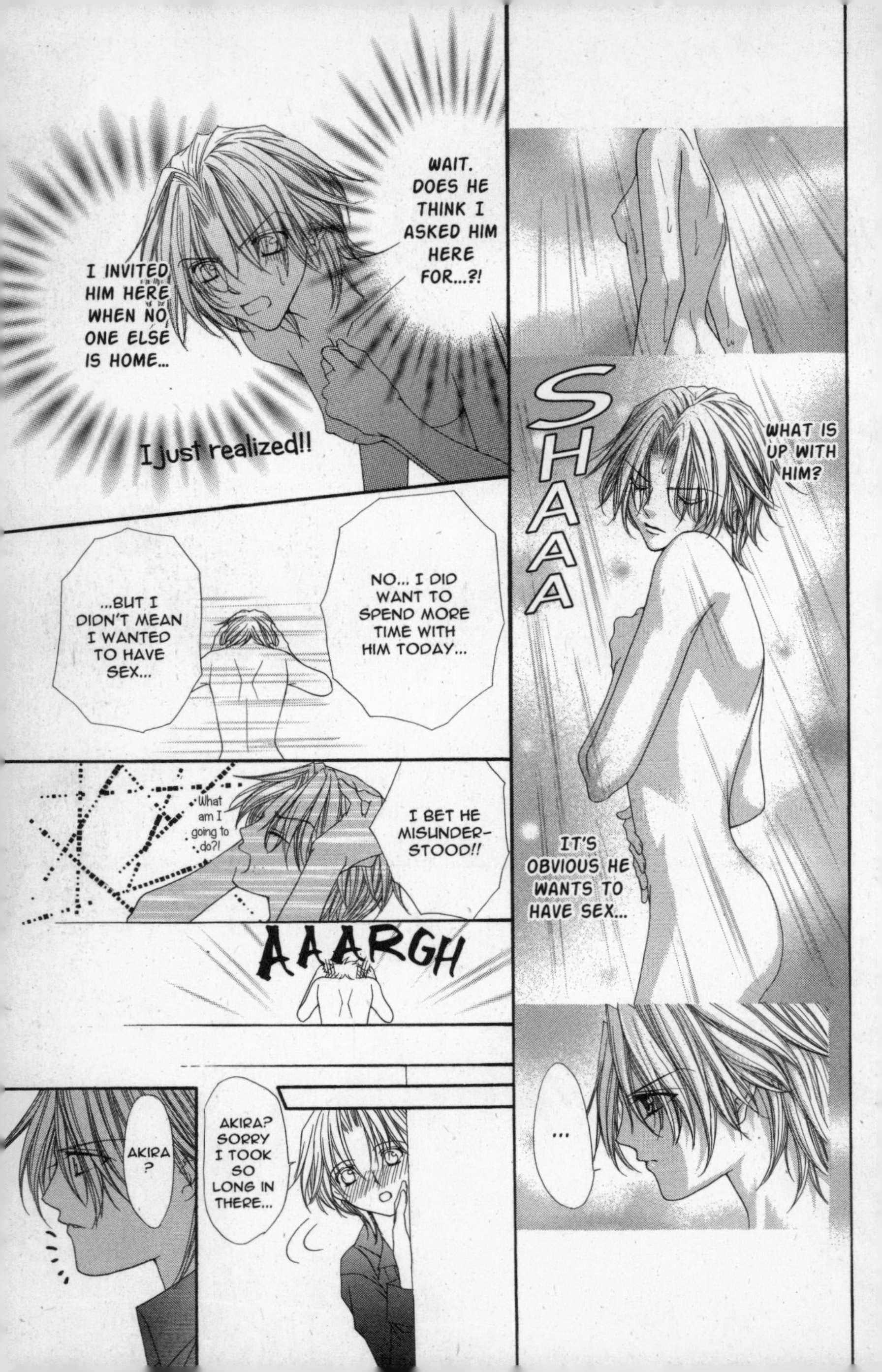
WHAT IS UP WITH HIM?
SHAAA
IT'S OBVIOUS HE WANTS TO HAVE SEX...
...
WAIT. DOES HE THINK I ASKED HIM HERE FOR...?!
I INVITED HIM HERE WHEN NO ONE ELSE IS HOME...
I just realized!!
NO... I DID WANT TO SPEND MORE TIME WITH HIM TODAY...
...BUT I DIDN'T MEAN I WANTED TO HAVE SEX...
I BET HE MISUNDERSTOOD!!
What am I going to do?!
AAARGH
AKIRA? SORRY I TOOK SO LONG IN THERE...
AKIRA?

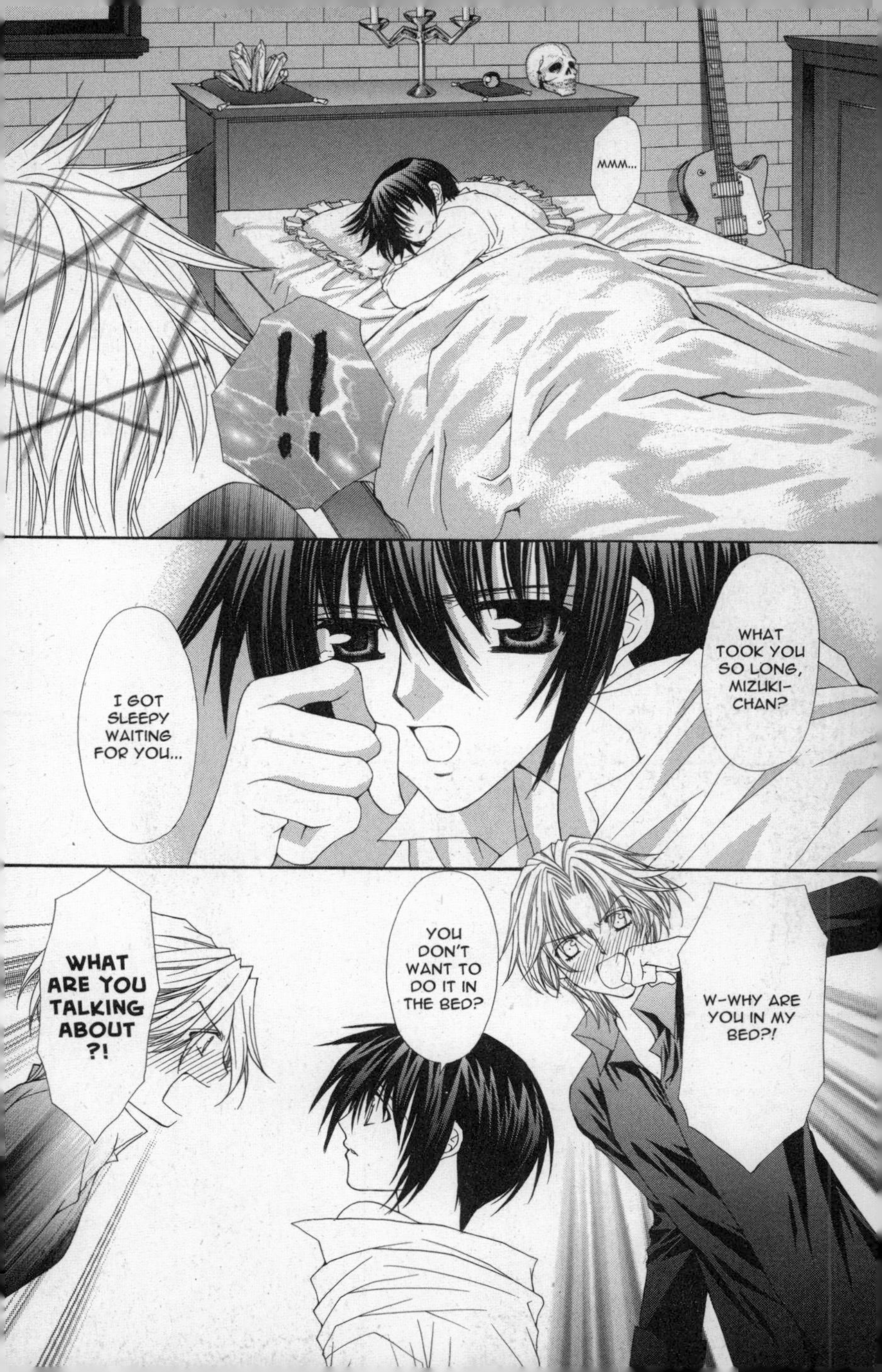
MMM...
!!
WHAT TOOK YOU SO LONG, MIZUKI-CHAN?
I GOT SLEEPY WAITING FOR YOU...
W-WHY ARE YOU IN MY BED?!
YOU DON'T WANT TO DO IT IN THE BED?
WHAT ARE YOU TALKING ABOUT ?!

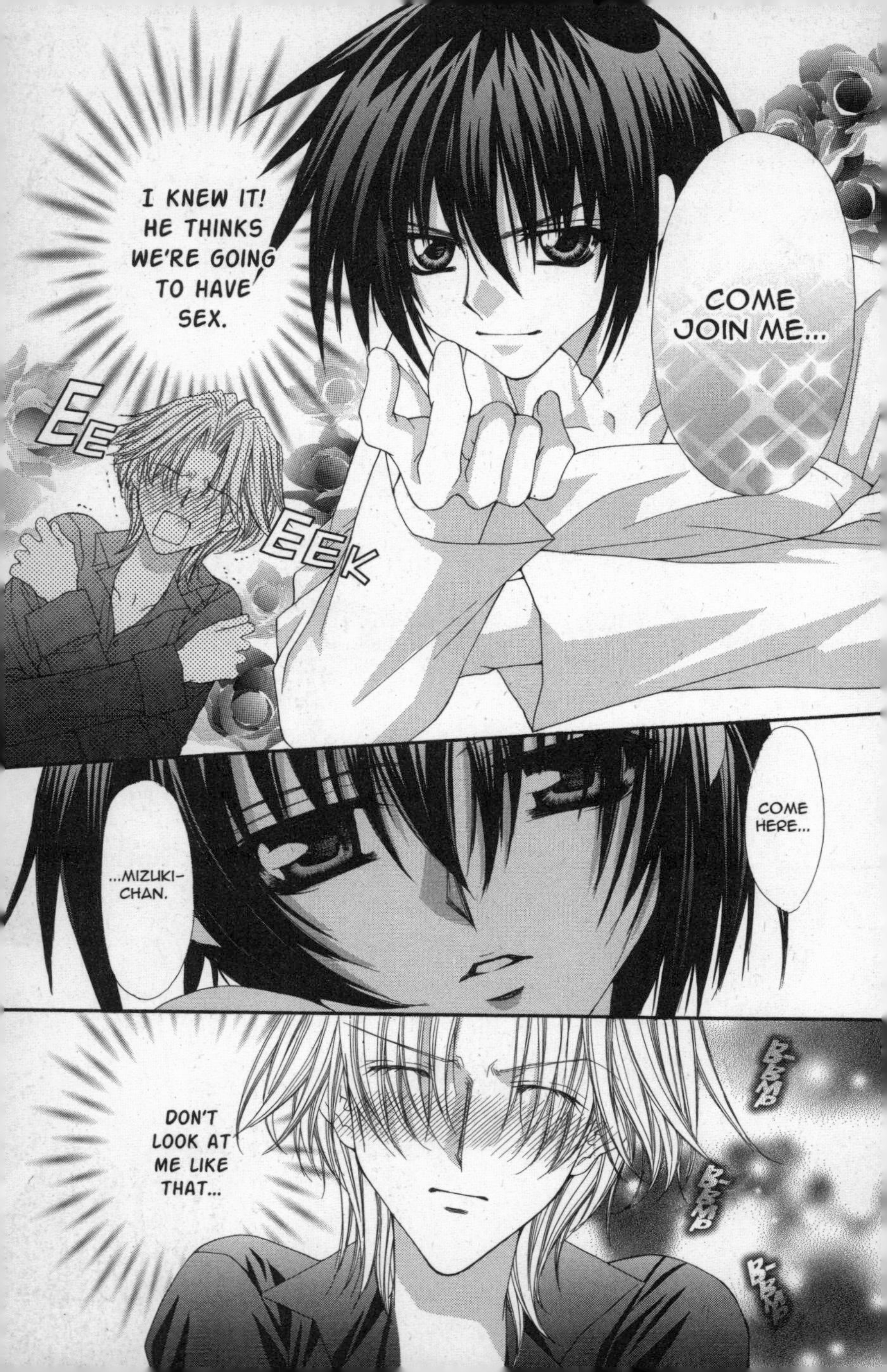
COME JOIN ME...
I KNEW IT! HE THINKS WE'RE GOING TO HAVE SEX.
EE
EEEK
COME HERE...
...MIZUKI-CHAN.
DON'T LOOK AT ME LIKE THAT...

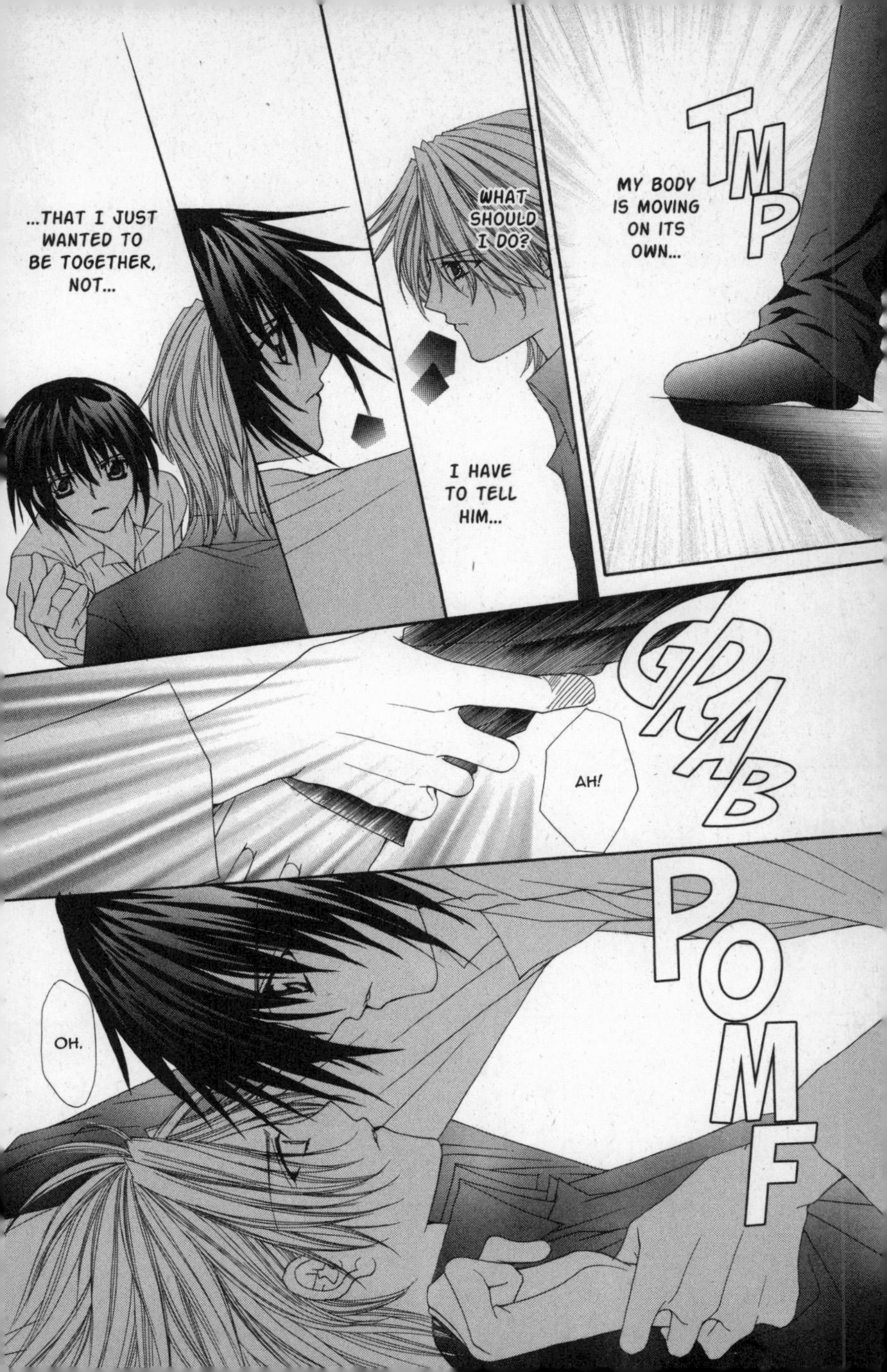
TMP
MY BODY IS MOVING ON ITS OWN...
WHAT SHOULD I DO?
I HAVE TO TELL HIM...
...THAT I JUST WANTED TO BE TOGETHER, NOT...
GRAB
AH!
POMF
OH.

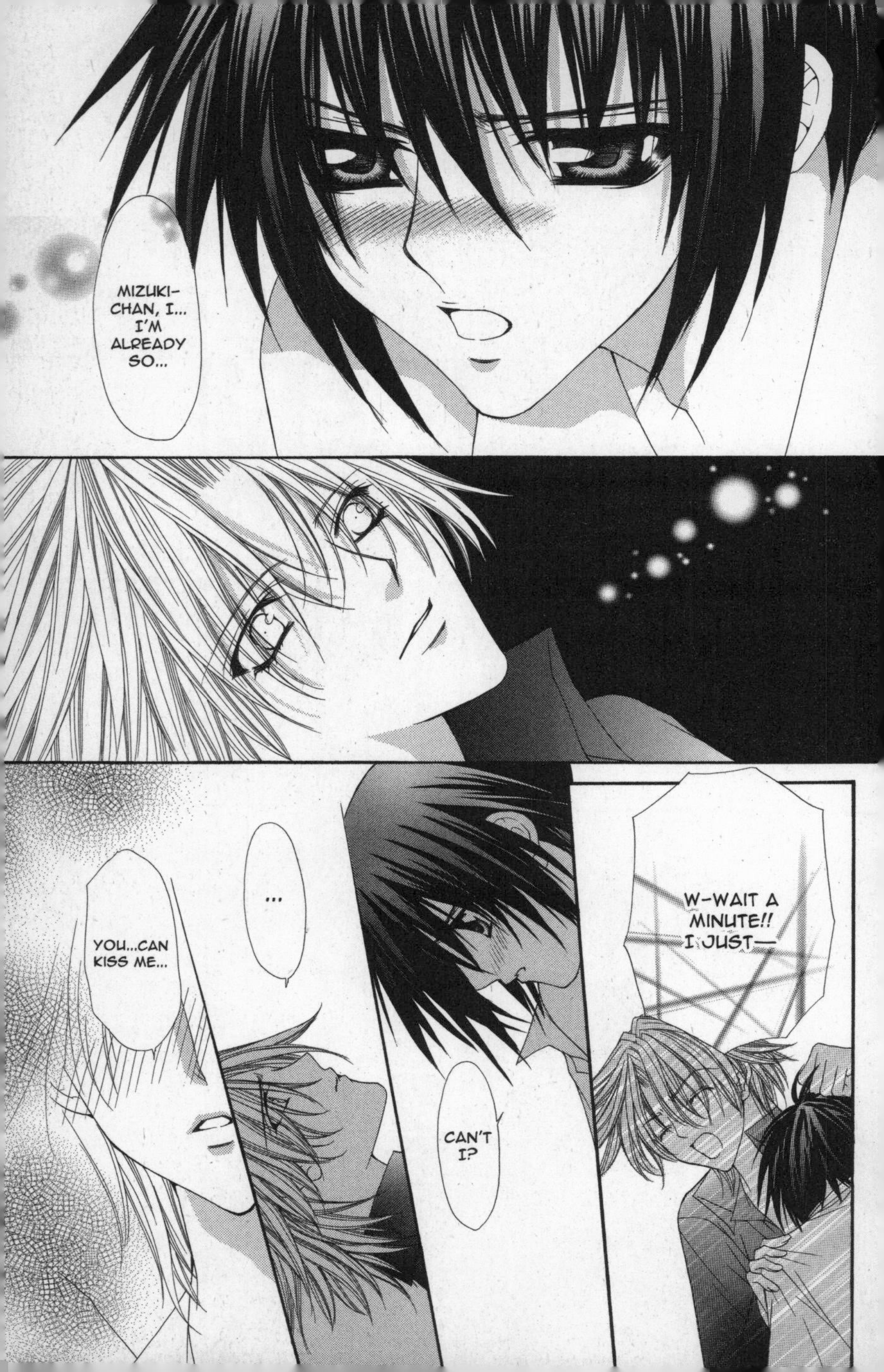
MIZUKI-CHAN, I... I'M ALREADY SO...
W-WAIT A MINUTE!! I JUST—
CAN'T I?
...
YOU...CAN KISS ME...

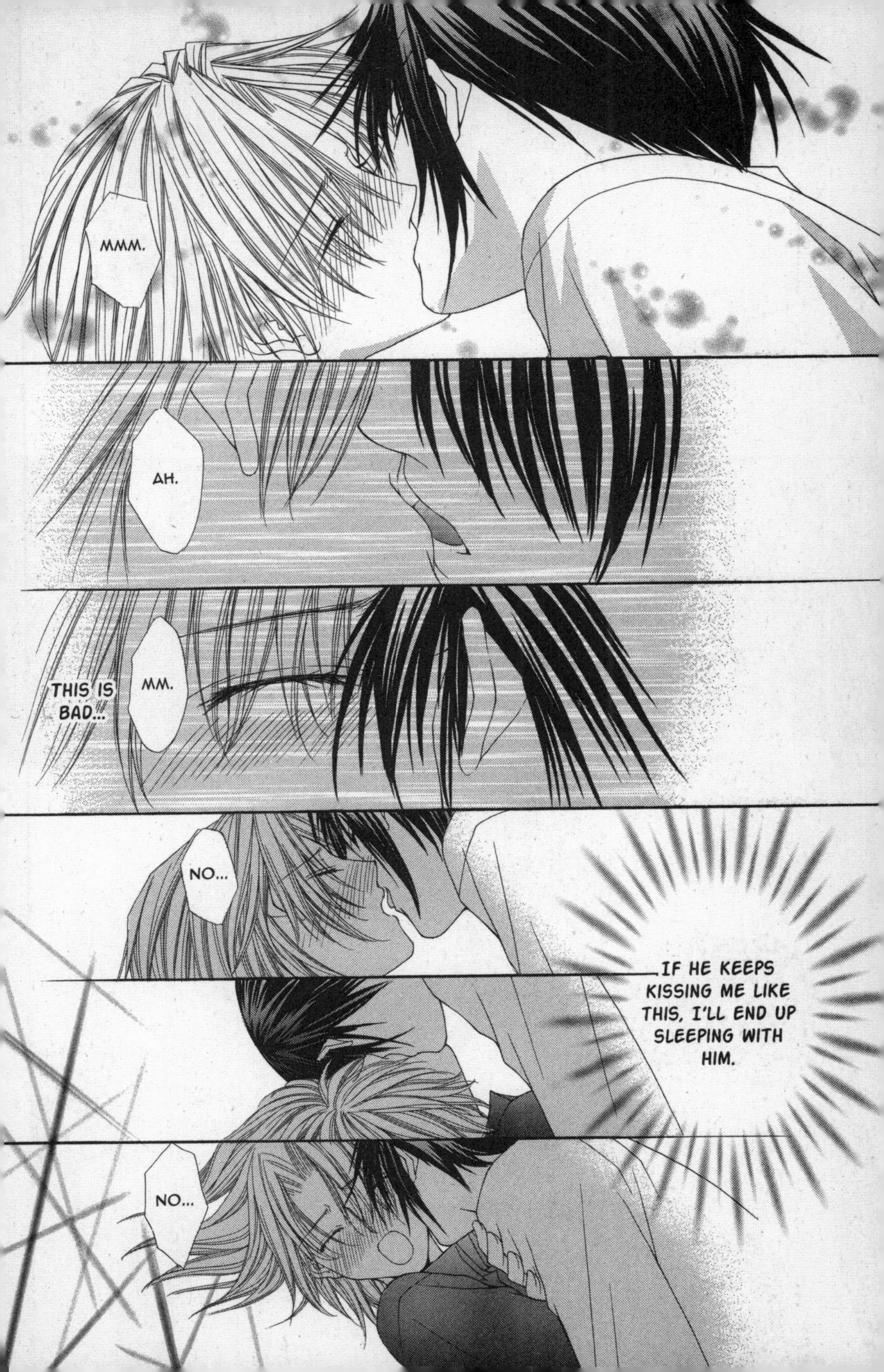
MMM.
AH.
MM.
THIS IS BAD...
NO...
...IF HE KEEPS KISSING ME LIKE THIS, I'LL END UP SLEEPING WITH HIM.
NO...

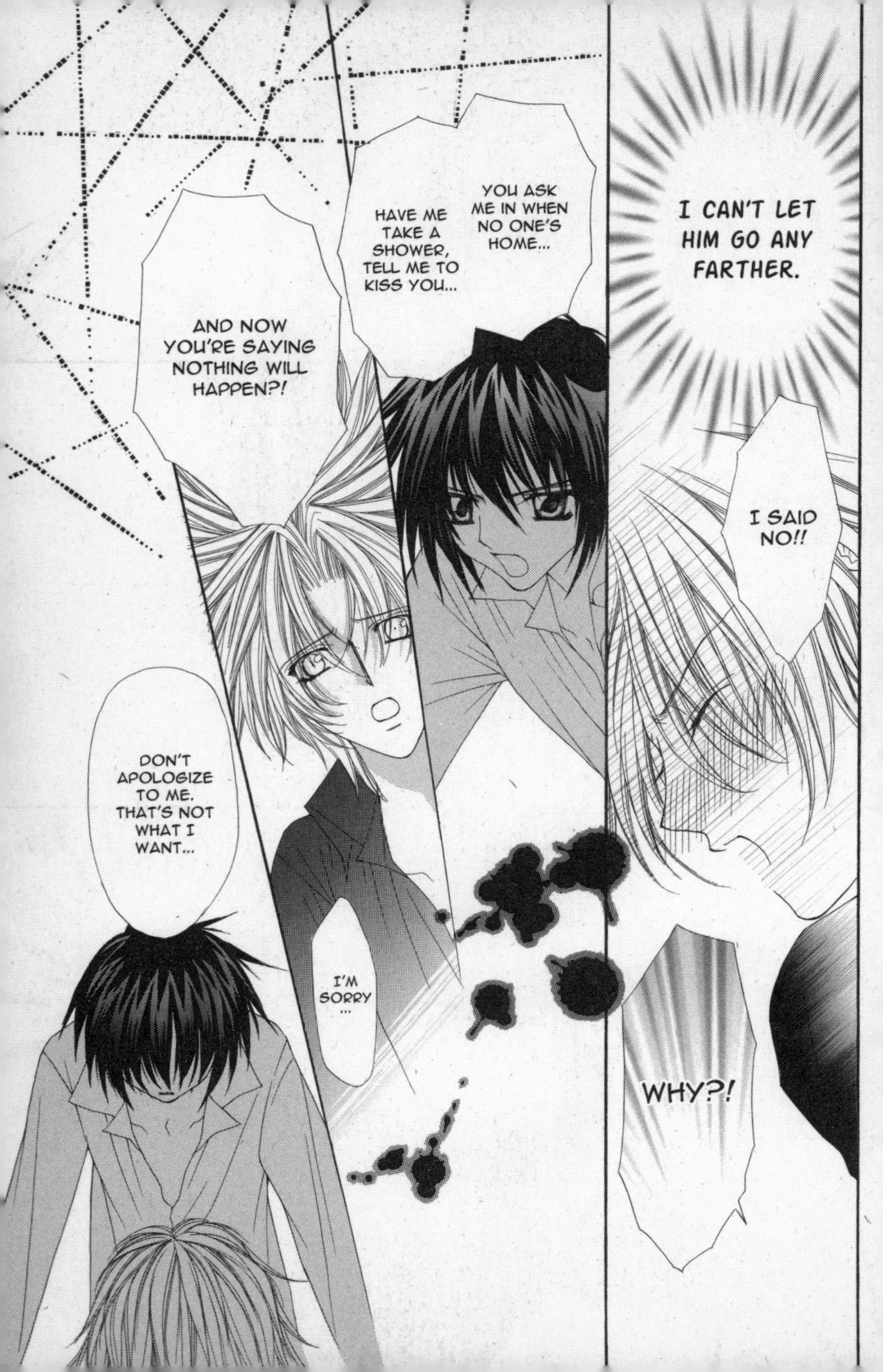
I CAN'T LET HIM GO ANY FARTHER.
I SAID NO!!
WHY?!
YOU ASK ME IN WHEN NO ONE'S HOME...
HAVE ME TAKE A SHOWER, TELL ME TO KISS YOU...
AND NOW YOU'RE SAYING NOTHING WILL HAPPEN?!
I'M SORRY...
DON'T APOLOGIZE TO ME. THAT'S NOT WHAT I WANT...

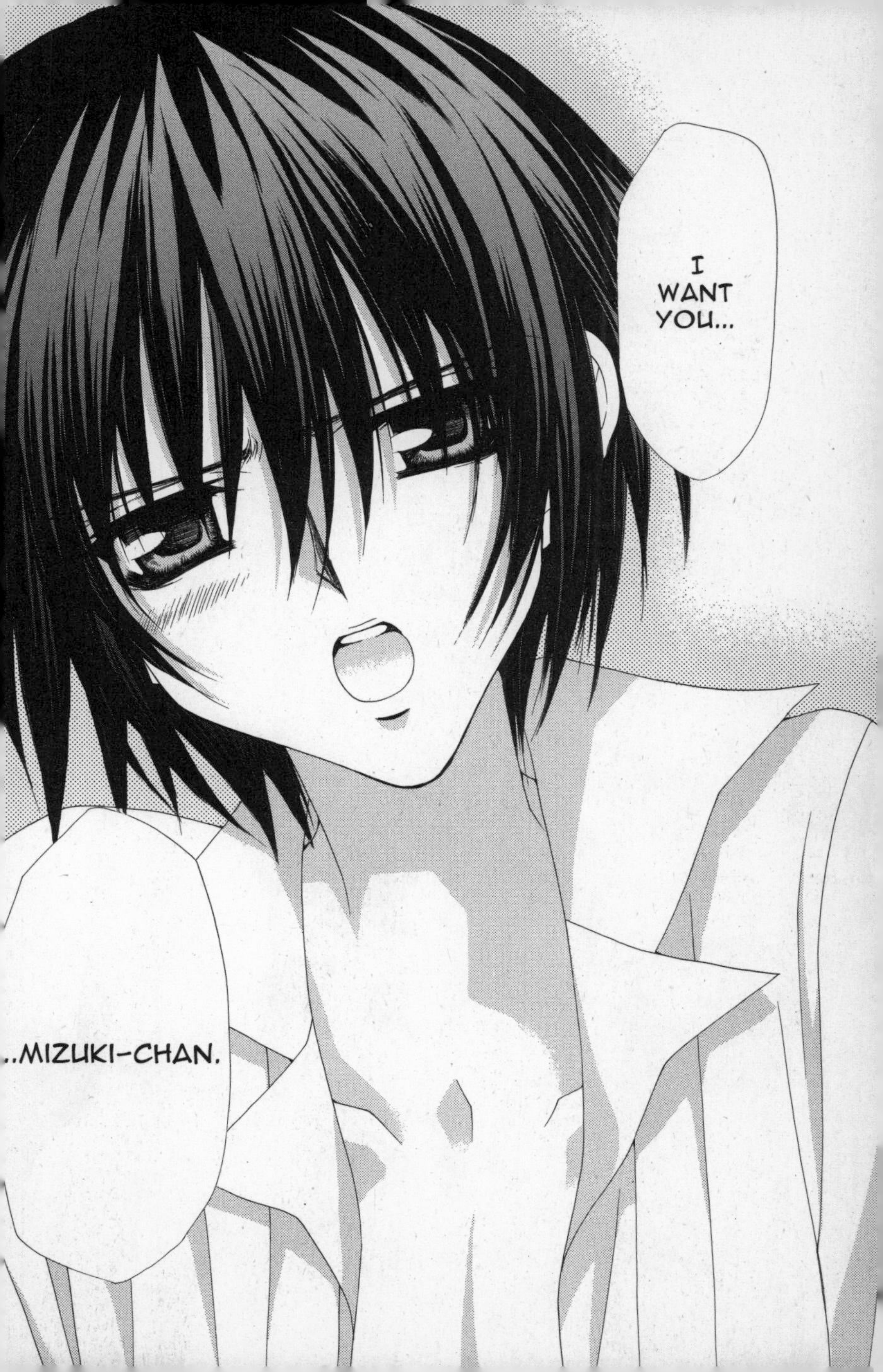
I WANT YOU...
...MIZUKI-CHAN.

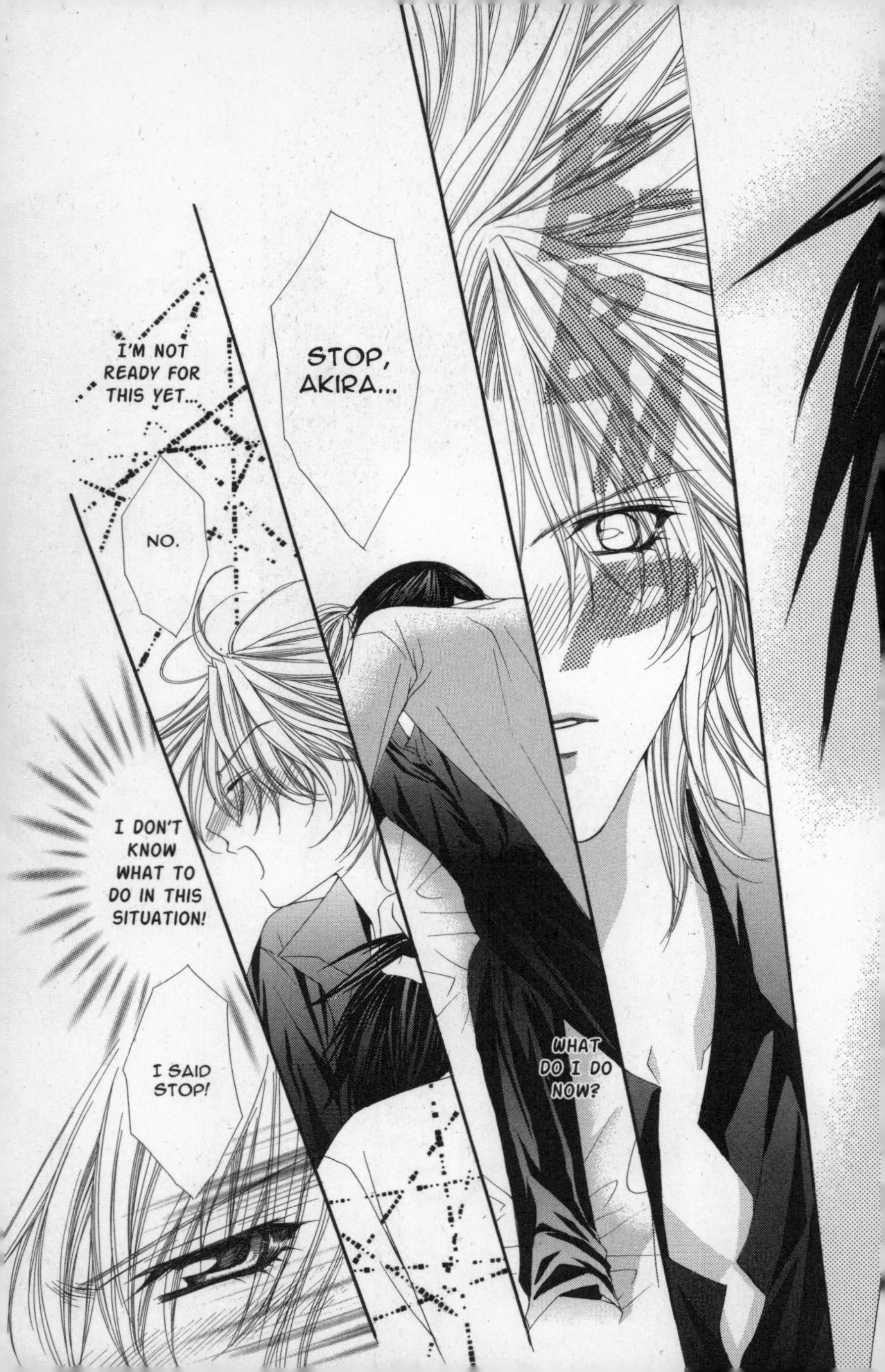
STOP, AKIRA...
I'M NOT READY FOR THIS YET...
NO.
I DON'T KNOW WHAT TO DO IN THIS SITUATION!
I SAID STOP!
WHAT DO I DO NOW?

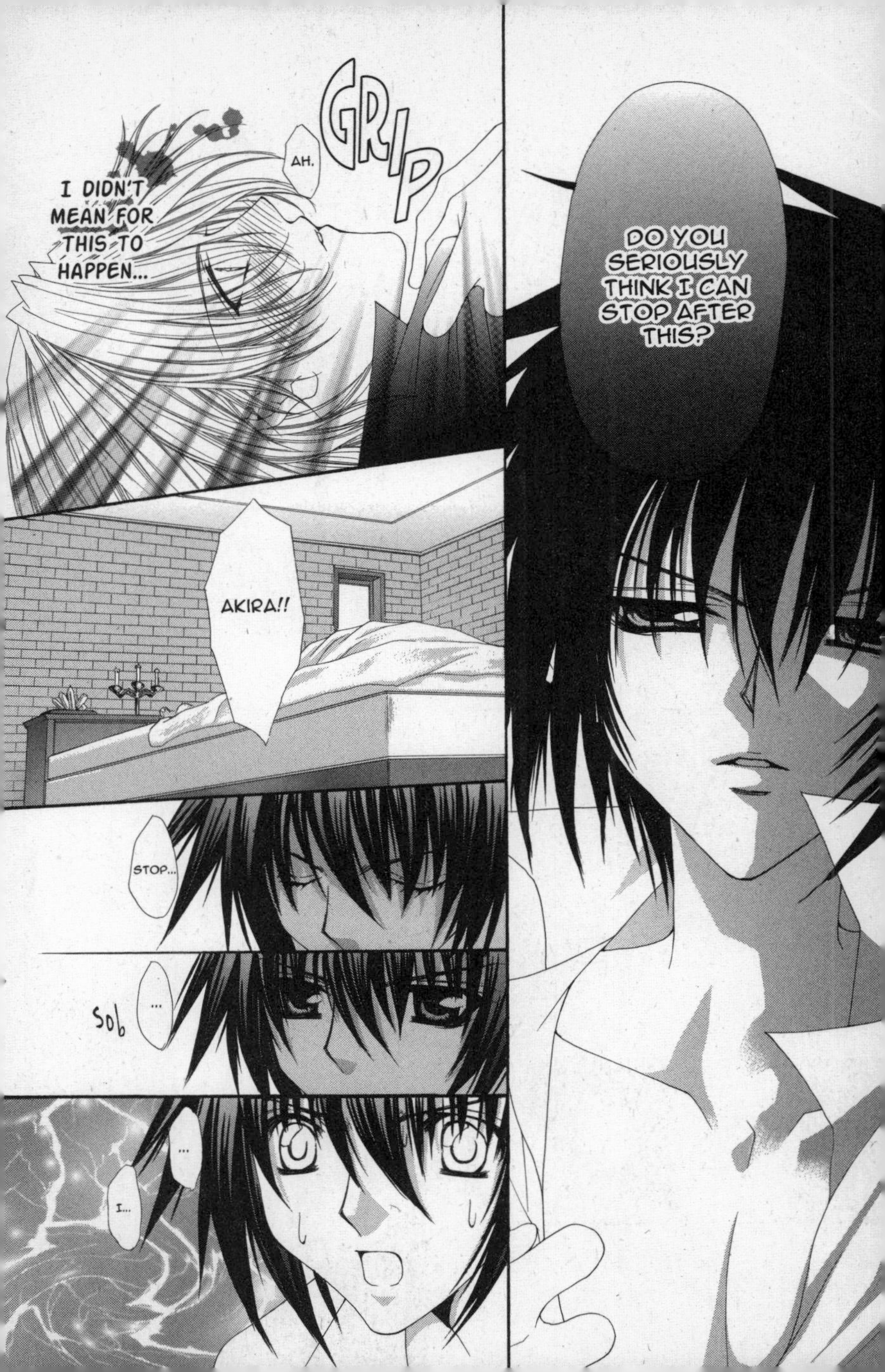
DO YOU SERIOUSLY THINK I CAN STOP AFTER THIS?
GRIP
AH.
I DIDN'T MEAN FOR THIS TO HAPPEN...
AKIRA!!
STOP...
...
Sob
...
I...

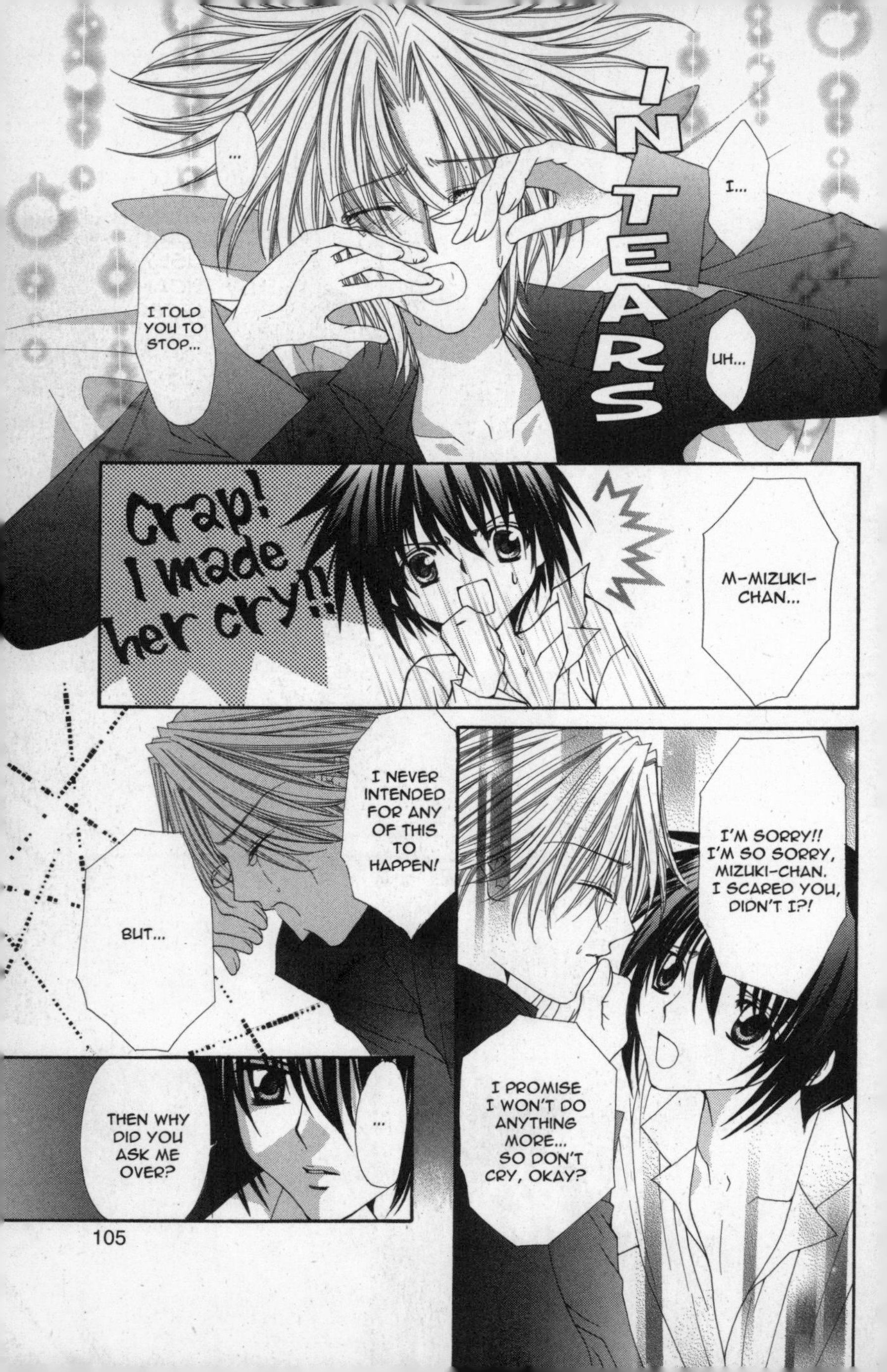
I...
UH...
IN TEARS
...
I TOLD YOU TO STOP...
M-MIZUKI-CHAN...
Crap! I made her cry!!
I'M SORRY!! I'M SO SORRY, MIZUKI-CHAN. I SCARED YOU, DIDN'T I?!
I PROMISE I WON'T DO ANYTHING MORE... SO DON'T CRY, OKAY?
I NEVER INTENDED FOR ANY OF THIS TO HAPPEN!
BUT...
...
THEN WHY DID YOU ASK ME OVER?

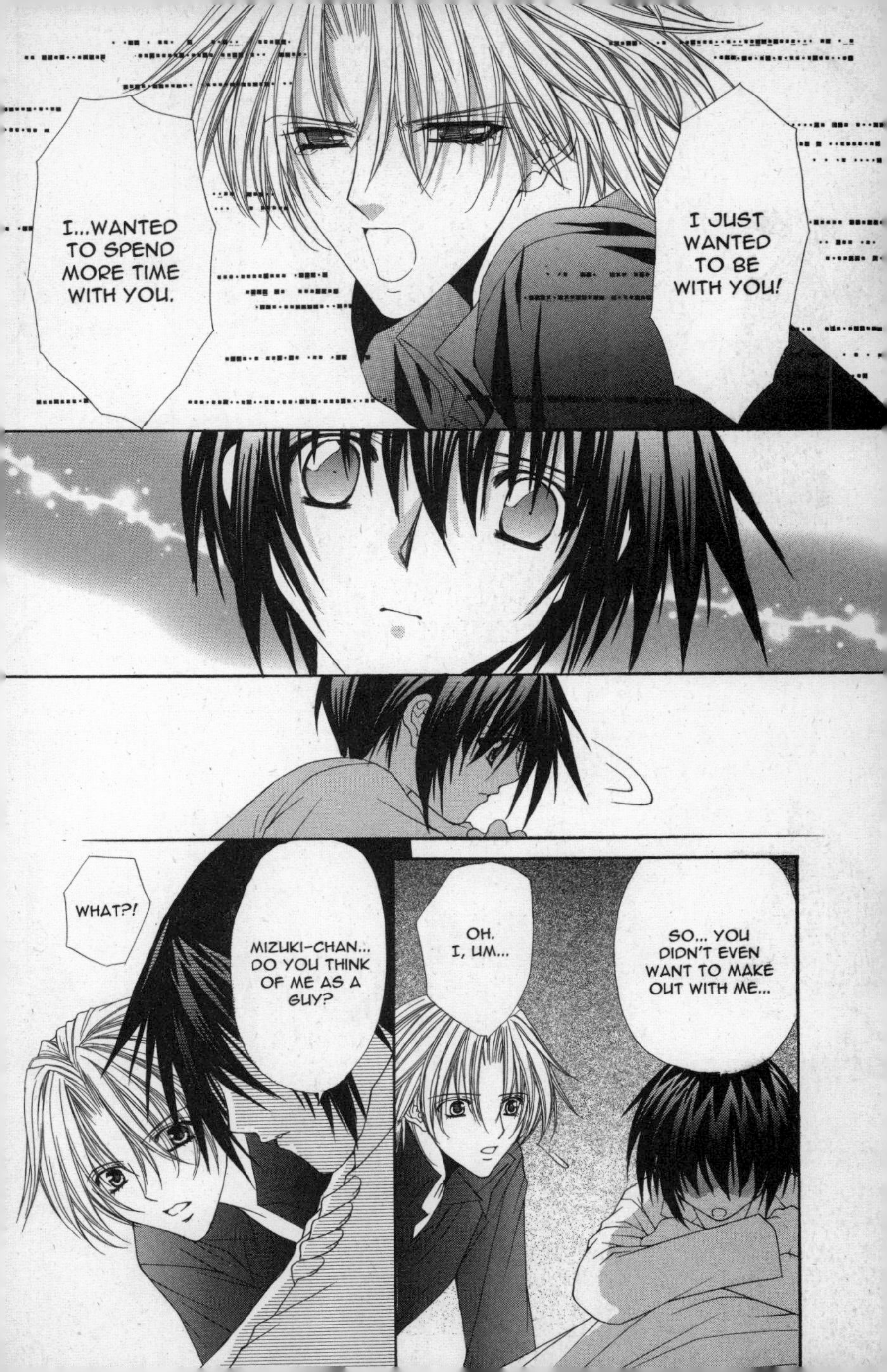
I JUST WANTED TO BE WITH YOU!
I...WANTED TO SPEND MORE TIME WITH YOU.
SO... YOU DIDN'T EVEN WANT TO MAKE OUT WITH ME...
OH. I, UM...
MIZUKI-CHAN... DO YOU THINK OF ME AS A GUY?
WHAT?!

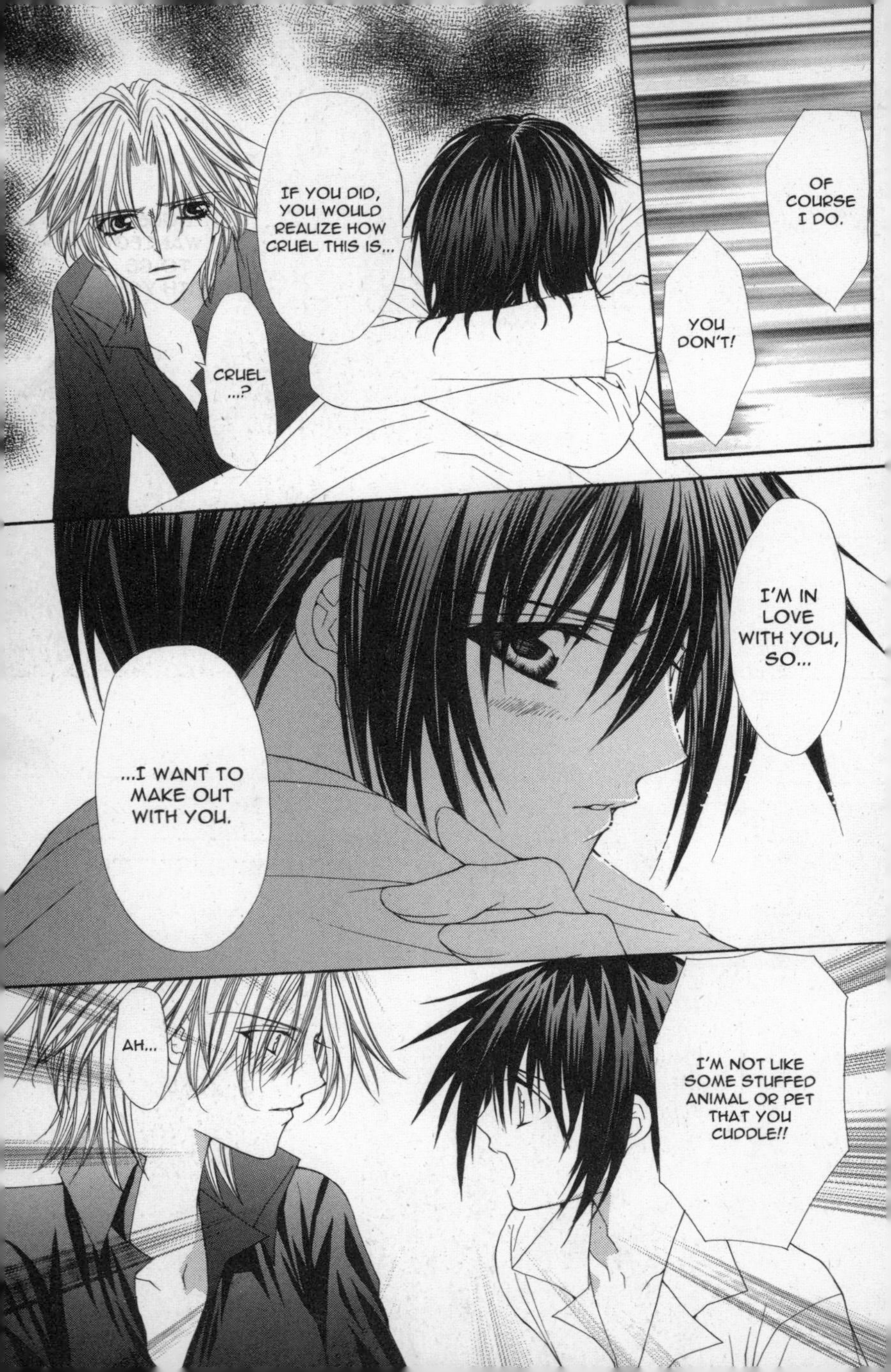
OF COURSE I DO.
YOU DON'T!
IF YOU DID, YOU WOULD REALIZE HOW CRUEL THIS IS...
CRUEL ...?
I'M IN LOVE WITH YOU, SO...
...I WANT TO MAKE OUT WITH YOU.
I'M NOT LIKE SOME STUFFED ANIMAL OR PET THAT YOU CUDDLE!!
AH...

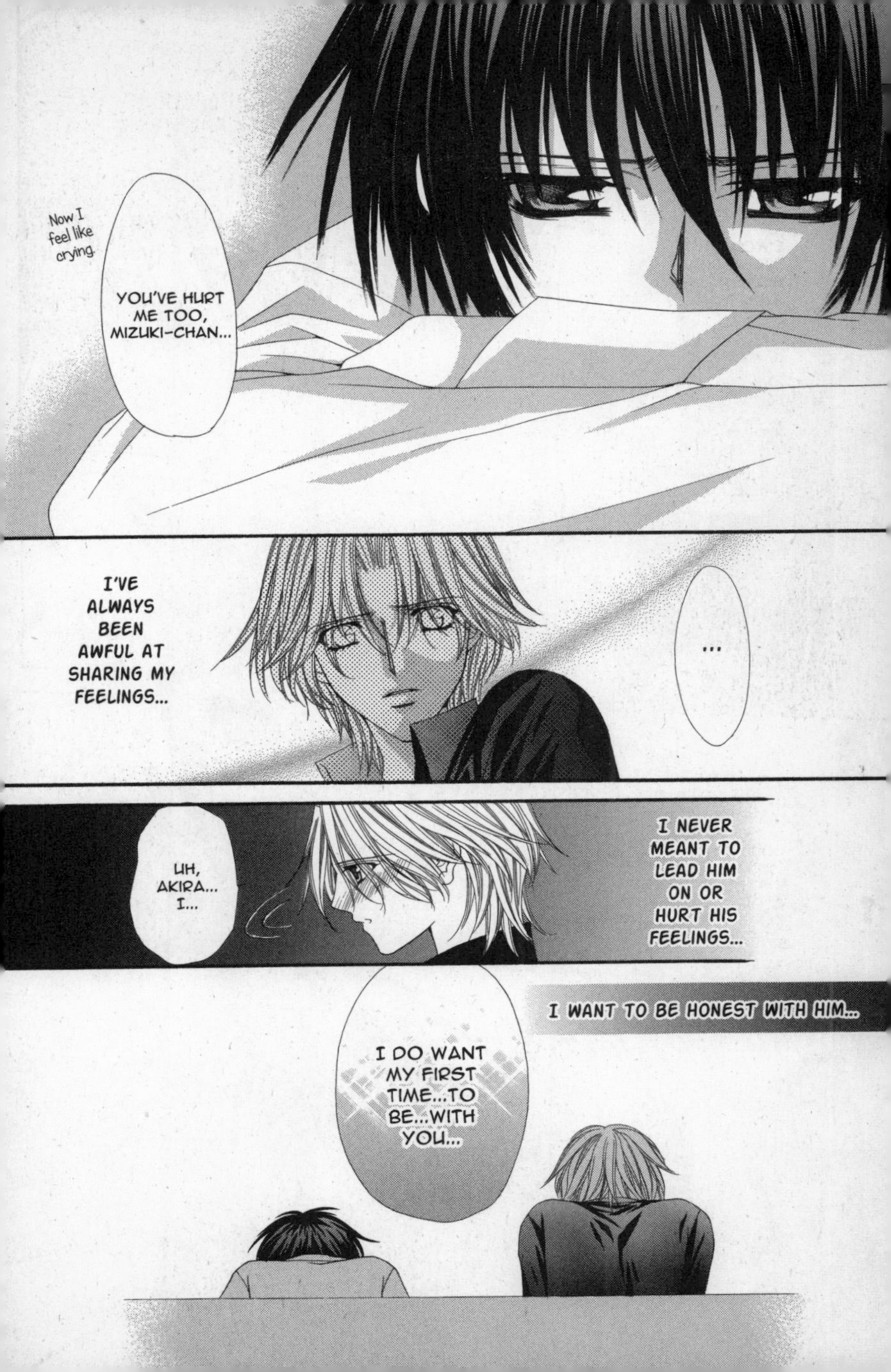
YOU'VE HURT ME TOO, MIZUKI-CHAN...
Now I feel like crying.
...
I'VE ALWAYS BEEN AWFUL AT SHARING MY FEELINGS...
I NEVER MEANT TO LEAD HIM ON OR HURT HIS FEELINGS...
UH, AKIRA... I...
I WANT TO BE HONEST WITH HIM...
I DO WANT MY FIRST TIME...TO BE...WITH YOU...

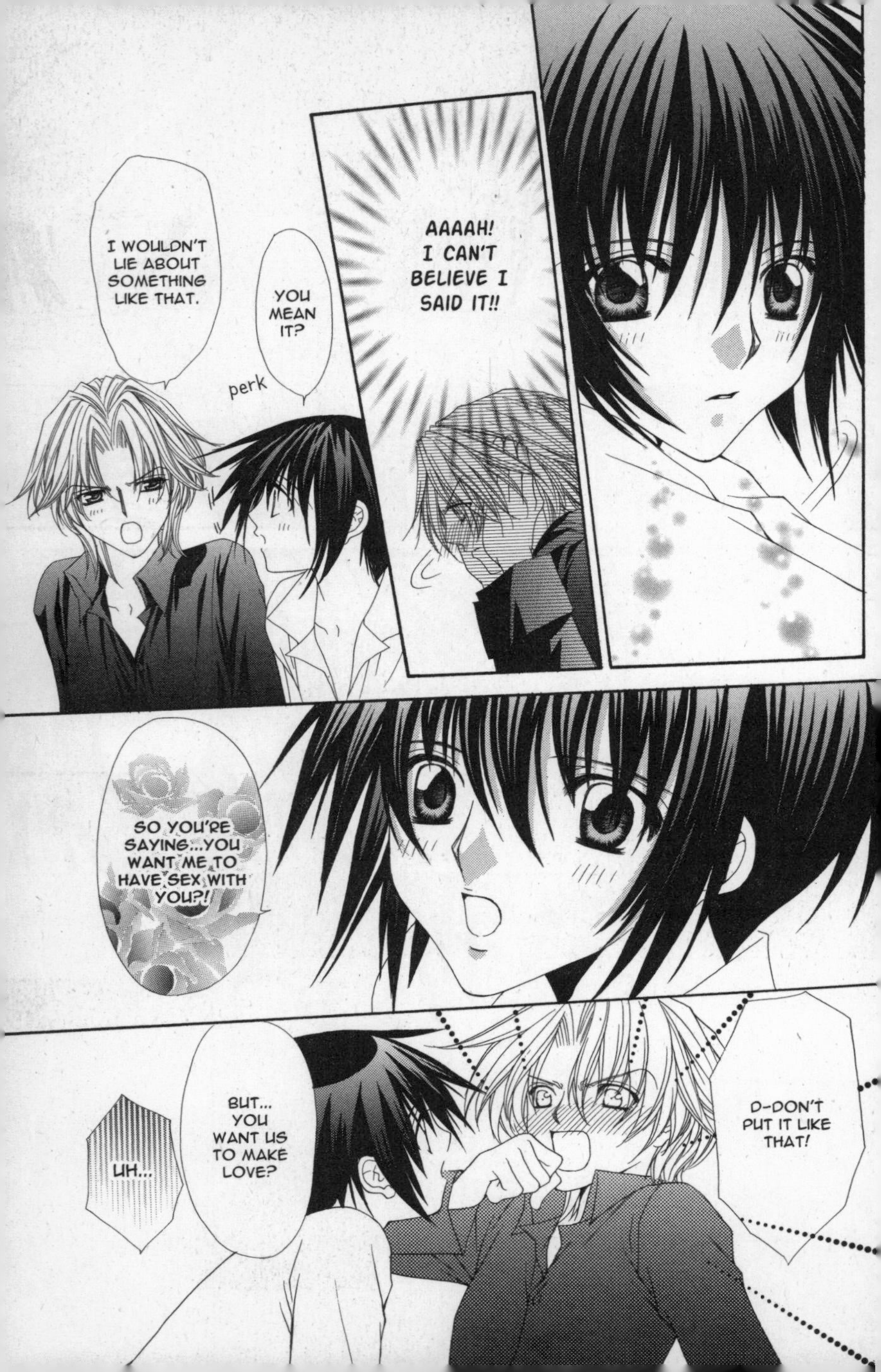
AAAAH! I CAN'T BELIEVE I SAID IT!!
YOU MEAN IT?
perk
I WOULDN'T LIE ABOUT SOMETHING LIKE THAT.
SO YOU'RE SAYING...YOU WANT ME TO HAVE SEX WITH YOU?!
D-DON'T PUT IT LIKE THAT!
BUT... YOU WANT US TO MAKE LOVE?
UH...

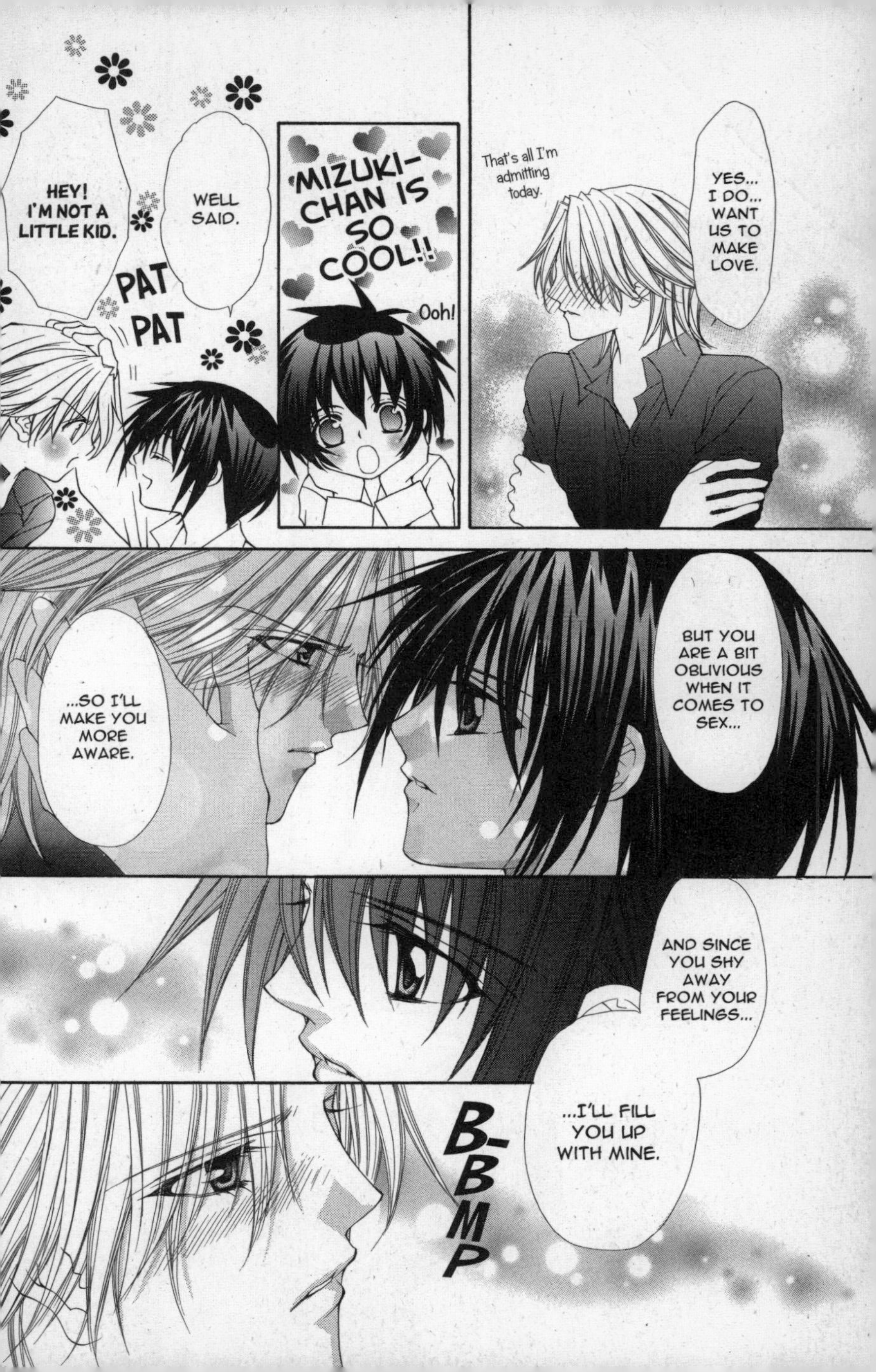
YES... I DO... WANT US TO MAKE LOVE.
That's all I'm admitting today.
'MIZUKI-CHAN IS SO COOL!!
Ooh!
WELL SAID.
HEY! I'M NOT A LITTLE KID.
PAT PAT
BUT YOU ARE A BIT OBLIVIOUS WHEN IT COMES TO SEX...
...SO I'LL MAKE YOU MORE AWARE.
AND SINCE YOU SHY AWAY FROM YOUR FEELINGS...
...I'LL FILL YOU UP WITH MINE.
B-BMP

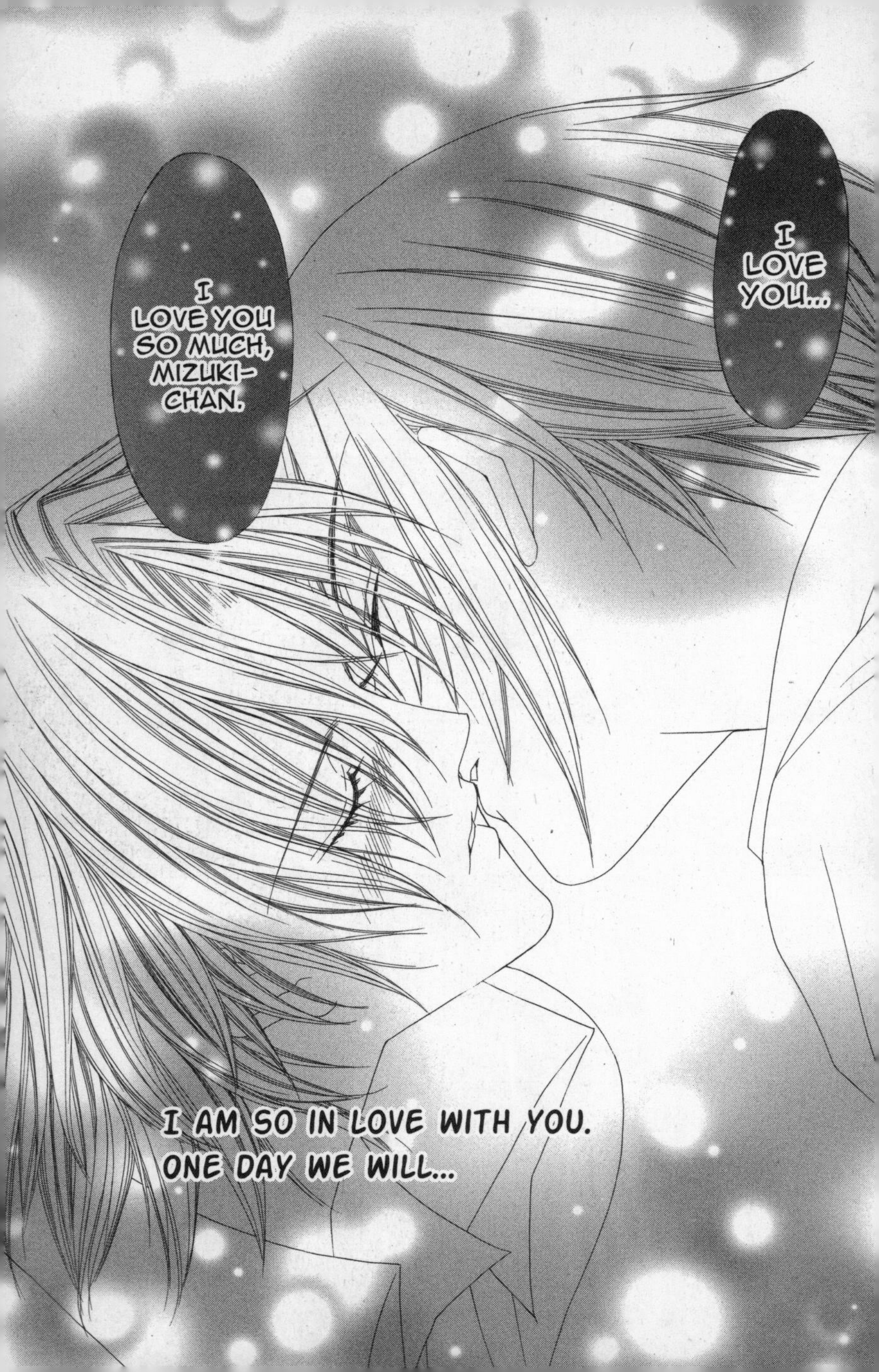
I LOVE YOU...
I LOVE YOU SO MUCH, MIZUKI-CHAN.
I AM SO IN LOVE WITH YOU. ONE DAY WE WILL...

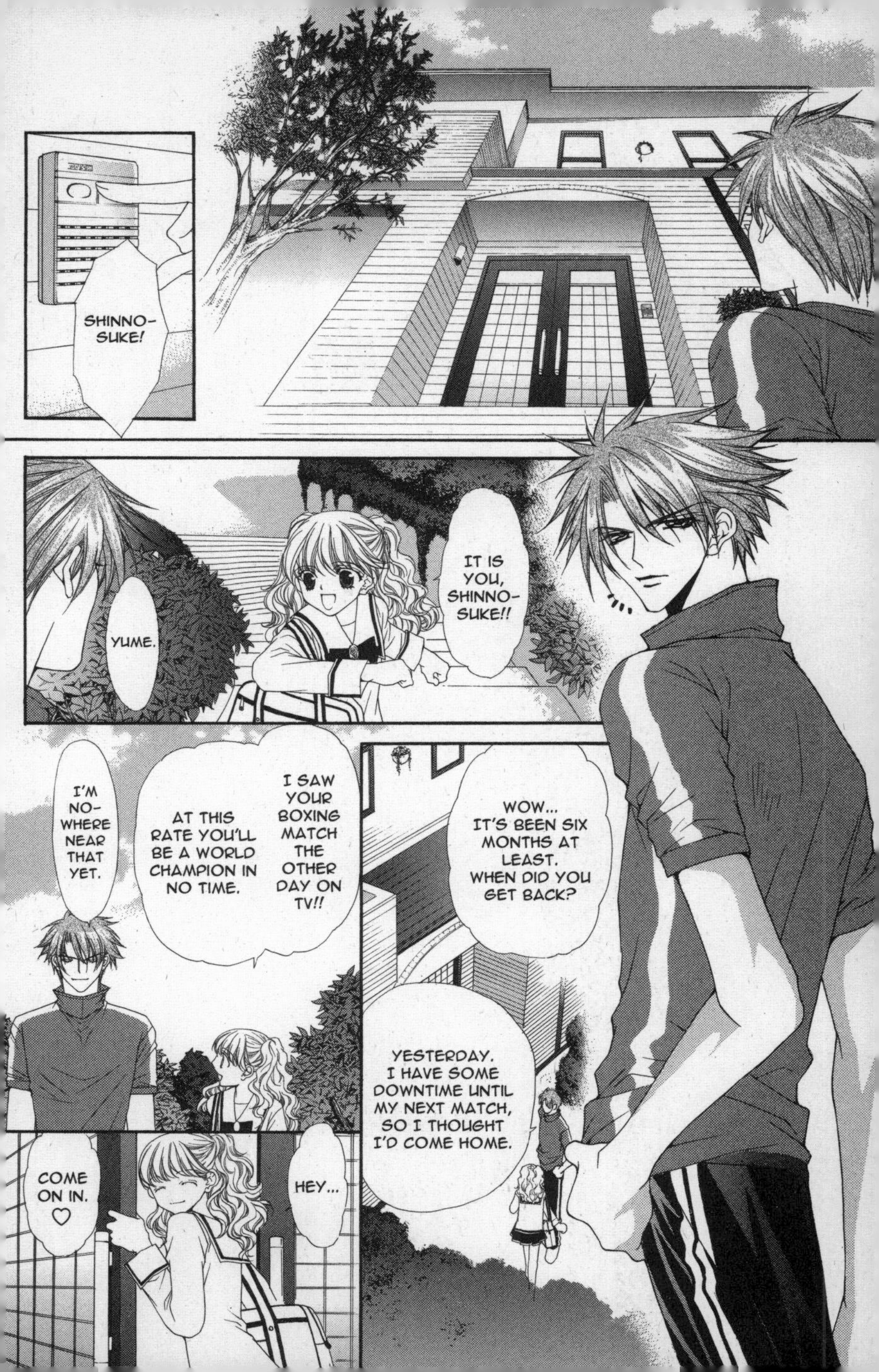
SHINNO-SUKE!
IT IS YOU, SHINNO-SUKE!!
YUME.
WOW... IT'S BEEN SIX MONTHS AT LEAST. WHEN DID YOU GET BACK?
YESTERDAY. I HAVE SOME DOWNTIME UNTIL MY NEXT MATCH, SO I THOUGHT I'D COME HOME.
I SAW YOUR BOXING MATCH THE OTHER DAY ON TV!!
AT THIS RATE YOU'LL BE A WORLD CHAMPION IN NO TIME.
I'M NO-WHERE NEAR THAT YET.
HEY...
COME ON IN. ♡

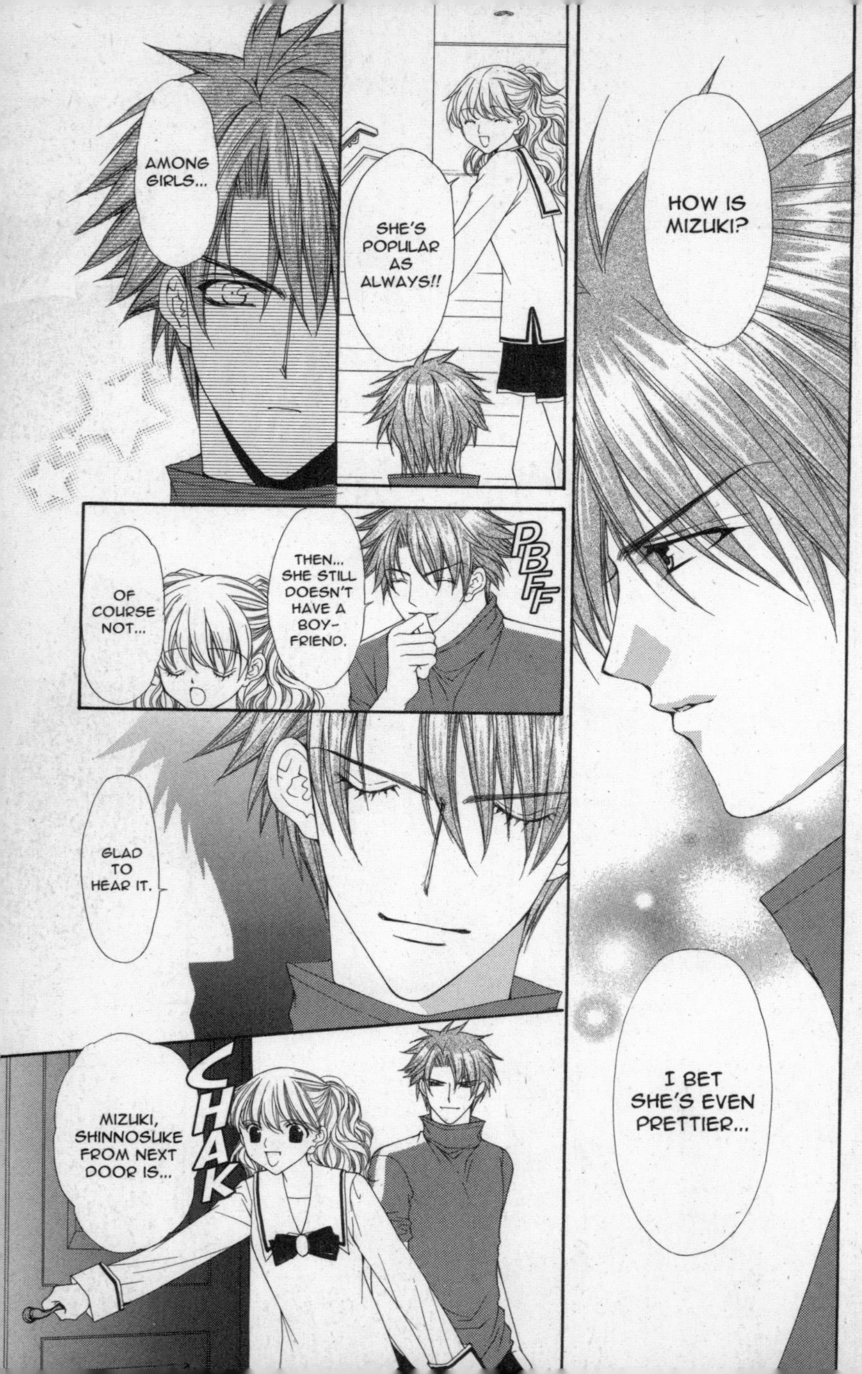
HOW IS MIZUKI?
I BET SHE'S EVEN PRETTIER...
SHE'S POPULAR AS ALWAYS!!
AMONG GIRLS...
PBFF
THEN... SHE STILL DOESN'T HAVE A BOY-FRIEND.
OF COURSE NOT...
GLAD TO HEAR IT.
CHAK
MIZUKI, SHINNOSUKE FROM NEXT DOOR IS...

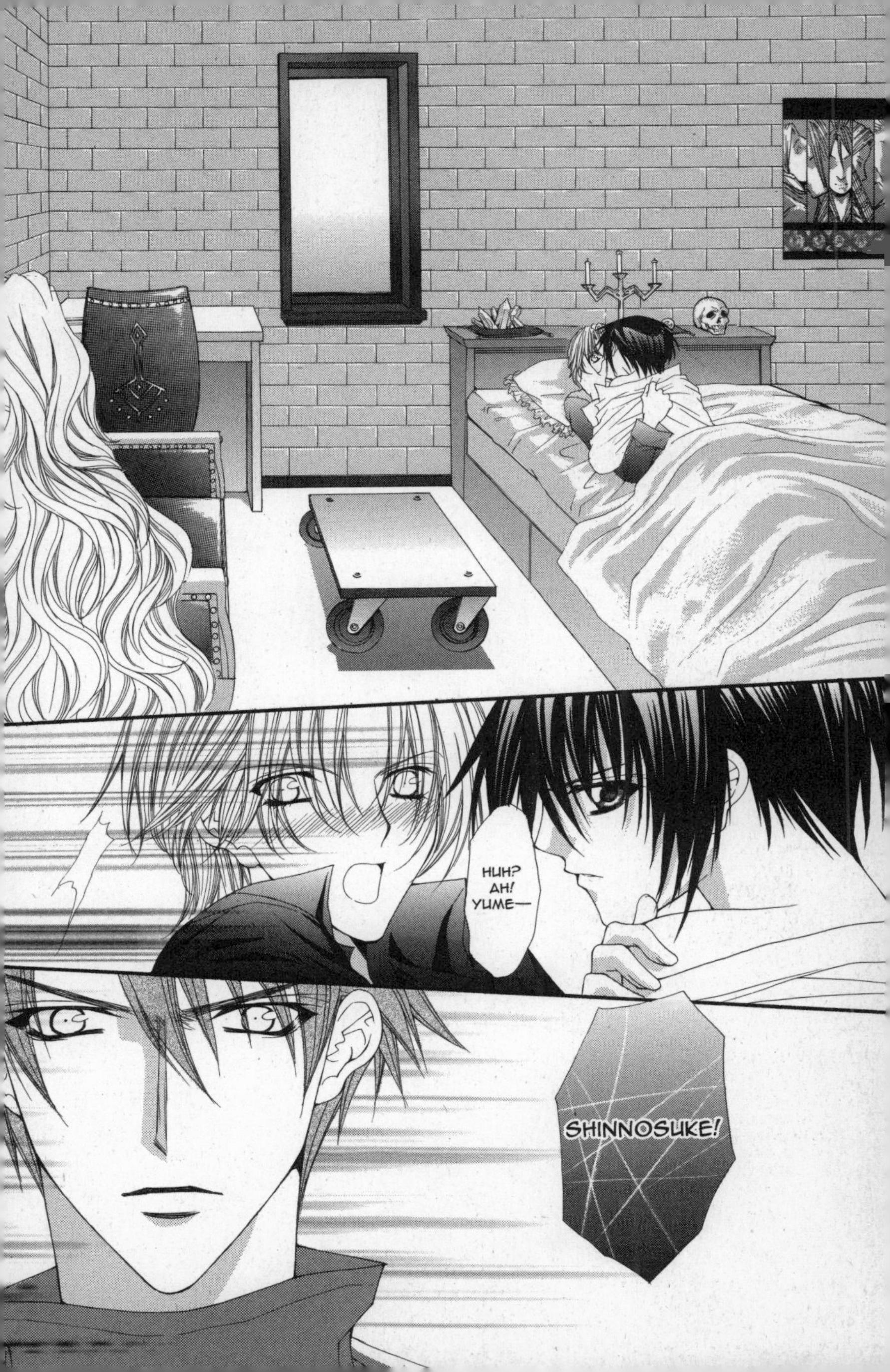
HUH? AH! YUME—
SHINNOSUKE!

AI ORE!

Love Me

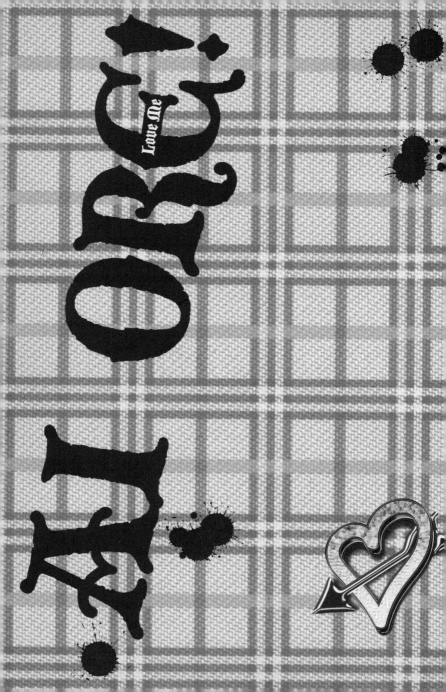

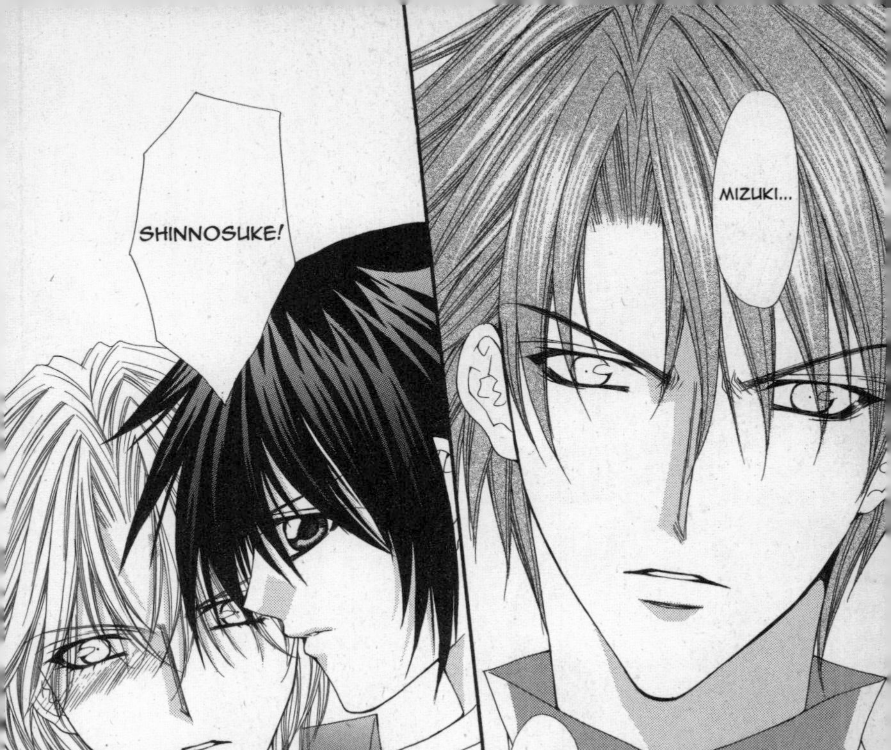
MIZUKI...
YOU...
SHINNOSUKE!

Answer me!! Mizuki ♡

Q3: What about Akira do you like best?

A3: Um... I like how he gets straight to the point. He's honest, straightforward, and true to himself.
How do I describe it...? He's a very pure person.

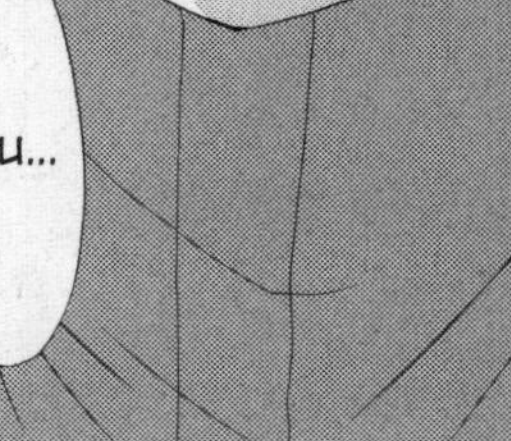

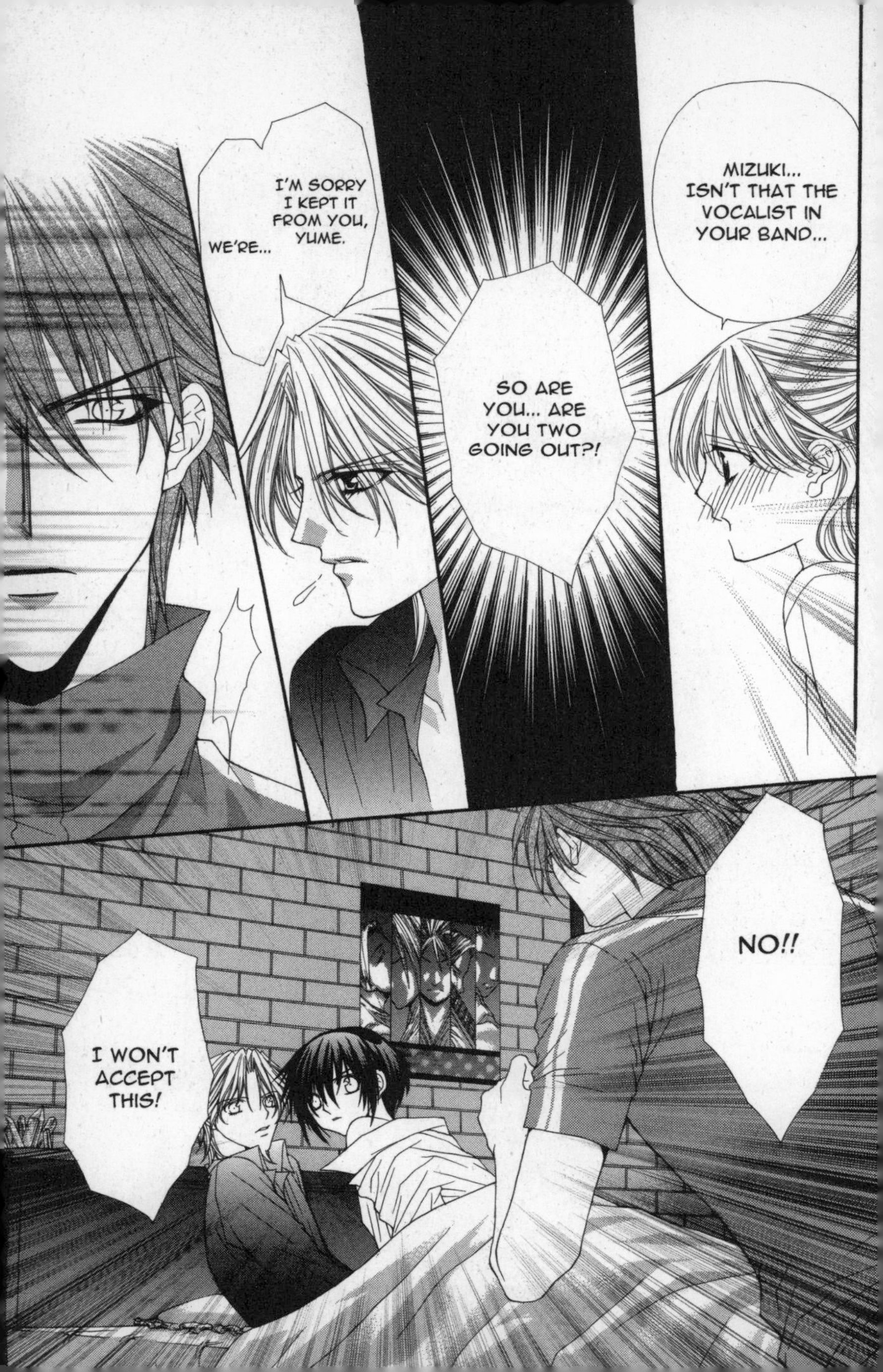
MIZUKI... ISN'T THAT THE VOCALIST IN YOUR BAND...
SO ARE YOU... ARE YOU TWO GOING OUT?!
I'M SORRY I KEPT IT FROM YOU, YUME.
WE'RE...
NO!!
I WON'T ACCEPT THIS!

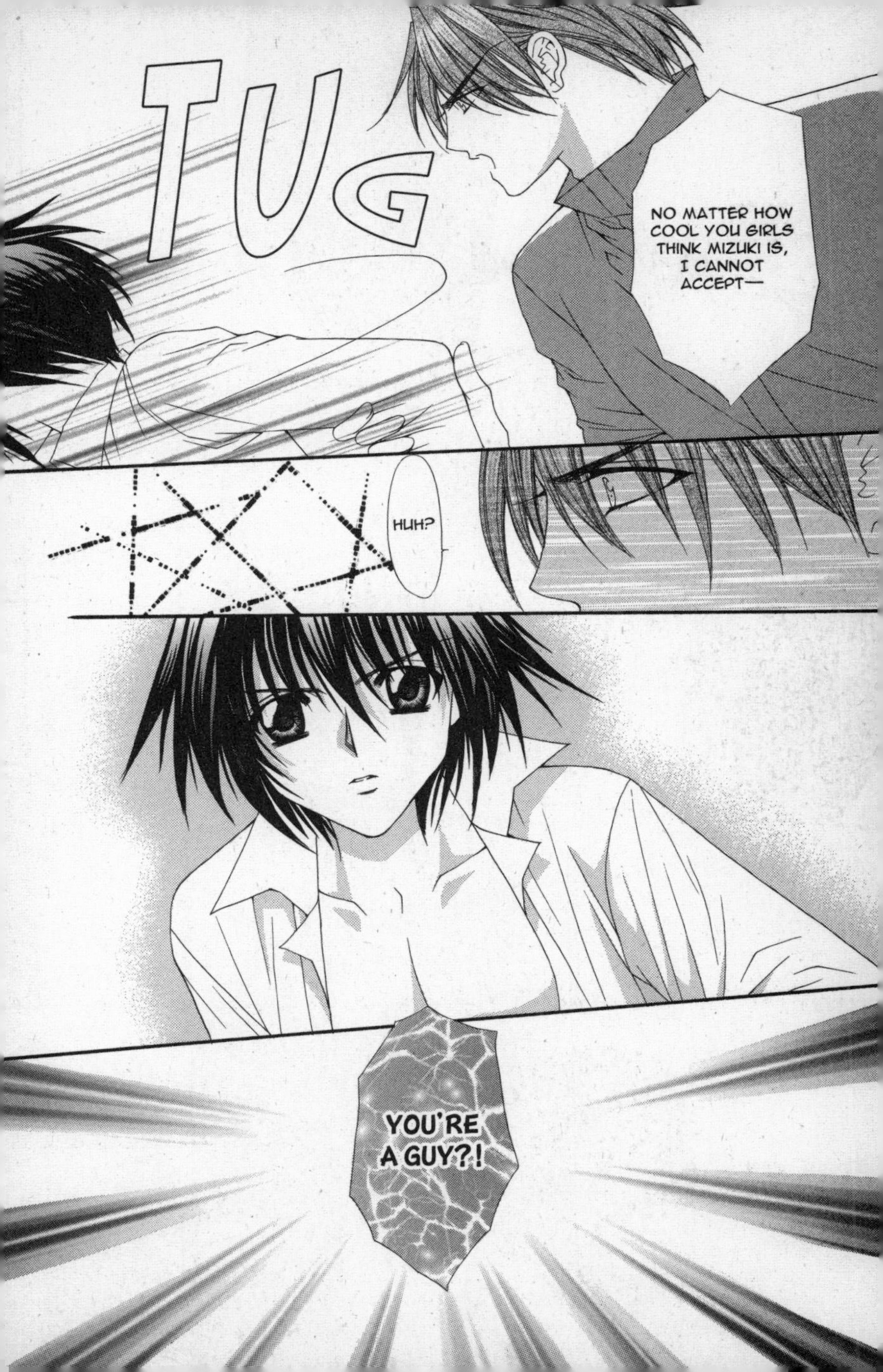
TUG
NO MATTER HOW COOL YOU GIRLS THINK MIZUKI IS, I CANNOT ACCEPT—
HUH?
YOU'RE A GUY?!

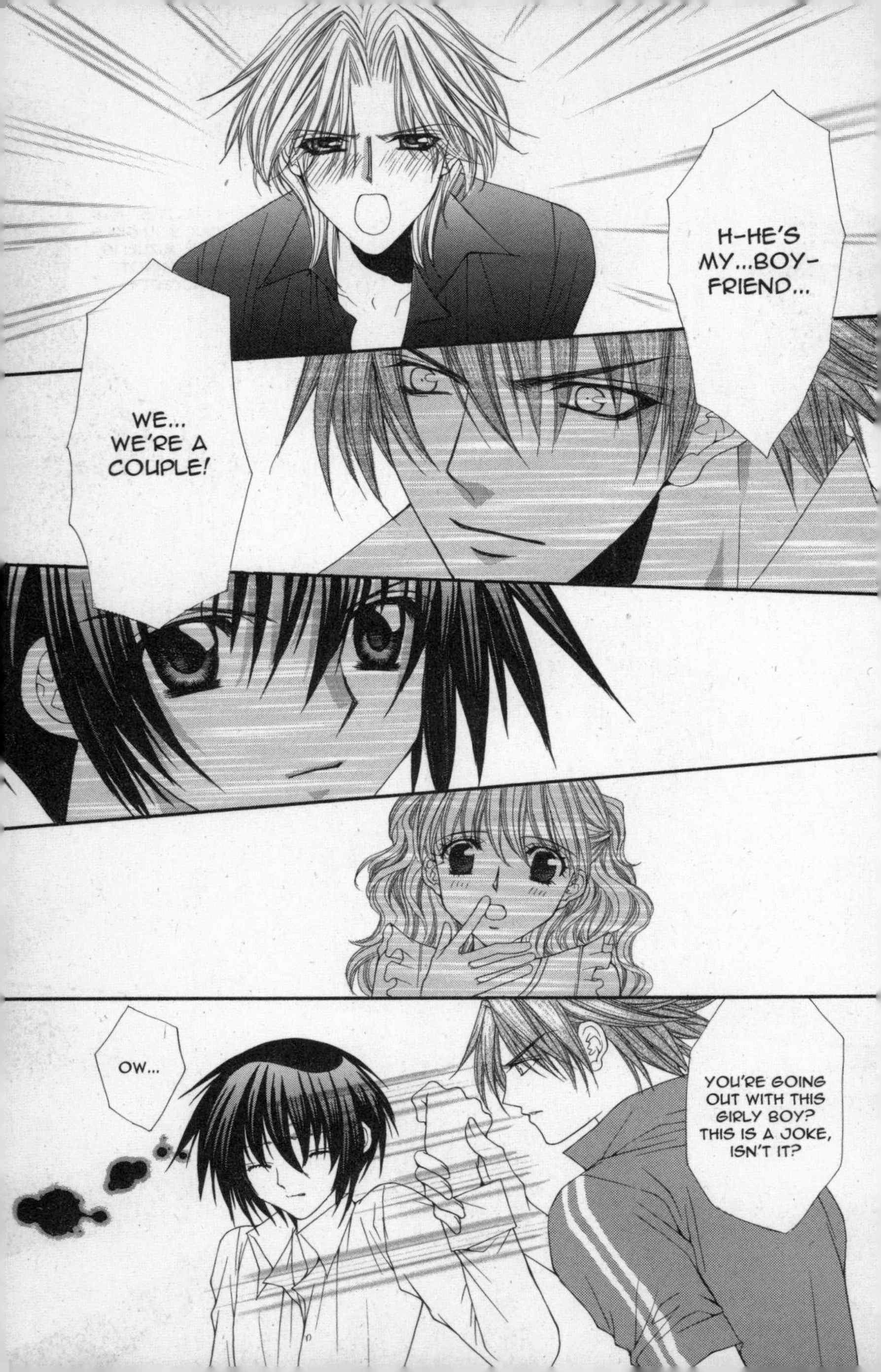
H-HE'S MY...BOY-FRIEND...
WE... WE'RE A COUPLE!
YOU'RE GOING OUT WITH THIS GIRLY BOY? THIS IS A JOKE, ISN'T IT?
OW...

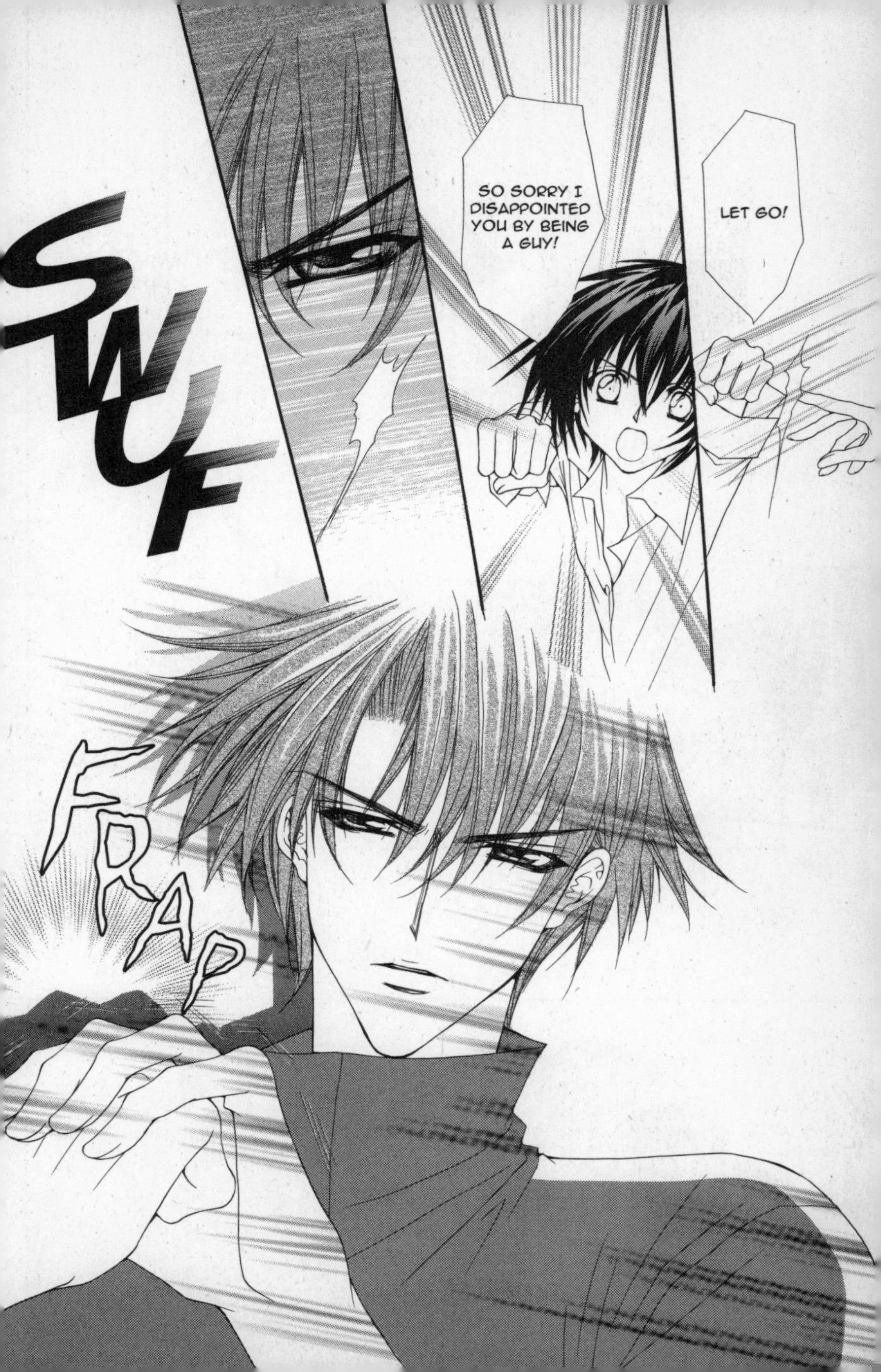
LET GO!
SO SORRY I DISAPPOINTED YOU BY BEING A GUY!
SWUF
FRAP

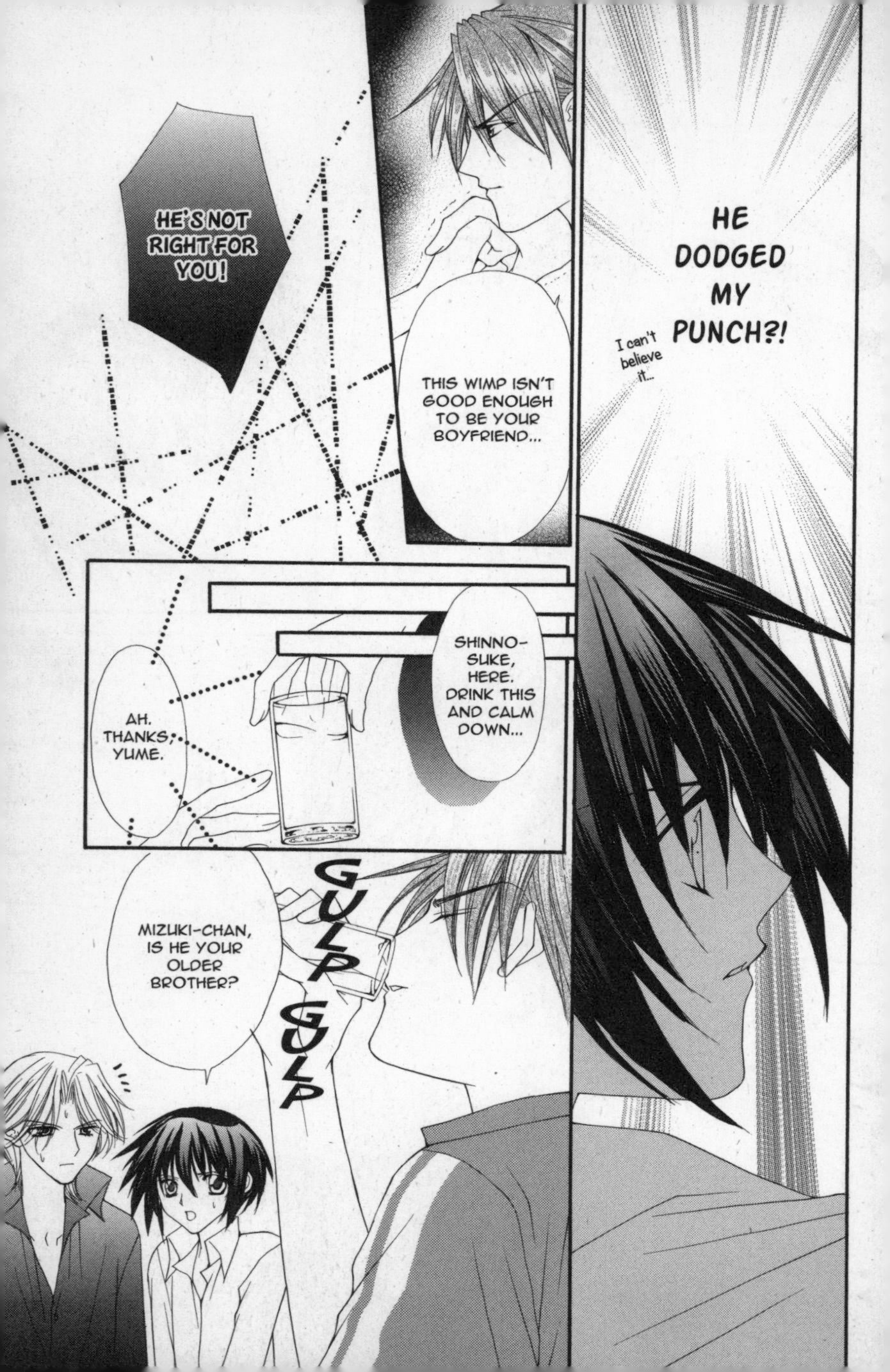
HE DODGED MY PUNCH?!
I can't believe it...
THIS WIMP ISN'T GOOD ENOUGH TO BE YOUR BOYFRIEND...
HE'S NOT RIGHT FOR YOU!
SHINNO-SUKE, HERE. DRINK THIS AND CALM DOWN...
AH. THANKS, YUME.
GULP GULP GULP
MIZUKI-CHAN, IS HE YOUR OLDER BROTHER?

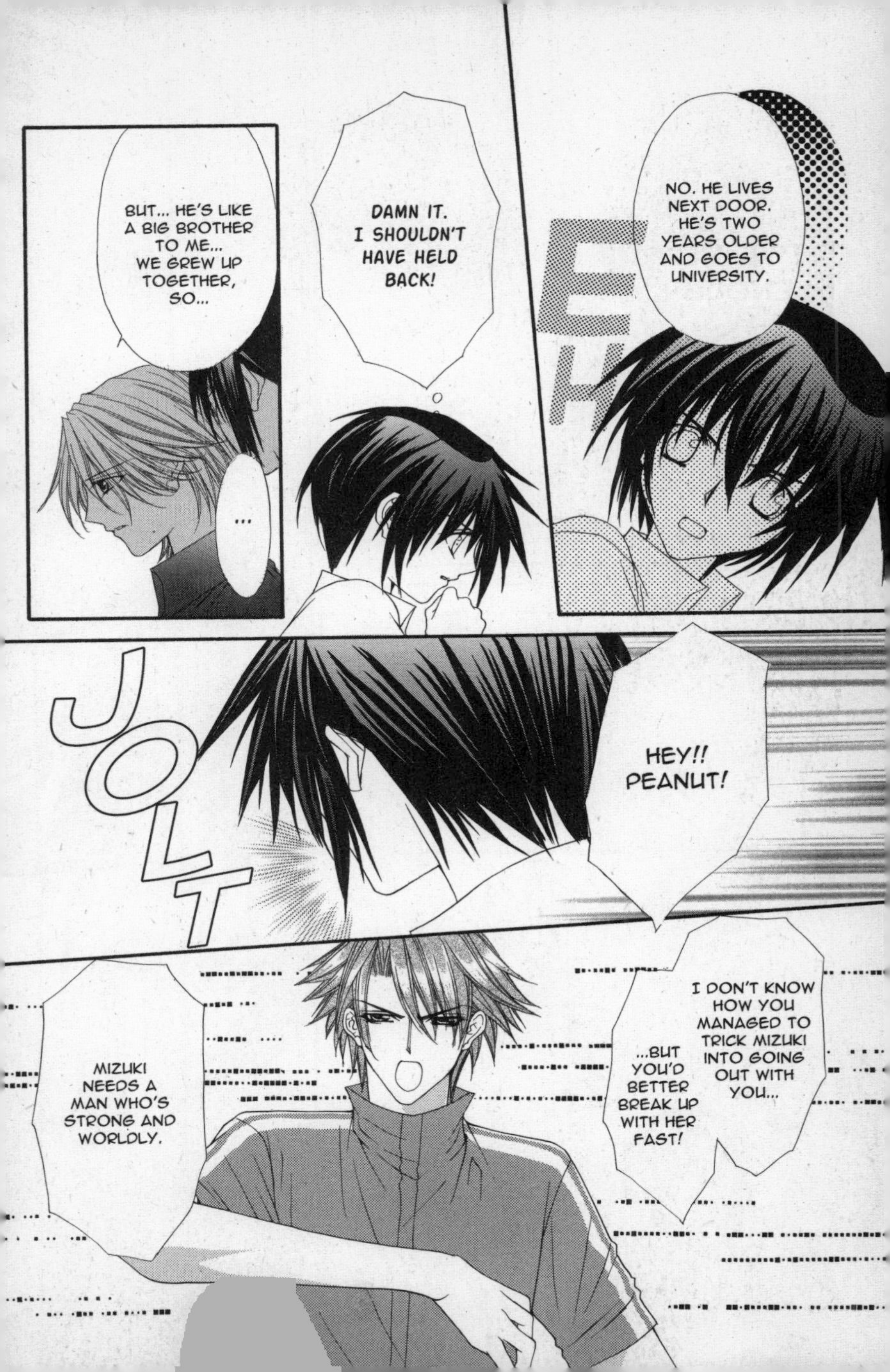
NO. HE LIVES NEXT DOOR. HE'S TWO YEARS OLDER AND GOES TO UNIVERSITY.
EH
DAMN IT. I SHOULDN'T HAVE HELD BACK!
BUT... HE'S LIKE A BIG BROTHER TO ME... WE GREW UP TOGETHER, SO...
...
HEY!! PEANUT!
JOLT
I DON'T KNOW HOW YOU MANAGED TO TRICK MIZUKI INTO GOING OUT WITH YOU...
...BUT YOU'D BETTER BREAK UP WITH HER FAST!
MIZUKI NEEDS A MAN WHO'S STRONG AND WORLDLY.

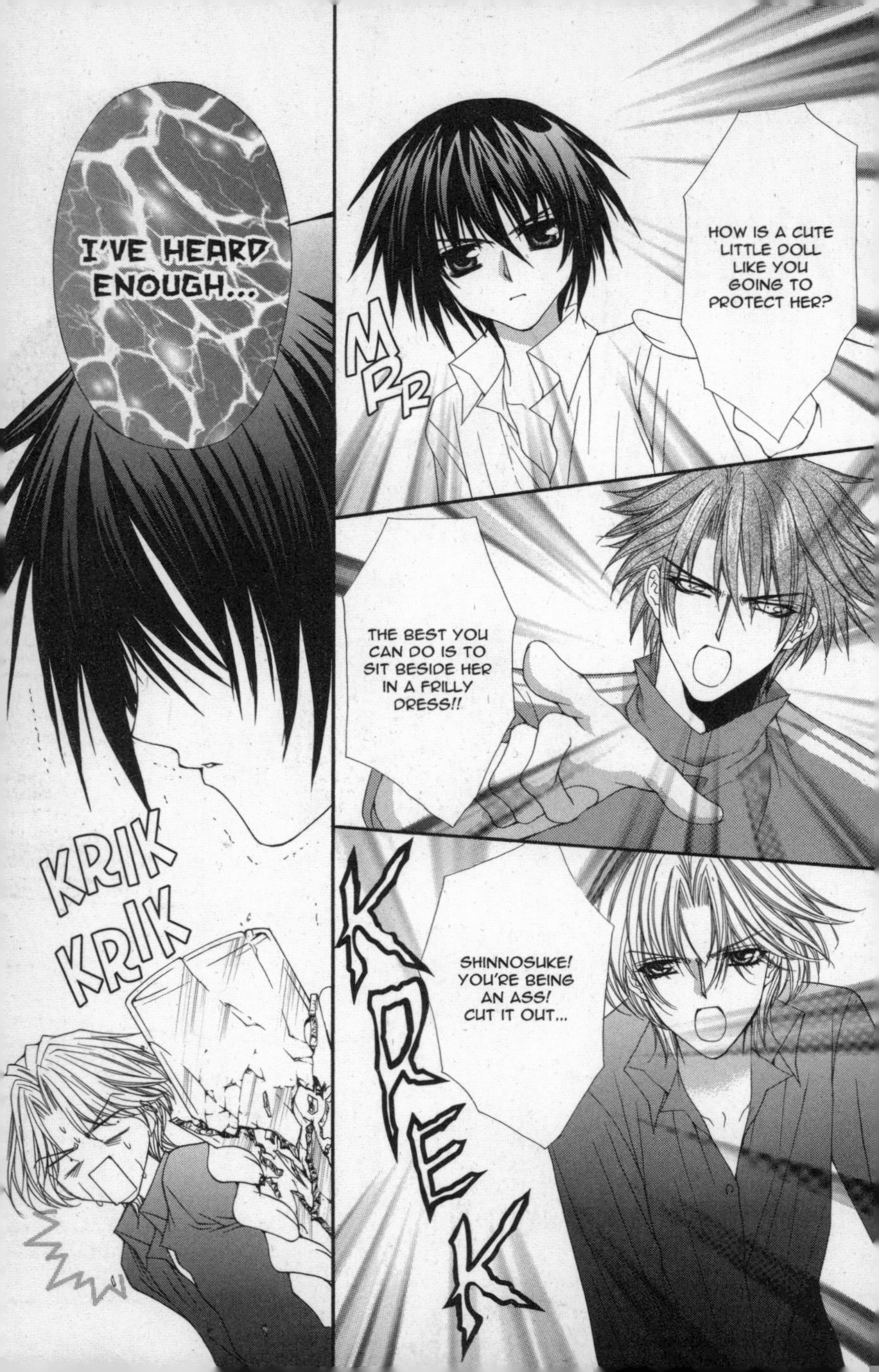
MRR
HOW IS A CUTE LITTLE DOLL LIKE YOU GOING TO PROTECT HER?
THE BEST YOU CAN DO IS TO SIT BESIDE HER IN A FRILLY DRESS!!
KREEK
SHINNOSUKE! YOU'RE BEING AN ASS! CUT IT OUT...
I'VE HEARD ENOUGH...
KRIK KRIK

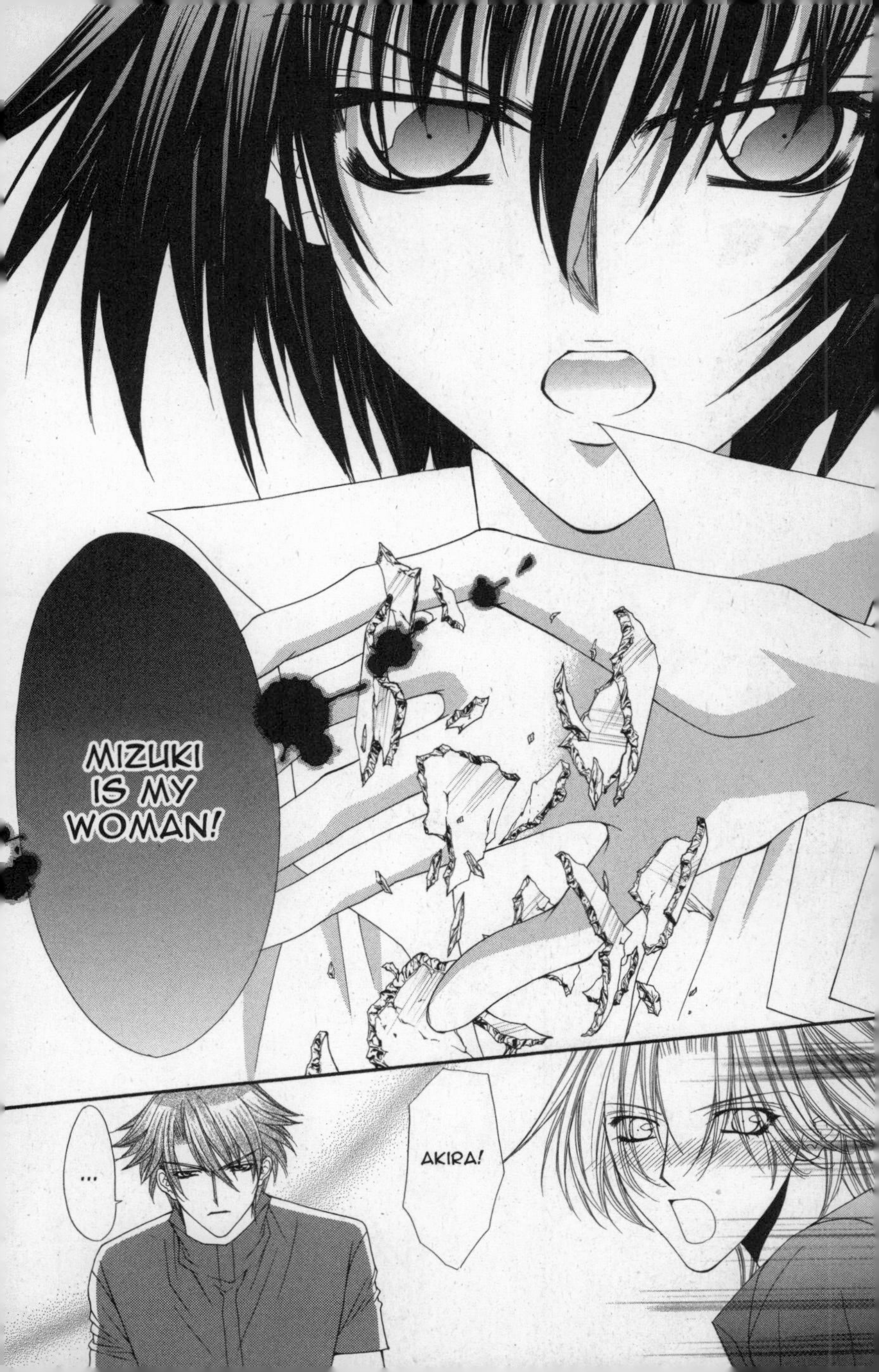
MIZUKI IS MY WOMAN!
AKIRA!
...

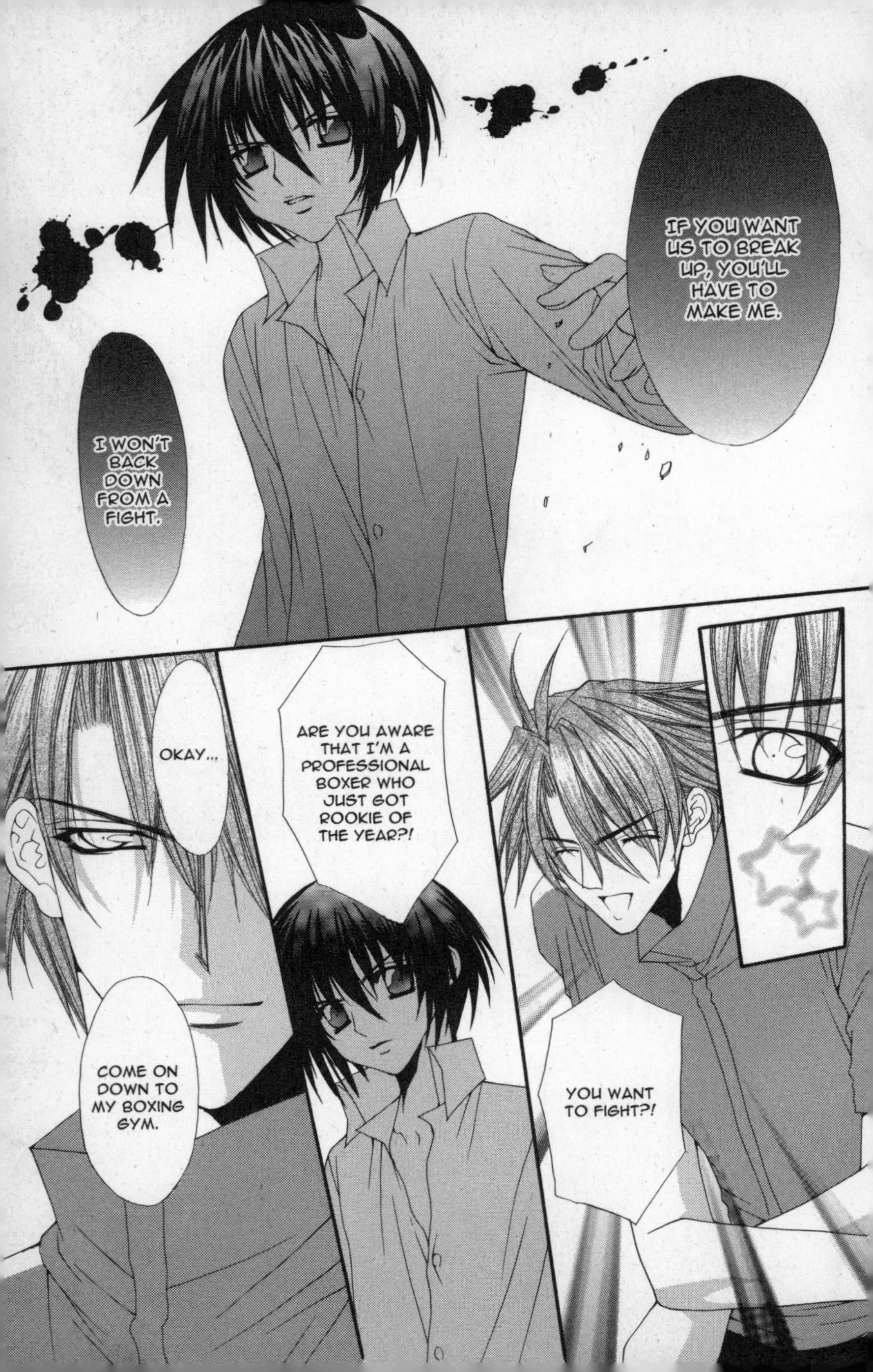

IF YOU WANT US TO BREAK UP, YOU'LL HAVE TO MAKE ME.
I WON'T BACK DOWN FROM A FIGHT.
YOU WANT TO FIGHT?!
ARE YOU AWARE THAT I'M A PROFESSIONAL BOXER WHO JUST GOT ROOKIE OF THE YEAR?!
OKAY...
COME ON DOWN TO MY BOXING GYM.

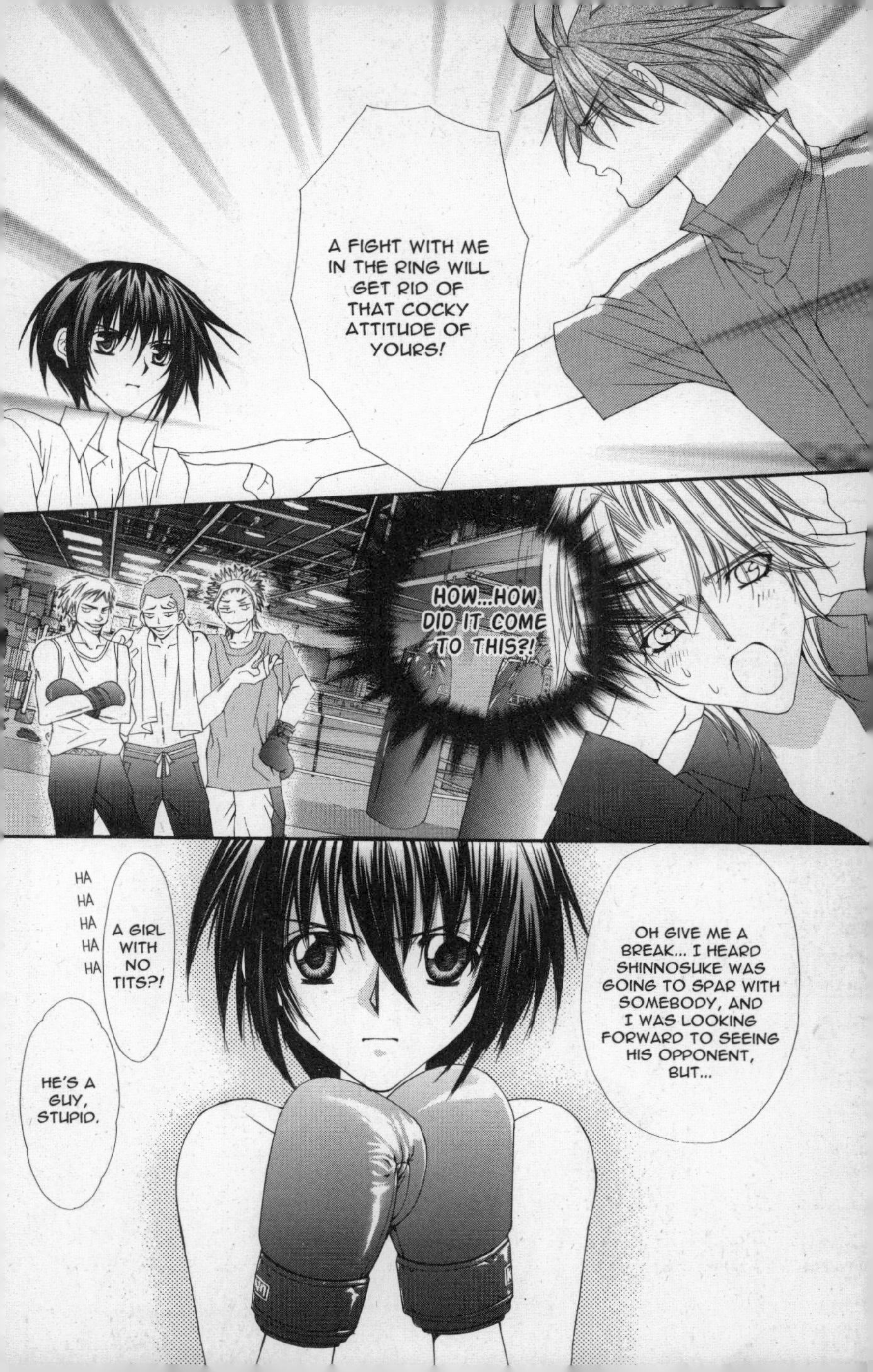
A FIGHT WITH ME IN THE RING WILL GET RID OF THAT COCKY ATTITUDE OF YOURS!
HOW...HOW DID IT COME TO THIS?!
OH GIVE ME A BREAK... I HEARD SHINNOSUKE WAS GOING TO SPAR WITH SOMEBODY, AND I WAS LOOKING FORWARD TO SEEING HIS OPPONENT, BUT...
A GIRL WITH NO TITS?!
HA HA HA HA HA
HE'S A GUY, STUPID.

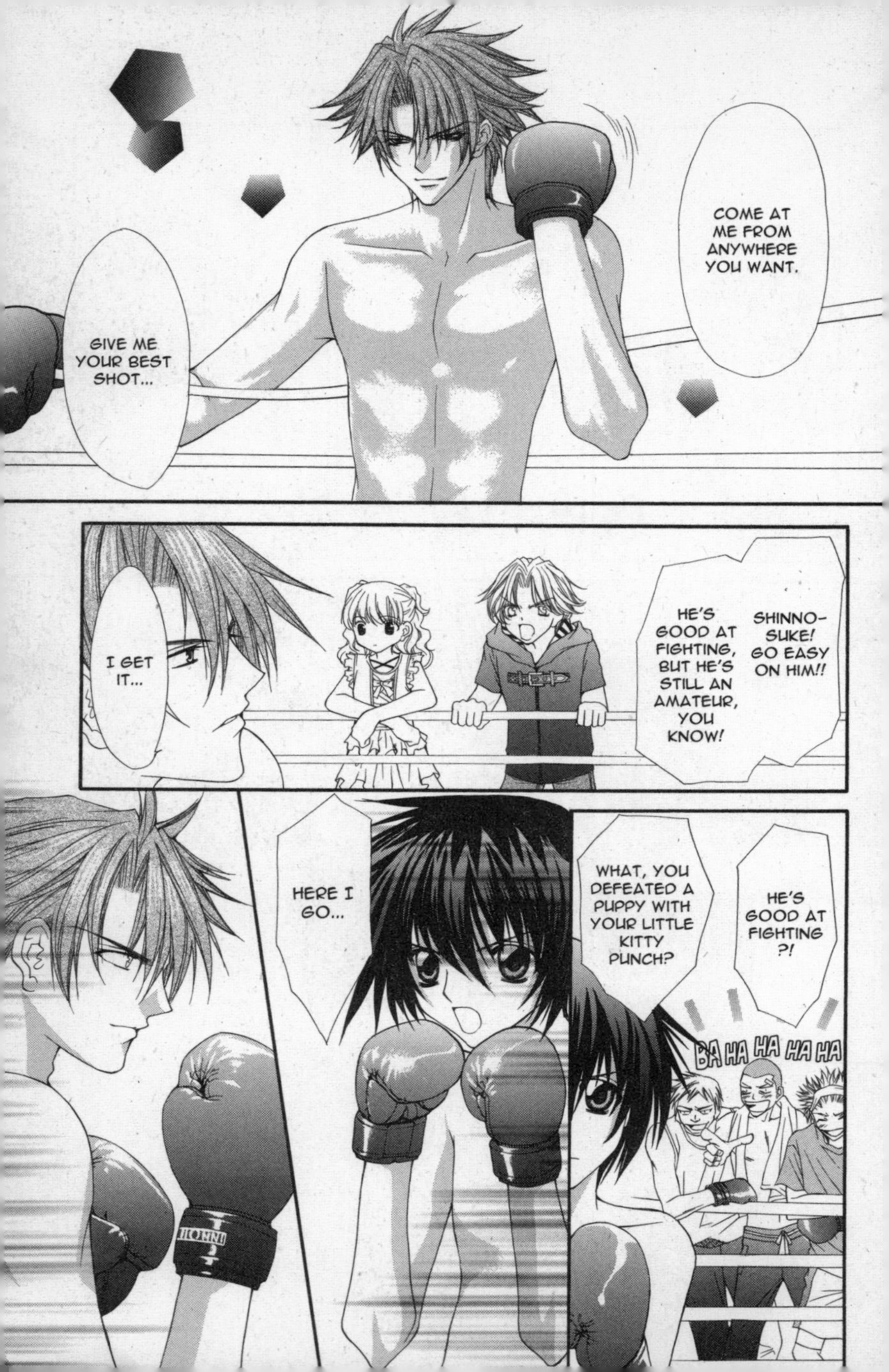
COME AT ME FROM ANYWHERE YOU WANT.
GIVE ME YOUR BEST SHOT...
SHINNO-SUKE! GO EASY ON HIM!!
HE'S GOOD AT FIGHTING, BUT HE'S STILL AN AMATEUR, YOU KNOW!
I GET IT...
HE'S GOOD AT FIGHTING ?!
WHAT, YOU DEFEATED A PUPPY WITH YOUR LITTLE KITTY PUNCH?
BA HA HA HA HA
HERE I GO...

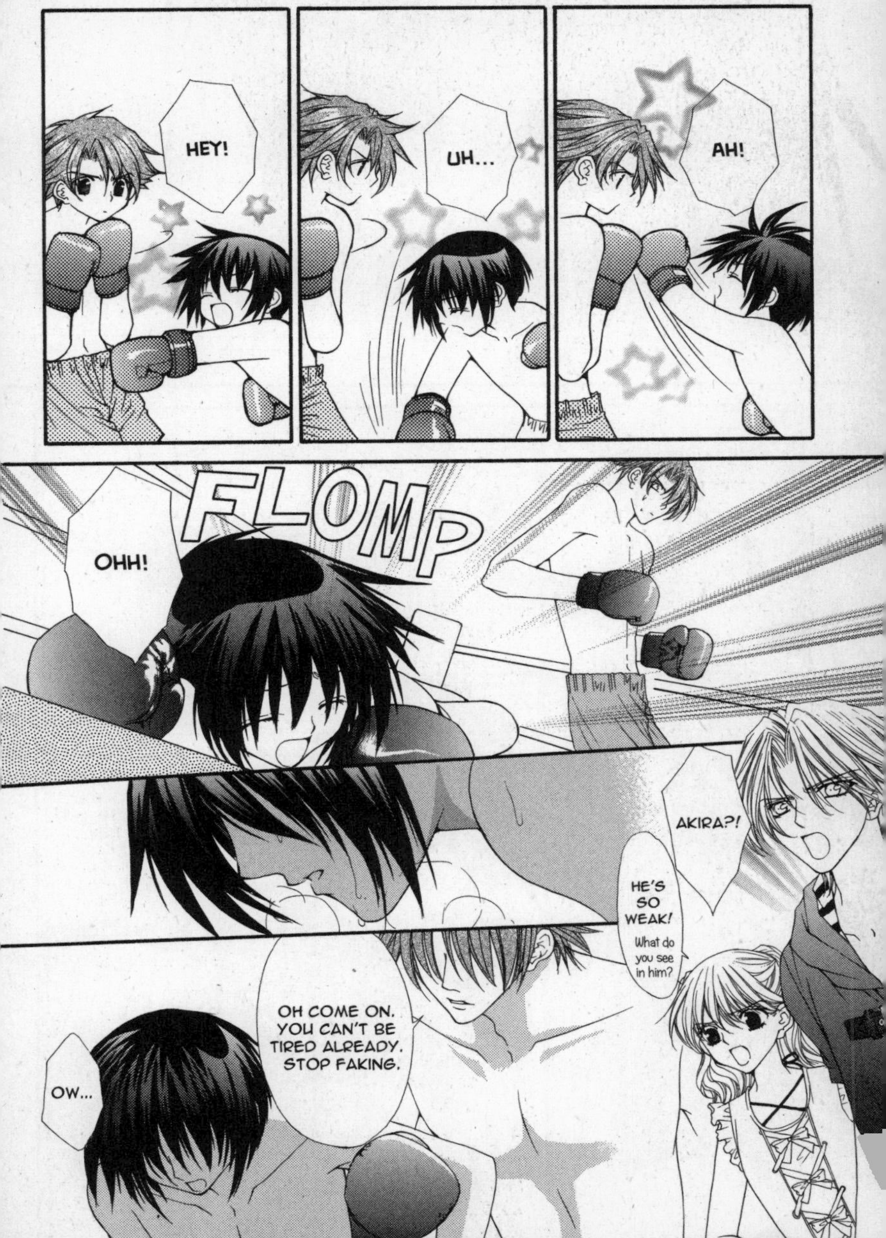
AH!
UH...
HEY!
FLOMP
OHH!
AKIRA?!
HE'S SO WEAK!
What do you see in him?
OH COME ON. YOU CAN'T BE TIRED ALREADY. STOP FAKING.
OW...

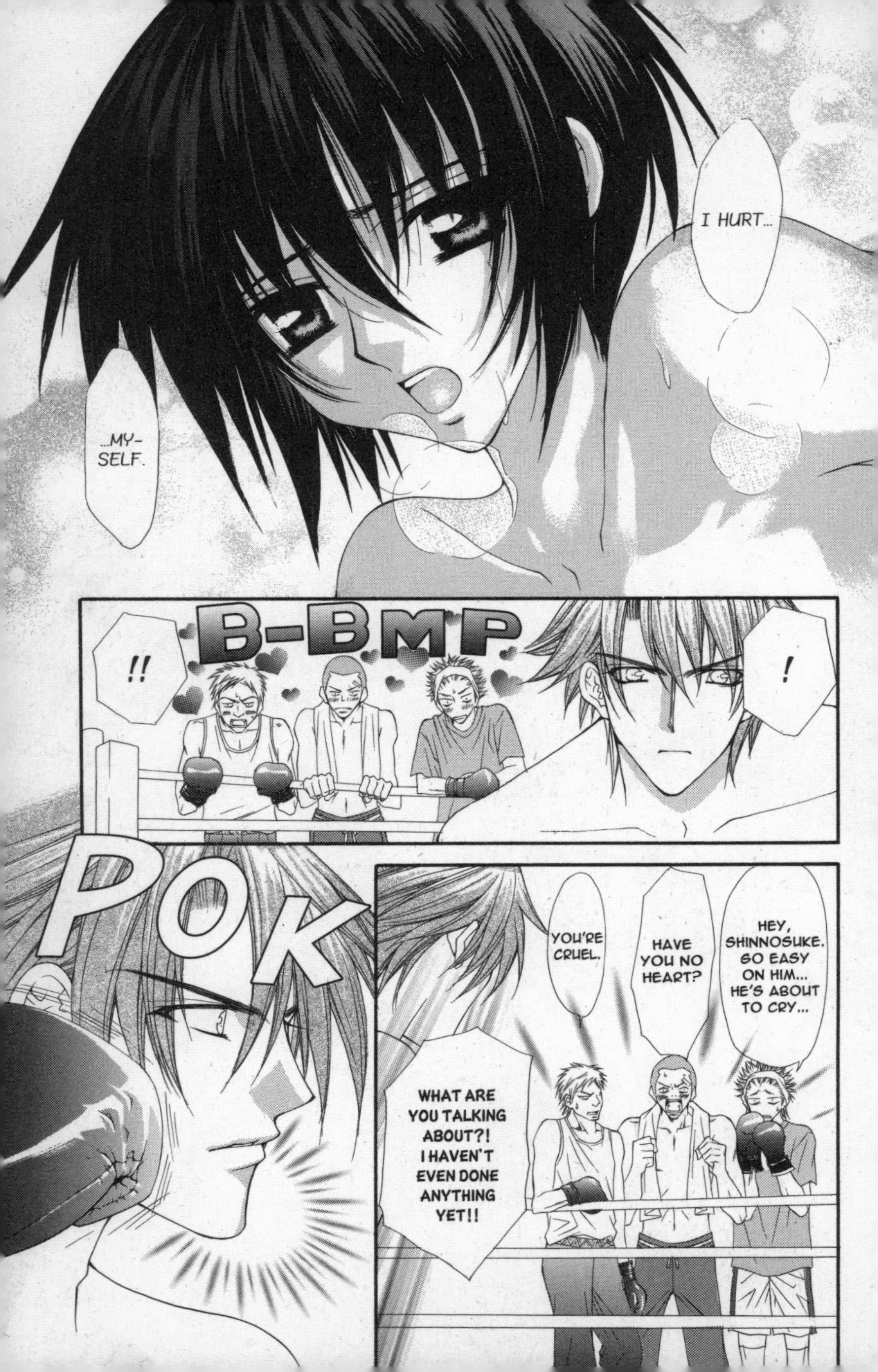
I HURT...
...MY-SELF.
!
B-BMP
!!
HEY, SHINNOSUKE. GO EASY ON HIM... HE'S ABOUT TO CRY...
HAVE YOU NO HEART?
YOU'RE CRUEL.
WHAT ARE YOU TALKING ABOUT?! I HAVEN'T EVEN DONE ANYTHING YET!!
POK

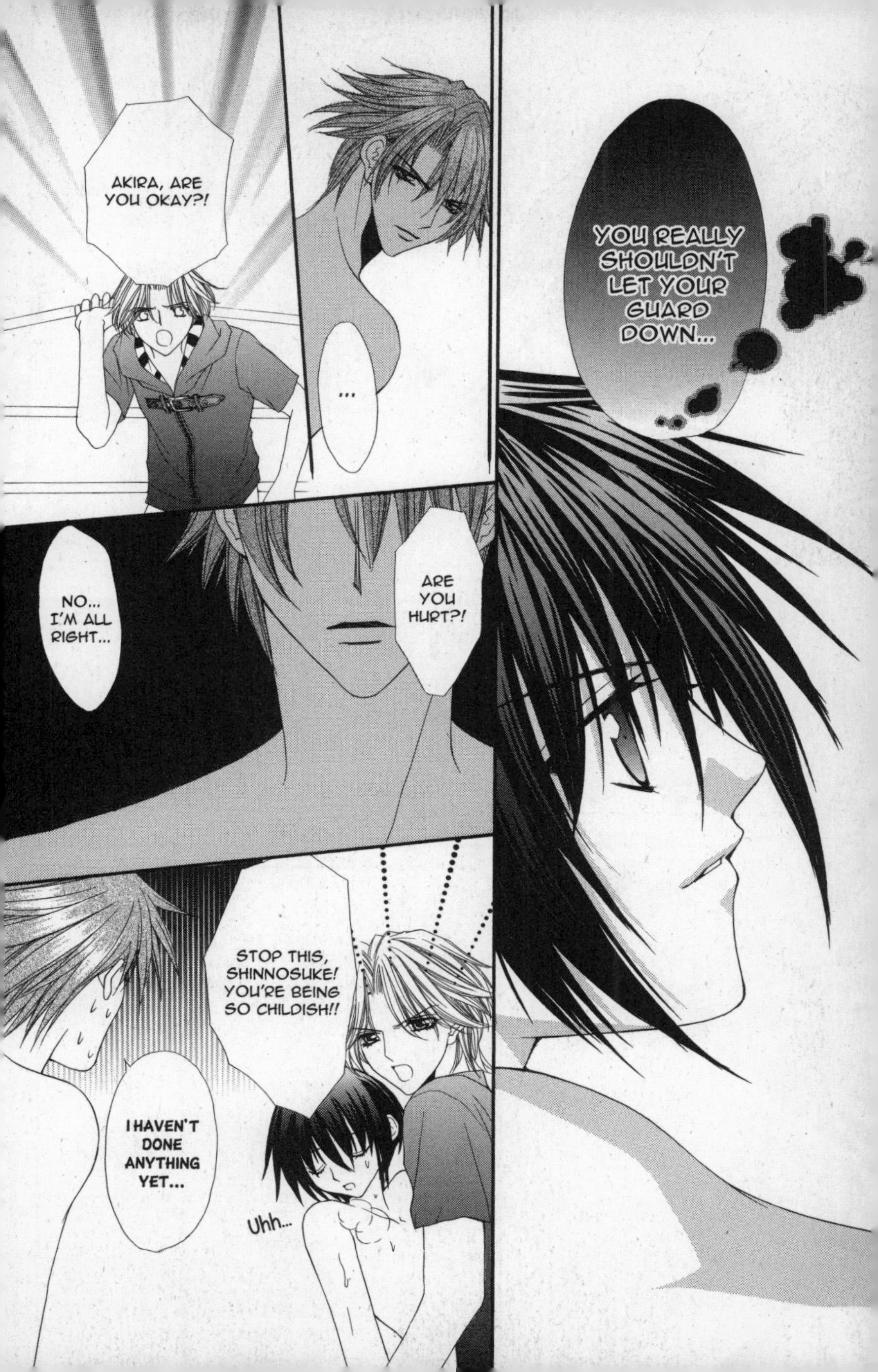
YOU REALLY SHOULDN'T LET YOUR GUARD DOWN...
...
AKIRA, ARE YOU OKAY?!
ARE YOU HURT?!
NO... I'M ALL RIGHT...
STOP THIS, SHINNOSUKE! YOU'RE BEING SO CHILDISH!!
I HAVEN'T DONE ANYTHING YET...
Uhh...

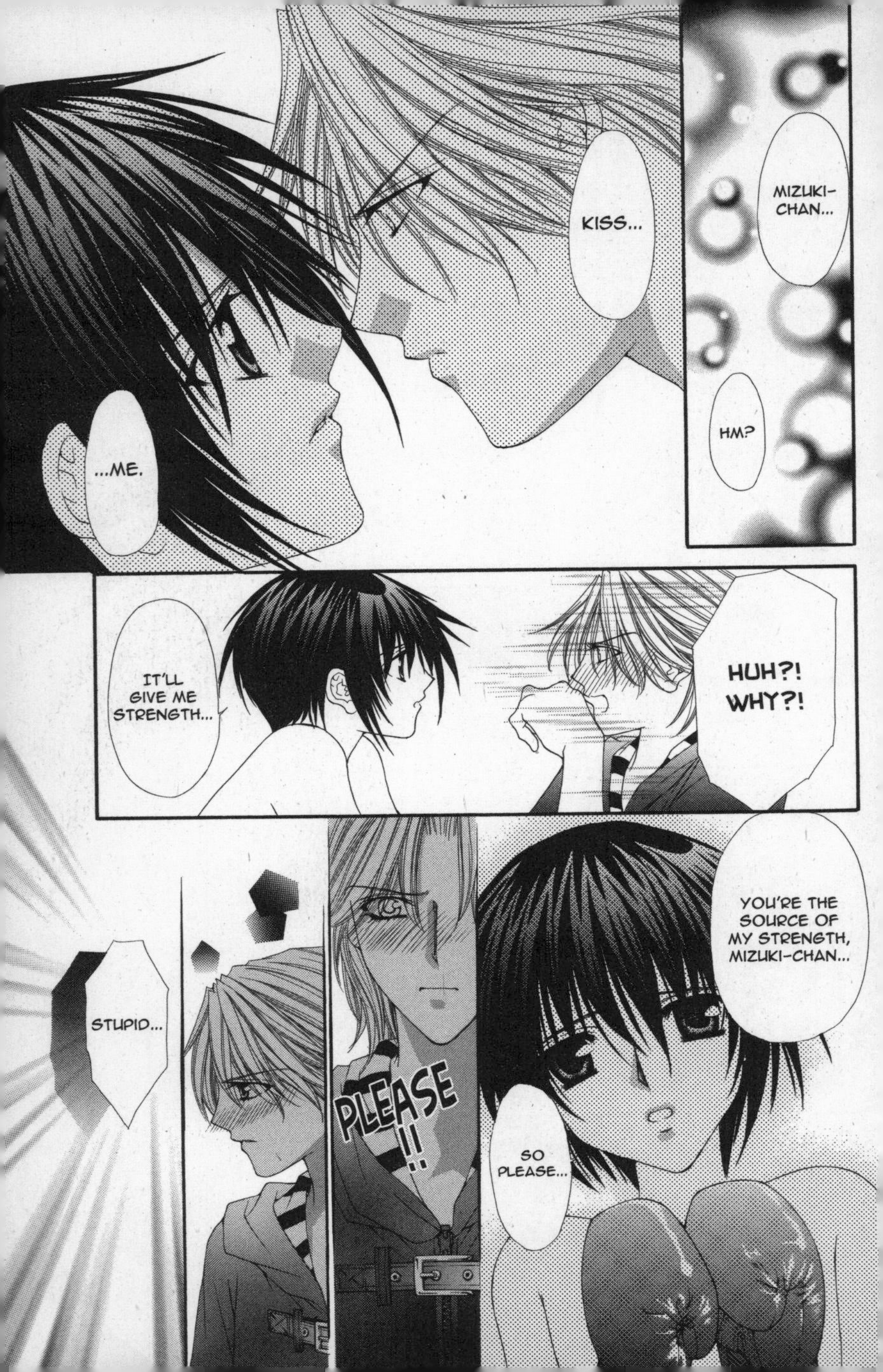
MIZUKI-CHAN...
HM?
KISS...
...ME.
HUH?! WHY?!
IT'LL GIVE ME STRENGTH...
YOU'RE THE SOURCE OF MY STRENGTH, MIZUKI-CHAN...
SO PLEASE...
PLEASE!!
STUPID...

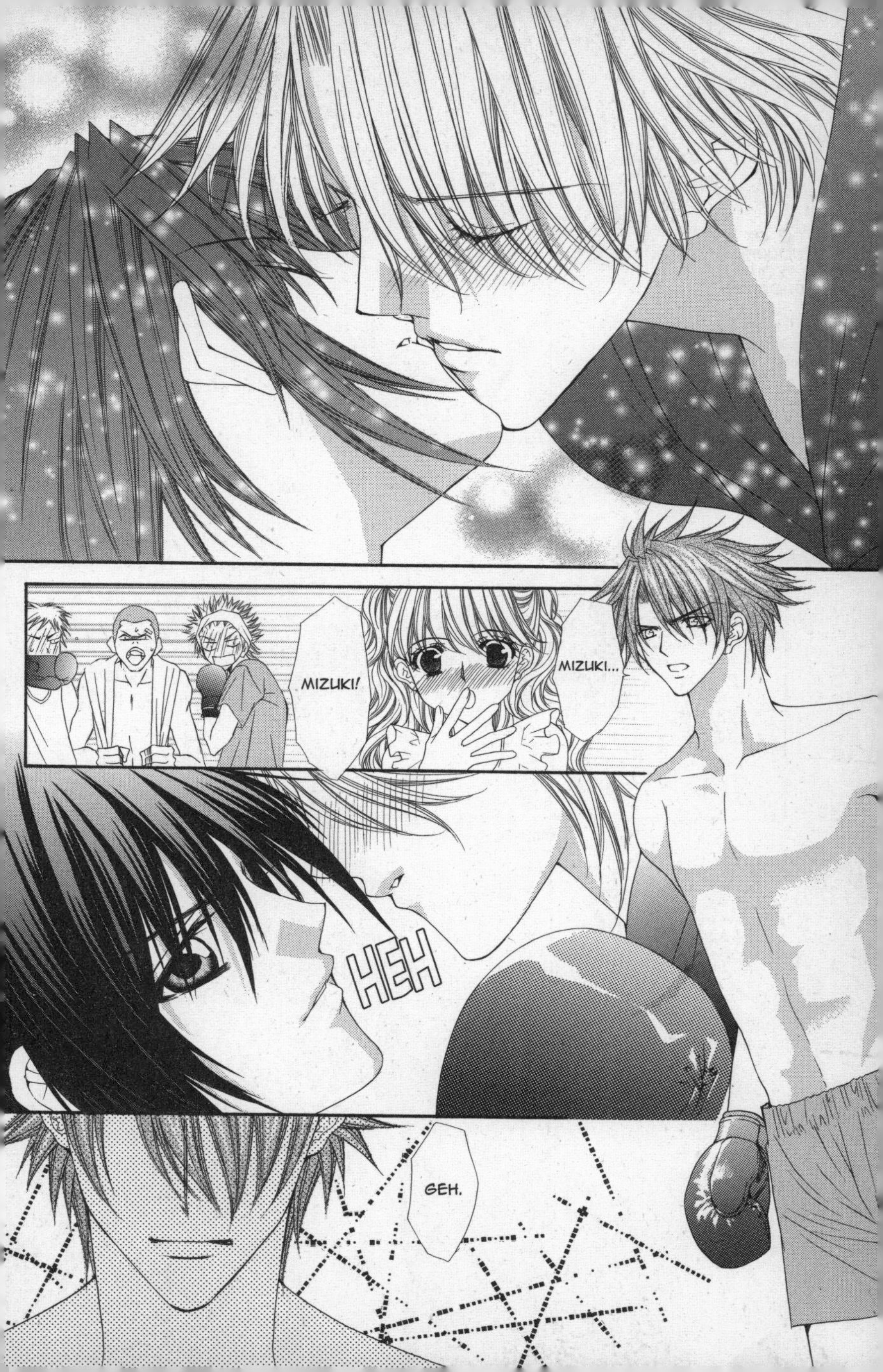
MIZUKI...
MIZUKI!
HEH
GEH.

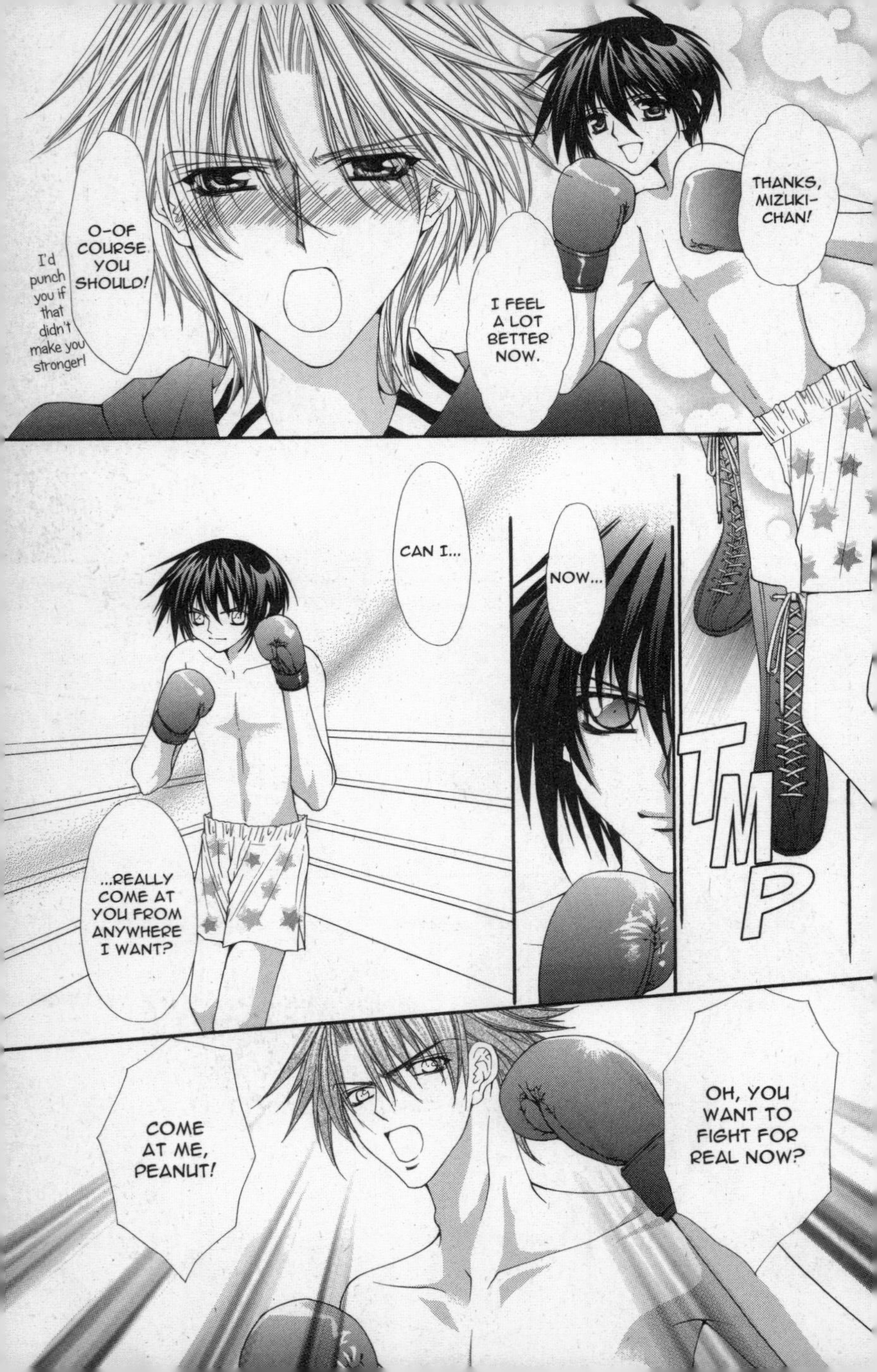
THANKS, MIZUKI-CHAN!
I FEEL A LOT BETTER NOW.
O-OF COURSE YOU SHOULD!
I'd punch you if that didn't make you stronger!
NOW...
TMP
CAN I...
...REALLY COME AT YOU FROM ANYWHERE I WANT?
OH, YOU WANT TO FIGHT FOR REAL NOW?
COME AT ME, PEANUT!

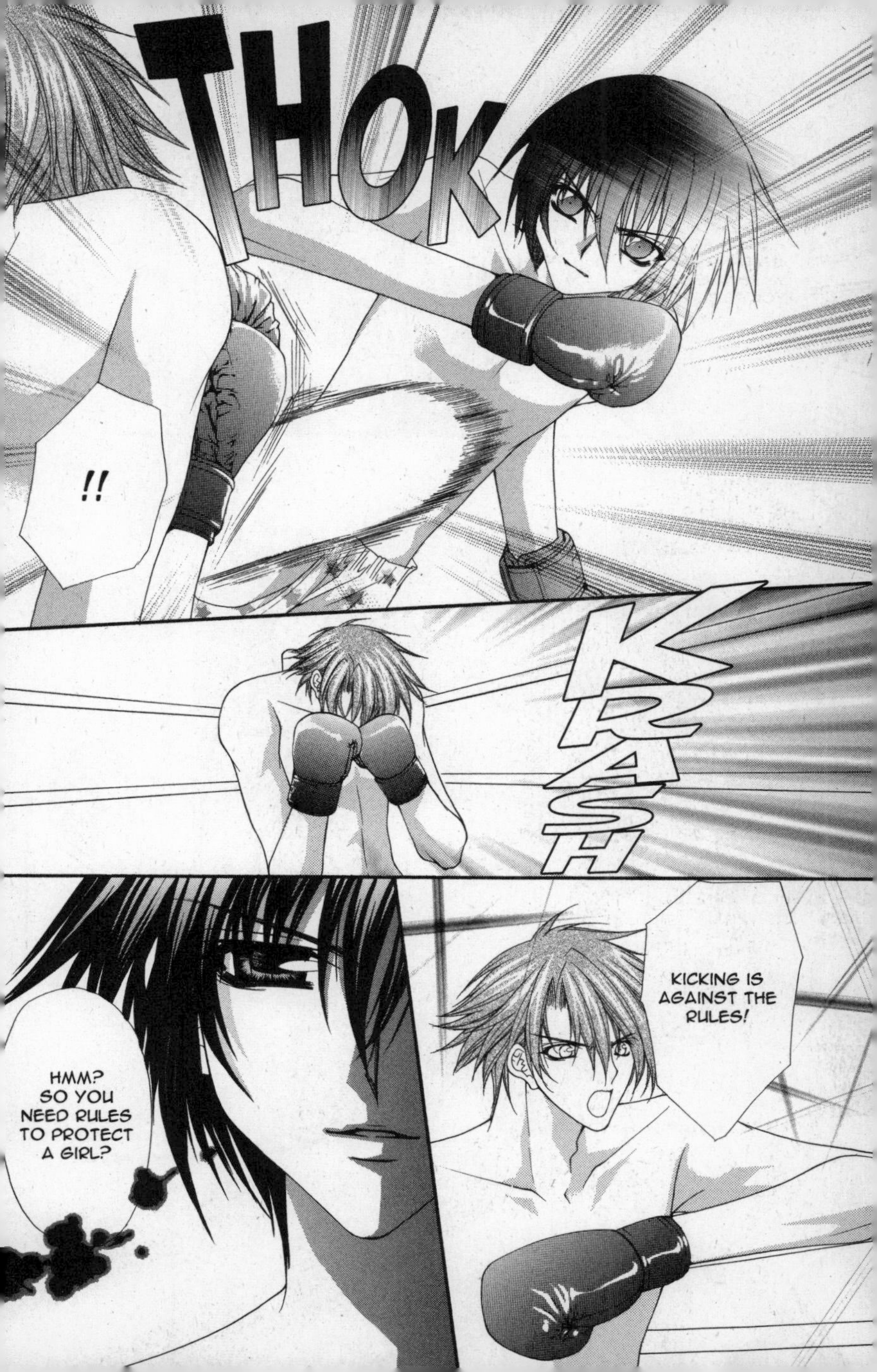
THOK
!!
KRASH
KICKING IS AGAINST THE RULES!
HMM? SO YOU NEED RULES TO PROTECT A GIRL?

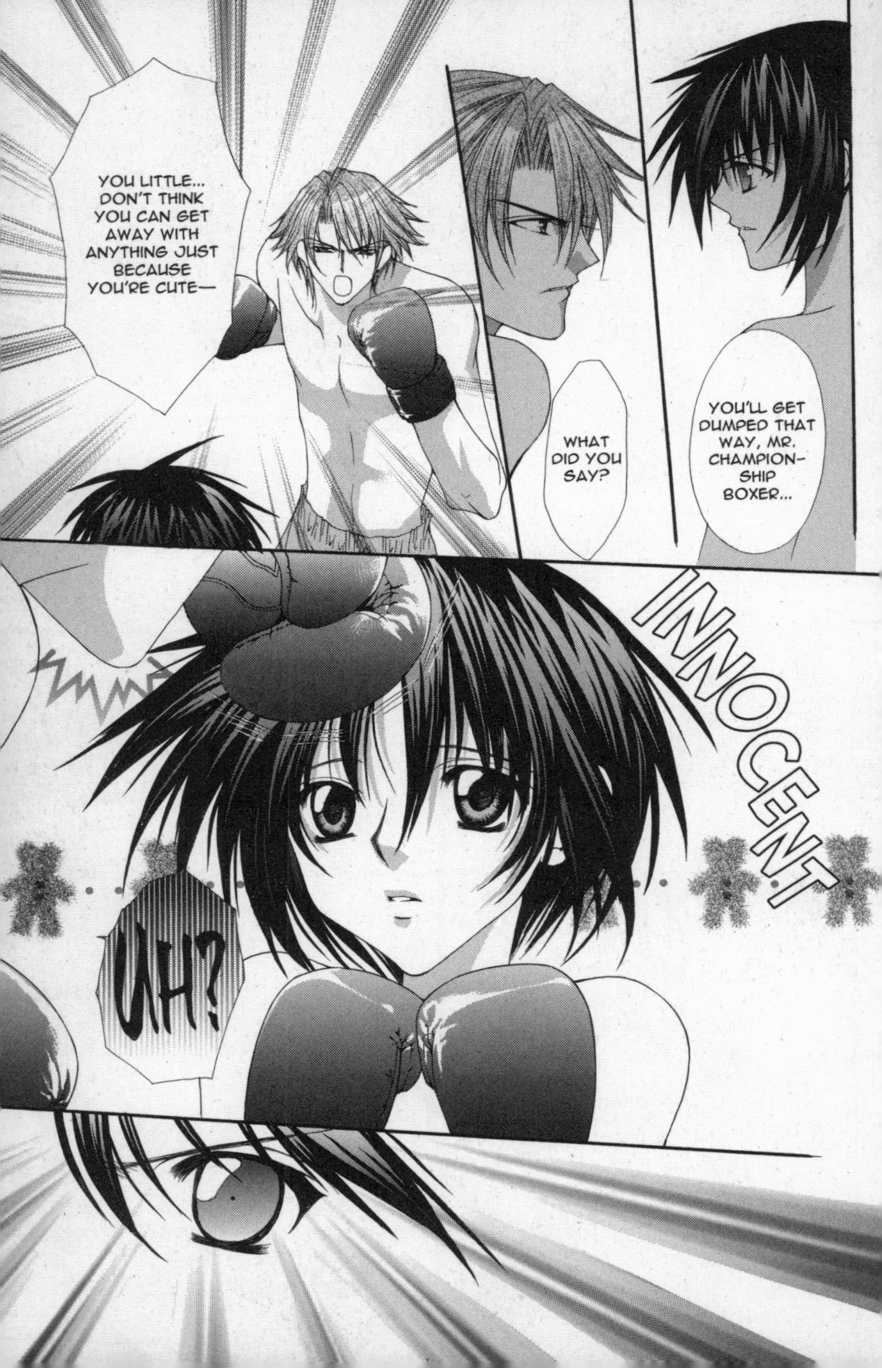
YOU'LL GET DUMPED THAT WAY, MR. CHAMPION-SHIP BOXER...
WHAT DID YOU SAY?
YOU LITTLE... DON'T THINK YOU CAN GET AWAY WITH ANYTHING JUST BECAUSE YOU'RE CUTE—
INNOCENT
UH?

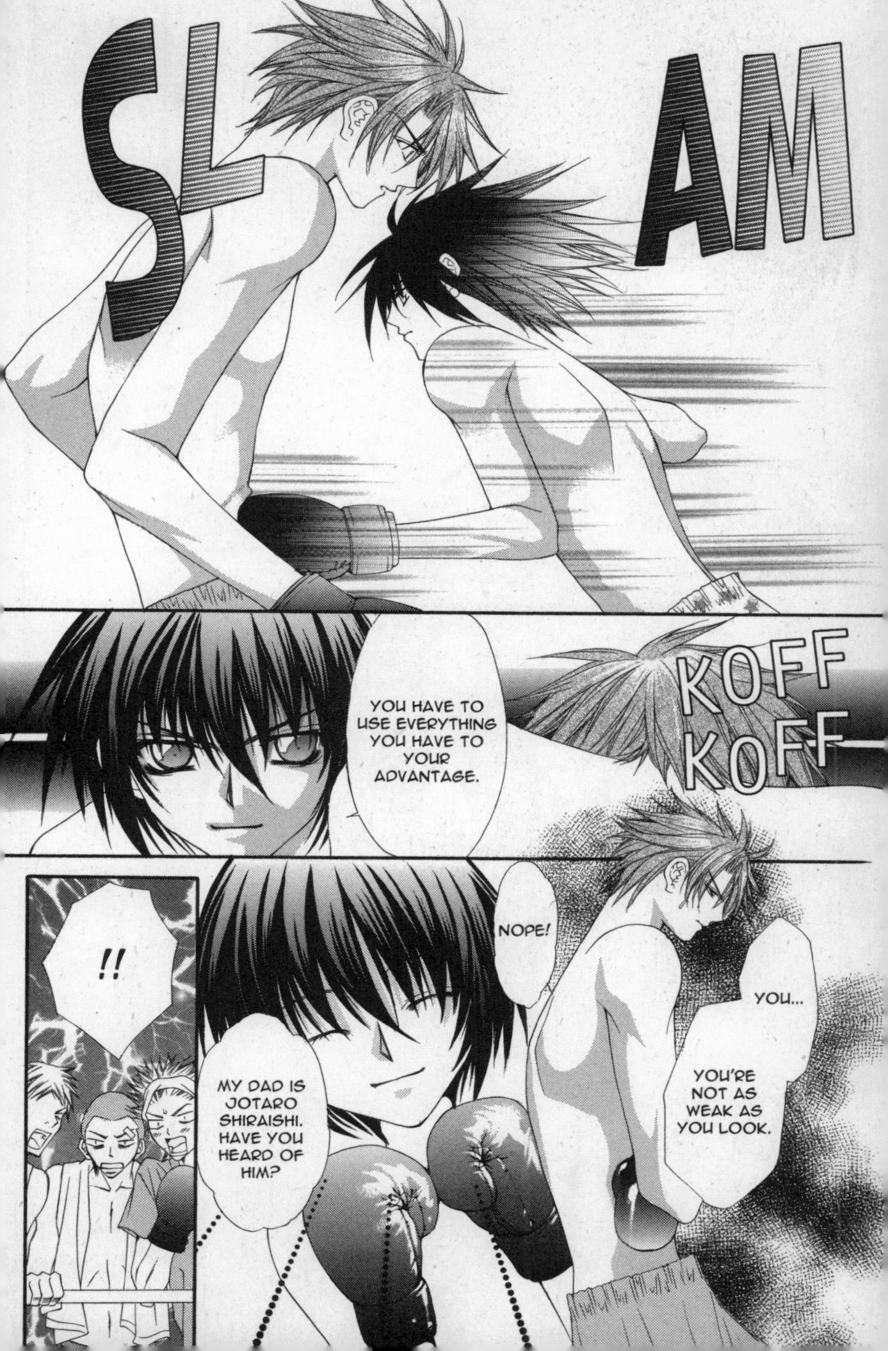
SLAM
KOFF KOFF
YOU HAVE TO USE EVERYTHING YOU HAVE TO YOUR ADVANTAGE.
YOU...
YOU'RE NOT AS WEAK AS YOU LOOK.
NOPE!
MY DAD IS JOTARO SHIRAISHI. HAVE YOU HEARD OF HIM?
!!

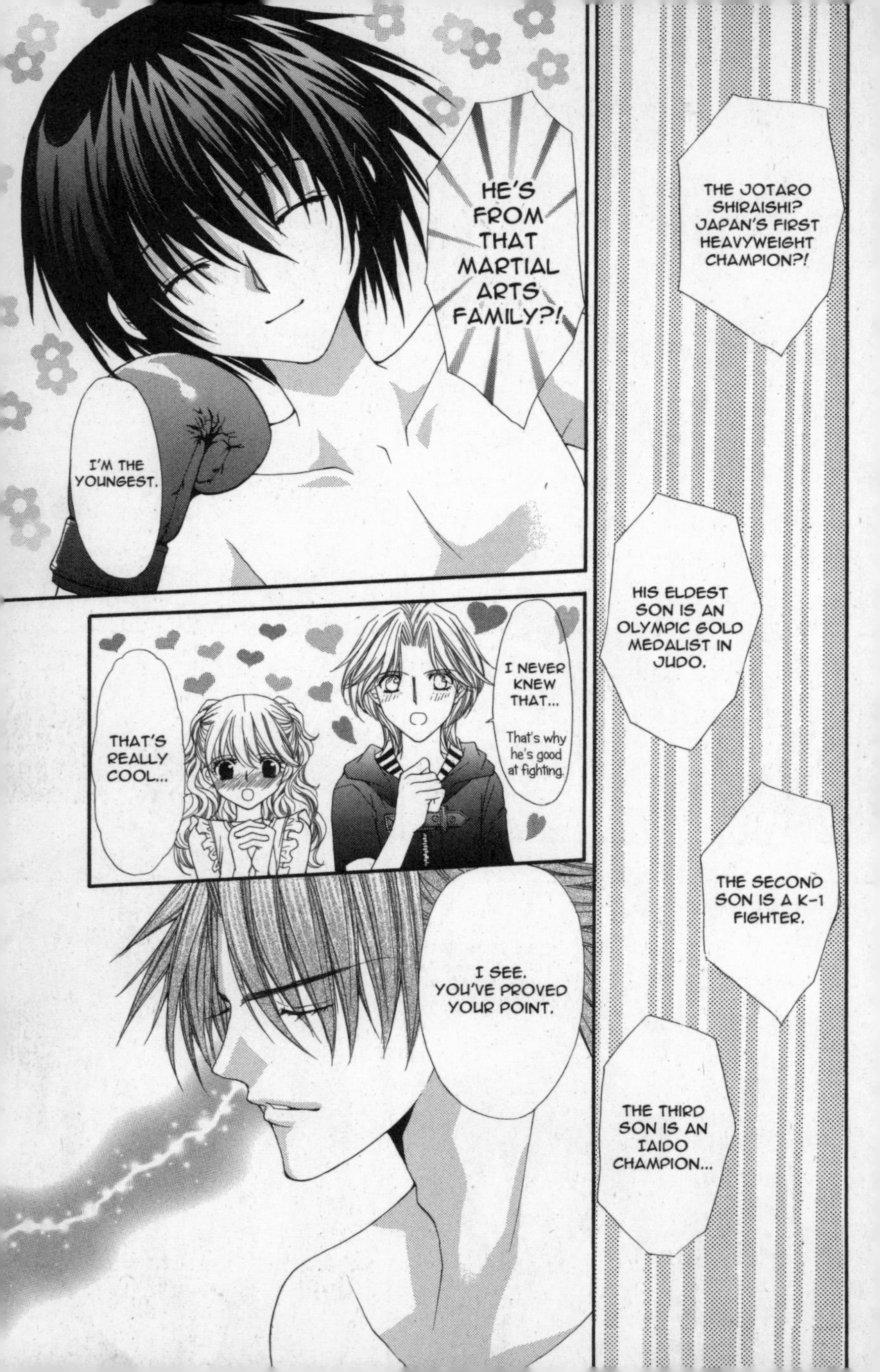
THE JOTARO SHIRAISHI? JAPAN'S FIRST HEAVYWEIGHT CHAMPION?!
HIS ELDEST SON IS AN OLYMPIC GOLD MEDALIST IN JUDO.
THE SECOND SON IS A K-1 FIGHTER.
THE THIRD SON IS AN IAIDO CHAMPION...
HE'S FROM THAT MARTIAL ARTS FAMILY?!
I'M THE YOUNGEST.
I NEVER KNEW THAT...
That's why he's good at fighting.
THAT'S REALLY COOL...
I SEE. YOU'VE PROVED YOUR POINT.

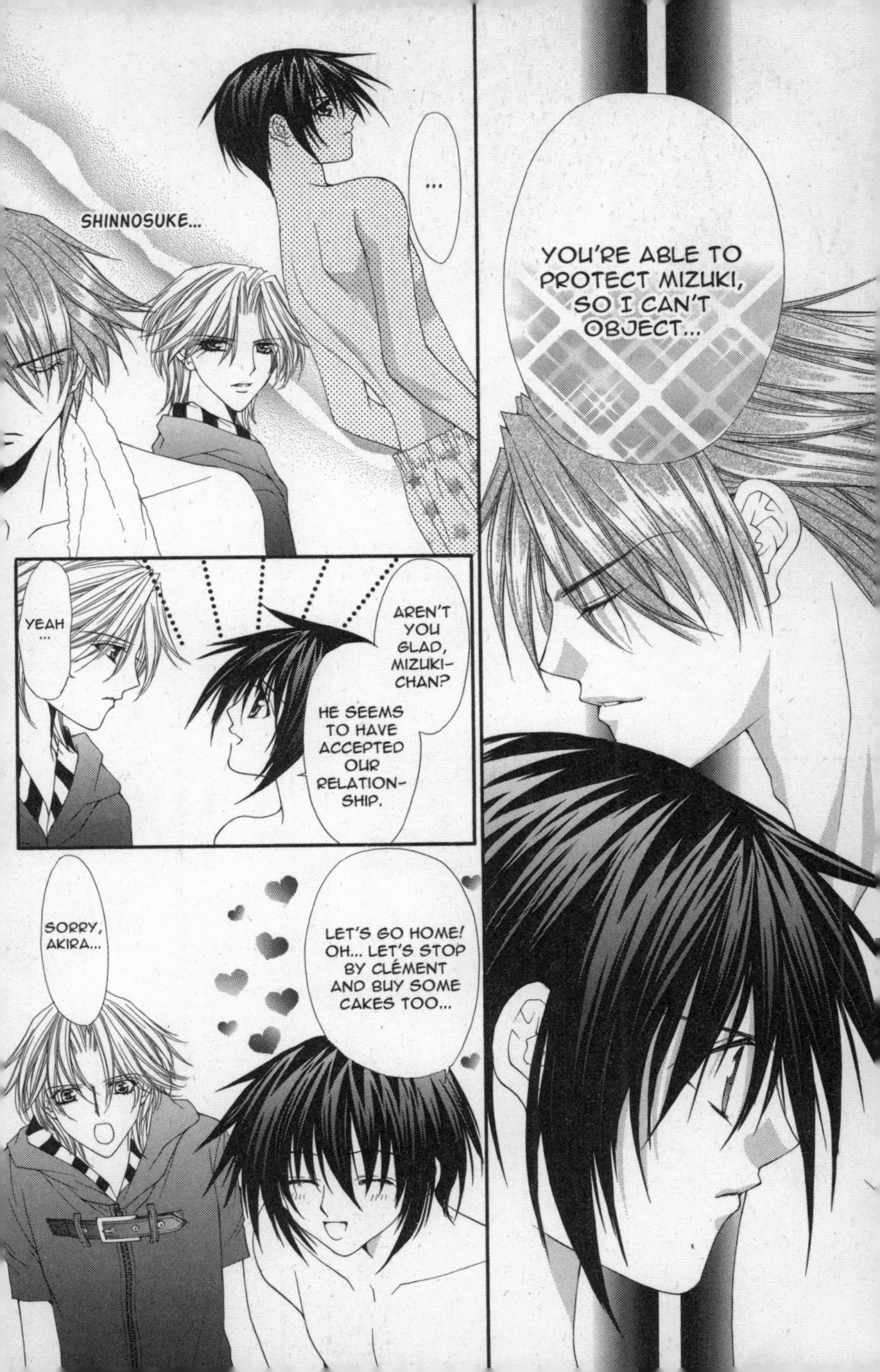
YOU'RE ABLE TO PROTECT MIZUKI, SO I CAN'T OBJECT...
...
SHINNOSUKE...
AREN'T YOU GLAD, MIZUKI-CHAN?
HE SEEMS TO HAVE ACCEPTED OUR RELATIONSHIP.
YEAH ...
LET'S GO HOME! OH... LET'S STOP BY CLÉMENT AND BUY SOME CAKES TOO...
SORRY, AKIRA...

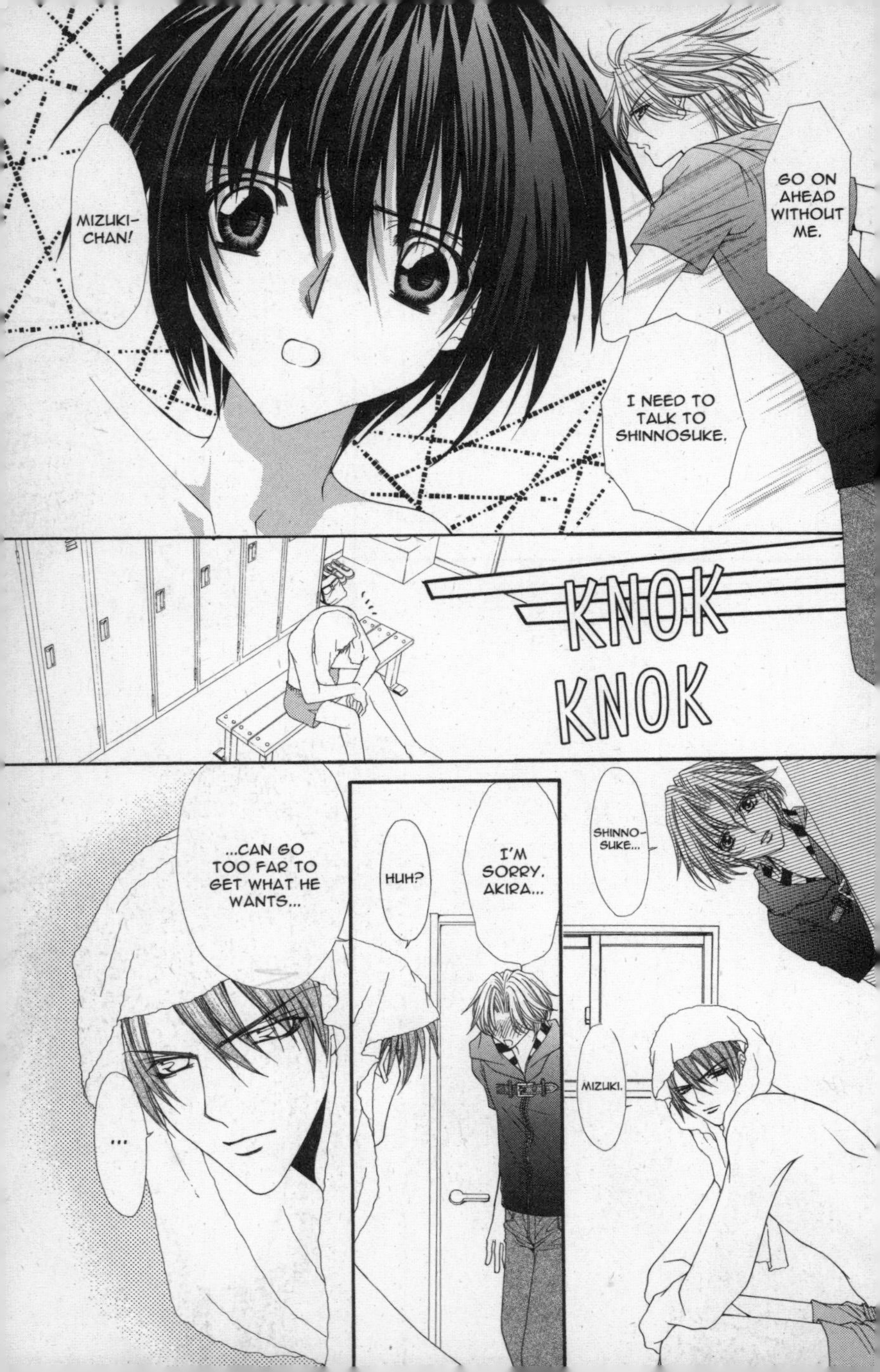
GO ON AHEAD WITHOUT ME.
I NEED TO TALK TO SHINNOSUKE.
MIZUKI-CHAN!
KNOK
KNOK
SHINNOSUKE...
MIZUKI.
I'M SORRY. AKIRA...
HUH?
...CAN GO TOO FAR TO GET WHAT HE WANTS...
...

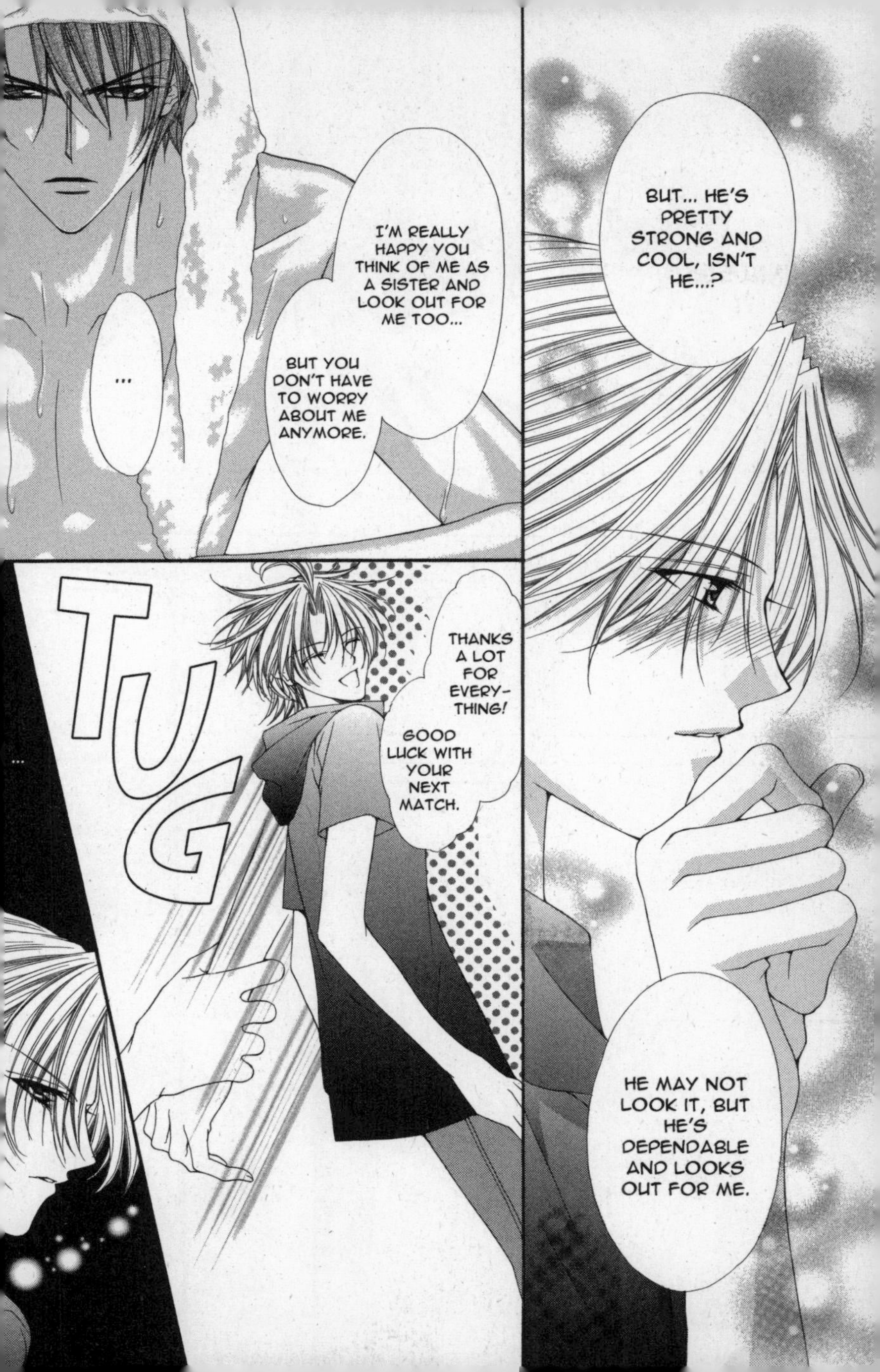
BUT... HE'S PRETTY STRONG AND COOL, ISN'T HE...?
HE MAY NOT LOOK IT, BUT HE'S DEPENDABLE AND LOOKS OUT FOR ME.
I'M REALLY HAPPY YOU THINK OF ME AS A SISTER AND LOOK OUT FOR ME TOO...
BUT YOU DON'T HAVE TO WORRY ABOUT ME ANYMORE.
...
THANKS A LOT FOR EVERY-THING!
GOOD LUCK WITH YOUR NEXT MATCH.
TUG

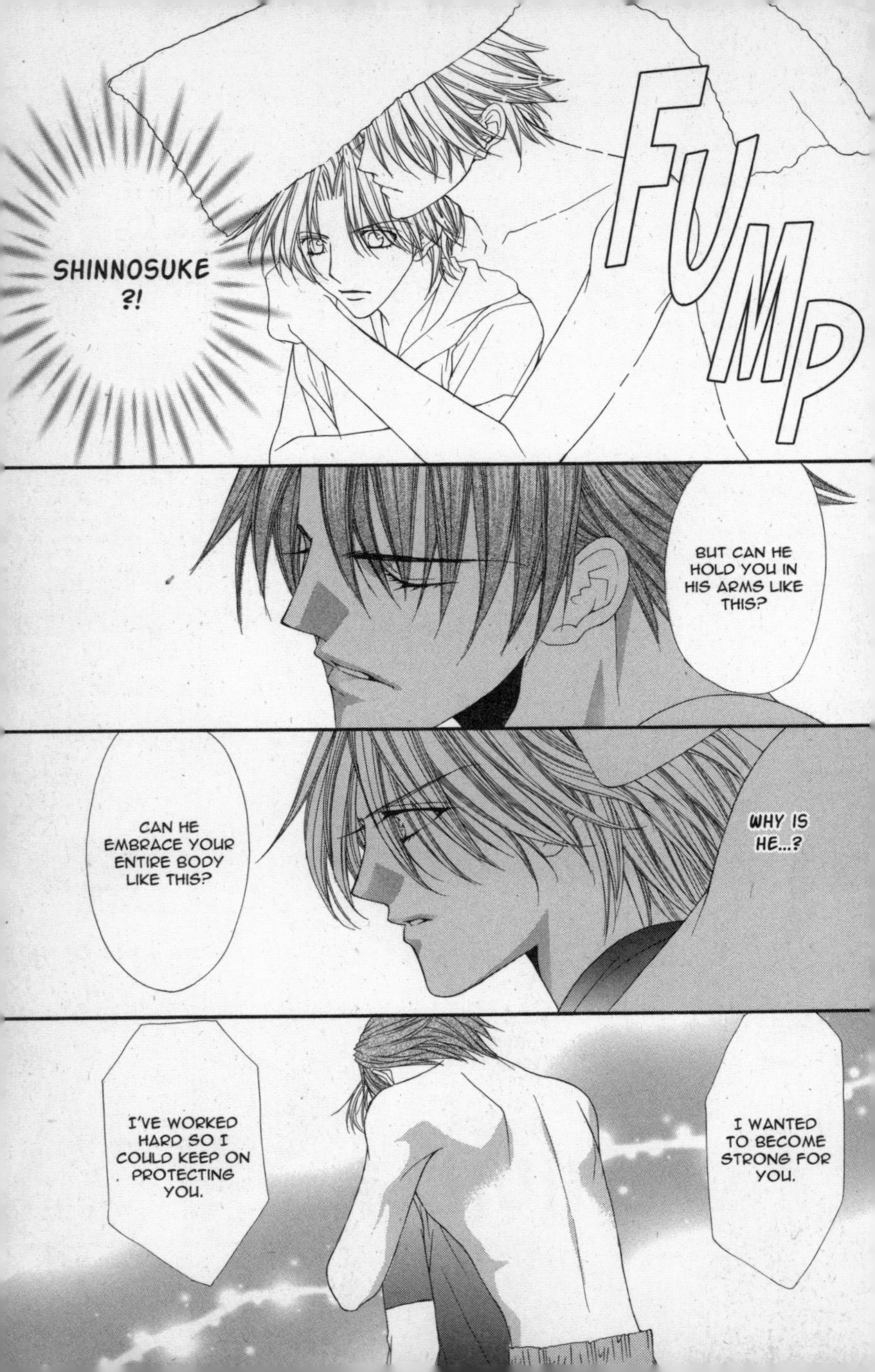
FUMP
SHINNOSUKE ?!
BUT CAN HE HOLD YOU IN HIS ARMS LIKE THIS?
WHY IS HE...?
CAN HE EMBRACE YOUR ENTIRE BODY LIKE THIS?
I WANTED TO BECOME STRONG FOR YOU.
I'VE WORKED HARD SO I COULD KEEP ON PROTECTING YOU.

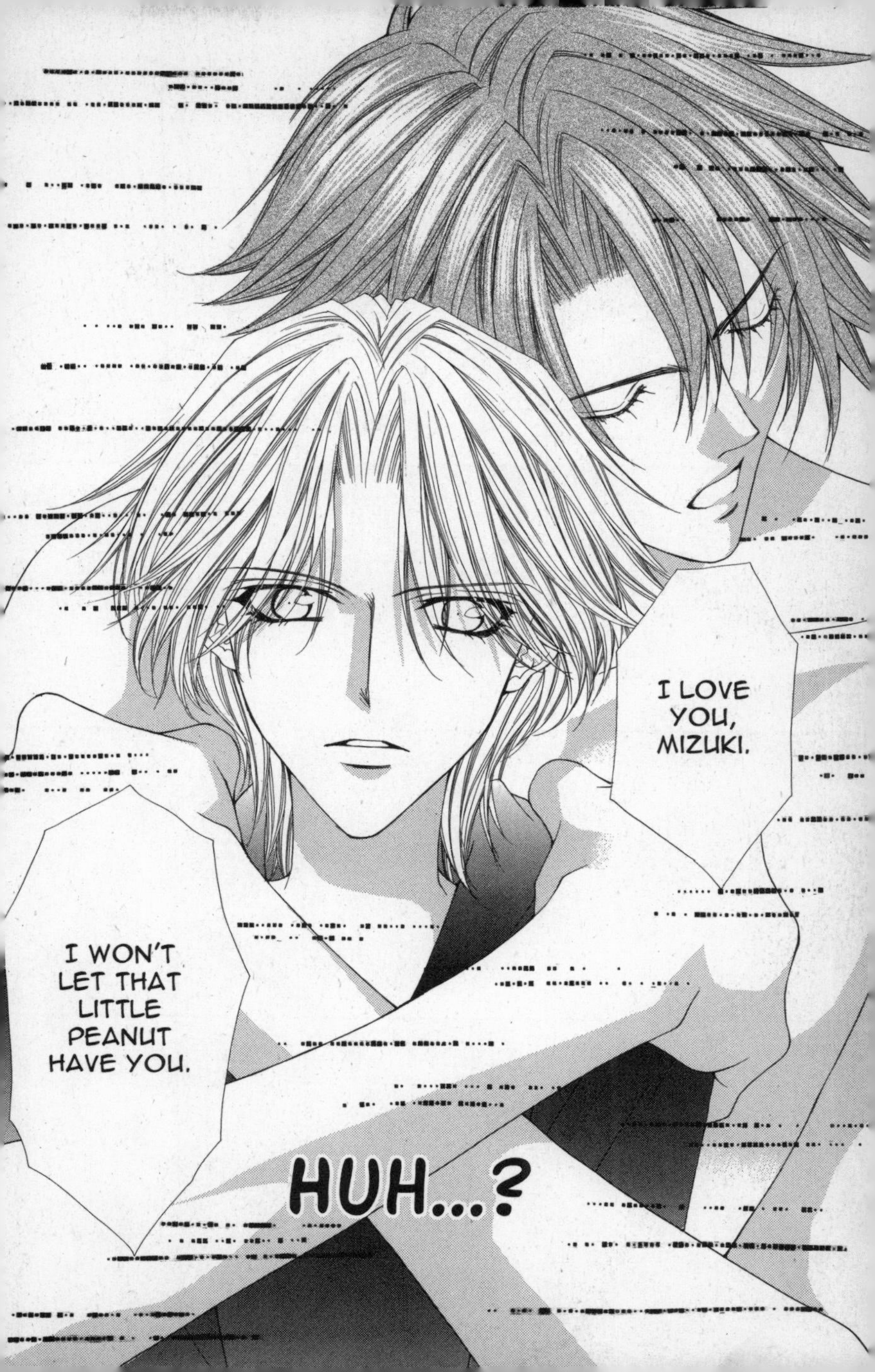
I LOVE YOU, MIZUKI.
I WON'T LET THAT LITTLE PEANUT HAVE YOU.
HUH...?

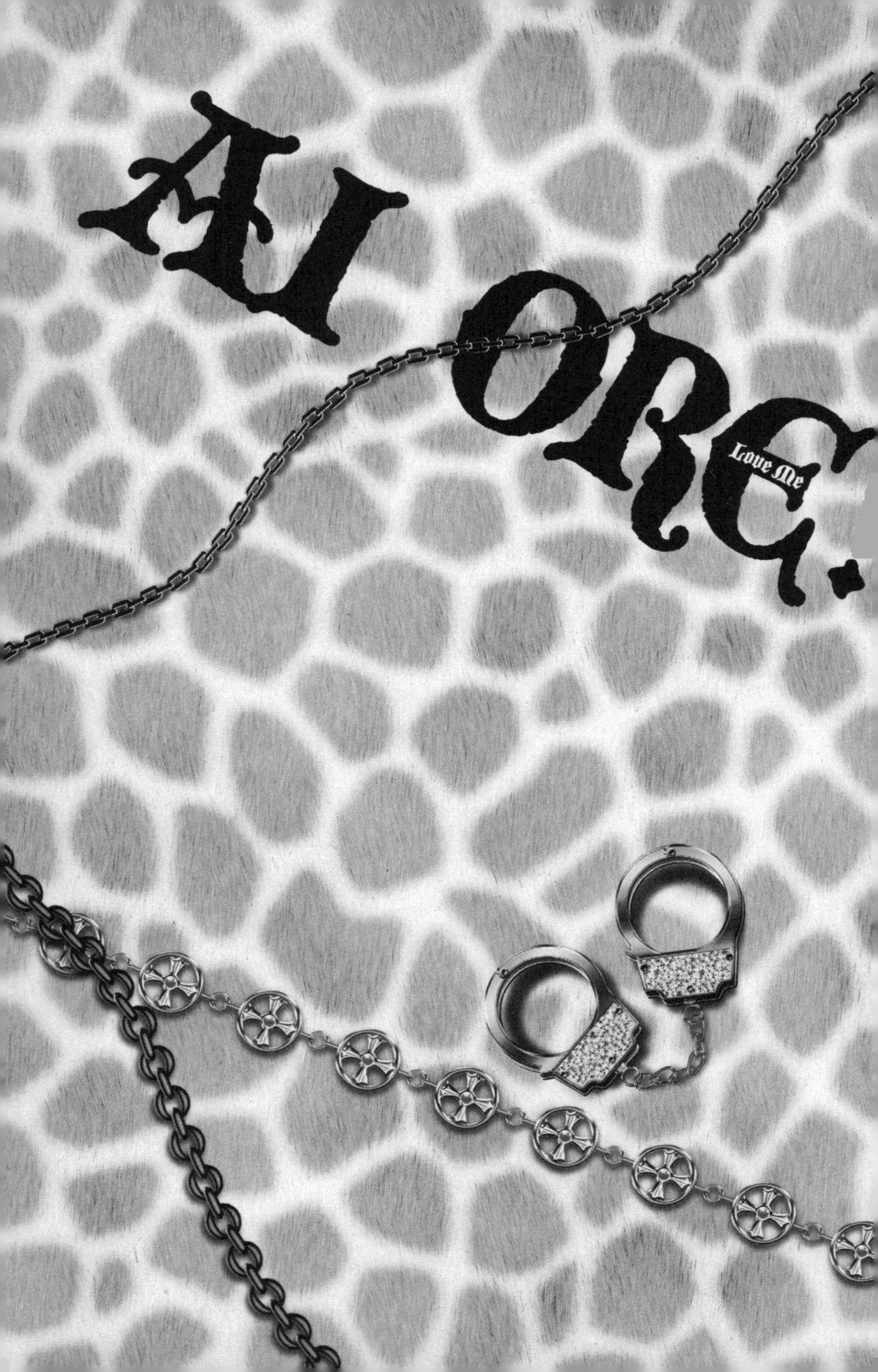
AI ORE.
Love Me

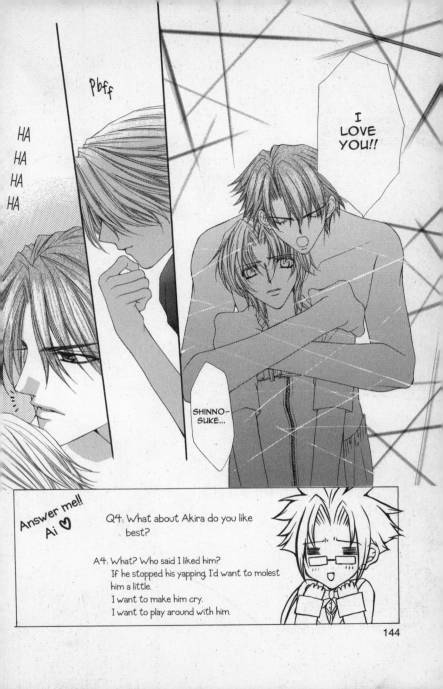

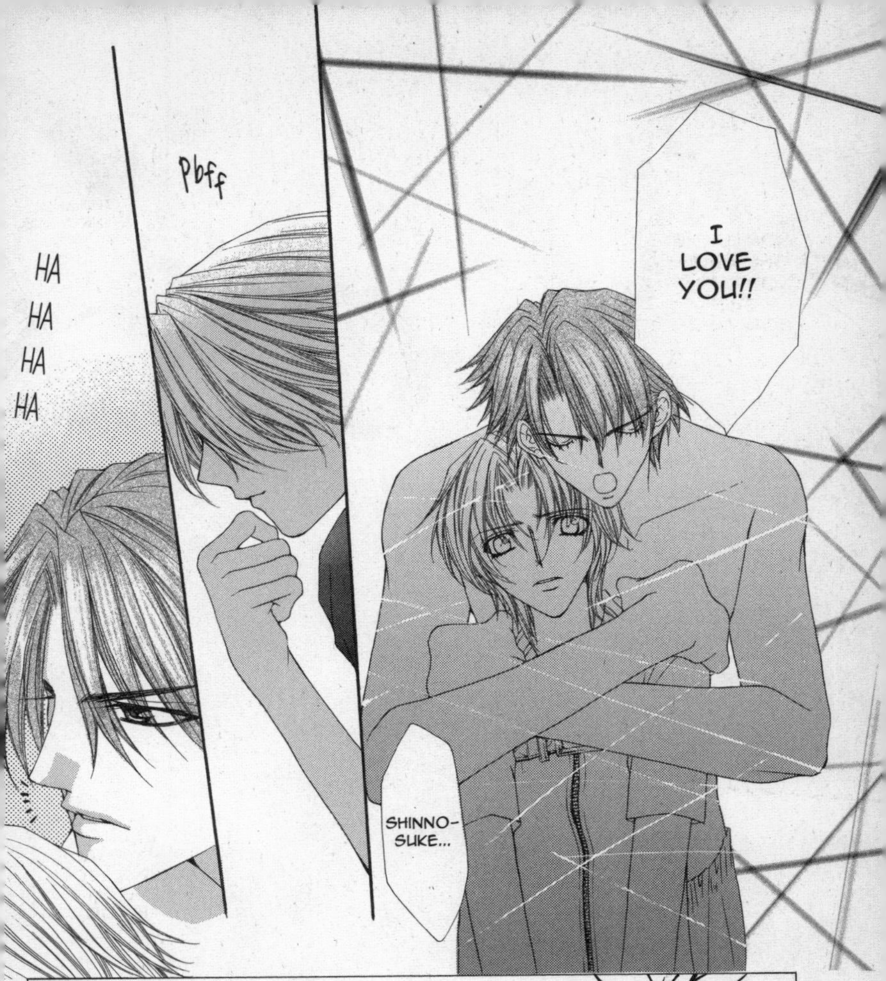
I LOVE YOU!!
SHINNO-SUKE...
Pbff
HA HA HA HA

Answer me!! Ai ♡

Q4: What about Akira do you like best?

A4: What? Who said I liked him?
If he stopped his yapping, I'd want to molest him a little.
I want to make him cry.
I want to play around with him.

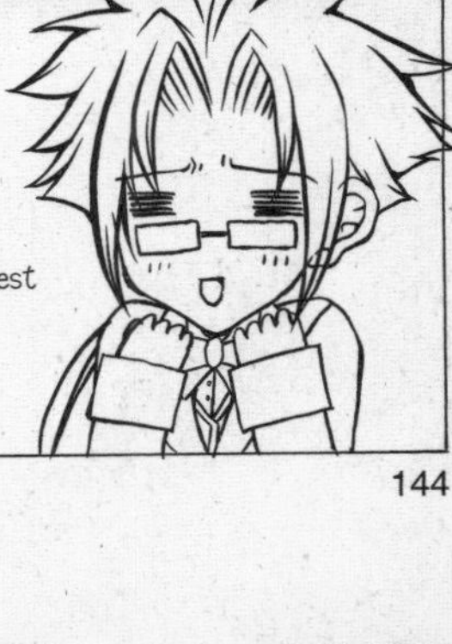

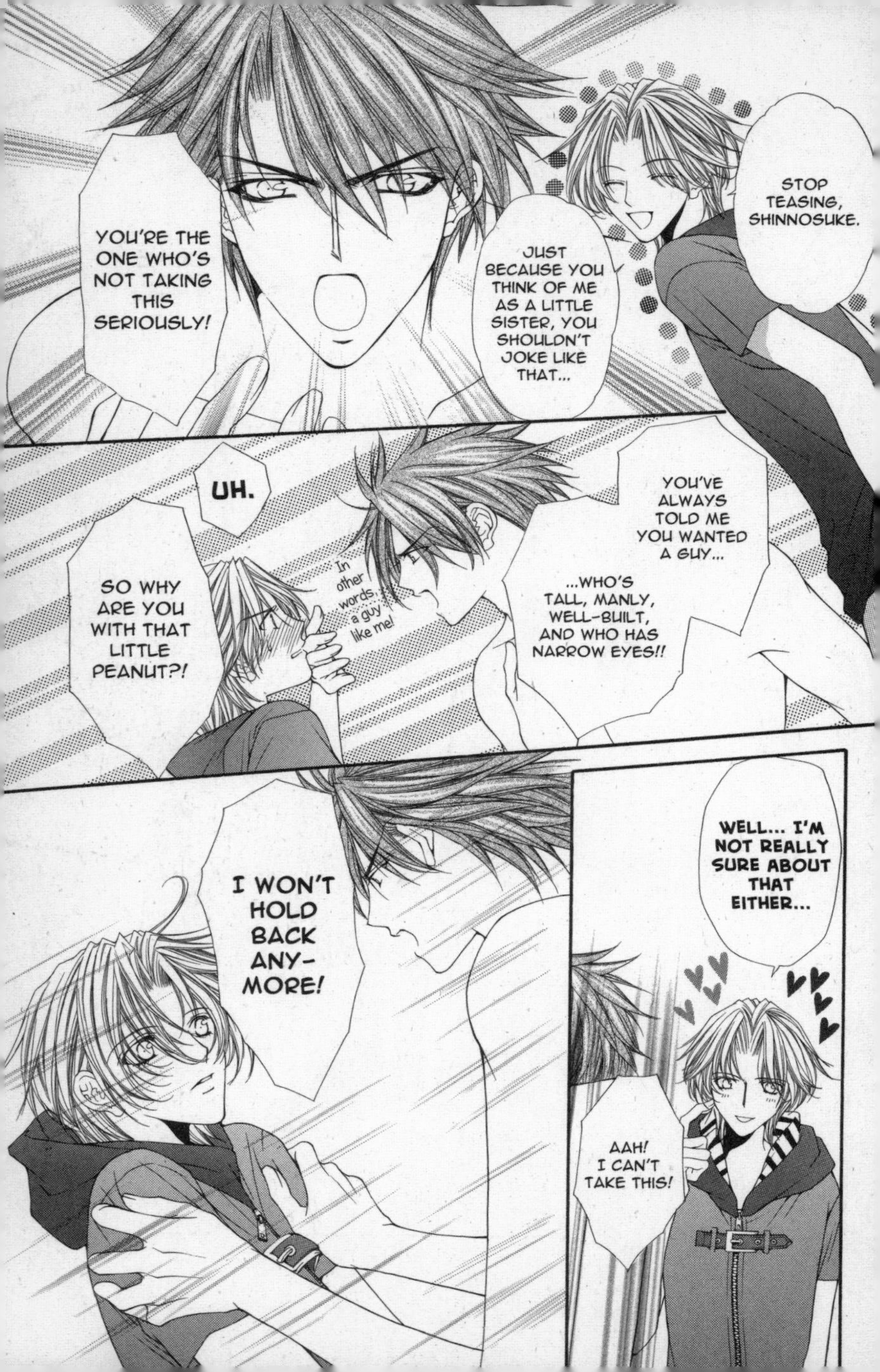
STOP TEASING, SHINNOSUKE.
JUST BECAUSE YOU THINK OF ME AS A LITTLE SISTER, YOU SHOULDN'T JOKE LIKE THAT...
YOU'RE THE ONE WHO'S NOT TAKING THIS SERIOUSLY!
YOU'VE ALWAYS TOLD ME YOU WANTED A GUY...
...WHO'S TALL, MANLY, WELL-BUILT, AND WHO HAS NARROW EYES!!
In other words, a guy like me!
UH.
SO WHY ARE YOU WITH THAT LITTLE PEANUT?!
WELL... I'M NOT REALLY SURE ABOUT THAT EITHER...
AAH! I CAN'T TAKE THIS!
I WON'T HOLD BACK ANY-MORE!

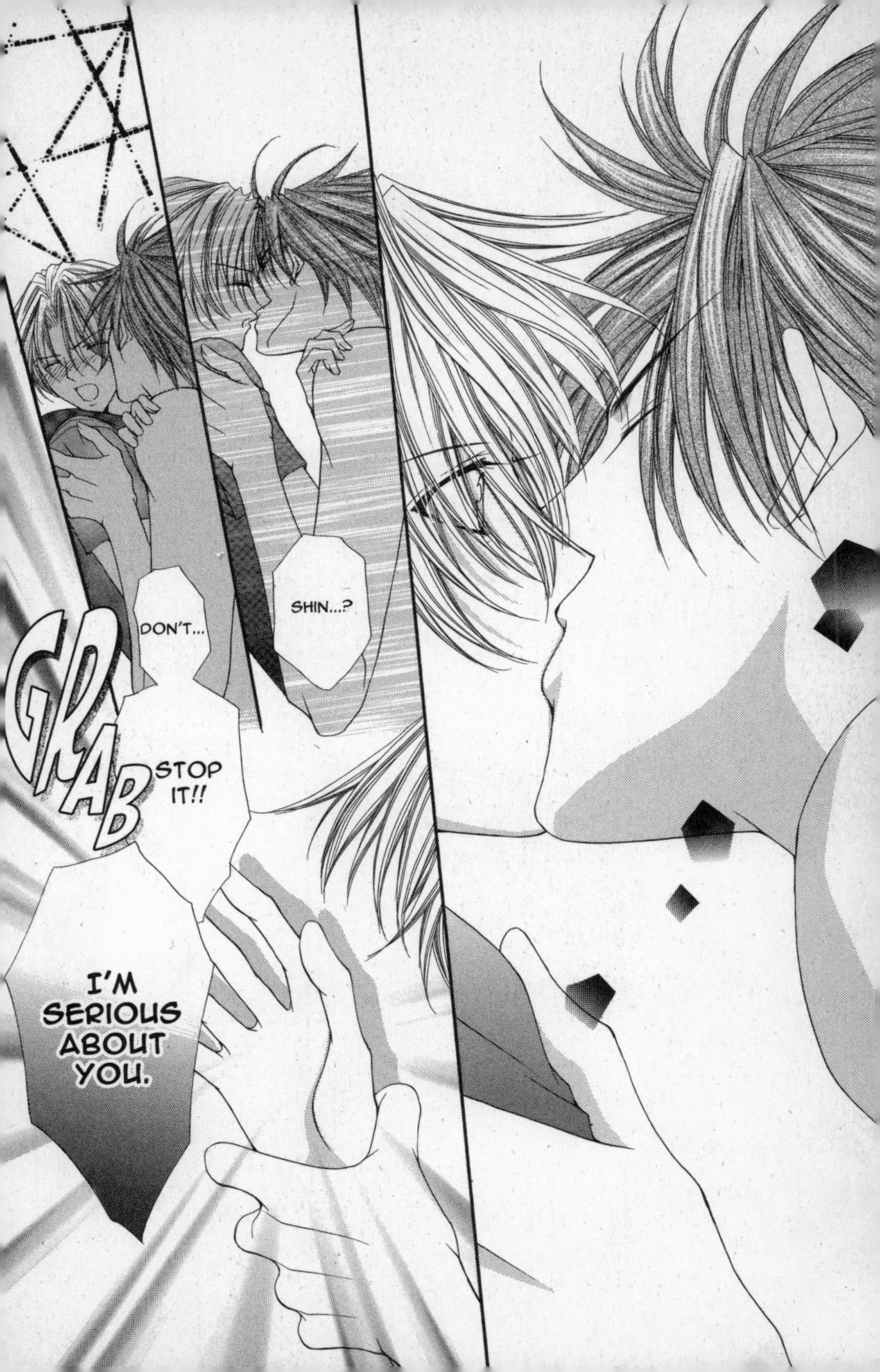
SHIN...?
DON'T...
GRAB
STOP IT!!
I'M SERIOUS ABOUT YOU.

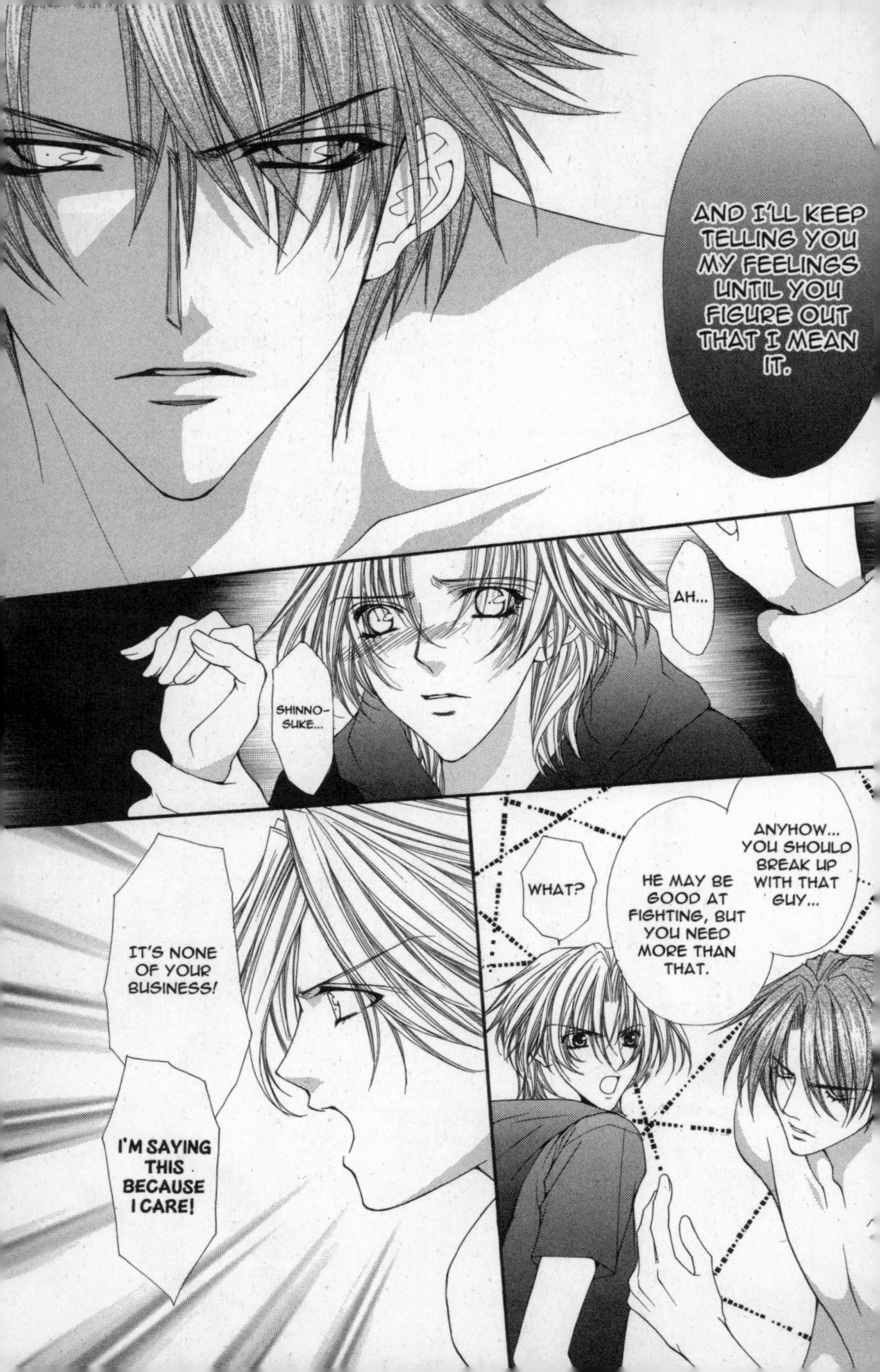
AND I'LL KEEP TELLING YOU MY FEELINGS UNTIL YOU FIGURE OUT THAT I MEAN IT.
AH...
SHINNO-SUKE...
ANYHOW... YOU SHOULD BREAK UP WITH THAT GUY...
HE MAY BE GOOD AT FIGHTING, BUT YOU NEED MORE THAN THAT.
WHAT?
IT'S NONE OF YOUR BUSINESS!
I'M SAYING THIS BECAUSE I CARE!

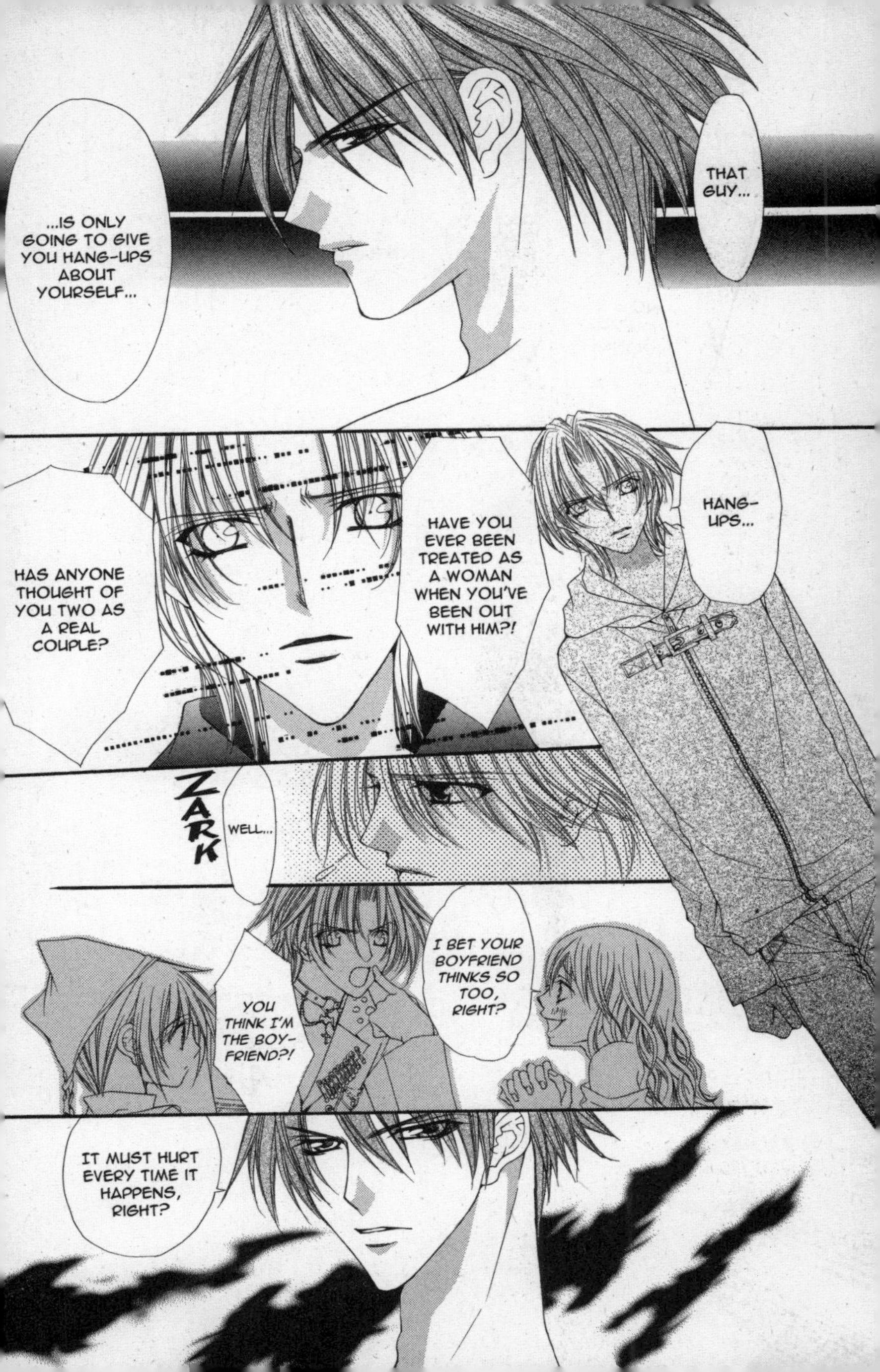
THAT GUY...
...IS ONLY GOING TO GIVE YOU HANG-UPS ABOUT YOURSELF...
HANG-UPS...
HAVE YOU EVER BEEN TREATED AS A WOMAN WHEN YOU'VE BEEN OUT WITH HIM?!
HAS ANYONE THOUGHT OF YOU TWO AS A REAL COUPLE?
WELL...
ZARK
I BET YOUR BOYFRIEND THINKS SO TOO, RIGHT?
YOU THINK I'M THE BOY-FRIEND?!
IT MUST HURT EVERY TIME IT HAPPENS, RIGHT?

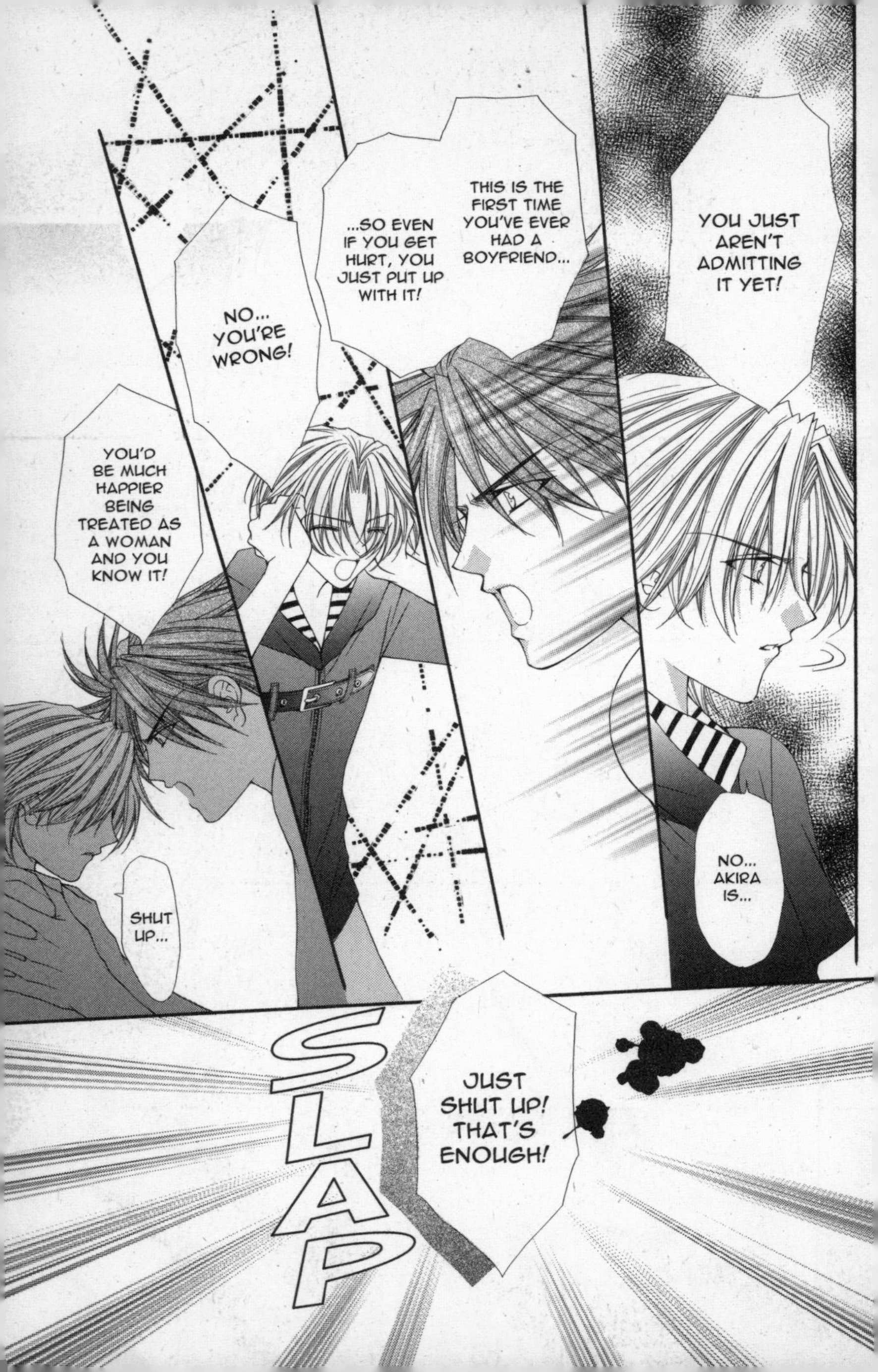
YOU JUST AREN'T ADMITTING IT YET!
NO... AKIRA IS...
THIS IS THE FIRST TIME YOU'VE EVER HAD A BOYFRIEND...
...SO EVEN IF YOU GET HURT, YOU JUST PUT UP WITH IT!
NO... YOU'RE WRONG!
YOU'D BE MUCH HAPPIER BEING TREATED AS A WOMAN AND YOU KNOW IT!
SHUT UP...
JUST SHUT UP! THAT'S ENOUGH!
SLAP

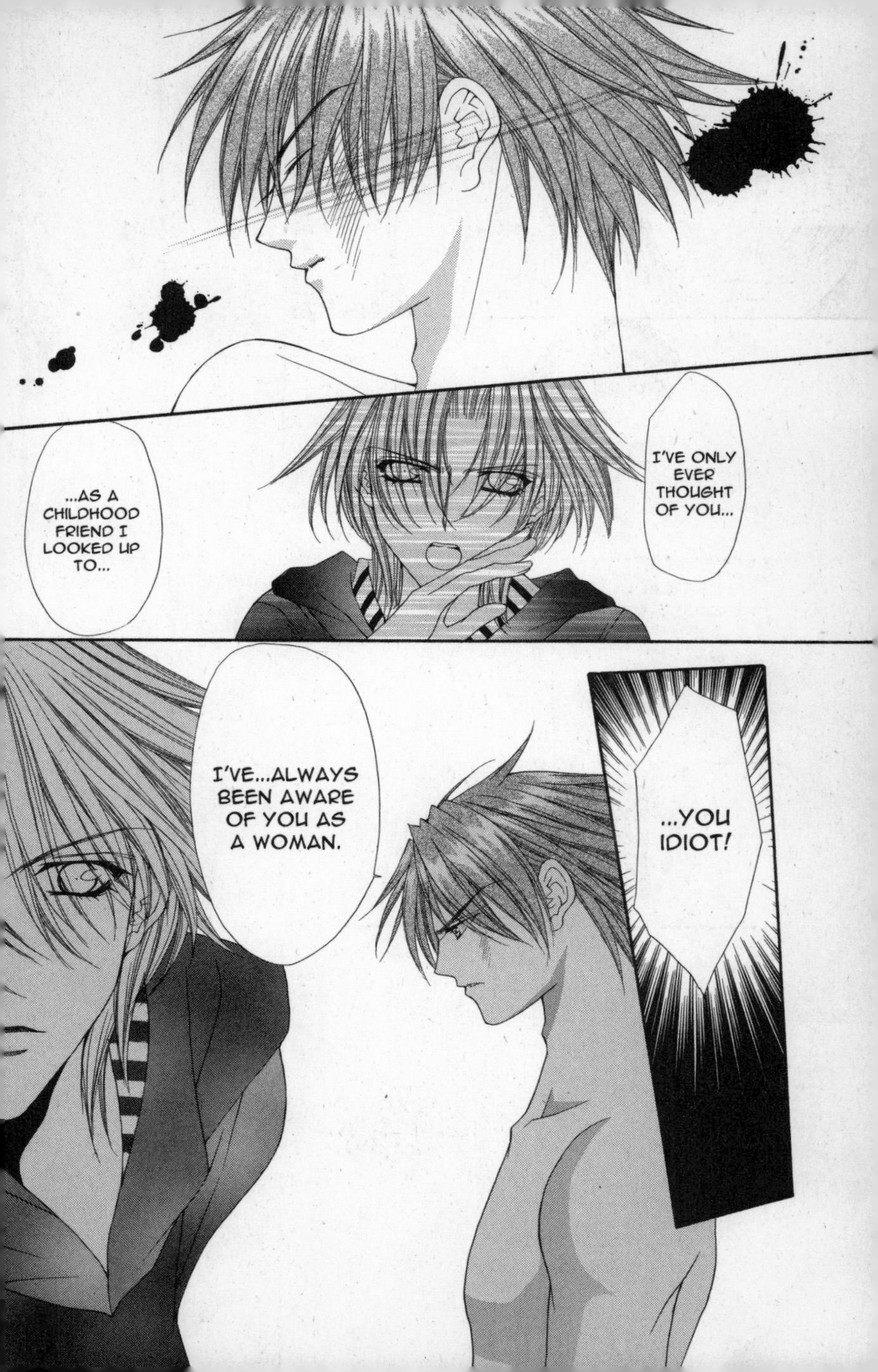
I'VE ONLY EVER THOUGHT OF YOU...
...AS A CHILDHOOD FRIEND I LOOKED UP TO...
I'VE...ALWAYS BEEN AWARE OF YOU AS A WOMAN.
...YOU IDIOT!

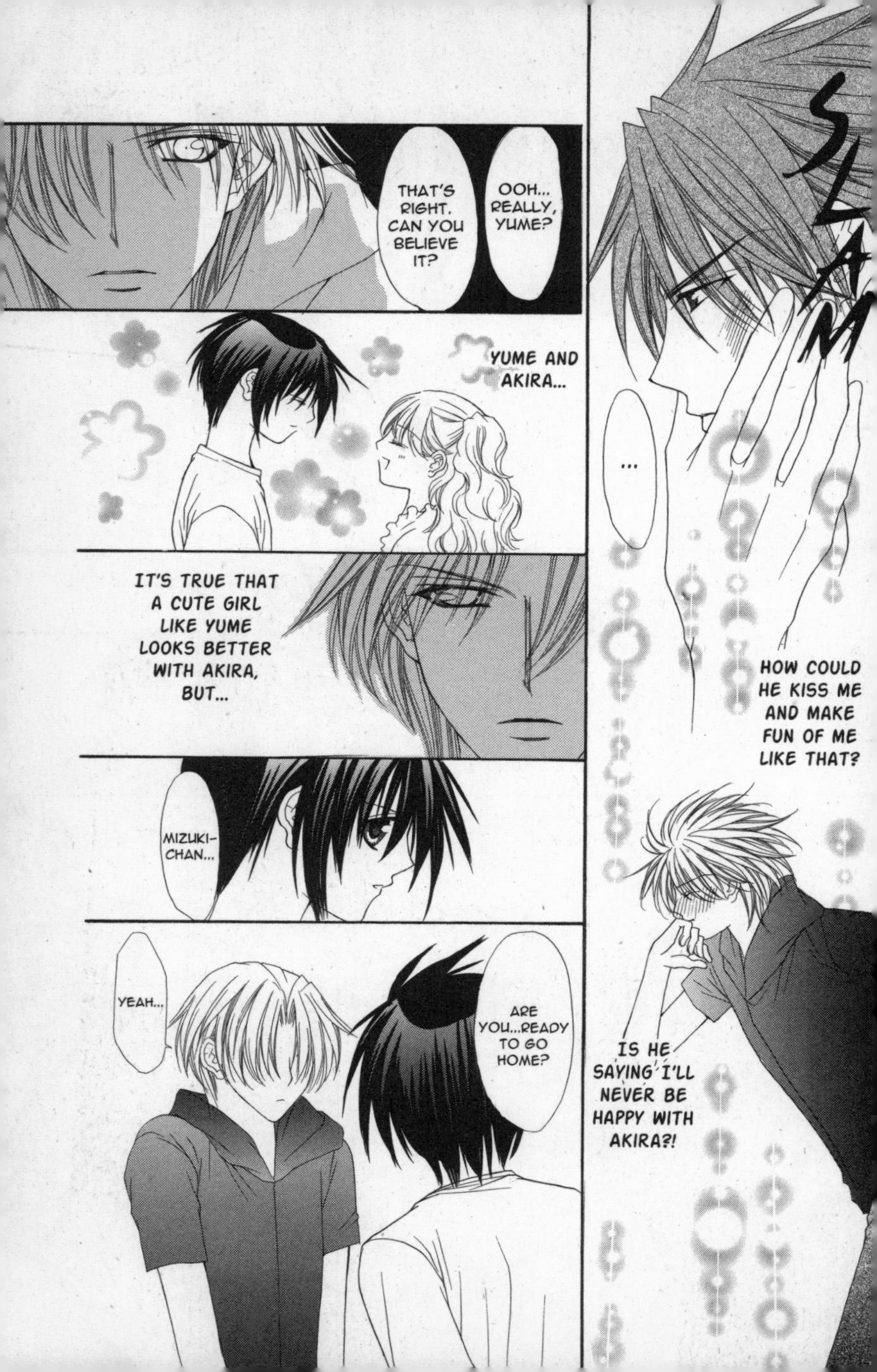
SLAM
...
HOW COULD HE KISS ME AND MAKE FUN OF ME LIKE THAT?
IS HE SAYING I'LL NEVER BE HAPPY WITH AKIRA?!
OOH... REALLY, YUME?
THAT'S RIGHT. CAN YOU BELIEVE IT?
YUME AND AKIRA...
IT'S TRUE THAT A CUTE GIRL LIKE YUME LOOKS BETTER WITH AKIRA, BUT...
MIZUKI-CHAN...
ARE YOU...READY TO GO HOME?
YEAH...

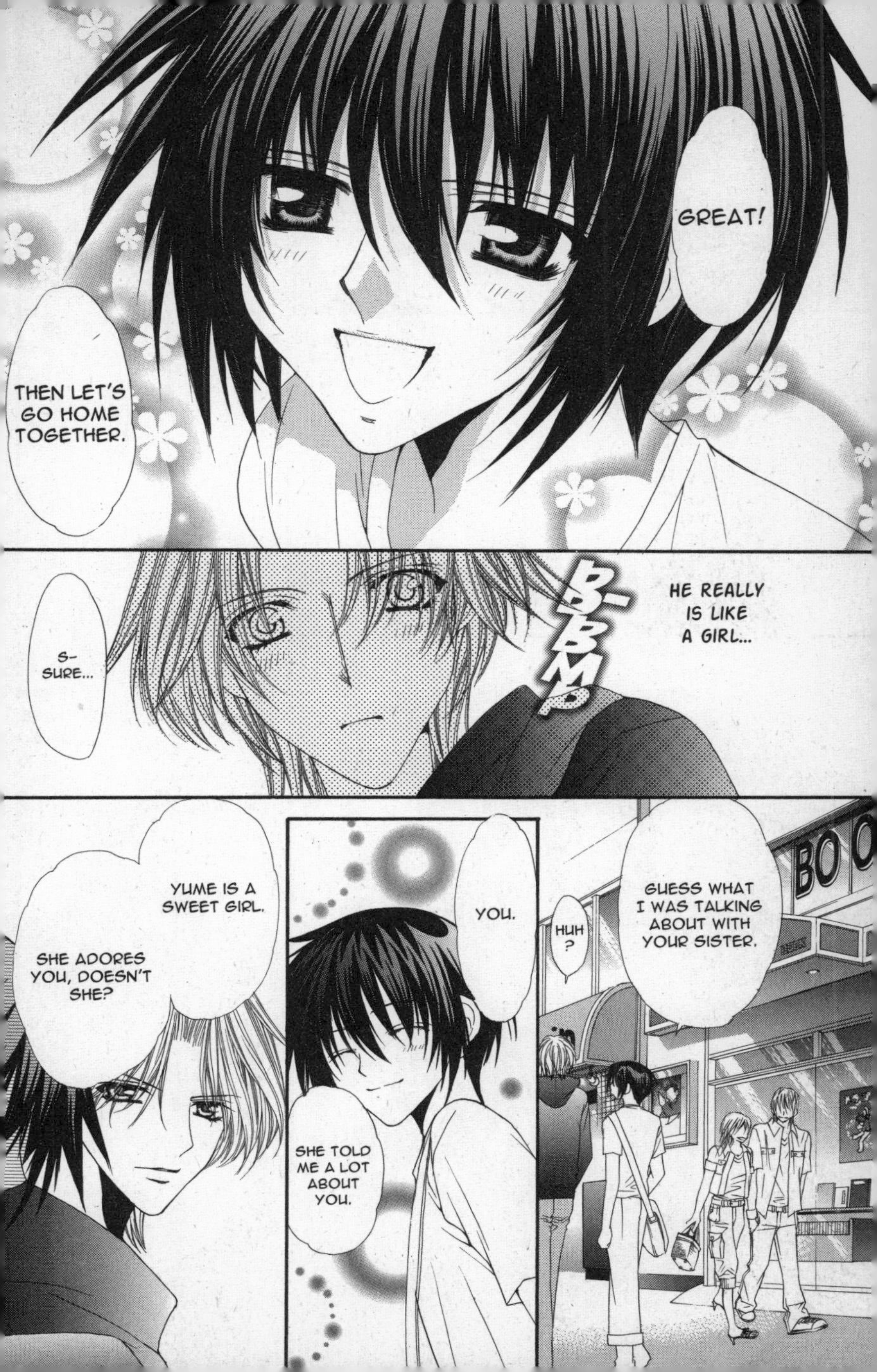
GREAT!
THEN LET'S GO HOME TOGETHER.
HE REALLY IS LIKE A GIRL...
B-BMP
S-SURE...
GUESS WHAT I WAS TALKING ABOUT WITH YOUR SISTER.
HUH?
YOU.
SHE TOLD ME A LOT ABOUT YOU.
YUME IS A SWEET GIRL.
SHE ADORES YOU, DOESN'T SHE?

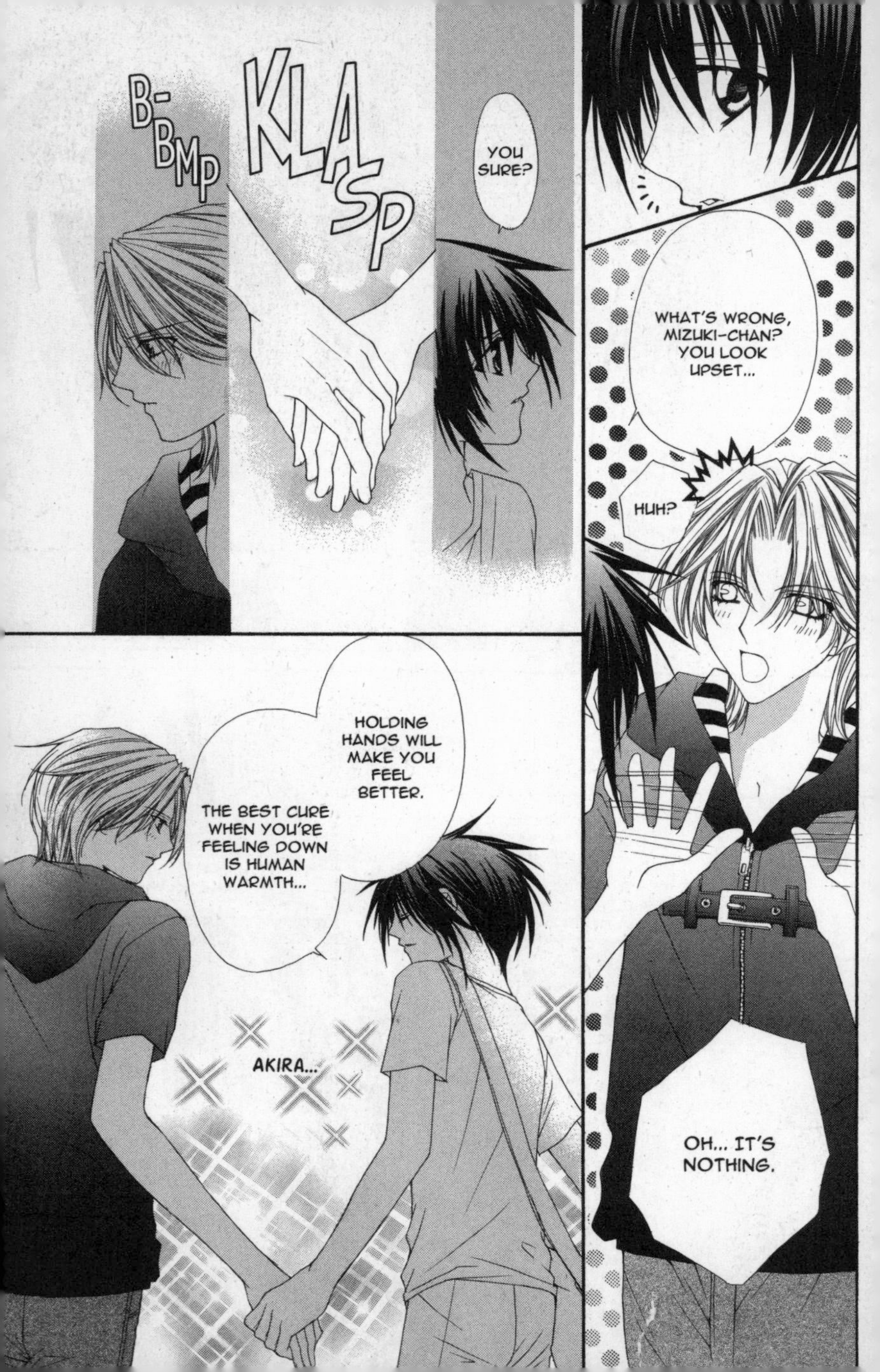
WHAT'S WRONG, MIZUKI-CHAN? YOU LOOK UPSET...
HUH?
OH... IT'S NOTHING.
YOU SURE?
KLASP
B-BMP
HOLDING HANDS WILL MAKE YOU FEEL BETTER.
THE BEST CURE WHEN YOU'RE FEELING DOWN IS HUMAN WARMTH...
AKIRA...

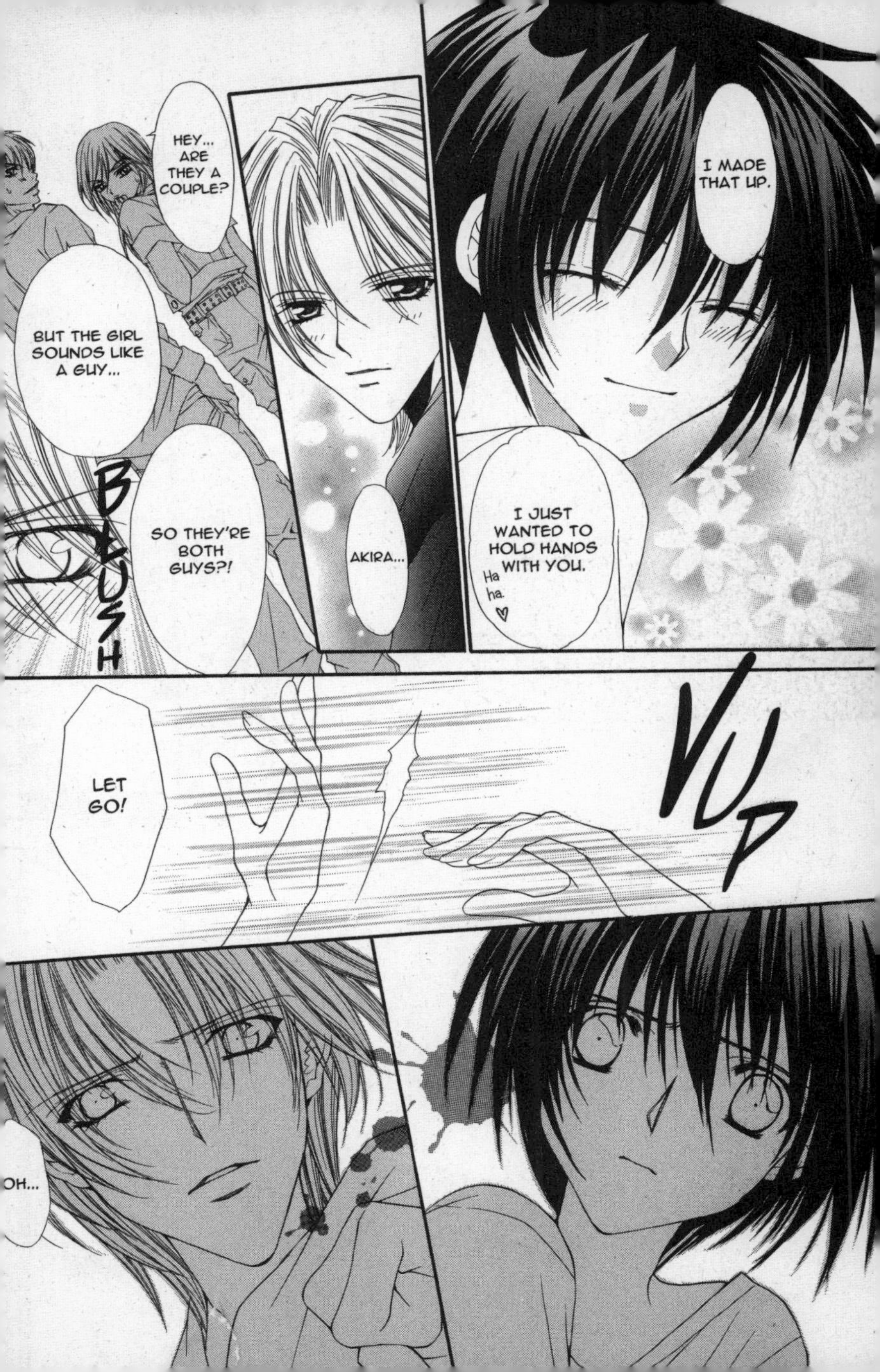
I MADE THAT UP.
I JUST WANTED TO HOLD HANDS WITH YOU.
Ha ha. ♥
AKIRA...
HEY... ARE THEY A COUPLE?
BUT THE GIRL SOUNDS LIKE A GUY...
SO THEY'RE BOTH GUYS?!
BLUSH
VUP
LET GO!
OH...

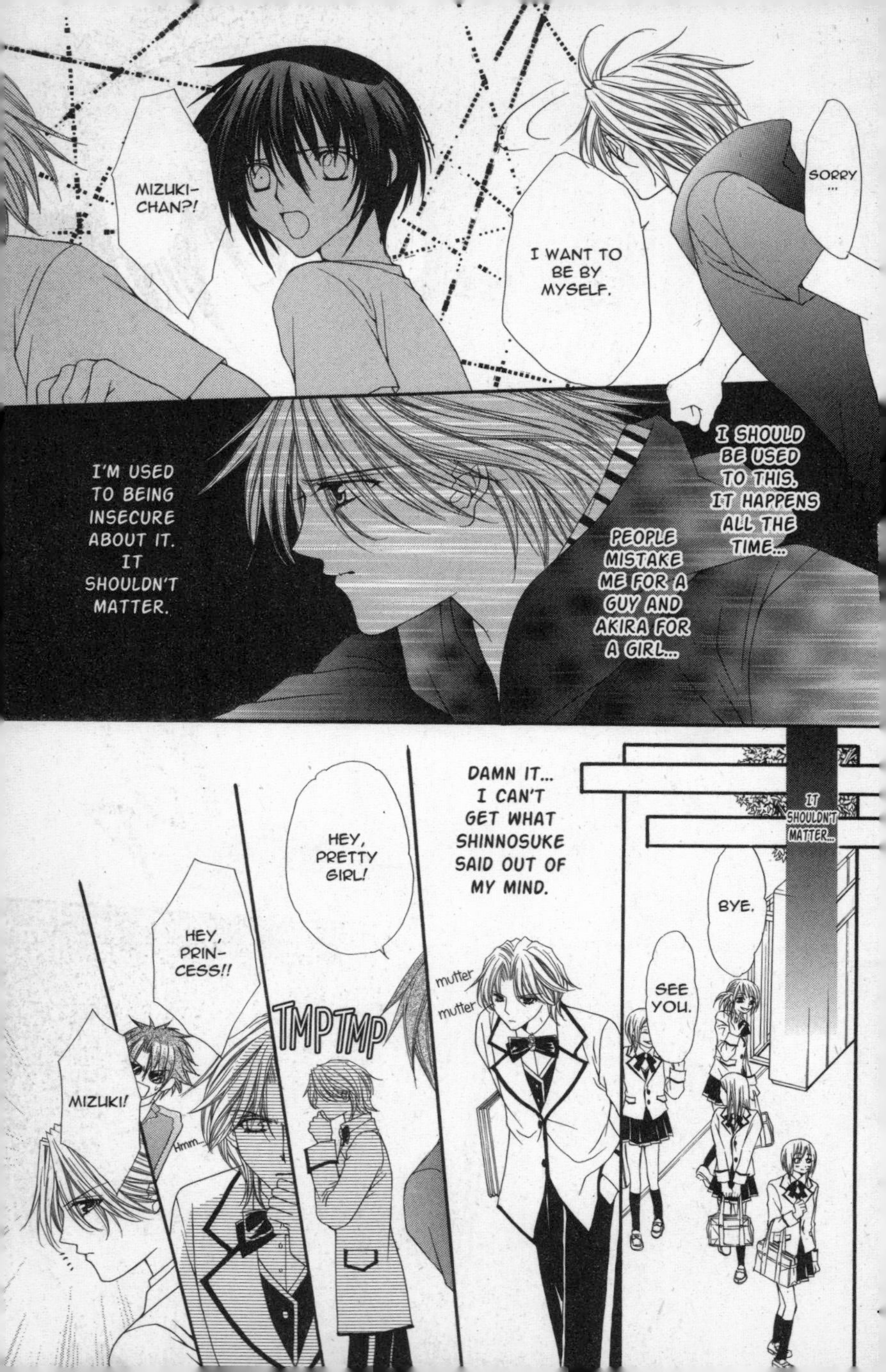
SORRY...
I WANT TO BE BY MYSELF.
MIZUKI-CHAN?!
I SHOULD BE USED TO THIS. IT HAPPENS ALL THE TIME...
PEOPLE MISTAKE ME FOR A GUY AND AKIRA FOR A GIRL...
I'M USED TO BEING INSECURE ABOUT IT. IT SHOULDN'T MATTER.
IT SHOULDN'T MATTER...
BYE.
SEE YOU.
DAMN IT... I CAN'T GET WHAT SHINNOSUKE SAID OUT OF MY MIND.
mutter mutter
HEY, PRETTY GIRL!
TMPTMP
HEY, PRIN-CESS!!
Hmm...
MIZUKI!

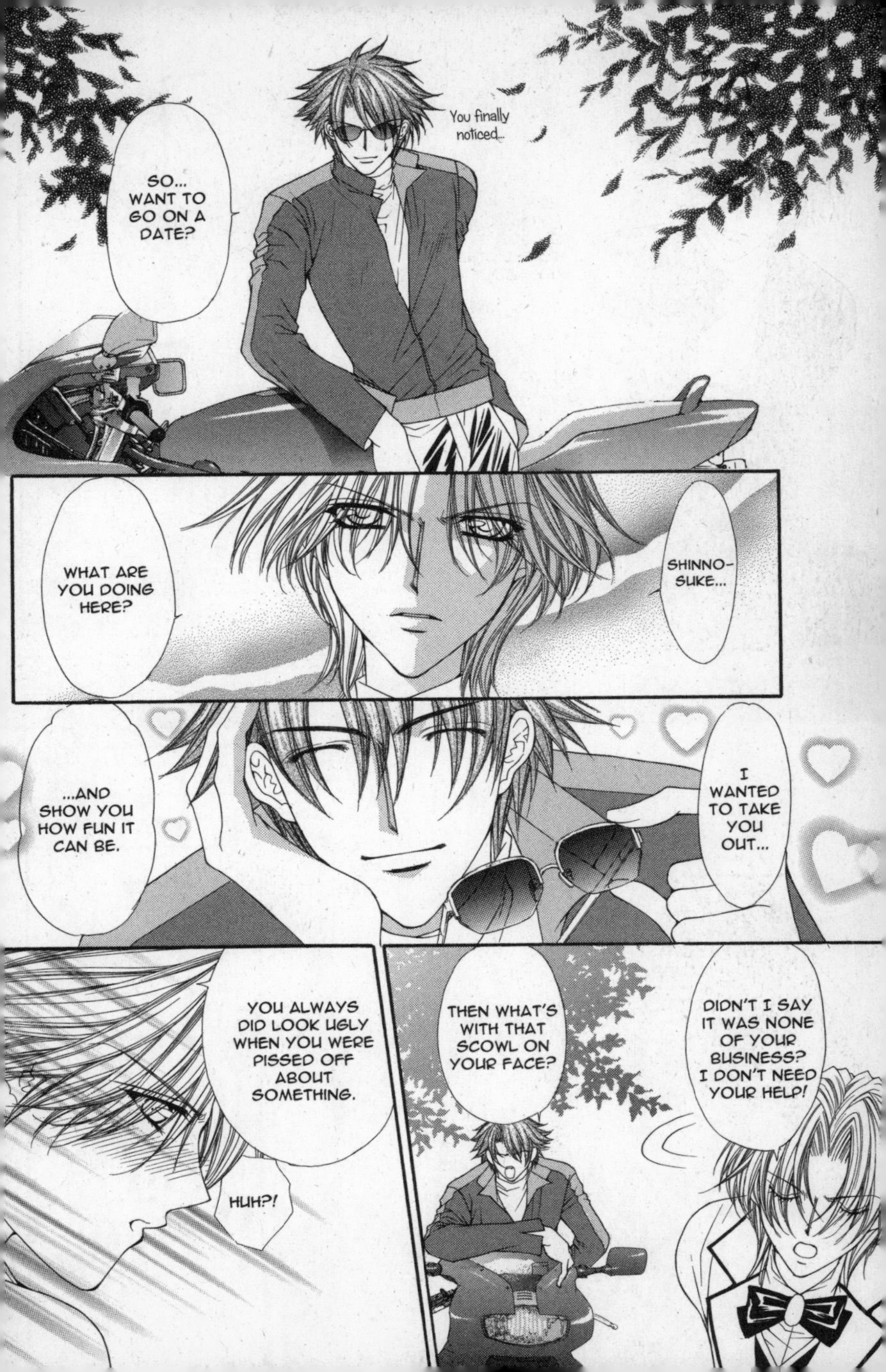
You finally noticed...
SO... WANT TO GO ON A DATE?
SHINNO-SUKE...
WHAT ARE YOU DOING HERE?
I WANTED TO TAKE YOU OUT...
...AND SHOW YOU HOW FUN IT CAN BE.
DIDN'T I SAY IT WAS NONE OF YOUR BUSINESS? I DON'T NEED YOUR HELP!
THEN WHAT'S WITH THAT SCOWL ON YOUR FACE?
YOU ALWAYS DID LOOK UGLY WHEN YOU WERE PISSED OFF ABOUT SOMETHING.
HUH?!

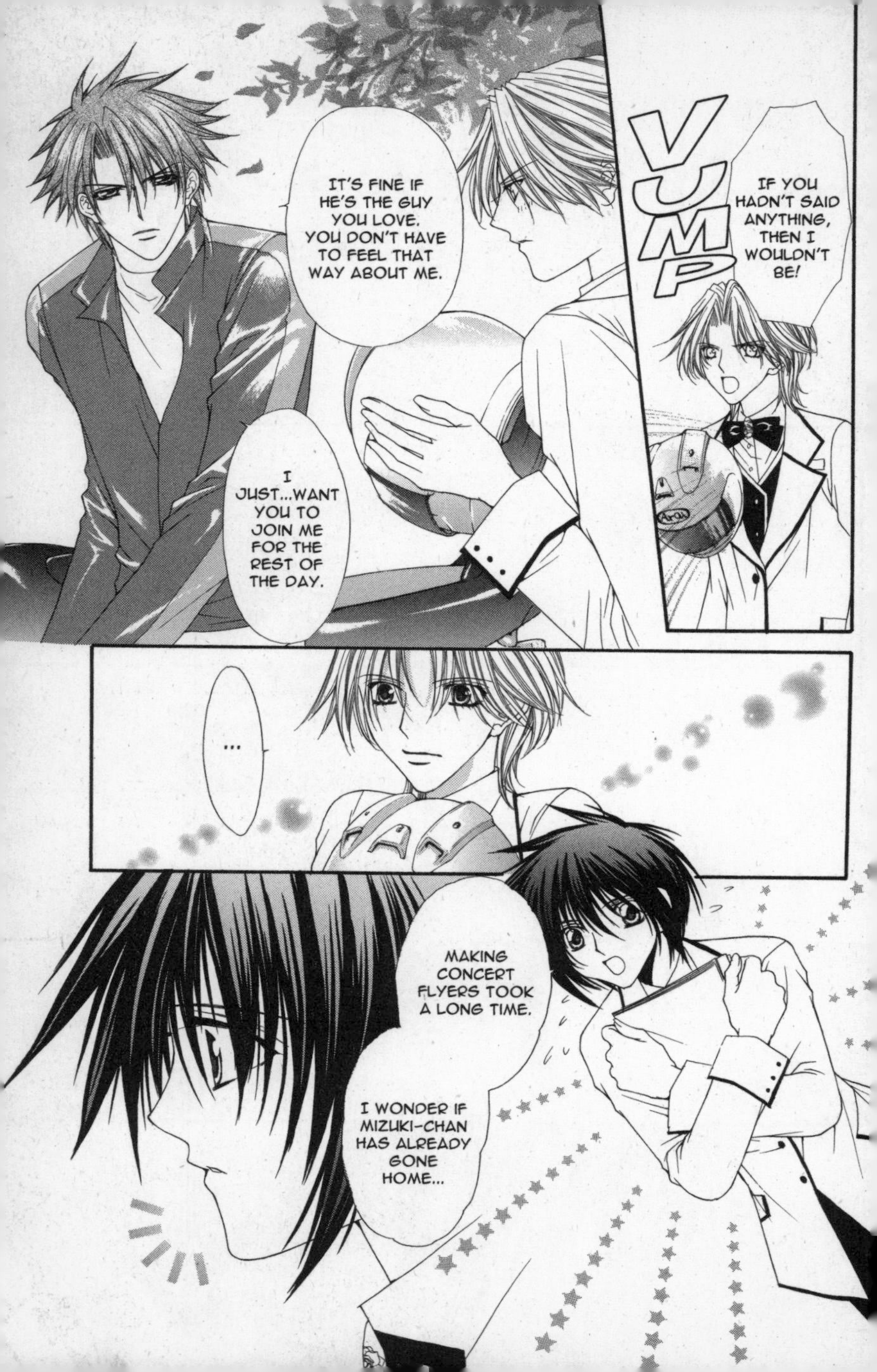
VUMP
IF YOU HADN'T SAID ANYTHING, THEN I WOULDN'T BE!
IT'S FINE IF HE'S THE GUY YOU LOVE. YOU DON'T HAVE TO FEEL THAT WAY ABOUT ME.
I JUST...WANT YOU TO JOIN ME FOR THE REST OF THE DAY.
...
MAKING CONCERT FLYERS TOOK A LONG TIME.
I WONDER IF MIZUKI-CHAN HAS ALREADY GONE HOME...

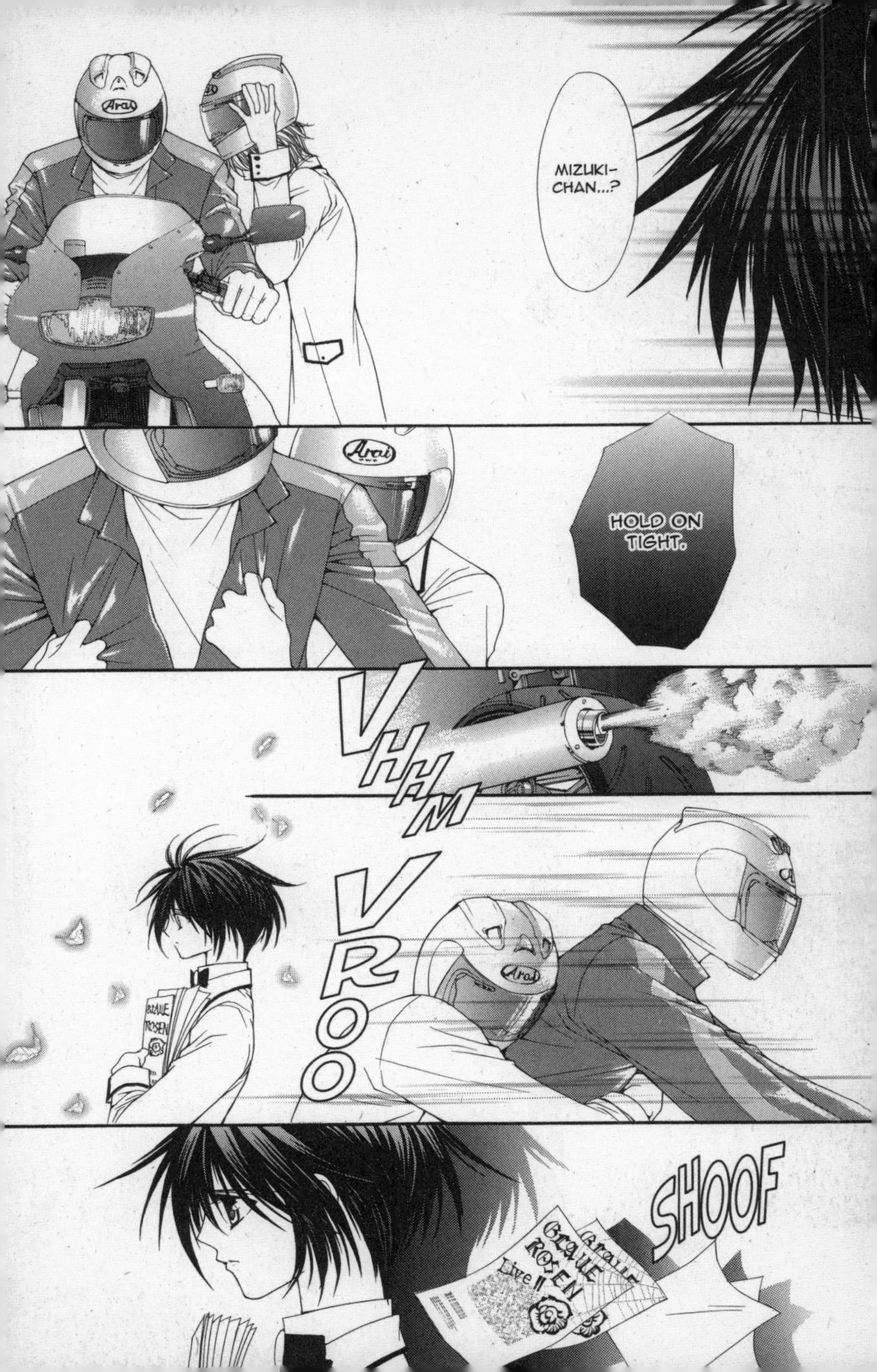
MIZUKI-CHAN...?
HOLD ON TIGHT.
VHHM
VROOO
SHOOF
GRAUE ROSEN Live!!

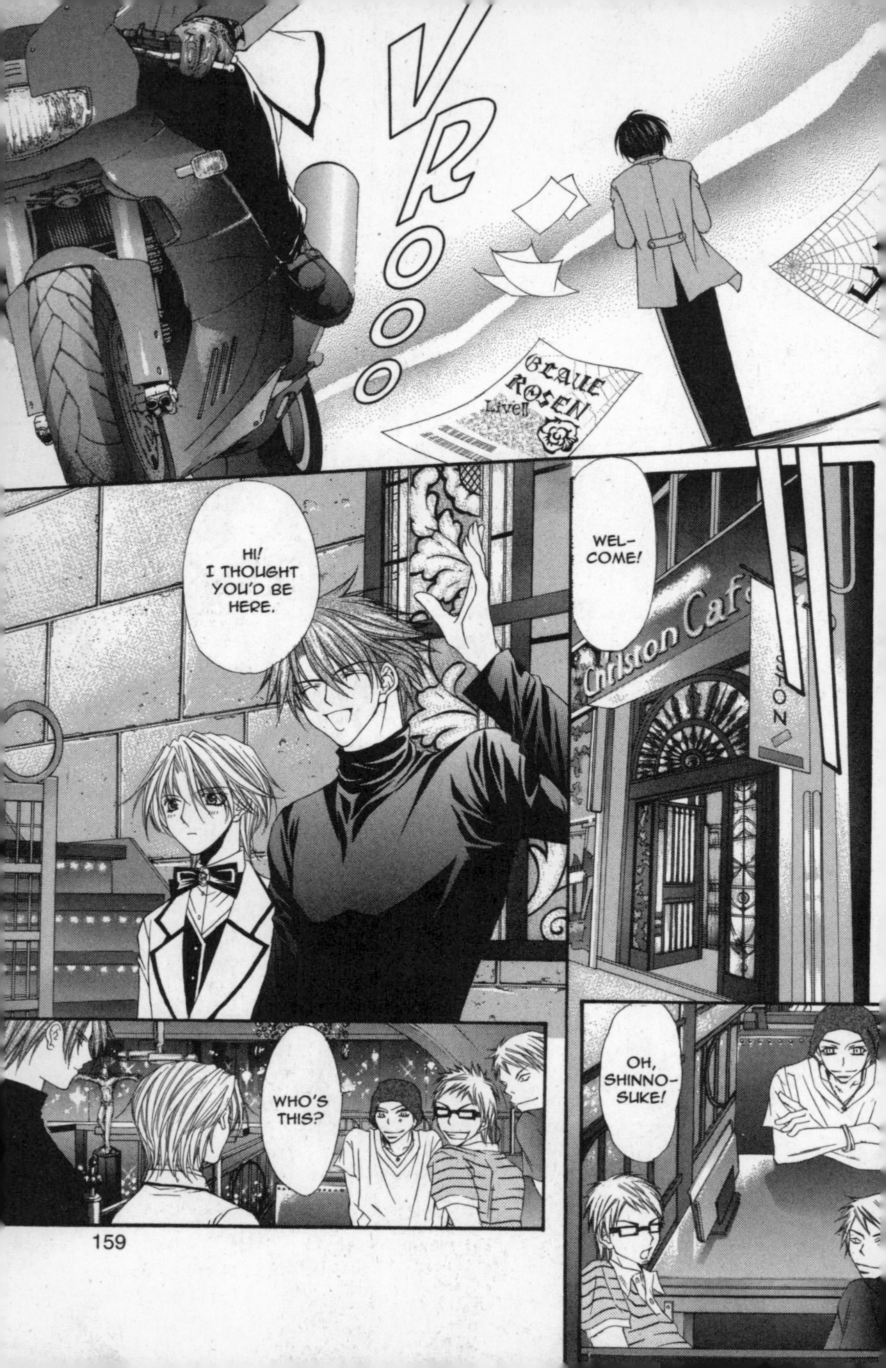
VROOOO
BLAUE ROSEN
Live!!
WEL-COME!
Christon Caf
STON
HI! I THOUGHT YOU'D BE HERE.
OH, SHINNO-SUKE!
WHO'S THIS?

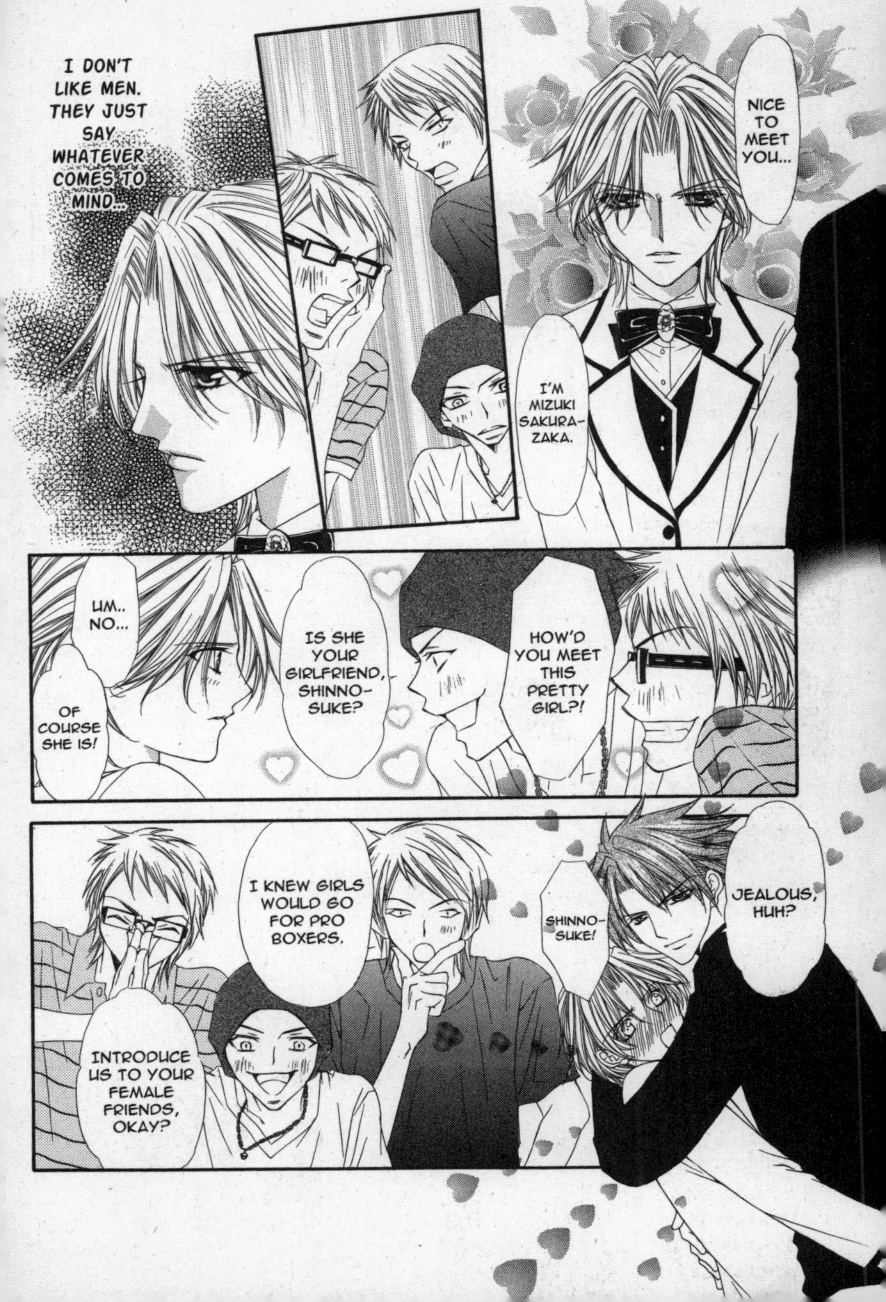
NICE TO MEET YOU...
I'M MIZUKI SAKURA-ZAKA.
I DON'T LIKE MEN. THEY JUST SAY WHATEVER COMES TO MIND...
HOW'D YOU MEET THIS PRETTY GIRL?!
IS SHE YOUR GIRLFRIEND, SHINNO-SUKE?
UM.. NO...
OF COURSE SHE IS!
JEALOUS, HUH?
SHINNO-SUKE!
I KNEW GIRLS WOULD GO FOR PRO BOXERS.
INTRODUCE US TO YOUR FEMALE FRIENDS, OKAY?

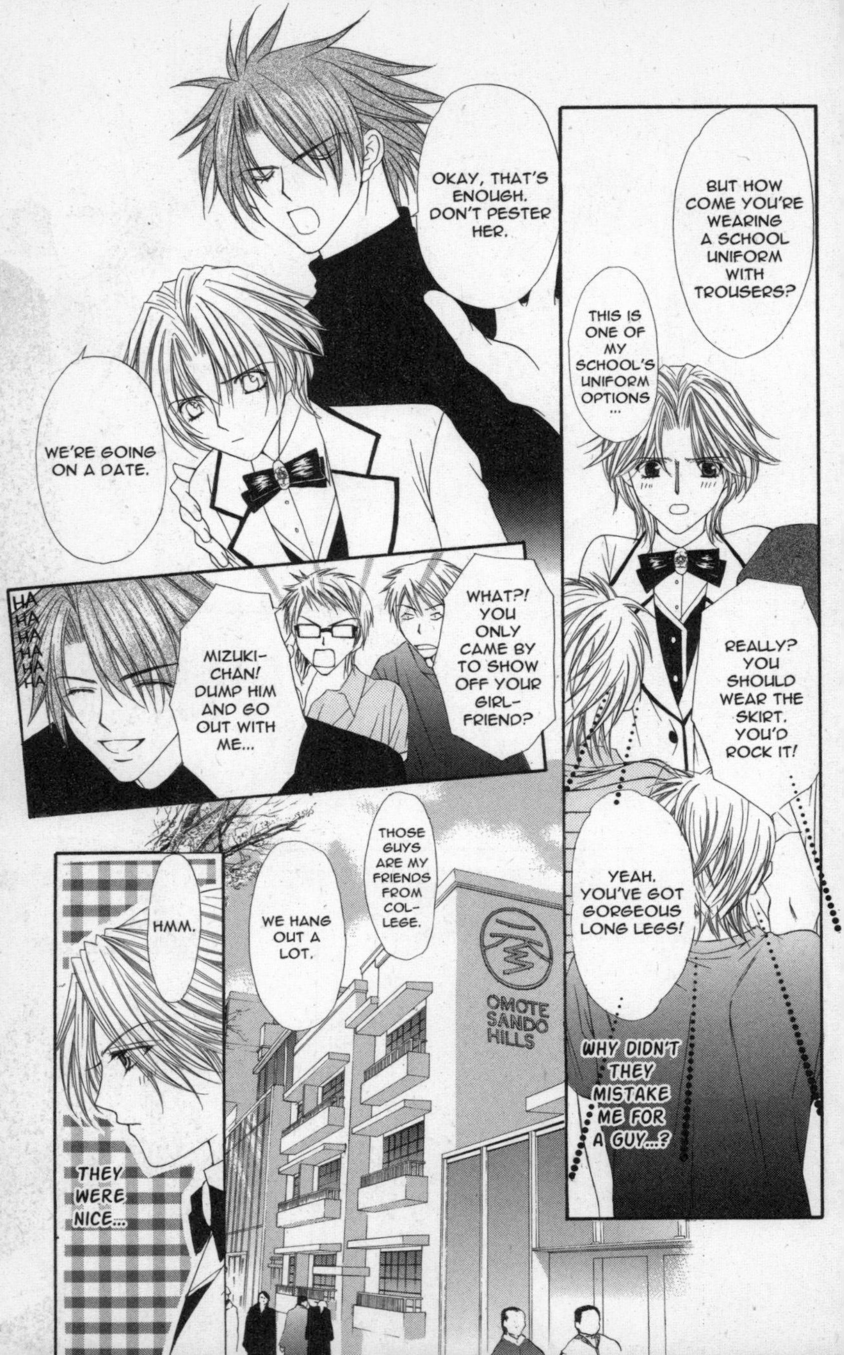

OKAY, THAT'S ENOUGH. DON'T PESTER HER.
WE'RE GOING ON A DATE.
WHAT?! YOU ONLY CAME BY TO SHOW OFF YOUR GIRL-FRIEND?
MIZUKI-CHAN! DUMP HIM AND GO OUT WITH ME...
HA HA HA HA HA HA
BUT HOW COME YOU'RE WEARING A SCHOOL UNIFORM WITH TROUSERS?
THIS IS ONE OF MY SCHOOL'S UNIFORM OPTIONS...
REALLY? YOU SHOULD WEAR THE SKIRT. YOU'D ROCK IT!
YEAH. YOU'VE GOT GORGEOUS LONG LEGS!
WHY DIDN'T THEY MISTAKE ME FOR A GUY...?
THOSE GUYS ARE MY FRIENDS FROM COL-LEGE.
WE HANG OUT A LOT.
OMOTE SANDO HILLS
HMM.
THEY WERE NICE...

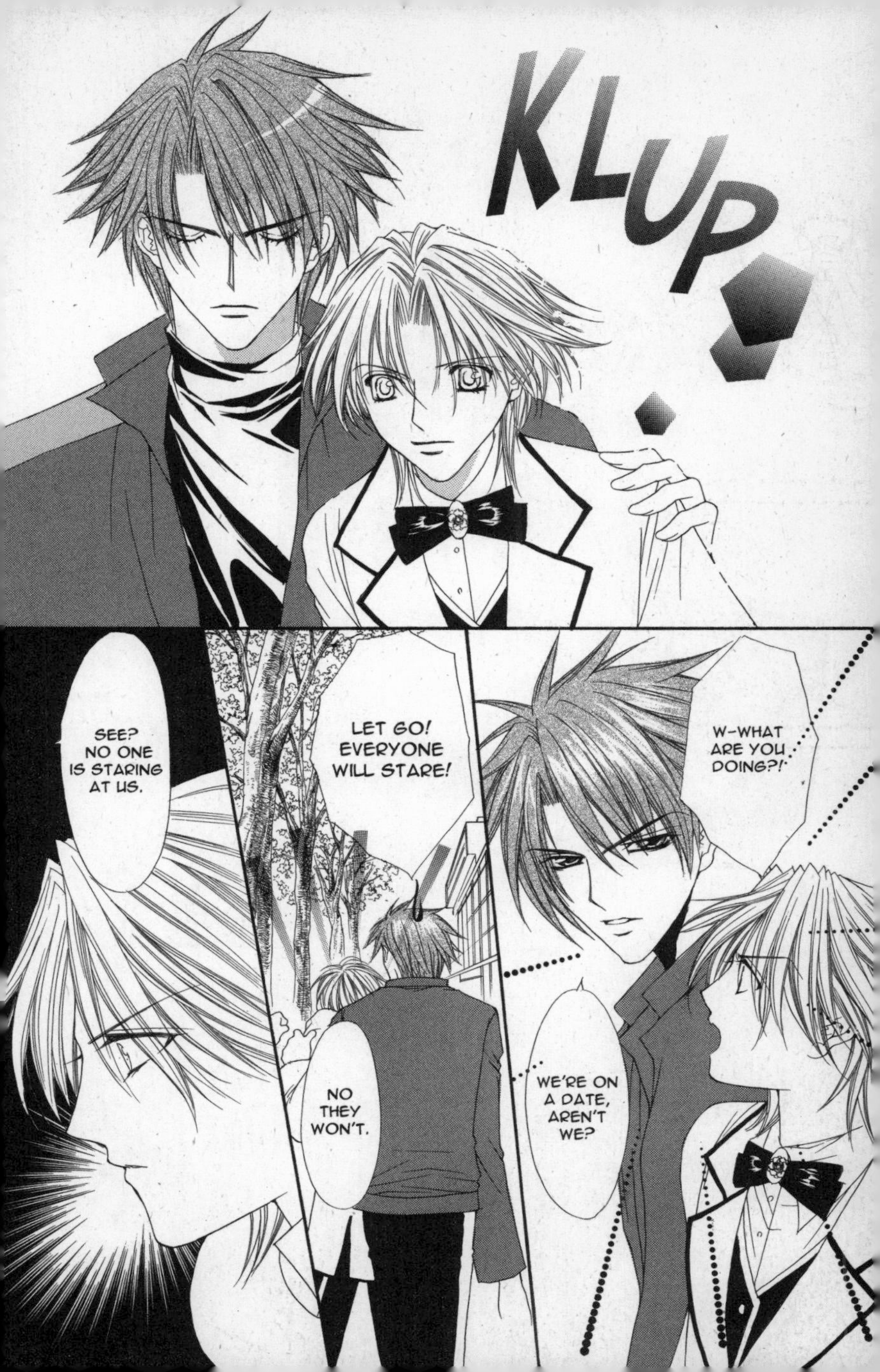
KLUP
W-WHAT ARE YOU DOING?!
WE'RE ON A DATE, AREN'T WE?
LET GO! EVERYONE WILL STARE!
NO THEY WON'T.
SEE? NO ONE IS STARING AT US.

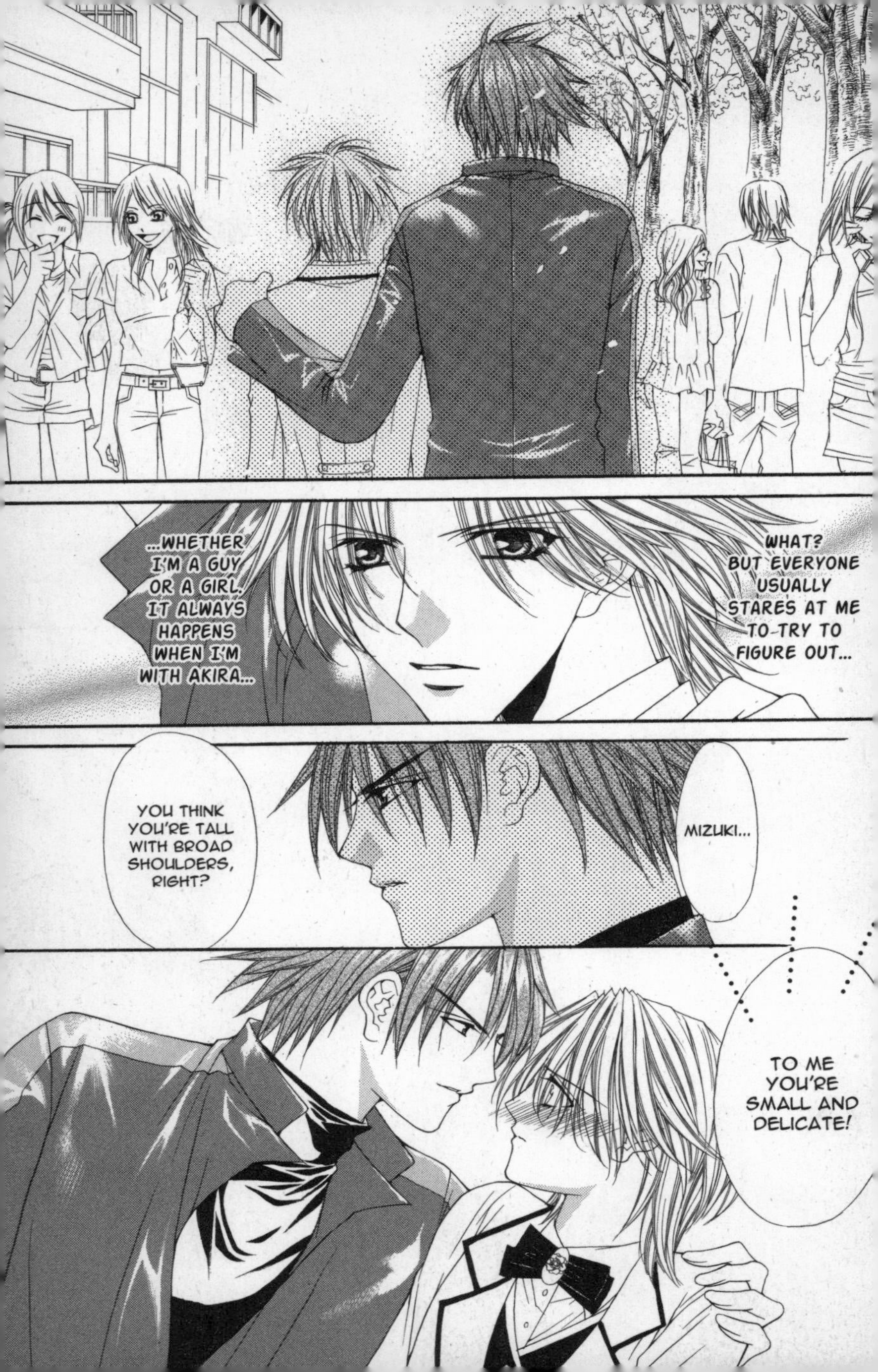
WHAT? BUT EVERYONE USUALLY STARES AT ME TO TRY TO FIGURE OUT...
...WHETHER I'M A GUY OR A GIRL. IT ALWAYS HAPPENS WHEN I'M WITH AKIRA...
MIZUKI...
YOU THINK YOU'RE TALL WITH BROAD SHOULDERS, RIGHT?
...
TO ME YOU'RE SMALL AND DELICATE!

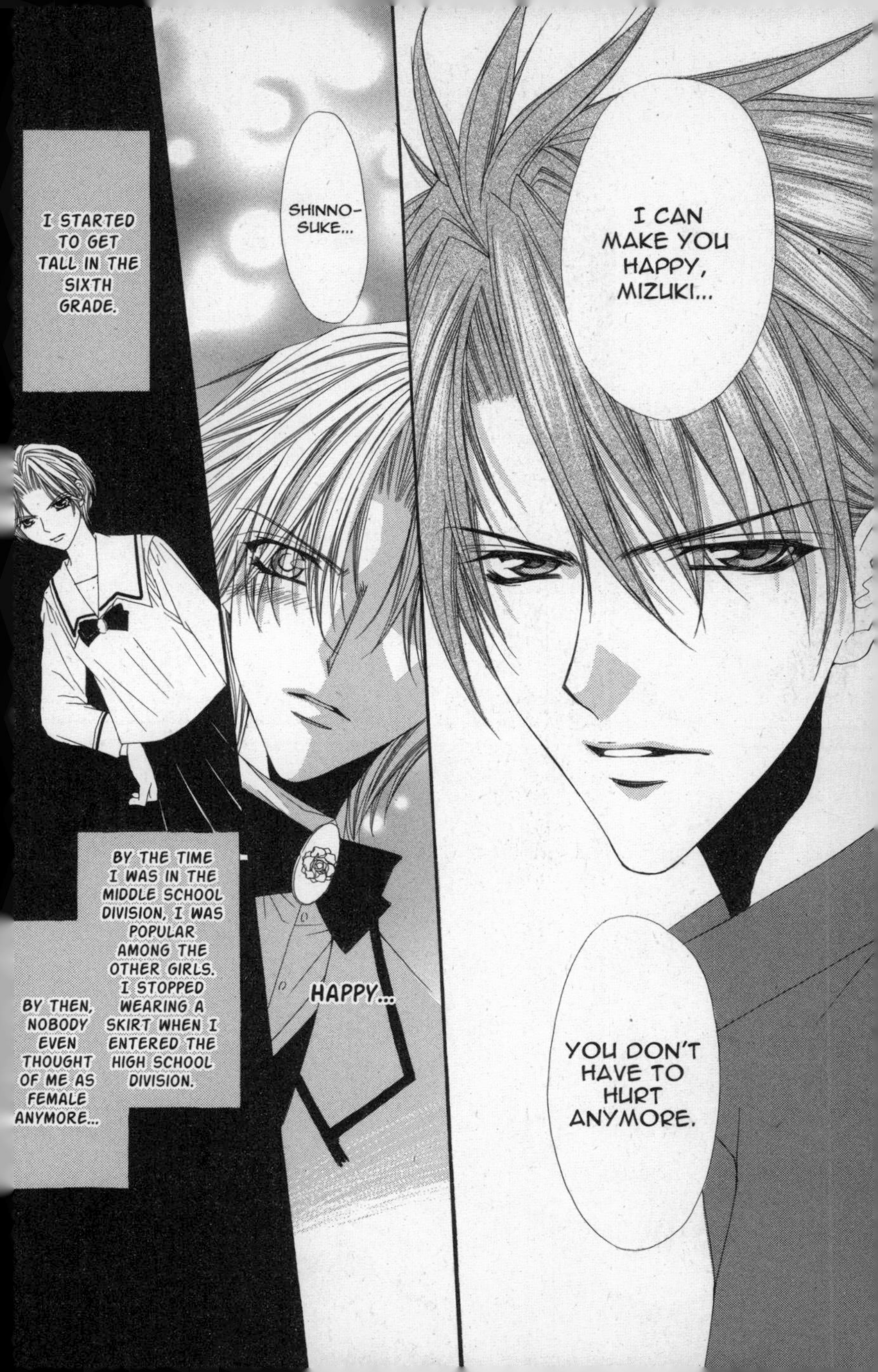
I CAN MAKE YOU HAPPY, MIZUKI...
YOU DON'T HAVE TO HURT ANYMORE.
SHINNO-SUKE...
HAPPY...
I STARTED TO GET TALL IN THE SIXTH GRADE.
BY THE TIME I WAS IN THE MIDDLE SCHOOL DIVISION, I WAS POPULAR AMONG THE OTHER GIRLS. I STOPPED WEARING A SKIRT WHEN I ENTERED THE HIGH SCHOOL DIVISION.
BY THEN, NOBODY EVEN THOUGHT OF ME AS FEMALE ANYMORE...

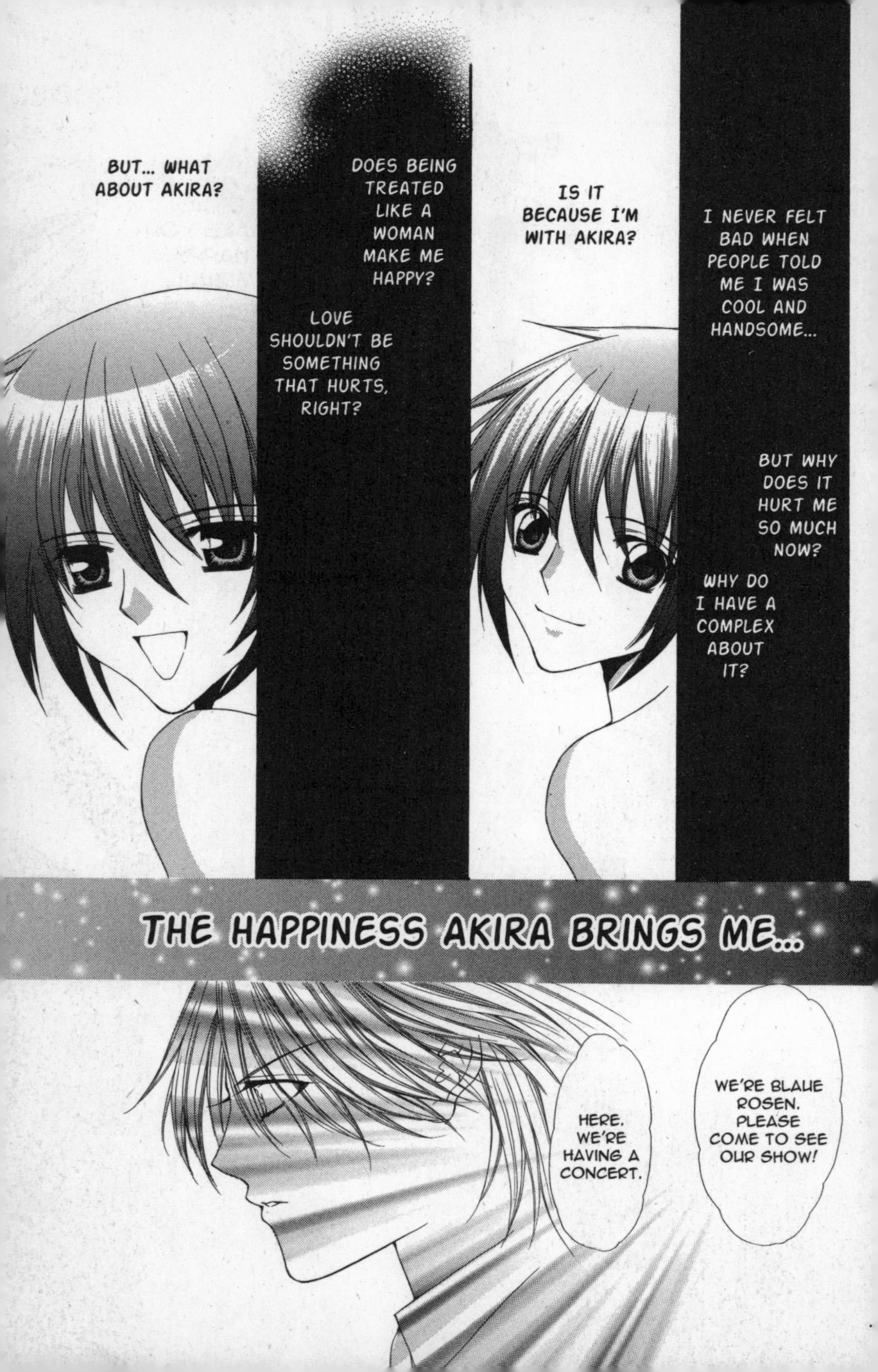
I NEVER FELT BAD WHEN PEOPLE TOLD ME I WAS COOL AND HANDSOME...
BUT WHY DOES IT HURT ME SO MUCH NOW?
WHY DO I HAVE A COMPLEX ABOUT IT?
IS IT BECAUSE I'M WITH AKIRA?
DOES BEING TREATED LIKE A WOMAN MAKE ME HAPPY?
LOVE SHOULDN'T BE SOMETHING THAT HURTS, RIGHT?
BUT... WHAT ABOUT AKIRA?
THE HAPPINESS AKIRA BRINGS ME...
WE'RE BLAUE ROSEN. PLEASE COME TO SEE OUR SHOW!
HERE. WE'RE HAVING A CONCERT.

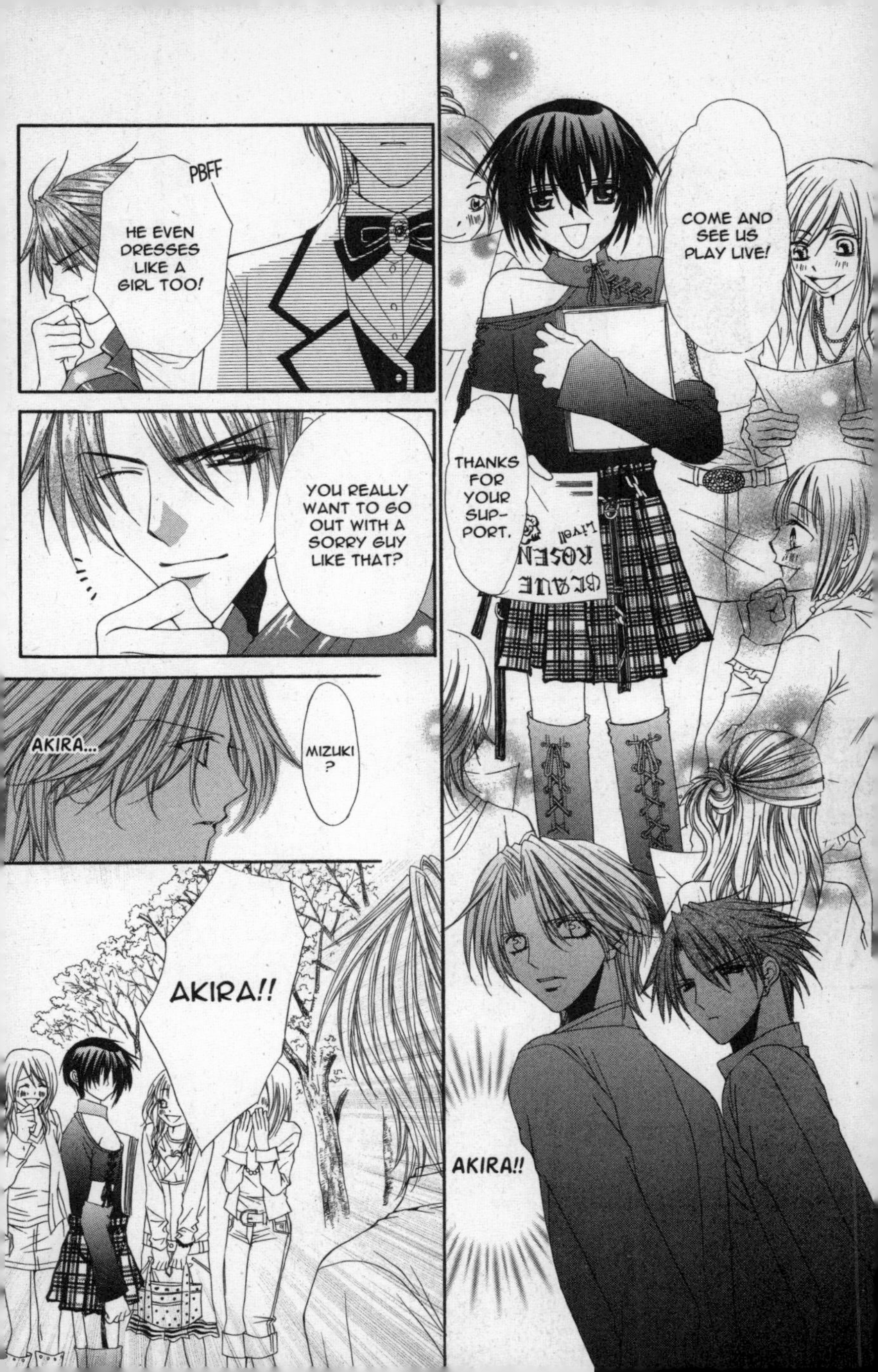
COME AND SEE US PLAY LIVE!
THANKS FOR YOUR SUP-PORT.
AKIRA!!
PBFF
HE EVEN DRESSES LIKE A GIRL TOO!
YOU REALLY WANT TO GO OUT WITH A SORRY GUY LIKE THAT?
MIZUKI?
AKIRA...
AKIRA!!

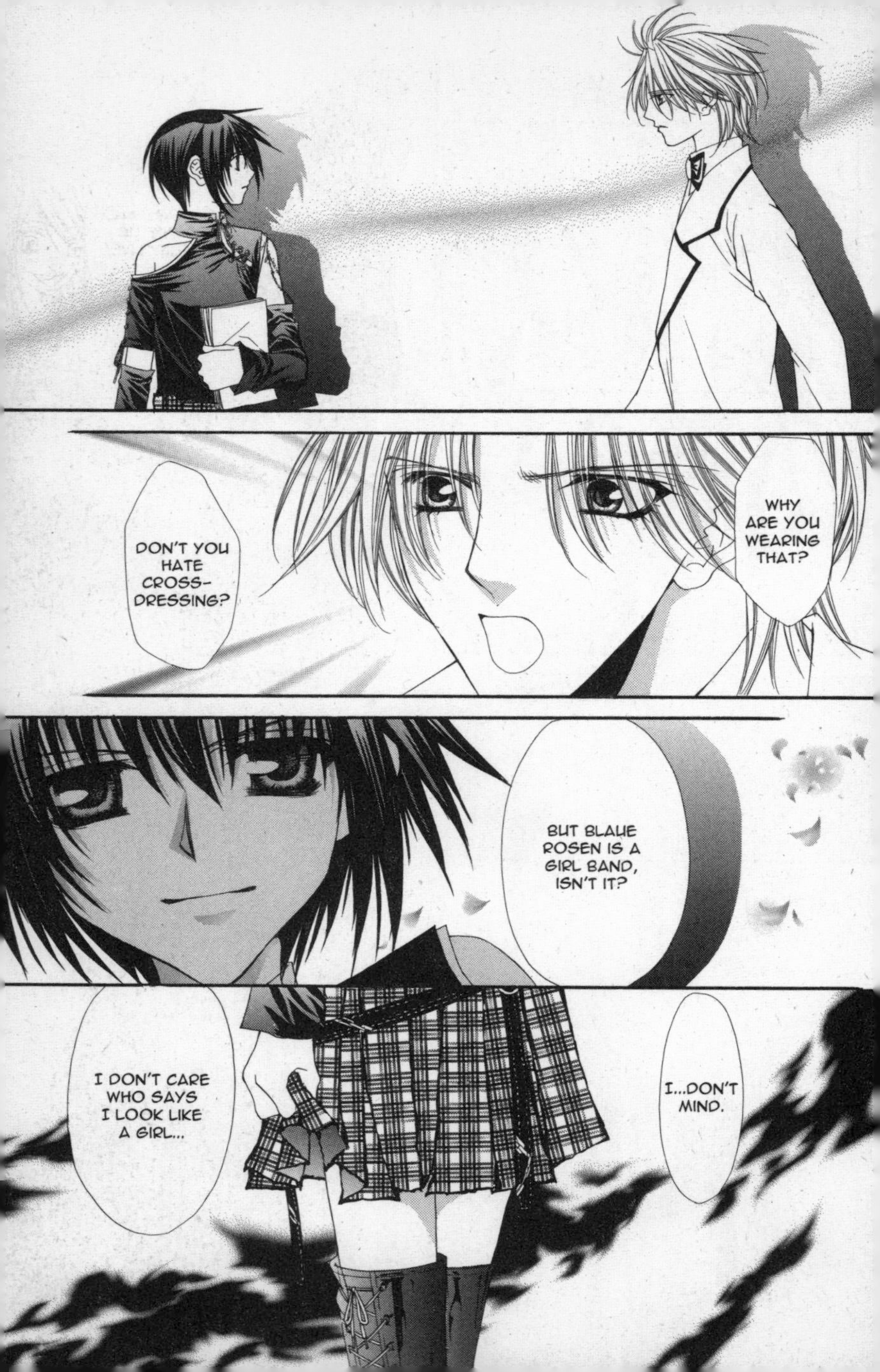
WHY ARE YOU WEARING THAT?
DON'T YOU HATE CROSS-DRESSING?
BUT BLAUE ROSEN IS A GIRL BAND, ISN'T IT?
I...DON'T MIND.
I DON'T CARE WHO SAYS I LOOK LIKE A GIRL...

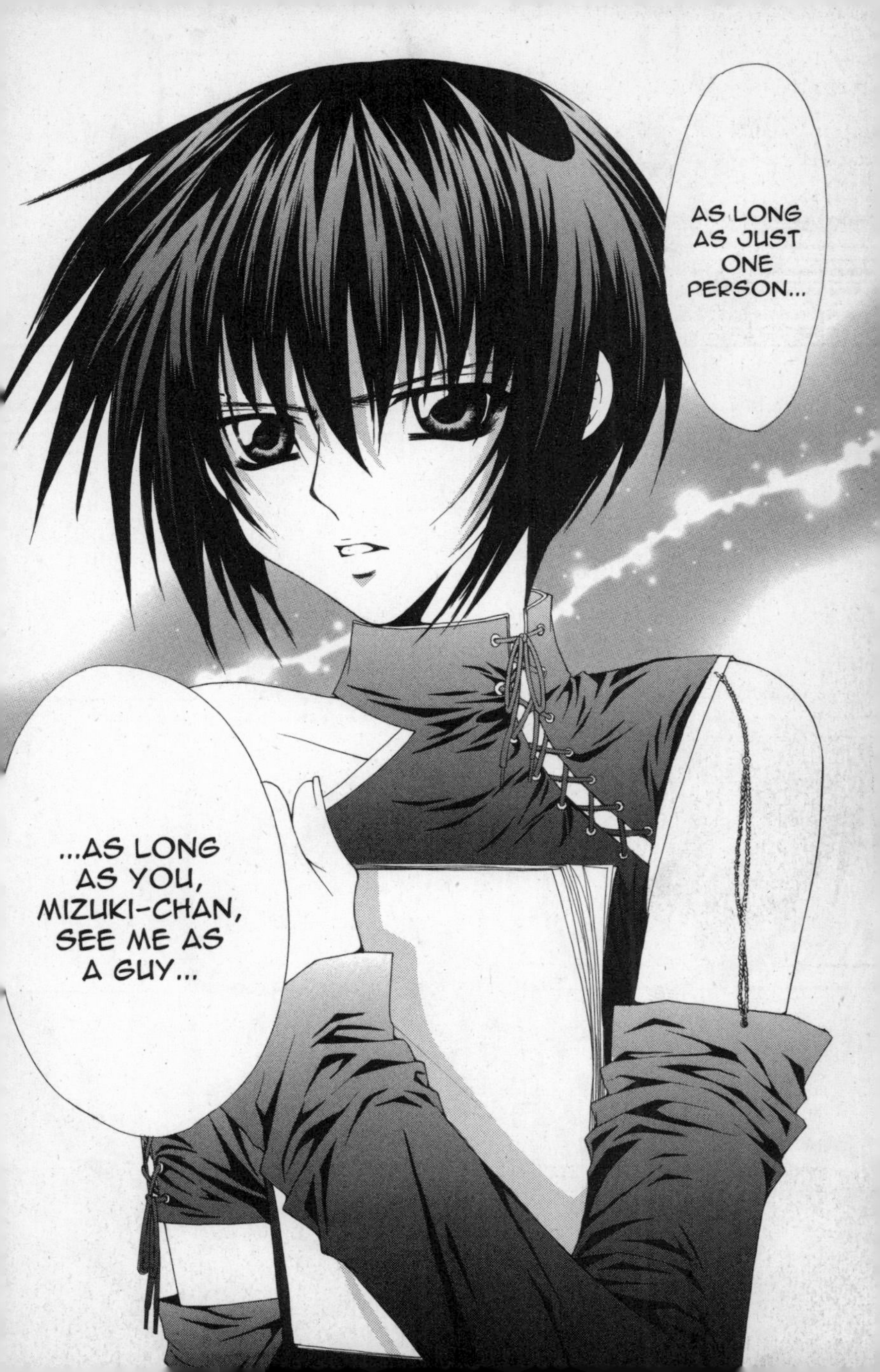
AS LONG AS JUST ONE PERSON...
...AS LONG AS YOU, MIZUKI-CHAN, SEE ME AS A GUY...

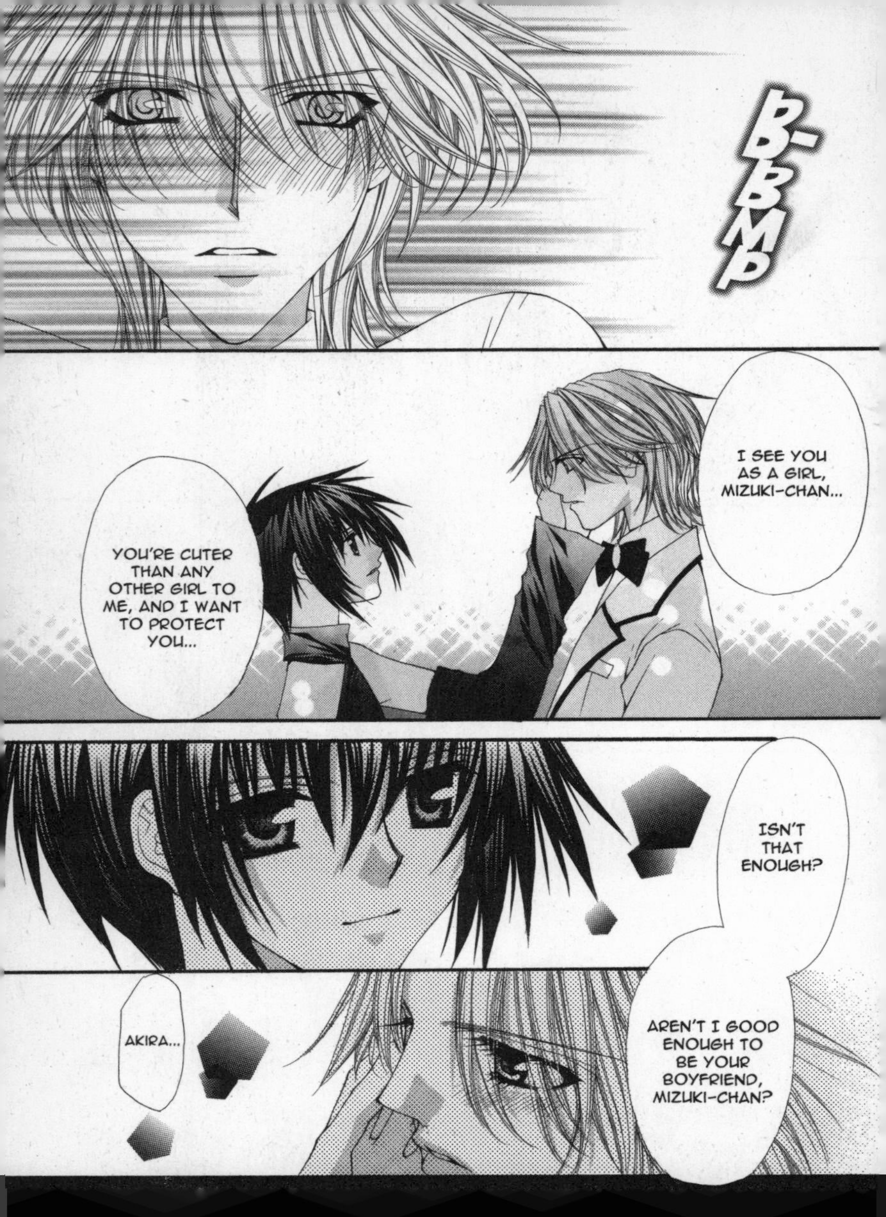
B-BMP
I SEE YOU AS A GIRL, MIZUKI-CHAN...
YOU'RE CUTER THAN ANY OTHER GIRL TO ME, AND I WANT TO PROTECT YOU...
ISN'T THAT ENOUGH?
AREN'T I GOOD ENOUGH TO BE YOUR BOYFRIEND, MIZUKI-CHAN?
AKIRA...

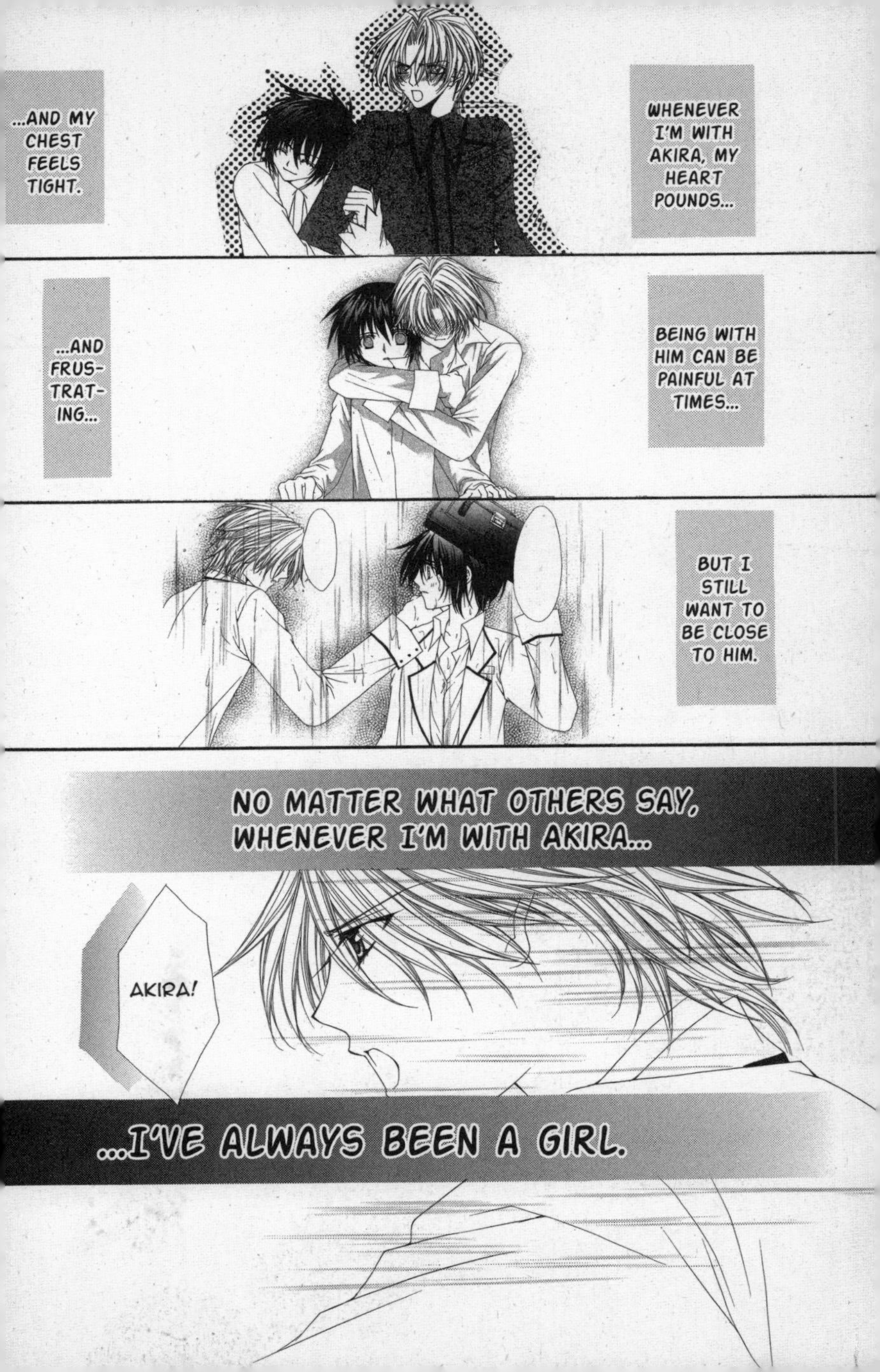
WHENEVER I'M WITH AKIRA, MY HEART POUNDS...
...AND MY CHEST FEELS TIGHT.
BEING WITH HIM CAN BE PAINFUL AT TIMES...
...AND FRUS-TRAT-ING...
BUT I STILL WANT TO BE CLOSE TO HIM.
NO MATTER WHAT OTHERS SAY, WHENEVER I'M WITH AKIRA...
AKIRA!
...I'VE ALWAYS BEEN A GIRL.

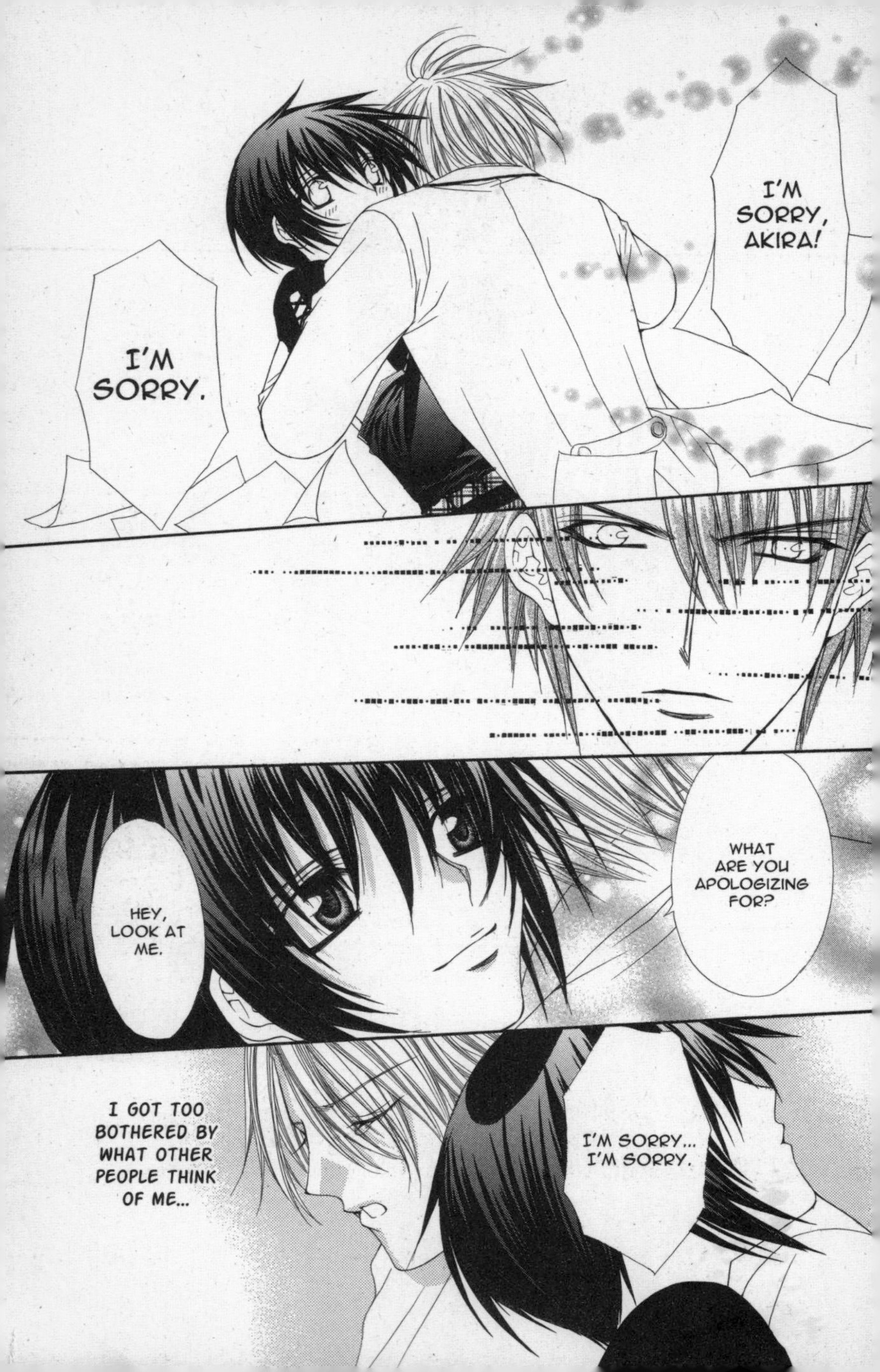
I'M SORRY, AKIRA!
I'M SORRY.
WHAT ARE YOU APOLOGIZING FOR?
HEY, LOOK AT ME.
I'M SORRY... I'M SORRY.
I GOT TOO BOTHERED BY WHAT OTHER PEOPLE THINK OF ME...

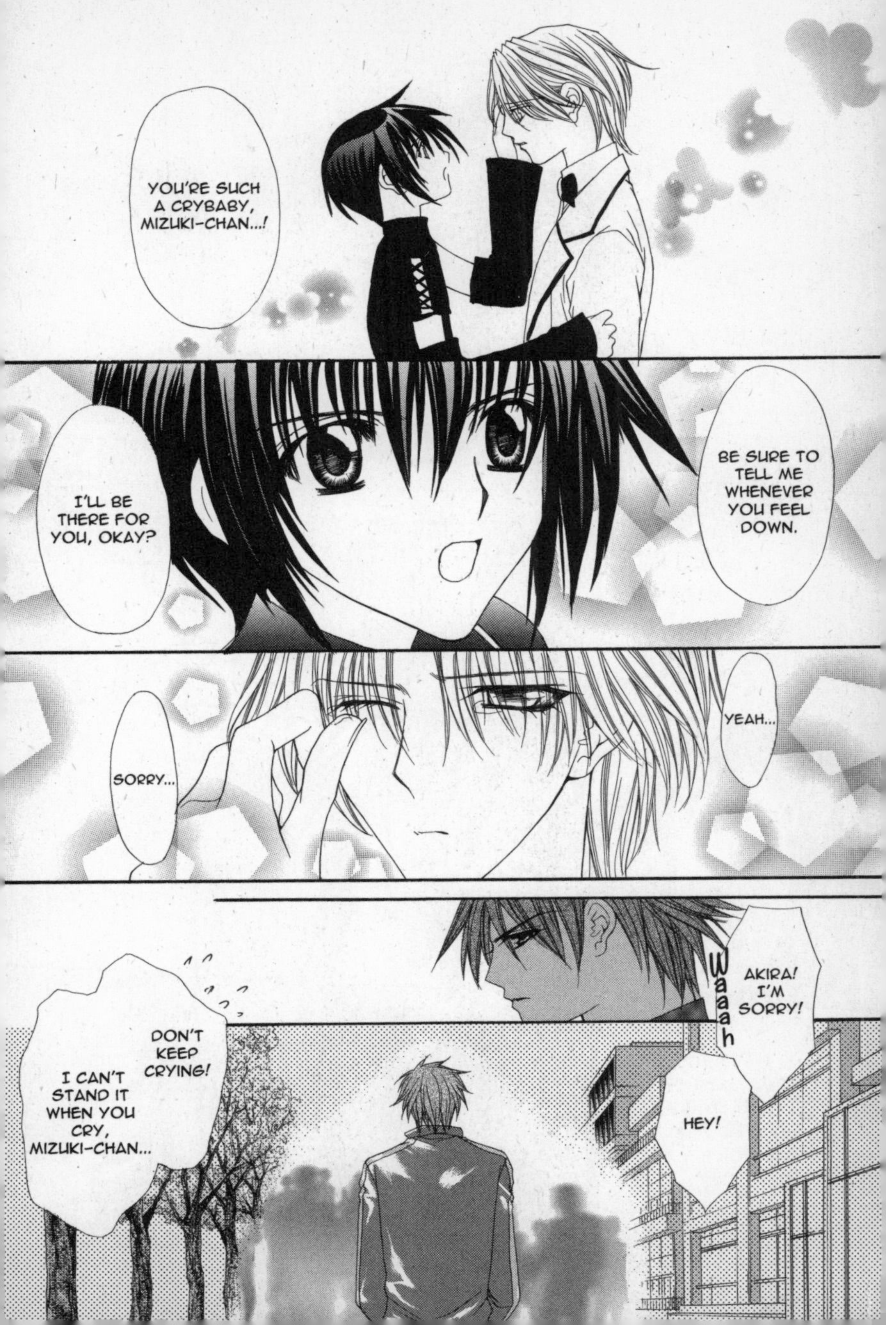
YOU'RE SUCH A CRYBABY, MIZUKI-CHAN...!
BE SURE TO TELL ME WHENEVER YOU FEEL DOWN.
I'LL BE THERE FOR YOU, OKAY?
YEAH...
SORRY...
AKIRA! I'M SORRY!
Waaah
HEY!
DON'T KEEP CRYING!
I CAN'T STAND IT WHEN YOU CRY, MIZUKI-CHAN...

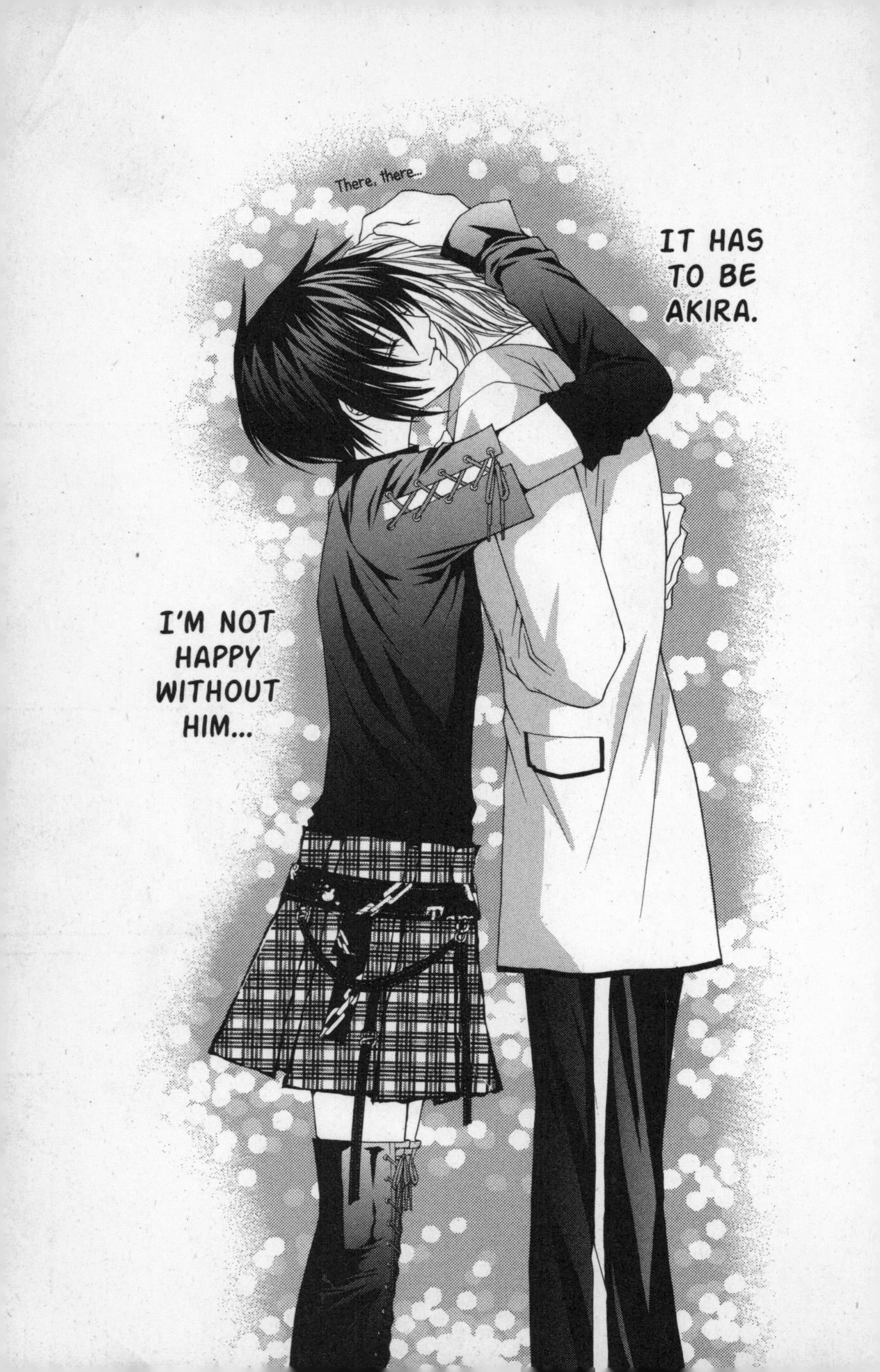
There, there...
IT HAS TO BE AKIRA.
I'M NOT HAPPY WITHOUT HIM...

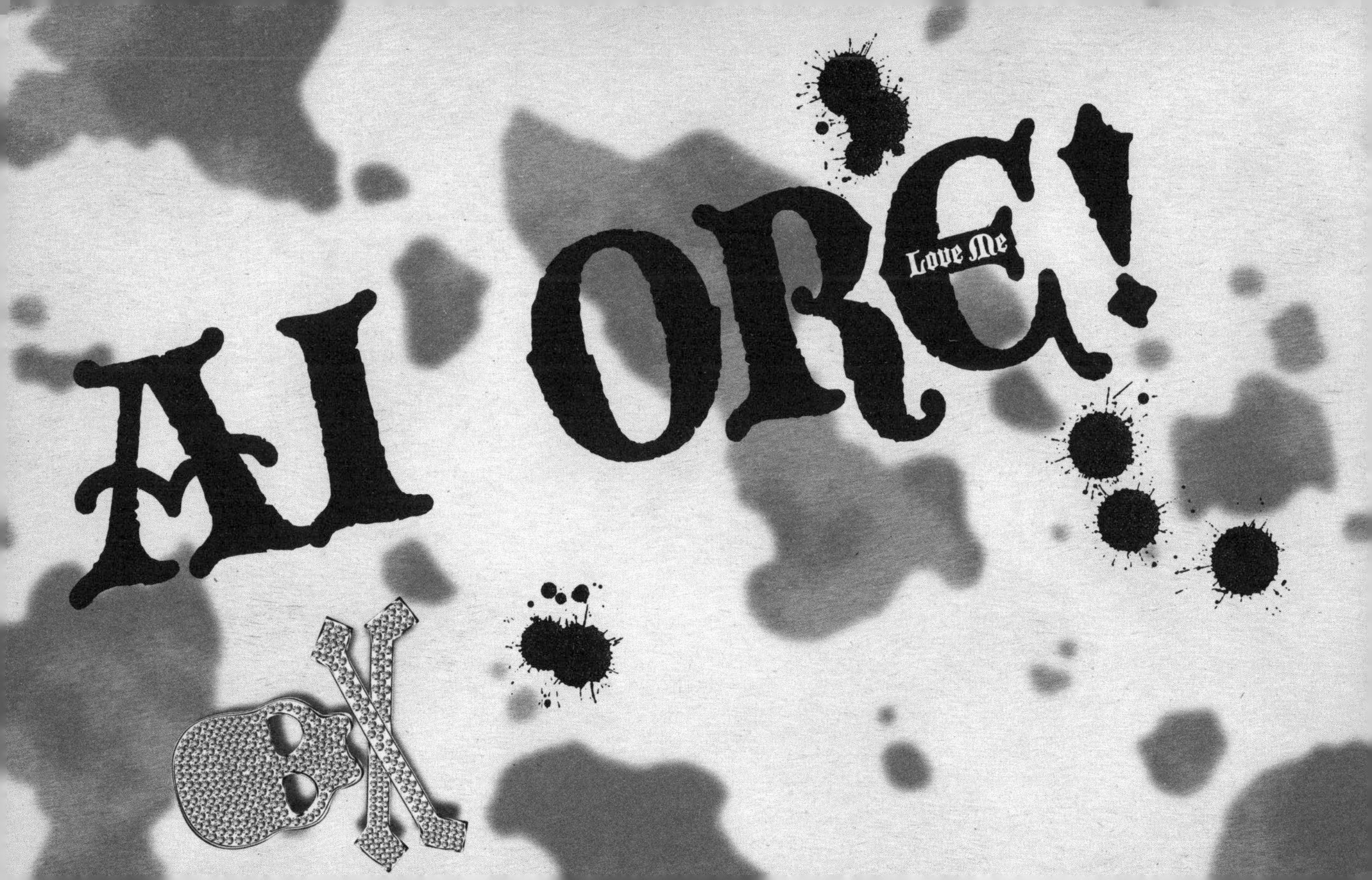
AI ORE!
Love Me

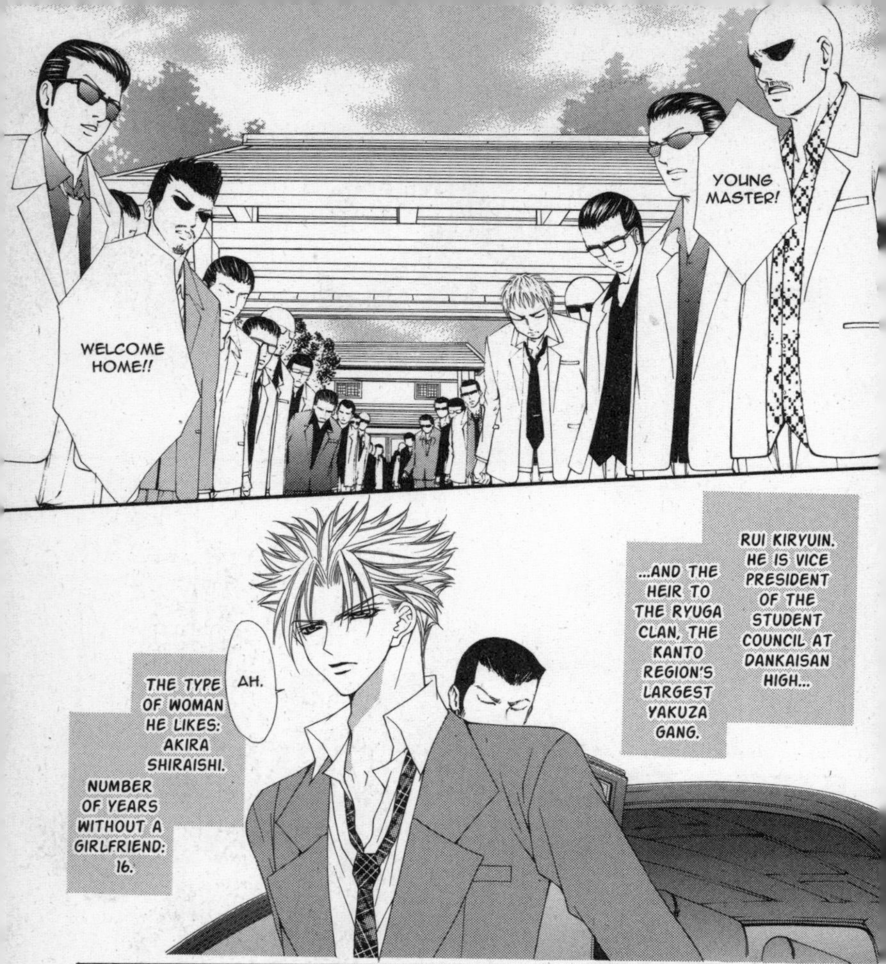
YOUNG MASTER!
WELCOME HOME!!
RUI KIRYUIN. HE IS VICE PRESIDENT OF THE STUDENT COUNCIL AT DANKAISAN HIGH...
...AND THE HEIR TO THE RYUGA CLAN, THE KANTO REGION'S LARGEST YAKUZA GANG.
AH.
THE TYPE OF WOMAN HE LIKES: AKIRA SHIRAISHI.
NUMBER OF YEARS WITHOUT A GIRLFRIEND: 16.

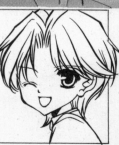

Answer me!! Mizuki ♥

Q5: How do you feel about people mistaking you for a guy?

A5: I don't mind the girls at school being my fans, but I don't like to be mistaken for a guy... I just want to be a cool-looking girl!!

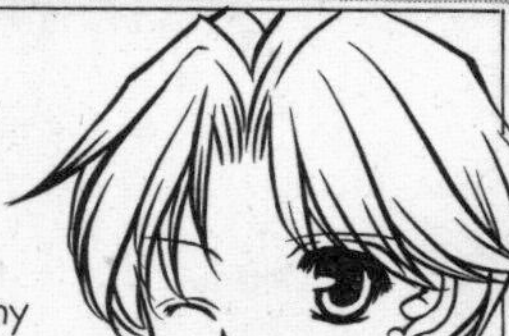

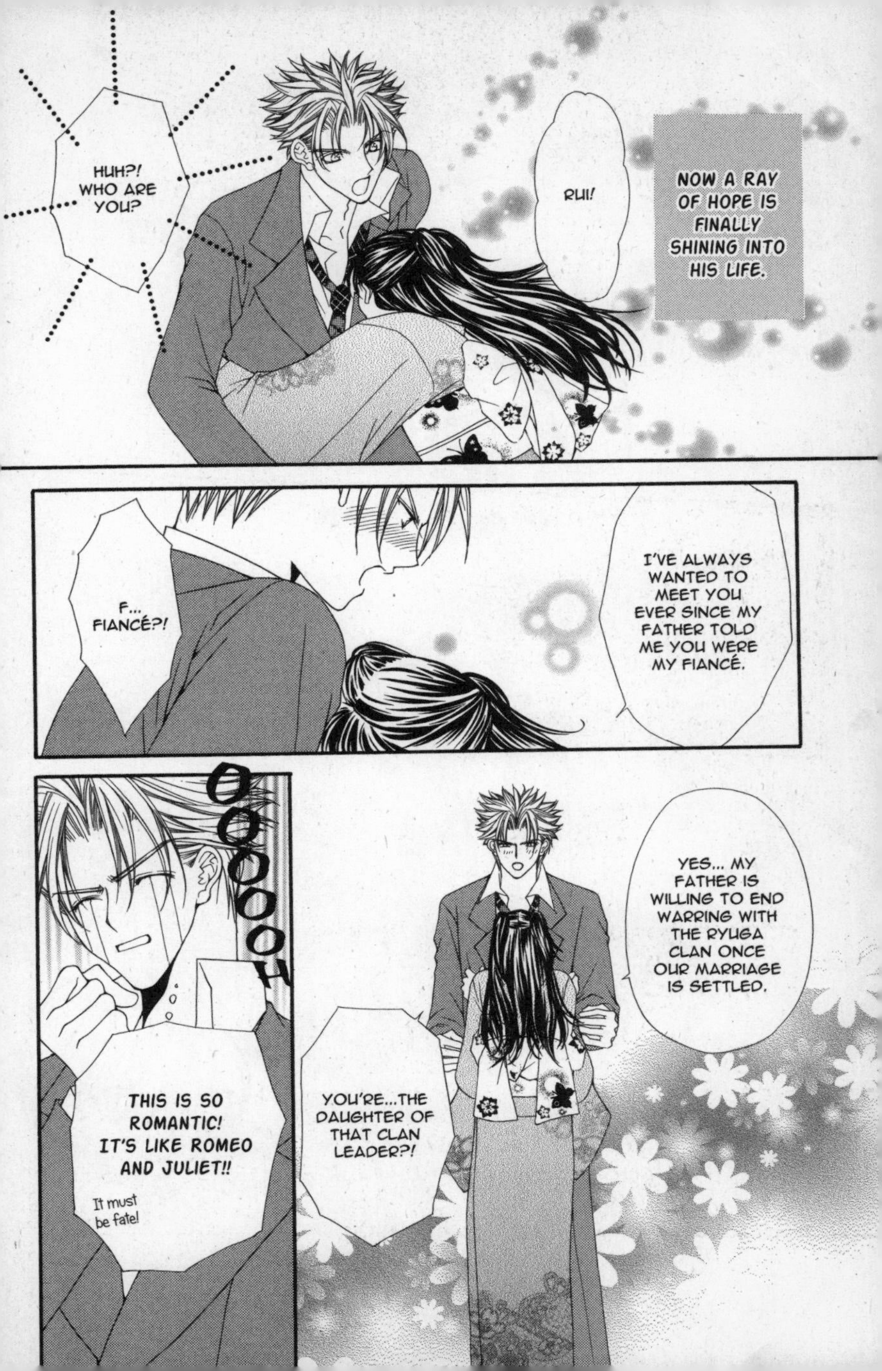
NOW A RAY OF HOPE IS FINALLY SHINING INTO HIS LIFE.
RUI!
HUH?! WHO ARE YOU?
I'VE ALWAYS WANTED TO MEET YOU EVER SINCE MY FATHER TOLD ME YOU WERE MY FIANCÉ.
F... FIANCÉ?!
YES... MY FATHER IS WILLING TO END WARRING WITH THE RYUGA CLAN ONCE OUR MARRIAGE IS SETTLED.
YOU'RE...THE DAUGHTER OF THAT CLAN LEADER?!
OOOOOOH
THIS IS SO ROMANTIC! IT'S LIKE ROMEO AND JULIET!!
It must be fate!

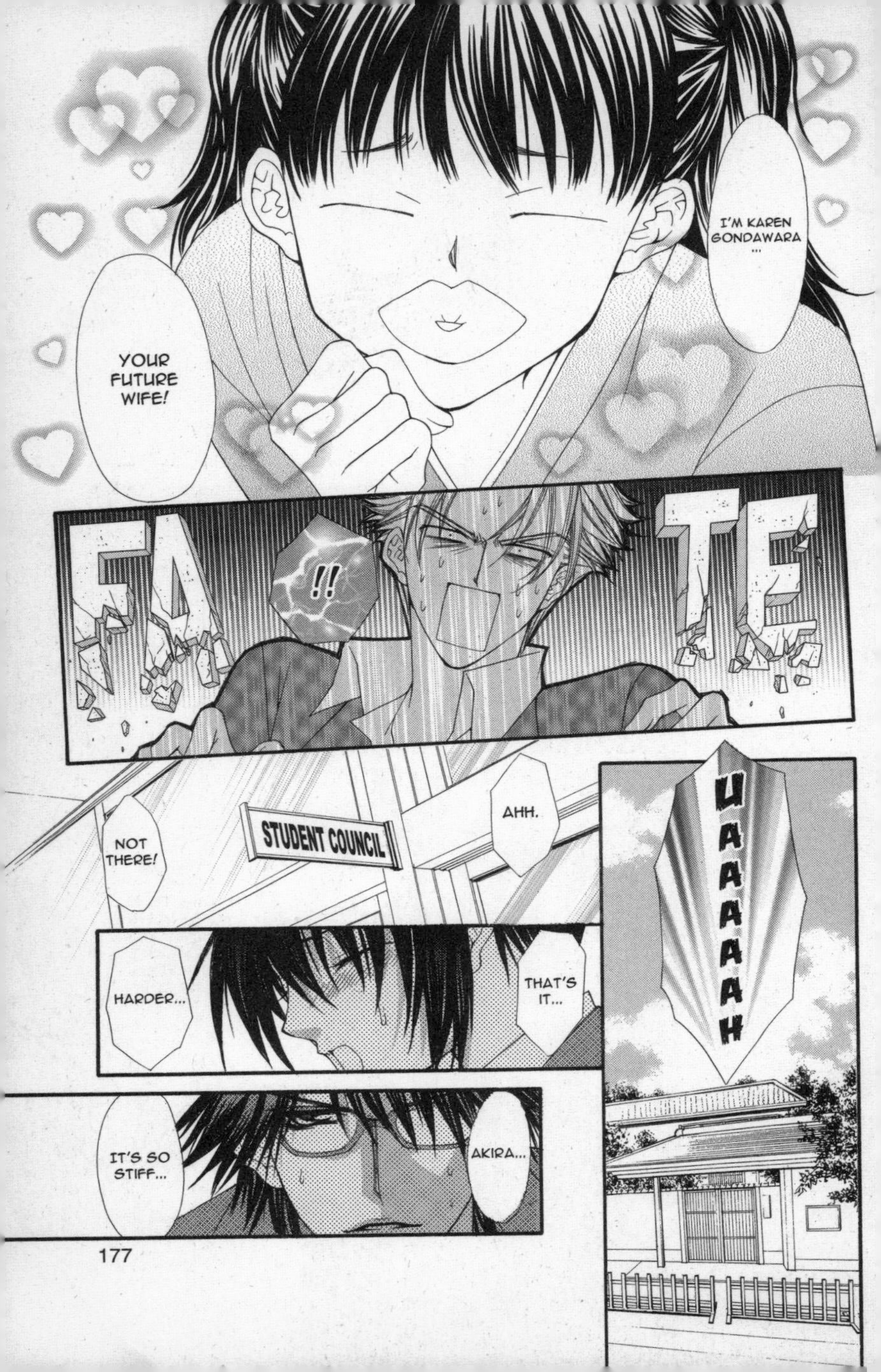
I'M KAREN GONDAWARA ...
YOUR FUTURE WIFE!
FA
TE
!!
UAAAAAAH
STUDENT COUNCIL
AHH.
NOT THERE!
THAT'S IT...
HARDER...
AKIRA...
IT'S SO STIFF...

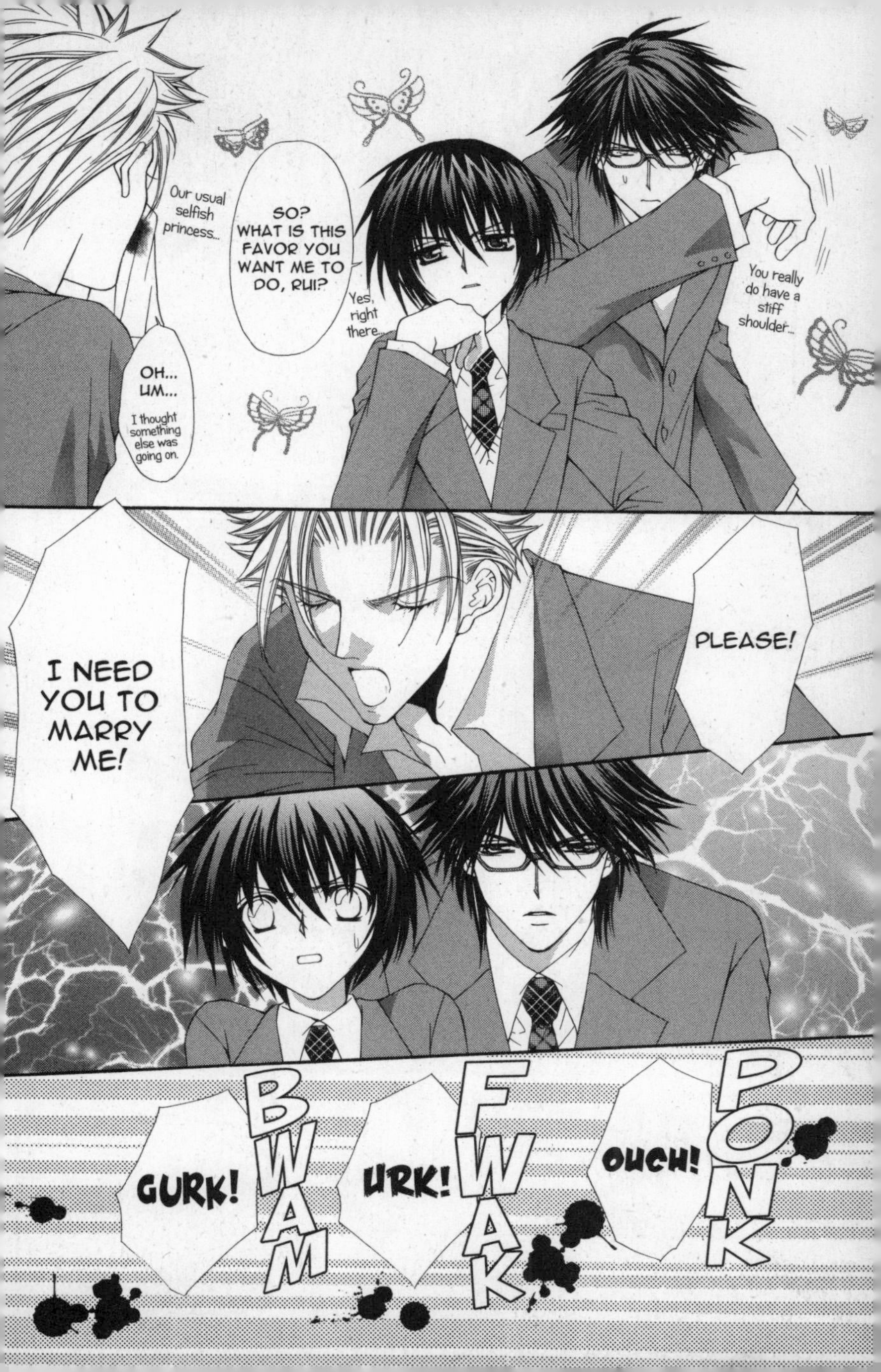
You really do have a stiff shoulder...
Yes, right there...
SO? WHAT IS THIS FAVOR YOU WANT ME TO DO, RUI?
Our usual selfish princess...
OH... UM...
I thought something else was going on.
PLEASE!
I NEED YOU TO MARRY ME!
PONK
OUCH!
FWAK
URK!
BWAM
GURK!

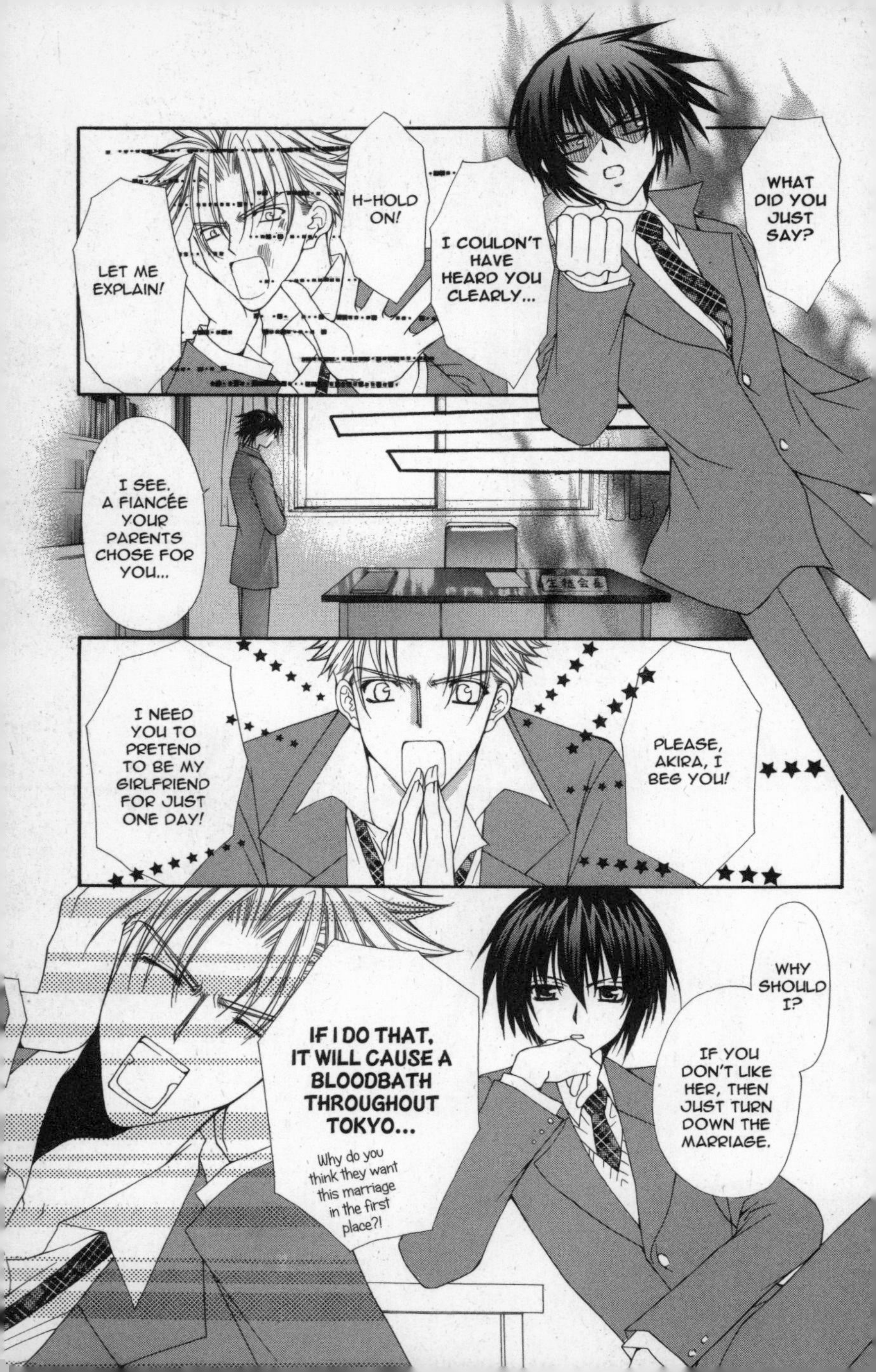
WHAT DID YOU JUST SAY?
I COULDN'T HAVE HEARD YOU CLEARLY...
H-HOLD ON!
LET ME EXPLAIN!
I SEE. A FIANCÉE YOUR PARENTS CHOSE FOR YOU...
PLEASE, AKIRA, I BEG YOU!
I NEED YOU TO PRETEND TO BE MY GIRLFRIEND FOR JUST ONE DAY!
WHY SHOULD I?
IF YOU DON'T LIKE HER, THEN JUST TURN DOWN THE MARRIAGE.
IF I DO THAT, IT WILL CAUSE A BLOODBATH THROUGHOUT TOKYO...
Why do you think they want this marriage in the first place?!

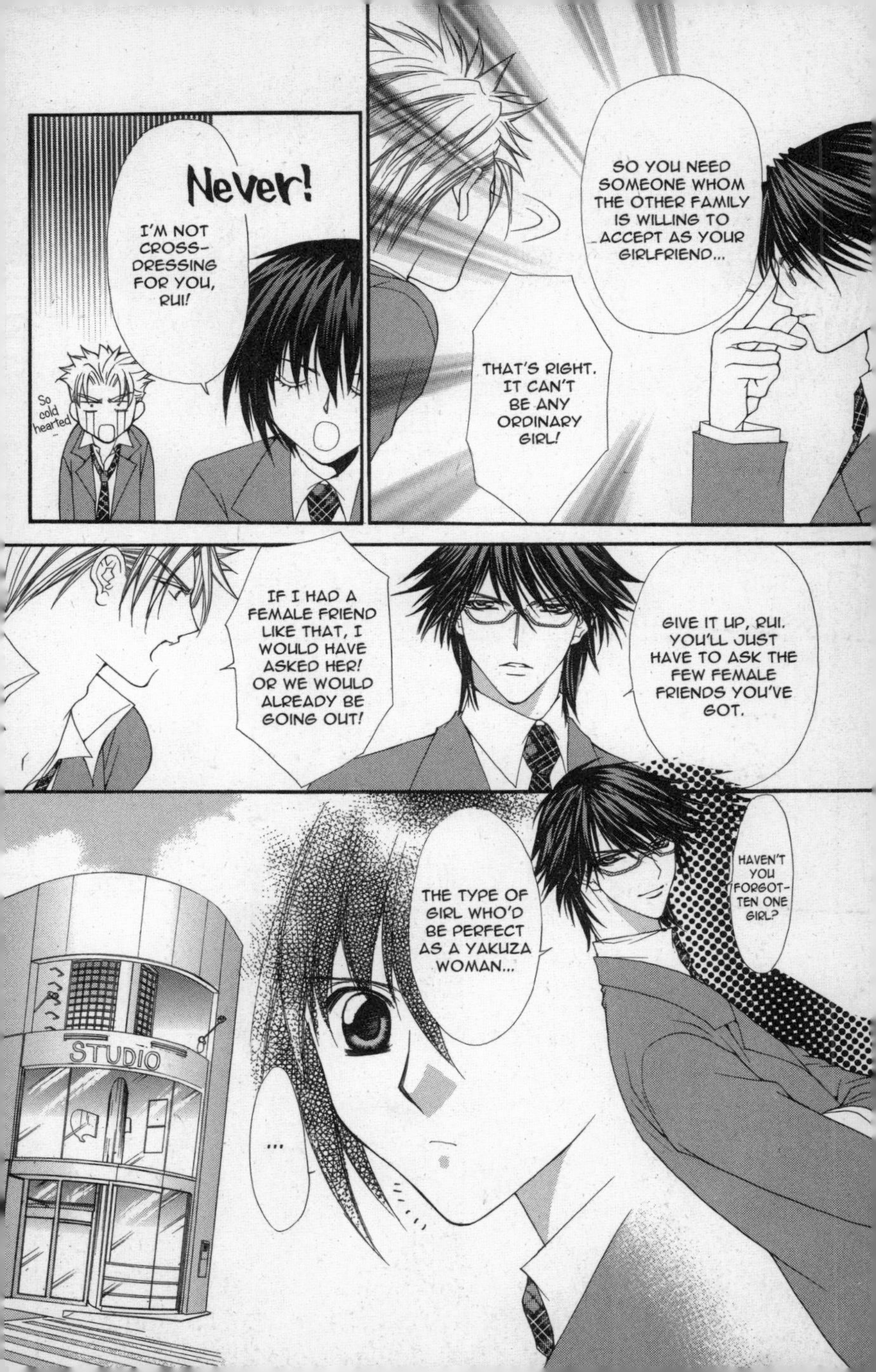
SO YOU NEED SOMEONE WHOM THE OTHER FAMILY IS WILLING TO ACCEPT AS YOUR GIRLFRIEND...
THAT'S RIGHT. IT CAN'T BE ANY ORDINARY GIRL!
Never!
I'M NOT CROSS-DRESSING FOR YOU, RUI!
So cold hearted...
GIVE IT UP, RUI. YOU'LL JUST HAVE TO ASK THE FEW FEMALE FRIENDS YOU'VE GOT.
IF I HAD A FEMALE FRIEND LIKE THAT, I WOULD HAVE ASKED HER! OR WE WOULD ALREADY BE GOING OUT!
HAVEN'T YOU FORGOT-TEN ONE GIRL?
THE TYPE OF GIRL WHO'D BE PERFECT AS A YAKUZA WOMAN...
...
STUDIO

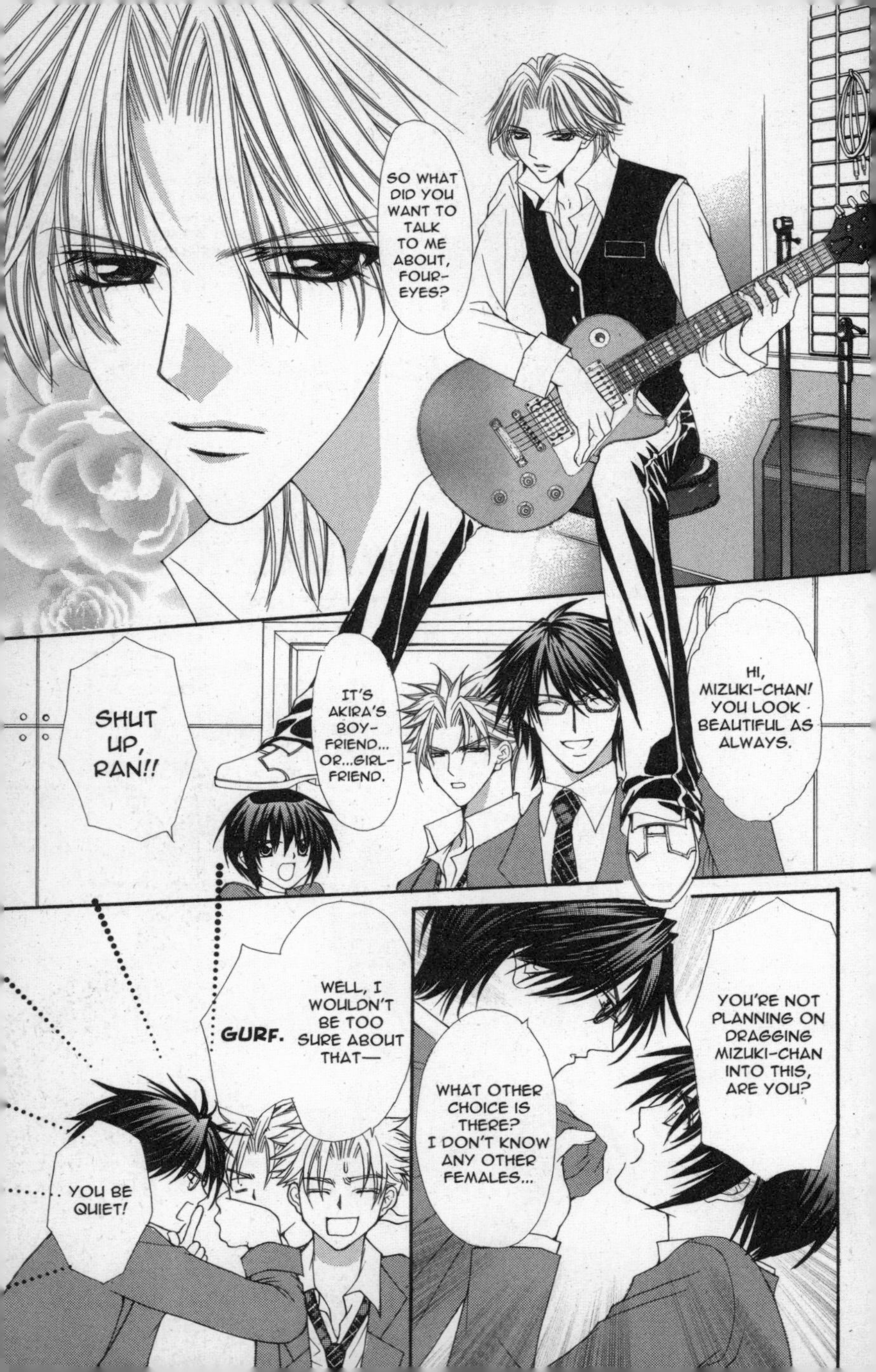
SO WHAT DID YOU WANT TO TALK TO ME ABOUT, FOUR-EYES?
HI, MIZUKI-CHAN! YOU LOOK BEAUTIFUL AS ALWAYS.
IT'S AKIRA'S BOY-FRIEND... OR...GIRL-FRIEND.
SHUT UP, RAN!!
YOU'RE NOT PLANNING ON DRAGGING MIZUKI-CHAN INTO THIS, ARE YOU?
WHAT OTHER CHOICE IS THERE? I DON'T KNOW ANY OTHER FEMALES...
WELL, I WOULDN'T BE TOO SURE ABOUT THAT—
GURF.
YOU BE QUIET!

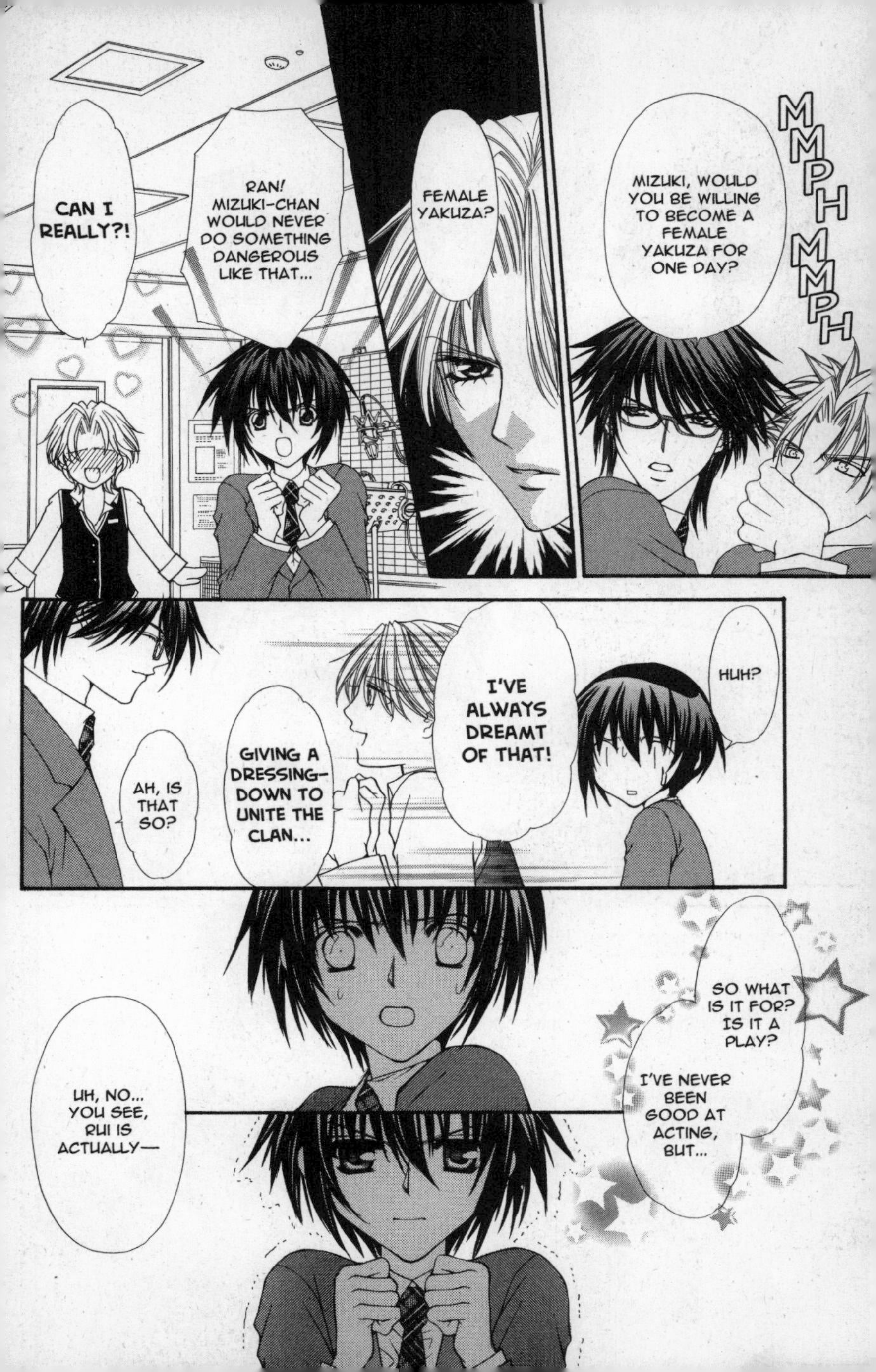
MMPH MMPH
MIZUKI, WOULD YOU BE WILLING TO BECOME A FEMALE YAKUZA FOR ONE DAY?
FEMALE YAKUZA?
RAN! MIZUKI-CHAN WOULD NEVER DO SOMETHING DANGEROUS LIKE THAT...
CAN I REALLY?!
HUH?
I'VE ALWAYS DREAMT OF THAT!
GIVING A DRESSING-DOWN TO UNITE THE CLAN...
AH, IS THAT SO?
SO WHAT IS IT FOR? IS IT A PLAY?
I'VE NEVER BEEN GOOD AT ACTING, BUT...
UH, NO... YOU SEE, RUI IS ACTUALLY—

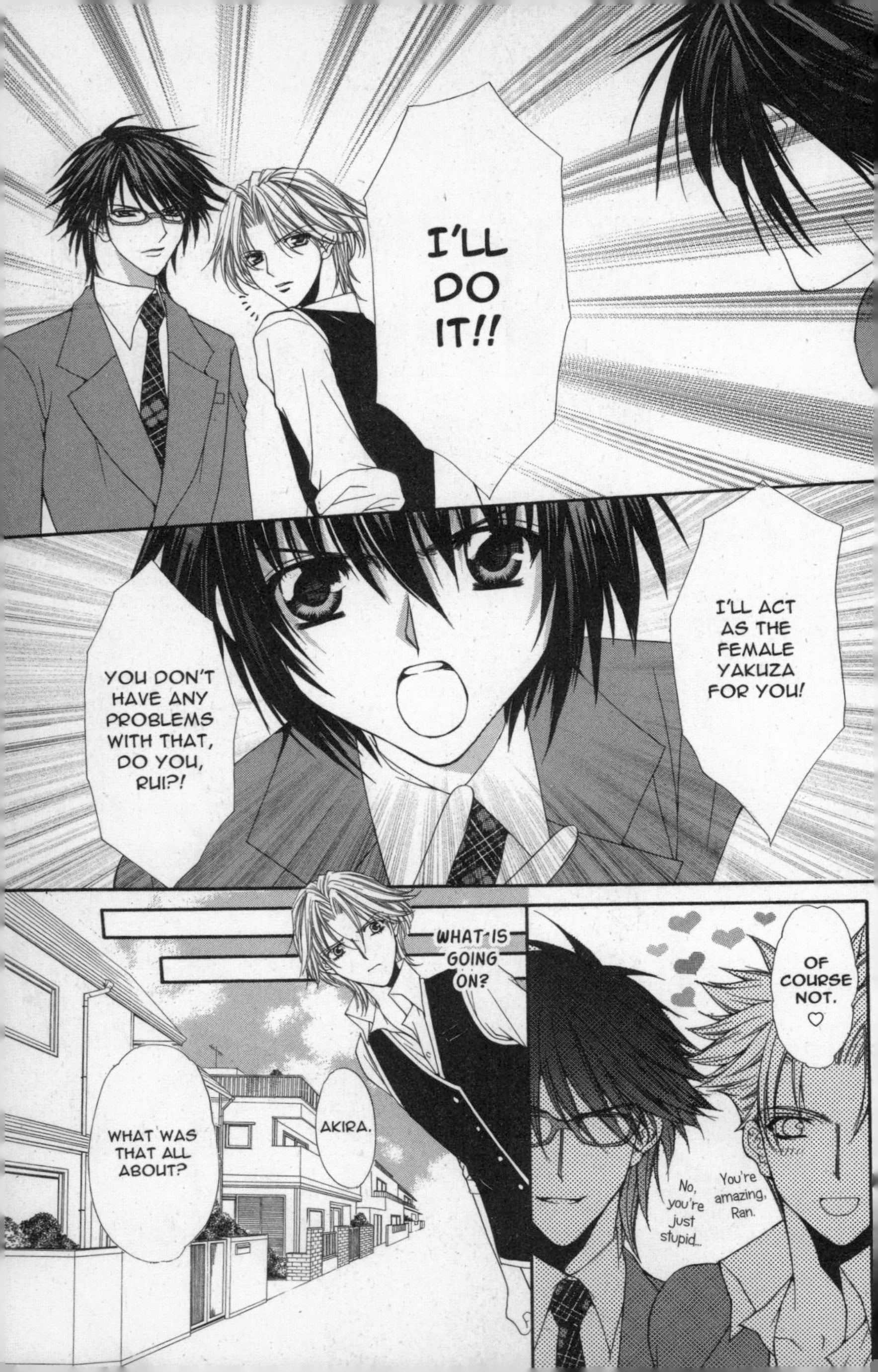
I'LL DO IT!!
I'LL ACT AS THE FEMALE YAKUZA FOR YOU!
YOU DON'T HAVE ANY PROBLEMS WITH THAT, DO YOU, RUI?!
OF COURSE NOT. ♡
You're amazing, Ran.
No, you're just stupid...
WHAT IS GOING ON?
AKIRA.
WHAT WAS THAT ALL ABOUT?

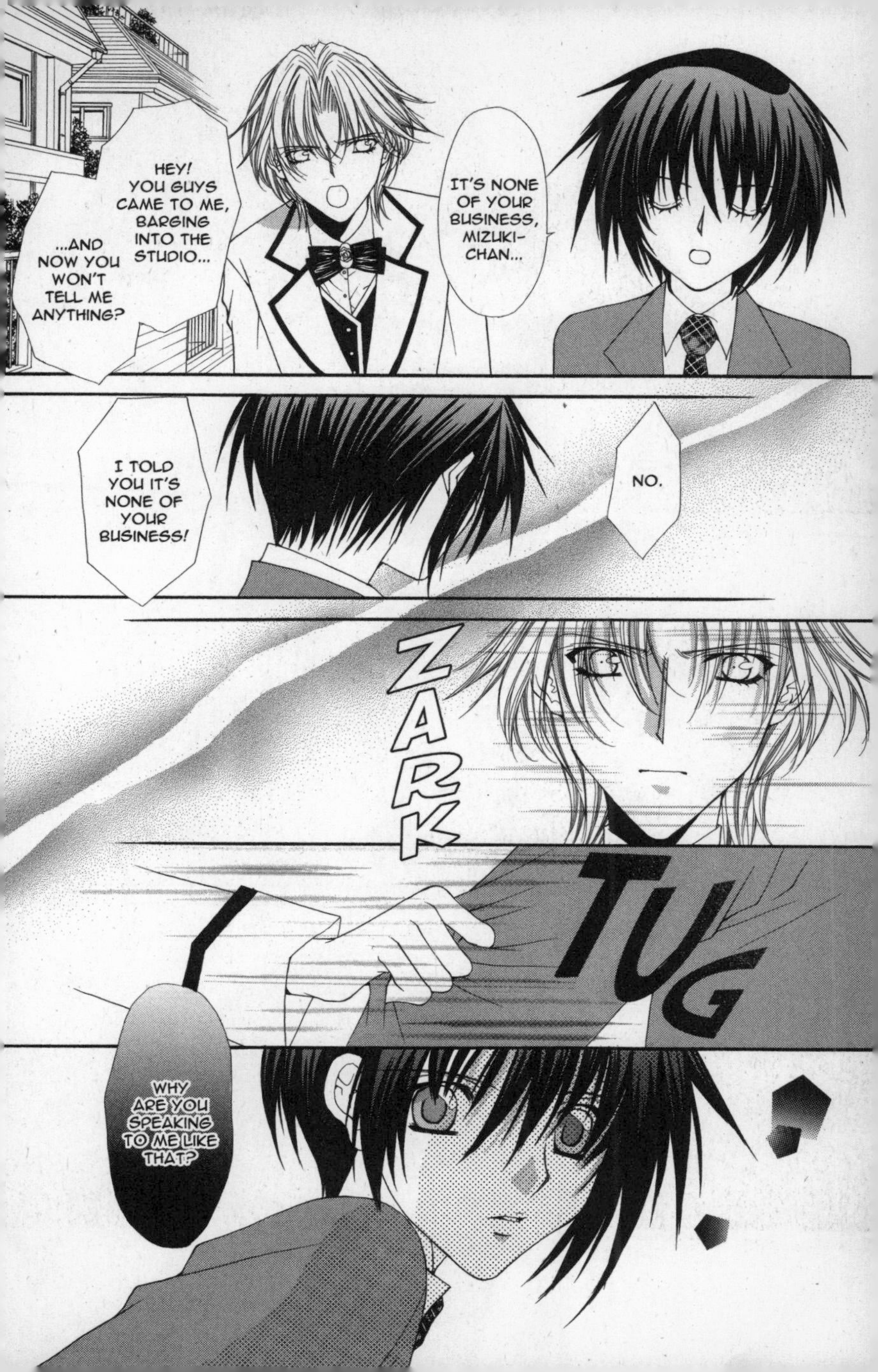
IT'S NONE OF YOUR BUSINESS, MIZUKI-CHAN...
HEY! YOU GUYS CAME TO ME, BARGING INTO THE STUDIO...
...AND NOW YOU WON'T TELL ME ANYTHING?
NO.
I TOLD YOU IT'S NONE OF YOUR BUSINESS!
ZARK
TUG
WHY ARE YOU SPEAKING TO ME LIKE THAT?

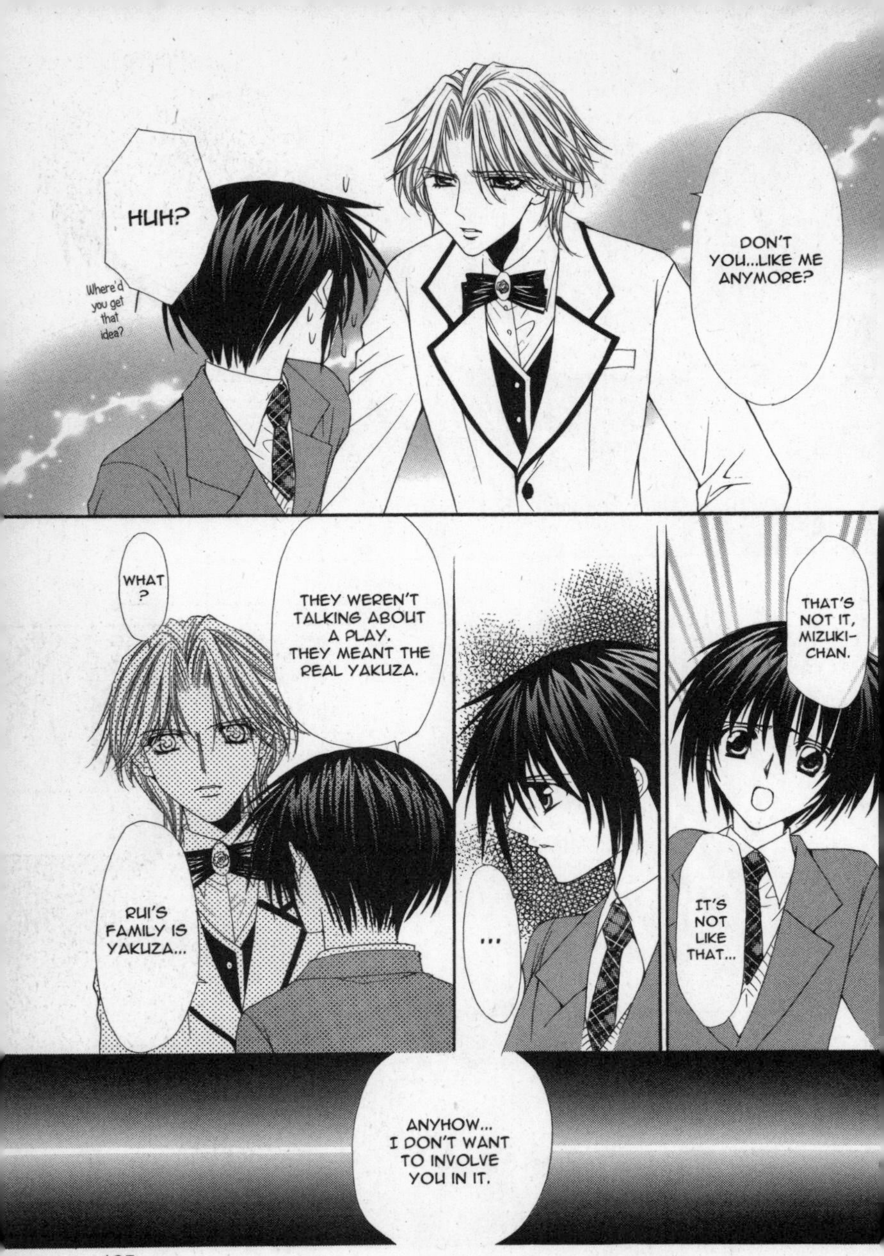
DON'T YOU...LIKE ME ANYMORE?
HUH?
Where'd you get that idea?
THAT'S NOT IT, MIZUKI-CHAN.
IT'S NOT LIKE THAT...
...
THEY WEREN'T TALKING ABOUT A PLAY. THEY MEANT THE REAL YAKUZA.
WHAT?
RUI'S FAMILY IS YAKUZA...
ANYHOW... I DON'T WANT TO INVOLVE YOU IN IT.

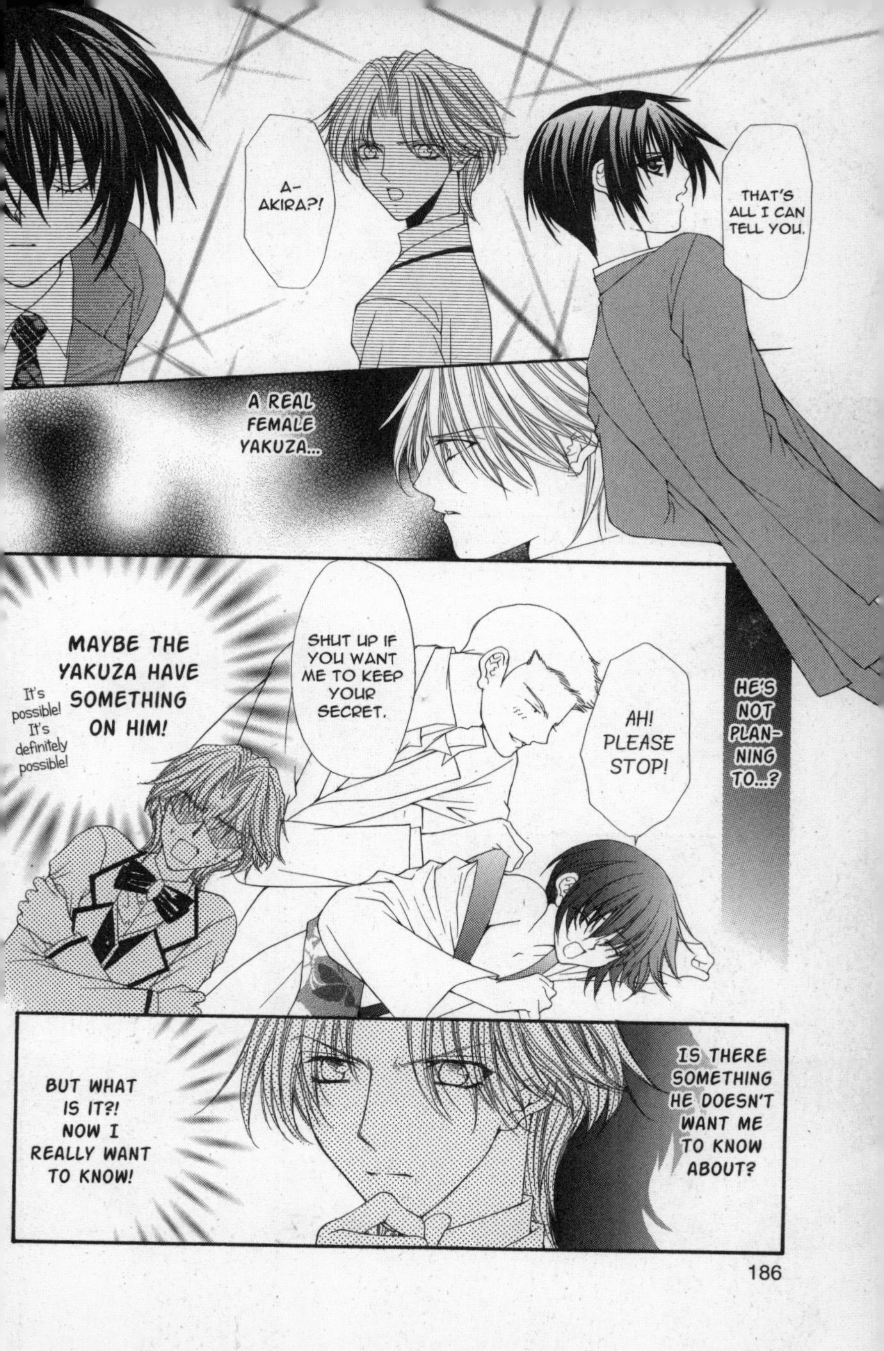
THAT'S ALL I CAN TELL YOU.
A- AKIRA?!
A REAL FEMALE YAKUZA...
HE'S NOT PLAN-NING TO...?
AH! PLEASE STOP!
SHUT UP IF YOU WANT ME TO KEEP YOUR SECRET.
MAYBE THE YAKUZA HAVE SOMETHING ON HIM!
It's possible! It's definitely possible!
IS THERE SOMETHING HE DOESN'T WANT ME TO KNOW ABOUT?
BUT WHAT IS IT?! NOW I REALLY WANT TO KNOW!

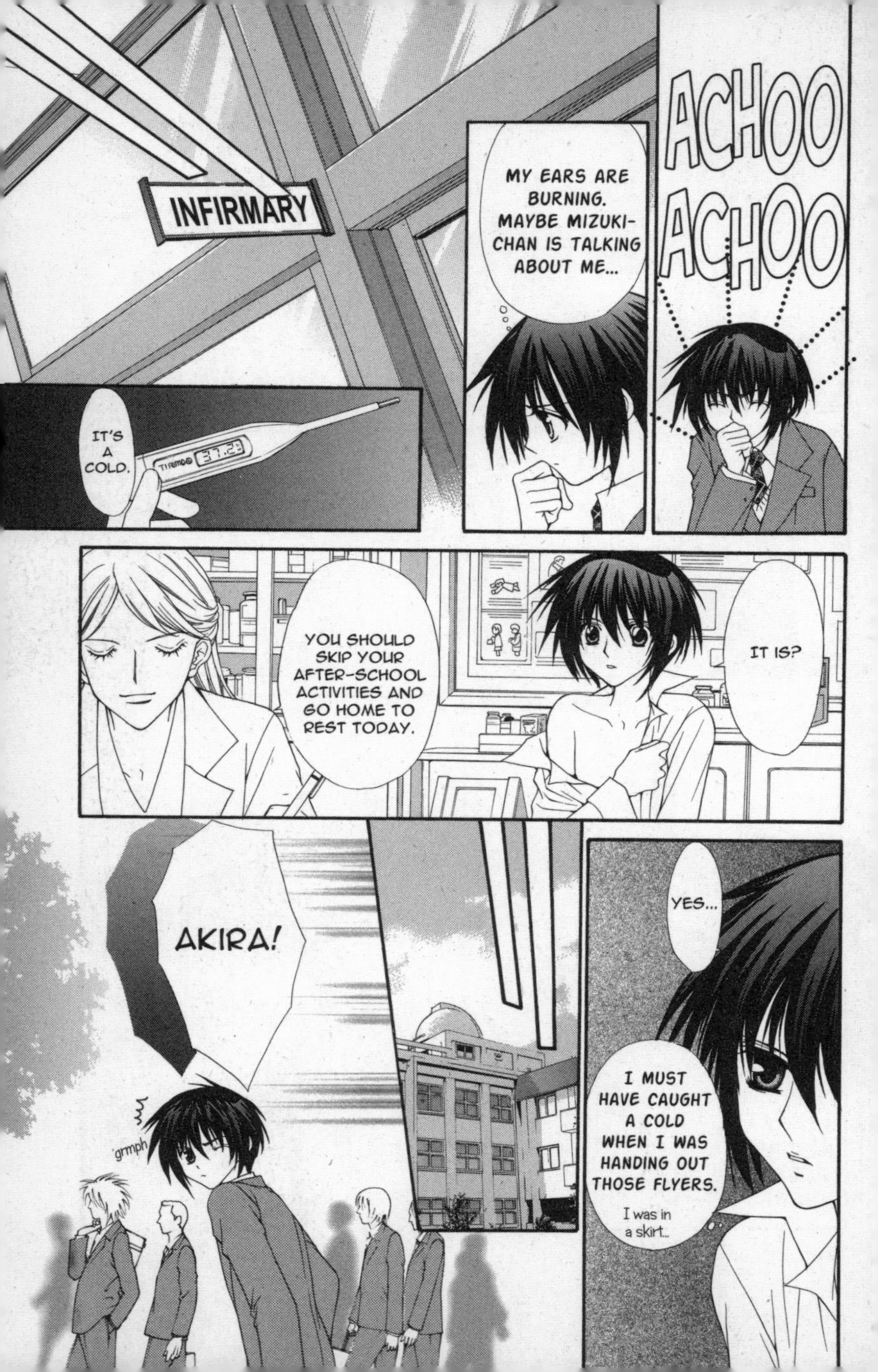
ACHOO ACHOO
MY EARS ARE BURNING. MAYBE MIZUKI-CHAN IS TALKING ABOUT ME...
INFIRMARY
IT'S A COLD.
IT IS?
YOU SHOULD SKIP YOUR AFTER-SCHOOL ACTIVITIES AND GO HOME TO REST TODAY.
YES...
I MUST HAVE CAUGHT A COLD WHEN I WAS HANDING OUT THOSE FLYERS.
I was in a skirt...
AKIRA!
grmph

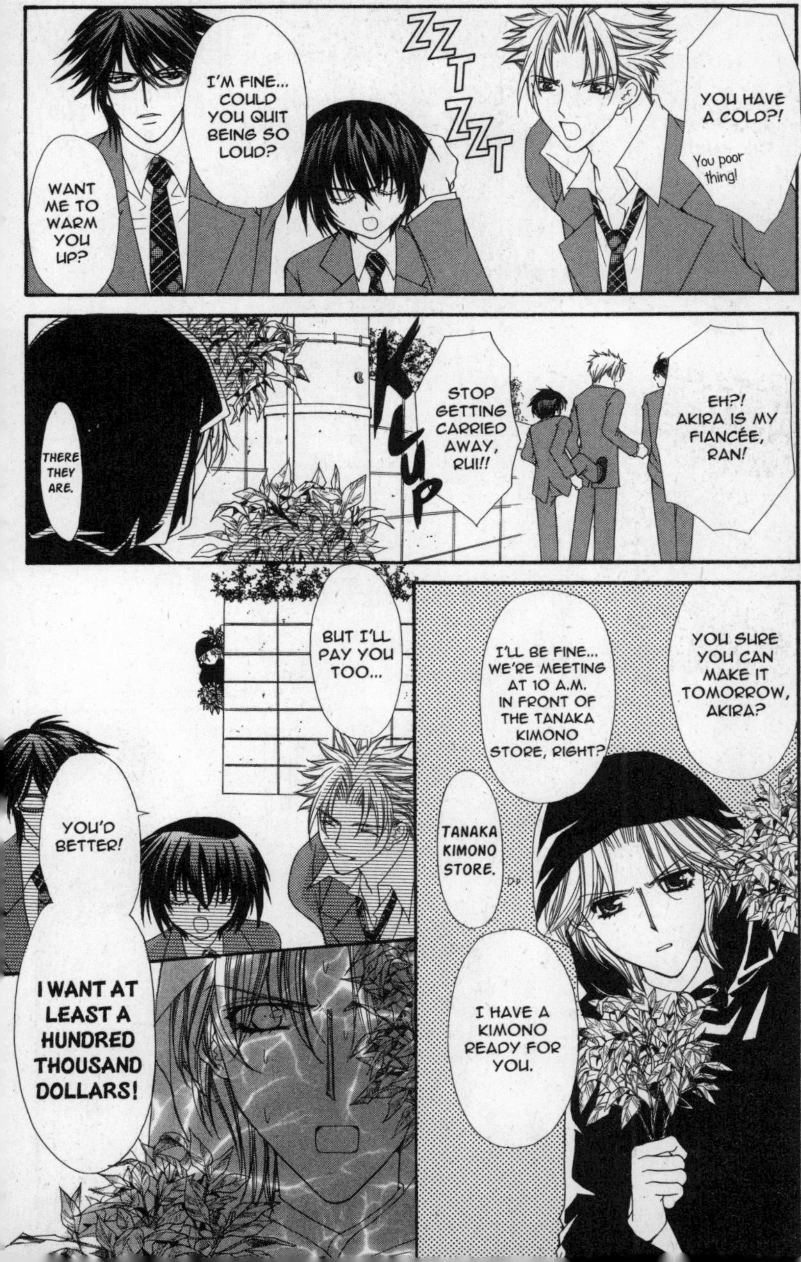
YOU HAVE A COLD?!
You poor thing!
ZZZT ZZZT
I'M FINE... COULD YOU QUIT BEING SO LOUD?
WANT ME TO WARM YOU UP?
EH?! AKIRA IS MY FIANCÉE, RAN!
STOP GETTING CARRIED AWAY, RUI!!
KLUP
THERE THEY ARE.
YOU SURE YOU CAN MAKE IT TOMORROW, AKIRA?
I'LL BE FINE... WE'RE MEETING AT 10 A.M. IN FRONT OF THE TANAKA KIMONO STORE, RIGHT?
TANAKA KIMONO STORE.
I HAVE A KIMONO READY FOR YOU.
BUT I'LL PAY YOU TOO...
YOU'D BETTER!
I WANT AT LEAST A HUNDRED THOUSAND DOLLARS!

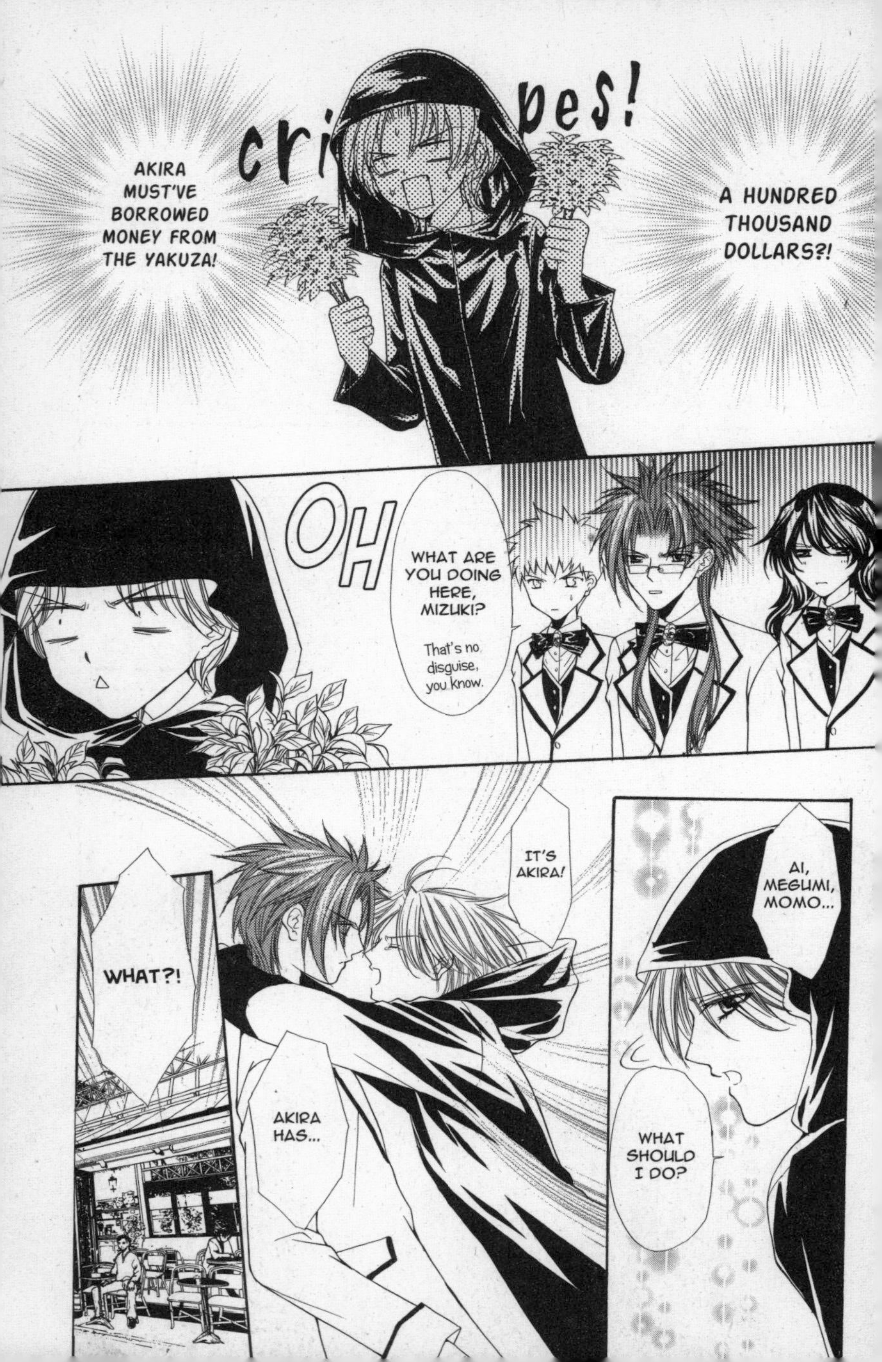
A HUNDRED THOUSAND DOLLARS?!
cri pes!
AKIRA MUST'VE BORROWED MONEY FROM THE YAKUZA!
WHAT ARE YOU DOING HERE, MIZUKI?
That's no disguise, you know.
OH
AI, MEGUMI, MOMO...
WHAT SHOULD I DO?
IT'S AKIRA!
AKIRA HAS...
WHAT?!

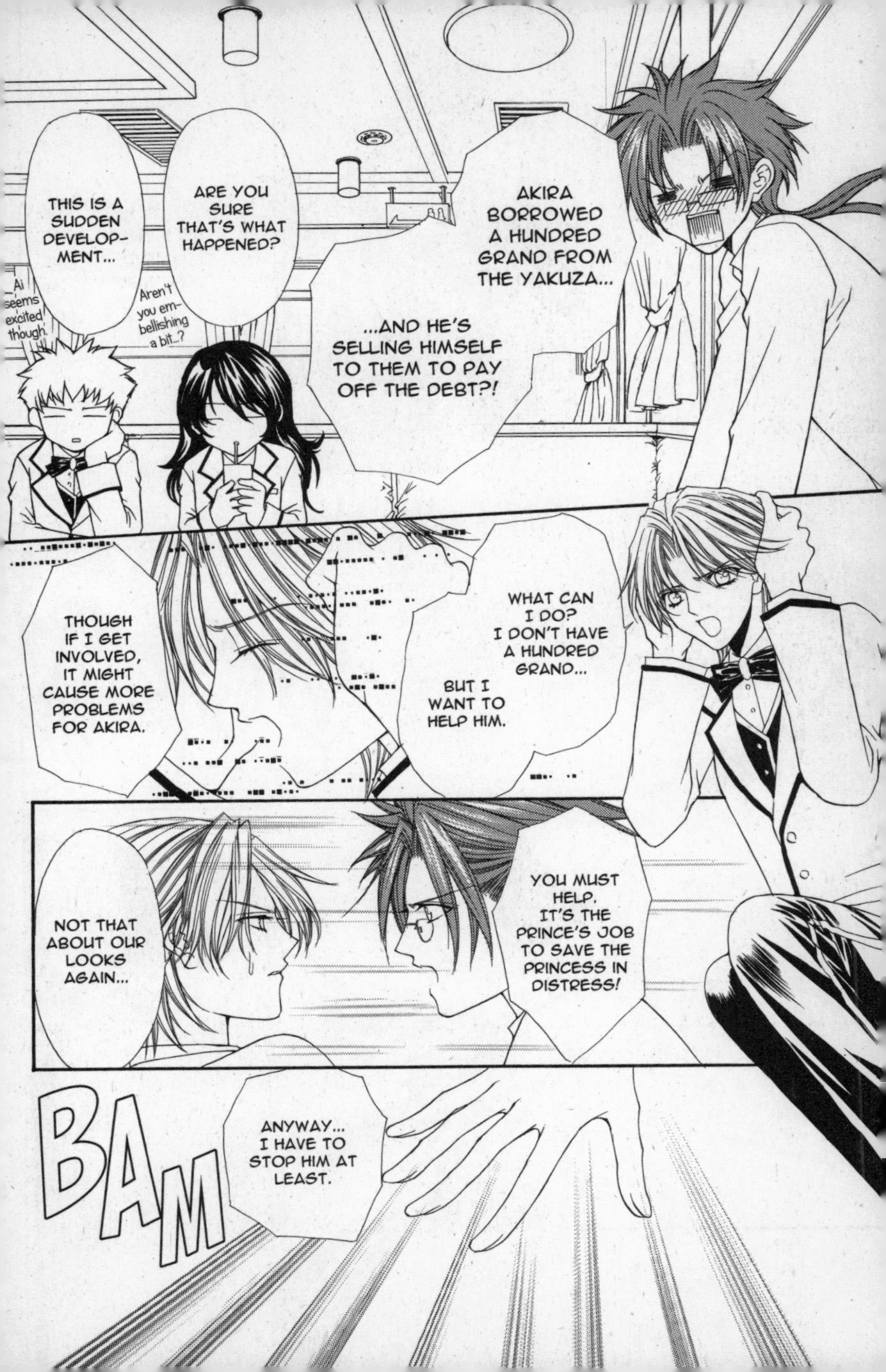
AKIRA BORROWED A HUNDRED GRAND FROM THE YAKUZA...
...AND HE'S SELLING HIMSELF TO THEM TO PAY OFF THE DEBT?!
ARE YOU SURE THAT'S WHAT HAPPENED?
Aren't you embellishing a bit..?
THIS IS A SUDDEN DEVELOPMENT...
Ai seems excited though.
WHAT CAN I DO? I DON'T HAVE A HUNDRED GRAND...
BUT I WANT TO HELP HIM.
THOUGH IF I GET INVOLVED, IT MIGHT CAUSE MORE PROBLEMS FOR AKIRA.
YOU MUST HELP. IT'S THE PRINCE'S JOB TO SAVE THE PRINCESS IN DISTRESS!
NOT THAT ABOUT OUR LOOKS AGAIN...
ANYWAY... I HAVE TO STOP HIM AT LEAST.
BAM

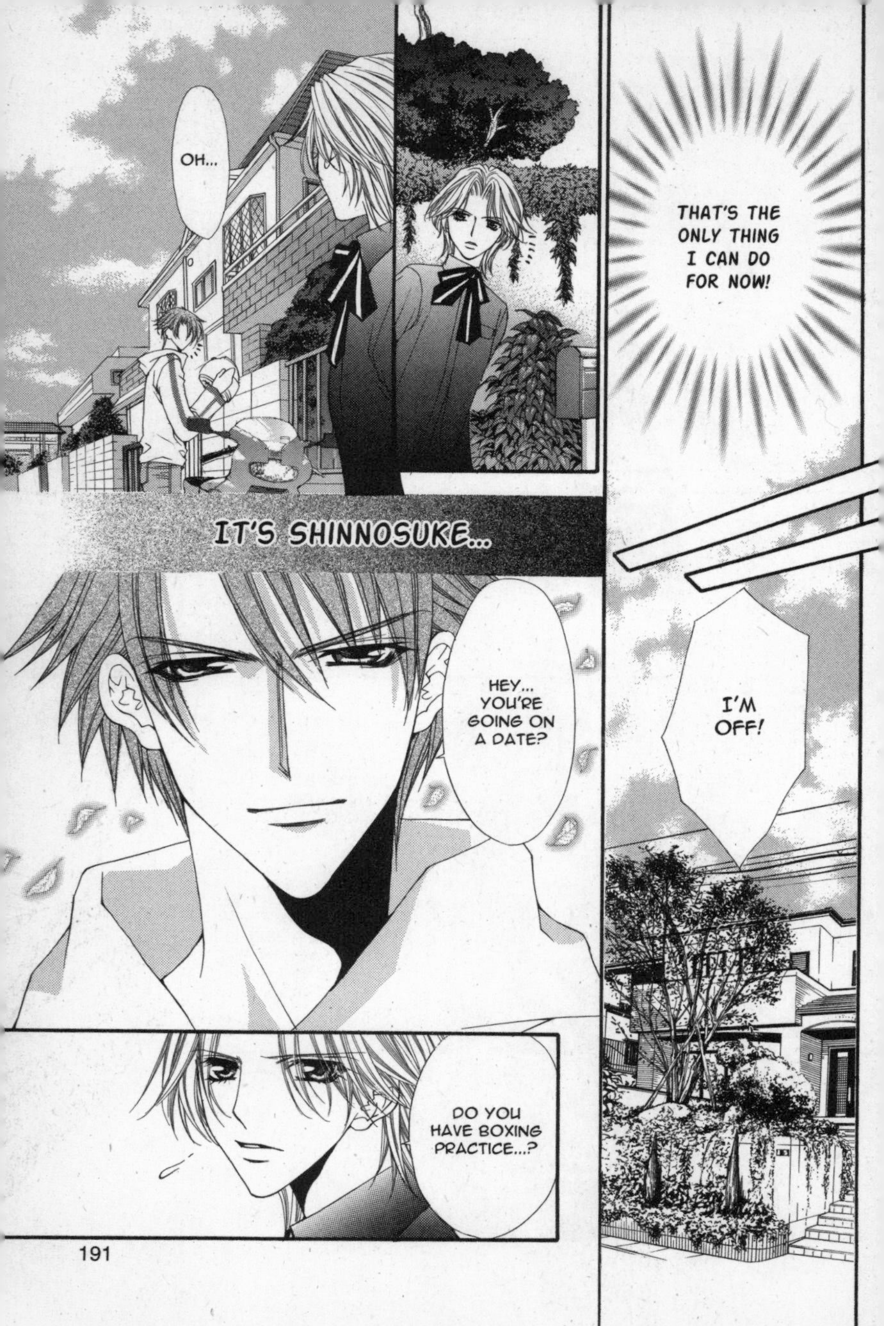
THAT'S THE ONLY THING I CAN DO FOR NOW!
I'M OFF!
OH...
IT'S SHINNOSUKE...
HEY... YOU'RE GOING ON A DATE?
DO YOU HAVE BOXING PRACTICE...?

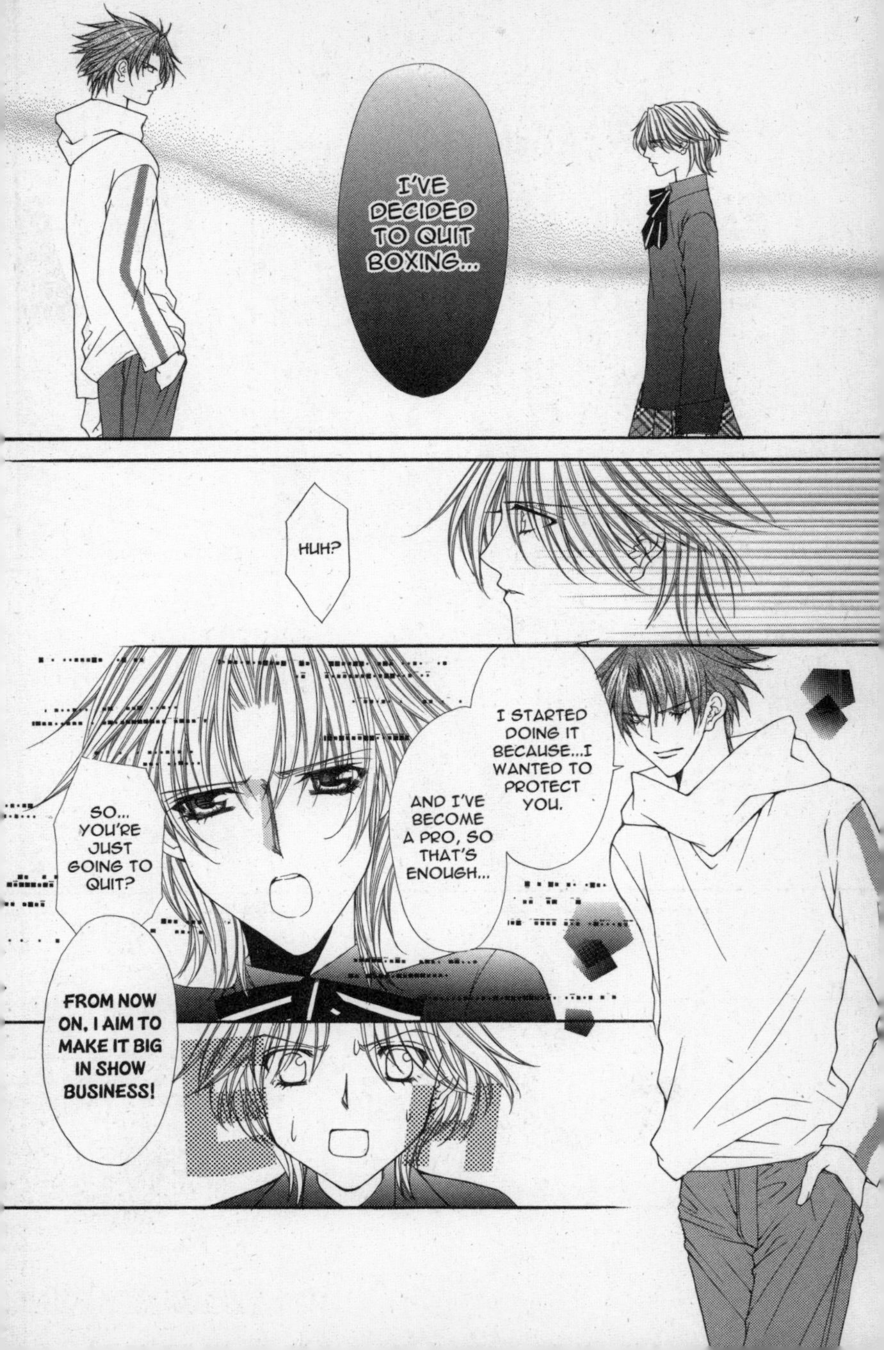
I'VE DECIDED TO QUIT BOXING...
HUH?
I STARTED DOING IT BECAUSE...I WANTED TO PROTECT YOU.
AND I'VE BECOME A PRO, SO THAT'S ENOUGH...
SO... YOU'RE JUST GOING TO QUIT?
FROM NOW ON, I AIM TO MAKE IT BIG IN SHOW BUSINESS!

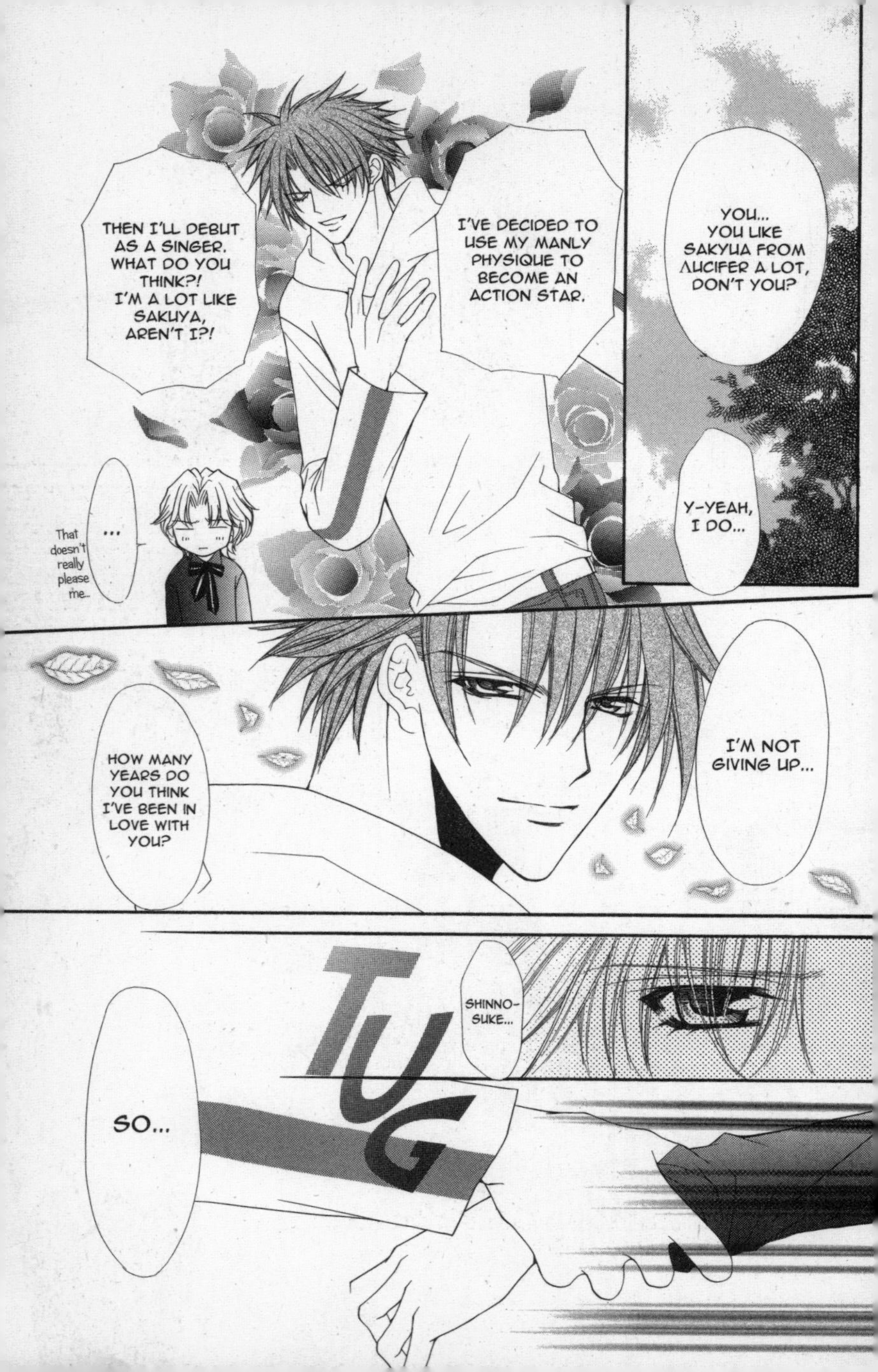
YOU... YOU LIKE SAKYUA FROM ΛUCIFER A LOT, DON'T YOU?
Y-YEAH, I DO...
I'VE DECIDED TO USE MY MANLY PHYSIQUE TO BECOME AN ACTION STAR.
THEN I'LL DEBUT AS A SINGER. WHAT DO YOU THINK?! I'M A LOT LIKE SAKUYA, AREN'T I?!
...
That doesn't really please me..
I'M NOT GIVING UP...
HOW MANY YEARS DO YOU THINK I'VE BEEN IN LOVE WITH YOU?
SHINNO-SUKE...
TUG
SO...

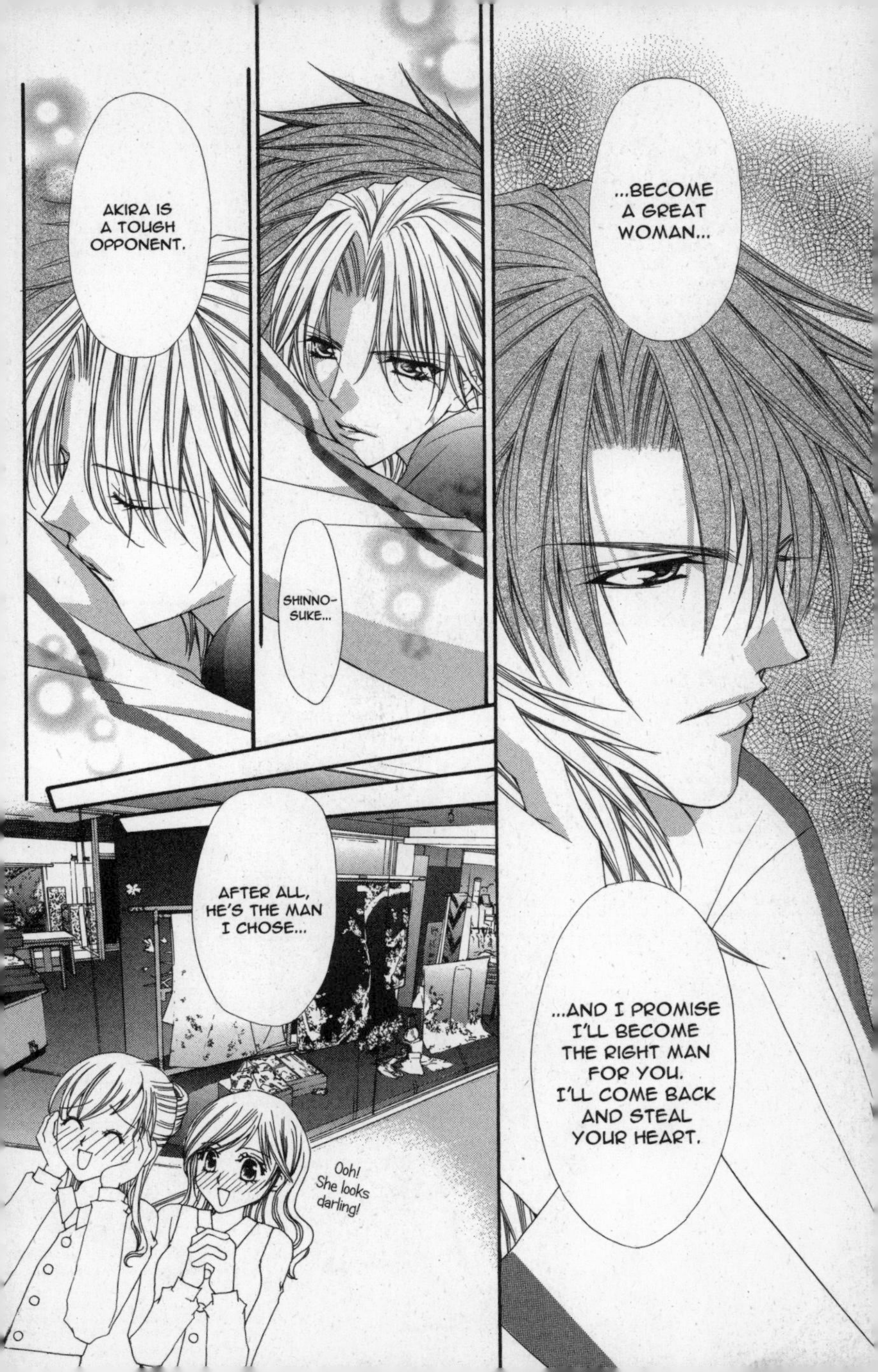
...BECOME A GREAT WOMAN...
...AND I PROMISE I'LL BECOME THE RIGHT MAN FOR YOU. I'LL COME BACK AND STEAL YOUR HEART.
SHINNO-SUKE...
AKIRA IS A TOUGH OPPONENT.
AFTER ALL, HE'S THE MAN I CHOSE...
Ooh! She looks darling!

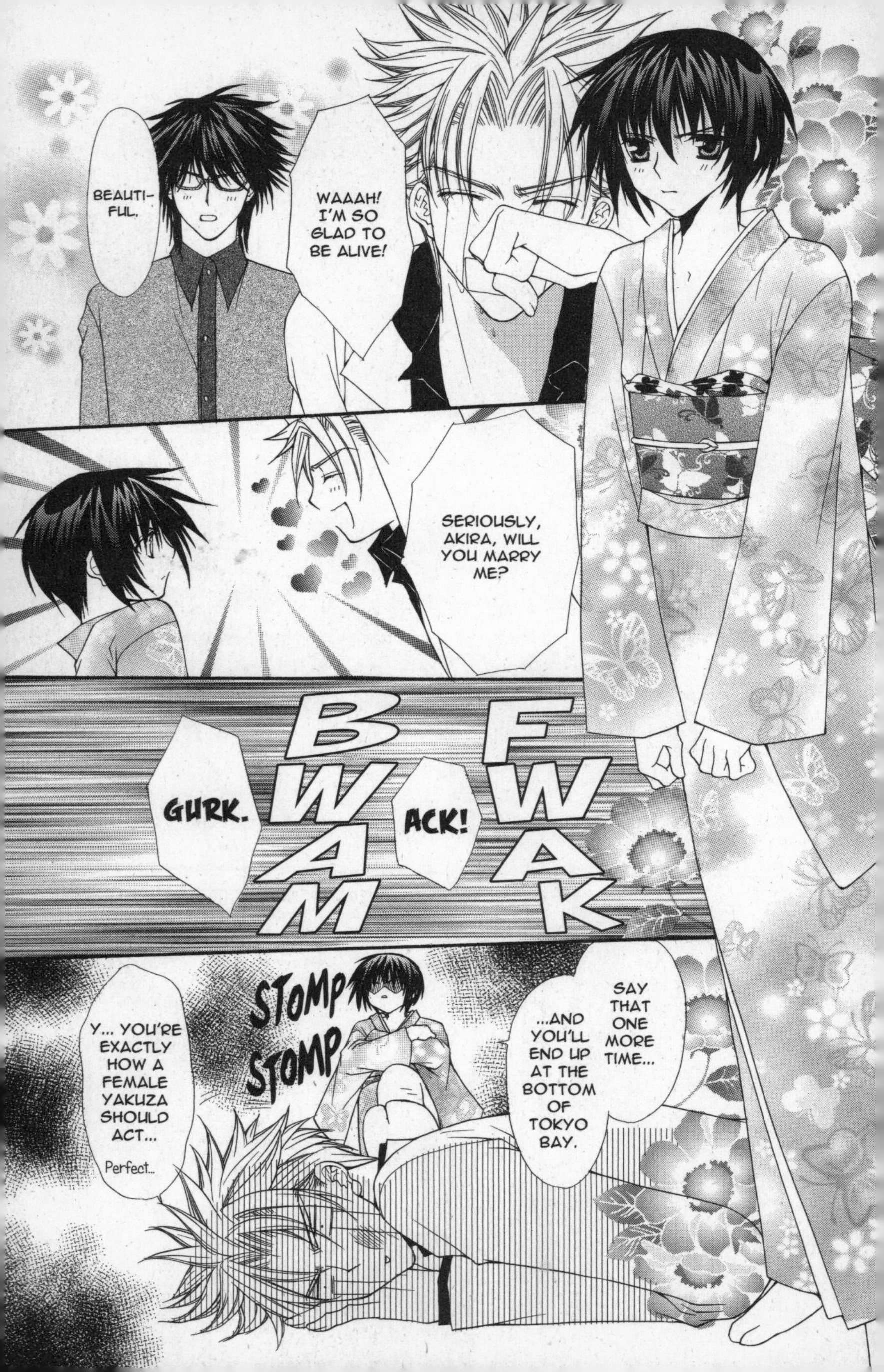
WAAAH! I'M SO GLAD TO BE ALIVE!
BEAUTI-FUL.
SERIOUSLY, AKIRA, WILL YOU MARRY ME?
FWAK
ACK!
BWAM
GURK.
SAY THAT ONE MORE TIME...
...AND YOU'LL END UP AT THE BOTTOM OF TOKYO BAY.
STOMP STOMP
Y... YOU'RE EXACTLY HOW A FEMALE YAKUZA SHOULD ACT...
Perfect...

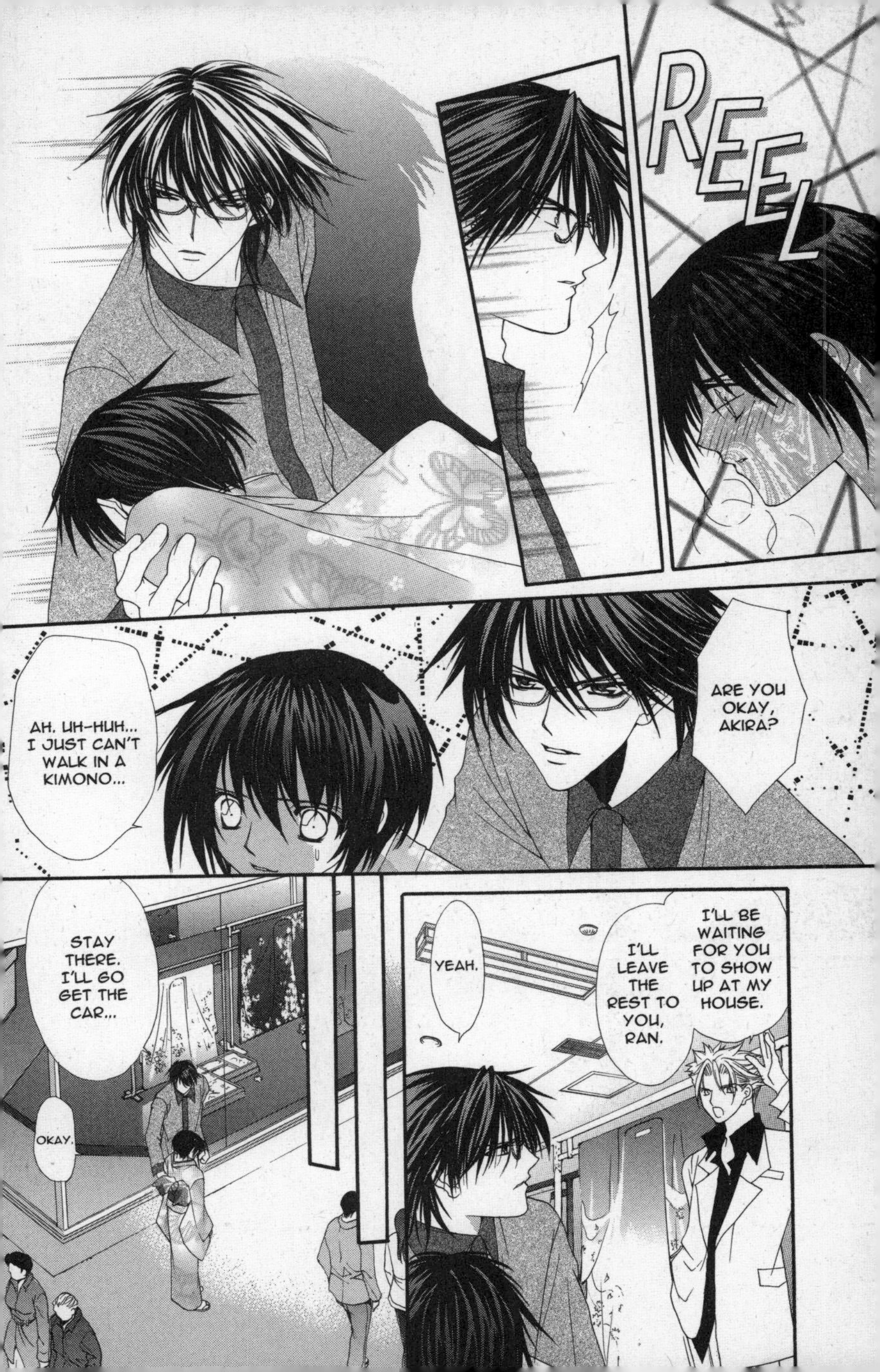
REEL
ARE YOU OKAY, AKIRA?
AH, UH-HUH... I JUST CAN'T WALK IN A KIMONO...
I'LL BE WAITING FOR YOU TO SHOW UP AT MY HOUSE.
I'LL LEAVE THE REST TO YOU, RAN.
YEAH.
STAY THERE. I'LL GO GET THE CAR...
OKAY.

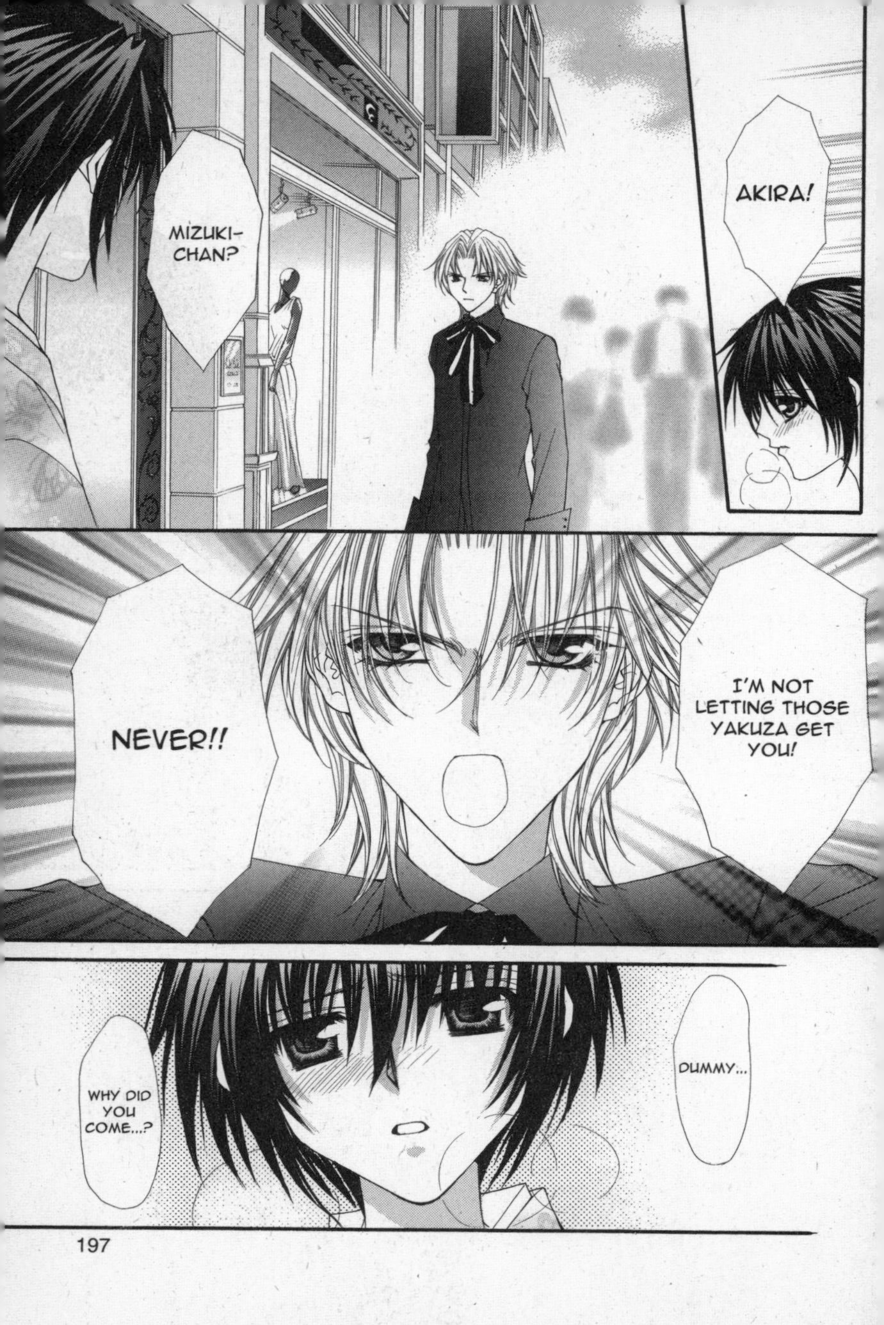
AKIRA!
MIZUKI-CHAN?
I'M NOT LETTING THOSE YAKUZA GET YOU!
NEVER!!
DUMMY...
WHY DID YOU COME...?

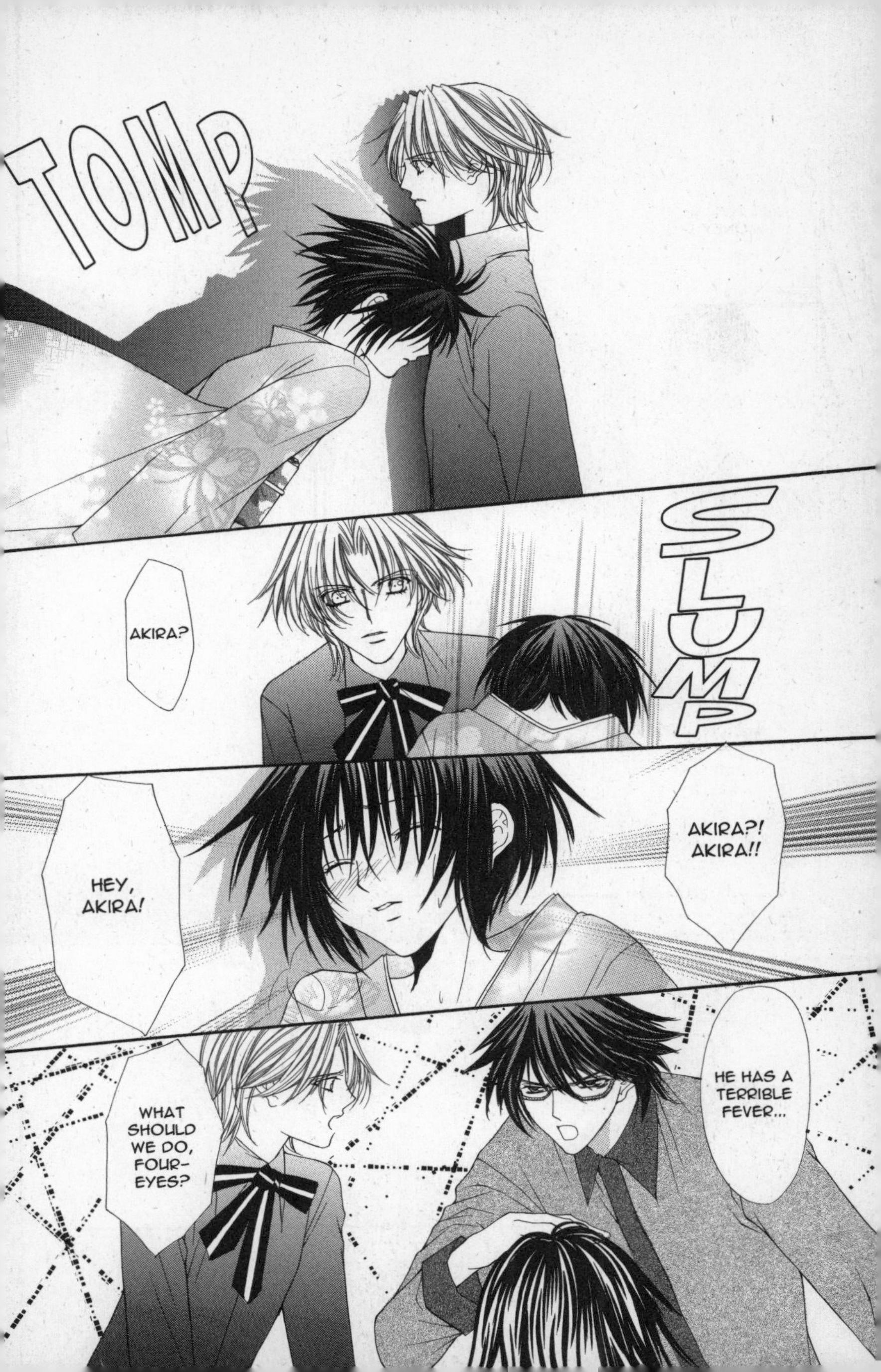
TOMP
SLUMP
AKIRA?
AKIRA?! AKIRA!!
HEY, AKIRA!
HE HAS A TERRIBLE FEVER...
WHAT SHOULD WE DO, FOUR-EYES?

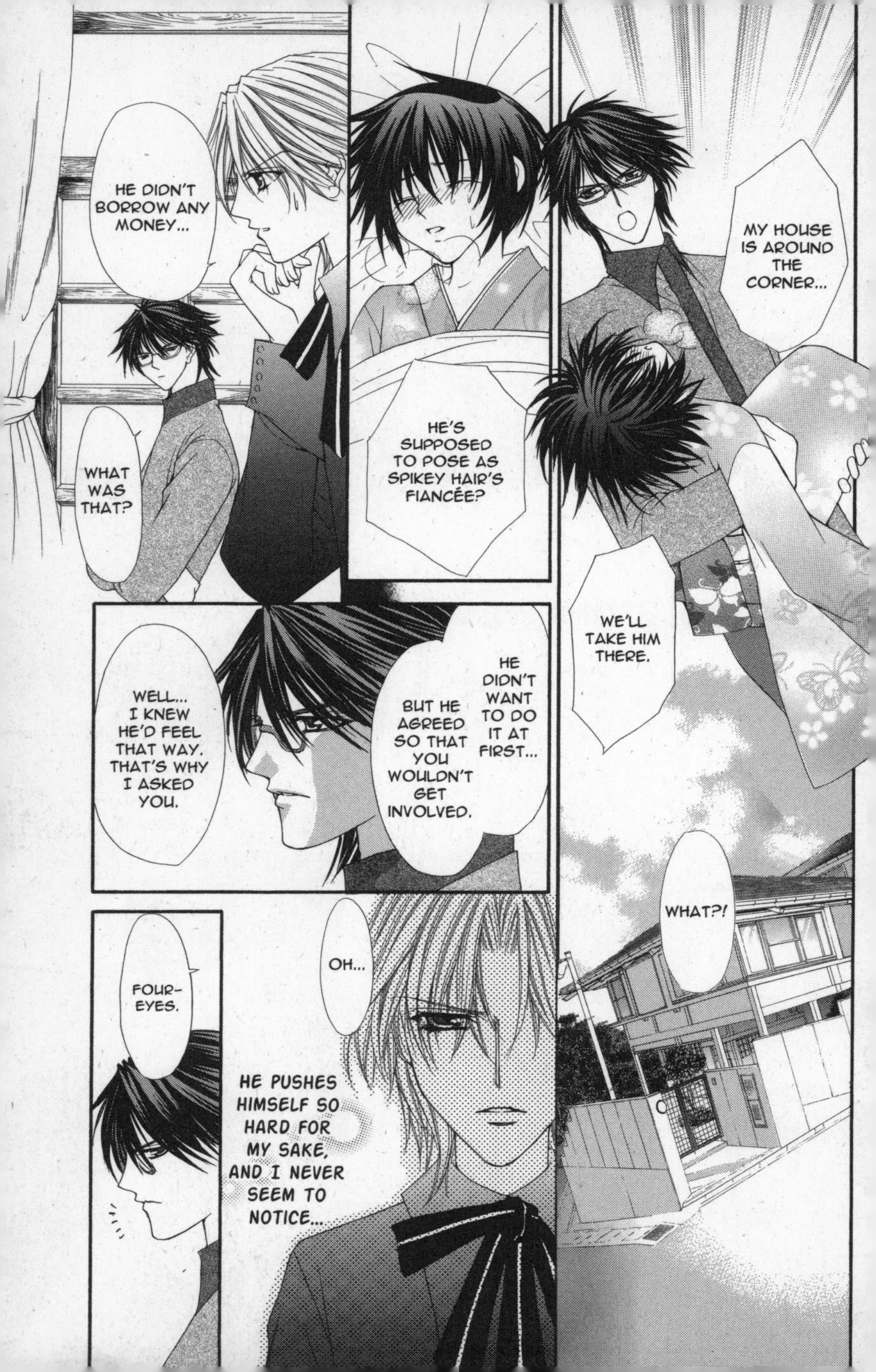
MY HOUSE IS AROUND THE CORNER...
WE'LL TAKE HIM THERE.
WHAT?!
HE'S SUPPOSED TO POSE AS SPIKEY HAIR'S FIANCÉE?
HE DIDN'T BORROW ANY MONEY...
WHAT WAS THAT?
HE DIDN'T WANT TO DO IT AT FIRST...
BUT HE AGREED SO THAT YOU WOULDN'T GET INVOLVED.
WELL... I KNEW HE'D FEEL THAT WAY. THAT'S WHY I ASKED YOU.
OH...
HE PUSHES HIMSELF SO HARD FOR MY SAKE, AND I NEVER SEEM TO NOTICE...
FOUR-EYES.

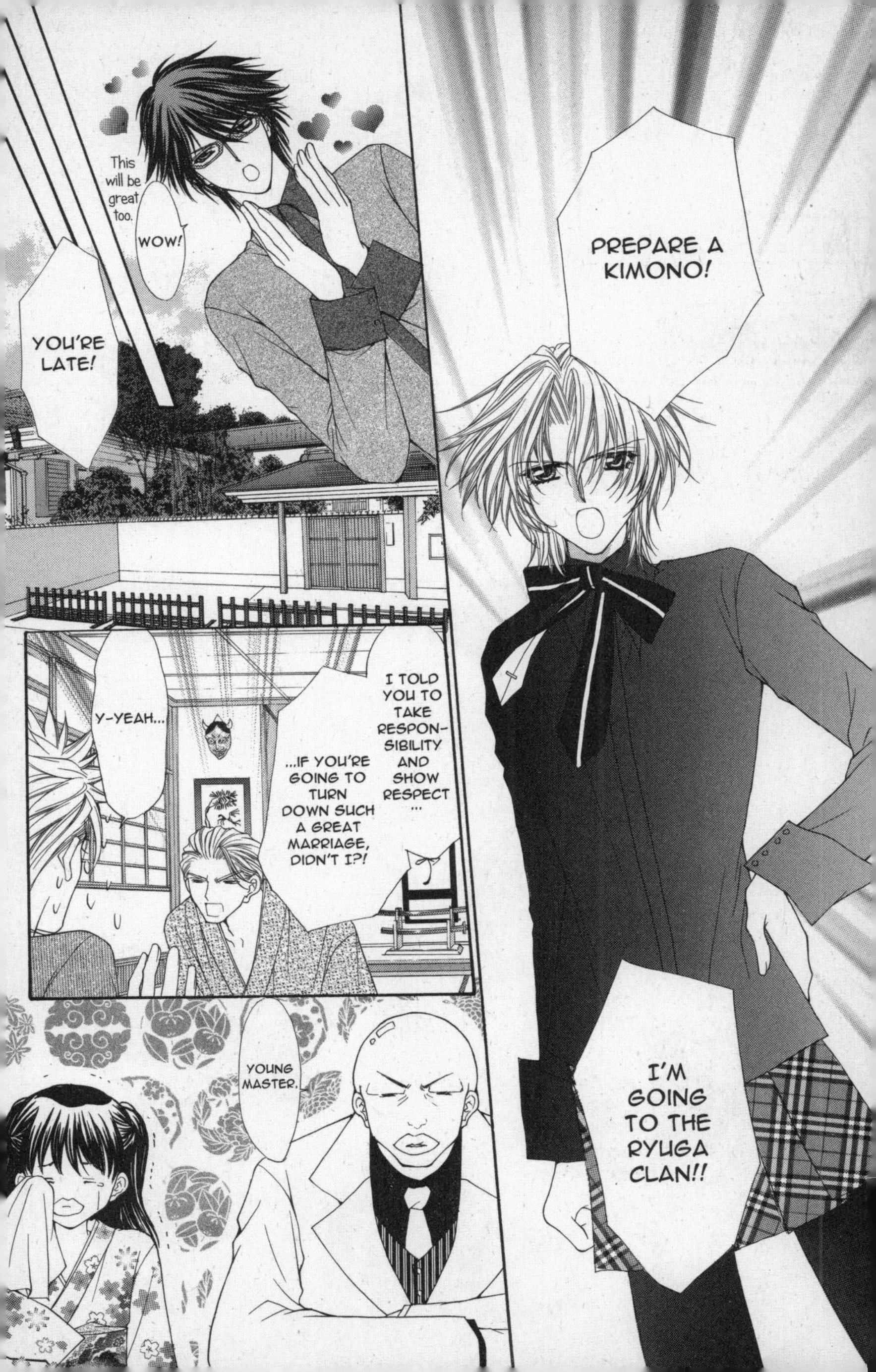
PREPARE A KIMONO!
I'M GOING TO THE RYUGA CLAN!!
WOW!
This will be great too.
YOU'RE LATE!
I TOLD YOU TO TAKE RESPONSIBILITY AND SHOW RESPECT ...
...IF YOU'RE GOING TO TURN DOWN SUCH A GREAT MARRIAGE, DIDN'T I?!
Y-YEAH...
YOUNG MASTER.

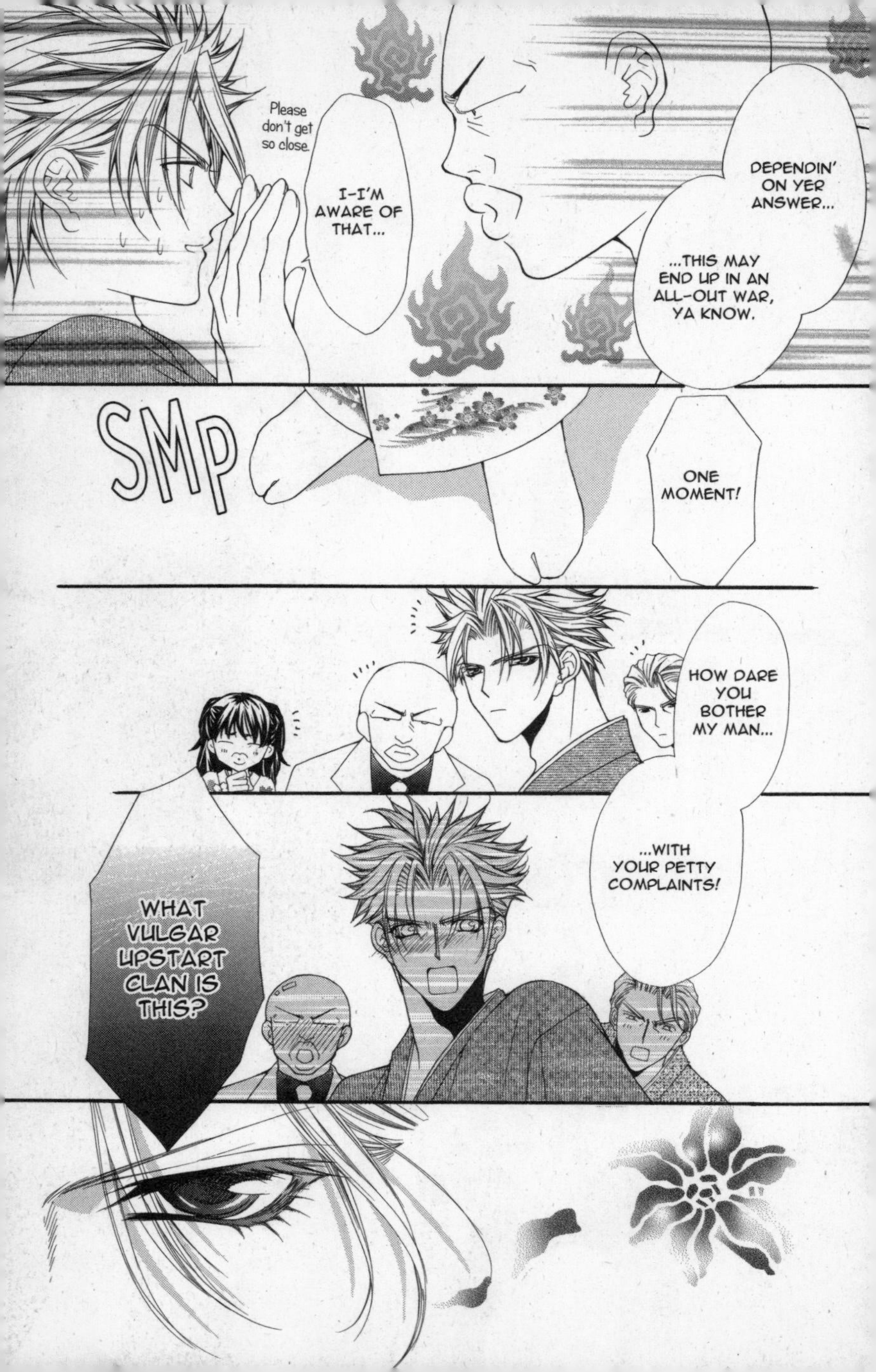
DEPENDIN' ON YER ANSWER...
...THIS MAY END UP IN AN ALL-OUT WAR, YA KNOW.
I-I'M AWARE OF THAT...
Please don't get so close.
ONE MOMENT!
SMP
HOW DARE YOU BOTHER MY MAN...
...WITH YOUR PETTY COMPLAINTS!
WHAT VULGAR UPSTART CLAN IS THIS?

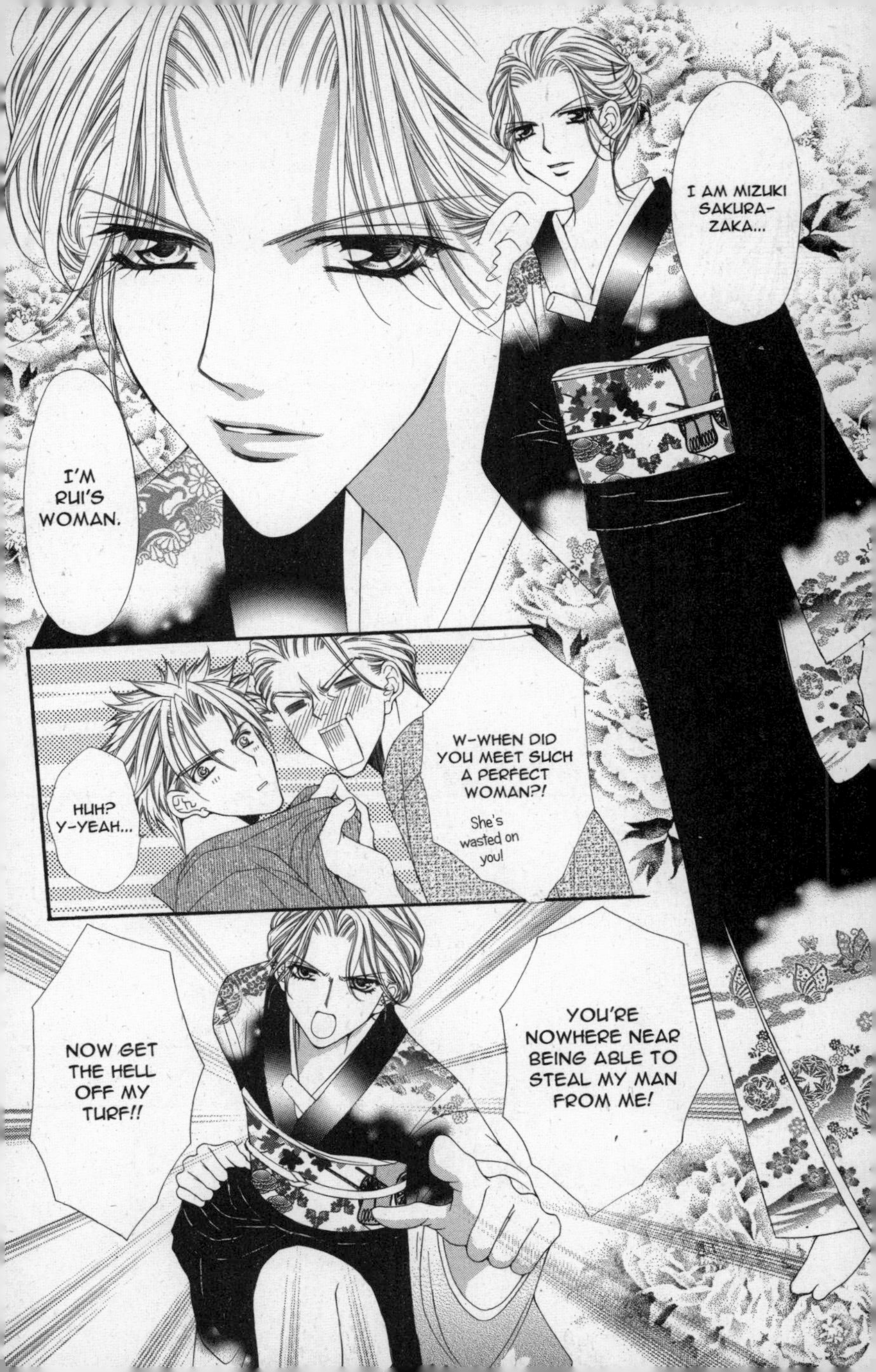
I AM MIZUKI SAKURA-ZAKA...
I'M RUI'S WOMAN.
W-WHEN DID YOU MEET SUCH A PERFECT WOMAN?!
She's wasted on you!
HUH? Y-YEAH...
YOU'RE NOWHERE NEAR BEING ABLE TO STEAL MY MAN FROM ME!
NOW GET THE HELL OFF MY TURF!!

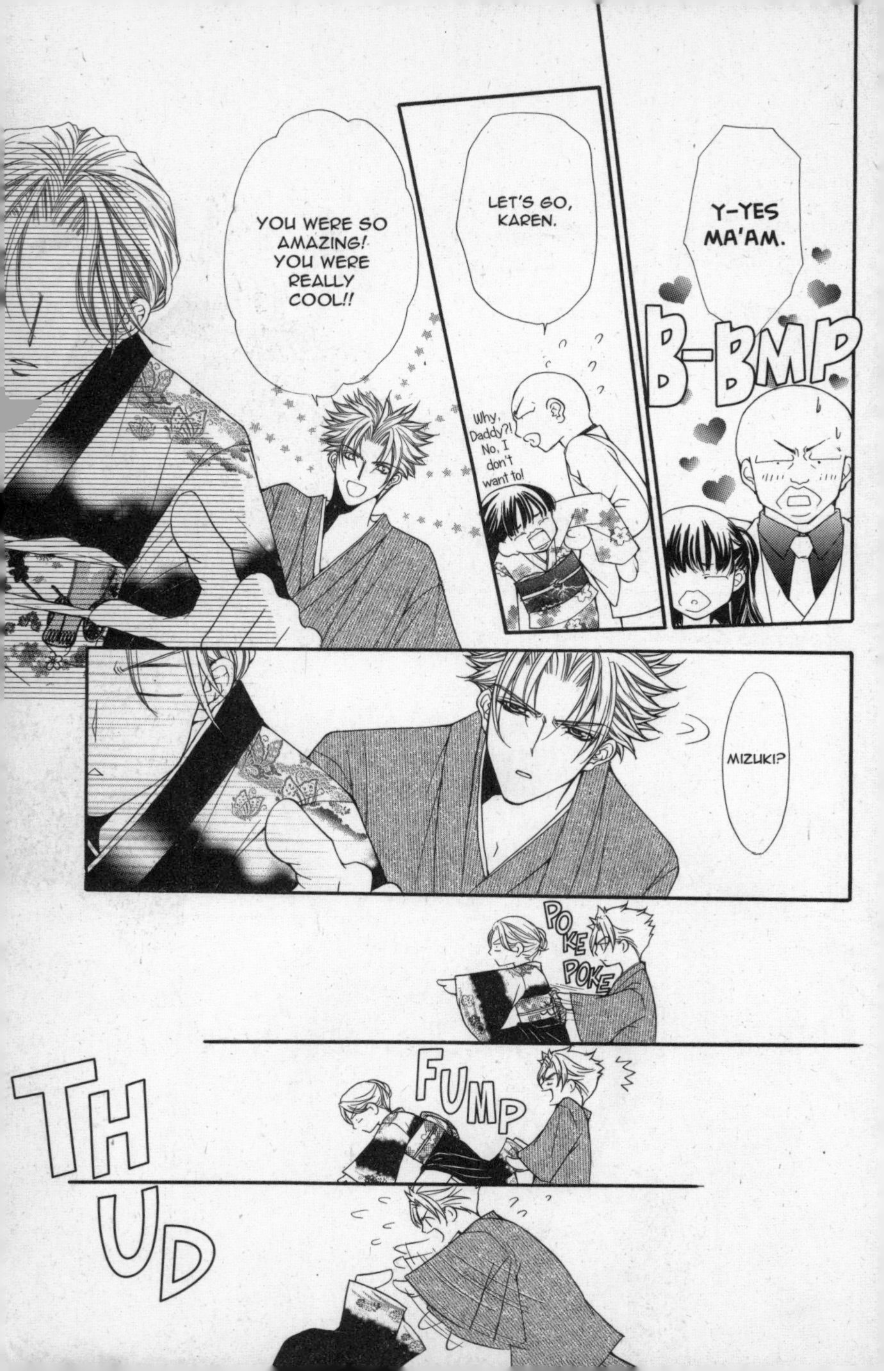
Y-YES MA'AM.
B-BMP
LET'S GO, KAREN.
Why, Daddy?! No, I don't want to!
YOU WERE SO AMAZING! YOU WERE REALLY COOL!!
MIZUKI?
POKE POKE
FUMP
THUD

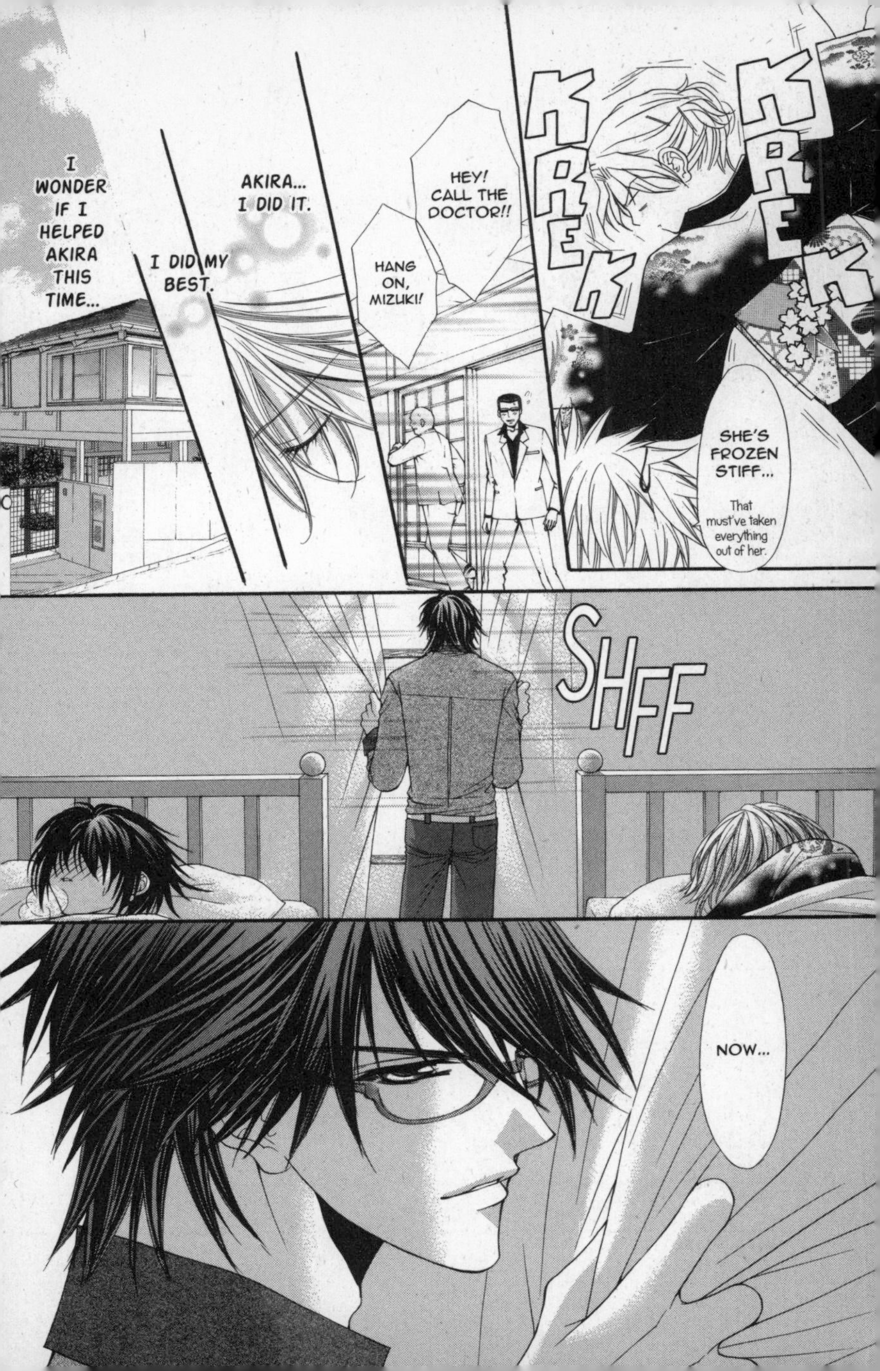
KREK
KREK
KREK
SHE'S FROZEN STIFF...
That must've taken everything out of her.
HEY! CALL THE DOCTOR!!
HANG ON, MIZUKI!
AKIRA... I DID IT.
I DID MY BEST.
I WONDER IF I HELPED AKIRA THIS TIME...
SHFF
NOW...

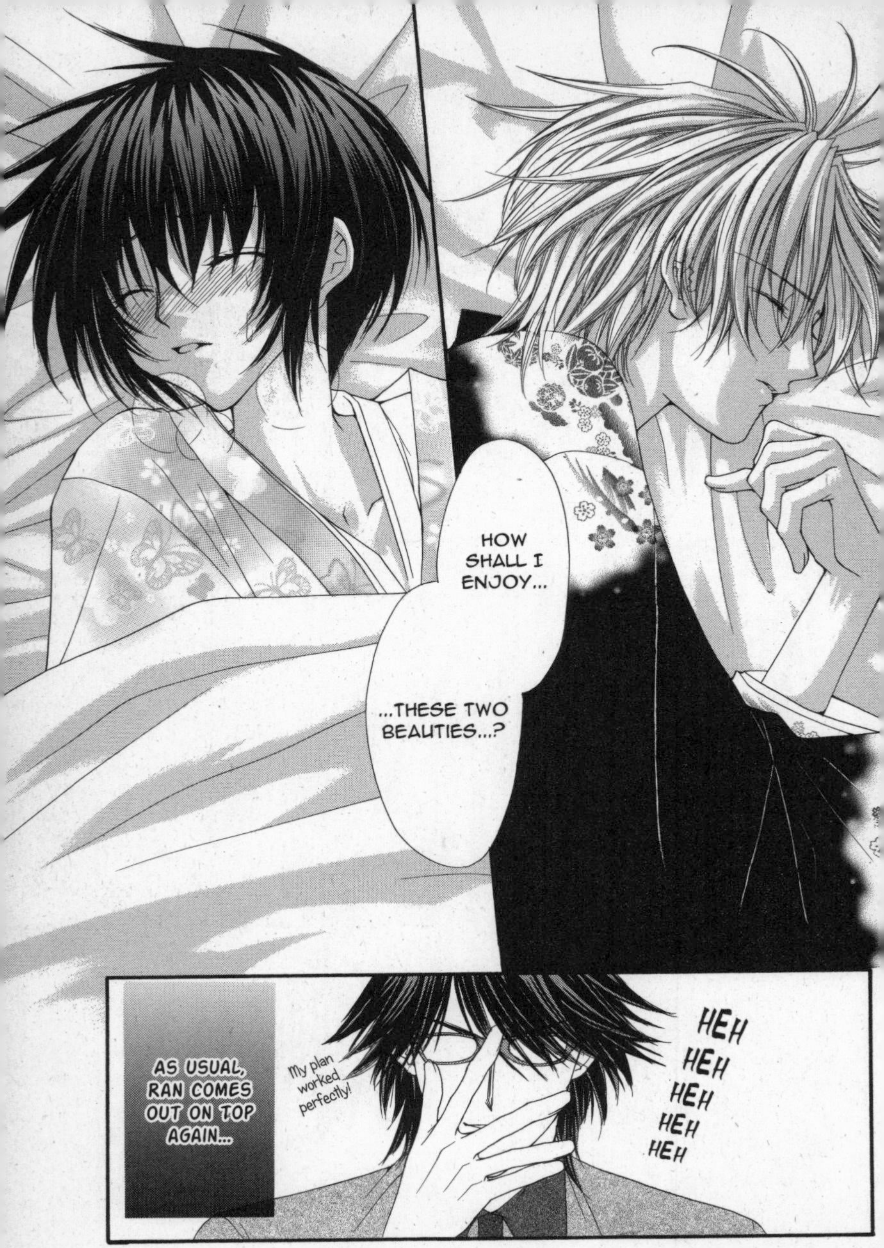
HOW SHALL I ENJOY...
...THESE TWO BEAUTIES...?
HEH HEH HEH HEH HEH
My plan worked perfectly!
AS USUAL, RAN COMES OUT ON TOP AGAIN...

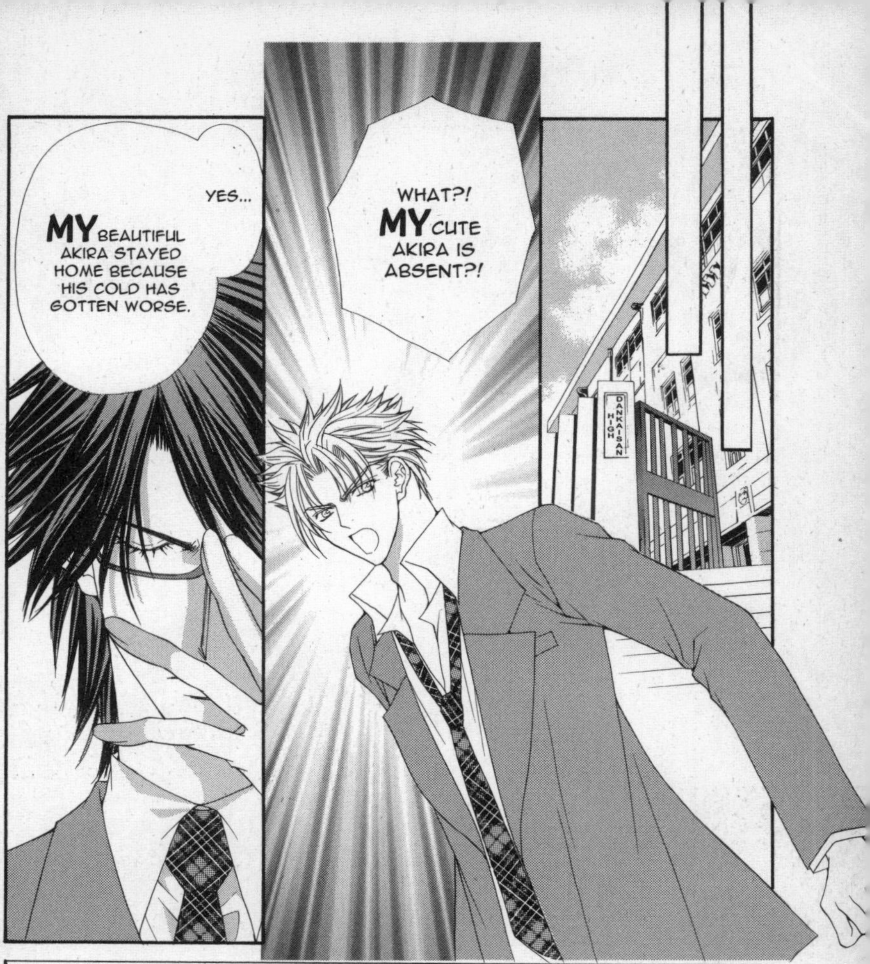
DANKAISAN HIGH
WHAT?! MY CUTE AKIRA IS ABSENT?!
YES... MY BEAUTIFUL AKIRA STAYED HOME BECAUSE HIS COLD HAS GOTTEN WORSE.

If you have any questions about the *Ai Ore* characters, please feel free to email me.
Questions for Shinjo are also accepted.
Here is the address!!

portier@mayutan.com

(The email won't reach Shinjo directly—the staff will read them first.)

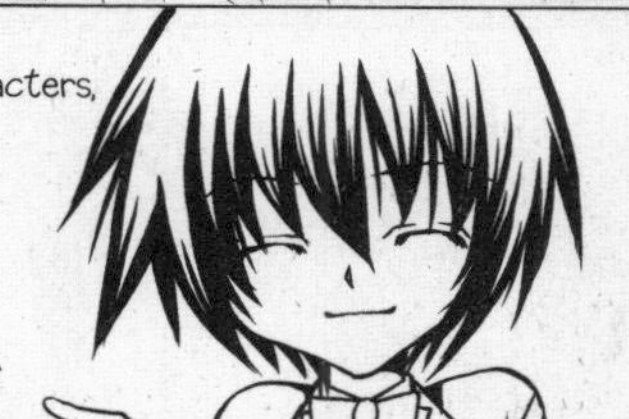

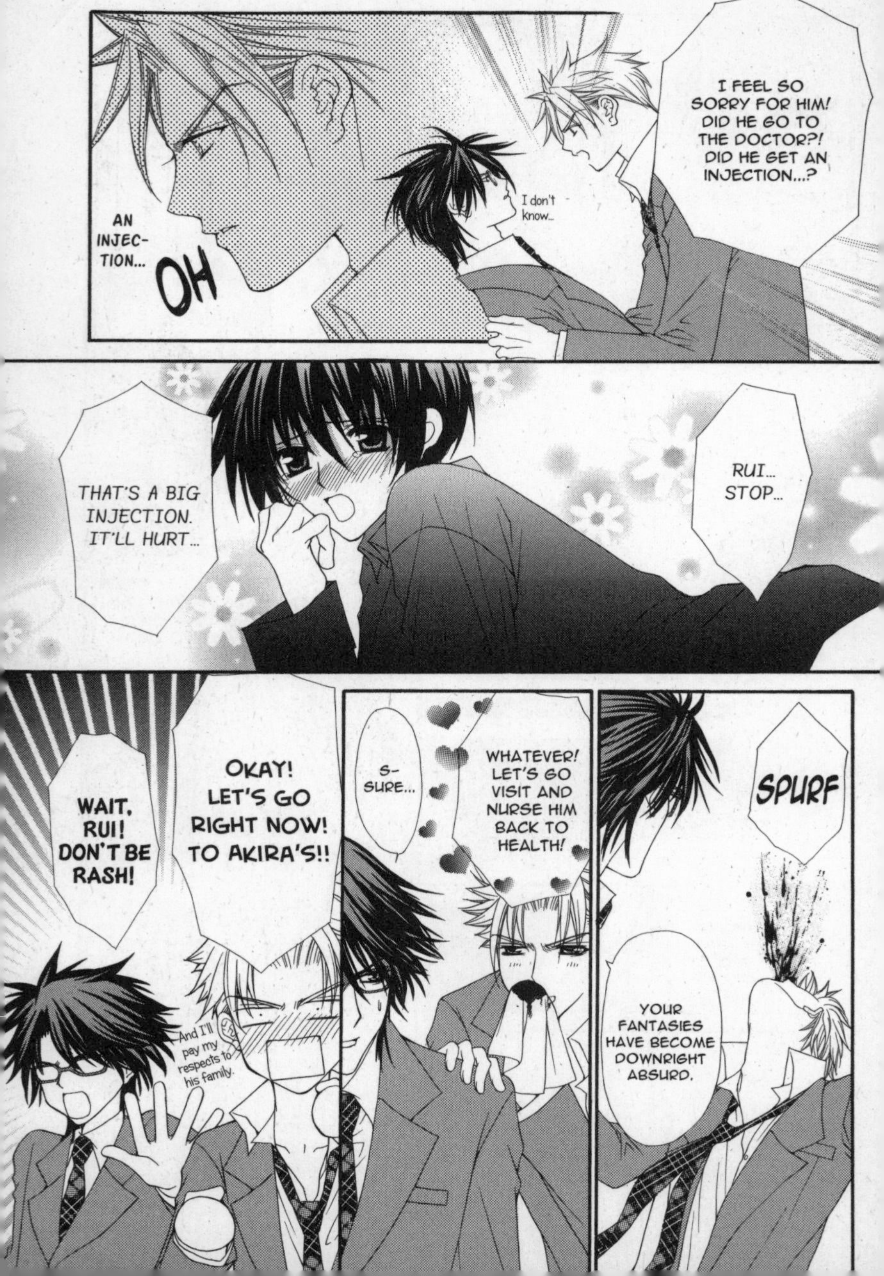
I FEEL SO SORRY FOR HIM! DID HE GO TO THE DOCTOR?! DID HE GET AN INJECTION...?
I don't know...
AN INJECTION...
OH
RUI... STOP...
THAT'S A BIG INJECTION. IT'LL HURT...
SPURF
YOUR FANTASIES HAVE BECOME DOWNRIGHT ABSURD.
WHATEVER! LET'S GO VISIT AND NURSE HIM BACK TO HEALTH!
S- SURE...
OKAY! LET'S GO RIGHT NOW! TO AKIRA'S!!
And I'll pay my respects to his family.
WAIT, RUI! DON'T BE RASH!

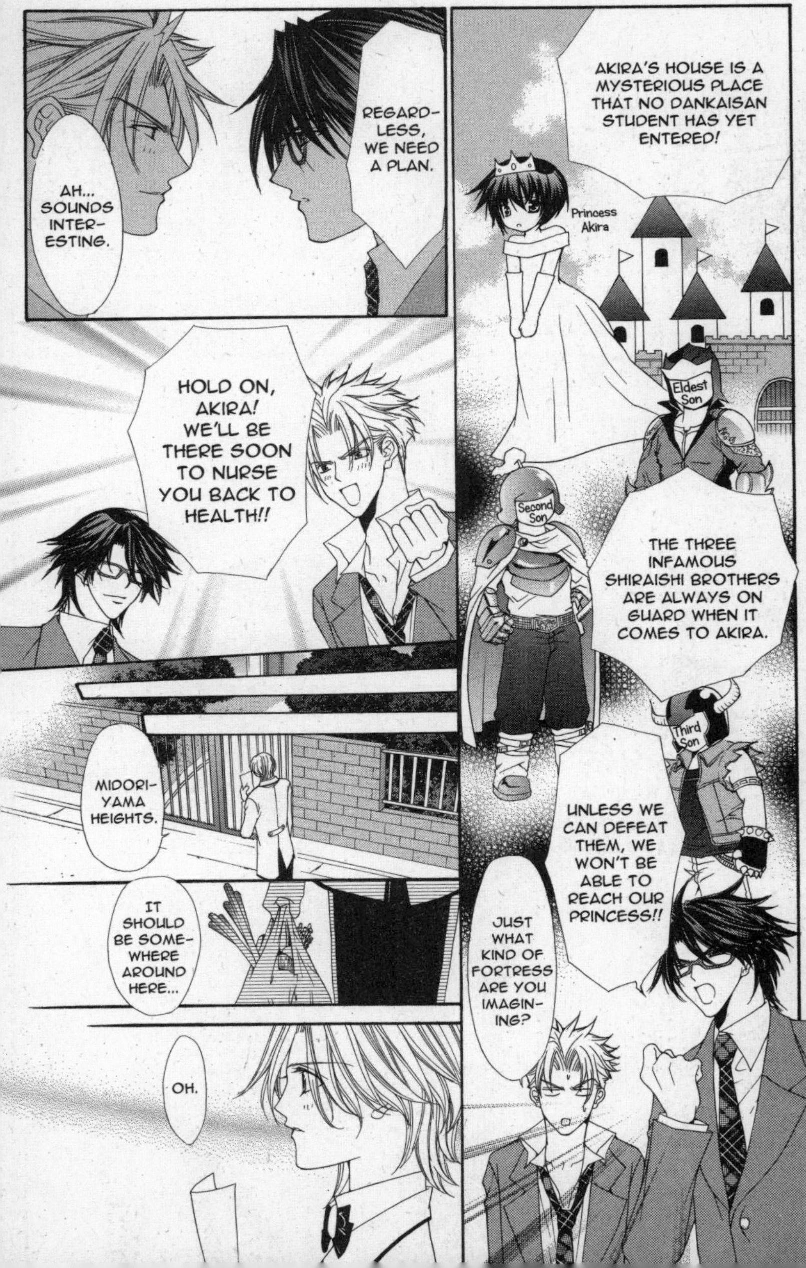
AKIRA'S HOUSE IS A MYSTERIOUS PLACE THAT NO DANKAISAN STUDENT HAS YET ENTERED!
Princess Akira
Eldest Son
Second Son
THE THREE INFAMOUS SHIRAISHI BROTHERS ARE ALWAYS ON GUARD WHEN IT COMES TO AKIRA.
Third Son
UNLESS WE CAN DEFEAT THEM, WE WON'T BE ABLE TO REACH OUR PRINCESS!!
JUST WHAT KIND OF FORTRESS ARE YOU IMAGINING?
REGARDLESS, WE NEED A PLAN.
AH... SOUNDS INTERESTING.
HOLD ON, AKIRA! WE'LL BE THERE SOON TO NURSE YOU BACK TO HEALTH!!
MIDORIYAMA HEIGHTS.
IT SHOULD BE SOMEWHERE AROUND HERE...
OH.

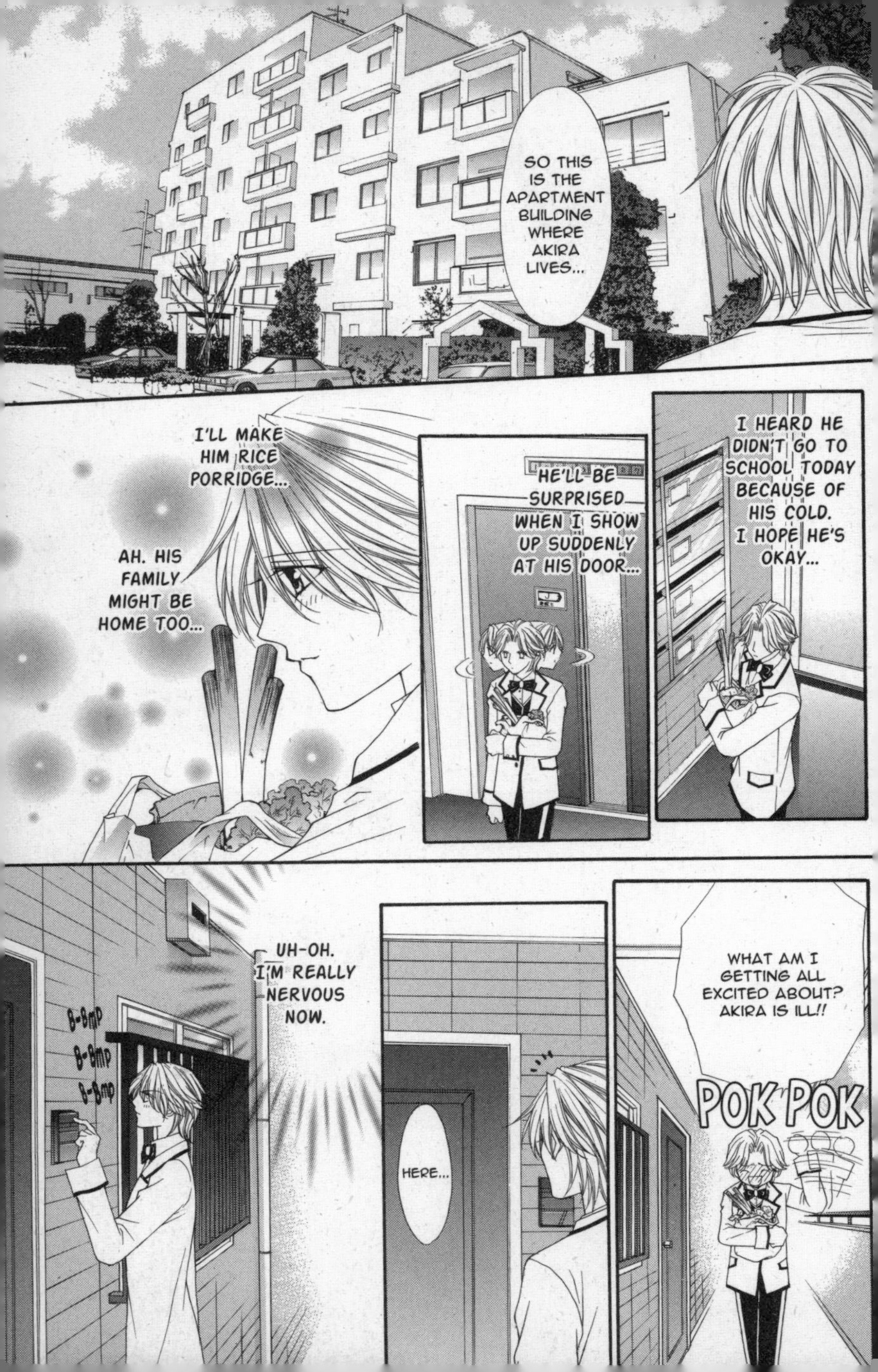
SO THIS IS THE APARTMENT BUILDING WHERE AKIRA LIVES...
I HEARD HE DIDN'T GO TO SCHOOL TODAY BECAUSE OF HIS COLD. I HOPE HE'S OKAY...
HE'LL BE SURPRISED WHEN I SHOW UP SUDDENLY AT HIS DOOR...
I'LL MAKE HIM RICE PORRIDGE...
AH. HIS FAMILY MIGHT BE HOME TOO...
WHAT AM I GETTING ALL EXCITED ABOUT? AKIRA IS ILL!!
POK POK
HERE...
UH-OH. I'M REALLY NERVOUS NOW.
B-BMP
B-BMP
B-BMP

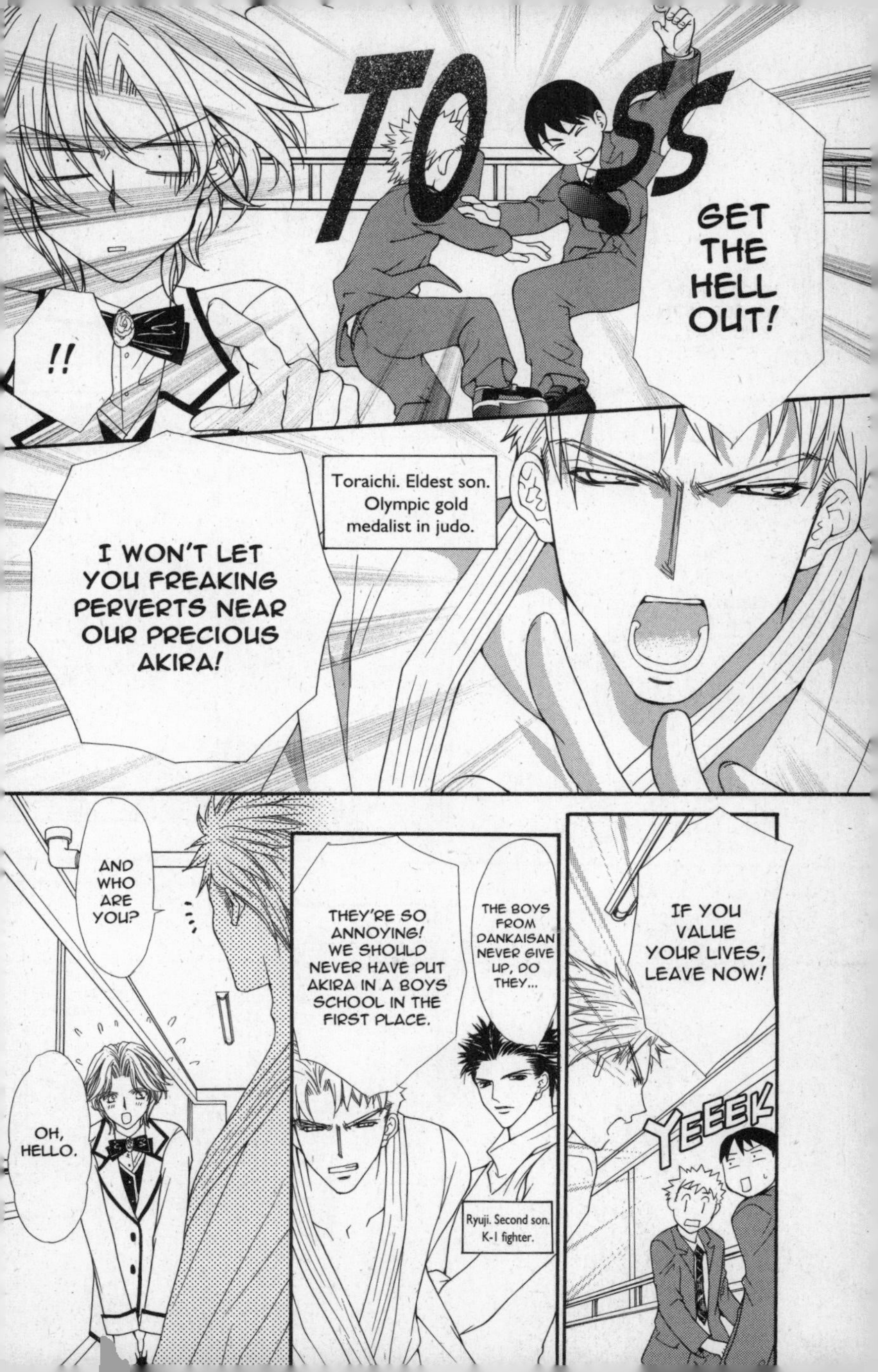
TOSS
GET THE HELL OUT!
!!
Toraichi. Eldest son. Olympic gold medalist in judo.
I WON'T LET YOU FREAKING PERVERTS NEAR OUR PRECIOUS AKIRA!
IF YOU VALUE YOUR LIVES, LEAVE NOW!
YEEEK
THE BOYS FROM DANKAISAN NEVER GIVE UP, DO THEY...
THEY'RE SO ANNOYING! WE SHOULD NEVER HAVE PUT AKIRA IN A BOYS SCHOOL IN THE FIRST PLACE.
Ryuji. Second son. K-1 fighter.
AND WHO ARE YOU?
OH, HELLO.

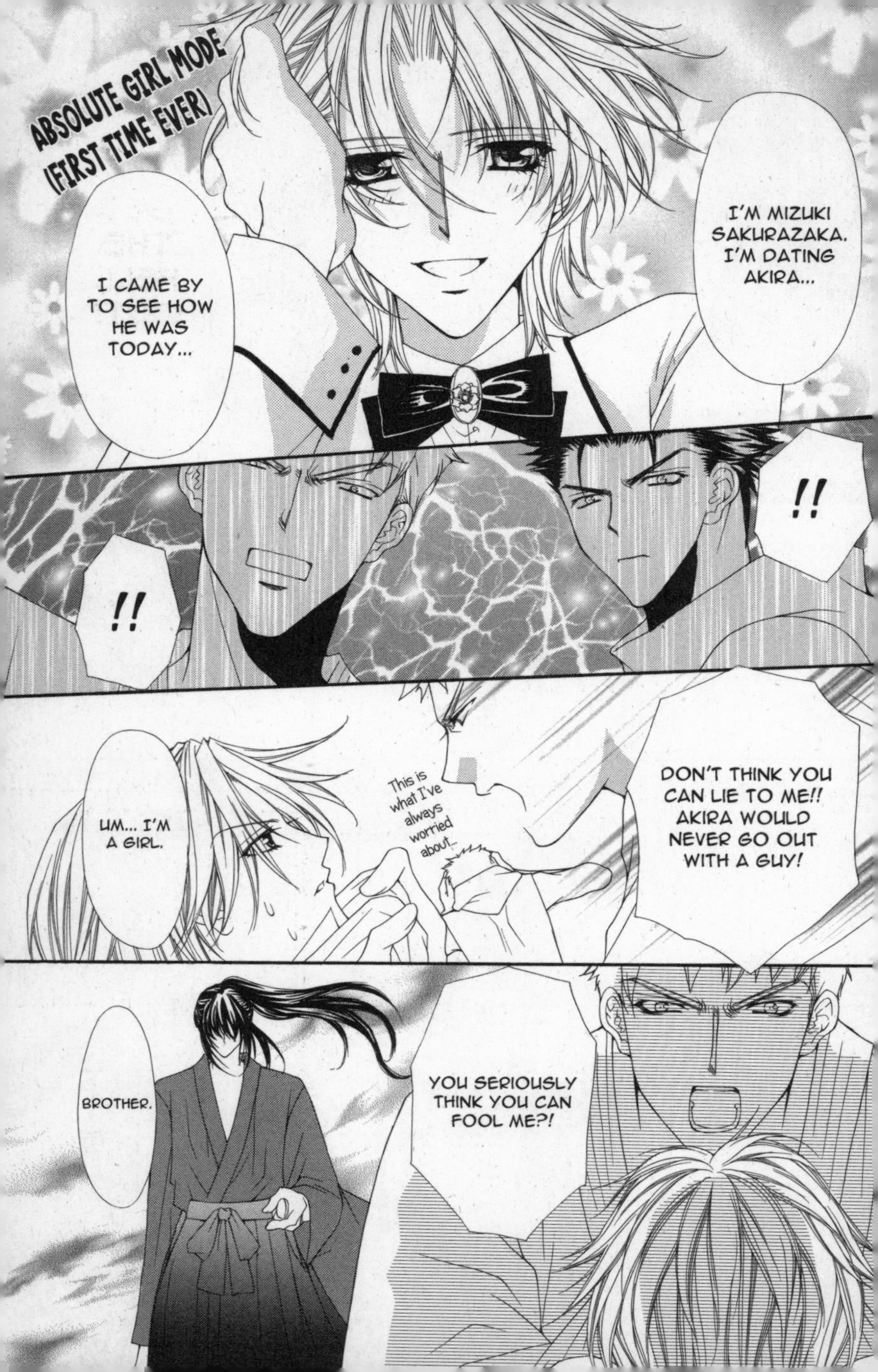
I'M MIZUKI SAKURAZAKA. I'M DATING AKIRA...
I CAME BY TO SEE HOW HE WAS TODAY...
ABSOLUTE GIRL MODE (FIRST TIME EVER)
!!
!!
DON'T THINK YOU CAN LIE TO ME!! AKIRA WOULD NEVER GO OUT WITH A GUY!
This is what I've always worried about...
UM... I'M A GIRL.
YOU SERIOUSLY THINK YOU CAN FOOL ME?!
BROTHER.

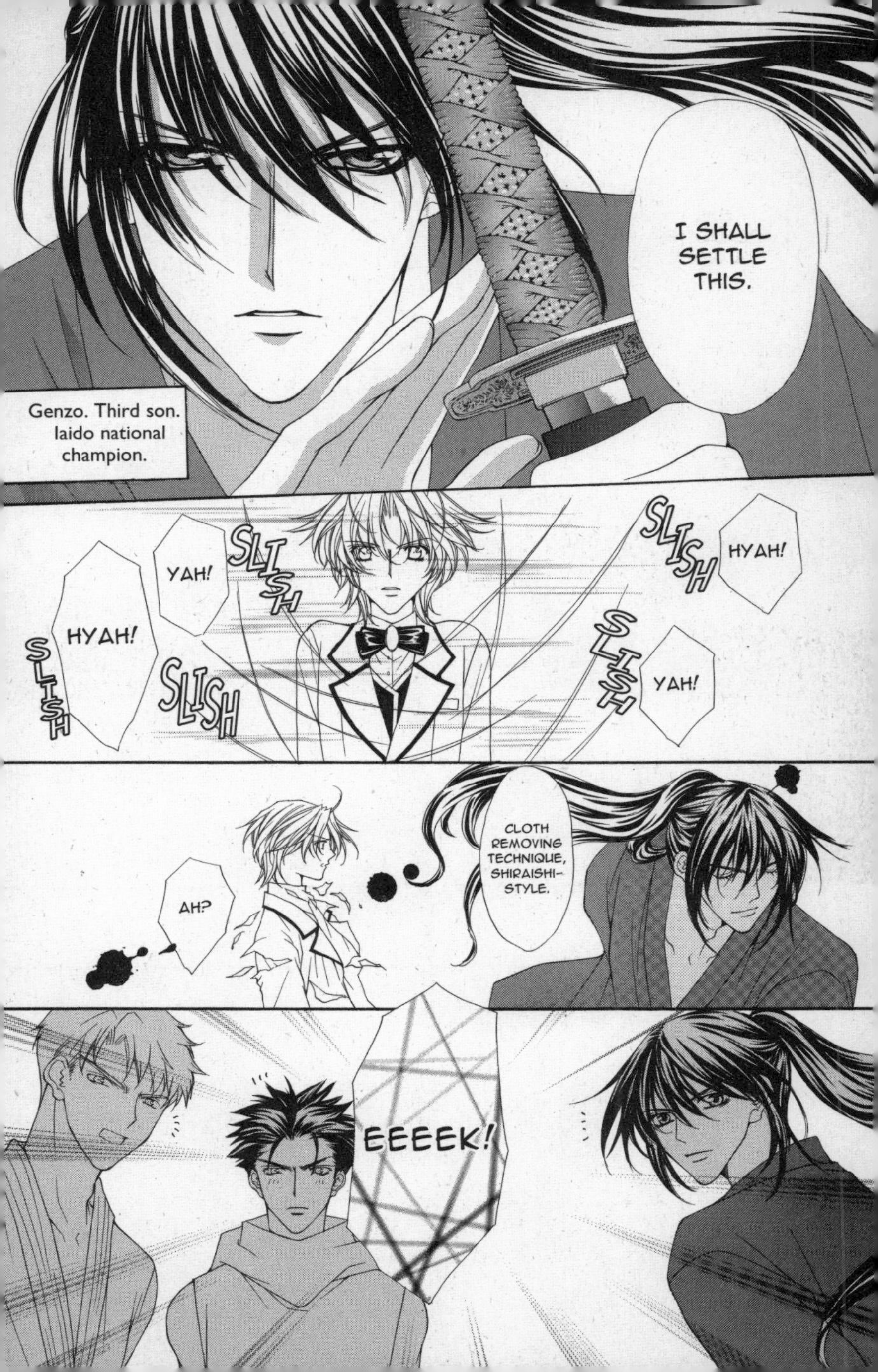

I SHALL SETTLE THIS.
Genzo. Third son. Iaido national champion.
SLISH
HYAH!
SLISH
YAH!
SLISH
YAH!
HYAH!
SLISH
SLISH
CLOTH REMOVING TECHNIQUE, SHIRAISHI-STYLE.
AH?
EEEEK!

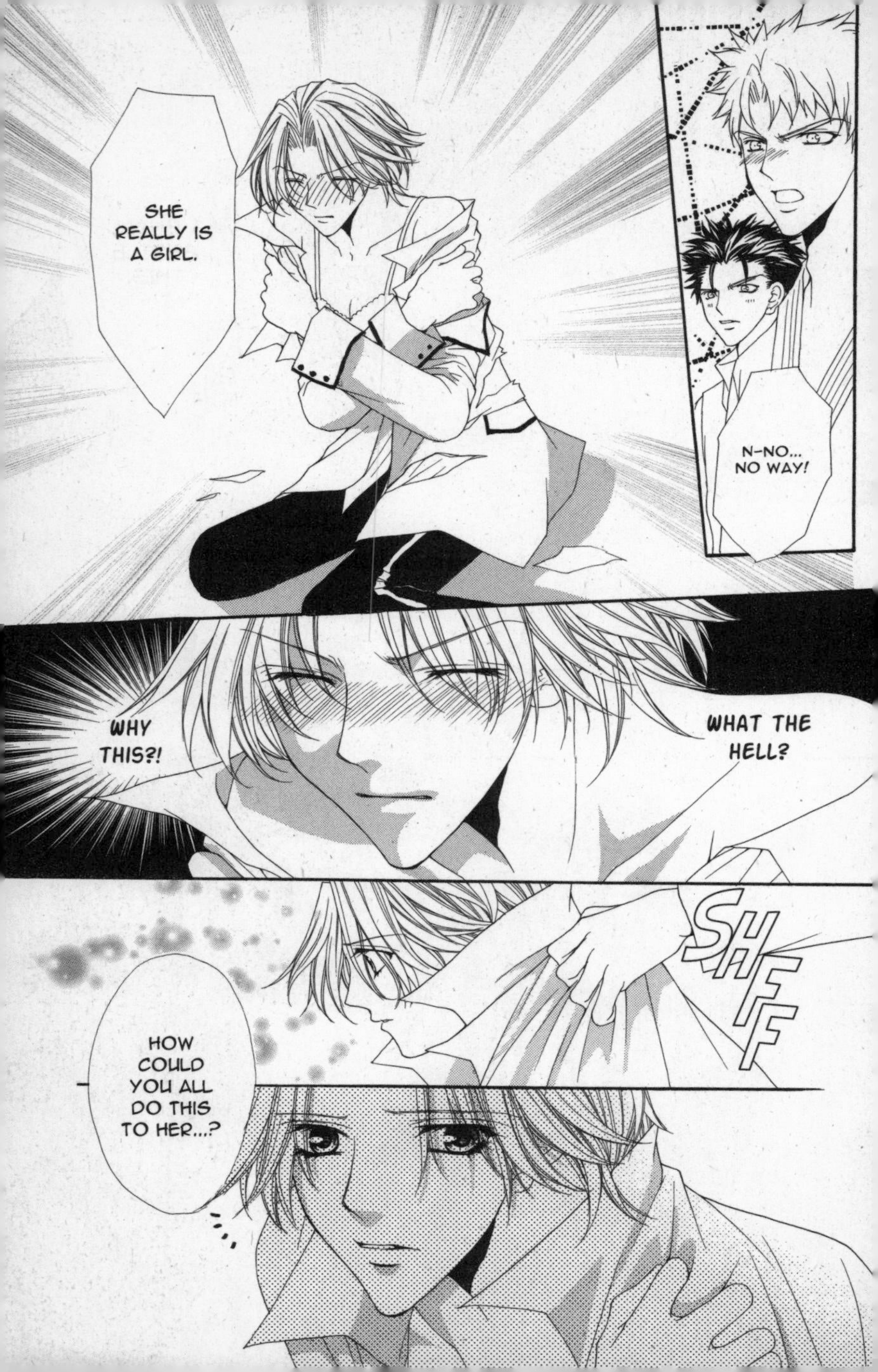
N-NO... NO WAY!
SHE REALLY IS A GIRL.
WHAT THE HELL?
WHY THIS?!
SHFF
HOW COULD YOU ALL DO THIS TO HER...?
...

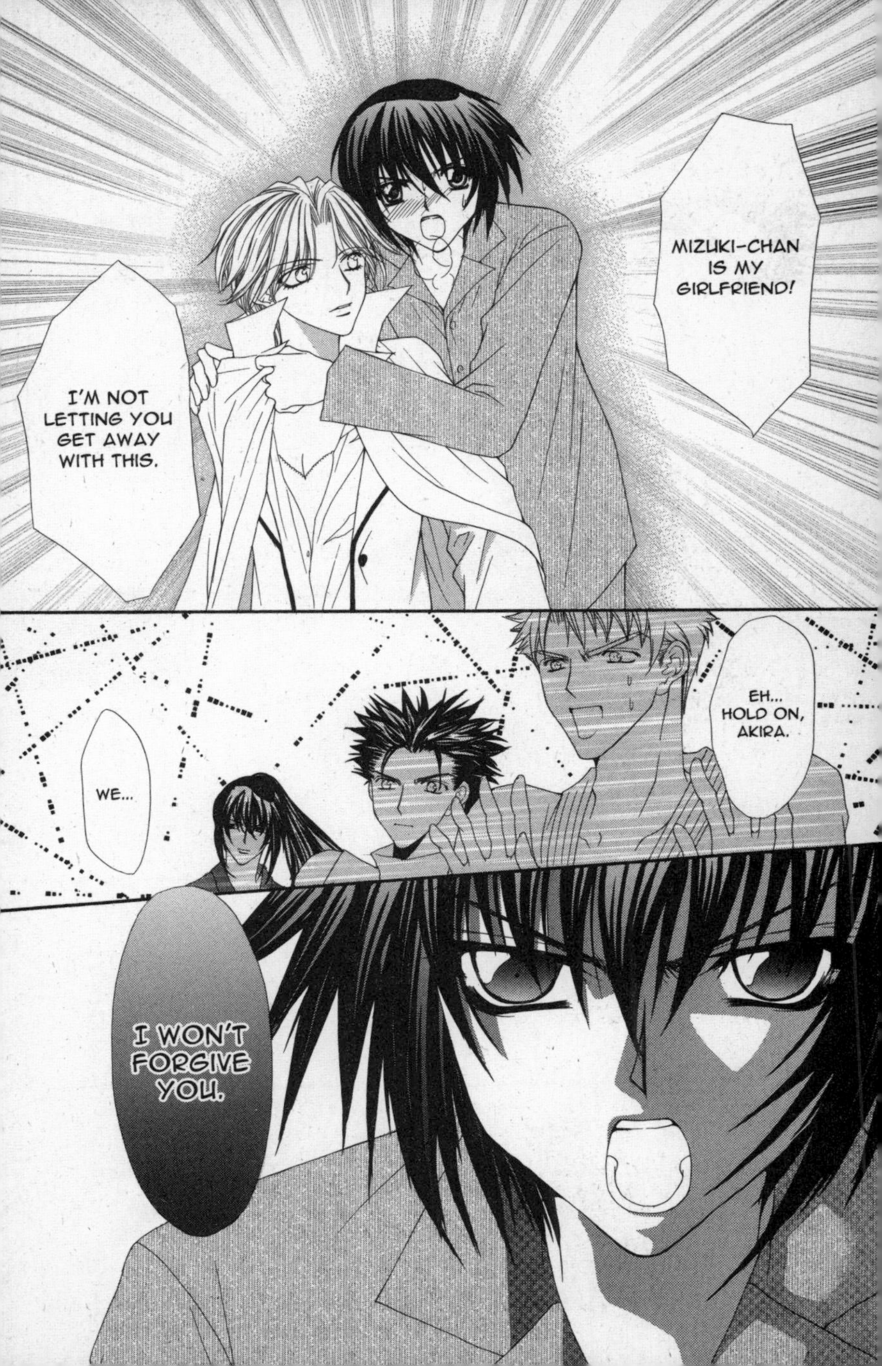
MIZUKI-CHAN IS MY GIRLFRIEND!
I'M NOT LETTING YOU GET AWAY WITH THIS.
EH... HOLD ON, AKIRA.
WE...
I WON'T FORGIVE YOU.

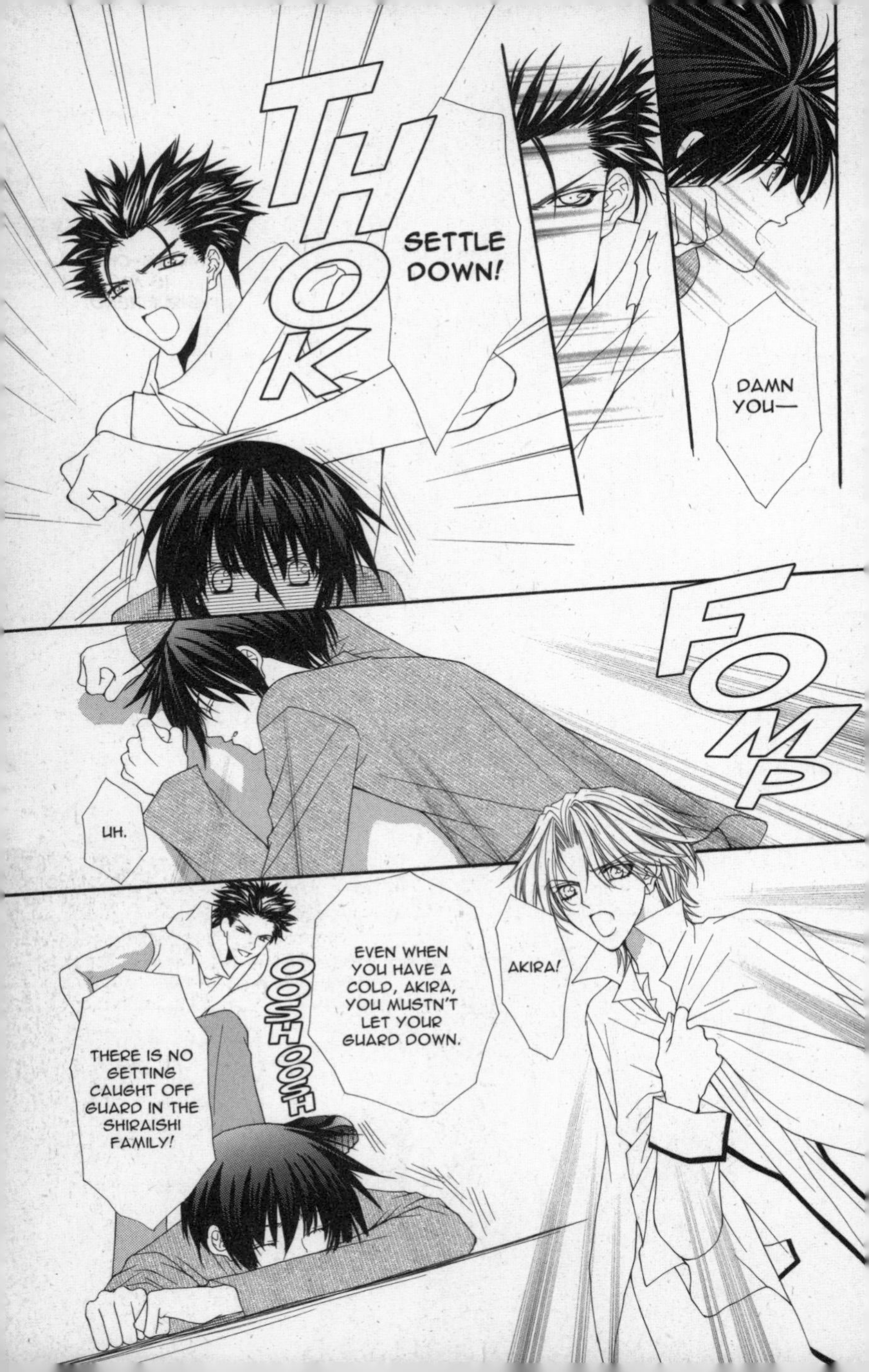
DAMN YOU—
THOK
SETTLE DOWN!
FOMP
UH.
AKIRA!
EVEN WHEN YOU HAVE A COLD, AKIRA, YOU MUSTN'T LET YOUR GUARD DOWN.
OOSHOOSH
THERE IS NO GETTING CAUGHT OFF GUARD IN THE SHIRAISHI FAMILY!

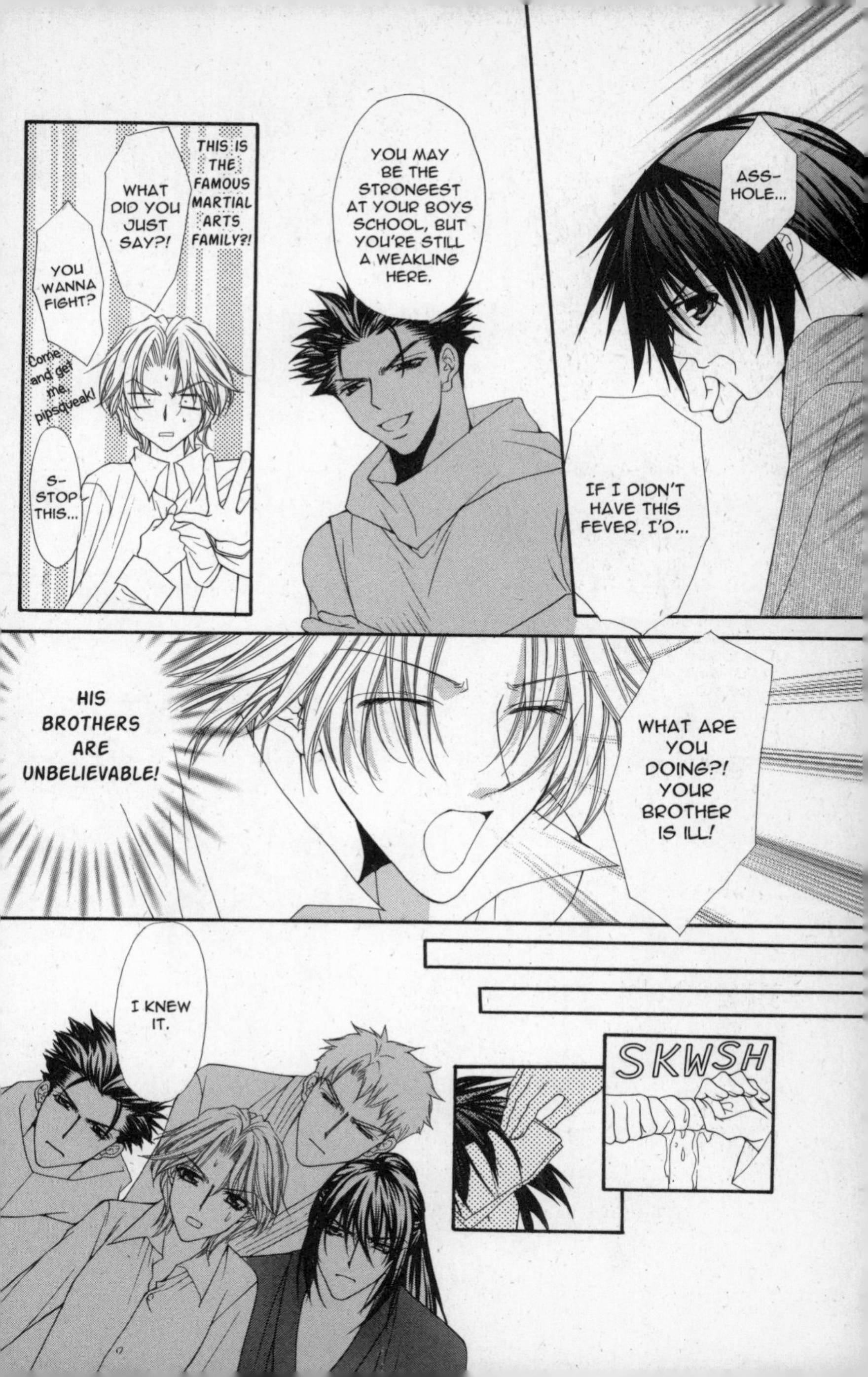
ASS-HOLE...
IF I DIDN'T HAVE THIS FEVER, I'D...
YOU MAY BE THE STRONGEST AT YOUR BOYS SCHOOL, BUT YOU'RE STILL A WEAKLING HERE.
THIS IS THE FAMOUS MARTIAL ARTS FAMILY?!
WHAT DID YOU JUST SAY?!
YOU WANNA FIGHT?
Come and get me, pipsqueak!
S-STOP THIS...
WHAT ARE YOU DOING?! YOUR BROTHER IS ILL!
HIS BROTHERS ARE UNBELIEVABLE!
SKWSH
I KNEW IT.

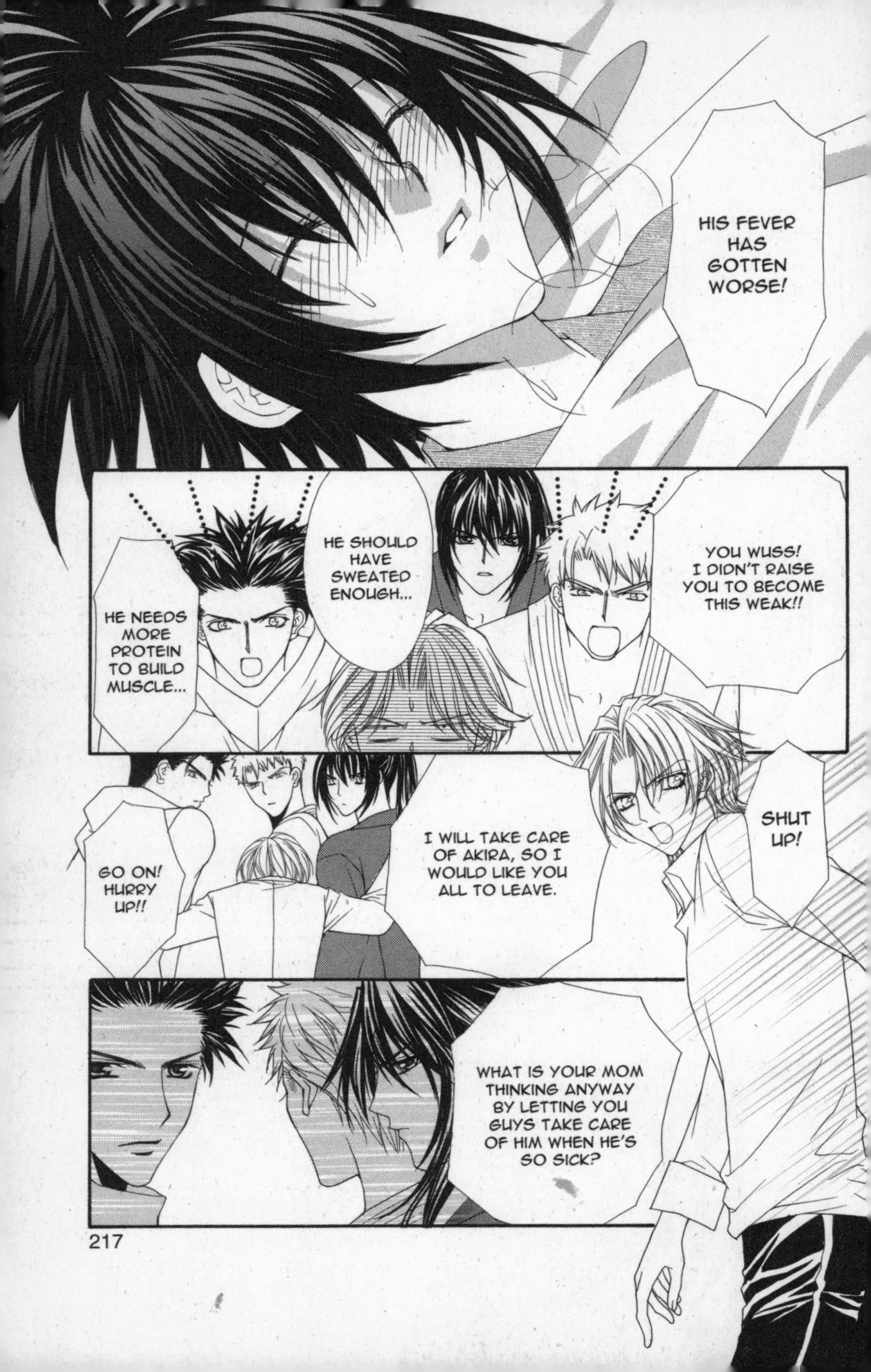
HIS FEVER HAS GOTTEN WORSE!
YOU WUSS! I DIDN'T RAISE YOU TO BECOME THIS WEAK!!
HE SHOULD HAVE SWEATED ENOUGH...
HE NEEDS MORE PROTEIN TO BUILD MUSCLE...
SHUT UP!
I WILL TAKE CARE OF AKIRA, SO I WOULD LIKE YOU ALL TO LEAVE.
GO ON! HURRY UP!!
WHAT IS YOUR MOM THINKING ANYWAY BY LETTING YOU GUYS TAKE CARE OF HIM WHEN HE'S SO SICK?

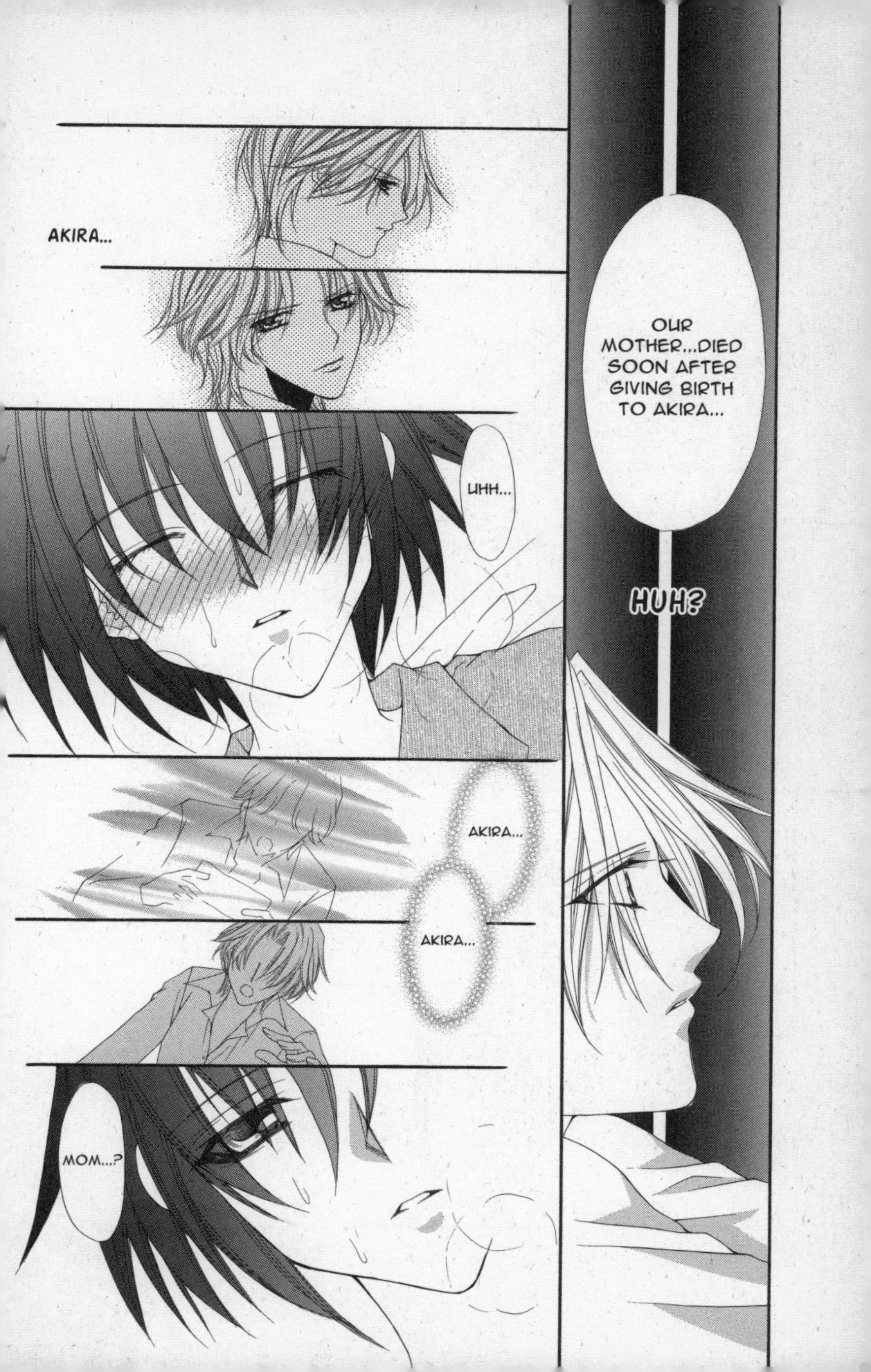
OUR MOTHER...DIED SOON AFTER GIVING BIRTH TO AKIRA...
HUH?
AKIRA...
UHH...
AKIRA...
AKIRA...
MOM...?

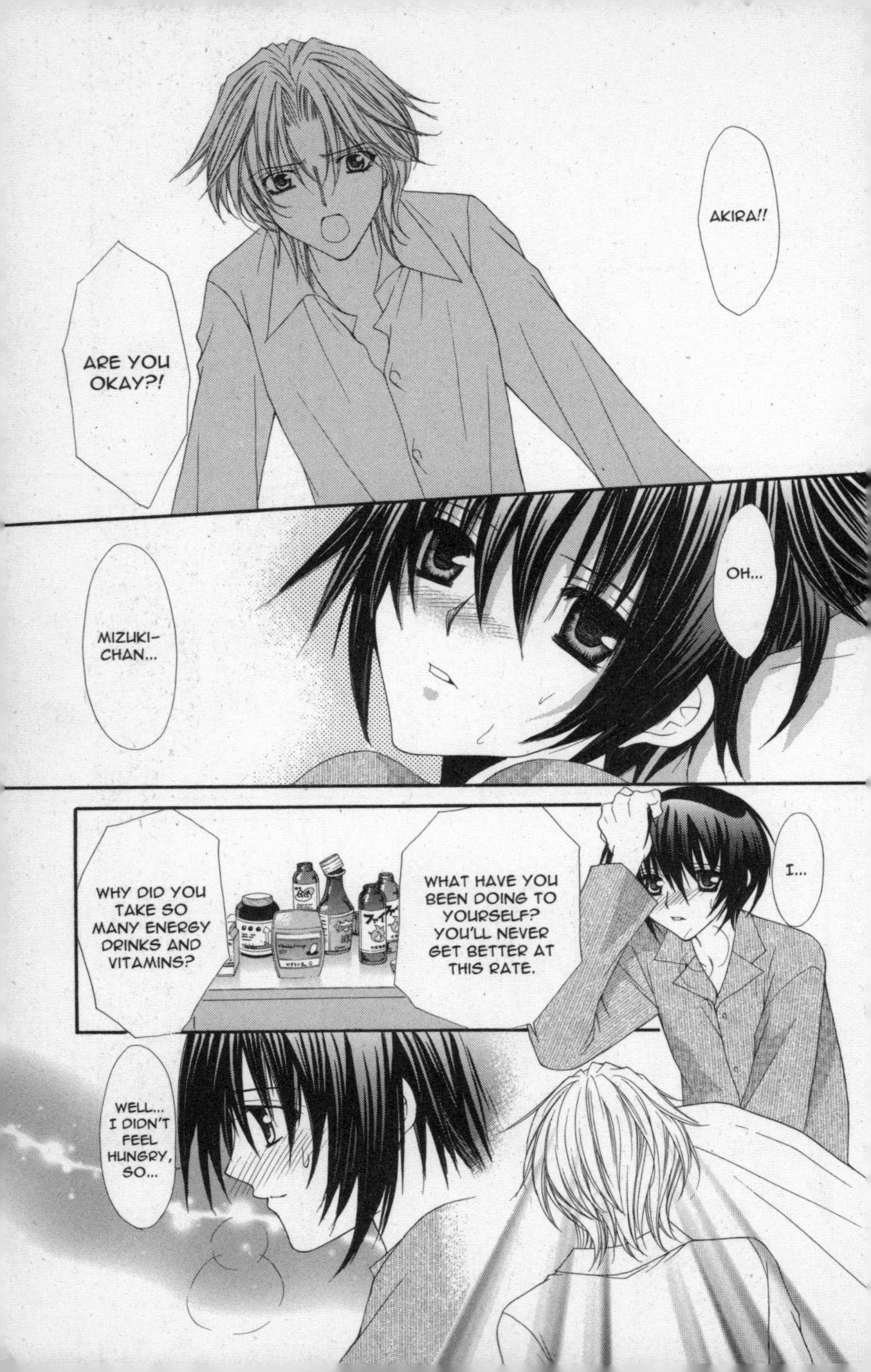
AKIRA!!
ARE YOU OKAY?!
OH...
MIZUKI-CHAN...
I...
WHAT HAVE YOU BEEN DOING TO YOURSELF? YOU'LL NEVER GET BETTER AT THIS RATE.
WHY DID YOU TAKE SO MANY ENERGY DRINKS AND VITAMINS?
WELL... I DIDN'T FEEL HUNGRY, SO...

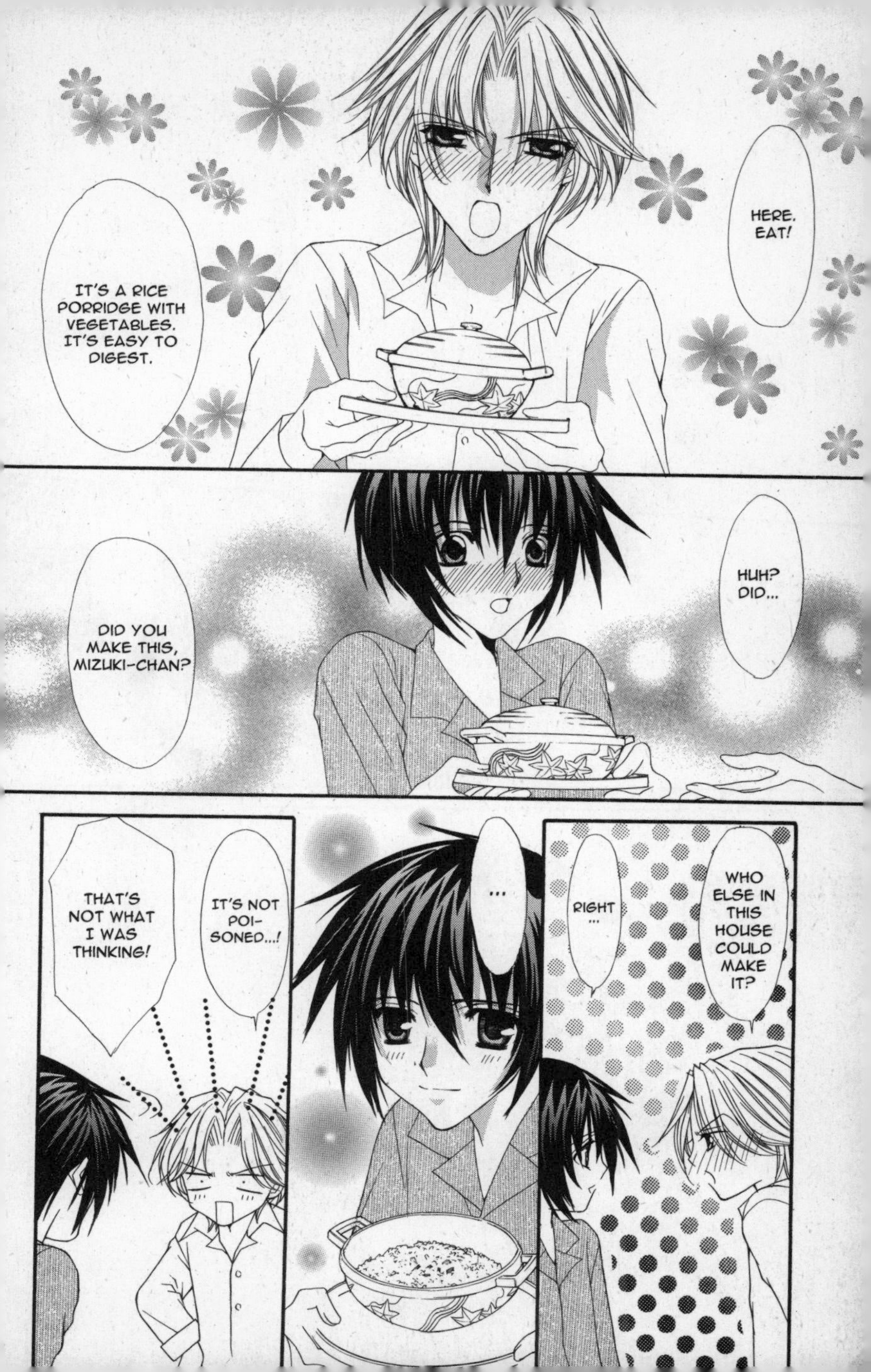
HERE. EAT!
IT'S A RICE PORRIDGE WITH VEGETABLES. IT'S EASY TO DIGEST.
HUH? DID...
DID YOU MAKE THIS, MIZUKI-CHAN?
WHO ELSE IN THIS HOUSE COULD MAKE IT?
RIGHT ...
...
IT'S NOT POI-SONED...!
THAT'S NOT WHAT I WAS THINKING!

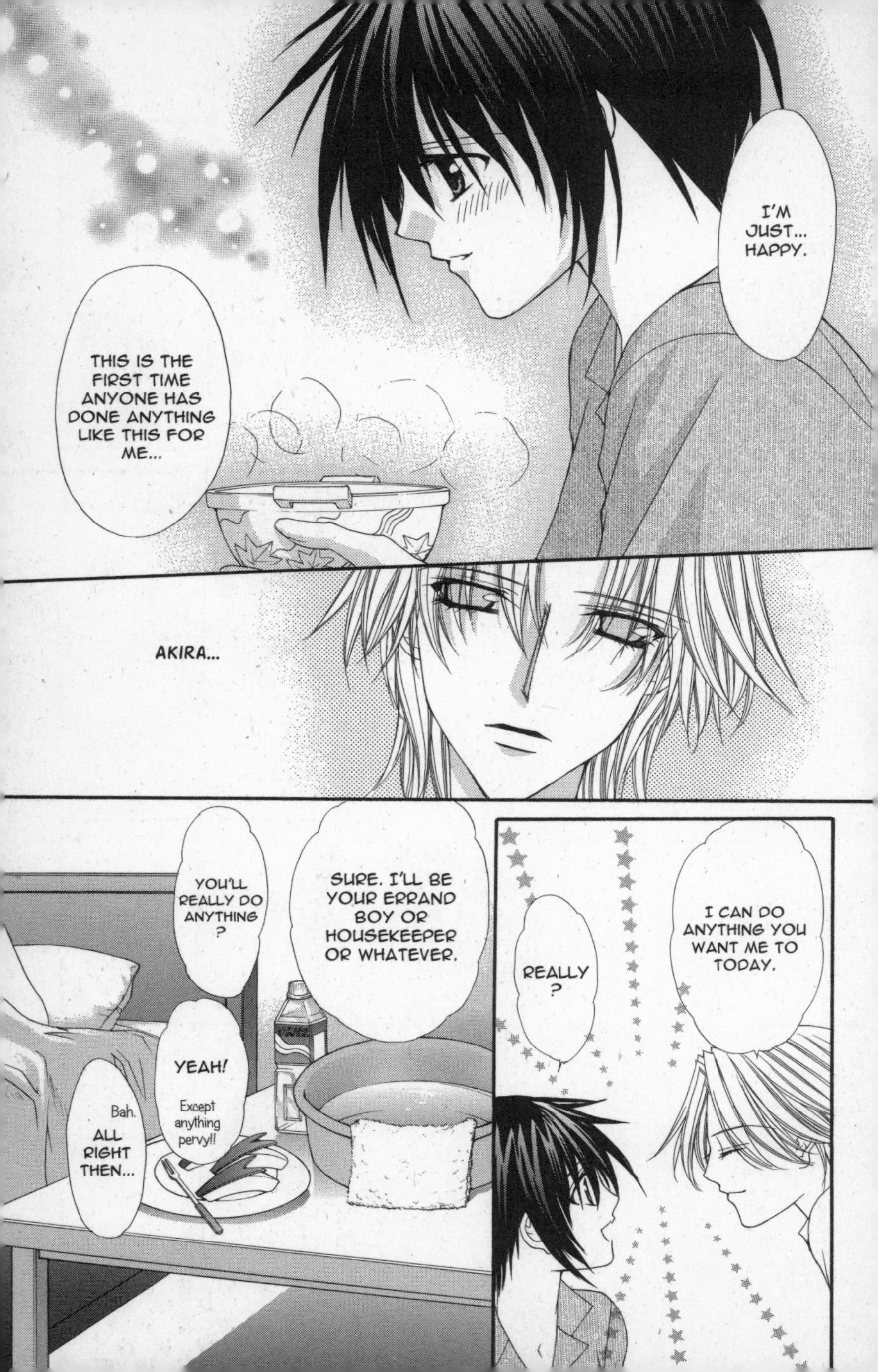
I'M JUST... HAPPY.
THIS IS THE FIRST TIME ANYONE HAS DONE ANYTHING LIKE THIS FOR ME...
AKIRA...
I CAN DO ANYTHING YOU WANT ME TO TODAY.
REALLY?
SURE. I'LL BE YOUR ERRAND BOY OR HOUSEKEEPER OR WHATEVER.
YOU'LL REALLY DO ANYTHING?
YEAH!
Except anything pervy!!
Bah.
ALL RIGHT THEN...

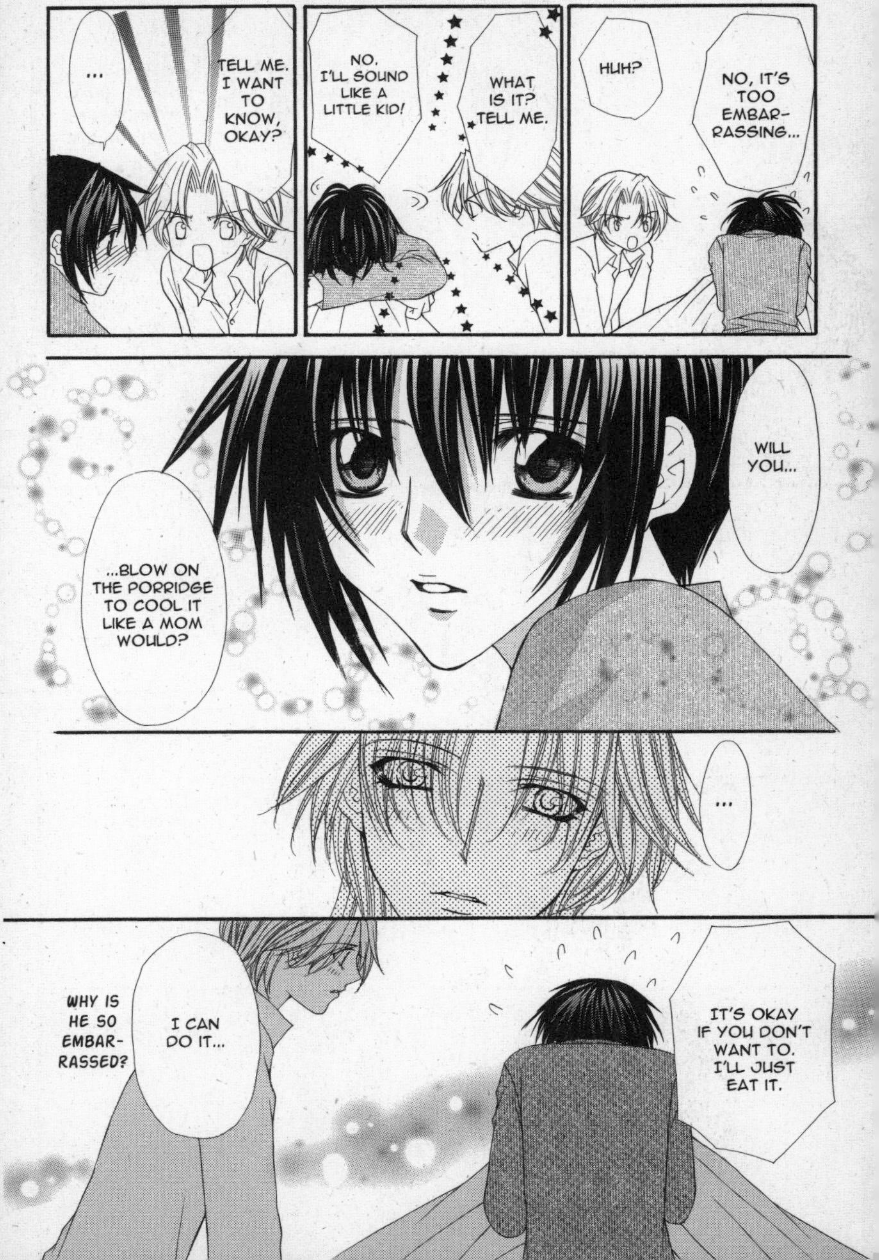
NO, IT'S TOO EMBAR-RASSING...
HUH?
WHAT IS IT? TELL ME.
NO. I'LL SOUND LIKE A LITTLE KID!
TELL ME. I WANT TO KNOW, OKAY?
...
WILL YOU...
...BLOW ON THE PORRIDGE TO COOL IT LIKE A MOM WOULD?
...
IT'S OKAY IF YOU DON'T WANT TO. I'LL JUST EAT IT.
I CAN DO IT...
WHY IS HE SO EMBAR-RASSED?

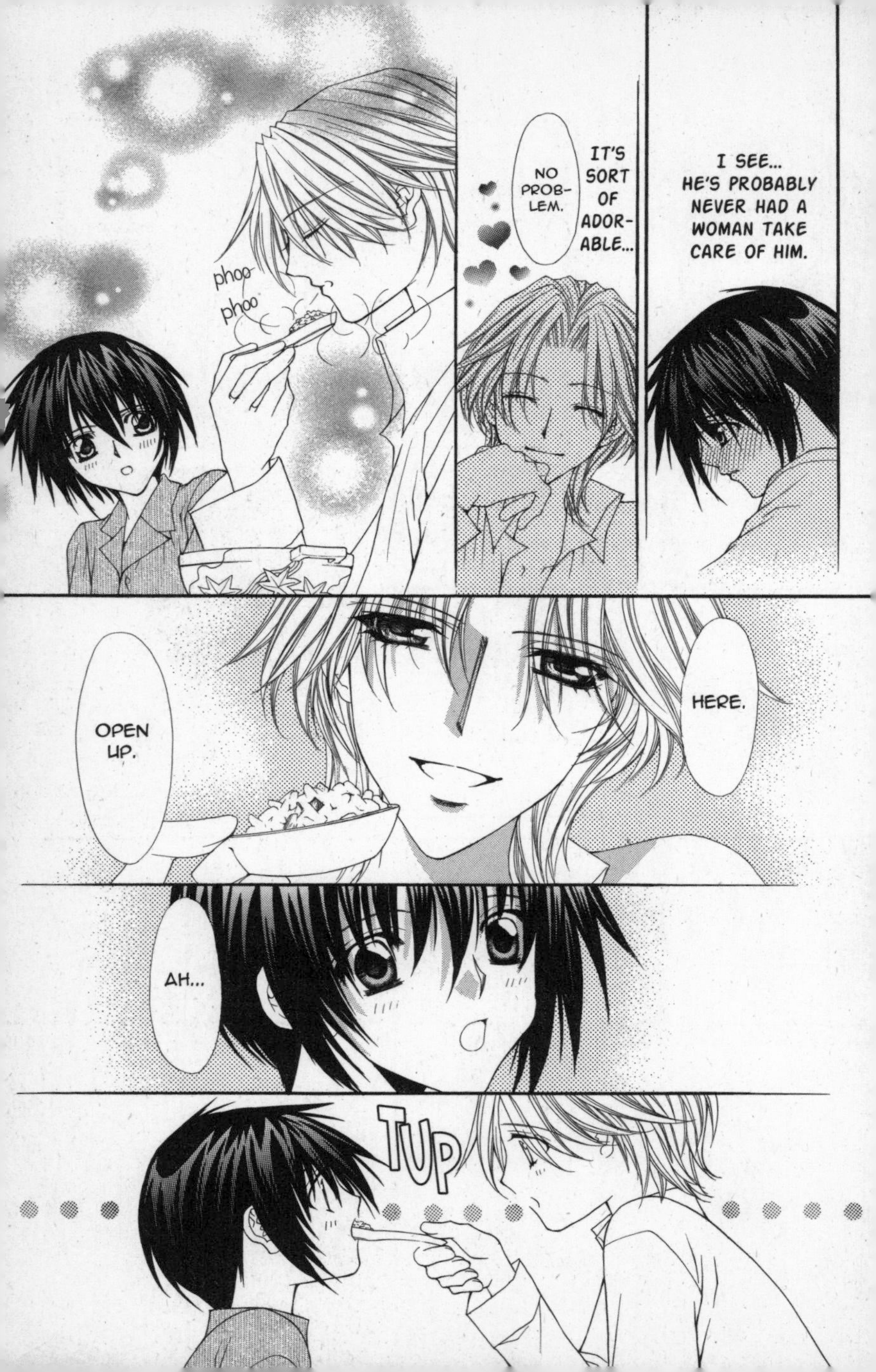
I SEE... HE'S PROBABLY NEVER HAD A WOMAN TAKE CARE OF HIM.
IT'S SORT OF ADOR-ABLE...
NO PROB-LEM.
phoo-phoo
HERE.
OPEN UP.
AH...
TUP

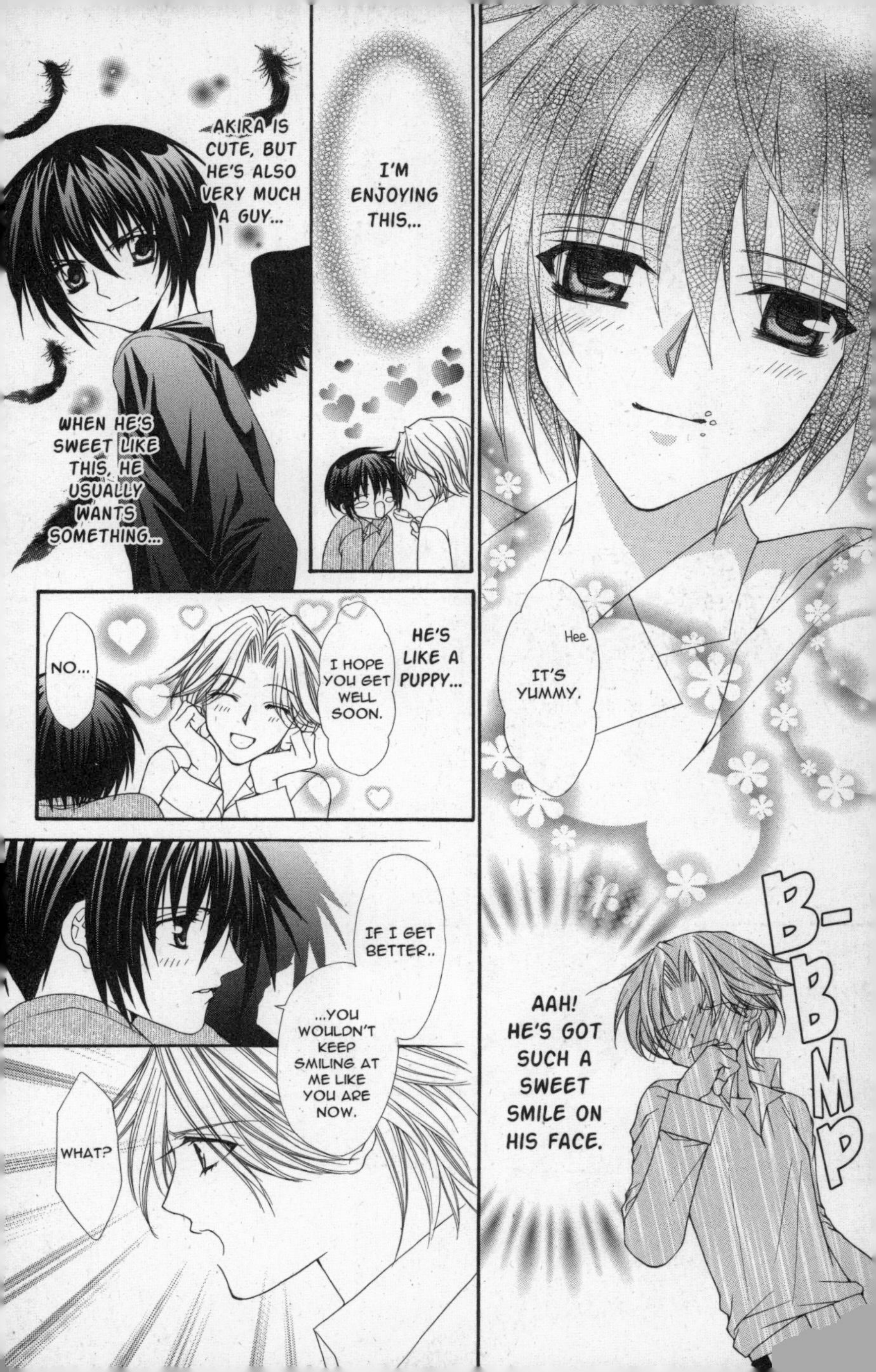
Hee.
IT'S YUMMY.
AAH! HE'S GOT SUCH A SWEET SMILE ON HIS FACE.
B-BBMP
I'M ENJOYING THIS...
AKIRA IS CUTE, BUT HE'S ALSO VERY MUCH A GUY...
WHEN HE'S SWEET LIKE THIS, HE USUALLY WANTS SOMETHING...
HE'S LIKE A PUPPY...
I HOPE YOU GET WELL SOON.
NO...
IF I GET BETTER..
...YOU WOULDN'T KEEP SMILING AT ME LIKE YOU ARE NOW.
WHAT?

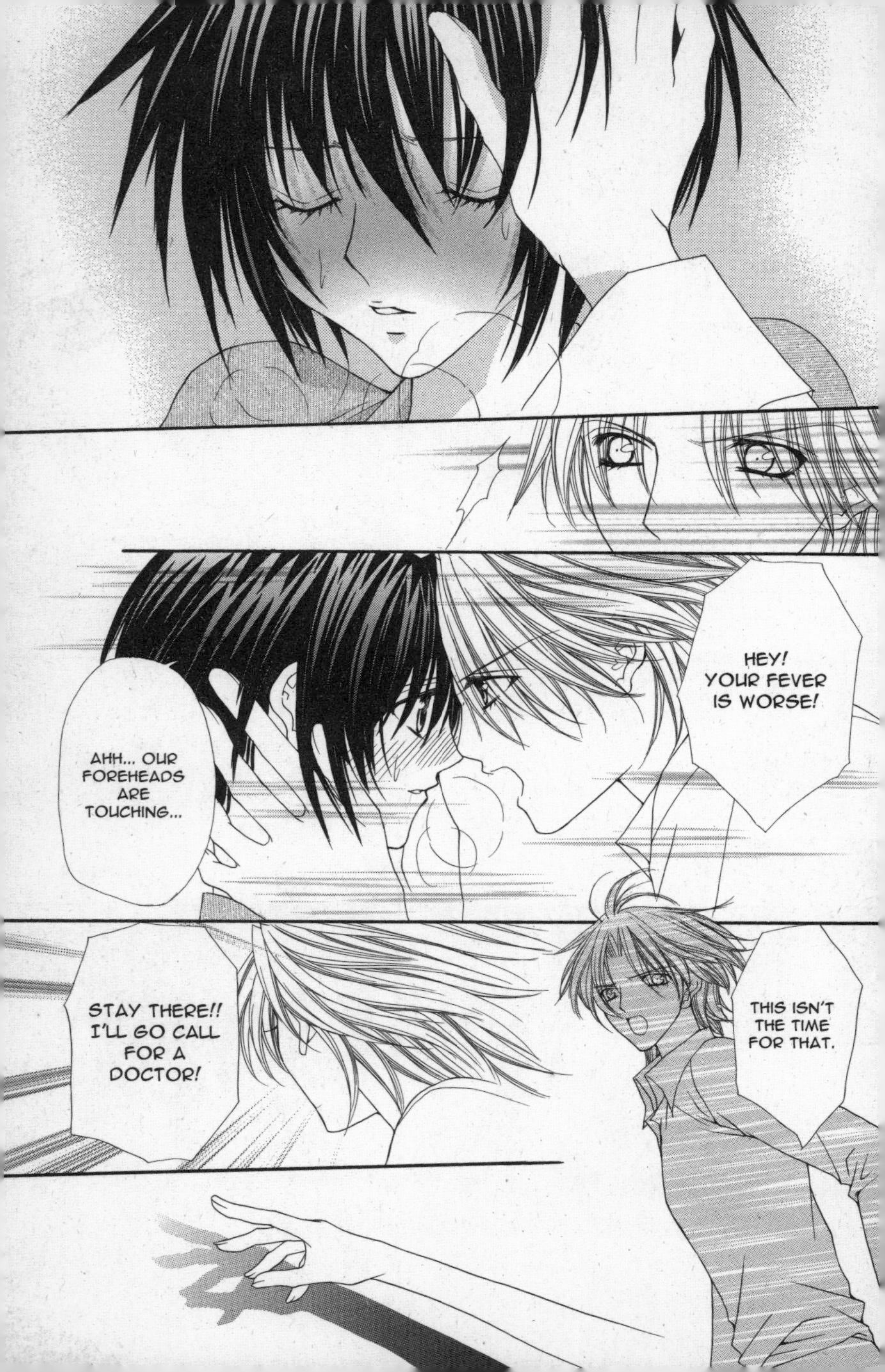
HEY! YOUR FEVER IS WORSE!
AHH... OUR FOREHEADS ARE TOUCHING...
THIS ISN'T THE TIME FOR THAT.
STAY THERE!! I'LL GO CALL FOR A DOCTOR!

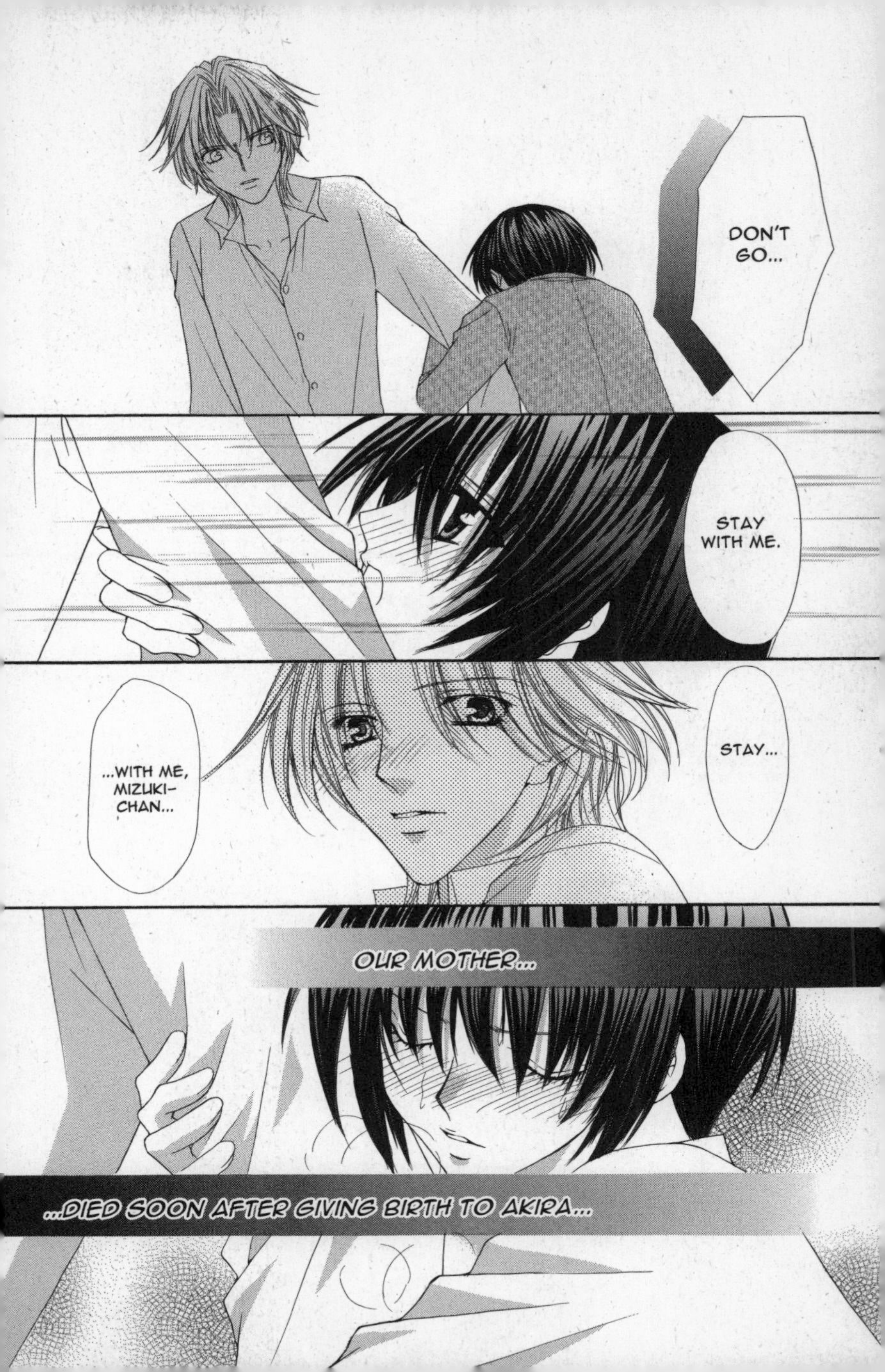
DON'T GO...
STAY WITH ME.
STAY...
...WITH ME, MIZUKI-CHAN...
OUR MOTHER...
...DIED SOON AFTER GIVING BIRTH TO AKIRA...

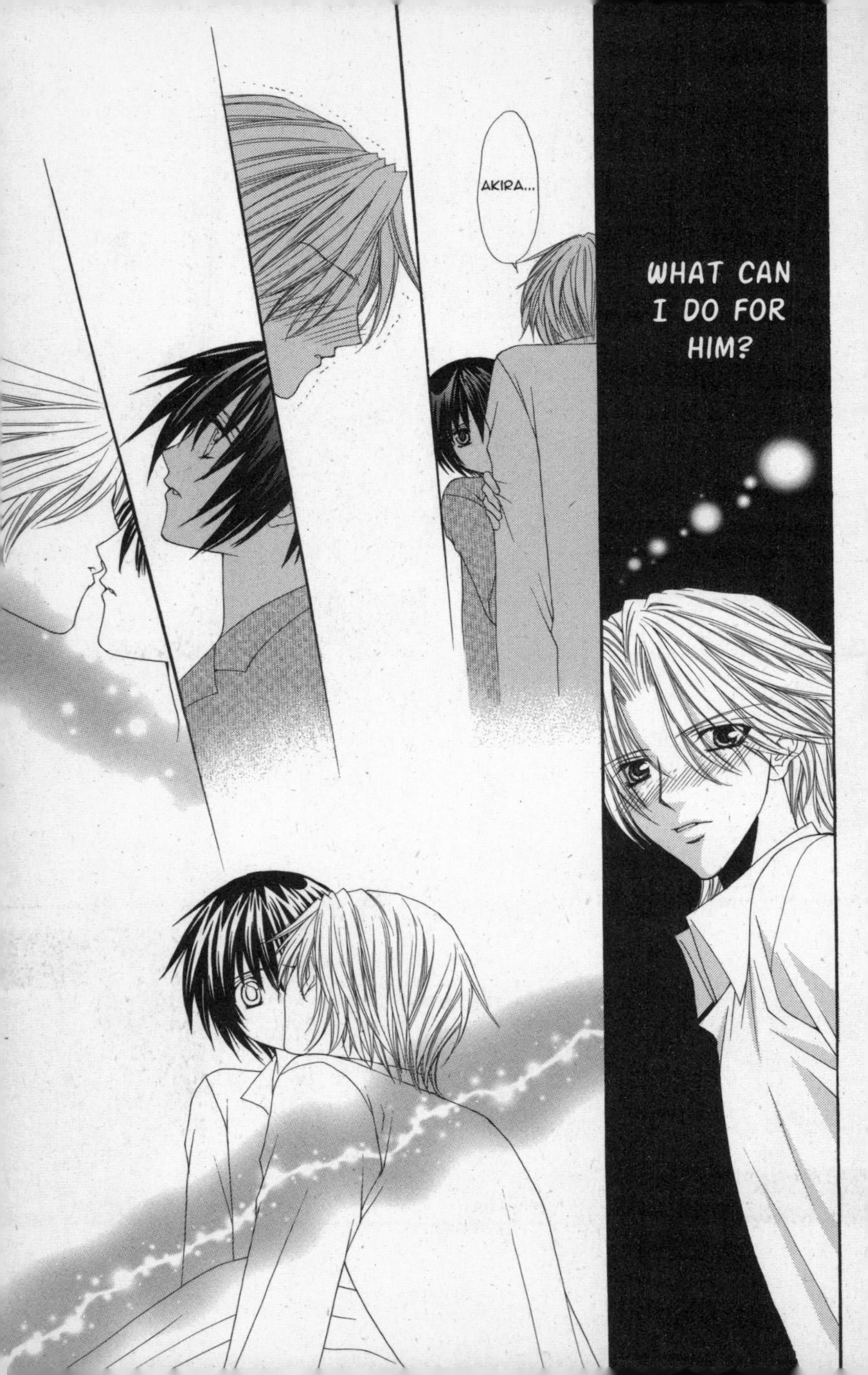
WHAT CAN I DO FOR HIM?
AKIRA...

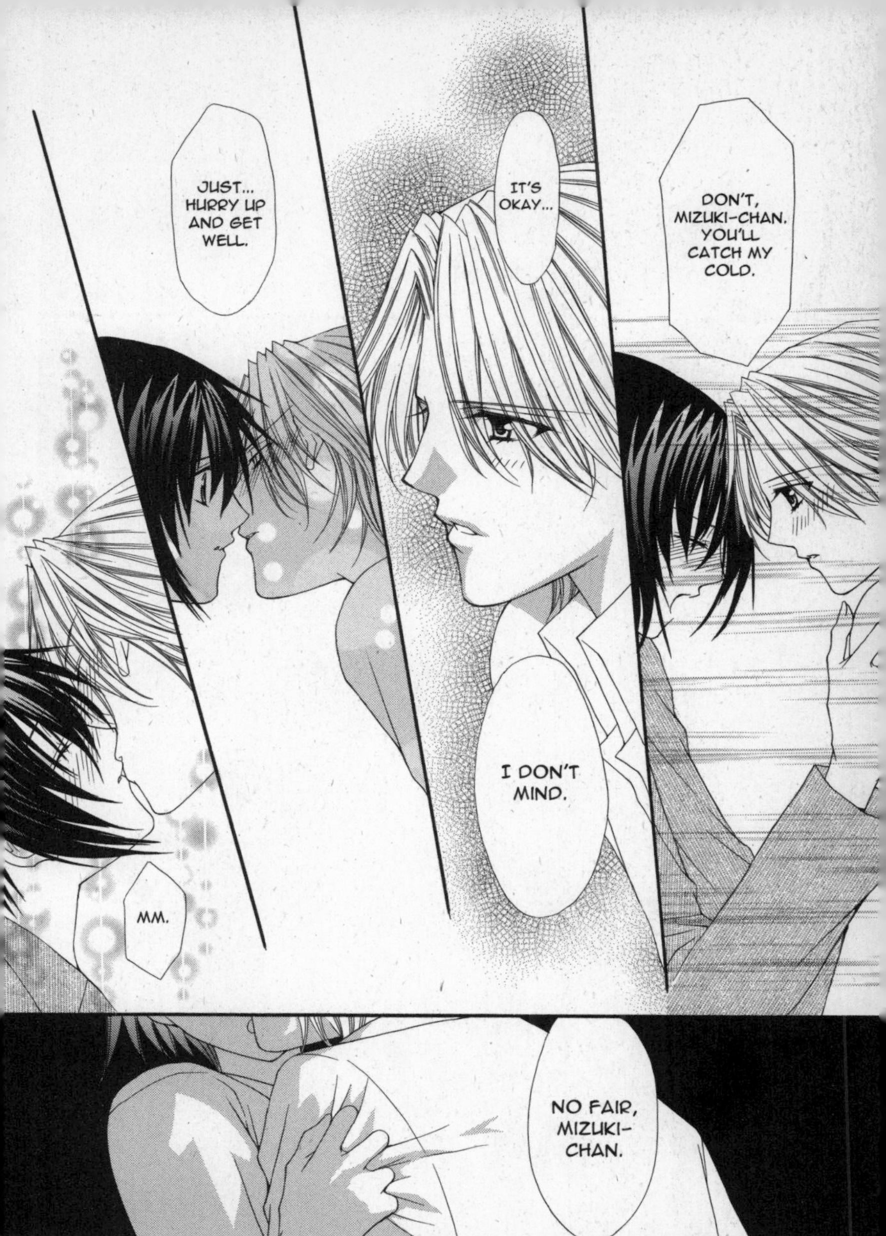
DON'T, MIZUKI-CHAN. YOU'LL CATCH MY COLD.
IT'S OKAY...
I DON'T MIND.
JUST... HURRY UP AND GET WELL.
MM.
NO FAIR, MIZUKI-CHAN.

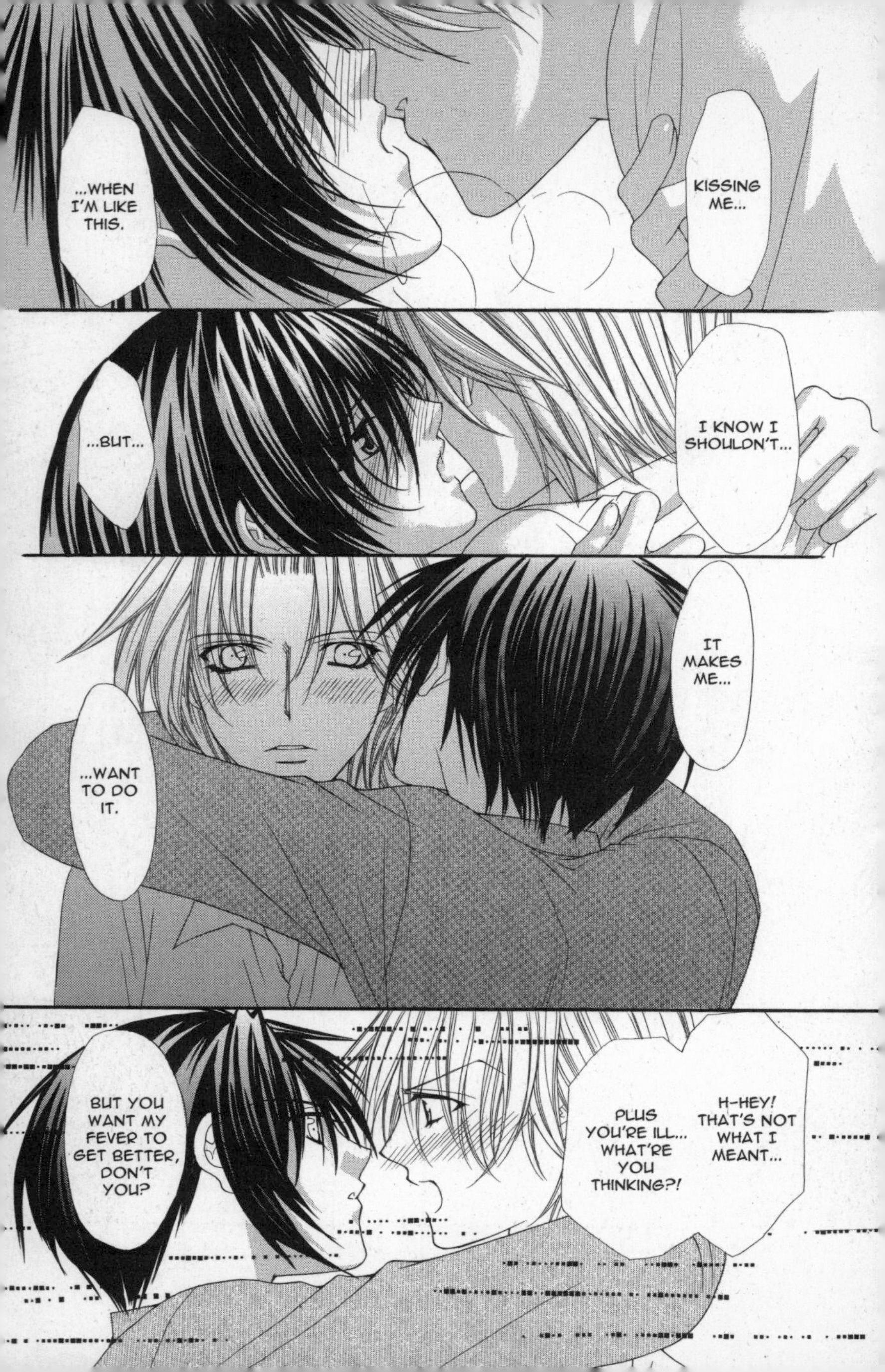
KISSING ME...
...WHEN I'M LIKE THIS.
I KNOW I SHOULDN'T...
...BUT...
IT MAKES ME...
...WANT TO DO IT.
H-HEY! THAT'S NOT WHAT I MEANT...
PLUS YOU'RE ILL... WHAT'RE YOU THINKING?!
BUT YOU WANT MY FEVER TO GET BETTER, DON'T YOU?

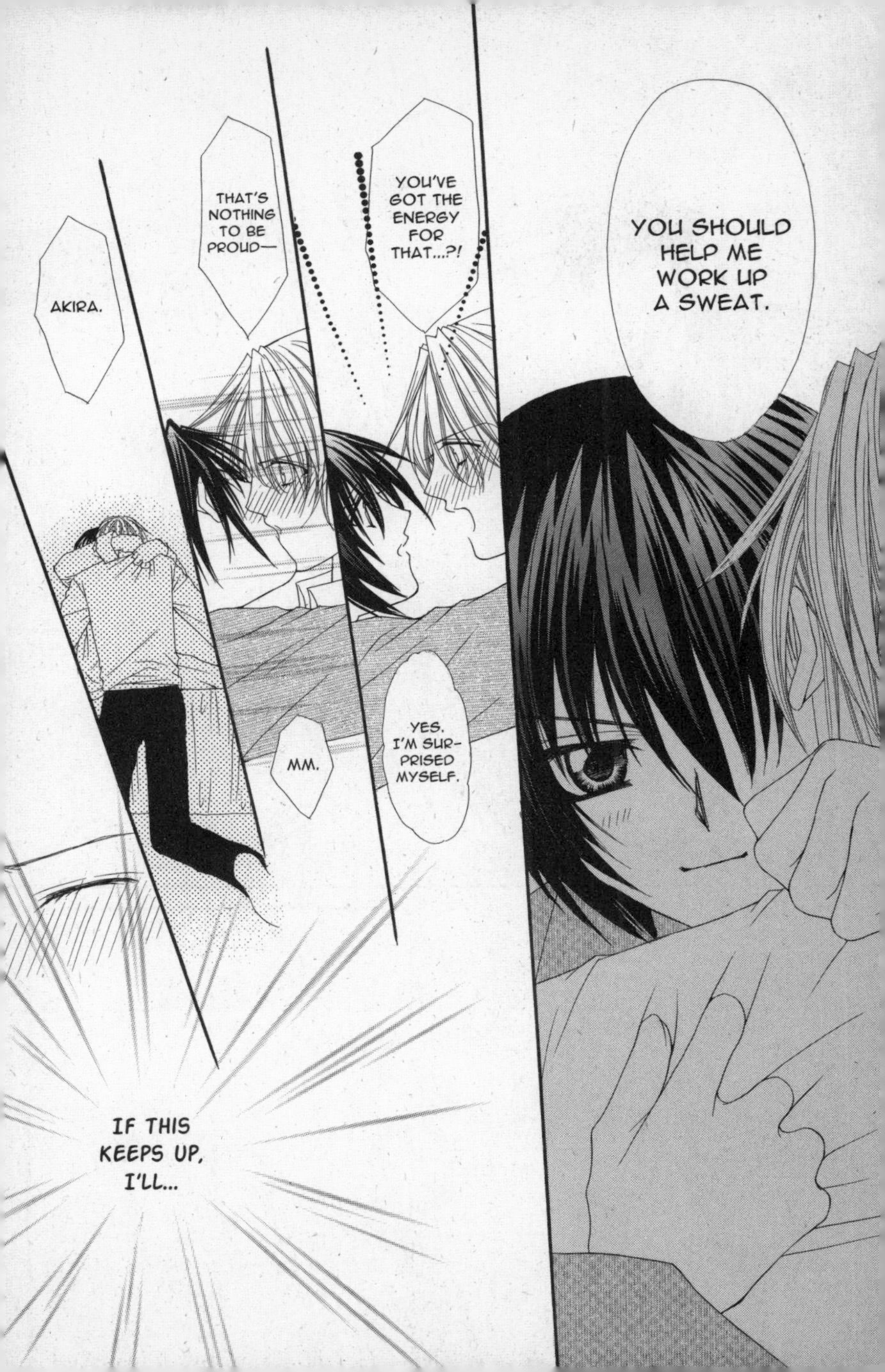
YOU SHOULD HELP ME WORK UP A SWEAT.
YOU'VE GOT THE ENERGY FOR THAT...?!
YES. I'M SUR-PRISED MYSELF.
THAT'S NOTHING TO BE PROUD—
MM.
AKIRA.
IF THIS KEEPS UP, I'LL...

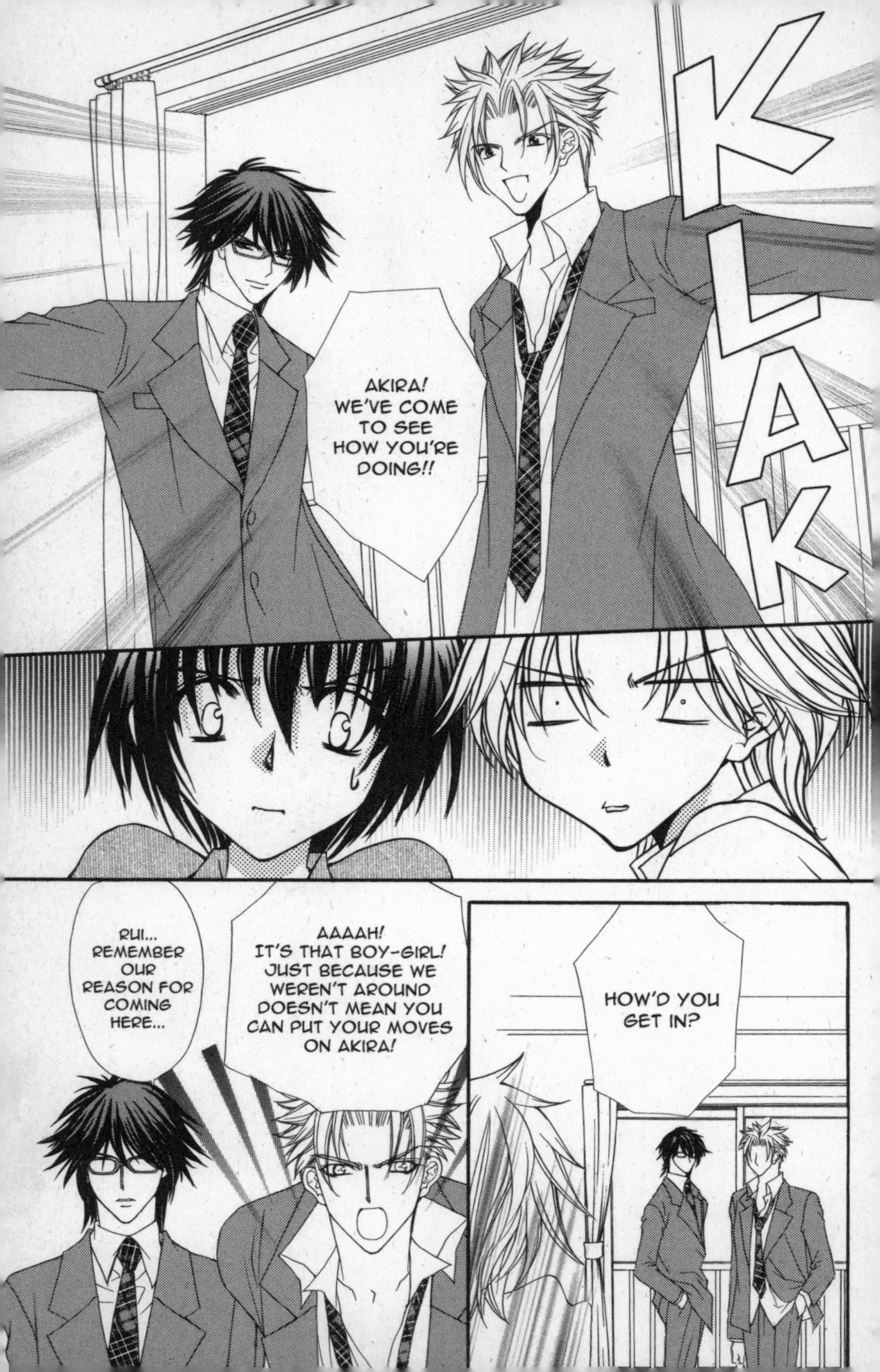
KLAK
AKIRA! WE'VE COME TO SEE HOW YOU'RE DOING!!
HOW'D YOU GET IN?
AAAAH! IT'S THAT BOY-GIRL! JUST BECAUSE WE WEREN'T AROUND DOESN'T MEAN YOU CAN PUT YOUR MOVES ON AKIRA!
RUI... REMEMBER OUR REASON FOR COMING HERE...

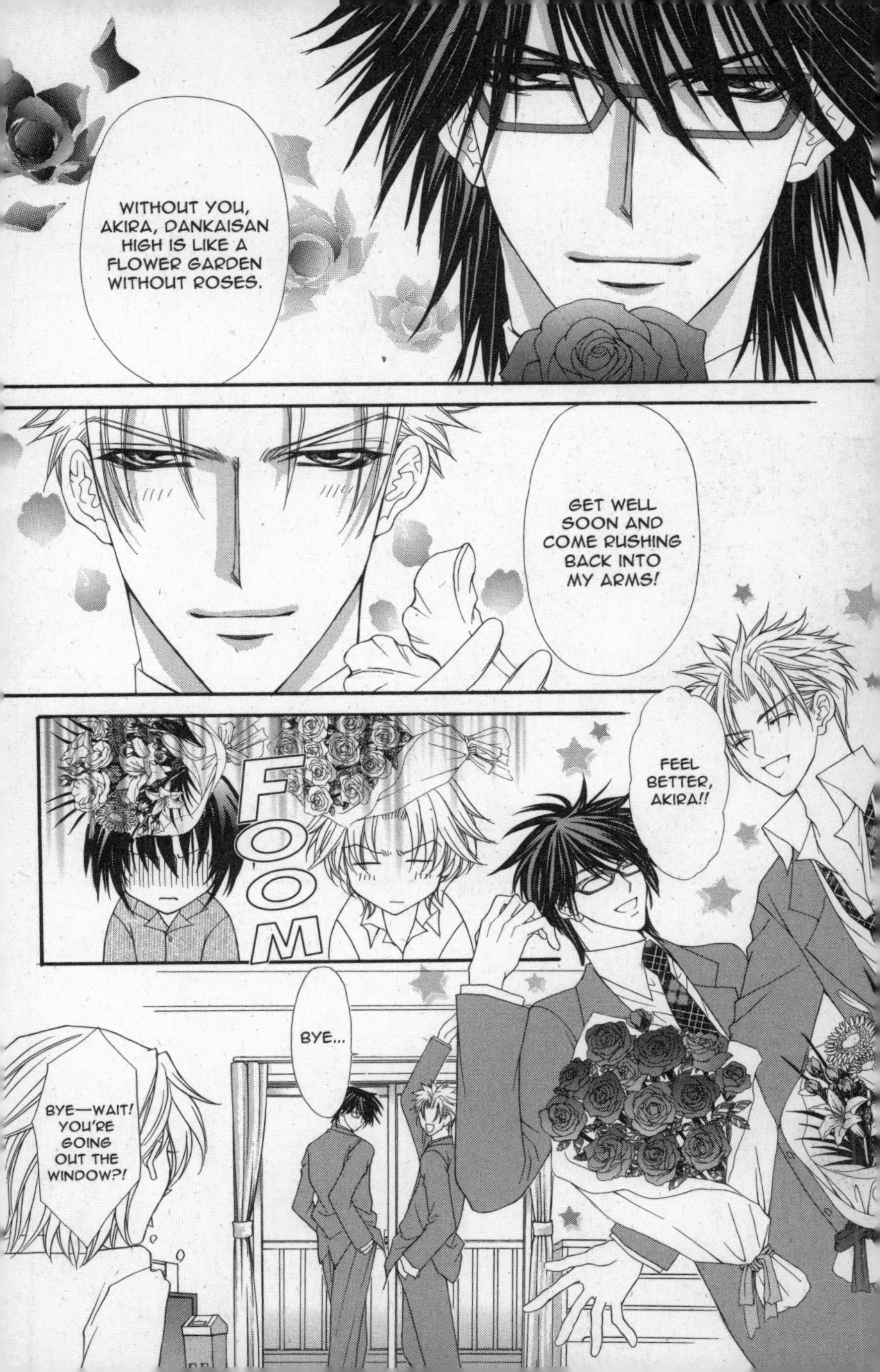
WITHOUT YOU, AKIRA, DANKAISAN HIGH IS LIKE A FLOWER GARDEN WITHOUT ROSES.
GET WELL SOON AND COME RUSHING BACK INTO MY ARMS!
FEEL BETTER, AKIRA!!
FOOOM
BYE...
BYE—WAIT! YOU'RE GOING OUT THE WINDOW?!

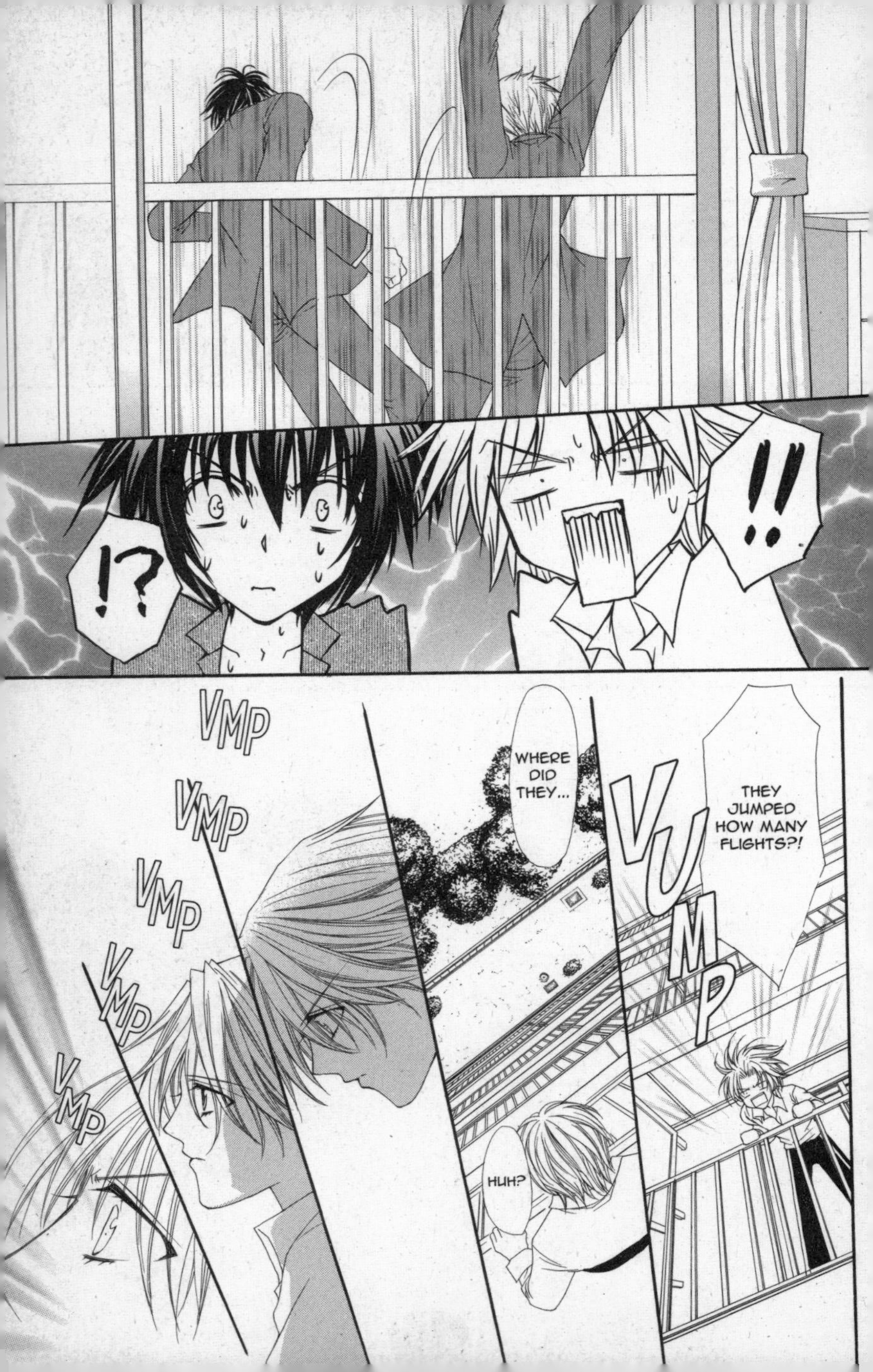
!!
!?
THEY JUMPED HOW MANY FLIGHTS?!
VUMP
WHERE DID THEY...
HUH?
VMP
VMP
VMP
VMP
VMP

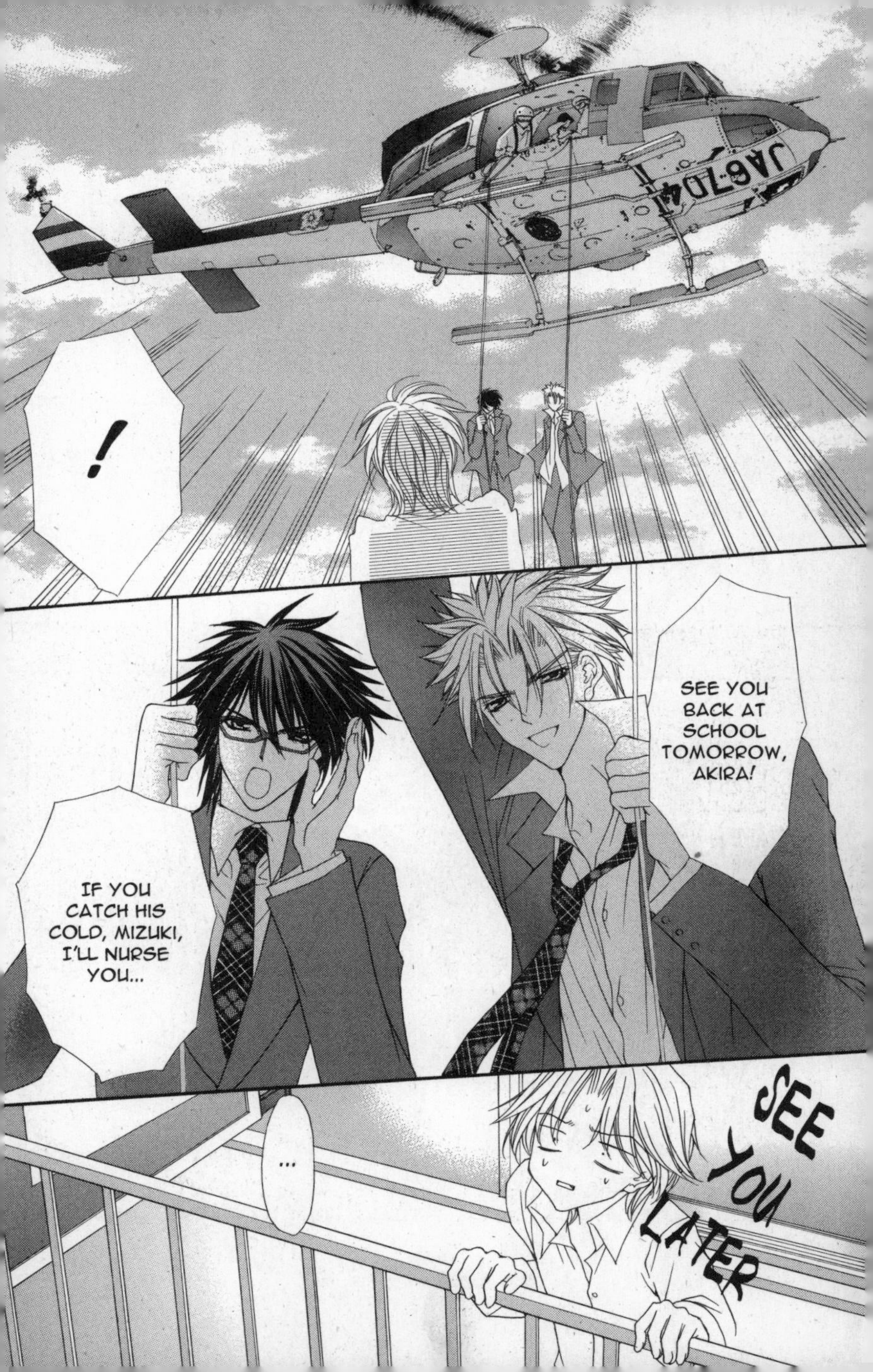
!
SEE YOU BACK AT SCHOOL TOMORROW, AKIRA!
IF YOU CATCH HIS COLD, MIZUKI, I'LL NURSE YOU...
SEE YOU LATER
...

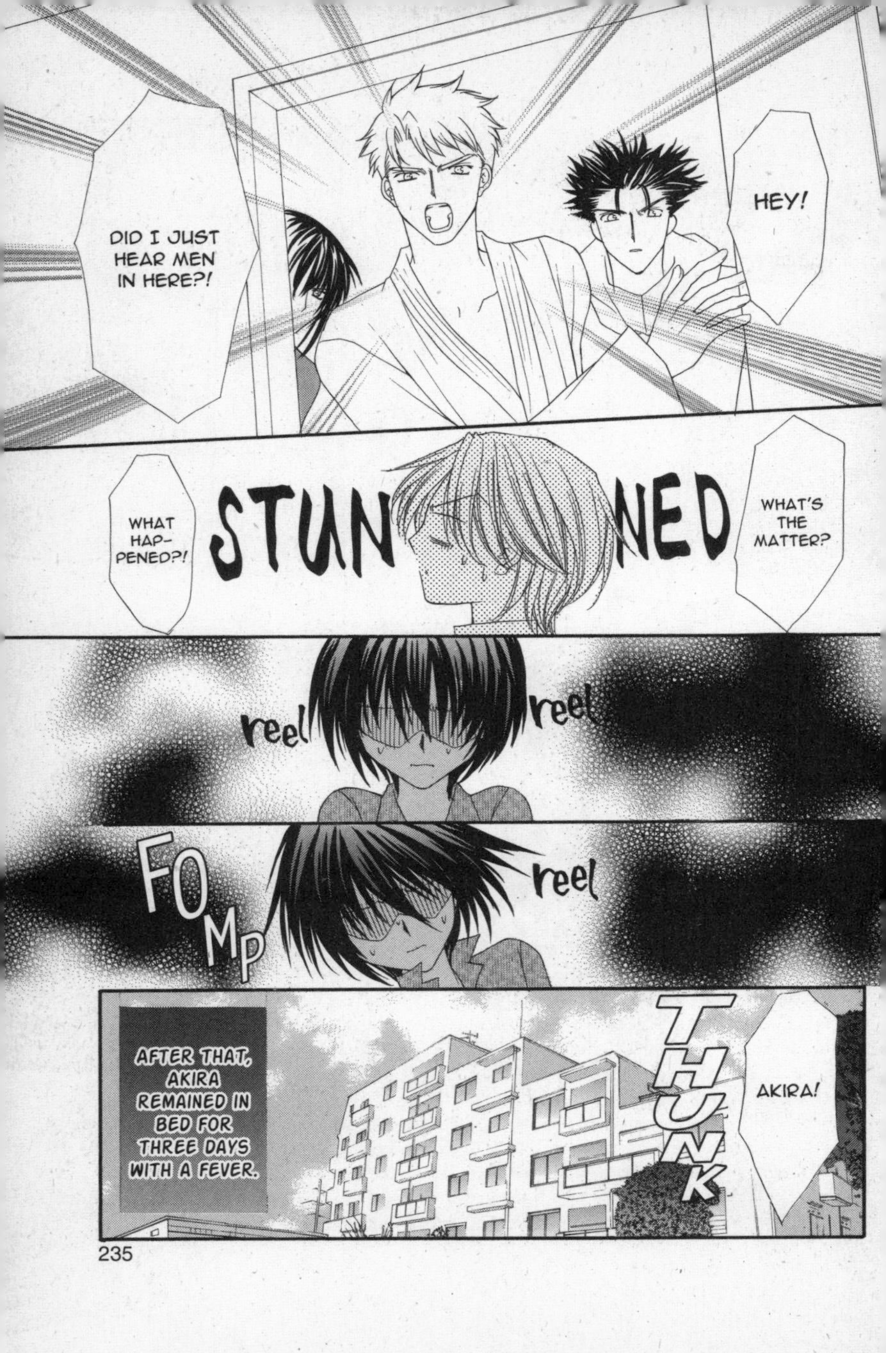
HEY!
DID I JUST HEAR MEN IN HERE?!
WHAT'S THE MATTER?
STUNNED
WHAT HAP-PENED?!
reel
reel
reel
FOMP
AKIRA!
THUNK
AFTER THAT, AKIRA REMAINED IN BED FOR THREE DAYS WITH A FEVER.

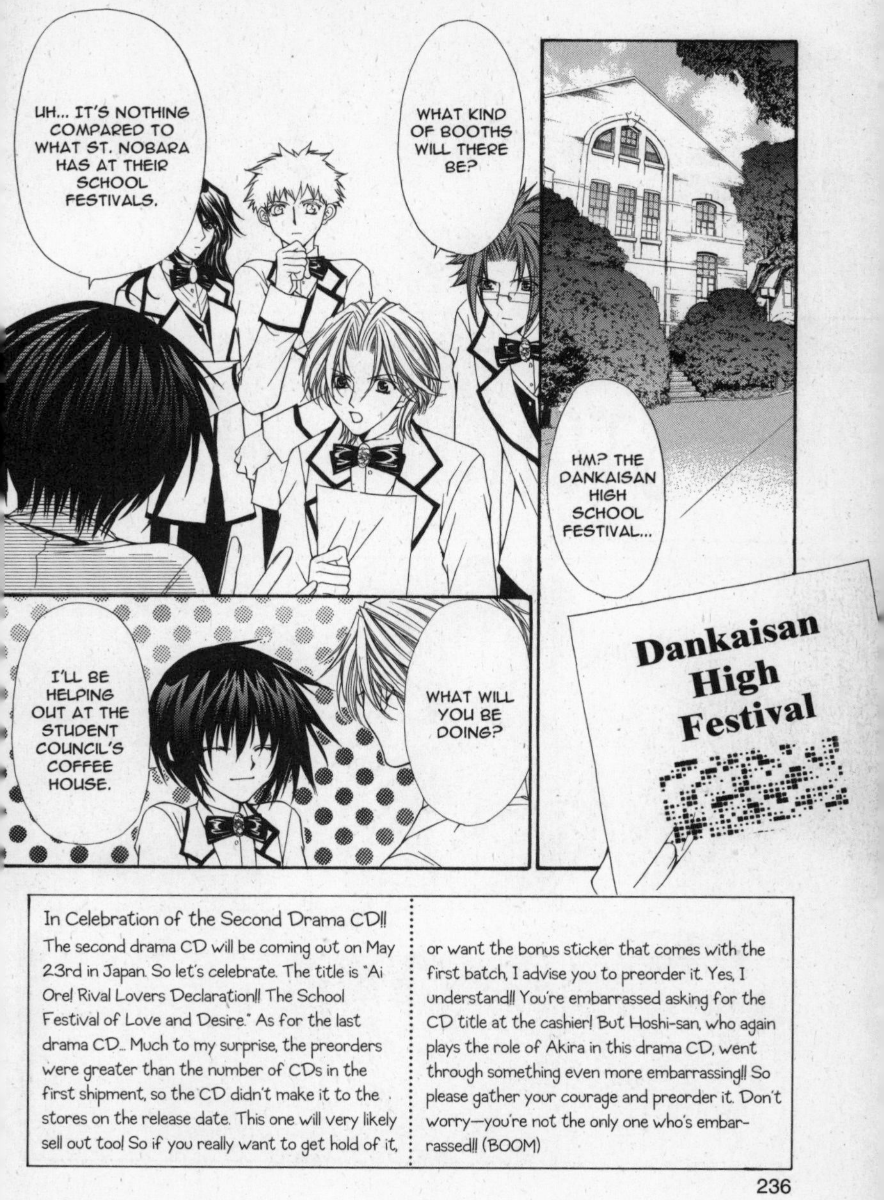
HM? THE DANKAISAN HIGH SCHOOL FESTIVAL...
Dankaisan High Festival
WHAT KIND OF BOOTHS WILL THERE BE?
UH... IT'S NOTHING COMPARED TO WHAT ST. NOBARA HAS AT THEIR SCHOOL FESTIVALS.
WHAT WILL YOU BE DOING?
I'LL BE HELPING OUT AT THE STUDENT COUNCIL'S COFFEE HOUSE.

In Celebration of the Second Drama CD!!

The second drama CD will be coming out on May 23rd in Japan. So let's celebrate. The title is "Ai Ore! Rival Lovers Declaration!! The School Festival of Love and Desire." As for the last drama CD... Much to my surprise, the preorders were greater than the number of CDs in the first shipment, so the CD didn't make it to the stores on the release date. This one will very likely sell out too! So if you really want to get hold of it, or want the bonus sticker that comes with the first batch, I advise you to preorder it. Yes, I understand!! You're embarrassed asking for the CD title at the cashier! But Hoshi-san, who again plays the role of Akira in this drama CD, went through something even more embarrassing!! So please gather your courage and preorder it. Don't worry—you're not the only one who's embarrassed!! (BOOM)

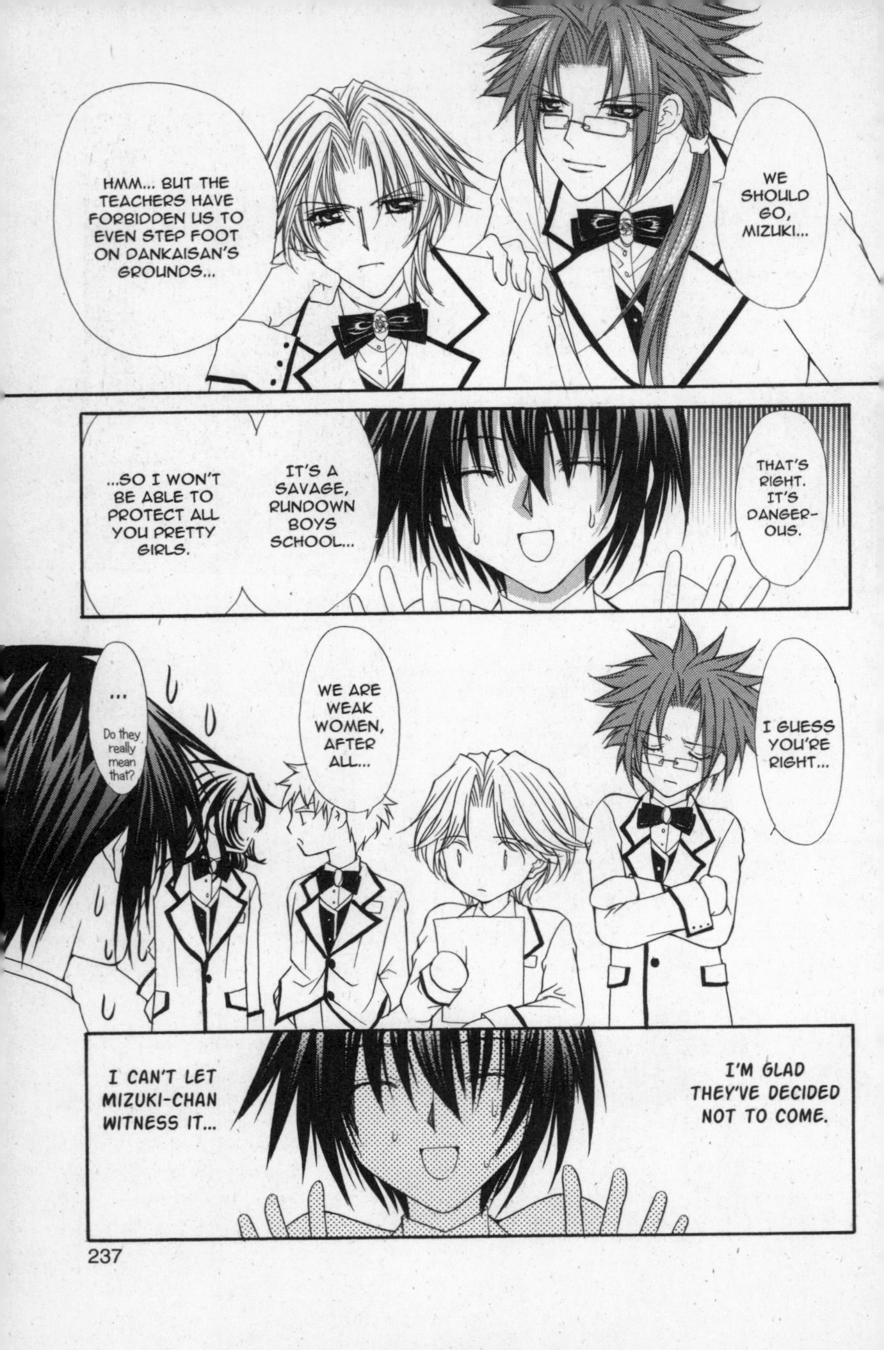
WE SHOULD GO, MIZUKI...
HMM... BUT THE TEACHERS HAVE FORBIDDEN US TO EVEN STEP FOOT ON DANKAISAN'S GROUNDS...
THAT'S RIGHT. IT'S DANGER-OUS.
IT'S A SAVAGE, RUNDOWN BOYS SCHOOL...
...SO I WON'T BE ABLE TO PROTECT ALL YOU PRETTY GIRLS.
I GUESS YOU'RE RIGHT...
WE ARE WEAK WOMEN, AFTER ALL...
...
Do they really mean that?
I'M GLAD THEY'VE DECIDED NOT TO COME.
I CAN'T LET MIZUKI-CHAN WITNESS IT...

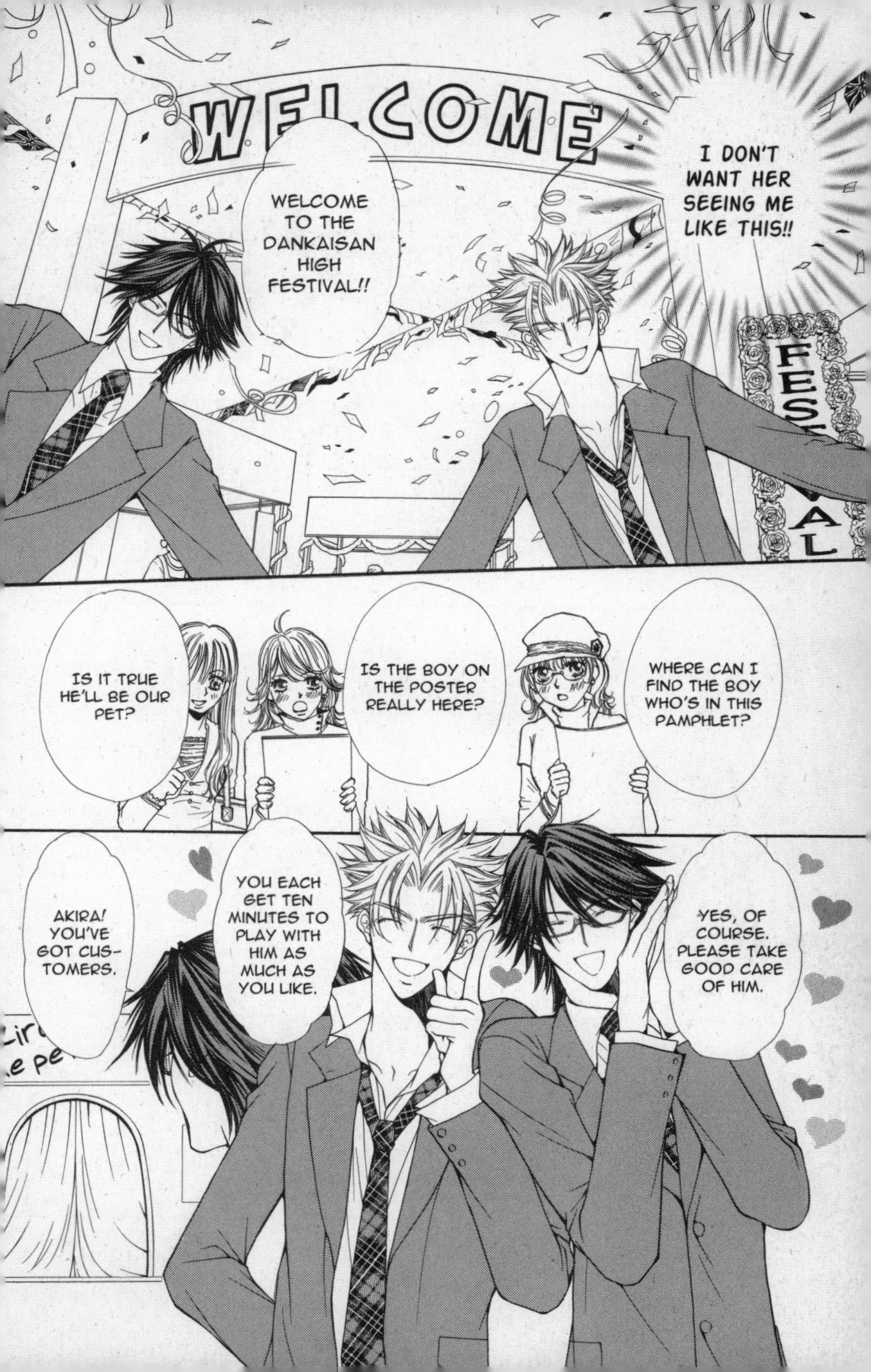
WELCOME
I DON'T WANT HER SEEING ME LIKE THIS!!
WELCOME TO THE DANKAISAN HIGH FESTIVAL!!
WHERE CAN I FIND THE BOY WHO'S IN THIS PAMPHLET?
IS THE BOY ON THE POSTER REALLY HERE?
IS IT TRUE HE'LL BE OUR PET?
YES, OF COURSE. PLEASE TAKE GOOD CARE OF HIM.
YOU EACH GET TEN MINUTES TO PLAY WITH HIM AS MUCH AS YOU LIKE.
AKIRA! YOU'VE GOT CUS- TOMERS.

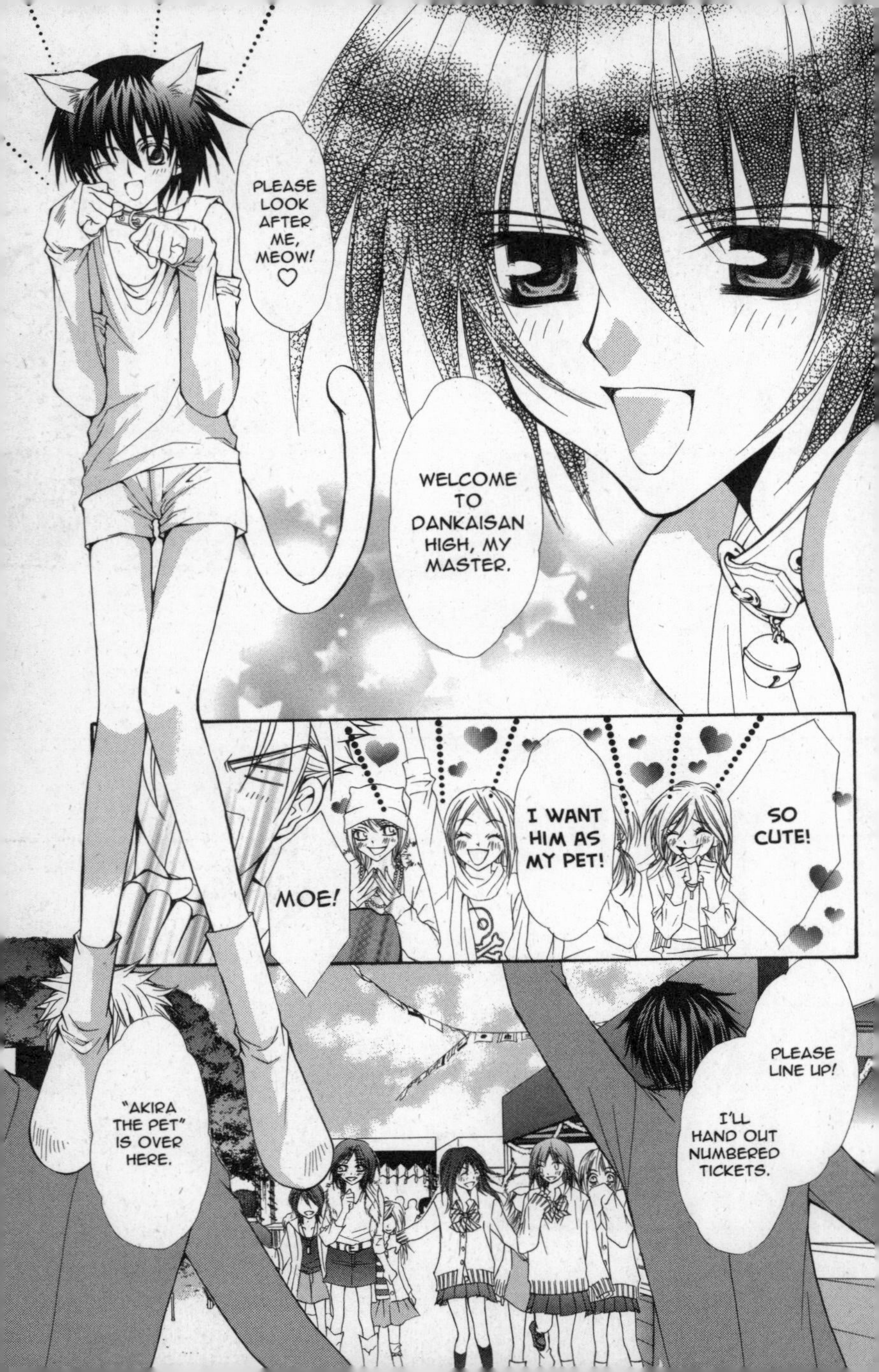
WELCOME TO DANKAISAN HIGH, MY MASTER.
PLEASE LOOK AFTER ME, MEOW! ♡
SO CUTE!
I WANT HIM AS MY PET!
MOE!
PLEASE LINE UP!
I'LL HAND OUT NUMBERED TICKETS.
"AKIRA THE PET" IS OVER HERE.

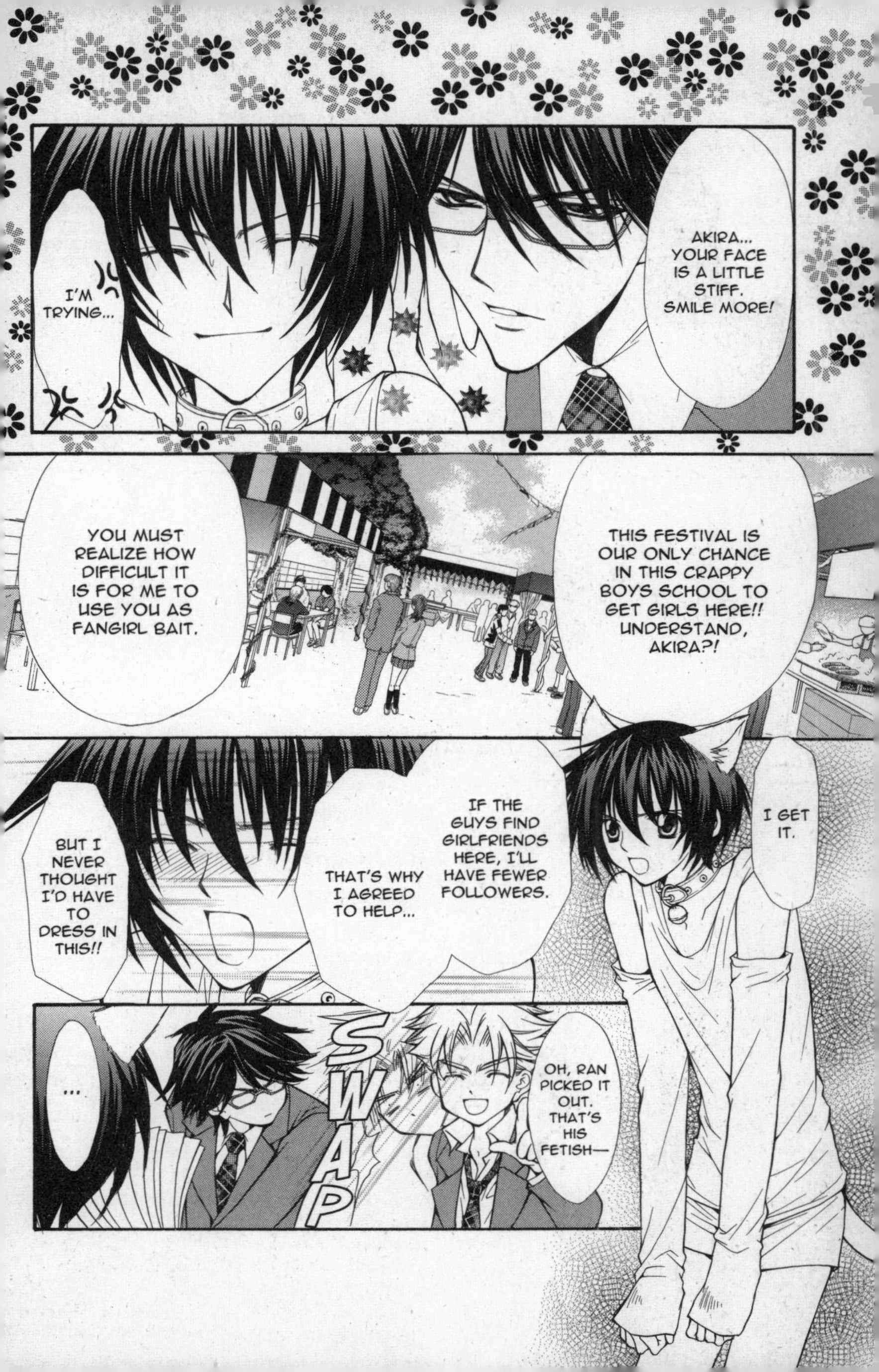
AKIRA... YOUR FACE IS A LITTLE STIFF. SMILE MORE!
I'M TRYING...
THIS FESTIVAL IS OUR ONLY CHANCE IN THIS CRAPPY BOYS SCHOOL TO GET GIRLS HERE!! UNDERSTAND, AKIRA?!
YOU MUST REALIZE HOW DIFFICULT IT IS FOR ME TO USE YOU AS FANGIRL BAIT.
I GET IT.
IF THE GUYS FIND GIRLFRIENDS HERE, I'LL HAVE FEWER FOLLOWERS.
THAT'S WHY I AGREED TO HELP...
BUT I NEVER THOUGHT I'D HAVE TO DRESS IN THIS!!
OH, RAN PICKED IT OUT. THAT'S HIS FETISH—
SWAP
...

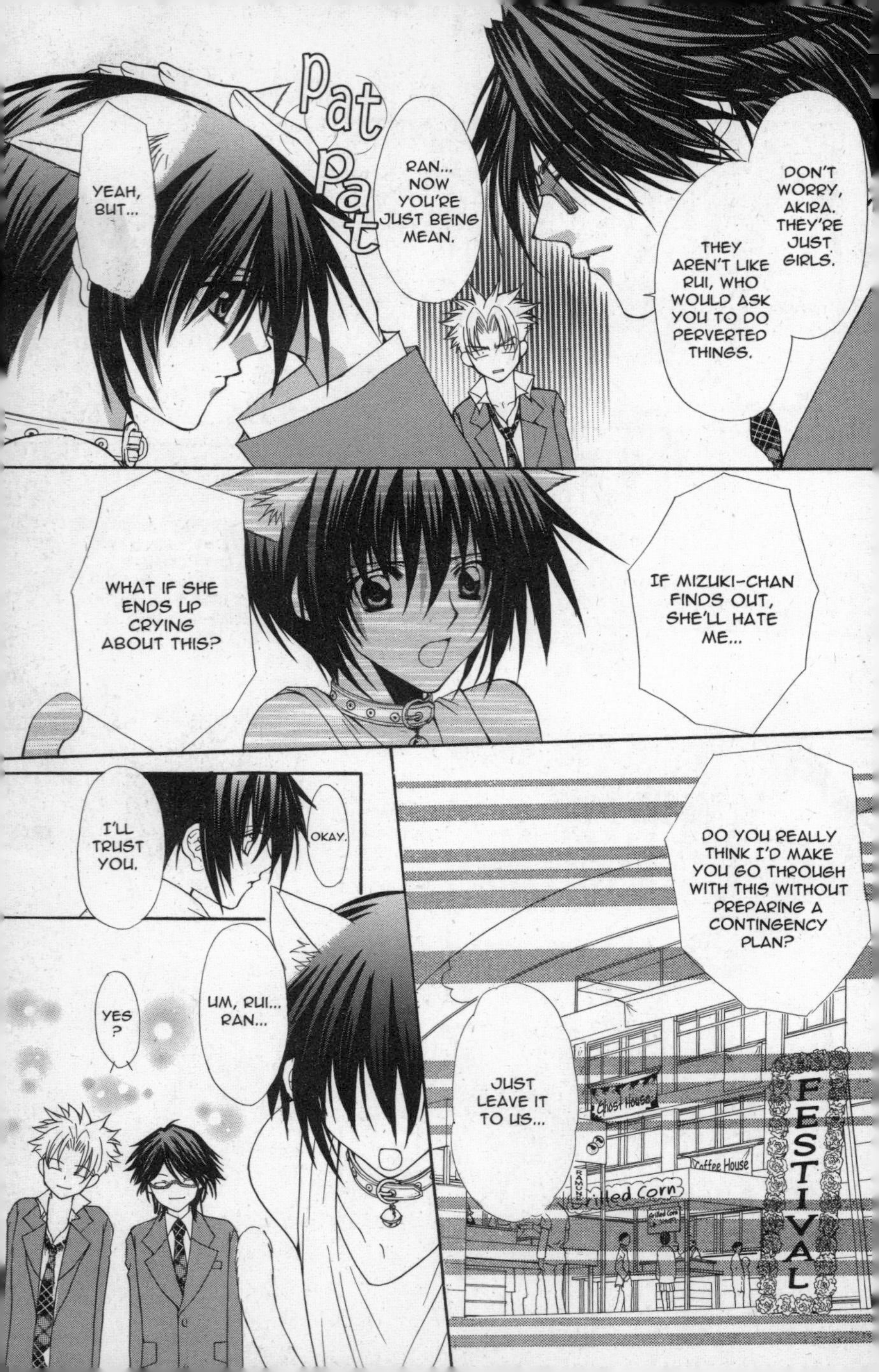
DON'T WORRY, AKIRA. THEY'RE JUST GIRLS.
THEY AREN'T LIKE RUI, WHO WOULD ASK YOU TO DO PERVERTED THINGS.
RAN... NOW YOU'RE JUST BEING MEAN.
Pat Pat
YEAH, BUT...
IF MIZUKI-CHAN FINDS OUT, SHE'LL HATE ME...
WHAT IF SHE ENDS UP CRYING ABOUT THIS?
DO YOU REALLY THINK I'D MAKE YOU GO THROUGH WITH THIS WITHOUT PREPARING A CONTINGENCY PLAN?
JUST LEAVE IT TO US...
FESTIVAL
Ghost House
Coffee House
RAMUNE
Grilled Corn
OKAY.
I'LL TRUST YOU.
UM, RUI... RAN...
YES?

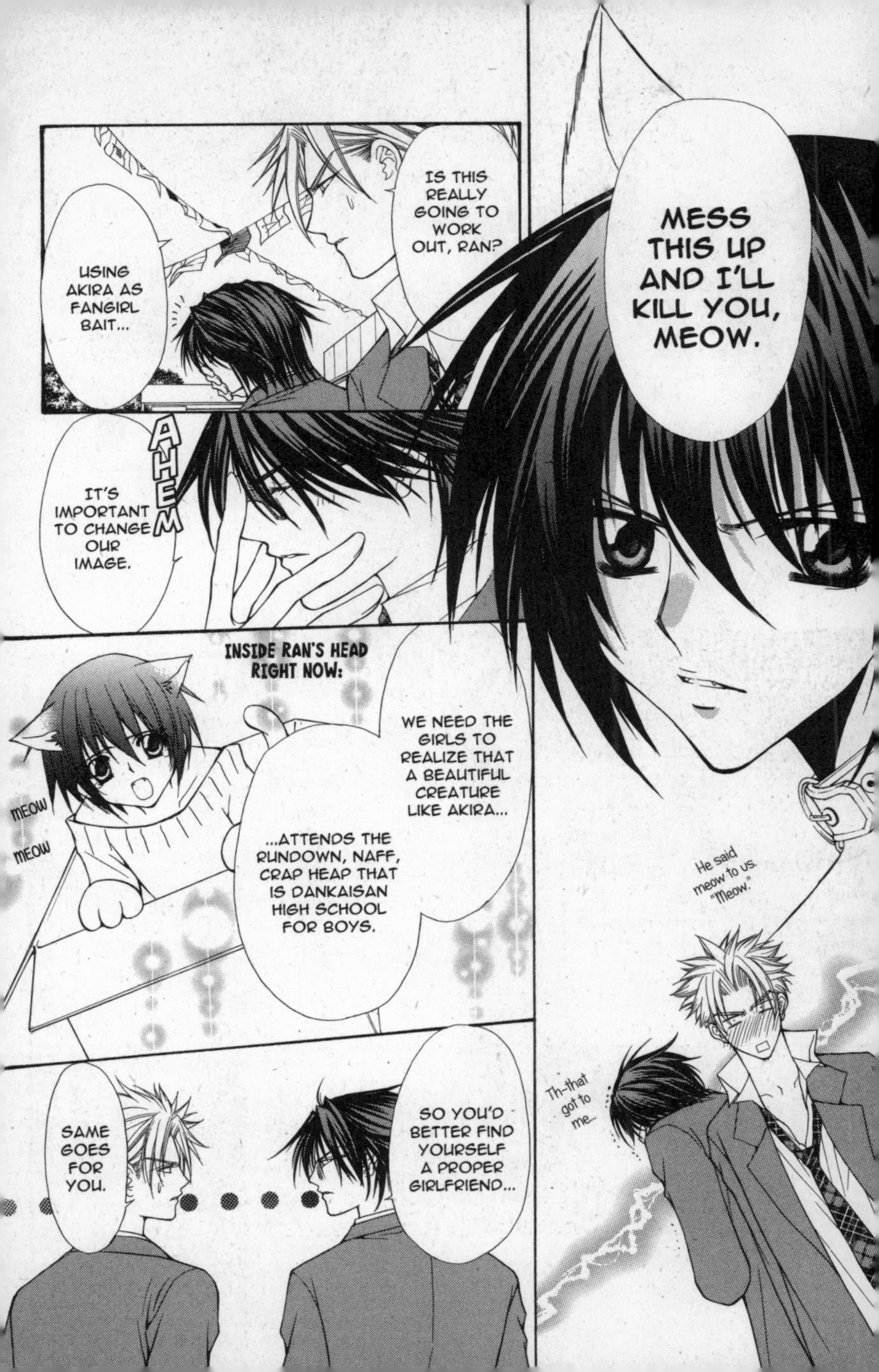

MESS THIS UP AND I'LL KILL YOU, MEOW.
He said meow to us. "Meow."
Th-that got to me...
IS THIS REALLY GOING TO WORK OUT, RAN?
USING AKIRA AS FANGIRL BAIT...
AHEM
IT'S IMPORTANT TO CHANGE OUR IMAGE.
INSIDE RAN'S HEAD RIGHT NOW:
WE NEED THE GIRLS TO REALIZE THAT A BEAUTIFUL CREATURE LIKE AKIRA...
...ATTENDS THE RUNDOWN, NAFF, CRAP HEAP THAT IS DANKAISAN HIGH SCHOOL FOR BOYS.
MEOW
MEOW
SO YOU'D BETTER FIND YOURSELF A PROPER GIRLFRIEND...
SAME GOES FOR YOU.

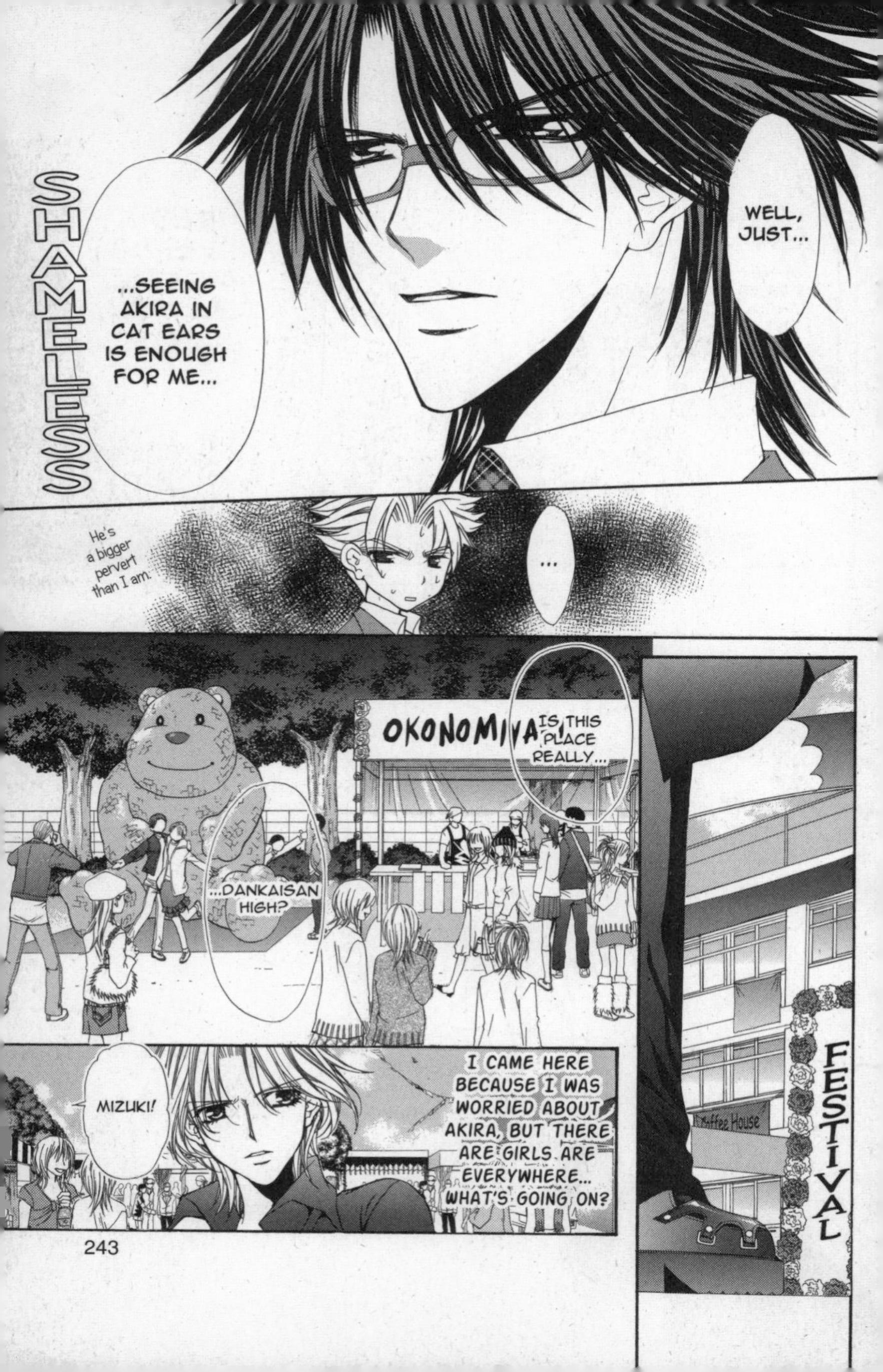
WELL, JUST...
...SEEING AKIRA IN CAT EARS IS ENOUGH FOR ME...
SHAMELESS
...
He's a bigger pervert than I am.
FESTIVAL
IS THIS PLACE REALLY...
...DANKAISAN HIGH?
I CAME HERE BECAUSE I WAS WORRIED ABOUT AKIRA, BUT THERE ARE GIRLS ARE EVERYWHERE... WHAT'S GOING ON?
MIZUKI!

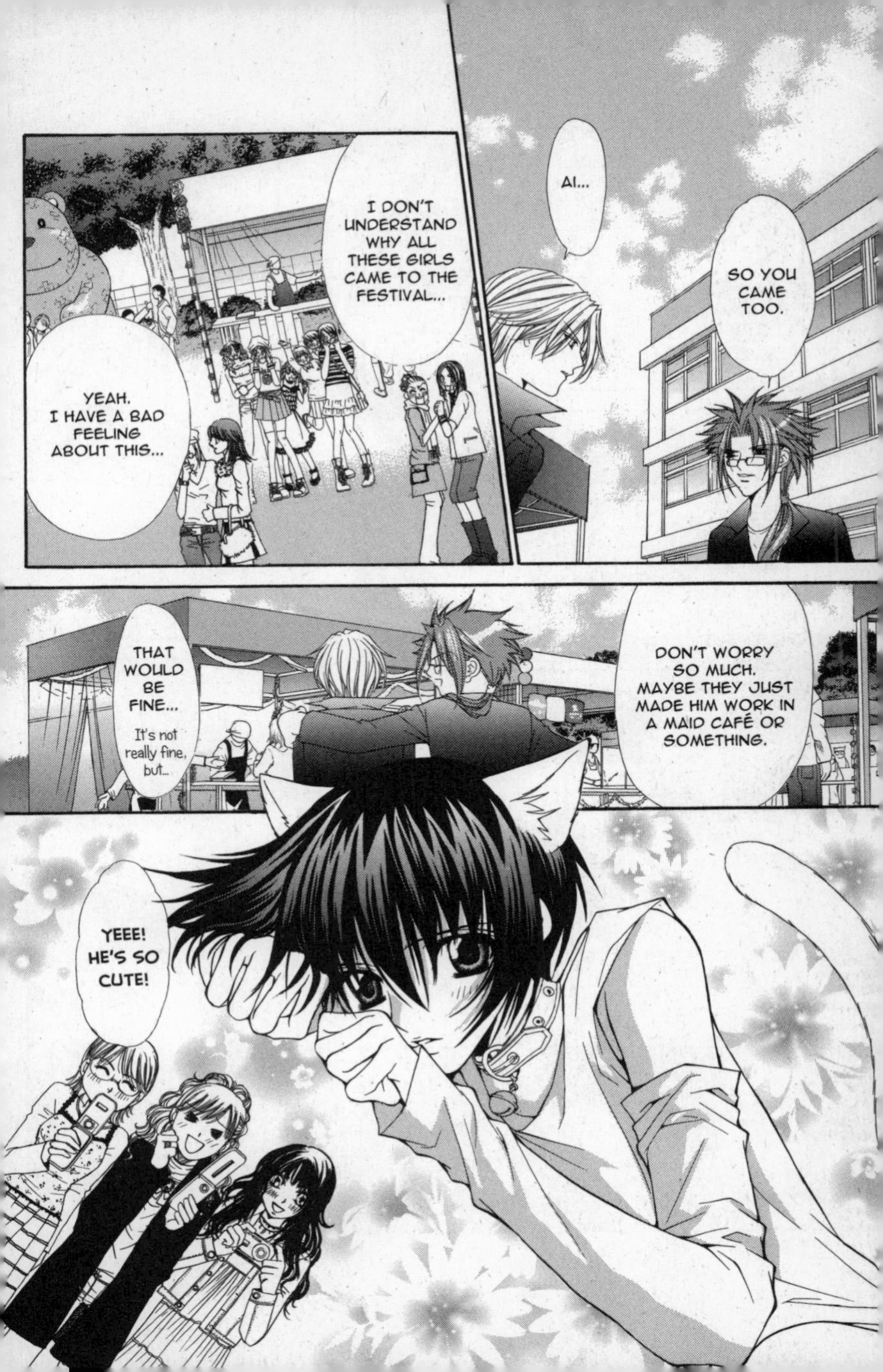
AI...
SO YOU CAME TOO.
I DON'T UNDERSTAND WHY ALL THESE GIRLS CAME TO THE FESTIVAL...
YEAH. I HAVE A BAD FEELING ABOUT THIS...
DON'T WORRY SO MUCH. MAYBE THEY JUST MADE HIM WORK IN A MAID CAFÉ OR SOMETHING.
THAT WOULD BE FINE...
It's not really fine, but...
YEEE! HE'S SO CUTE!

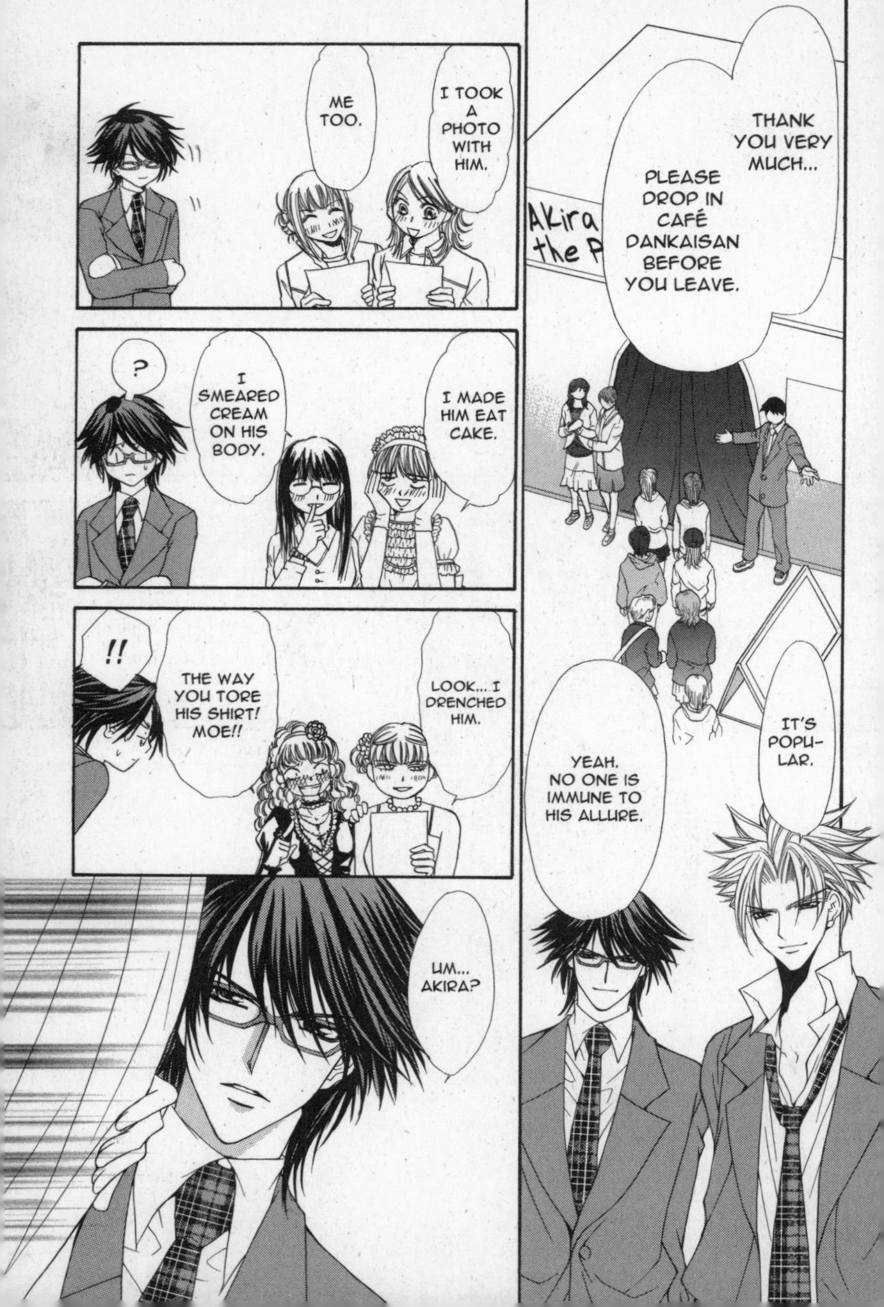
THANK YOU VERY MUCH...
PLEASE DROP IN CAFÉ DANKAISAN BEFORE YOU LEAVE.
Akira
IT'S POPU-LAR.
YEAH. NO ONE IS IMMUNE TO HIS ALLURE.
I TOOK A PHOTO WITH HIM.
ME TOO.
I MADE HIM EAT CAKE.
I SMEARED CREAM ON HIS BODY.
?
LOOK... I DRENCHED HIM.
THE WAY YOU TORE HIS SHIRT! MOE!!
!!
UM... AKIRA?

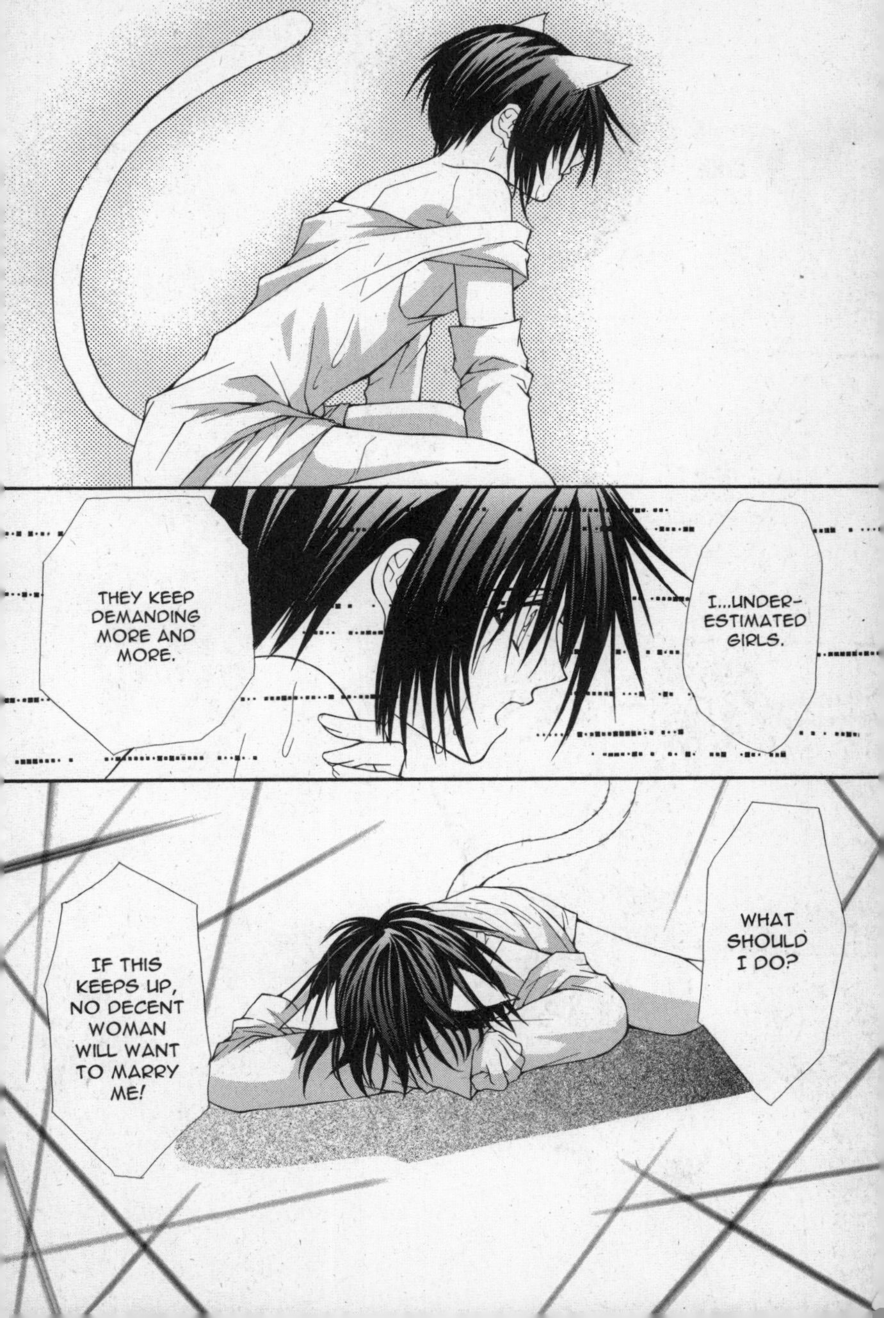
I...UNDER-ESTIMATED GIRLS.
THEY KEEP DEMANDING MORE AND MORE.
WHAT SHOULD I DO?
IF THIS KEEPS UP, NO DECENT WOMAN WILL WANT TO MARRY ME!

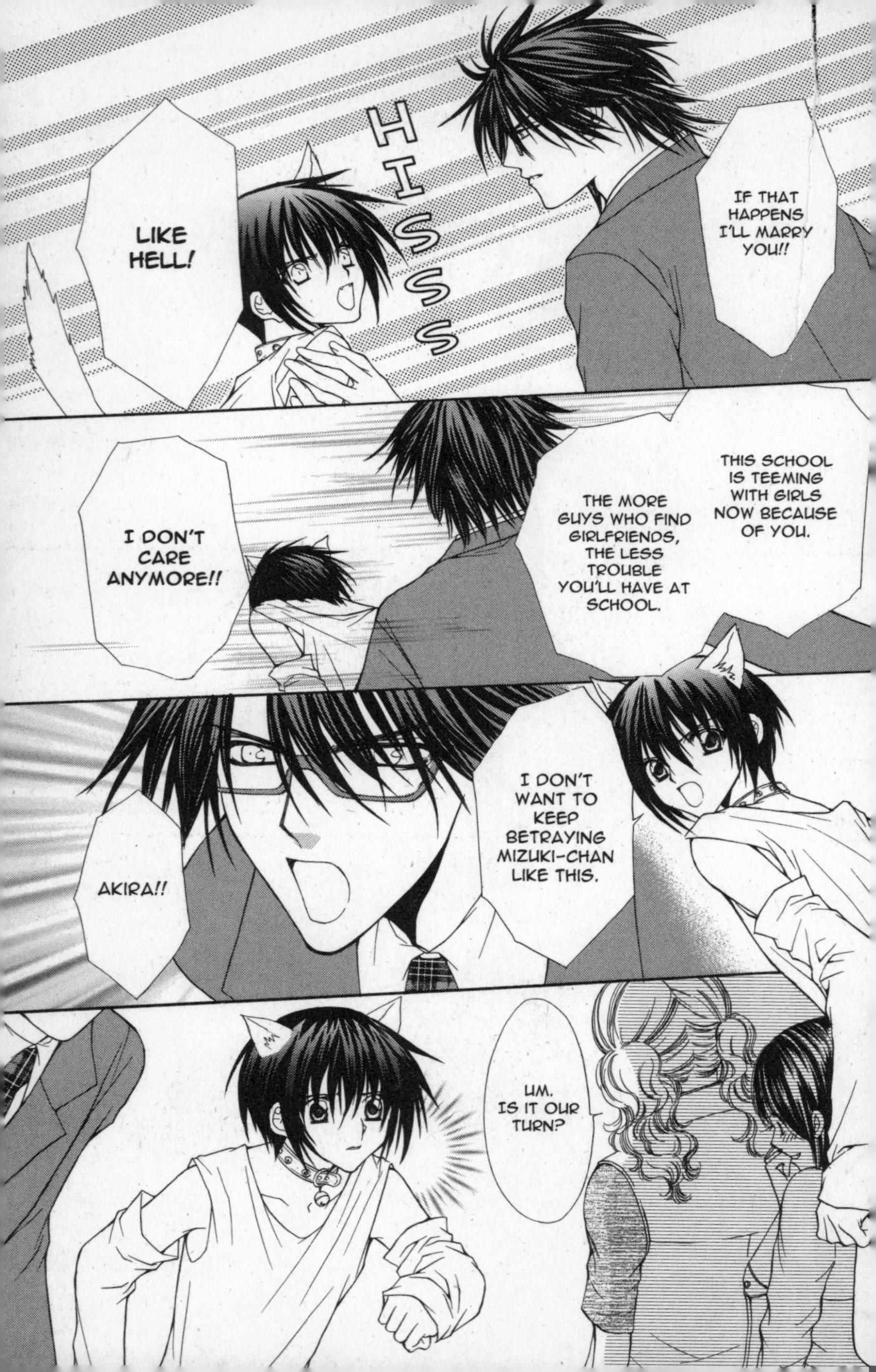
IF THAT HAPPENS I'LL MARRY YOU!!
HISSS
LIKE HELL!
THIS SCHOOL IS TEEMING WITH GIRLS NOW BECAUSE OF YOU.
THE MORE GUYS WHO FIND GIRLFRIENDS, THE LESS TROUBLE YOU'LL HAVE AT SCHOOL.
I DON'T CARE ANYMORE!!
I DON'T WANT TO KEEP BETRAYING MIZUKI-CHAN LIKE THIS.
AKIRA!!
UM. IS IT OUR TURN?

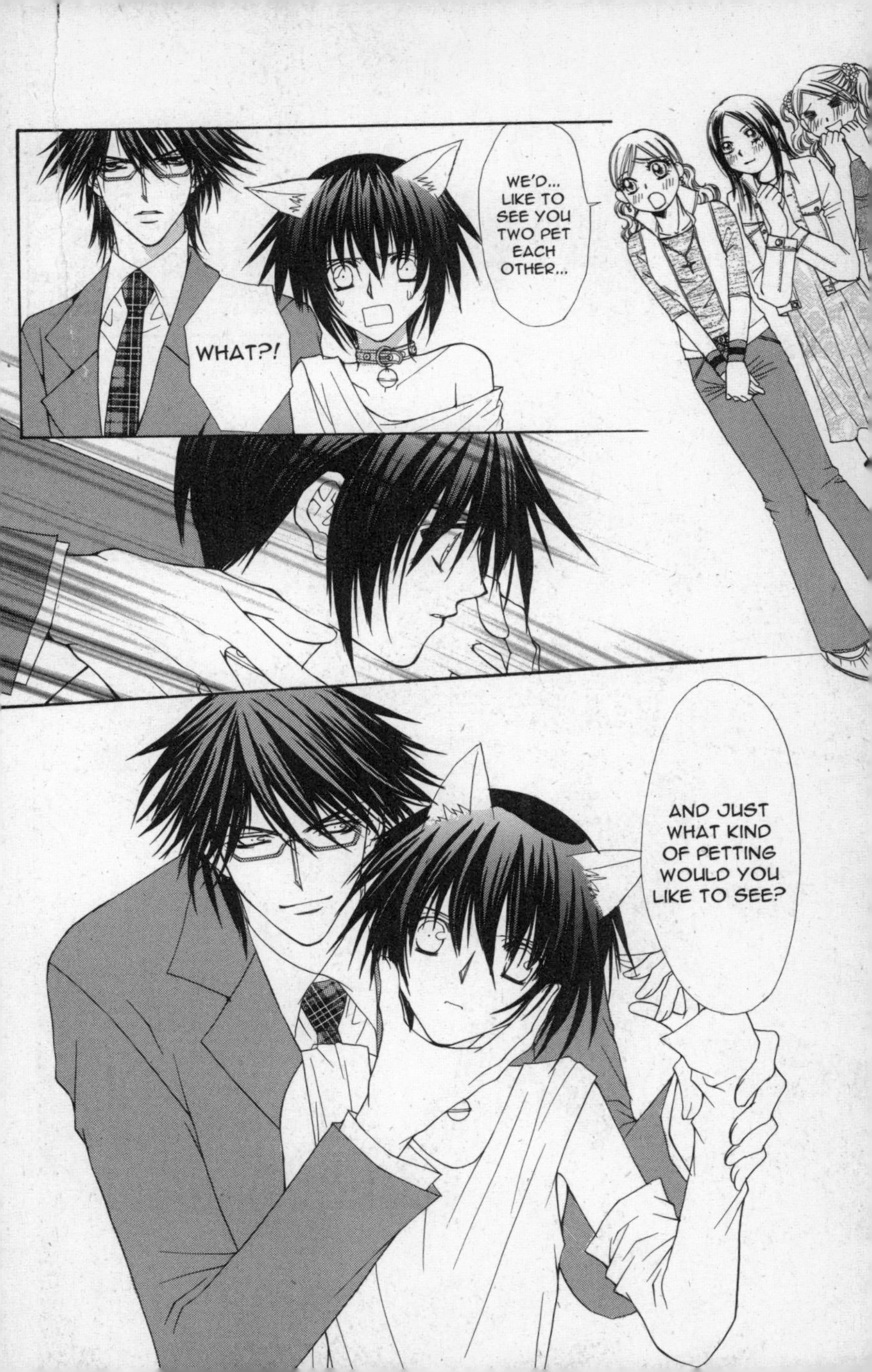
WE'D... LIKE TO SEE YOU TWO PET EACH OTHER...
WHAT?!
AND JUST WHAT KIND OF PETTING WOULD YOU LIKE TO SEE?

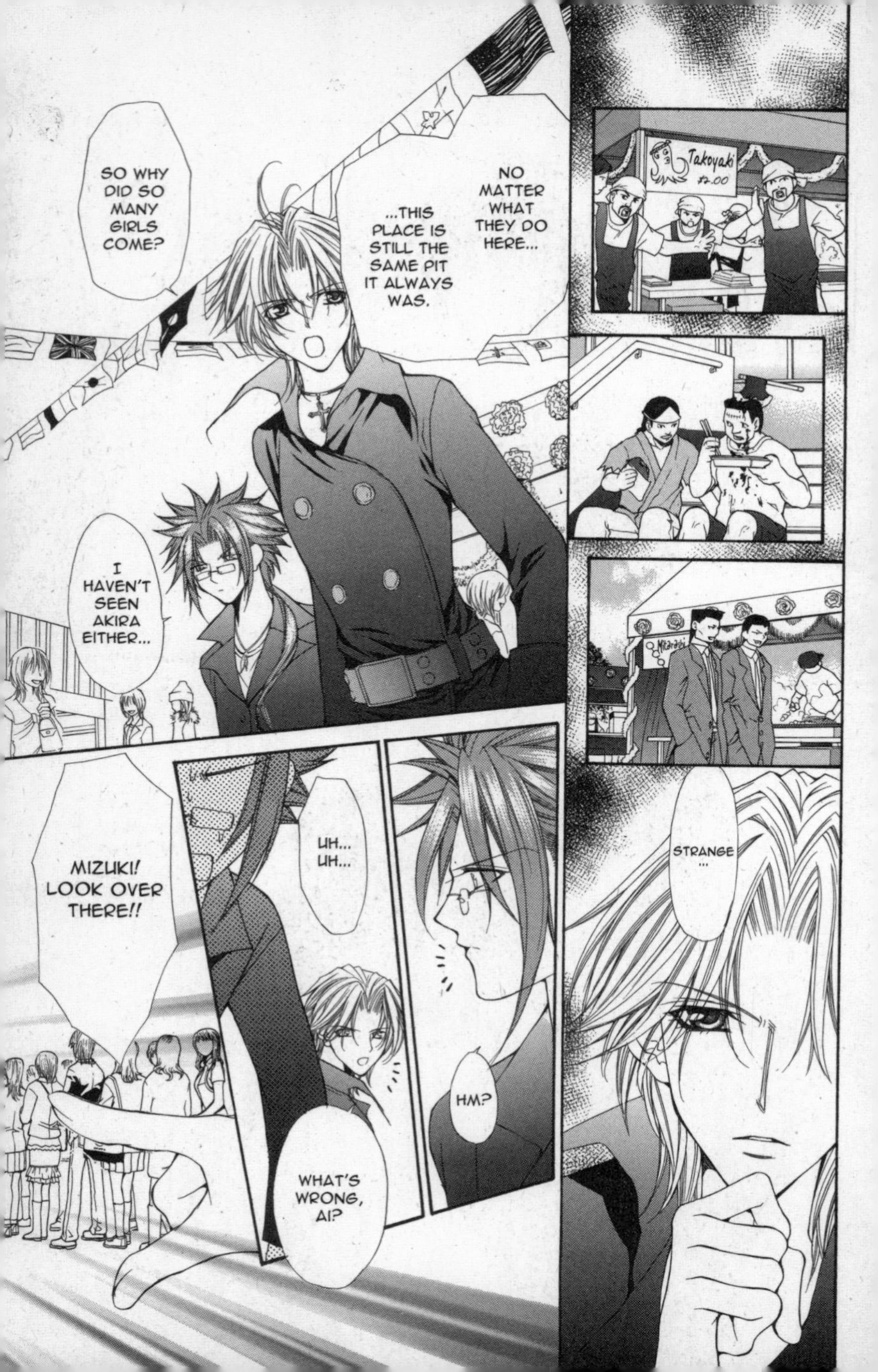

Takoyaki
$2.00
Mitarashi
NO MATTER WHAT THEY DO HERE...
...THIS PLACE IS STILL THE SAME PIT IT ALWAYS WAS.
SO WHY DID SO MANY GIRLS COME?
I HAVEN'T SEEN AKIRA EITHER...
STRANGE ...
HM?
WHAT'S WRONG, AI?
UH... UH...
MIZUKI! LOOK OVER THERE!!

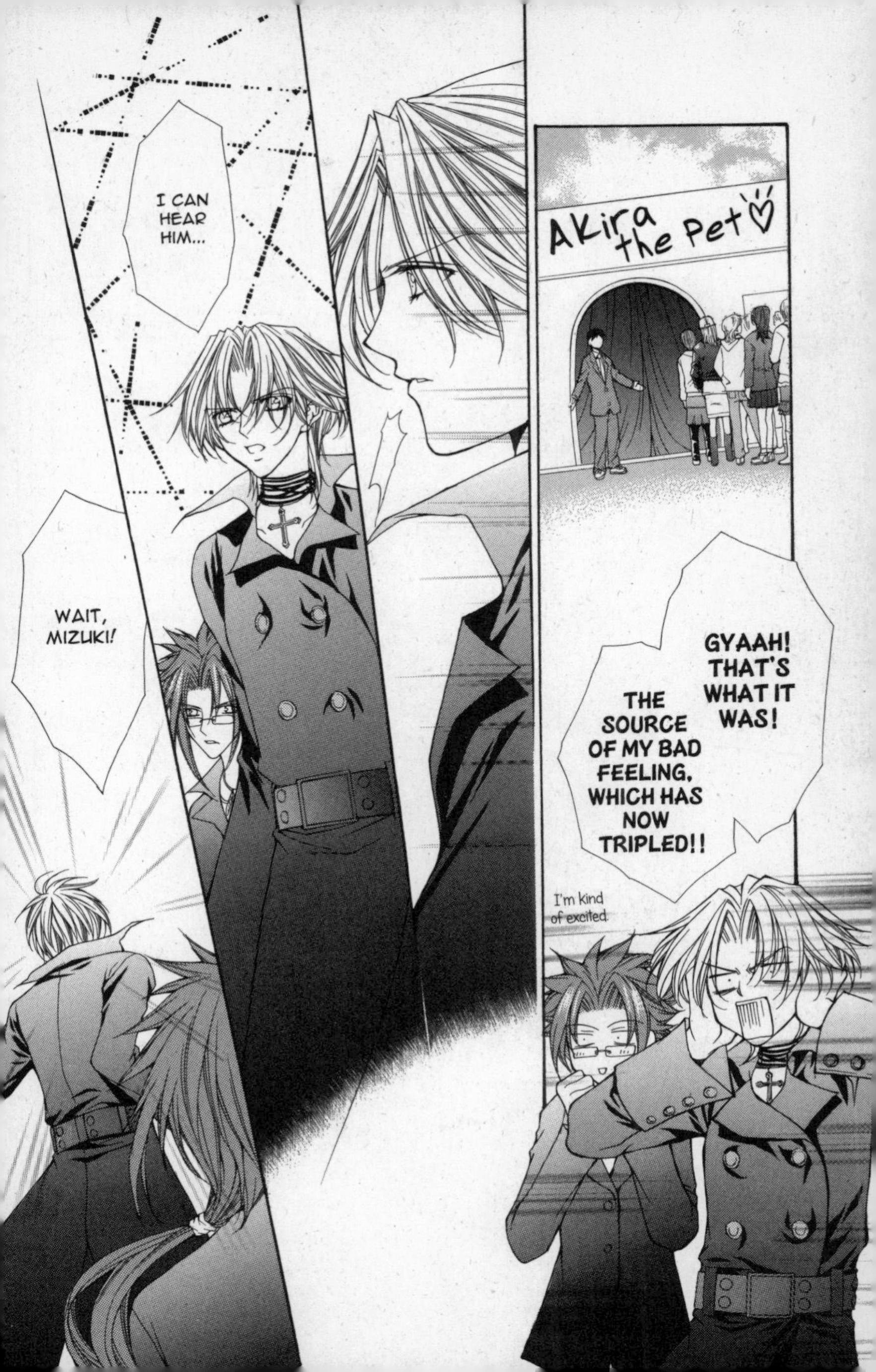
Akira the Pet
GYAAH! THAT'S WHAT IT WAS!
THE SOURCE OF MY BAD FEELING, WHICH HAS NOW TRIPLED!!
I'm kind of excited.
I CAN HEAR HIM...
WAIT, MIZUKI!

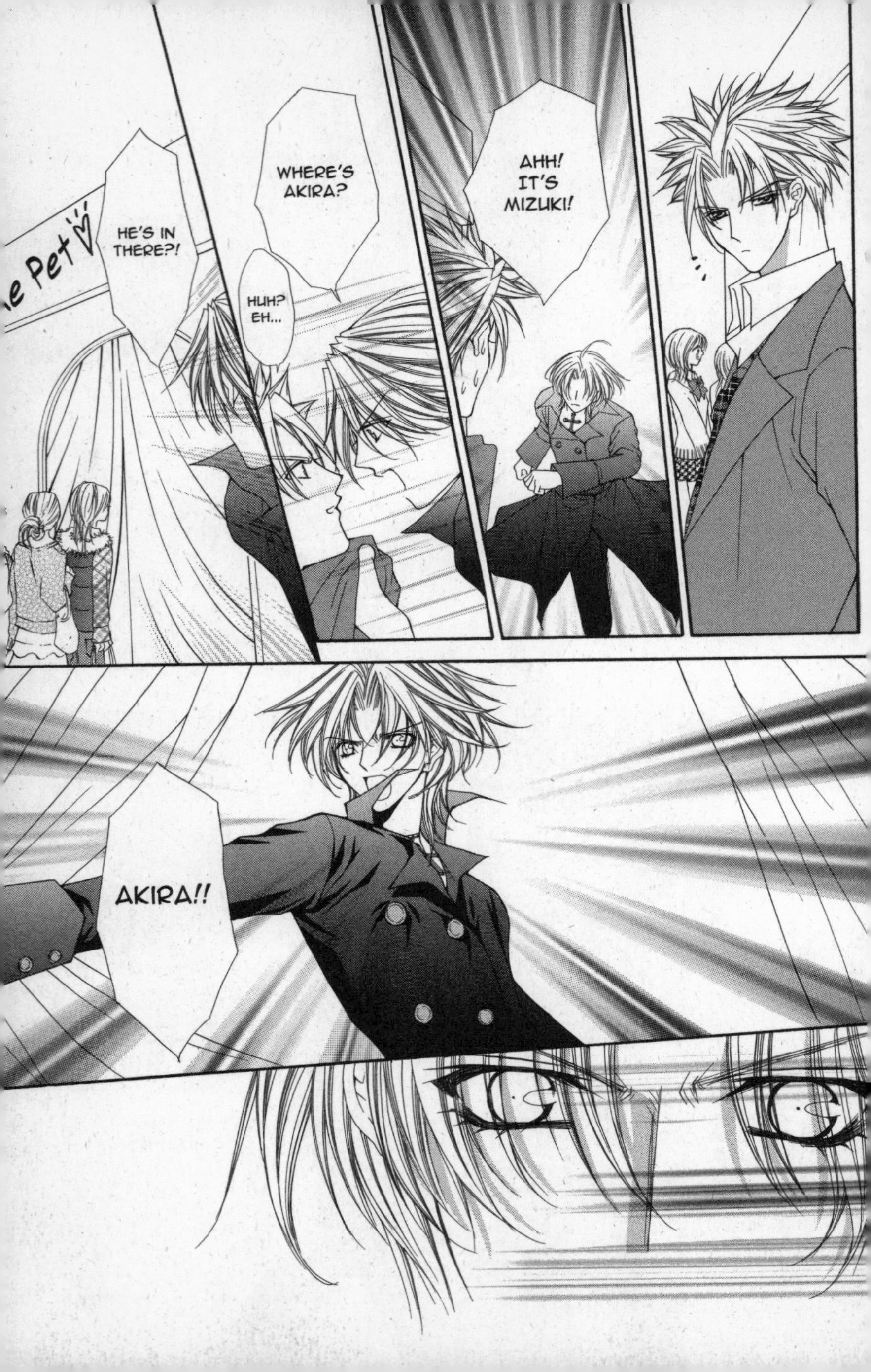
AHH! IT'S MIZUKI!
WHERE'S AKIRA?
HUH? EH...
HE'S IN THERE?!
e Pet
AKIRA!!

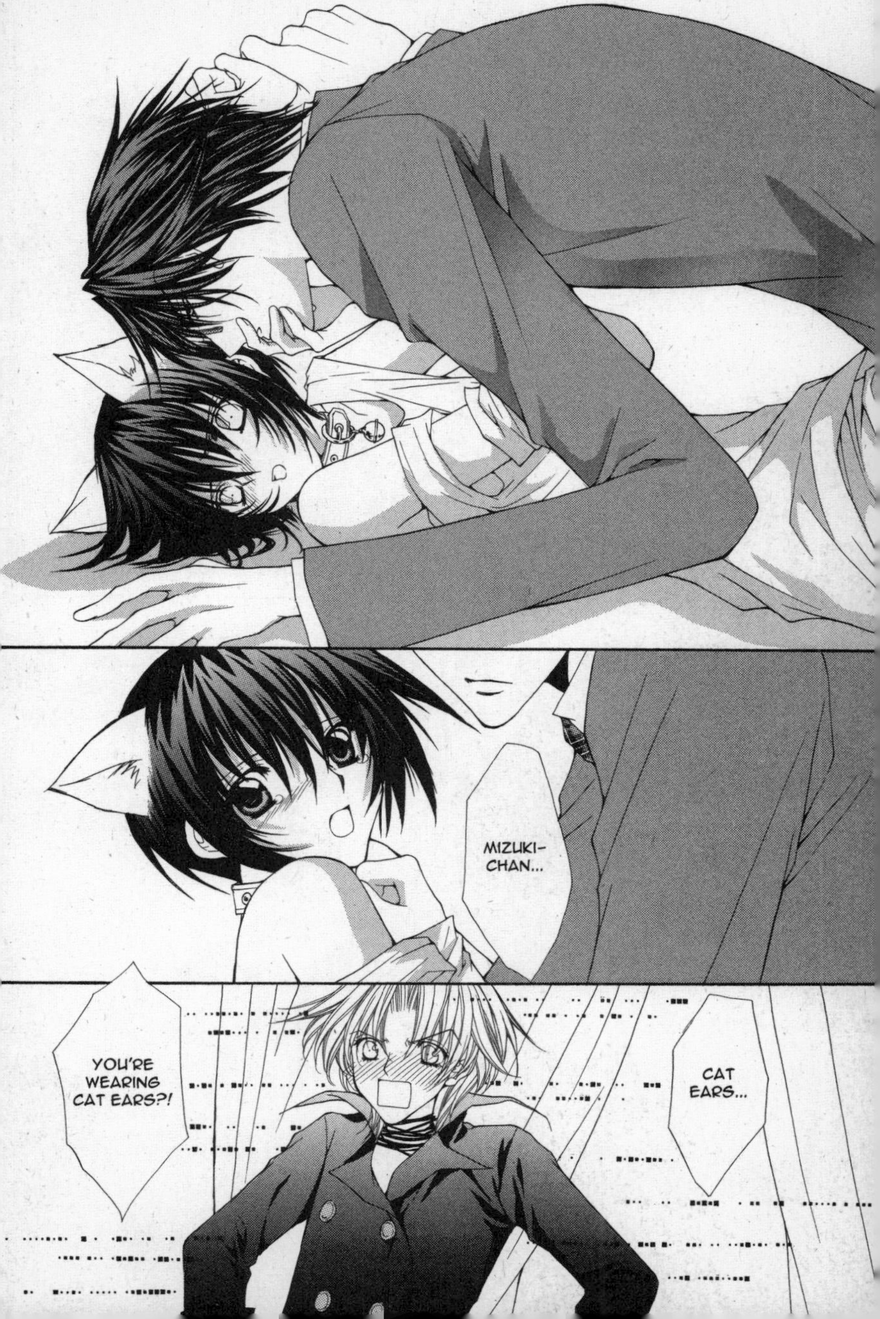
MIZUKI-CHAN...
CAT EARS...
YOU'RE WEARING CAT EARS?!

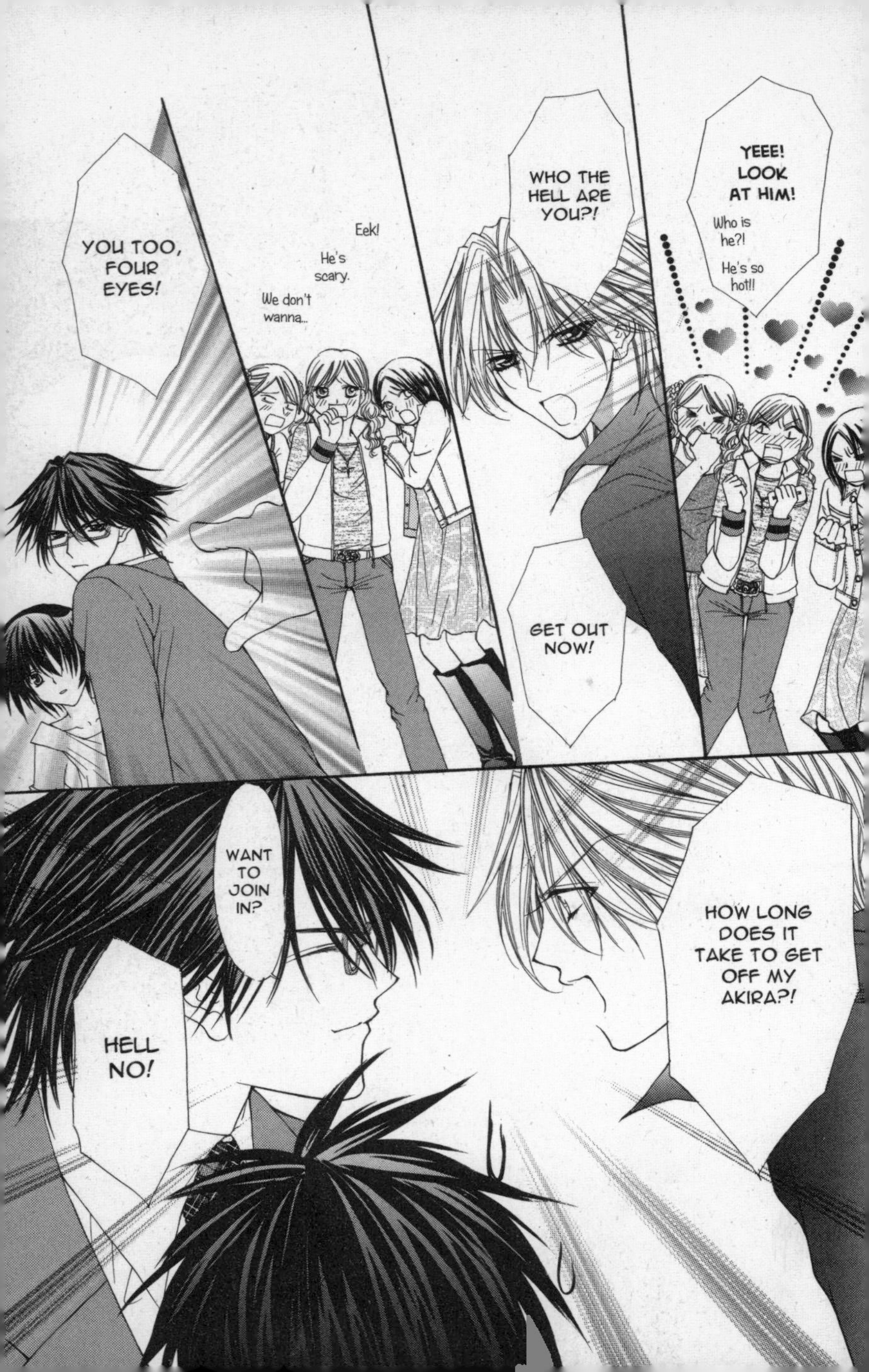
YEEE! LOOK AT HIM!
Who is he?!
He's so hot!!
WHO THE HELL ARE YOU?!
GET OUT NOW!
Eek!
He's scary.
We don't wanna...
YOU TOO, FOUR EYES!
HOW LONG DOES IT TAKE TO GET OFF MY AKIRA?!
WANT TO JOIN IN?
HELL NO!

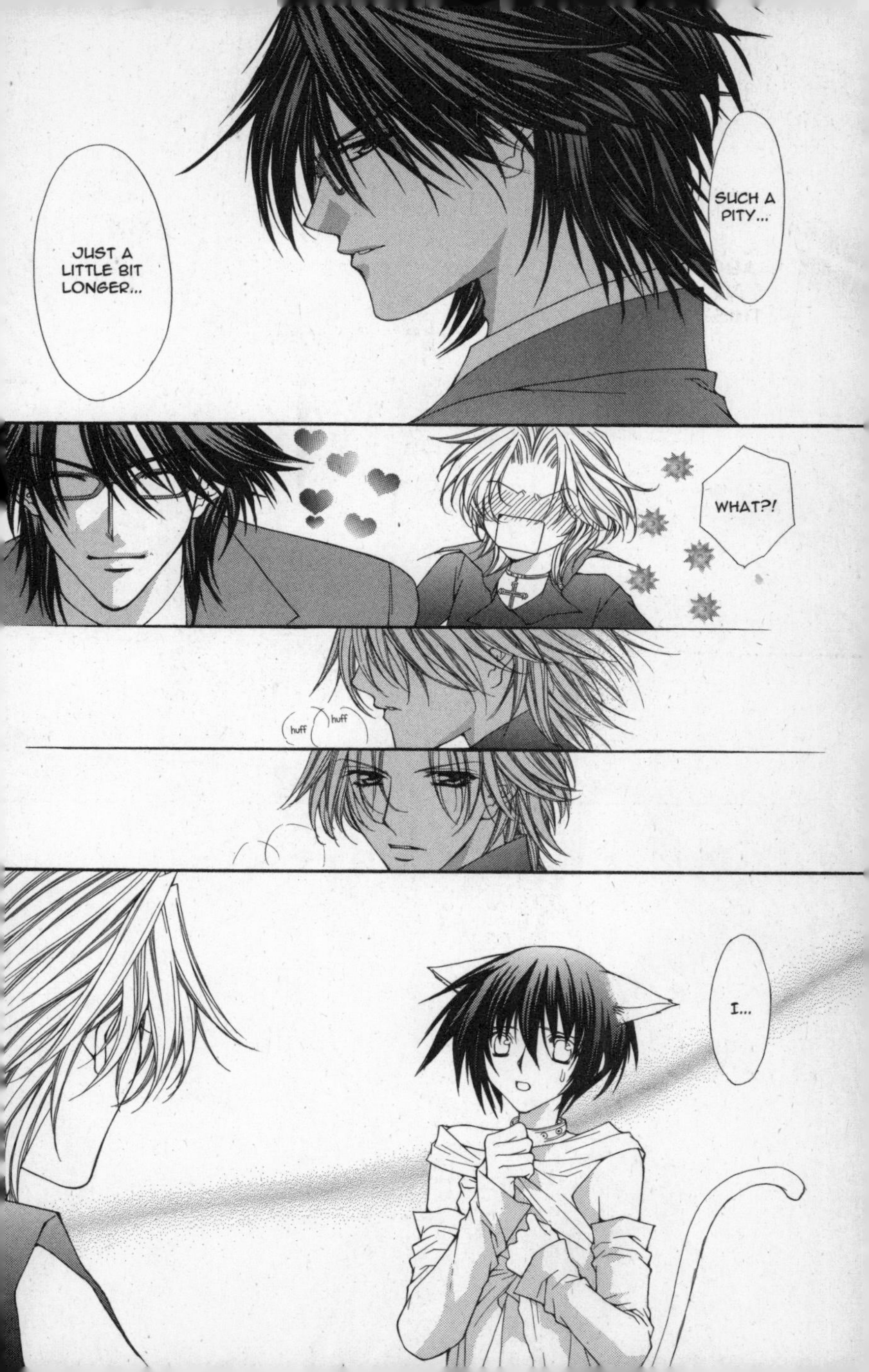
SUCH A PITY...
JUST A LITTLE BIT LONGER...
WHAT?!
huff
huff
I...

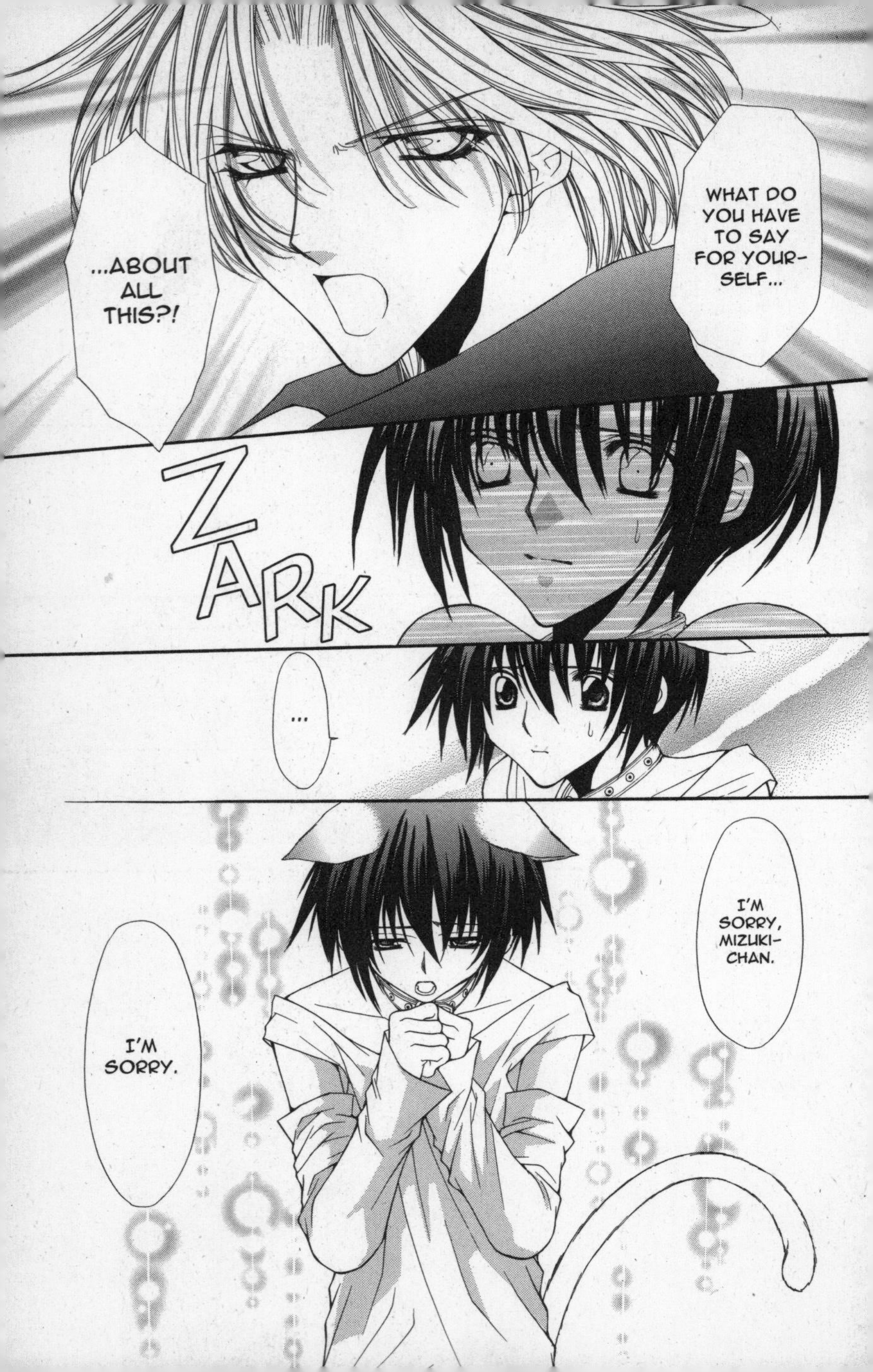
WHAT DO YOU HAVE TO SAY FOR YOUR-SELF...
...ABOUT ALL THIS?!
ZARK
...
I'M SORRY, MIZUKI-CHAN.
I'M SORRY.

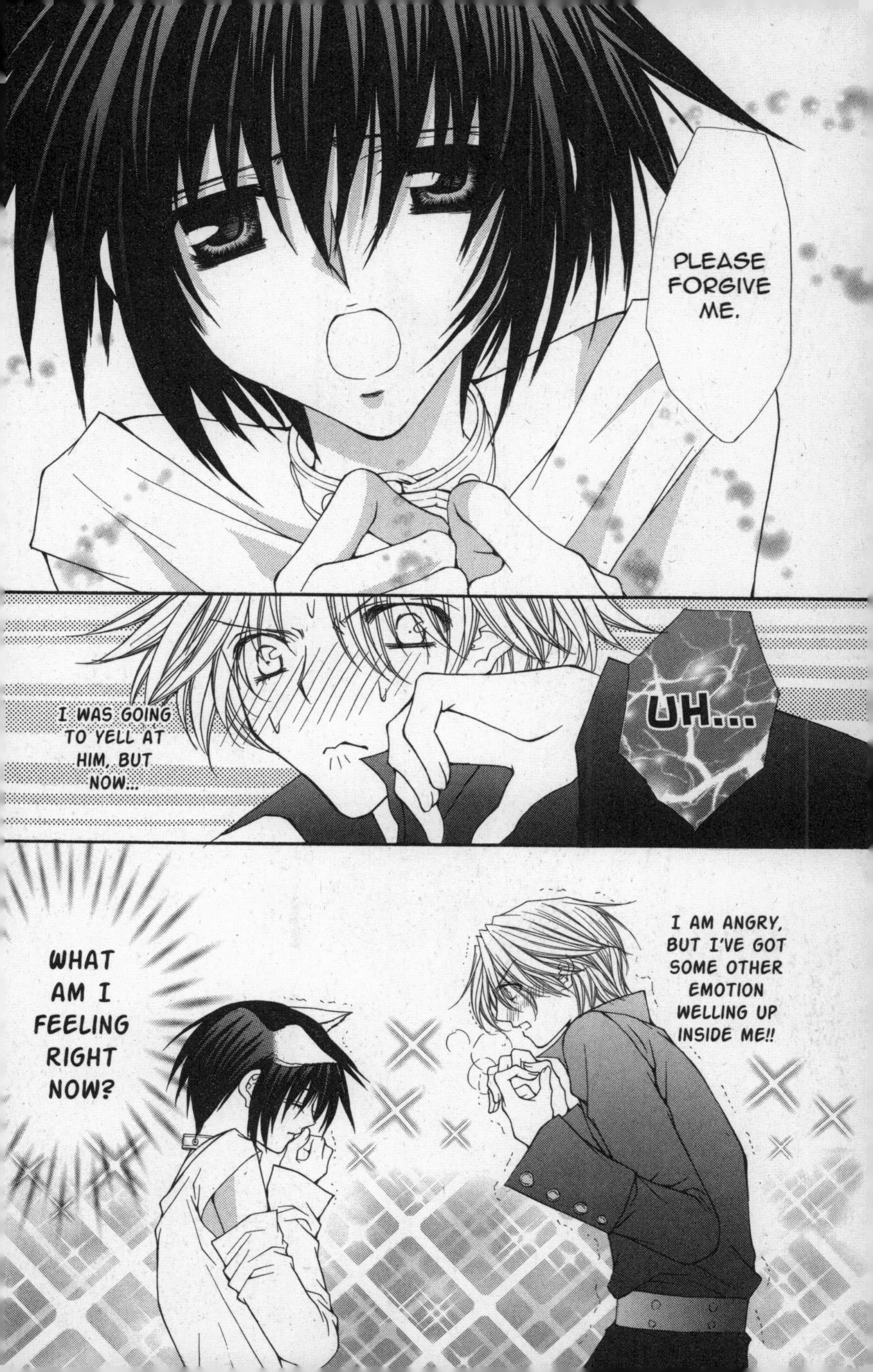
PLEASE FORGIVE ME.
UH...
I WAS GOING TO YELL AT HIM, BUT NOW...
I AM ANGRY, BUT I'VE GOT SOME OTHER EMOTION WELLING UP INSIDE ME!!
WHAT AM I FEELING RIGHT NOW?

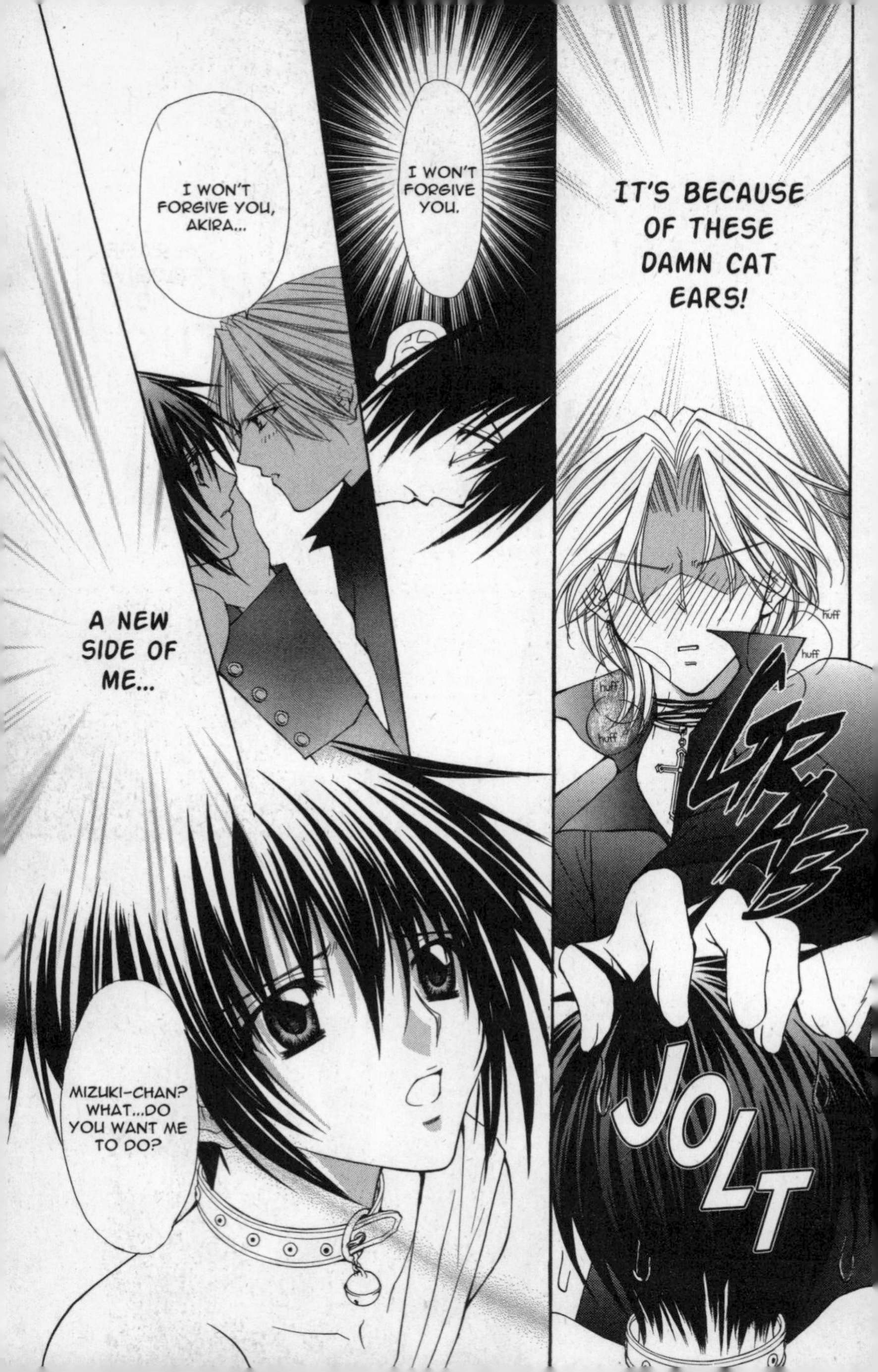
IT'S BECAUSE OF THESE DAMN CAT EARS!
huff
huff
huff
huff
GRAB
JOLT
I WON'T FORGIVE YOU.
I WON'T FORGIVE YOU, AKIRA...
A NEW SIDE OF ME...
MIZUKI-CHAN? WHAT...DO YOU WANT ME TO DO?

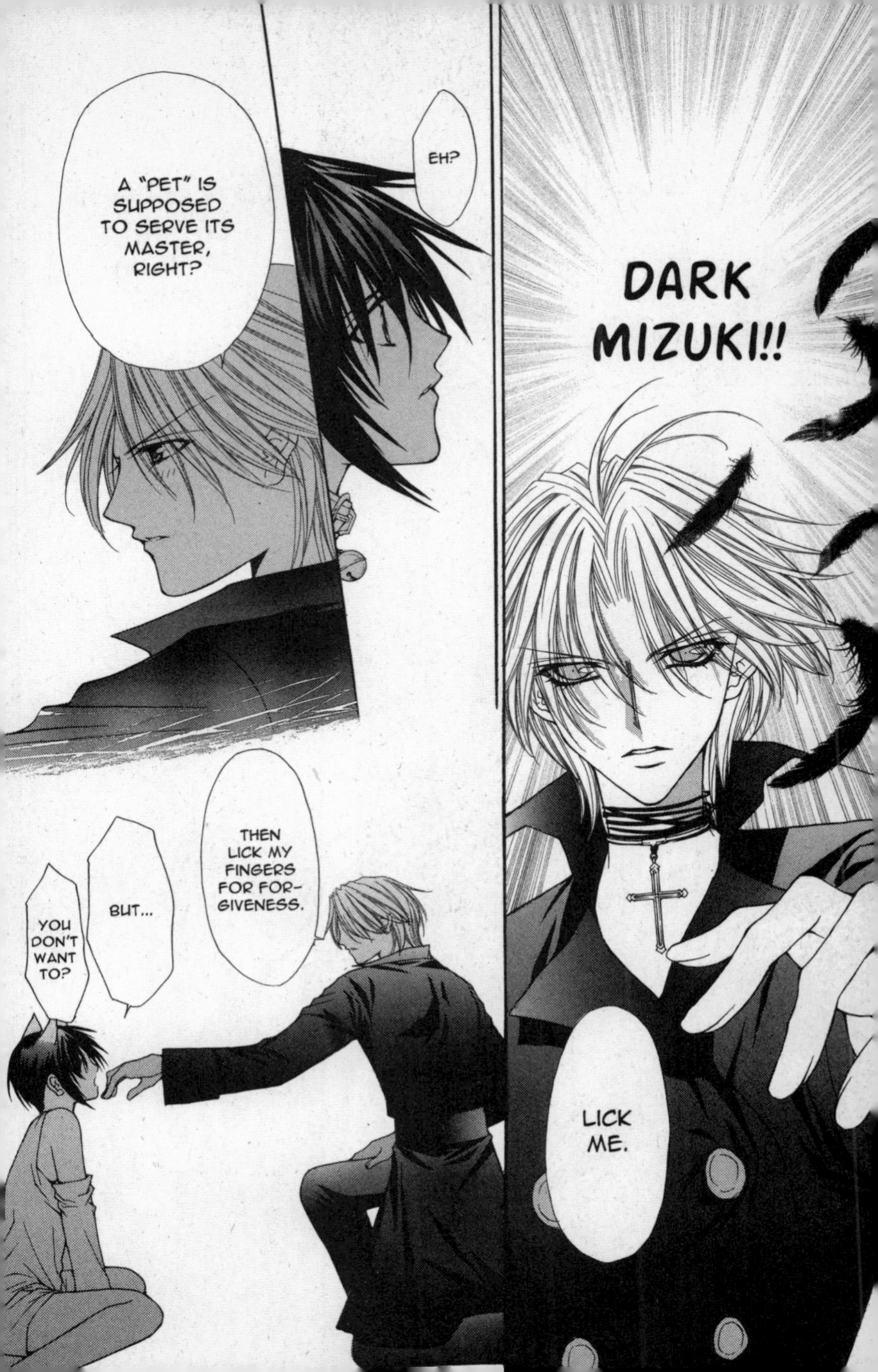
DARK MIZUKI!!
LICK ME.
A "PET" IS SUPPOSED TO SERVE ITS MASTER, RIGHT?
EH?
THEN LICK MY FINGERS FOR FOR-GIVENESS.
BUT...
YOU DON'T WANT TO?

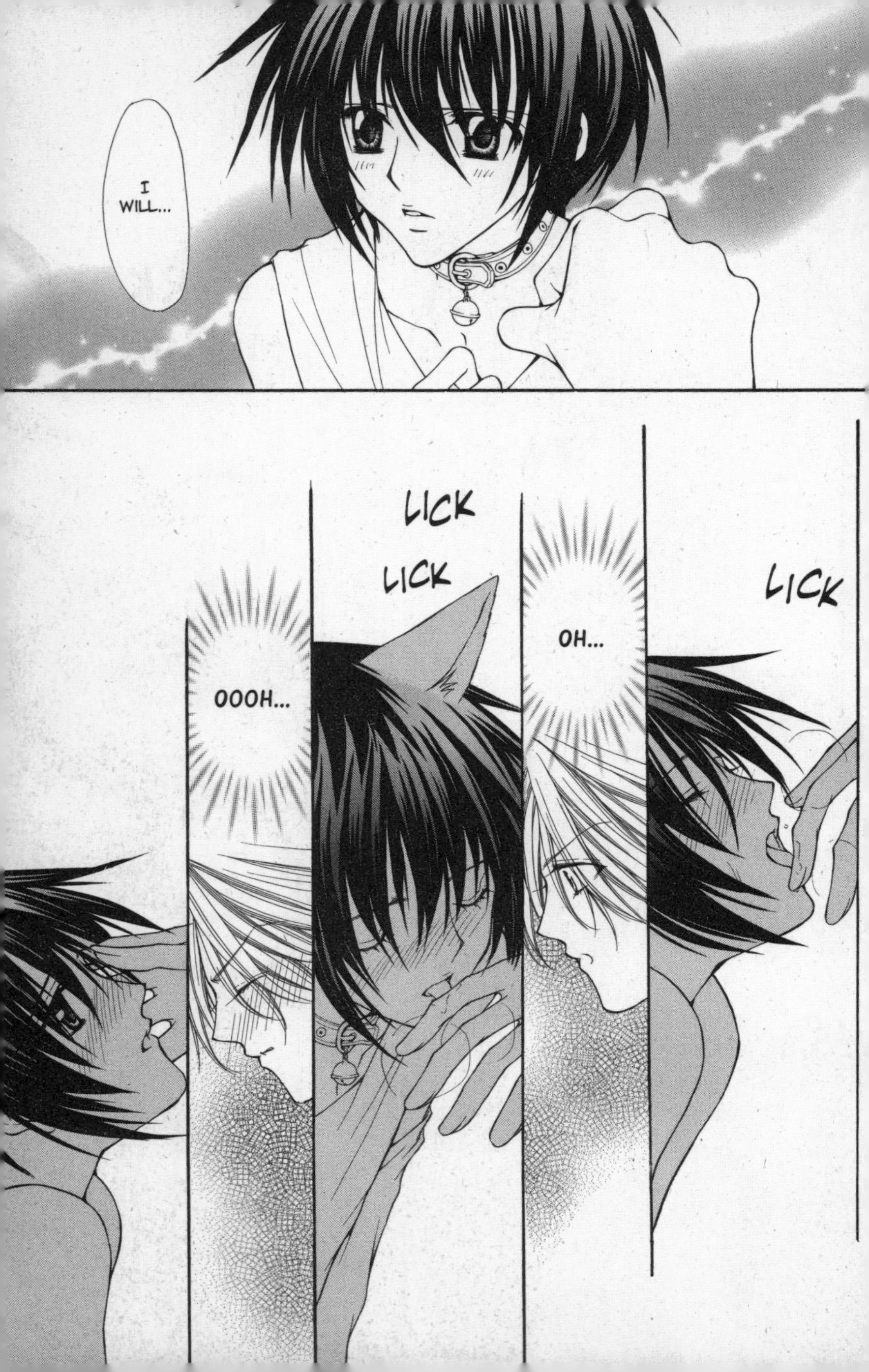
I WILL...
LICK
OH...
LICK
LICK
OOOH...

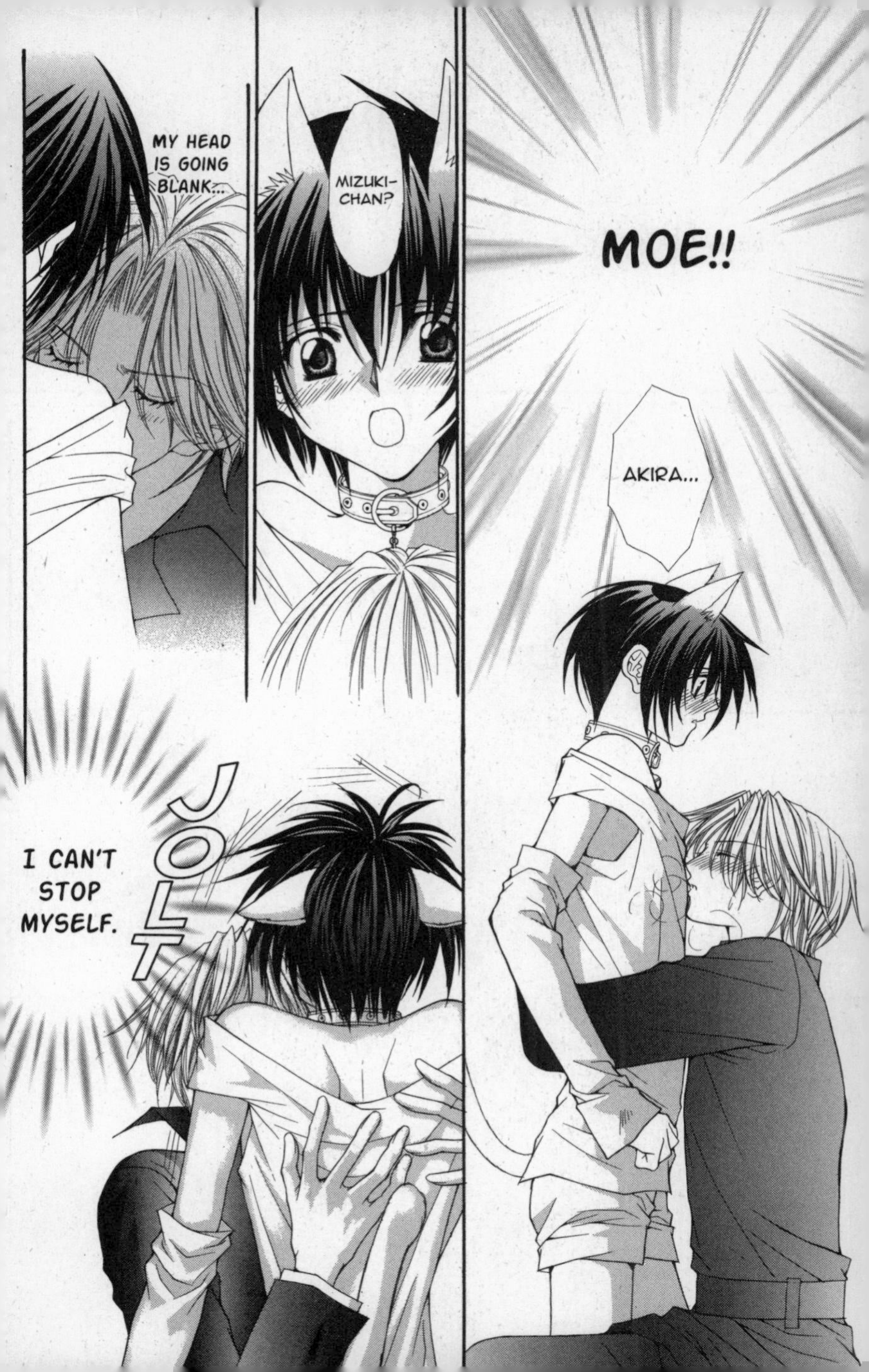
MOE!!
AKIRA...
MIZUKI-CHAN?
MY HEAD IS GOING BLANK...
JOLT
I CAN'T STOP MYSELF.

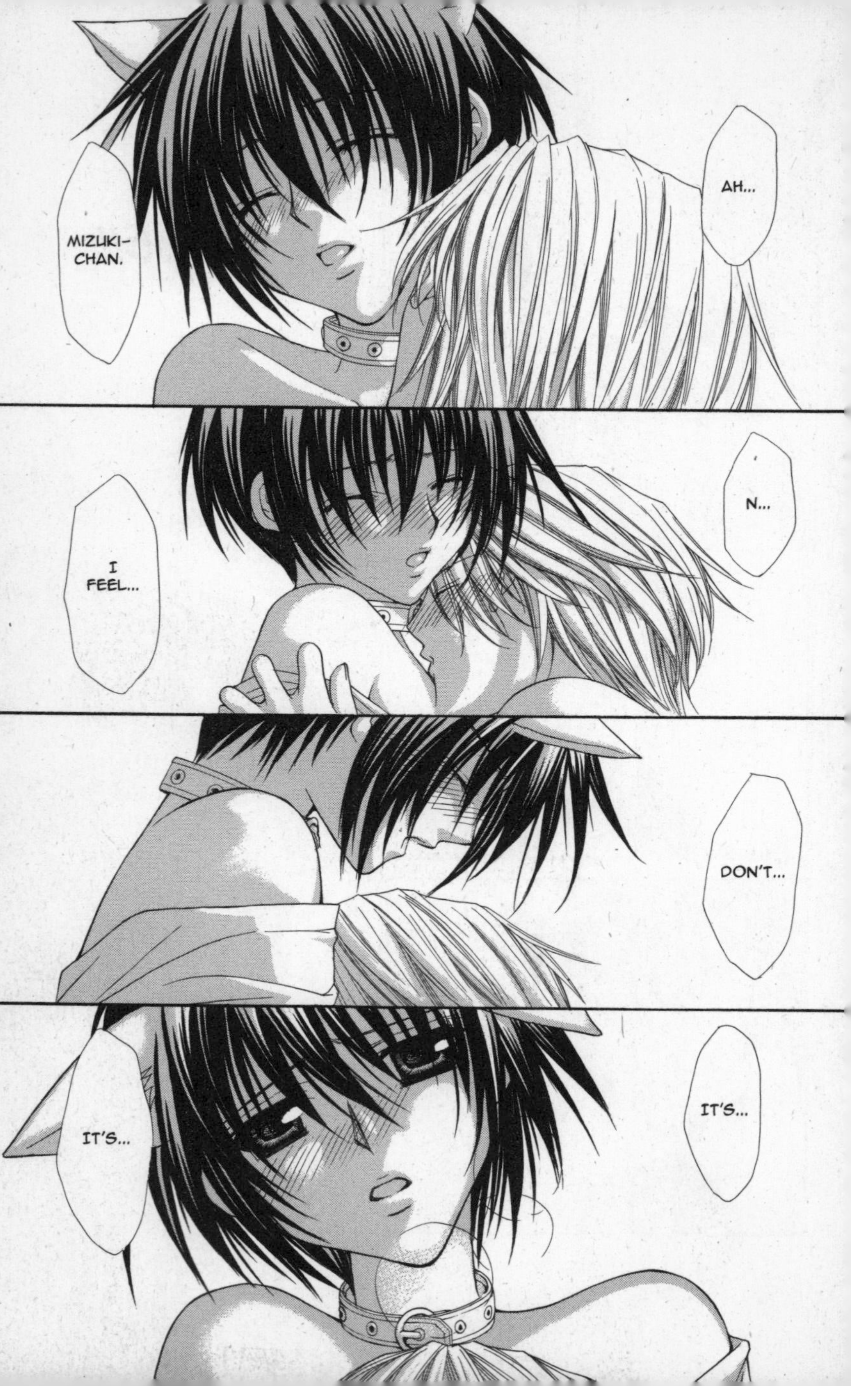
AH...
MIZUKI-CHAN.
N...
I FEEL...
DON'T...
IT'S...
IT'S...

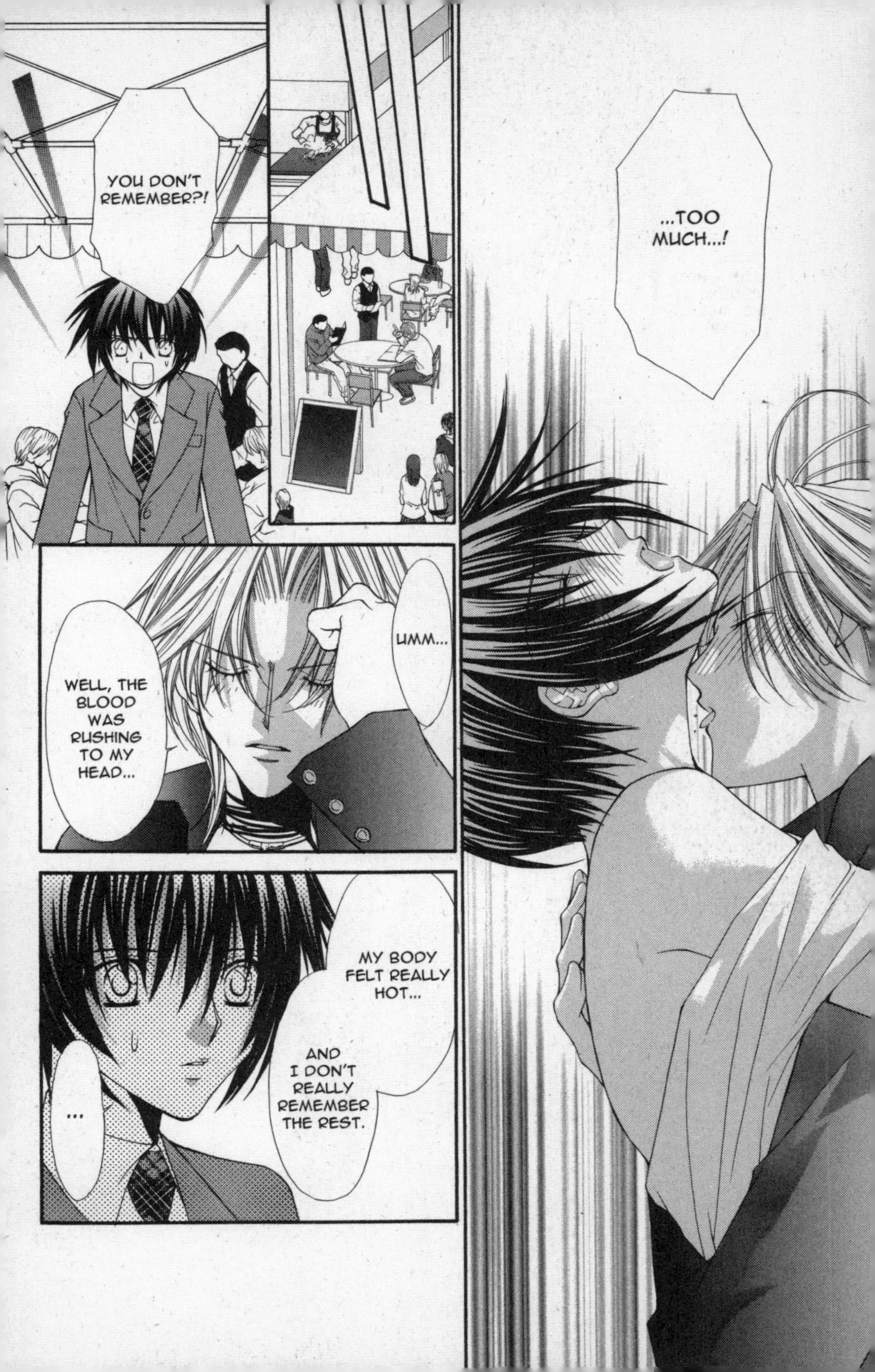
...TOO MUCH...!
YOU DON'T REMEMBER?!
UMM...
WELL, THE BLOOD WAS RUSHING TO MY HEAD...
MY BODY FELT REALLY HOT...
AND I DON'T REALLY REMEMBER THE REST.
...

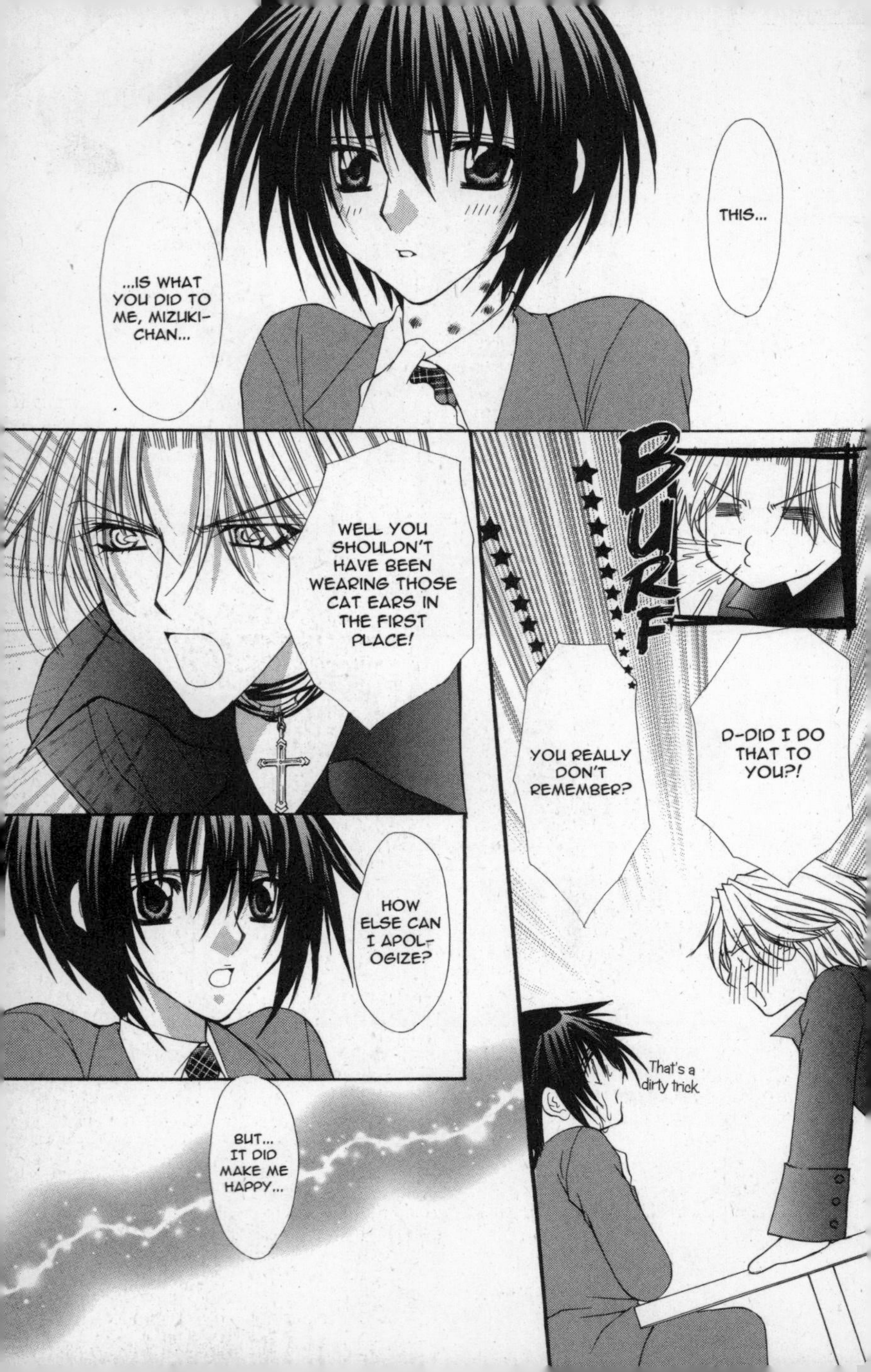
THIS...
...IS WHAT YOU DID TO ME, MIZUKI-CHAN...
BURF
D-DID I DO THAT TO YOU?!
YOU REALLY DON'T REMEMBER?
That's a dirty trick.
WELL YOU SHOULDN'T HAVE BEEN WEARING THOSE CAT EARS IN THE FIRST PLACE!
HOW ELSE CAN I APOLOGIZE?
BUT... IT DID MAKE ME HAPPY...

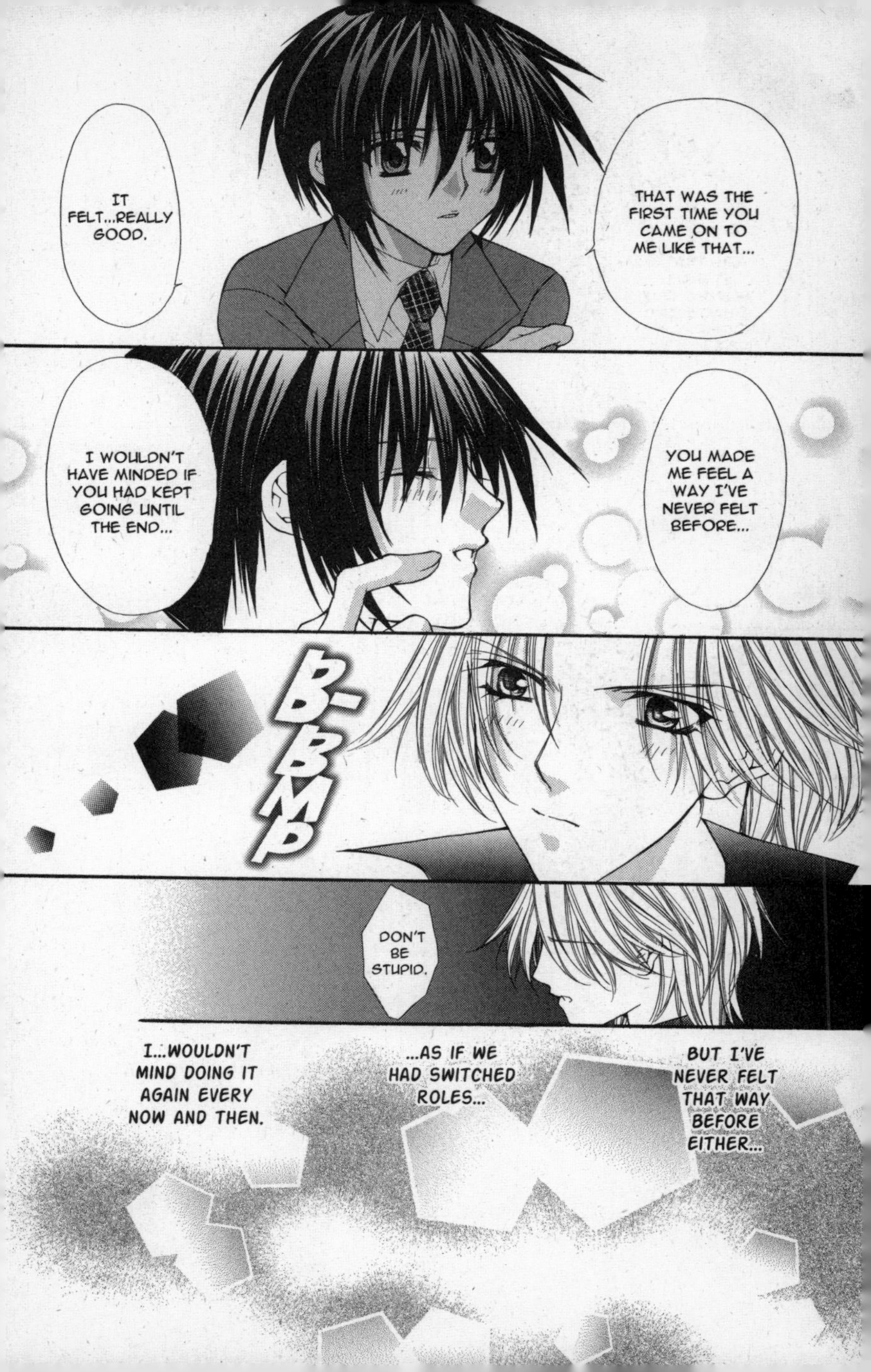
THAT WAS THE FIRST TIME YOU CAME ON TO ME LIKE THAT...
IT FELT...REALLY GOOD.
YOU MADE ME FEEL A WAY I'VE NEVER FELT BEFORE...
I WOULDN'T HAVE MINDED IF YOU HAD KEPT GOING UNTIL THE END...
B-BMP
DON'T BE STUPID.
BUT I'VE NEVER FELT THAT WAY BEFORE EITHER...
...AS IF WE HAD SWITCHED ROLES...
I...WOULDN'T MIND DOING IT AGAIN EVERY NOW AND THEN.

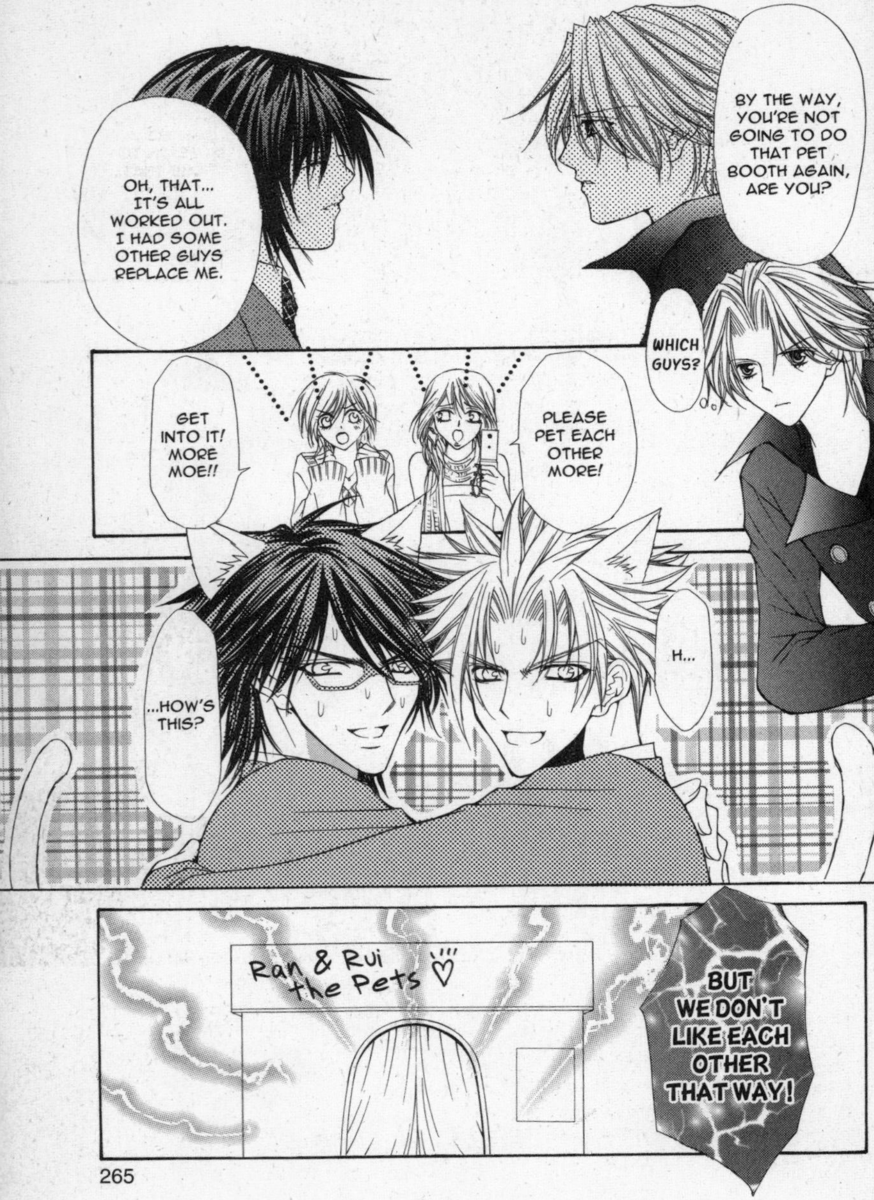
BY THE WAY, YOU'RE NOT GOING TO DO THAT PET BOOTH AGAIN, ARE YOU?
OH, THAT... IT'S ALL WORKED OUT. I HAD SOME OTHER GUYS REPLACE ME.
WHICH GUYS?
PLEASE PET EACH OTHER MORE!
GET INTO IT! MORE MOE!!
H...
...HOW'S THIS?
BUT WE DON'T LIKE EACH OTHER THAT WAY!
Ran & Rui the Pets

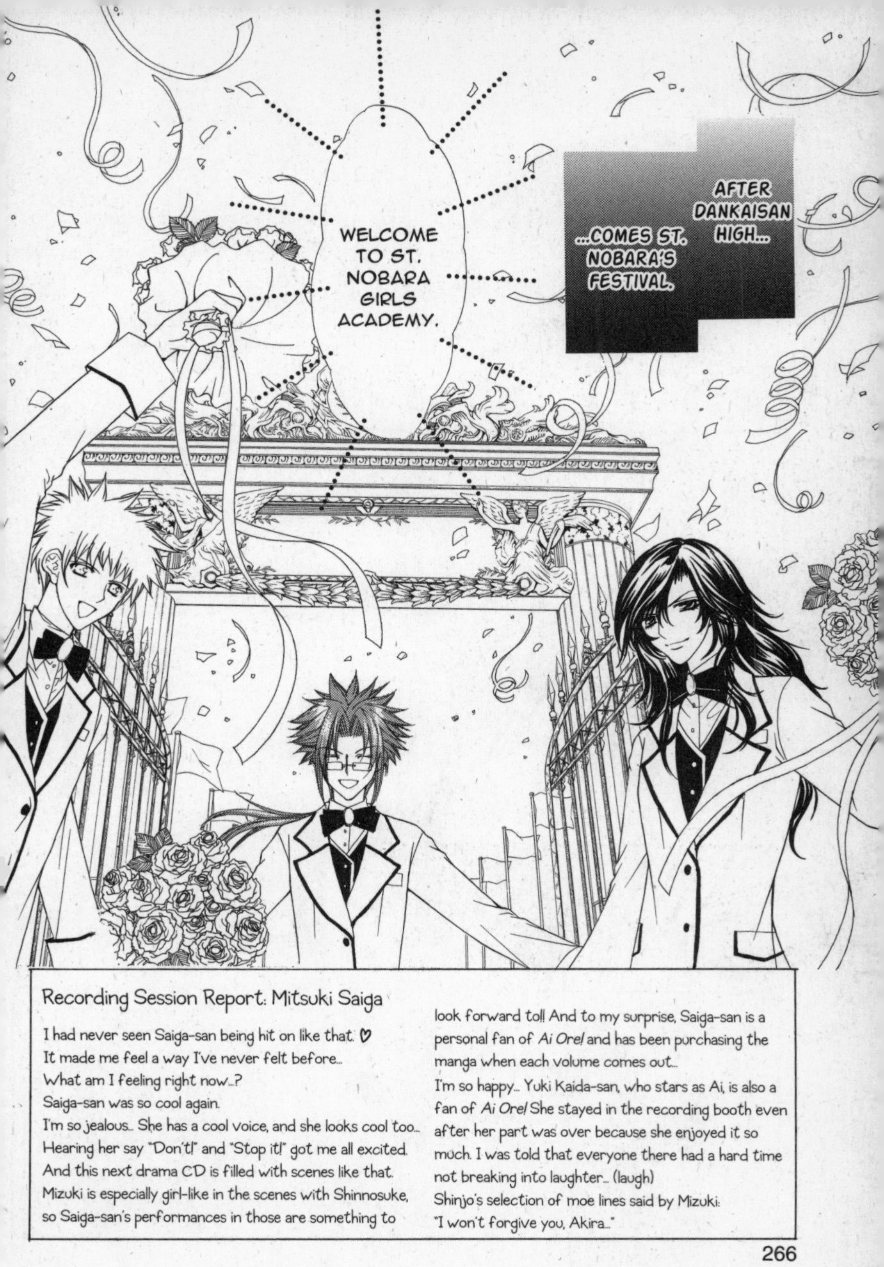
AFTER DANKAISAN HIGH...
...COMES ST. NOBARA'S FESTIVAL.
WELCOME TO ST. NOBARA GIRLS ACADEMY.

Recording Session Report: Mitsuki Saiga

I had never seen Saiga-san being hit on like that. ♡
It made me feel a way I've never felt before...
What am I feeling right now...?
Saiga-san was so cool again.
I'm so jealous... She has a cool voice, and she looks cool too...
Hearing her say "Don't!" and "Stop it!" got me all excited.
And this next drama CD is filled with scenes like that.
Mizuki is especially girl-like in the scenes with Shinnosuke, so Saiga-san's performances in those are something to look forward to!! And to my surprise, Saiga-san is a personal fan of *Ai Ore!* and has been purchasing the manga when each volume comes out...
I'm so happy... Yuki Kaida-san, who stars as Ai, is also a fan of *Ai Ore!* She stayed in the recording booth even after her part was over because she enjoyed it so much. I was told that everyone there had a hard time not breaking into laughter... (laugh)
Shinjo's selection of moe lines said by Mizuki:
"I won't forgive you, Akira..."

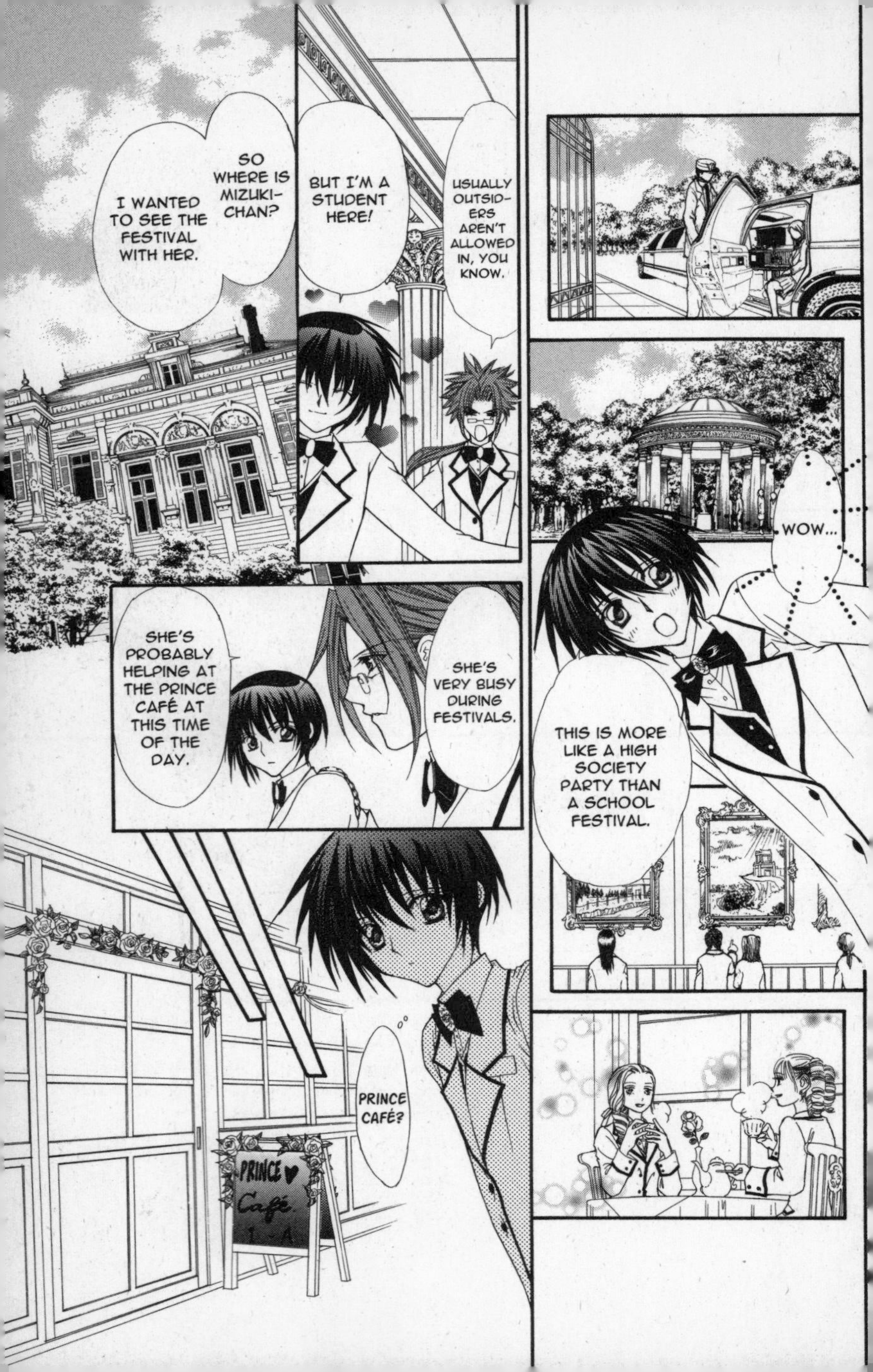
WOW...
THIS IS MORE LIKE A HIGH SOCIETY PARTY THAN A SCHOOL FESTIVAL.
USUALLY OUTSIDERS AREN'T ALLOWED IN, YOU KNOW.
BUT I'M A STUDENT HERE!
SO WHERE IS MIZUKI-CHAN?
I WANTED TO SEE THE FESTIVAL WITH HER.
SHE'S VERY BUSY DURING FESTIVALS.
SHE'S PROBABLY HELPING AT THE PRINCE CAFÉ AT THIS TIME OF THE DAY.
PRINCE CAFÉ?
PRINCE ♥ Café 1-A

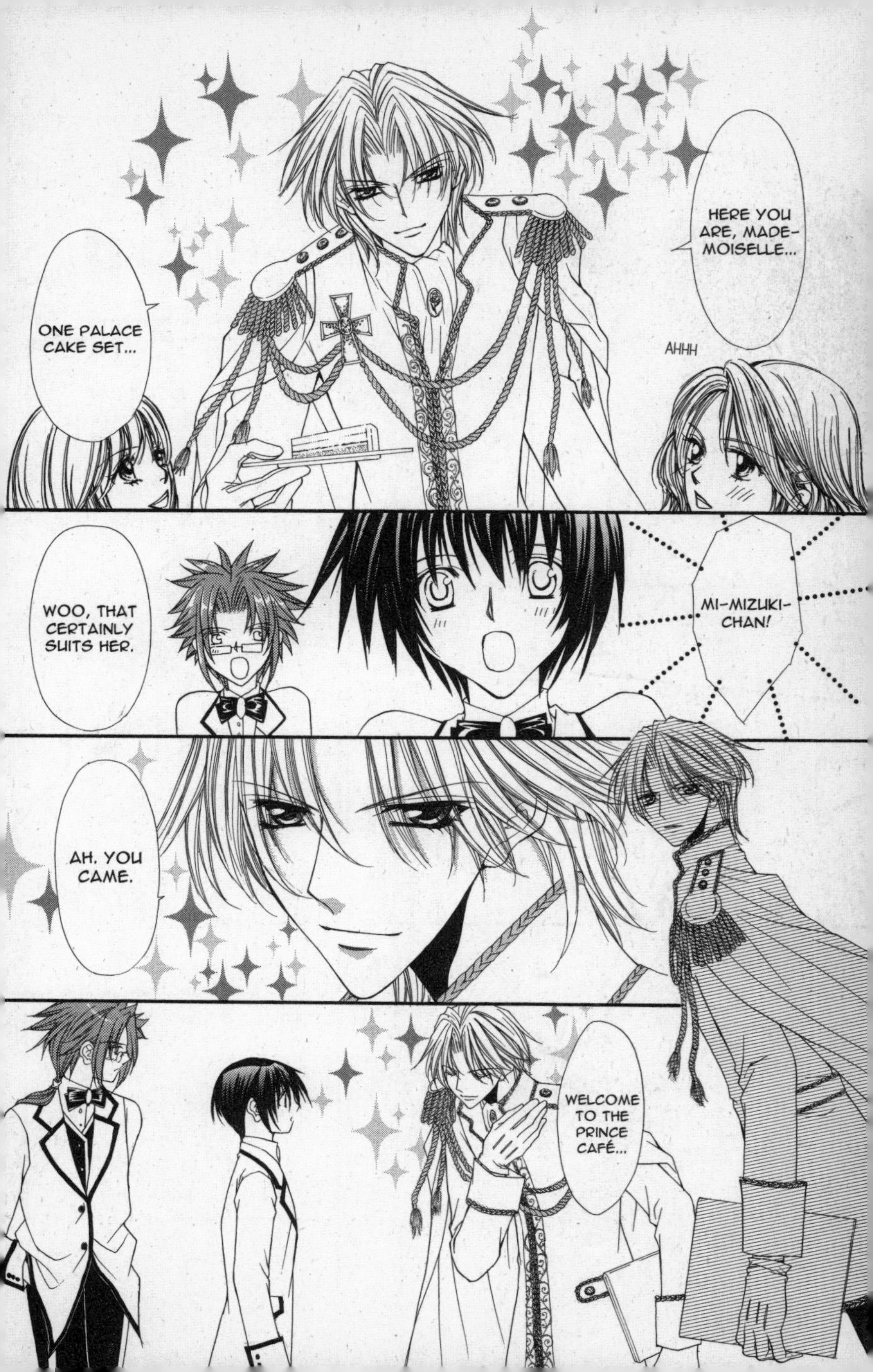

HERE YOU ARE, MADE-MOISELLE...
AHHH
ONE PALACE CAKE SET...
MI-MIZUKI-CHAN!
WOO, THAT CERTAINLY SUITS HER.
AH. YOU CAME.
WELCOME TO THE PRINCE CAFÉ...

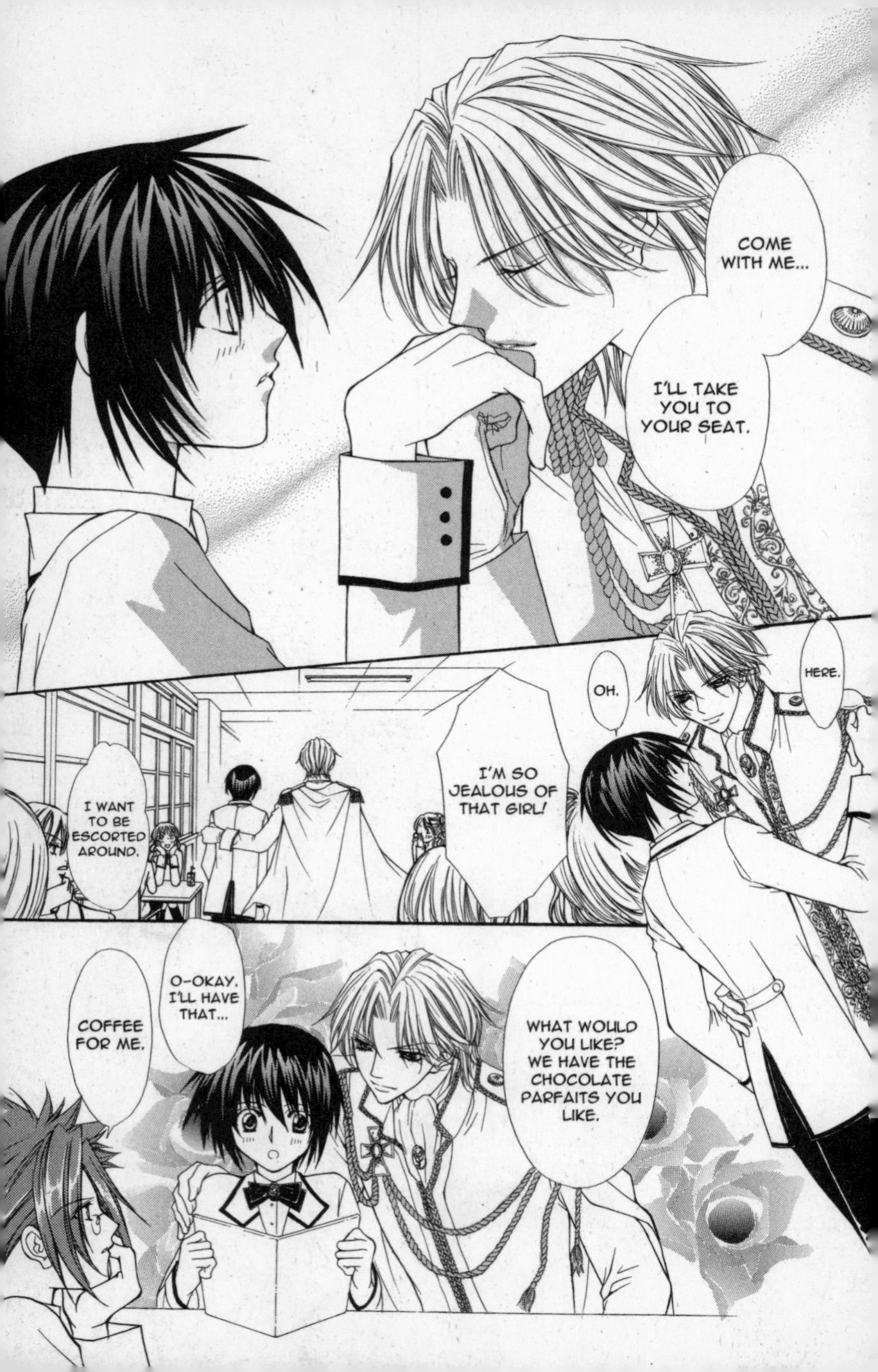
COME WITH ME...
I'LL TAKE YOU TO YOUR SEAT.
HERE.
OH.
I'M SO JEALOUS OF THAT GIRL!
I WANT TO BE ESCORTED AROUND.
WHAT WOULD YOU LIKE? WE HAVE THE CHOCOLATE PARFAITS YOU LIKE.
O-OKAY. I'LL HAVE THAT...
COFFEE FOR ME.

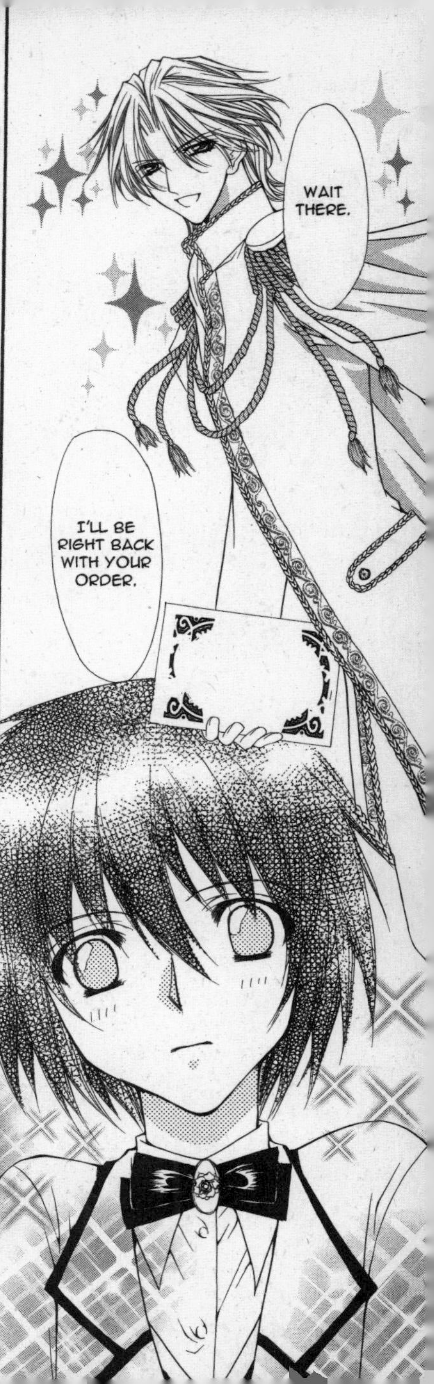
WAIT THERE.
I'LL BE RIGHT BACK WITH YOUR ORDER.

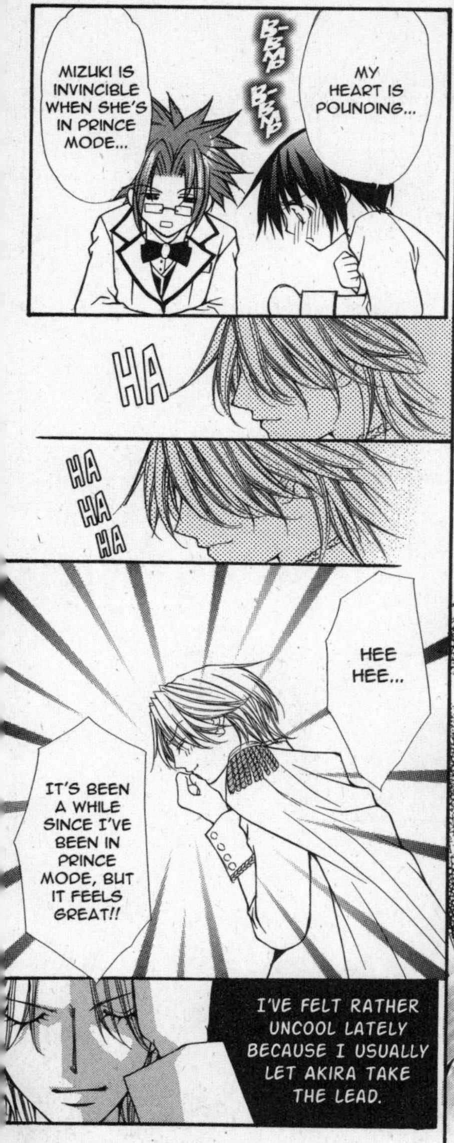
MY HEART IS POUNDING...
B-BMP B-BMP
MIZUKI IS INVINCIBLE WHEN SHE'S IN PRINCE MODE...
HA
HA HA HA
HEE HEE...
IT'S BEEN A WHILE SINCE I'VE BEEN IN PRINCE MODE, BUT IT FEELS GREAT!!
I'VE FELT RATHER UNCOOL LATELY BECAUSE I USUALLY LET AKIRA TAKE THE LEAD.

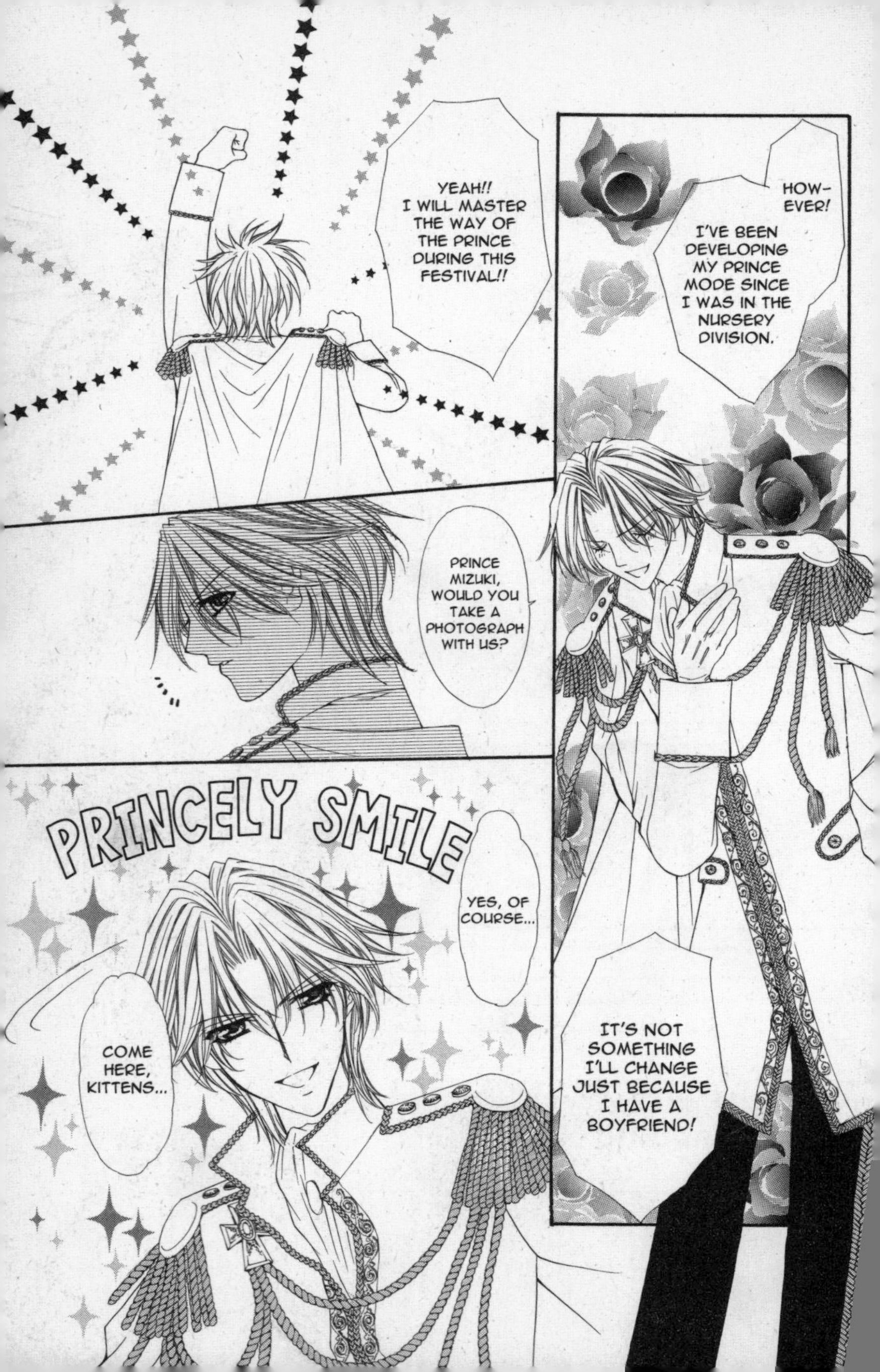
HOW-EVER!
I'VE BEEN DEVELOPING MY PRINCE MODE SINCE I WAS IN THE NURSERY DIVISION.
IT'S NOT SOMETHING I'LL CHANGE JUST BECAUSE I HAVE A BOYFRIEND!
YEAH!! I WILL MASTER THE WAY OF THE PRINCE DURING THIS FESTIVAL!!
PRINCE MIZUKI, WOULD YOU TAKE A PHOTOGRAPH WITH US?
...
PRINCELY SMILE
YES, OF COURSE...
COME HERE, KITTENS...

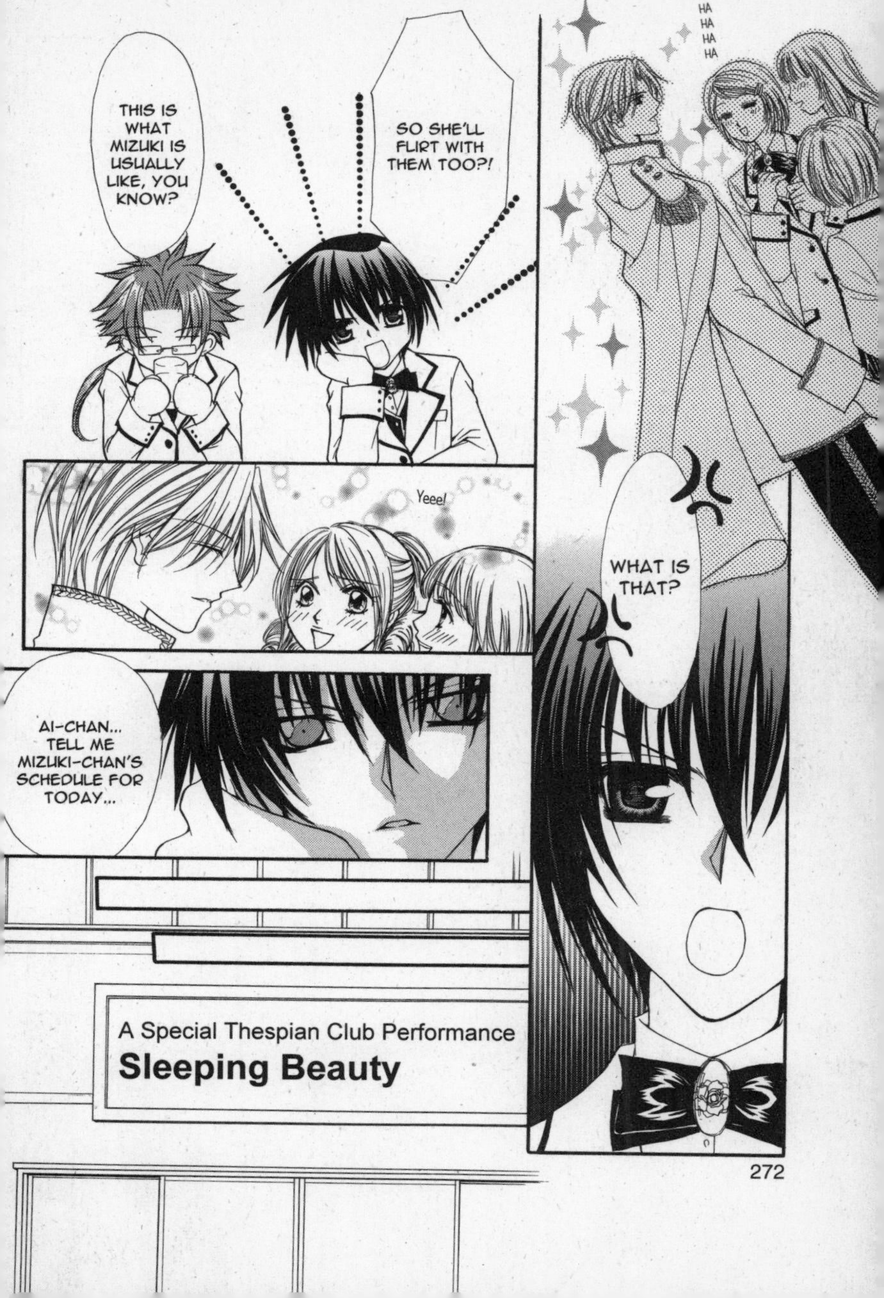
HA HA HA HA HA
WHAT IS THAT?
SO SHE'LL FLIRT WITH THEM TOO?!
THIS IS WHAT MIZUKI IS USUALLY LIKE, YOU KNOW?
Yeee!
AI-CHAN... TELL ME MIZUKI-CHAN'S SCHEDULE FOR TODAY...
A Special Thespian Club Performance
Sleeping Beauty

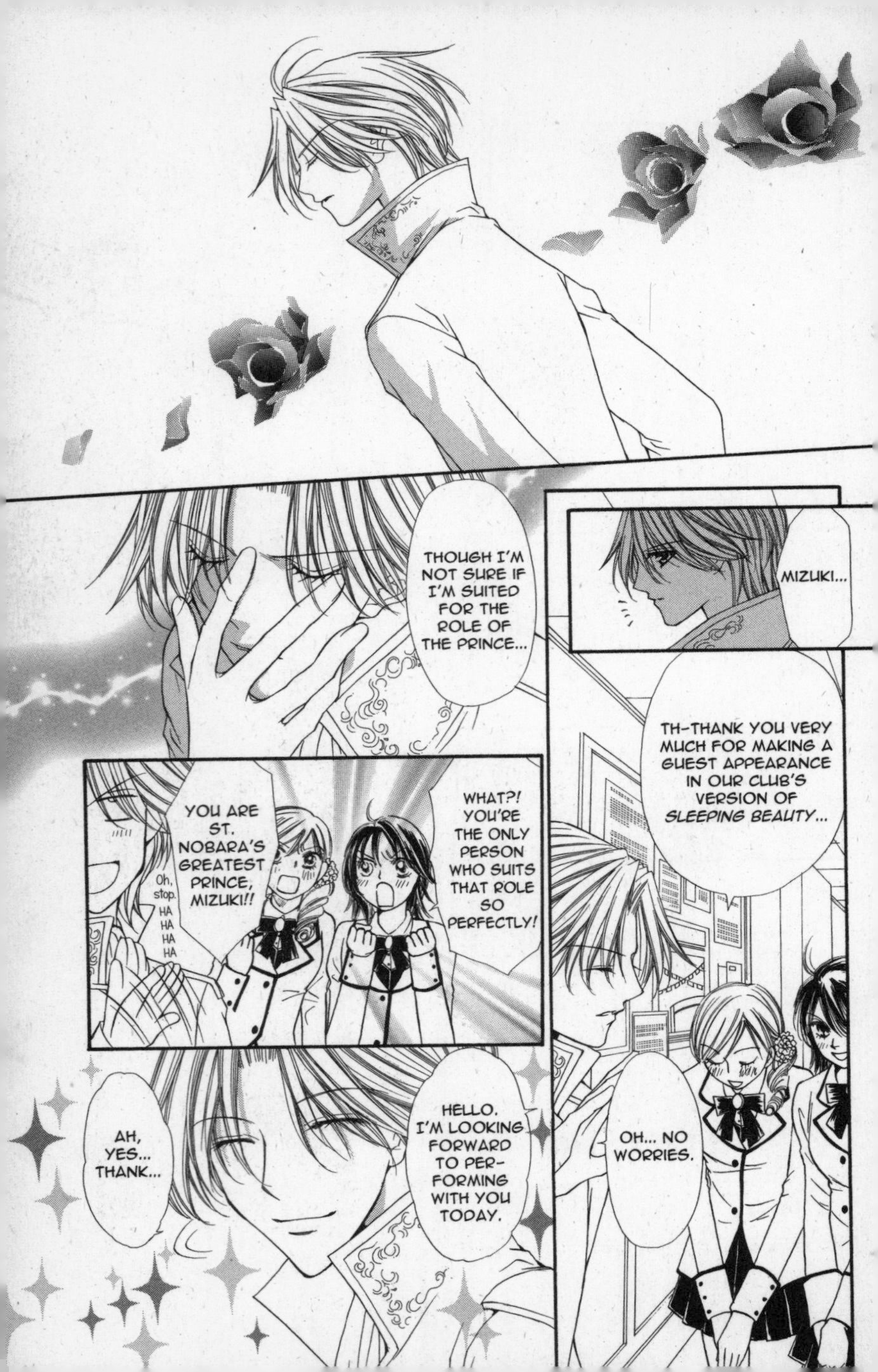
MIZUKI...
TH-THANK YOU VERY MUCH FOR MAKING A GUEST APPEARANCE IN OUR CLUB'S VERSION OF *SLEEPING BEAUTY*...
OH... NO WORRIES.
HELLO. I'M LOOKING FORWARD TO PER-FORMING WITH YOU TODAY.
AH, YES... THANK...
THOUGH I'M NOT SURE IF I'M SUITED FOR THE ROLE OF THE PRINCE...
WHAT?! YOU'RE THE ONLY PERSON WHO SUITS THAT ROLE SO PERFECTLY!
YOU ARE ST. NOBARA'S GREATEST PRINCE, MIZUKI!!
Oh, stop. HA HA HA HA

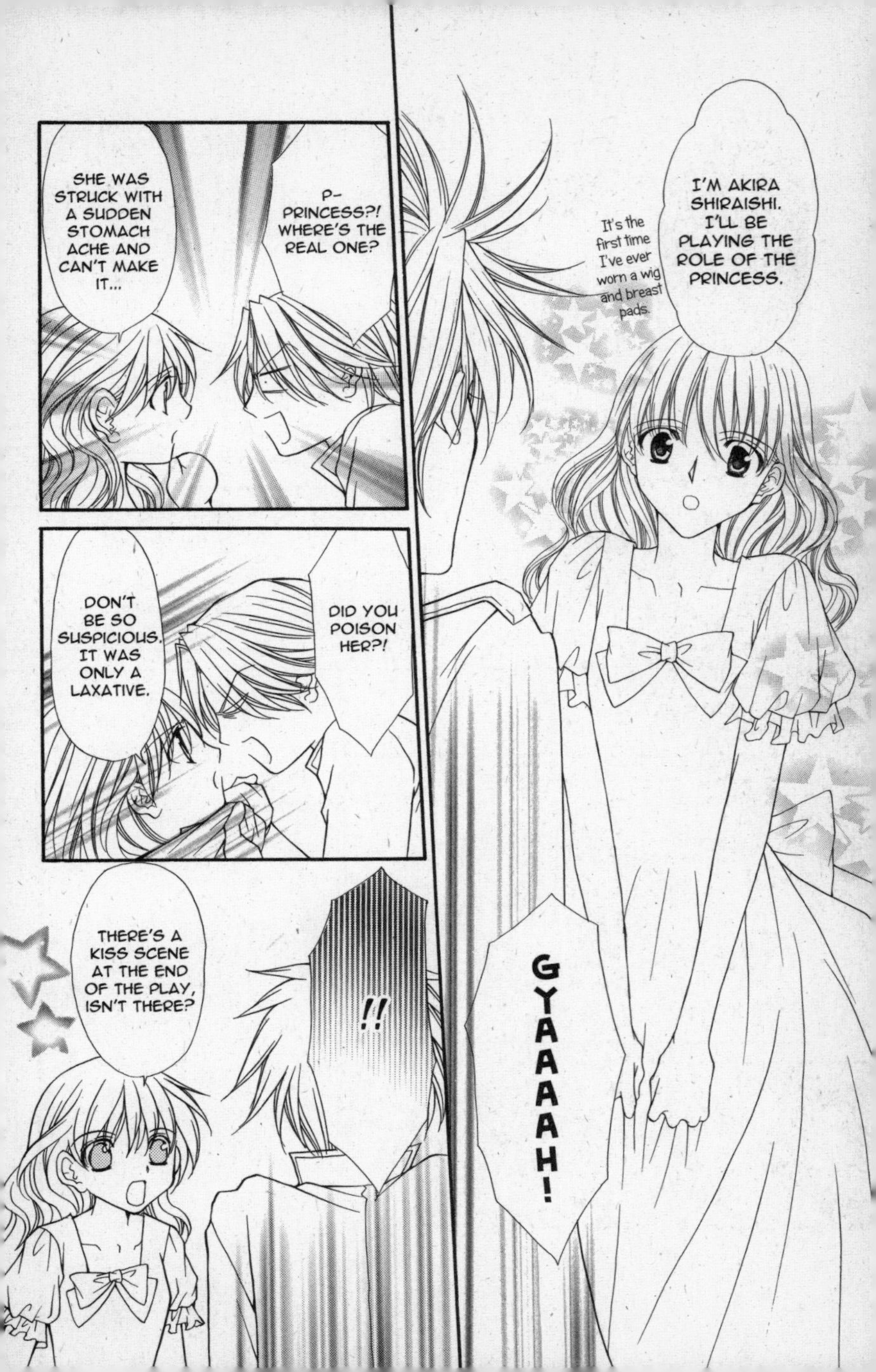
I'M AKIRA SHIRAISHI. I'LL BE PLAYING THE ROLE OF THE PRINCESS.
It's the first time I've ever worn a wig and breast pads.
GYAAAAH!
P-PRINCESS?! WHERE'S THE REAL ONE?
SHE WAS STRUCK WITH A SUDDEN STOMACH ACHE AND CAN'T MAKE IT...
DID YOU POISON HER?!
DON'T BE SO SUSPICIOUS. IT WAS ONLY A LAXATIVE.
THERE'S A KISS SCENE AT THE END OF THE PLAY, ISN'T THERE?
!!

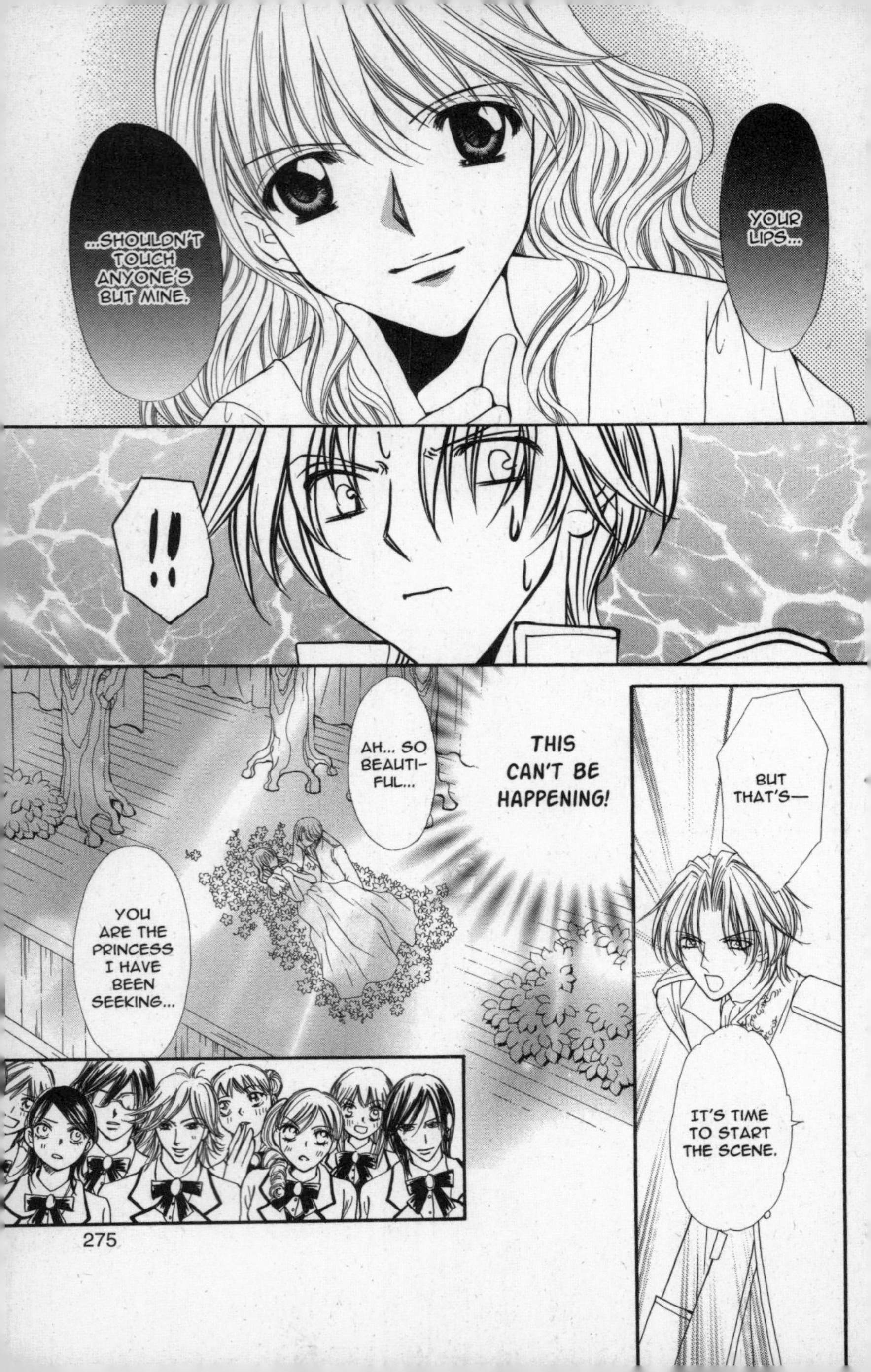
YOUR LIPS...
...SHOULDN'T TOUCH ANYONE'S BUT MINE.
!!
BUT THAT'S—
IT'S TIME TO START THE SCENE.
THIS CAN'T BE HAPPENING!
AH... SO BEAUTIFUL...
YOU ARE THE PRINCESS I HAVE BEEN SEEKING...

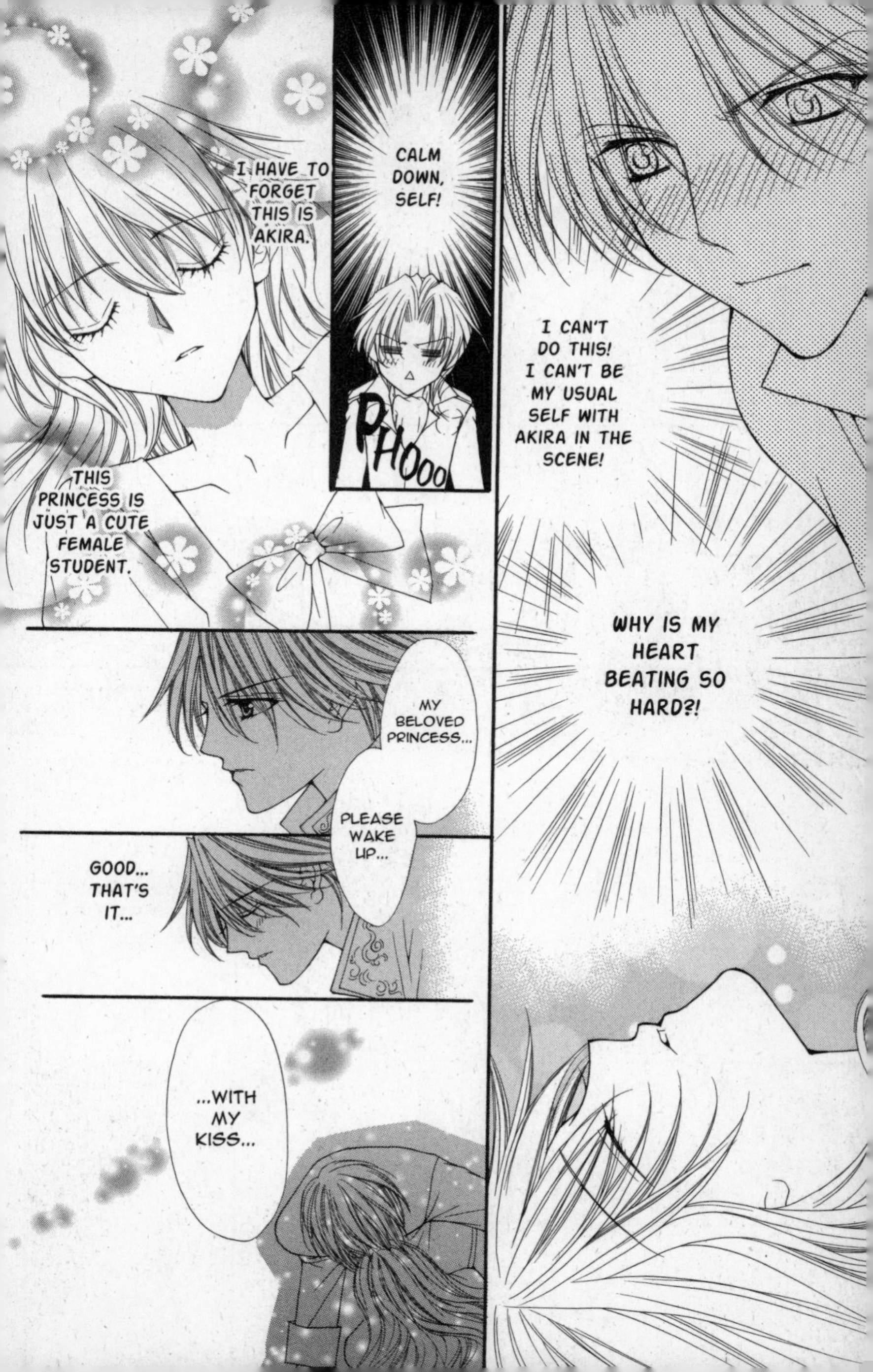
I CAN'T DO THIS! I CAN'T BE MY USUAL SELF WITH AKIRA IN THE SCENE!
WHY IS MY HEART BEATING SO HARD?!
CALM DOWN, SELF!
PHOOO
I HAVE TO FORGET THIS IS AKIRA.
THIS PRINCESS IS JUST A CUTE FEMALE STUDENT.
MY BELOVED PRINCESS...
PLEASE WAKE UP...
GOOD... THAT'S IT...
...WITH MY KISS...

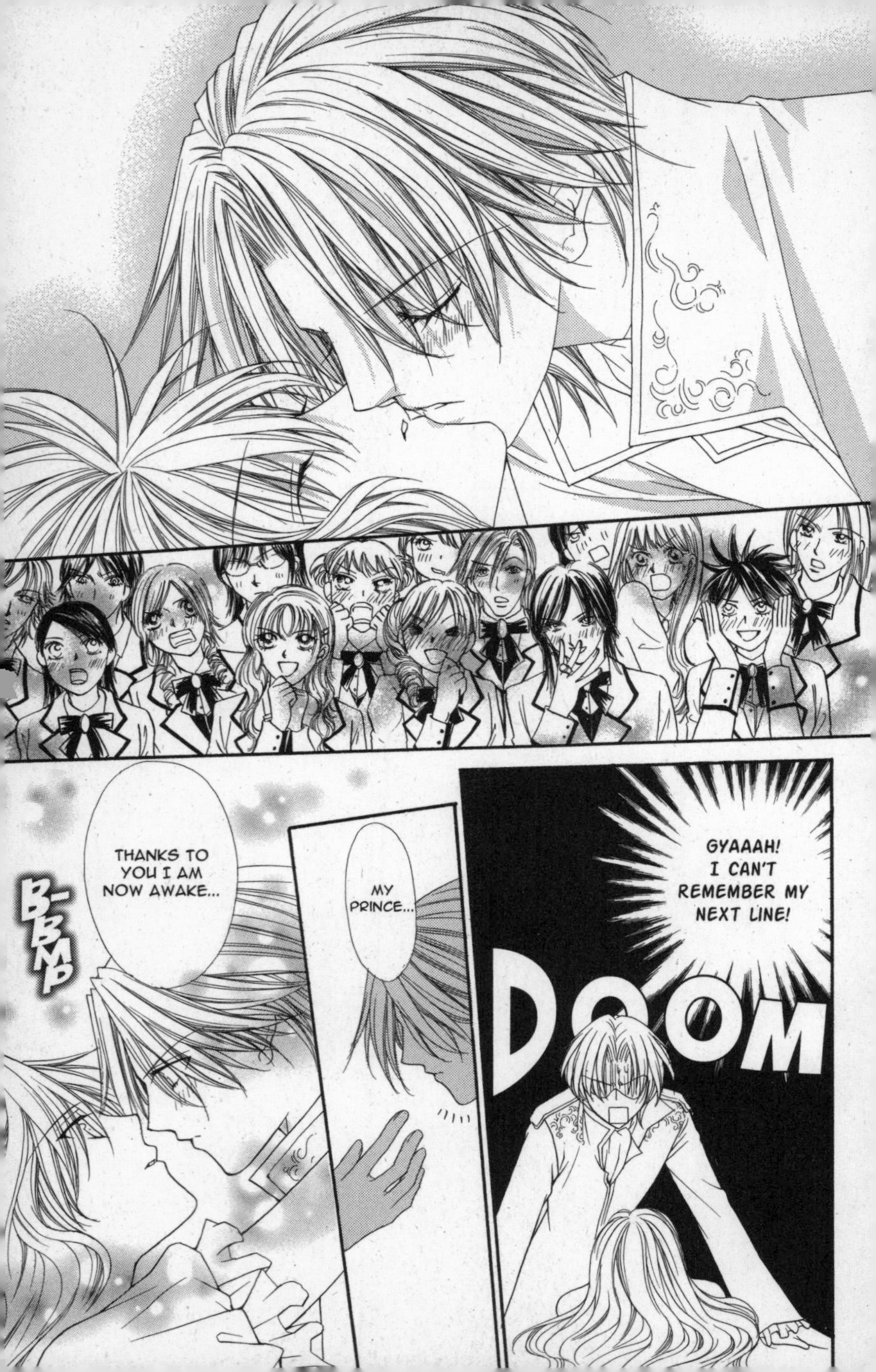
THANKS TO YOU I AM NOW AWAKE...
B-BMP
MY PRINCE...
GYAAAH! I CAN'T REMEMBER MY NEXT LINE!
DOOM

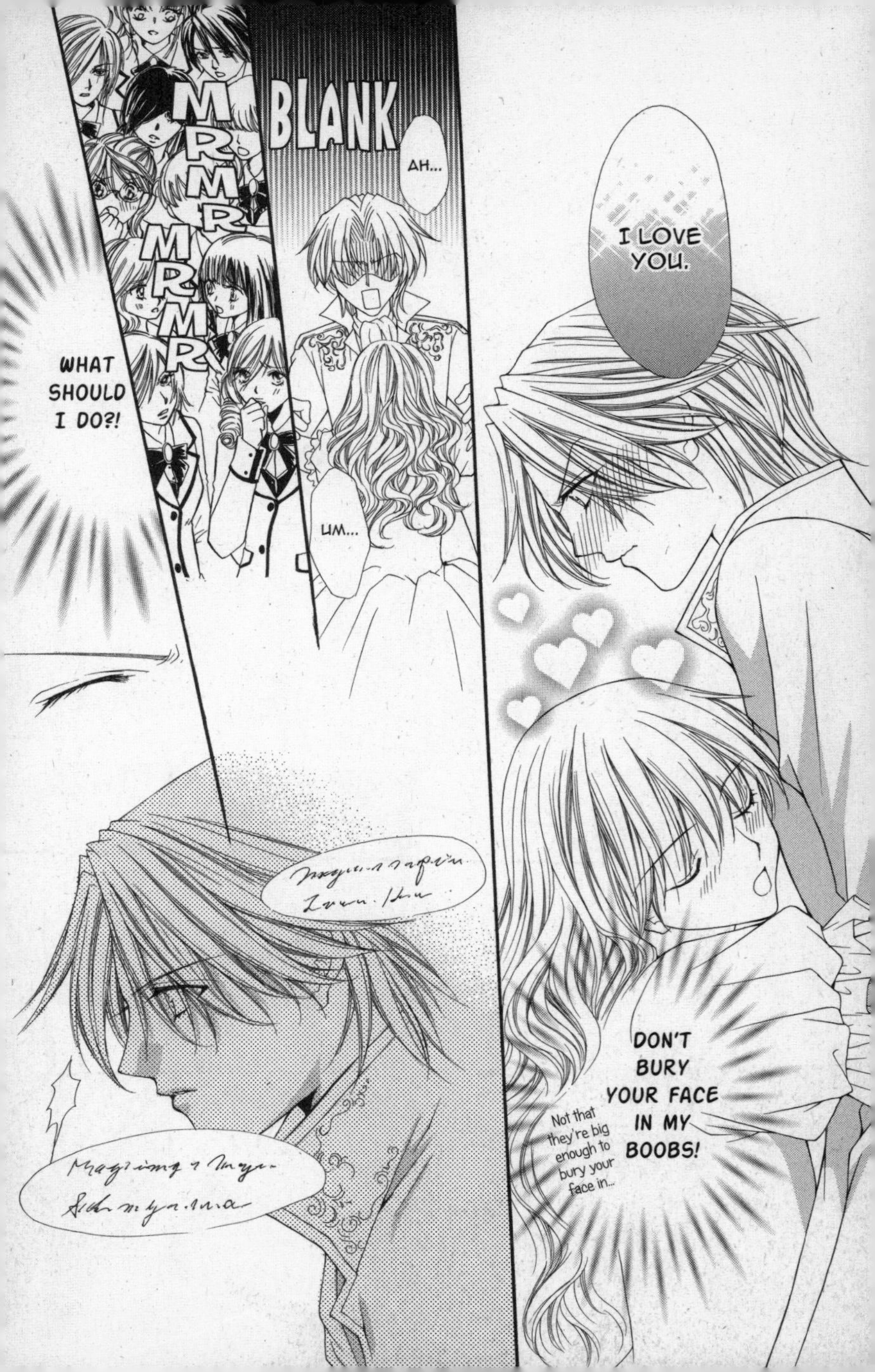
I LOVE YOU.
DON'T BURY YOUR FACE IN MY BOOBS!
Not that they're big enough to bury your face in...
BLANK
AH...
UM...
MRMR
MRMR
WHAT SHOULD I DO?!

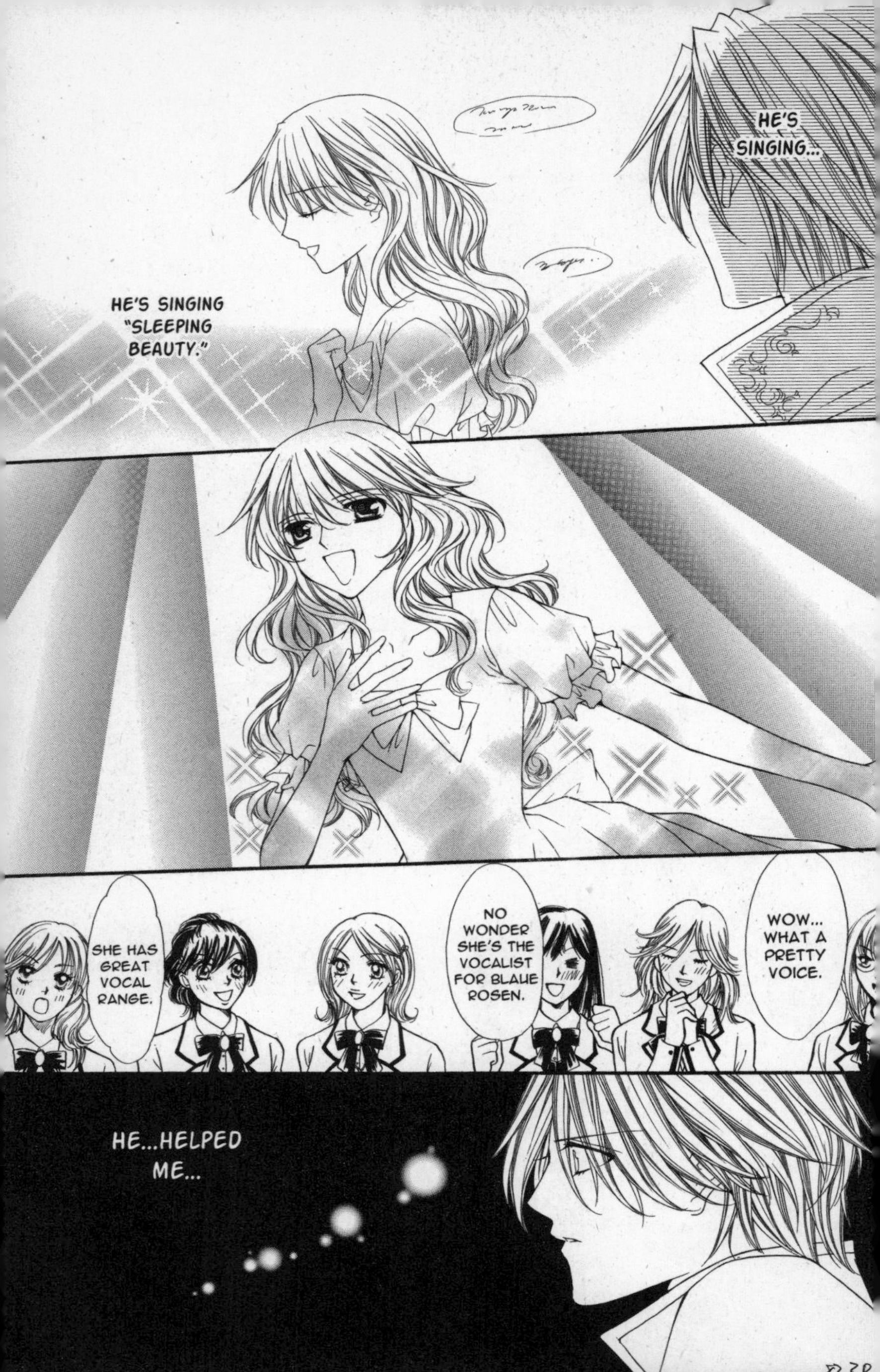
HE'S SINGING...
HE'S SINGING "SLEEPING BEAUTY."
WOW... WHAT A PRETTY VOICE.
NO WONDER SHE'S THE VOCALIST FOR BLAUE ROSEN.
SHE HAS GREAT VOCAL RANGE.
HE...HELPED ME...

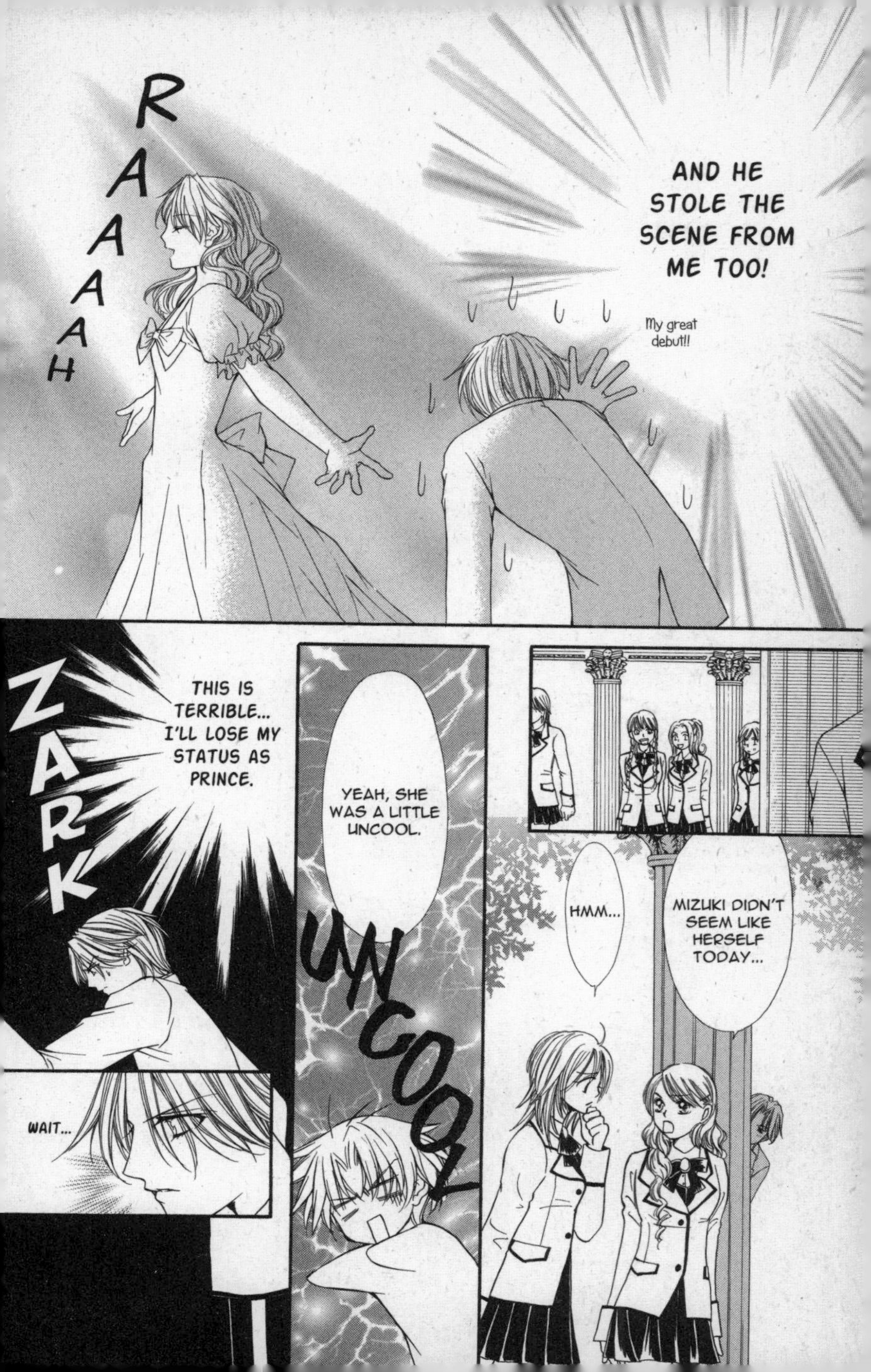
AND HE STOLE THE SCENE FROM ME TOO!
My great debut!!
RAAAAH
MIZUKI DIDN'T SEEM LIKE HERSELF TODAY...
HMM...
YEAH, SHE WAS A LITTLE UNCOOL.
UNCOOL
THIS IS TERRIBLE... I'LL LOSE MY STATUS AS PRINCE.
ZARK
WAIT...

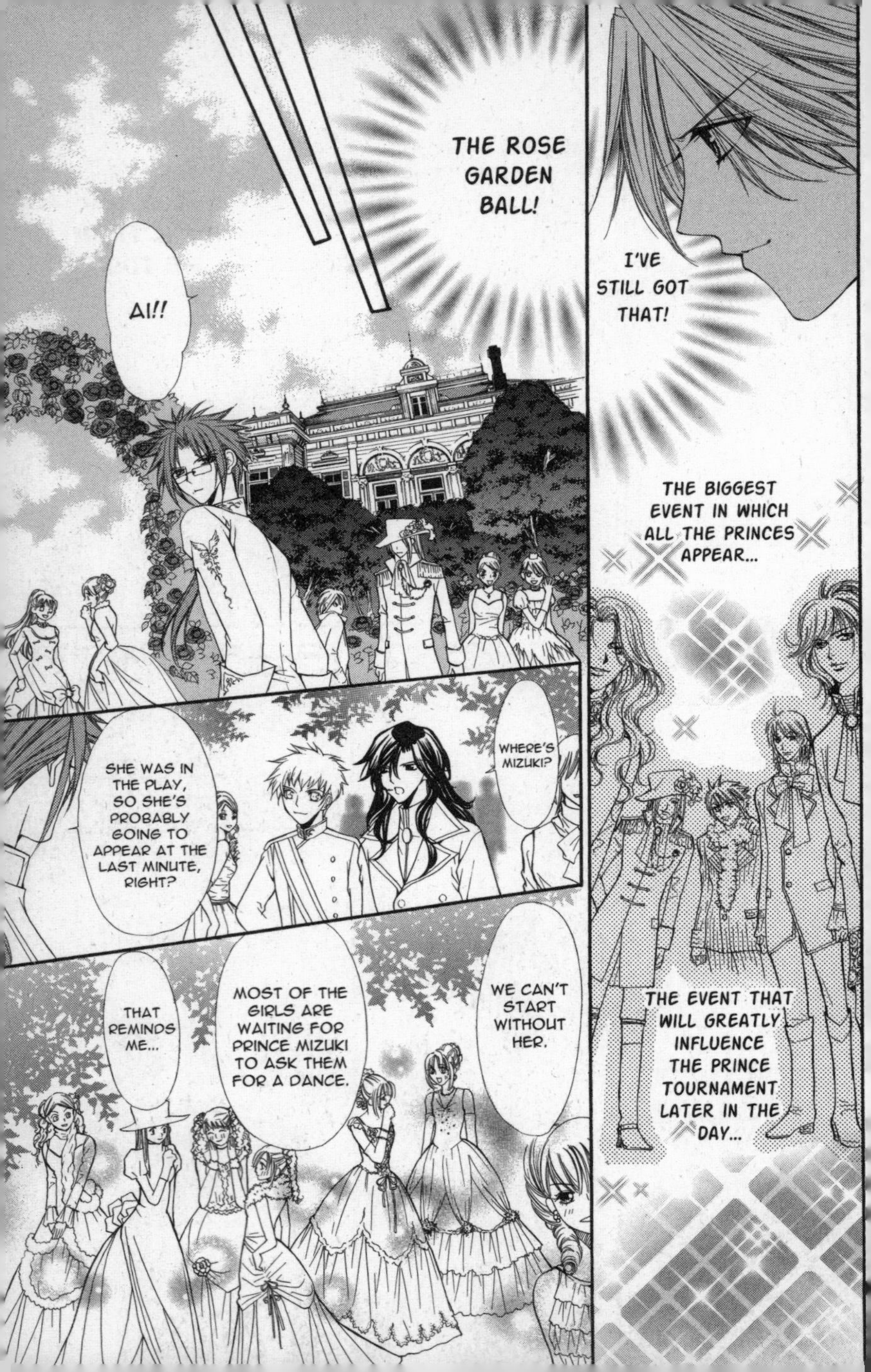
I'VE STILL GOT THAT!
THE ROSE GARDEN BALL!
AI!!
THE BIGGEST EVENT IN WHICH ALL THE PRINCES APPEAR...
THE EVENT THAT WILL GREATLY INFLUENCE THE PRINCE TOURNAMENT LATER IN THE DAY...
WHERE'S MIZUKI?
SHE WAS IN THE PLAY, SO SHE'S PROBABLY GOING TO APPEAR AT THE LAST MINUTE, RIGHT?
WE CAN'T START WITHOUT HER.
MOST OF THE GIRLS ARE WAITING FOR PRINCE MIZUKI TO ASK THEM FOR A DANCE.
THAT REMINDS ME...

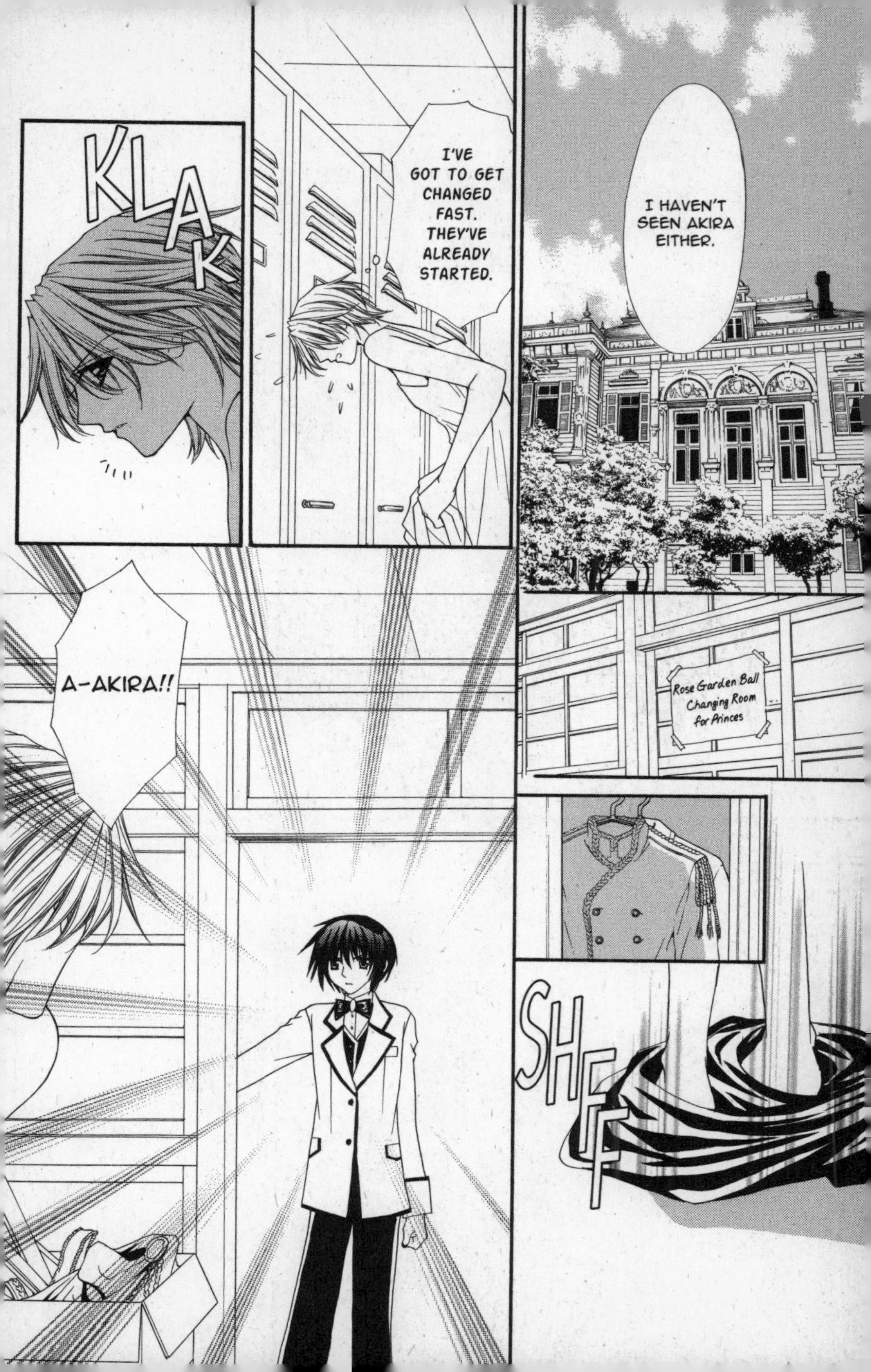
I HAVEN'T SEEN AKIRA EITHER.
I'VE GOT TO GET CHANGED FAST. THEY'VE ALREADY STARTED.
KLAK
Rose Garden Ball Changing Room for Princes
SHFF
A-AKIRA!!

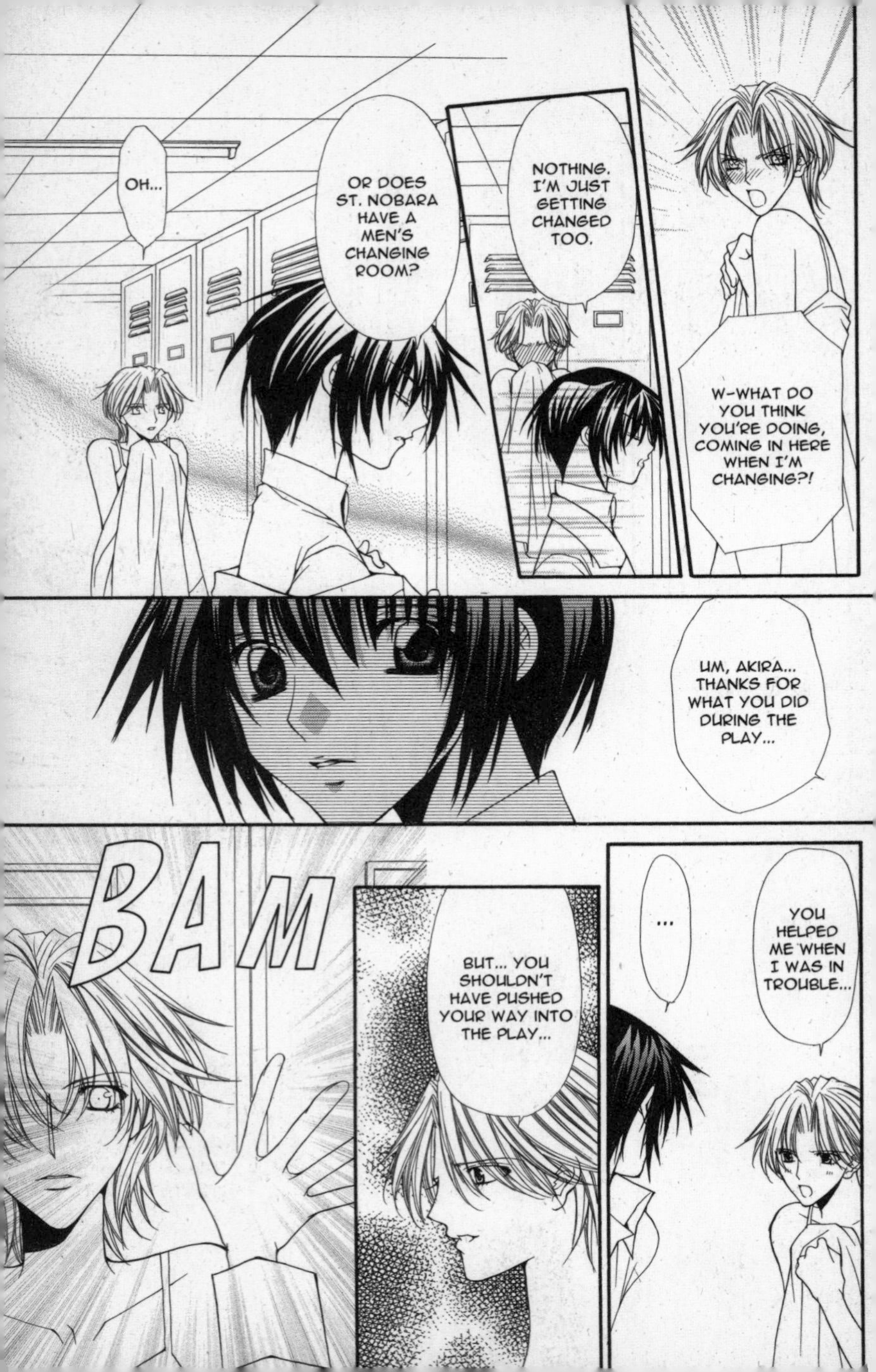
W-WHAT DO YOU THINK YOU'RE DOING, COMING IN HERE WHEN I'M CHANGING?!
NOTHING. I'M JUST GETTING CHANGED TOO.
OR DOES ST. NOBARA HAVE A MEN'S CHANGING ROOM?
OH...
UM, AKIRA... THANKS FOR WHAT YOU DID DURING THE PLAY...
YOU HELPED ME WHEN I WAS IN TROUBLE...
...
BUT... YOU SHOULDN'T HAVE PUSHED YOUR WAY INTO THE PLAY...
BAM

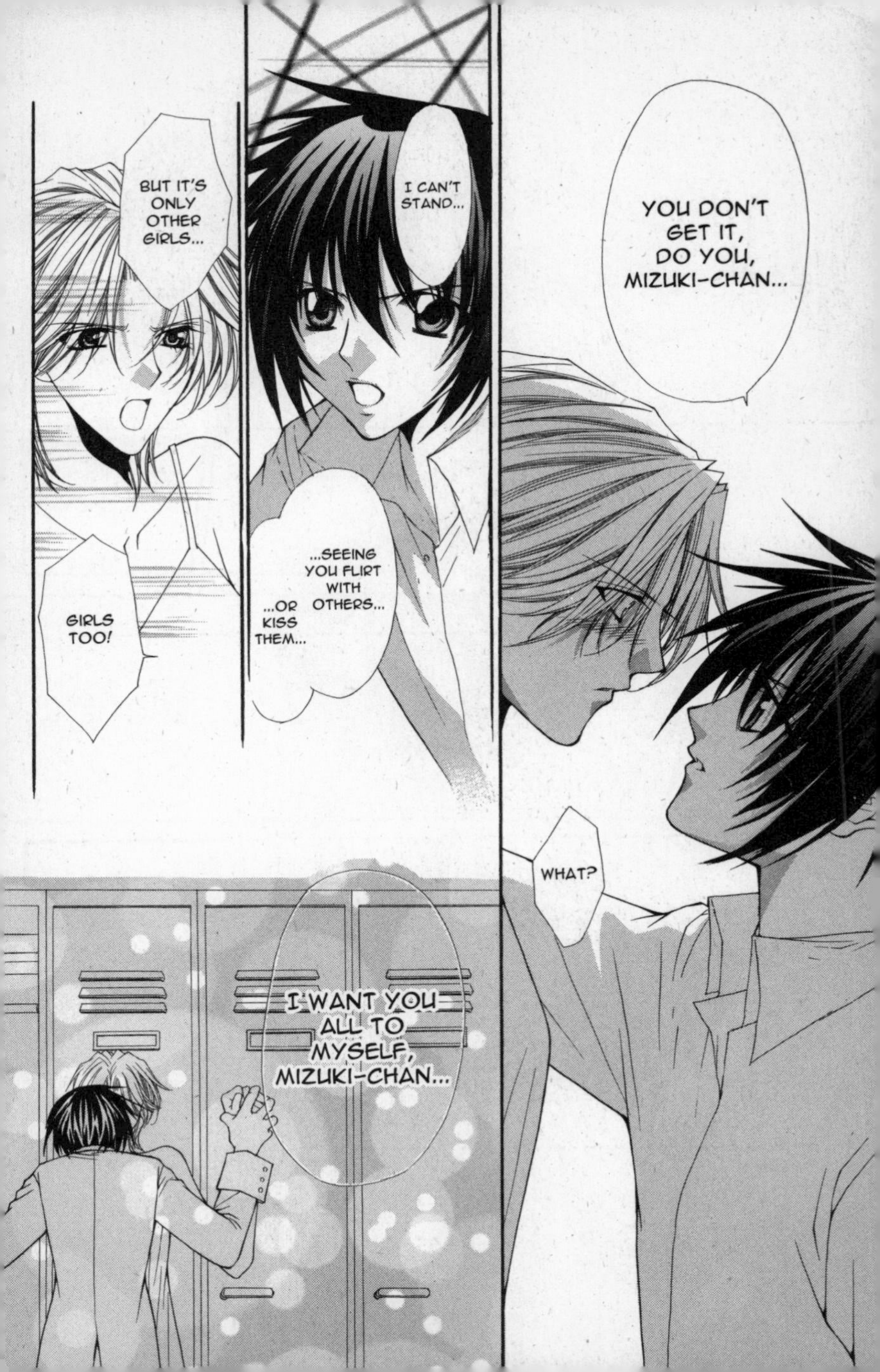
YOU DON'T GET IT, DO YOU, MIZUKI-CHAN...
WHAT?
I CAN'T STAND...
...SEEING YOU FLIRT WITH OTHERS...
...OR KISS THEM...
BUT IT'S ONLY OTHER GIRLS...
GIRLS TOO!
I WANT YOU ALL TO MYSELF, MIZUKI-CHAN...

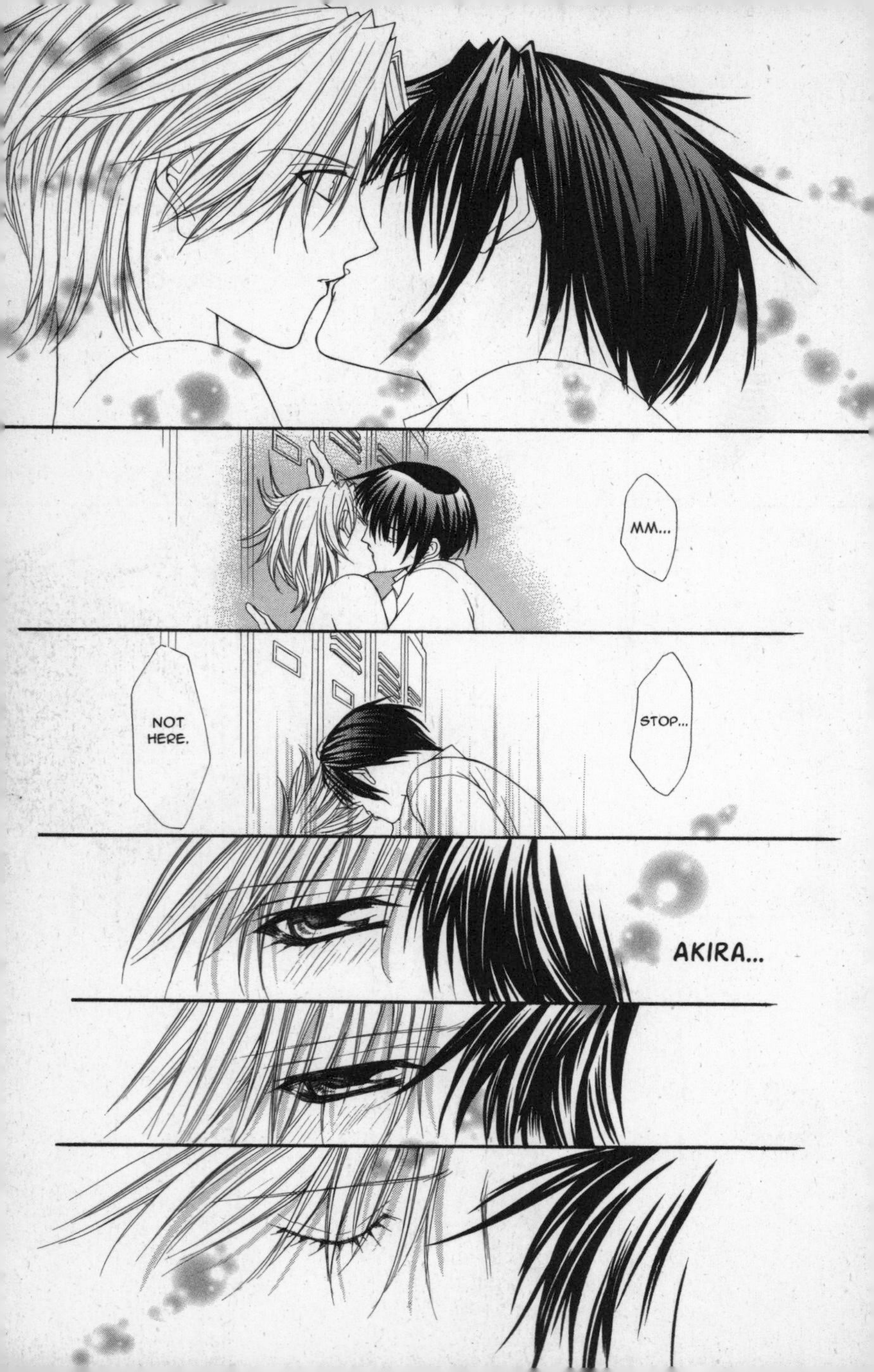
MM...
STOP...
NOT HERE.
AKIRA...

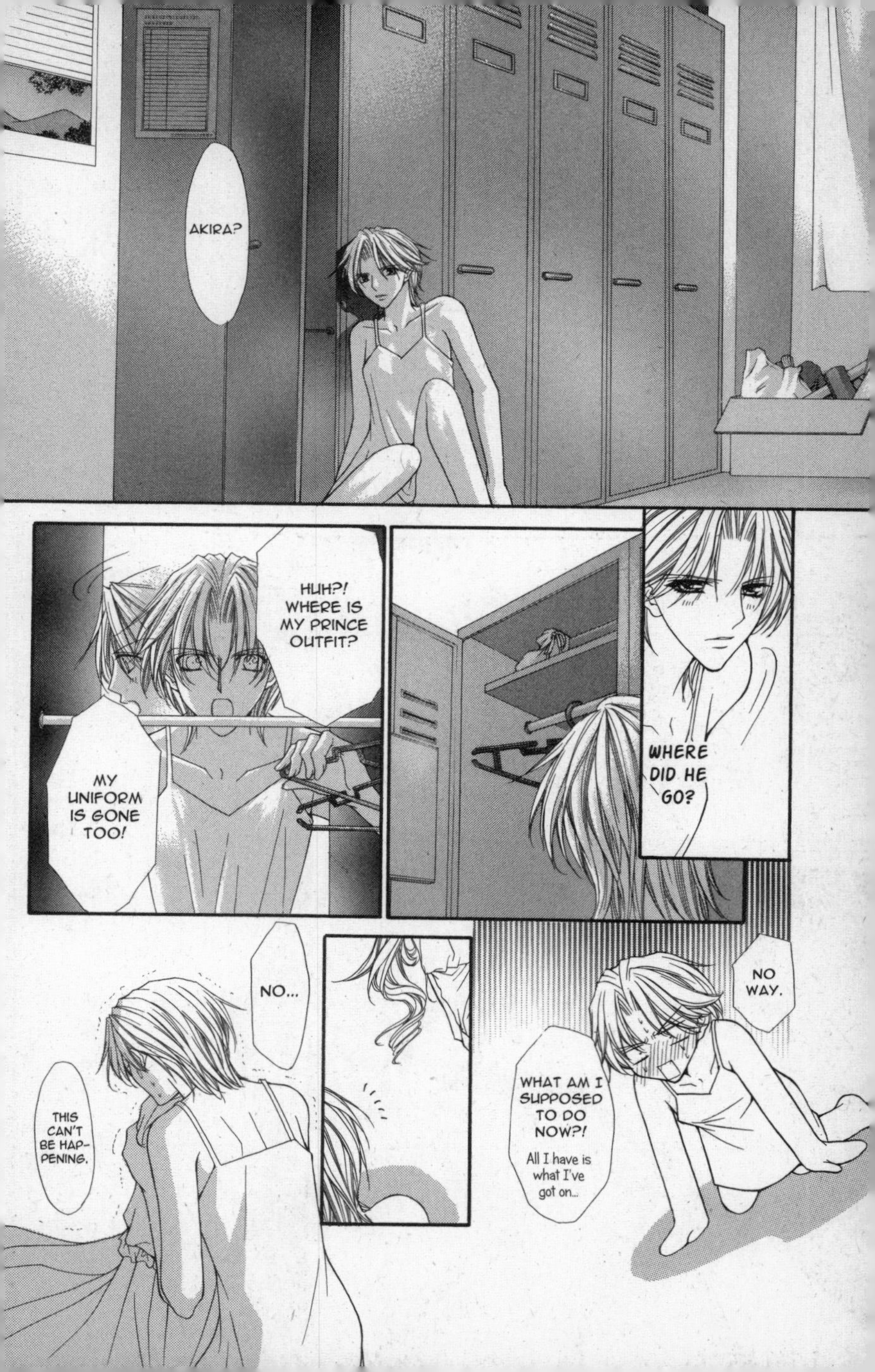
AKIRA?
WHERE DID HE GO?
HUH?! WHERE IS MY PRINCE OUTFIT?
MY UNIFORM IS GONE TOO!
NO WAY.
WHAT AM I SUPPOSED TO DO NOW?!
All I have is what I've got on...
NO...
THIS CAN'T BE HAP-PENING.

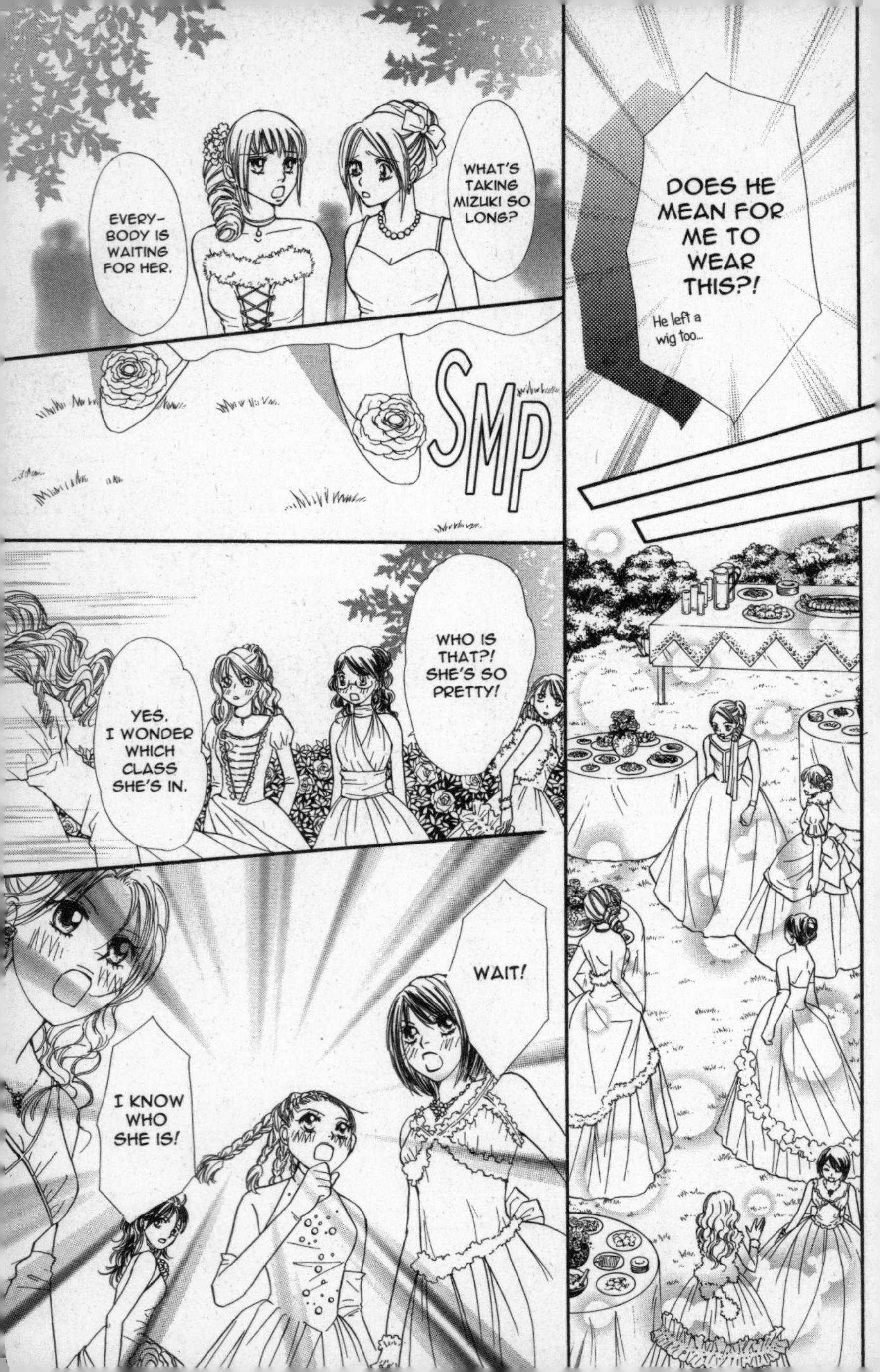
DOES HE MEAN FOR ME TO WEAR THIS?!
He left a wig too...
WHAT'S TAKING MIZUKI SO LONG?
EVERY-BODY IS WAITING FOR HER.
SMP
WHO IS THAT?! SHE'S SO PRETTY!
YES. I WONDER WHICH CLASS SHE'S IN.
WAIT!
I KNOW WHO SHE IS!

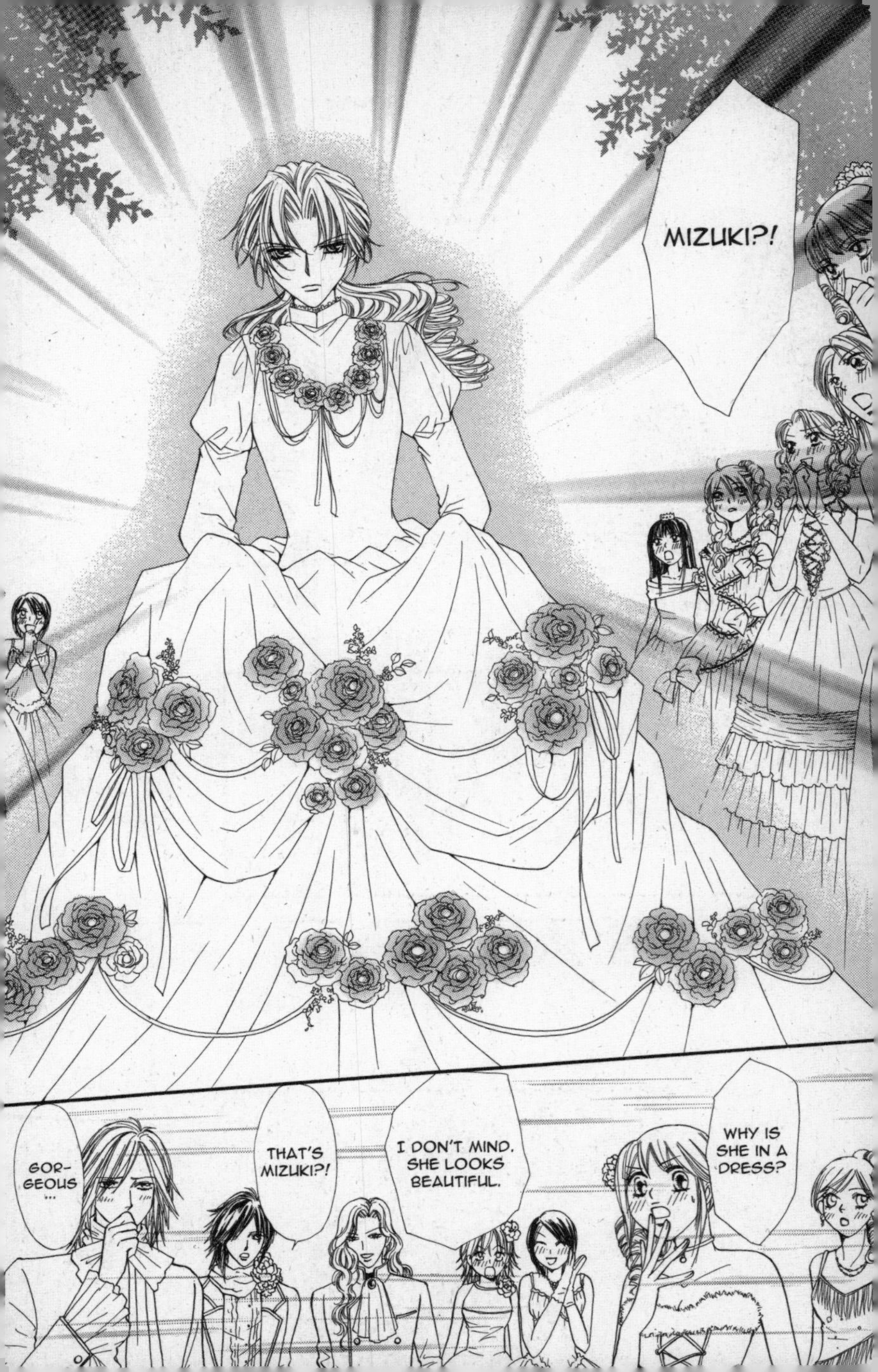
MIZUKI?!
WHY IS SHE IN A DRESS?
I DON'T MIND. SHE LOOKS BEAUTIFUL.
THAT'S MIZUKI?!
GOR-GEOUS...

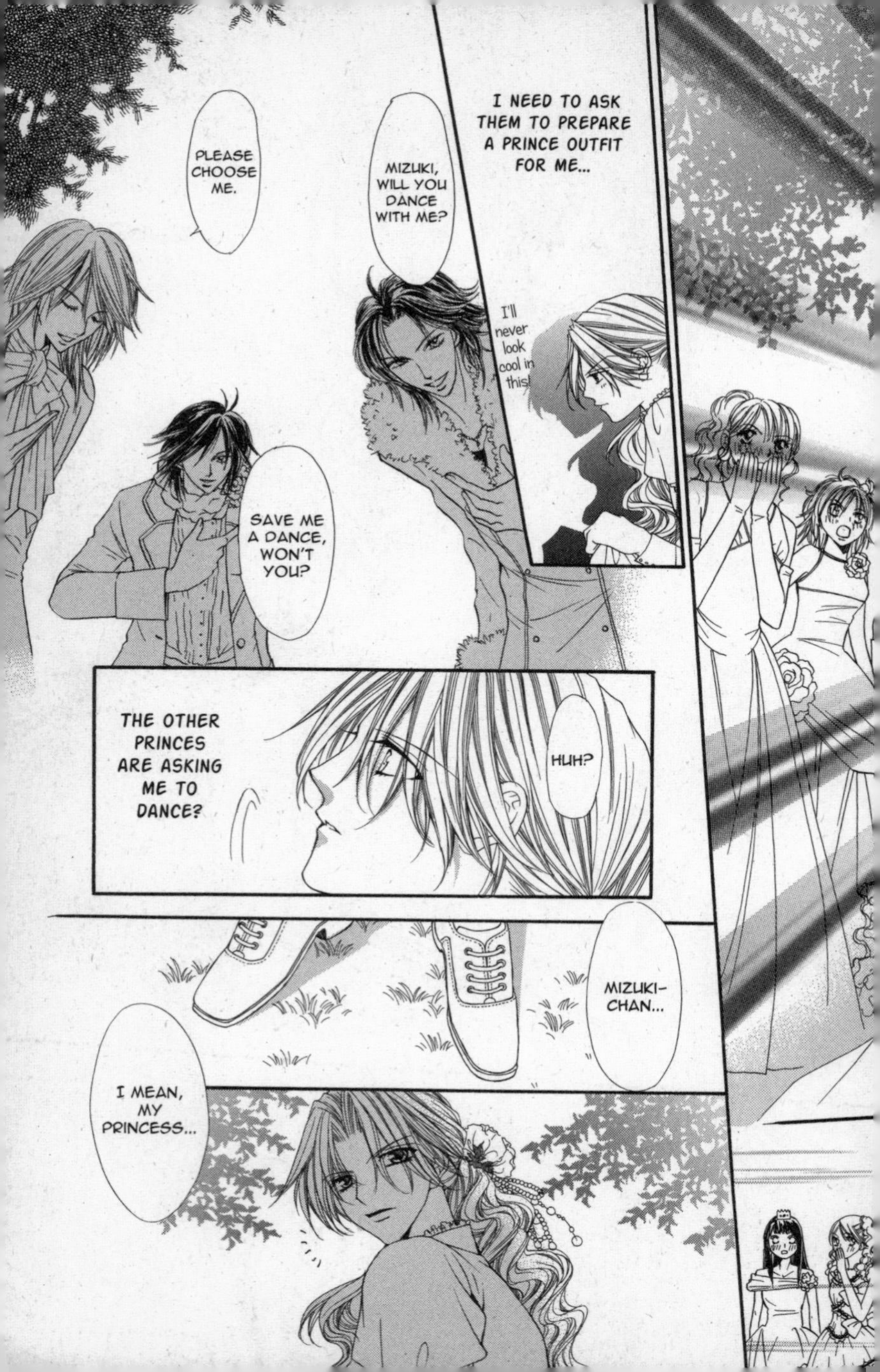
I NEED TO ASK THEM TO PREPARE A PRINCE OUTFIT FOR ME...
I'll never look cool in this!
MIZUKI, WILL YOU DANCE WITH ME?
PLEASE CHOOSE ME.
SAVE ME A DANCE, WON'T YOU?
HUH?
THE OTHER PRINCES ARE ASKING ME TO DANCE?
MIZUKI-CHAN...
I MEAN, MY PRINCESS...

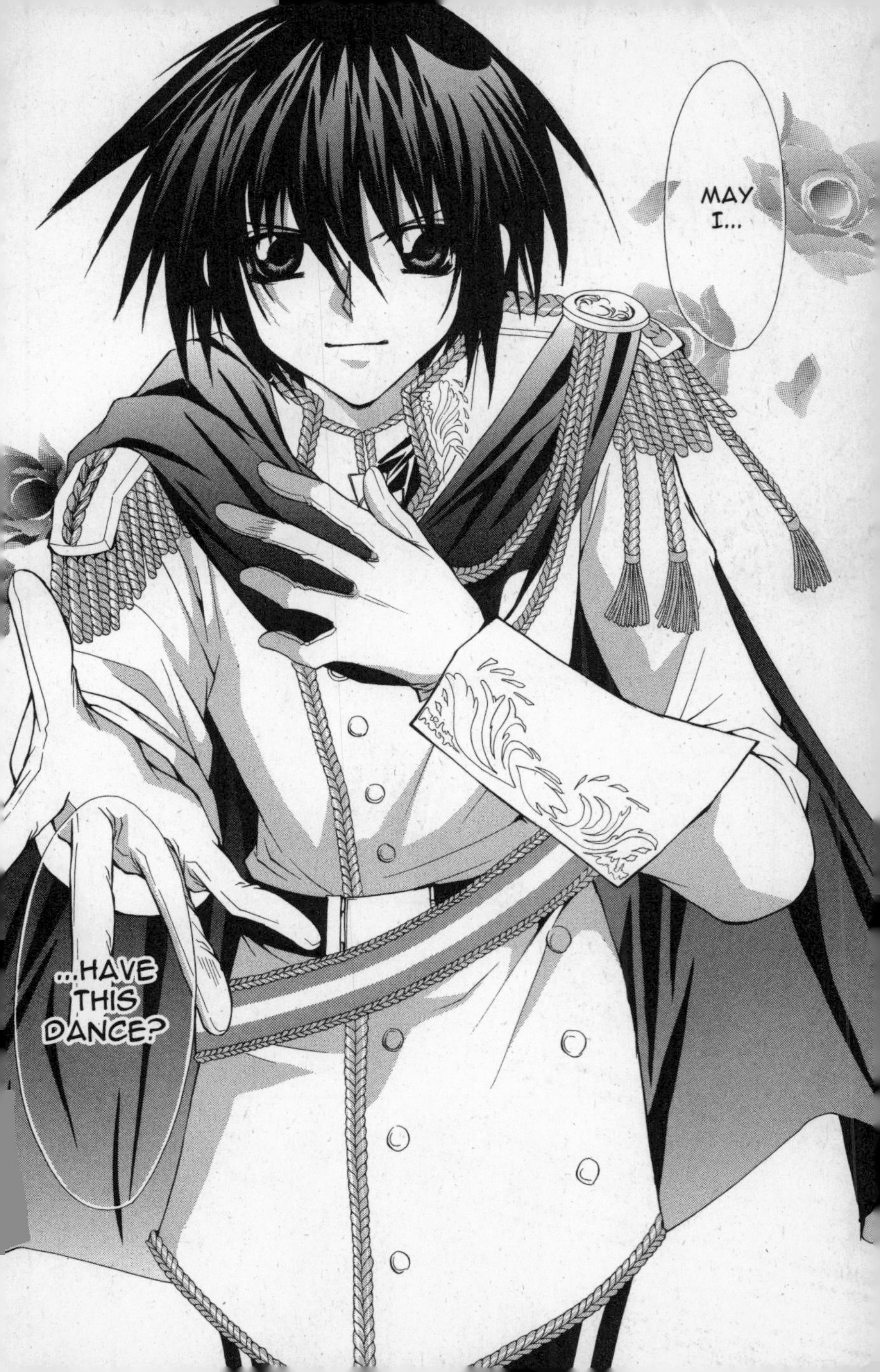
MAY I...
...HAVE THIS DANCE?

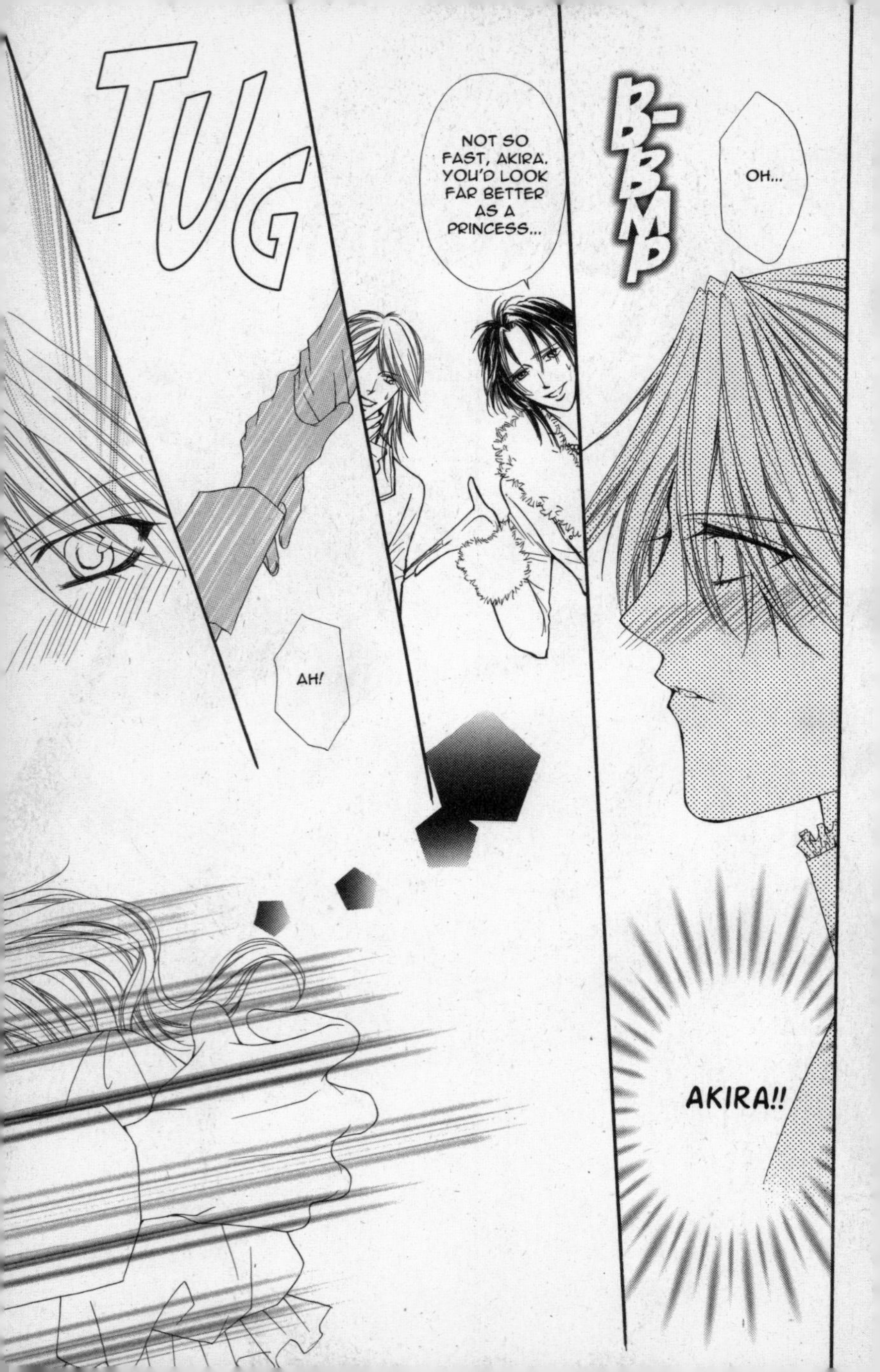
OH...
B-BUMP
AKIRA!!
NOT SO FAST, AKIRA. YOU'D LOOK FAR BETTER AS A PRINCESS...
TUG
AH!

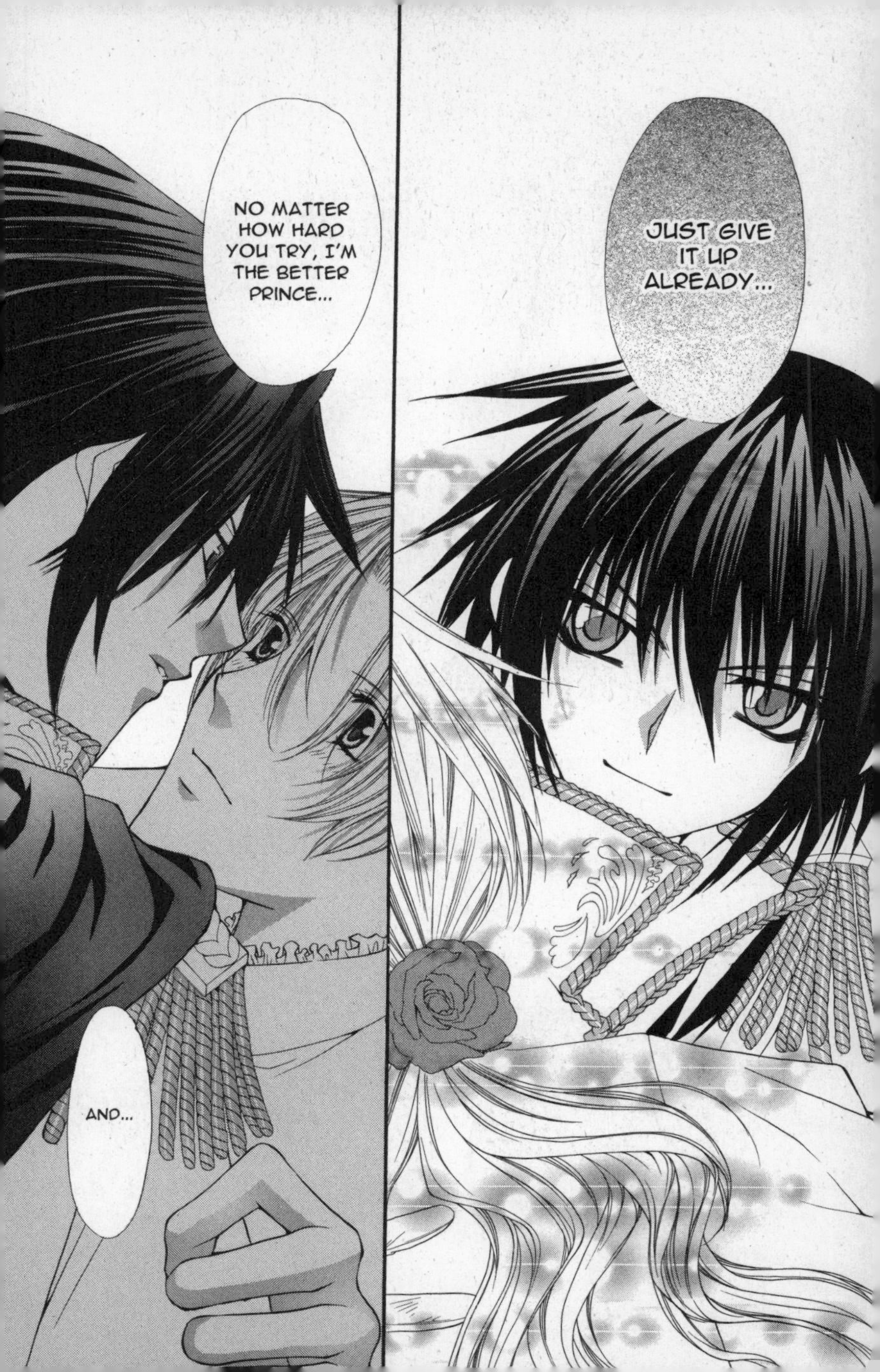
JUST GIVE IT UP ALREADY...
NO MATTER HOW HARD YOU TRY, I'M THE BETTER PRINCE...
AND...

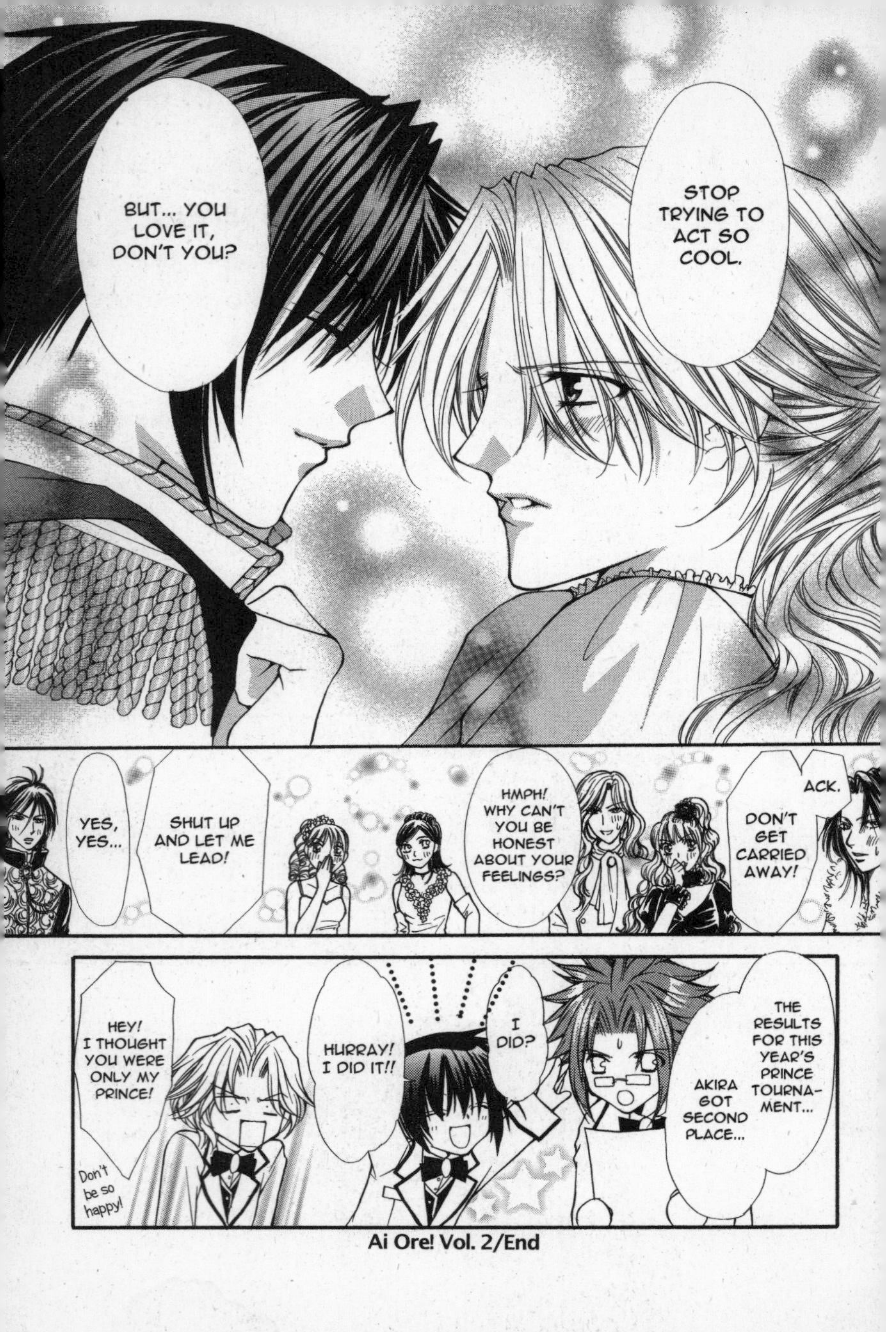
STOP TRYING TO ACT SO COOL.
BUT... YOU LOVE IT, DON'T YOU?
ACK.
DON'T GET CARRIED AWAY!
HMPH! WHY CAN'T YOU BE HONEST ABOUT YOUR FEELINGS?
SHUT UP AND LET ME LEAD!
YES, YES...
THE RESULTS FOR THIS YEAR'S PRINCE TOURNA-MENT...
AKIRA GOT SECOND PLACE...
I DID?
HURRAY! I DID IT!!
HEY! I THOUGHT YOU WERE ONLY MY PRINCE!
Don't be so happy!

Ai Ore! Vol. 2/End

Mayu Shinjo's...

First Experience in Voice Acting & Reunion with Takahiro Sakurai

Voice actors are really amazing...
Script

Eh... The second drama CD for *Ai Ore!* includes a short bonus story, and the nurse at the infirmary is played by...
Shinjo.
I was told I'd be appearing in a bit part, so I assumed it was going to be a line or two like "Say Aaaah..." or "Mizuki..." but I was given a proper role!
And I play around with Hoshi-san too!!
(Well... It's not Hoshi-san, but Akira...) Shock...
I had a conversation over drinks with the scriptwriter and others working on the CD about what to do with the bonus story. We were joking around saying, "Let's do this" and "Let's do that"... The next day, those jokes appeared in the script!!
Nooo! But I've got to do it!! But I was really busy with work!! So I turned up at the recording session without being able to practice first, and then they decided I should call out the title of the CD too...
My head was in such a panic that I don't remember a lot about it. (BAM!) The only thing I kept thinking was "I mustn't be any trouble!" Eh, I'm sorry if I was trouble...
After that, I was reunited with Sakurai-kun, whom I had not seen for several years. Now I have been reunited with every voice actor for Λucifer (in the anime). I was talking about how I had met Suzumura-kun too, and since we were being interviewed for a magazine, we started to reminisce... Sakurai-kun is famous for being a cool and handsome voice actor now, but back then he was really nerdy (laugh), and I thought he was some kind of country bumpkin...but he suddenly became so fashionable! (laugh)

His coke-bottle glasses and his rather long geeky hairstyle became fashionable, so I couldn't help asking him what had happened. According to him, his hair was cut too short one day, so a friend of his fixed it for him. Then he was advised to change his glasses as well... When he attended a party hosted by Shogakukan at the end of the year, the other mangaka kept asking, "Hey, who is that guy...?" Woo, he's amazing!
So I chatted with him about stuff like that.
I like it when Sakurai-kun is talking with his cool voice, but I absolutely love it when he's performing in a cheerful and comedic manner!! He will be playing Rui in the drama CD, but he was also one of the top choices for Ran. For a while he was in third place for voice actors for Rui, but he made a great comeback and rose up to first very quickly at the end. I was so happy when that happened. His over-the-top performance of Rui is just amazing! Ran and Rui's hyped-up, all-over-the-place conversation is a must-hear!!

Shinjo's selection of moe lines said by Rui:

"Hot spring with Akira! ♡ Hot spring with Akira! ♡... ♪"
"Take a shot! Take a photograph with your cell and use it as wallpaper!"
"Injection?! That's something I want to do to you!!"

Okay... Rui is all over the place...

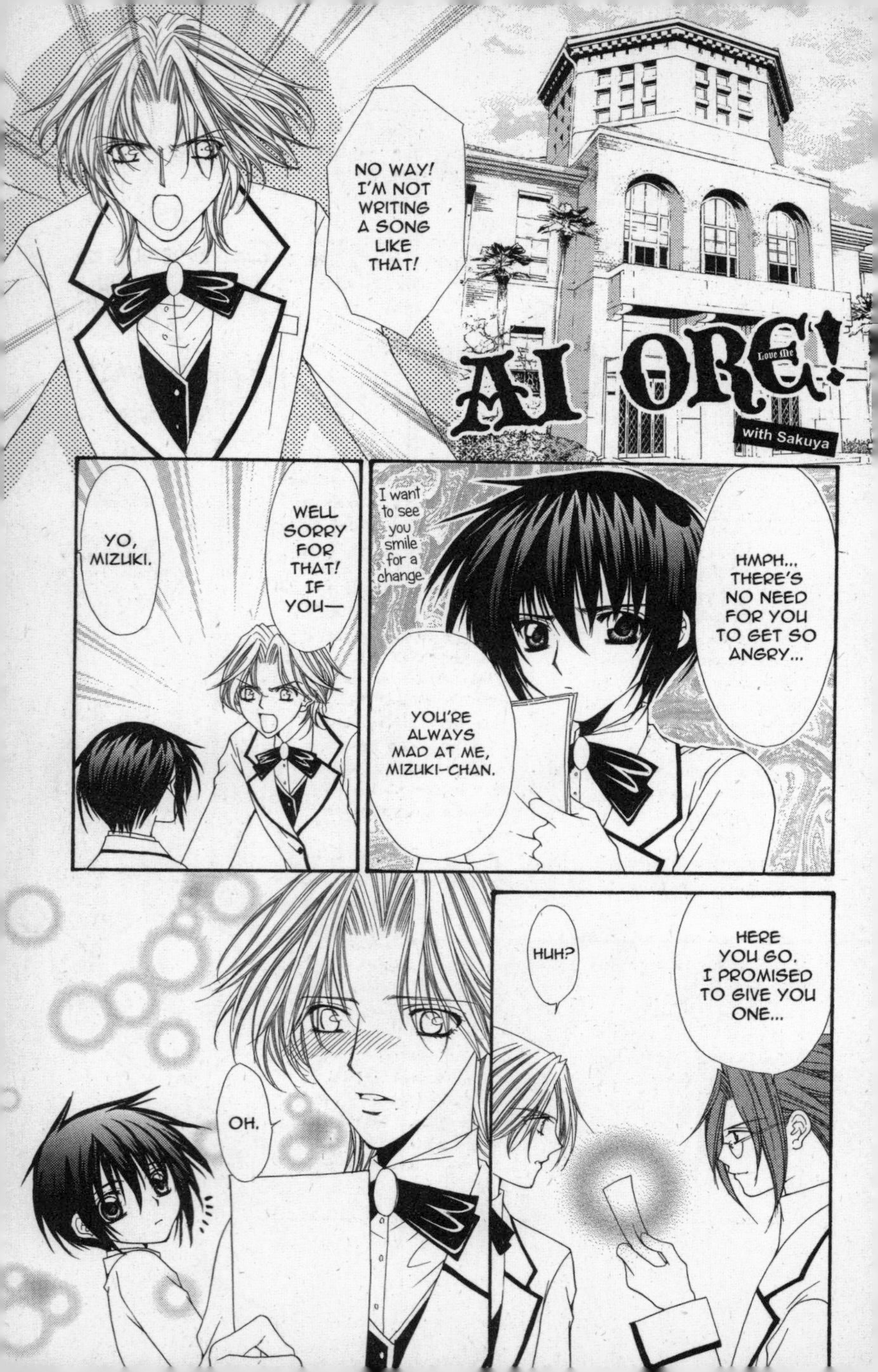
AI ORE!
Love Me
with Sakuya
NO WAY! I'M NOT WRITING A SONG LIKE THAT!
HMPH... THERE'S NO NEED FOR YOU TO GET SO ANGRY...
I want to see you smile for a change.
YOU'RE ALWAYS MAD AT ME, MIZUKI-CHAN.
WELL SORRY FOR THAT! IF YOU—
YO, MIZUKI.
HERE YOU GO. I PROMISED TO GIVE YOU ONE...
HUH?
OH.

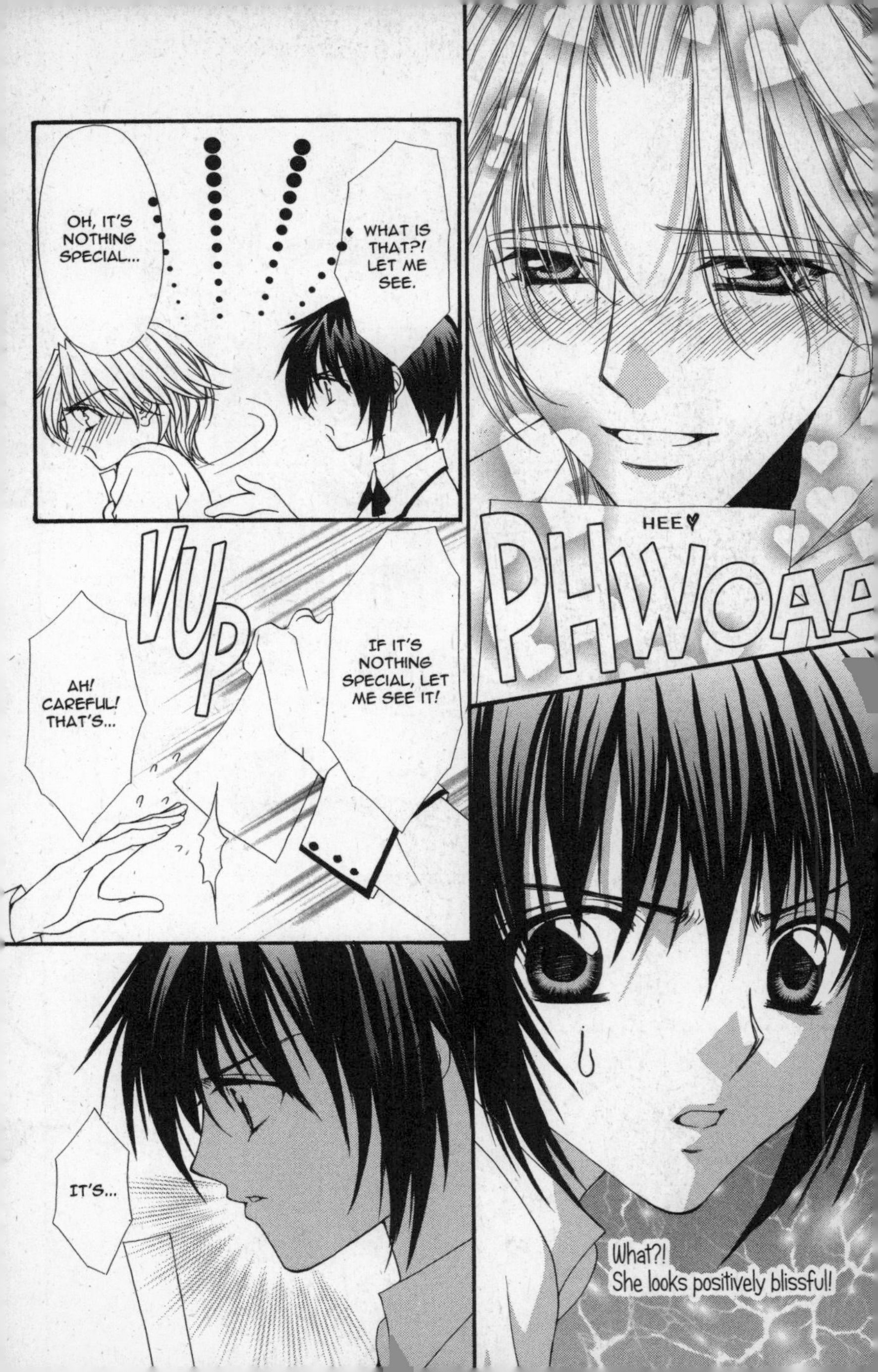
WHAT IS THAT?! LET ME SEE.
OH, IT'S NOTHING SPECIAL...
IF IT'S NOTHING SPECIAL, LET ME SEE IT!
VUP
AH! CAREFUL! THAT'S...
IT'S...
HEE♥
PHWOAA
What?! She looks positively blissful!

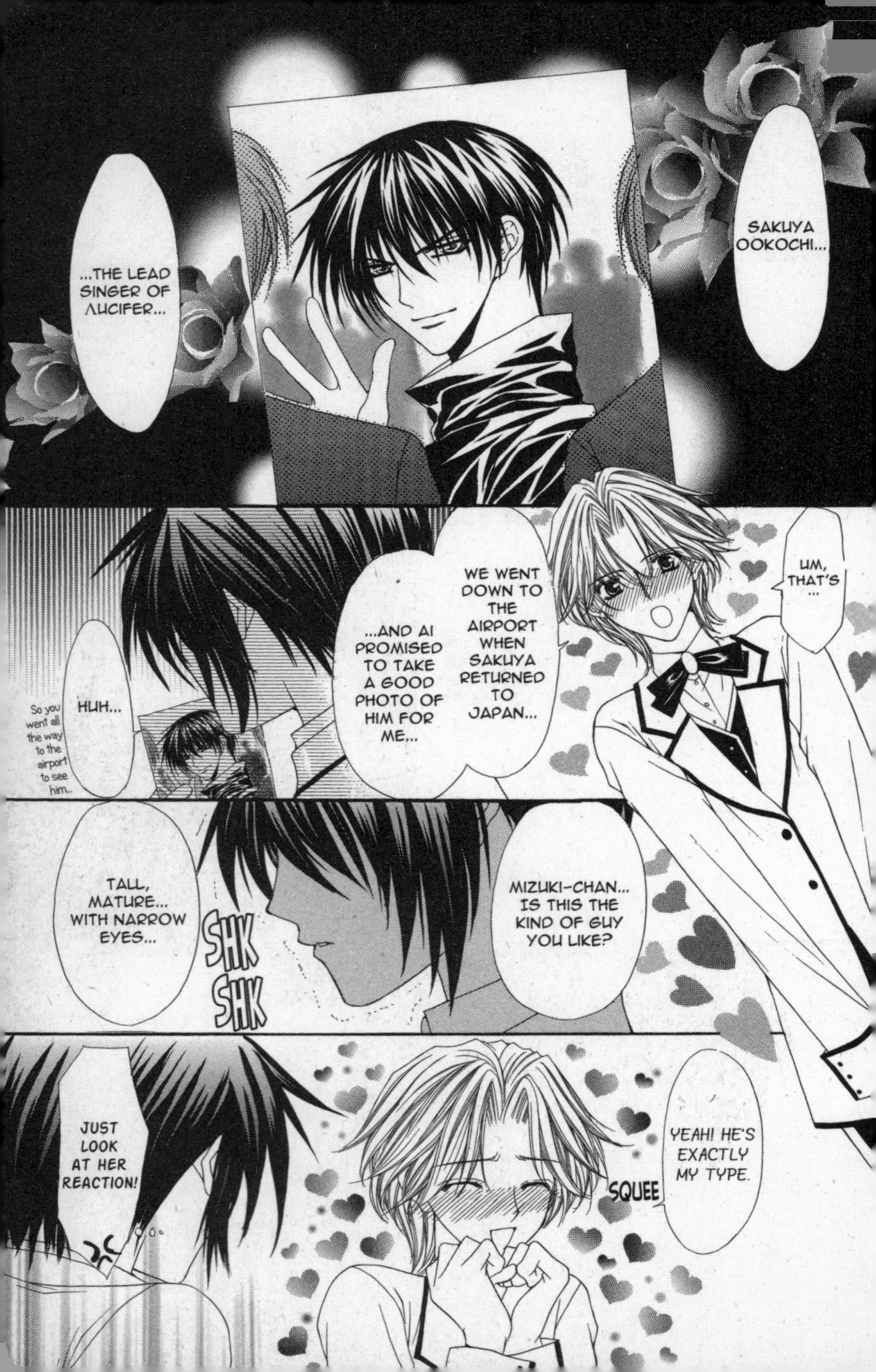
SAKUYA OOKOCHI...
...THE LEAD SINGER OF ΛUCIFER...
UM, THAT'S ...
WE WENT DOWN TO THE AIRPORT WHEN SAKUYA RETURNED TO JAPAN...
...AND AI PROMISED TO TAKE A GOOD PHOTO OF HIM FOR ME...
HUH...
So you went all the way to the airport to see him...
MIZUKI-CHAN... IS THIS THE KIND OF GUY YOU LIKE?
SHK SHK
TALL, MATURE... WITH NARROW EYES...
YEAH! HE'S EXACTLY MY TYPE.
SQUEE
JUST LOOK AT HER REACTION!

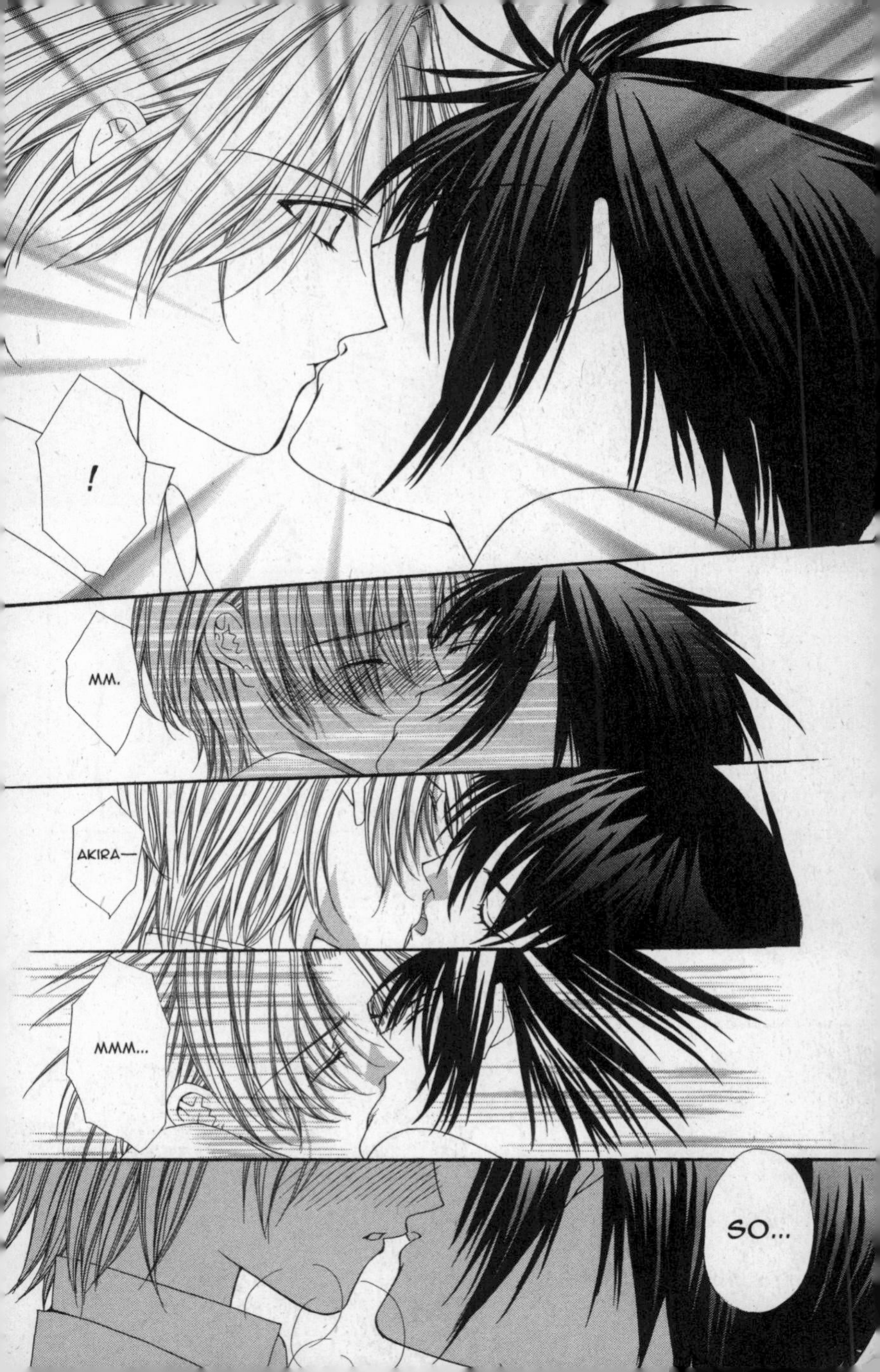
!
MM.
AKIRA—
MMM...
SO...

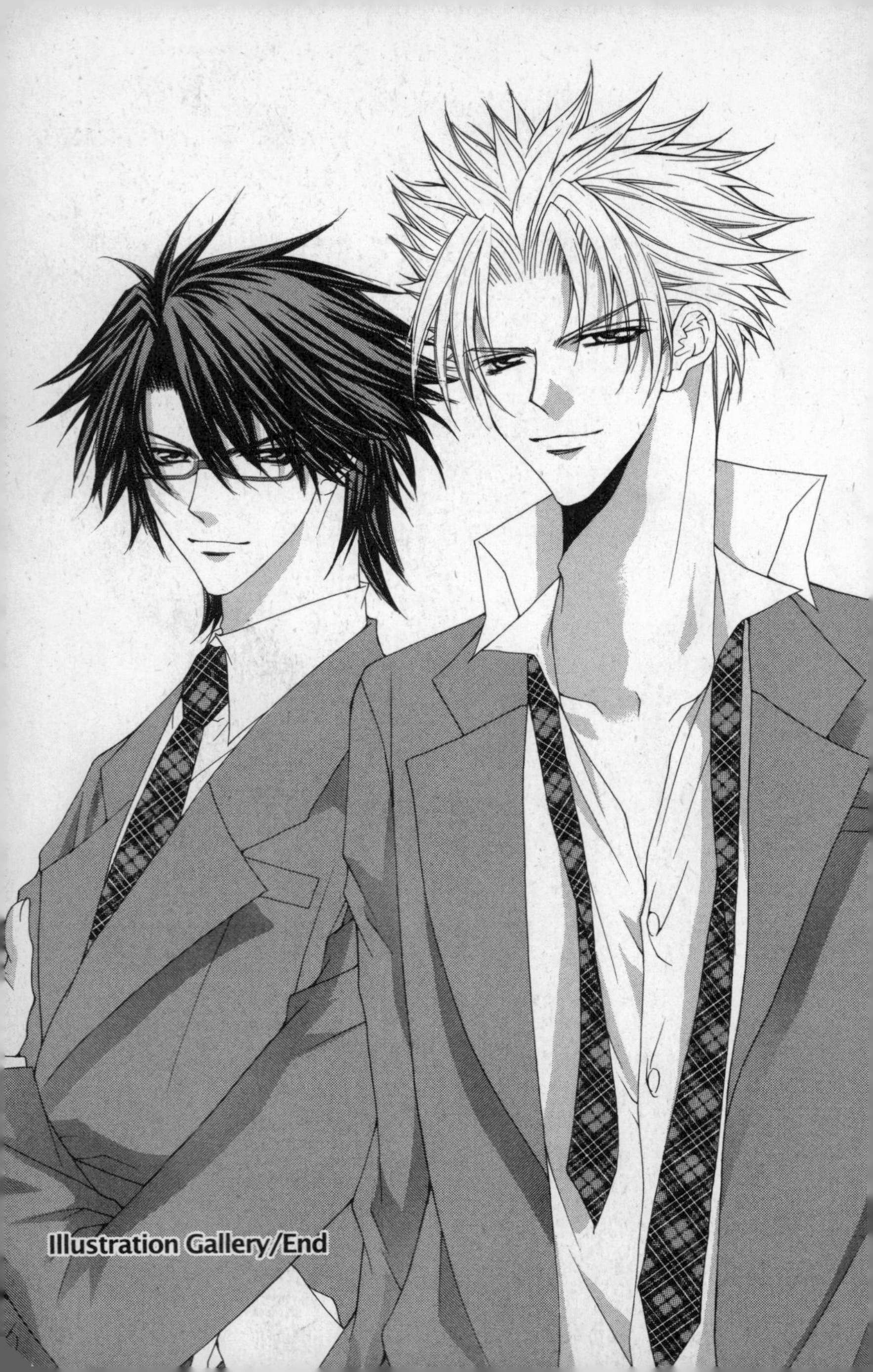
Illustration Gallery/End

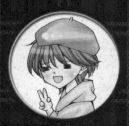

This was a time when a lot of things were happening around me, but I was able to relax whenever I was working on this. I didn't have any friends who stood by me, but I was able to continue creating this thanks to all my supportive fans. Now I have so many friends who support me. Thank you very much for loving this series!!

-Mayu Shinjo

Mayu Shinjo was born on January 26. She is a prolific writer of shojo manga, including the series *Sensual Phrase*. Her current series include *Ai-Ore!* and *Ayakashi Koi Emaki*. Her hobbies are cars, shopping and taking baths. Shinjo likes The Prodigy, Nirvana, U2 and Glay.

Ai Ore!

Volume 2
Shojo Beat Edition

STORY AND ART BY
MAYU SHINJO

Translation/Tetsuichiro Miyaki
Touch-up Art & Lettering/Inori Fukuda Trant
Design/Yukiko Whitley
Editor/Nancy Thistlethwaite

Aiwo Utauyori Oreni Oborero! Volume 2
© Mayu SHINJO 2010
First published in Japan in 2010 by KADOKAWA
SHOTEN Co., Ltd., Tokyo.
English translation rights arranged with
KADOKAWA SHOTEN Co., Ltd., Tokyo.

Printed in Canada

Published by VIZ Media, LLC
P.O. Box 77010
San Francisco, CA 94107

10 9 8 7 6 5 4 3 2 1
First printing, August 2011

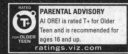

The World's Greatest Manga

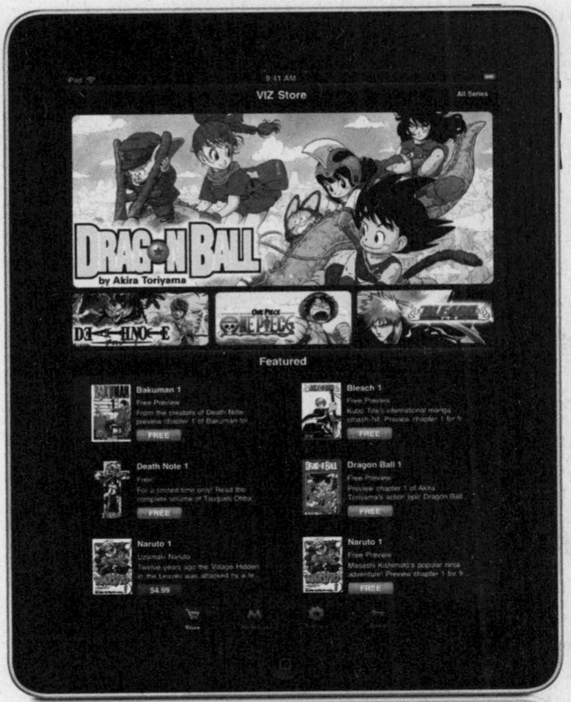
VIZ Store
All Series
DRAGON BALL
by Akira Toriyama
Featured
Bakuman 1
Bleach 1
Death Note 1
Dragon Ball 1
Naruto 1
Naruto 1
FREE
$4.99

Full of FREE previews and tons of new manga for you to explore

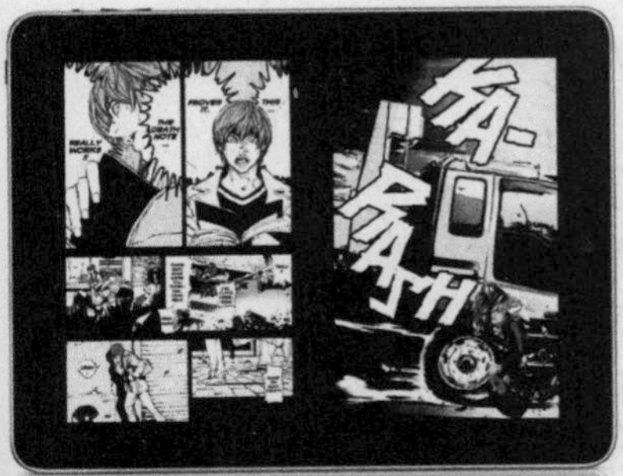

From legendary manga like *Dragon Ball* to *Bakuman。*, the newest series from the creators of *Death Note*, the best manga in the world is now available on the iPad through the official VIZ Manga app.

- Free App
- New content weekly
- Free chapter 1 previews